ART OF CHINA

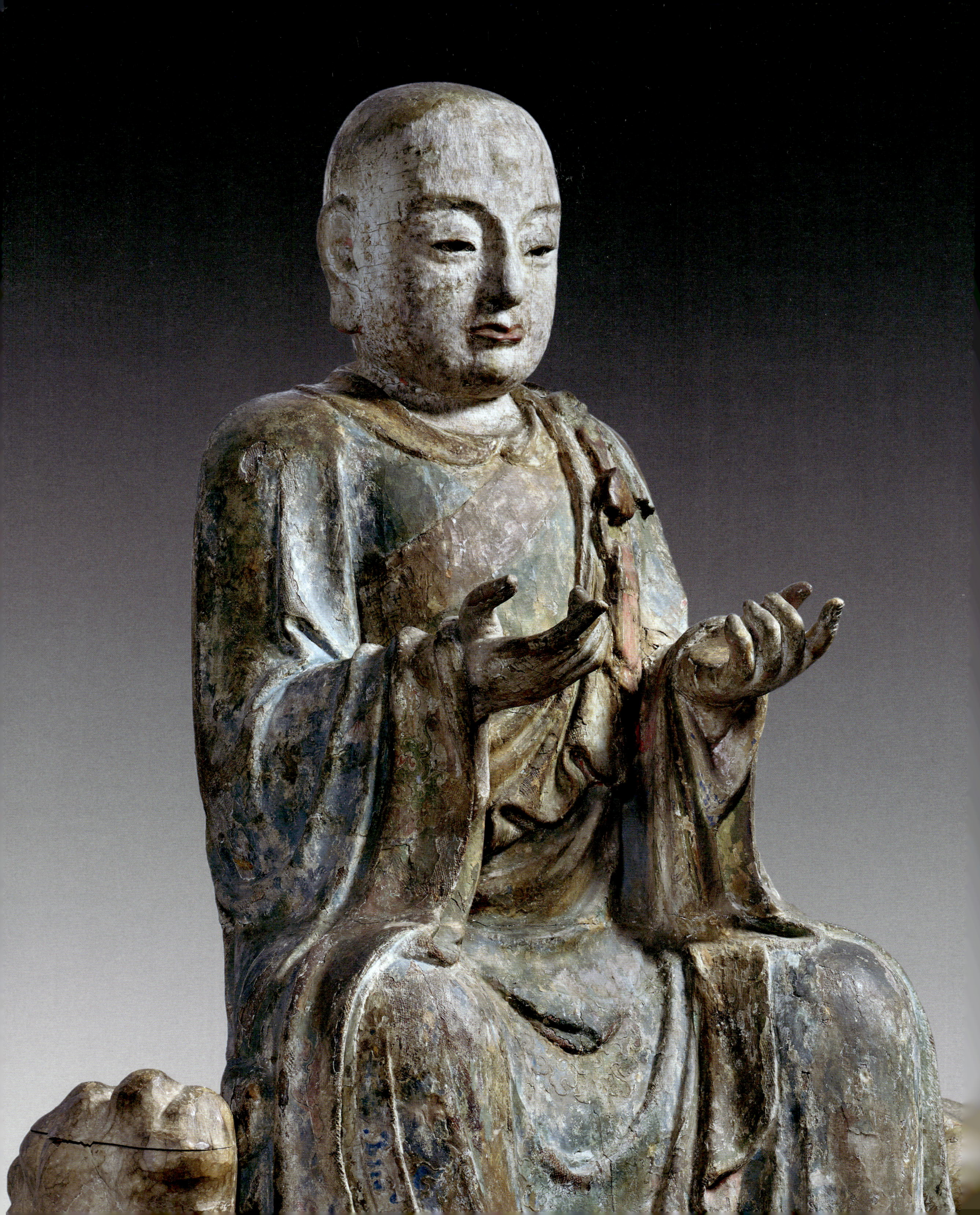

ART OF CHINA

Highlights from the Philadelphia Museum of Art

Edited by Hiromi Kinoshita

Essay by Hiromi Kinoshita
Contributions by Huang Xiaofeng, Hiromi Kinoshita,
Diandian Li, and John Vollmer

Philadelphia Museum of Art
in association with
Yale University Press, New Haven and London

Major support for this publication was provided by the E. Rhodes and Leona B. Carpenter Foundation, with additional funding from the Museum's endowment through The Gerry Lenfest Fund.

Produced by the Publishing Department
Philadelphia Museum of Art
Katie Reilly, The William T. Ranney Director of Publishing
2525 Pennsylvania Avenue
Philadelphia, PA 19130-2440 USA
philamuseum.org

Published in association with
Yale University Press
302 Temple Street
P.O. Box 209040
New Haven, CT 06520-9040
yalebooks.com/art

Edited by Kathleen Krattenmaker
Production by Richard Bonk
Photography by Philadelphia Museum of Art Photo Studio
Design by Rita Jules, Miko McGinty Inc.
Typesetting by Tina Henderson
Separations by Professional Graphics, Inc., Rockford, IL
Printed in Spain by Brizzolis, Madrid
Bound in Spain by Encuadernación Ramos, Madrid

Front cover: Insignia Badge for an Imperial Noble or Military Officer, late 17th–early 18th century (see no. 57)
Back cover: Panels from a Scholar's Study, late 18th century (see no. 88)
Frontispiece: Seated Luohan, 16th–17th century (see no. 51)

Library of Congress Cataloging-in-Publication Data

Names: Philadelphia Museum of Art, author. | Kinoshita, Hiromi, editor.
Title: Art of China : highlights from the Philadelphia Museum of Art / edited by Hiromi Kinoshita ; essay by Hiromi Kinoshita ; contributions by Huang Xiaofeng, Hiromi Kinoshita, Diandian Li, and John Vollmer.
Description: Philadelphia, PA : Philadelphia Museum of Art ; [New Haven, CT] : in association with Yale University Press, 2018. | Includes bibliographical references and index.
Identifiers: LCCN 2018031079 | ISBN 9780300237108 (hardback)
Subjects: LCSH: Art, Chinese—Catalogs. | Art—Pennsylvania—Philadelphia—Catalogs. | Philadelphia Museum of Art—Catalogs. | BISAC: ART / Asian. | ART / Collections, Catalogs, Exhibitions / Permanent Collections.
Classification: LCC N7342 .P38 2018 | DDC 700.951—dc23 LC record available at https://lccn.loc.gov/2018031079

Note to the Reader

Chinese and Japanese names are listed throughout with last name first, as is customary, except when those cited commonly use or used a Western name order. Dimensions are given in the order height by width by depth. For cylindrical or round objects, the two dimensions indicate height and diameter. The conventions for describing materials and techniques differ depending on the type of object. For instance, *color* is used to describe paint on silk, while *paint* or *painted decoration* is used for sculpture, furniture, and architecture. Materials were generally identified and are described by visual characteristics. In some cases, scientific analysis was done to further identify a material; for example, the inclusion of the scientific name in addition to the common name for a wood type indicates that microscopic wood identification was carried out. References cited in the object entries and the Documentation (pp. 244–51) are given in full under References, which are divided into exhibitions and their catalogues (pp. 252–54) and other types of publications (pp. 254–62).

Photography Credits

Photographs were supplied by the owners and/or the following:
Courtesy of Anhui Provincial Museum (reproduced from New York 2010–11, 288, fig. 351): fig. 35
© Ashmolean Library, Oxford University: fig. 43
Courtesy of Changzhou Museum (reproduced from Münster 2008, 106, pl. 15): fig. 31
© Freer Gallery of Art and Arthur M. Sackler Gallery, Smithsonian Institution, Washington, DC: figs. 48, 72, 74
Courtesy of Hubei Provincial Museum (reproduced from Liang 2007, vol. 2, col. pl. 21): fig. 36
The Metropolitan Museum of Art, New York: figs. 37, 52, 53, 71
© Minneapolis Institute of Art: fig. 73
© National Palace Museum, Taipei: figs. 44, 64
Courtesy of Osaka City Museum of Fine Arts, distributed under a CC-PD-Mark license: fig. 46
© Palace Museum, Beijing: figs. 32, 56, 57, 65, 69
© Shanghai Museum: fig. 66
Courtesy of Shanxi Institute of Archaeology (reproduced from Shanxi 2000, 11, fig. 5): fig. 26
Courtesy of Wenwu chubanshe (Wenwu Press), Beijing: figs. 25, 27, 28, 30, 33

Contents

FOREWORD

China has long been a source of fascination for the American people. On the far side of the world from our vantage point, China has been for much of our nation's history a place more imagined than known, and one about which we still are immensely curious.

Over time, this curiosity has manifested itself in a number of ways. It was the drive to open up new markets that led the Philadelphia merchant Robert Morris, one of the signers of the Declaration of Independence and the Constitution, to invest in the outfitting of the *Empress of China*, which in 1784 became the first American commercial vessel to sail to China. Another American merchant, Nathan Dunn, developed a passionate interest in Chinese art and material culture after arriving in 1818 in Canton (modern-day Guangzhou), the only Chinese port then open to foreign trade. In 1838, six years after returning to Philadelphia from a long sojourn abroad, Dunn opened the first museum in the United States devoted to this subject, publishing a catalogue of his extensive collection titled *Ten Thousand Chinese Things*. Later in the century, Philadelphians and visitors from all over the world were able to enjoy prominent displays of Chinese art and artifacts at the great Centennial Exposition of 1876.

It was an auspicious start. As Hiromi Kinoshita, our Hannah L. and J. Welles Henderson Associate Curator of Chinese Art, describes in detail in her essay for this catalogue, Philadelphia's avid and longstanding interest in China is perhaps best seen today in the Philadelphia Museum of Art's holdings of Chinese art. Taken as a whole, these are as varied as the tastes of the individuals whose benefactions helped form them. This important part of our collection also clearly reflects the expertise and diverse interests of the curators who oversaw its development, most prominently Langdon Warner, director of the Museum from 1917 to 1923, and Horace H. F. Jayne.

If the twentieth century was a time when museums were building their collections, then the twenty-first century will be the time for us to focus on their use. At the Philadelphia Museum of Art, much has been done over the past decade to reassess this area of our collection, to photograph all the objects and take advantage of new digital capabilities to provide access to them online, to review and improve our cataloguing records, and to renew the galleries where the collection is exhibited. This work was long overdue, and it is deeply gratifying to see it now come to fruition.

There has, likewise, long been a need for a publication like this, which presents highlights from a collection of Chinese art that numbers over seven thousand objects. It would not have been possible without the establishment of a new endowment, funded by trustee emerita Hannah L. Henderson and the former chair of our Board of Trustees, H. F. "Gerry" Lenfest, and his wife, Marguerite, which enabled us to add a new curatorial position in the field of Chinese art within our department of East Asian Art. Hiromi Kinoshita, the principal author of this book, joined the Museum in 2012 as the first to hold this permanently endowed position, bringing sustained attention to the collection, which has made an enormous difference. I am deeply grateful for the intelligence and energy she brought to this project as well as to the installation of our redesigned galleries of Chinese art, which are scheduled to be completed in early 2019.

I would also like to offer my deepest thanks to the many members of our East Asian Art Committee, a number of them long-serving trustees of this institution, for their support of this work, and to acknowledge with gratitude the funding we received from various individuals, foundations, and federal agencies to help with the documentation, care, and presentation of the collection. Without their assistance, the complex and interrelated activities that resulted in this publication would not have been possible.

Eight years ago, on the occasion of the late Gerry Lenfest's eightieth birthday, an endowment was established in his honor to fund a broad range of projects at the discretion of the director. When I asked him what he would like to see it used for first, Gerry replied without hesitation that we should publish—at long last—a catalogue of our collection of Chinese art. What he hoped for has now come to pass, and this publication is respectfully dedicated to his memory and all that he did to support the Philadelphia Museum of Art.

Timothy Rub
The George D. Widener Director and
Chief Executive Officer

ACKNOWLEDGMENTS

This book, the first in a series on highlights from the Philadelphia Museum of Art's collections, and written in conjunction with the renovation and reinstallation of the Chinese galleries, was made possible through the assistance and support of many individuals. My deepest thanks go to trustee emeritus H. F. "Gerry" Lenfest, who recognized the importance of further researching the Chinese collection and provided the means to accomplish this. It was through his unfailing interest and encouragement, as well as that of Timothy Rub, the Museum's George D. Widener Director and Chief Executive Officer, that this volume came to fruition.

Bringing to a broad audience a publication that aims to highlight the distinctive aspects of a collection scattered between various departments—including East Asian Art, South Asian Art, Contemporary Art, Costume and Textiles, European Decorative Art, American Art, and Prints, Drawings, and Photographs—could only be achieved through collective effort and cooperation, and I owe thanks to my associates throughout the Museum for their assistance and contributions to this project. Dilys Blum, Kristina Haugland, and Stephanie Pereira Feaster were generous with their time in coordinating access to the many costumes and textiles in their department for research and photography. I am particularly grateful to my colleagues in East Asian Art, especially Felice Fischer, and to our Conservation department for reviewing the text and the terminology used to describe the works included here. Nancy Ash, Sally Malenka, Melissa Meighan, Peggy Olley, Sara Reiter, and Behrooz Salimnejad also treated and conserved many of the Chinese pieces, along with Raina Chao and Kao Wei. Debra Breslin, Emily Brown, and Amanda Lepore beautifully conserved additional works, thanks to funding generously provided by the Women's Committee, in time for new photography. A picture is worth a thousand words: My appreciation goes to photographers Juan Arce, Joseph Hu, Lynn Rosenthal, Timothy Tiebout, Graydon Wood, and Michael Yoder for their patience and skill in capturing particular shots, and to Justyna Badach and Jessica Kwasniak for their coordinating efforts. Those who helped with researching the history of the collection and individual works include the indispensable Maxine Lewis, who delved into the history of the collector Mrs. Crozier and deciphered the handwriting in her diary; Susan Anderson Laquer, who assisted with locating archival materials, and Bertha Adams in Library and Archives; and interns and volunteers Yifan Zou, Lucy Yingxi Gong, and Mengnan Zhang. Thanks also go to the Museum's Marketing and Communications department and to Yale University Press for generating interest in the book.

Exchanges between colleagues in the wider scholarly community has been and continues to be a pleasurable and satisfying aspect of the field, and is especially welcome when researching such a diverse range of objects. I extend my gratitude to the following for kindly sharing their expertise, time, and thoughts and providing general support: Susan Beningson, Chen Yunru, Nicole Chiang, Dora Ching, Craig Clunas, Nicholas Grindley, Jessica Harrison-Hall, Jonathan Hay, Rose Kerr, Regina Krahl, James Lally, Peter Lam, Cary Liu, Colin Mackenzie, Carol Michaelson, Freda Murck, Susan Naquin, Katherine Paul, Pei Yajing, Jane Portal, Karolin Randhahn, Jessica Rawson, Joona Repo, David Sensabaugh, Hsueh-man Shen, Shih Ching-fei, Jenny So, Jan Stuart, Jason Sun, Susan Tai, Huei-chung Tsao, John Vollmer, Maggie Wan, Wang Le, Weng Yu-wen, Ming Wilson, Xu Xiaodong, Xu Zheng, Xue Jian, Yang Zhiguo, Josh Yiu, Yu Pei-chin, and Zhang Rong. Any errors or mistakes are my own, however, and feedback is welcome.

Wood analysis of works in the Museum's Chinese collection was carried out by Mechtild Mertz, Itoh Takao, Tazuru Suyako, and Sugiyama Junji; I much appreciate the expediting of their results for the works included in this volume (nos. 12, 26, 51). The J. S. Lee Memorial Fellowship Programme generously provided support to Huang Xiaofeng and Xu Zheng in 2014 so that they could research our Chinese paintings and sutra covers. Huang Xiaofeng, Diandian Li, and John Vollmer contributed interesting entries to this volume and were a pleasure to work with. Diandian Li also ably assisted in researching the collection and offered invaluable help throughout; I am grateful for her compilation of the documentation and the map, and for the clearing of image rights, along with editor Kathleen Krattenmaker, who worked tirelessly, asking great questions while coaxing the text and publication into shape. The idea for a highlights catalogue began with Sherry Babbitt, and thanks go to Sarah Noreika, Katie Reilly, and Richard Bonk in Publishing for carrying it forward. Rita Jules and Miko McGinty are responsible for the book's beautiful design.

Generous support for the publication came from the E. Rhodes and Leona B. Carpenter Foundation. Finally, I would especially like to thank the members of the East Asian Art Committee and the individuals who have given gifts of art and supported the Museum's Chinese collection all these years. It is through their generosity that the department, the Museum, and the Museum's many visitors have been and will continue to be inspired by a rich and thought-provoking collection.

Hiromi Kinoshita
The Hannah L. and J. Welles Henderson Associate
Curator of Chinese Art

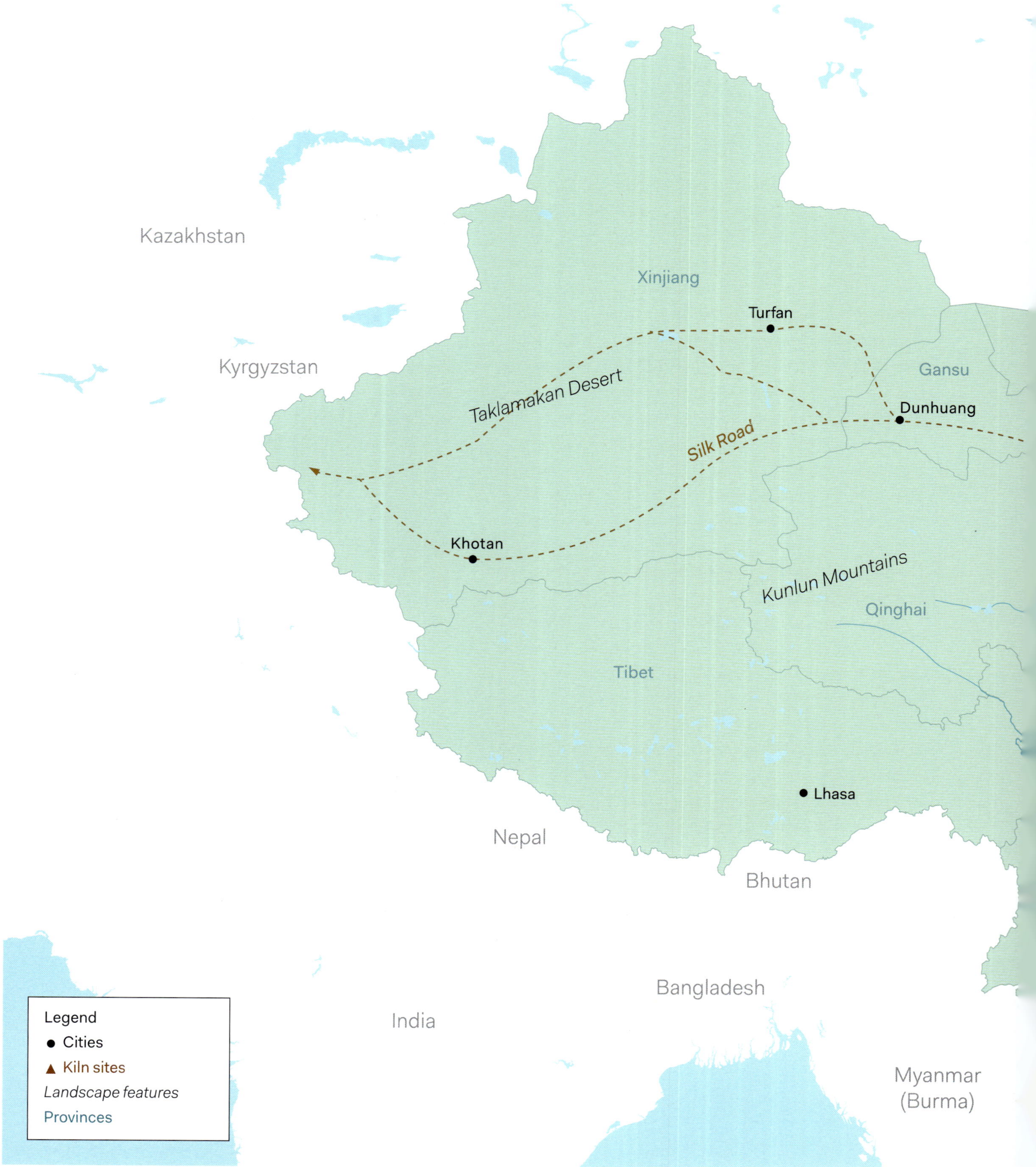
Kazakhstan
Xinjiang
Turfan
Kyrgyzstan
Gansu
Taklamakan Desert
Dunhuang
Silk Road
Khotan
Kunlun Mountains
Qinghai
Tibet
Lhasa
Nepal
Bhutan
Bangladesh
India
Myanmar (Burma)
Legend
Cities
Kiln sites
Landscape features
Provinces

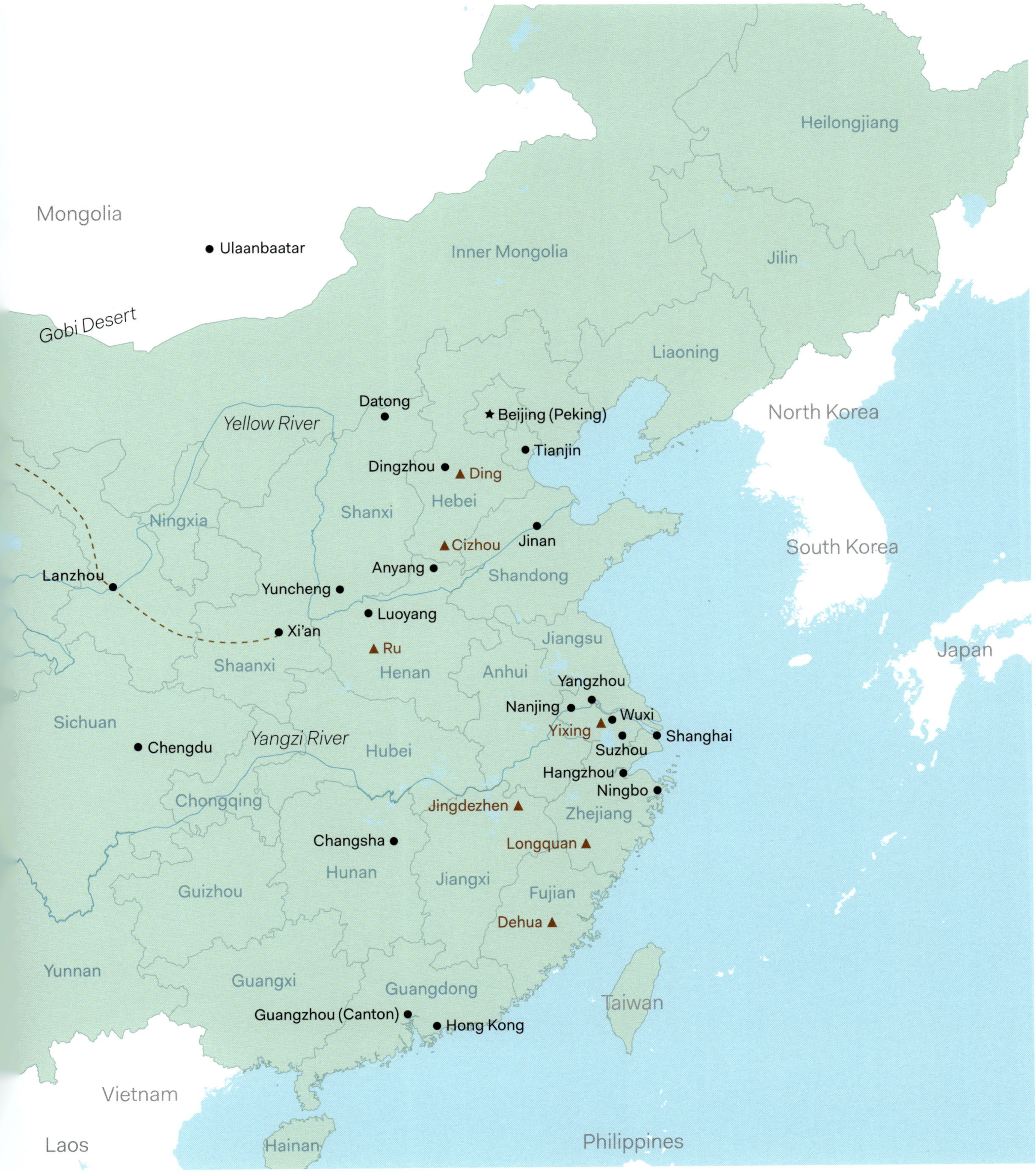

Mongolia
Ulaanbaatar
Gobi Desert
Inner Mongolia
Heilongjiang
Jilin
Liaoning
North Korea
South Korea
Japan
Datong
Beijing (Peking)
Tianjin
Yellow River
Dingzhou
Ding
Hebei
Shanxi
Ningxia
Cizhou
Jinan
Anyang
Shandong
Lanzhou
Yuncheng
Luoyang
Xi'an
Ru
Jiangsu
Shaanxi
Henan
Anhui
Yangzhou
Nanjing
Wuxi
Yixing
Shanghai
Suzhou
Sichuan
Chengdu
Yangzi River
Hubei
Hangzhou
Ningbo
Chongqing
Jingdezhen
Zhejiang
Changsha
Longquan
Hunan
Jiangxi
Guizhou
Fujian
Dehua
Yunnan
Guangxi
Guangdong
Taiwan
Guangzhou (Canton)
Hong Kong
Vietnam
Laos
Hainan
Philippines

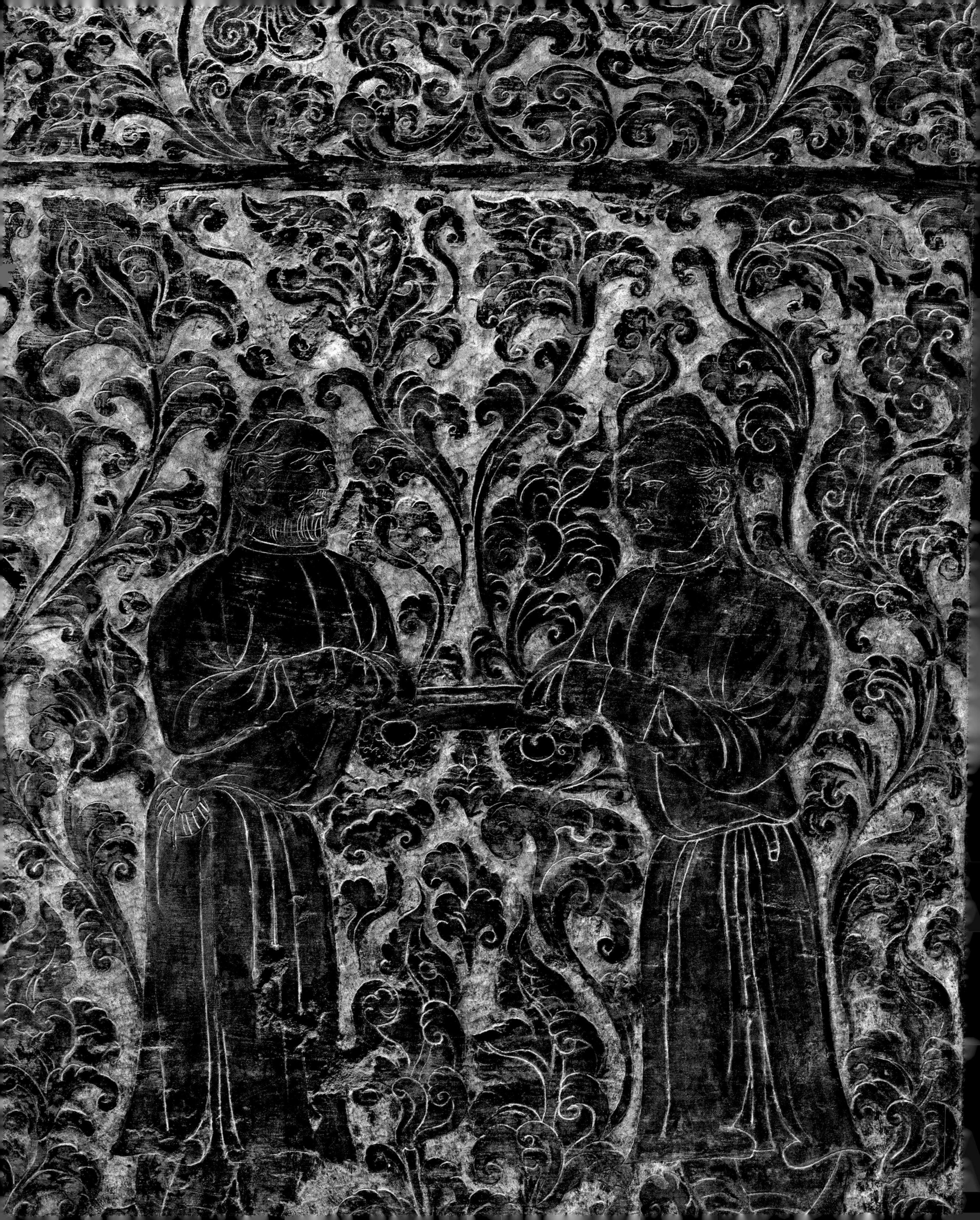

COLLECTING CHINA

AT THE PHILADELPHIA MUSEUM OF ART

Hiromi Kinoshita

Philadelphia, site of the Continental Congress and first capital of the United States, is not surprisingly a city of firsts. Among these was the Chinese Museum, established in 1838 by Nathan Dunn (1782–1844), a Quaker merchant involved in the China trade. Displaying some ten thousand Chinese cultural artifacts and works of art, the museum—also known as Ten Thousand Chinese Things—aimed to impress, entertain, and educate the American people during its brief run (in 1842 Dunn moved the collection to London).[1] Among public institutions, the Philadelphia Museum of Art was one of the first in the nation to begin systematically collecting art from China,[2] in the latter part of the nineteenth century (fig. 1). Originally called the Pennsylvania Museum and School of Industrial Art (renamed the Philadelphia Museum of Art in 1934), it was founded in 1876 to improve and promote the industrial arts in the state for both educational and economic purposes. The museum's core collection was acquired from the Centennial Exhibition, a world's fair held in Philadelphia in 1876 to celebrate one hundred years of American independence. Attracting more than ten million visitors over six months, the exhibition showcased the industrial and innovative prowess of the United States and included art for sale from around the world. A two-hundred-page catalogue with the lengthy title *Gems of the Centennial Exhibition: Consisting of Illustrated Descriptions of Objects of an Artistic Character, in the Exhibits of the United States, Great Britain, France, Spain, Italy, Germany, Belgium, Norway, Sweden, Denmark, Hungary, Russia, Japan, China, Egypt, Turkey, India, etc. etc.* was designed to entice private collectors in particular. China's successful exhibit garnered praise, as not only were China-trade materials such as lacquer, ivory, silk, and porcelain available for purchase, but cloisonné, bamboo, wood carvings, bronzes, silver, fans, paintings, and jades ranging from the modern to the antique were also for sale (fig. 2).[3] The appealing, "exotic," and novel objects captivated the American audience, resulting in the Pennsylvania Museum purchasing twenty pieces from Hu Kwang-yung (Hu Guangyong, 1825–1885),[4] a banker, merchant, and official whose notable clients included William and Henry Walters of Baltimore, founders of the Walters Art Museum. Included in the group were "Century furniture" (Canton blackwood) chairs, a pair of cloisonné vases, a wood screen by the renowned Chinese craftsman Sung Sing Kung from Ningbo, and an eighteenth-century enameled porcelain vase (fig. 3).[5] The latter depicts a historical event, the tour of the Grand Canal connecting Peking (modern-day Beijing) with Hangzhou after it was completed by the Sui emperor Yangdi (r. 604–17/18).[6] The representation was understood in China as a commentary on the excesses of rulership and power,

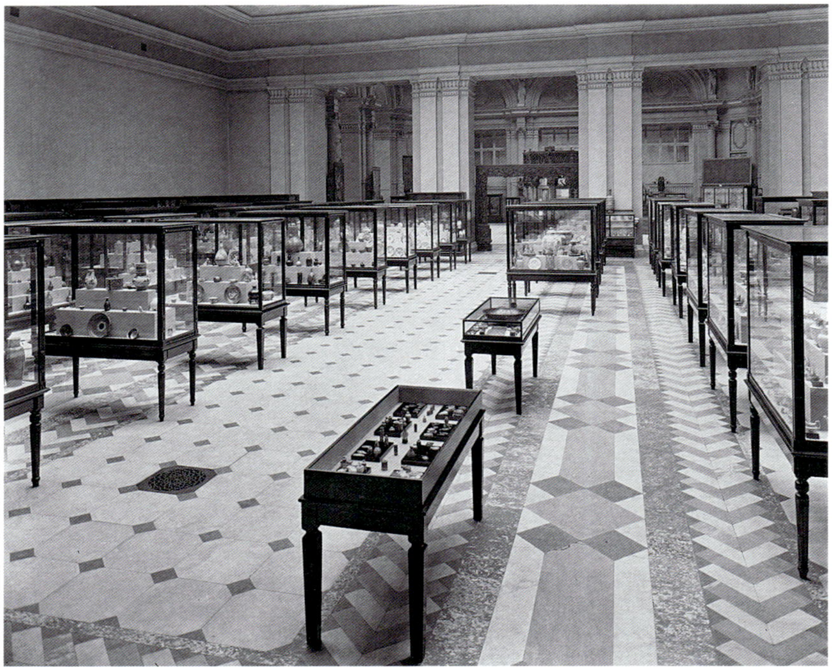

Fig. 1. The Ceramic Room, Memorial Hall, late 19th–early 20th century. Philadelphia Museum of Art, Library and Archives

Fig. 2. Side gateway of the Chinese exhibit, Centennial Exhibition, 1876. Centennial Photographic Company Collection. Print and Picture Collection, Free Library of Philadelphia

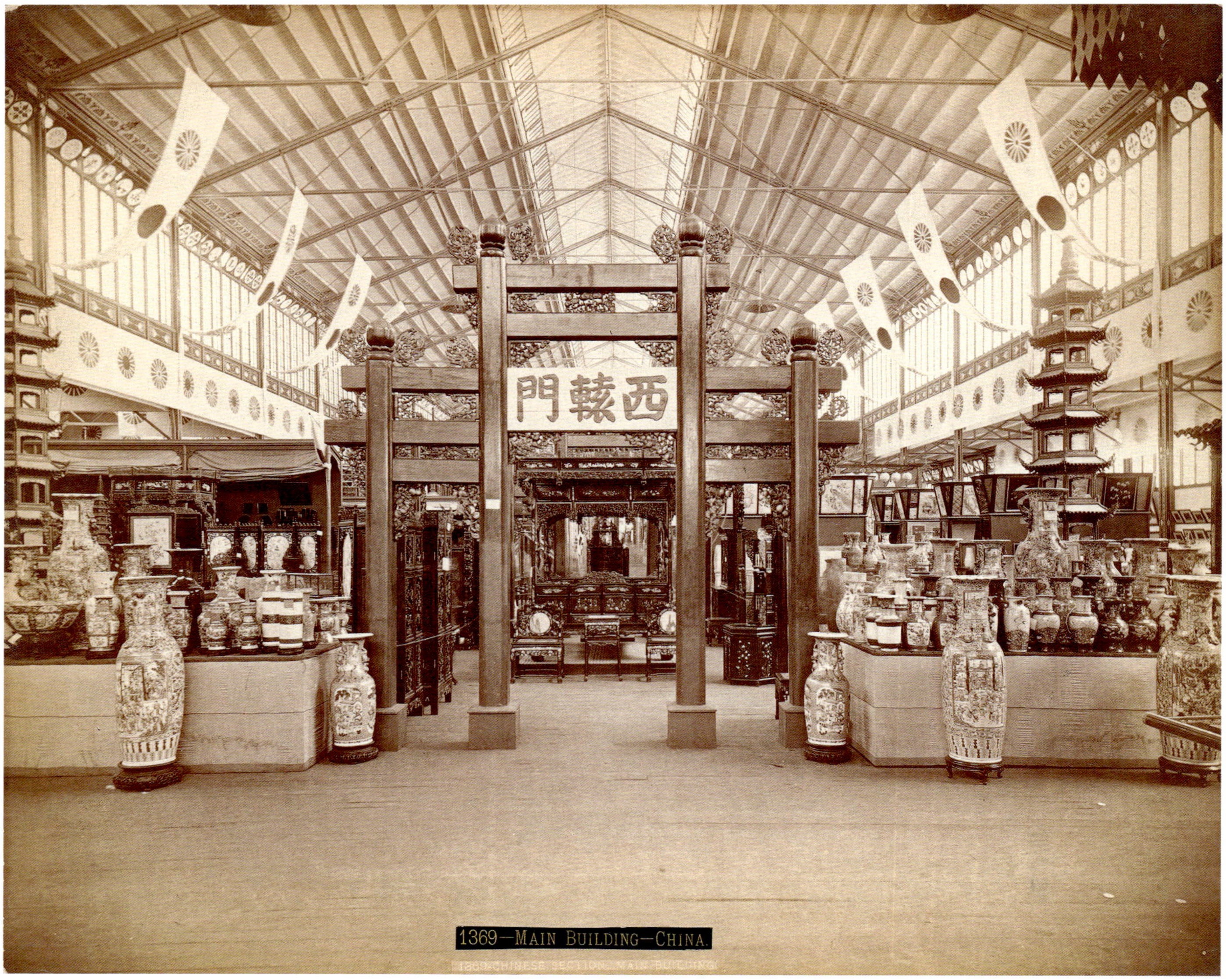

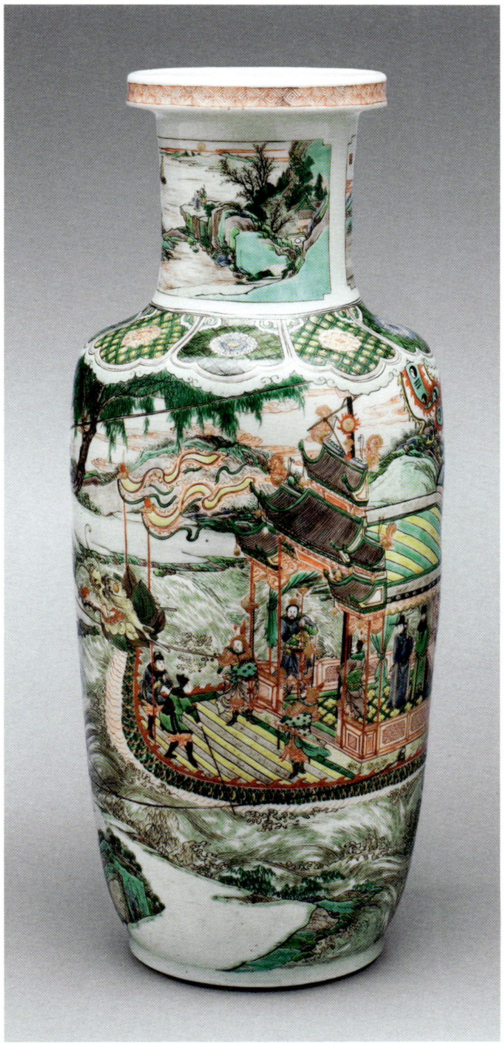

Fig. 3. Vase with the Sui Emperor Touring the Grand Canal. Qing dynasty (1644–1911), Kangxi period (1662–1722). Porcelain with overglaze enamel and gilded decoration, $17\frac{7}{8} \times 7\frac{5}{16}$ inches (45.4 x 18.5 cm). Philadelphia Museum of Art. Purchased with Museum funds, 1876-1486

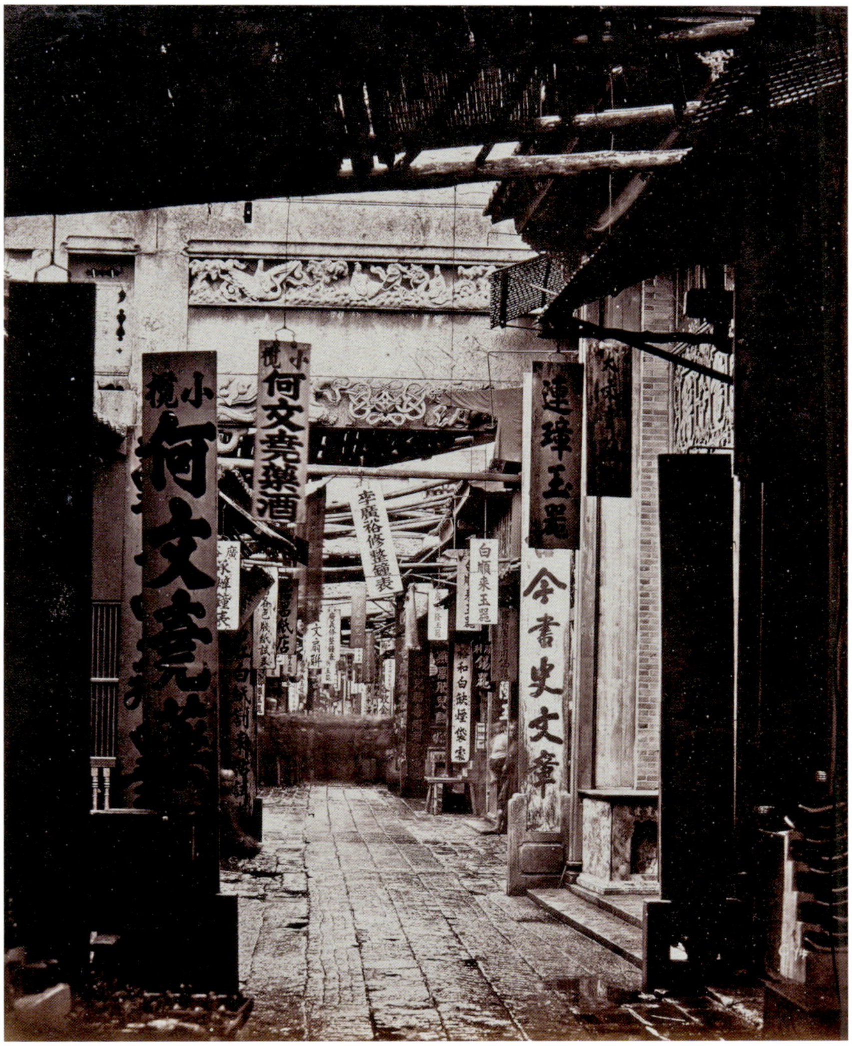

Fig. 4. Felice Beato (English, b. Italy, 1825–1909). *Treasury Street, Canton, April 1860*. Albumen silver print; image and sheet 12 x 10 inches (30.5 x 25.4 cm). Philadelphia Museum of Art. Purchased with funds contributed by Dr. Chaoying Fang, Harvey S. Shipley Miller and J. Randall Plummer, and with the Alice Newton Osborn Fund, 1978-148-1(69)

but this didactic message would have been lost on American viewers, who simply appreciated the colorful and detailed historical scene.

Over the next few decades the museum's Chinese collection expanded significantly, mainly through gifts from Philadelphians keen to support their local institution. At the end of the nineteenth and beginning of the twentieth century, well-off Philadelphians, like their European counterparts, were avidly collecting Chinese porcelains, furniture, and other objects to decorate their homes and lend an air of sophistication and cosmopolitanism.[7] Yet the collecting of Chinese art in the West was still in a nascent stage, since the works favored by Westerners for their aesthetic and technical achievement[8] did not reflect the taste of Chinese collectors, who preferred archaic bronzes, jades, and paintings of historical value.

Philadelphians' first direct contact with China came through trade at the end of the nineteenth century. But the type of art Americans were exposed to and were able to acquire was limited, as China was still closed to outsiders, with foreign traders only allowed into select port cities. One of these ports was Canton (modern-day Guangzhou; fig. 4), which had specialty shops that sold lacquer furniture, porcelains, oil and reverse glass paintings, ivory carvings (fig. 5), and brilliant watercolors

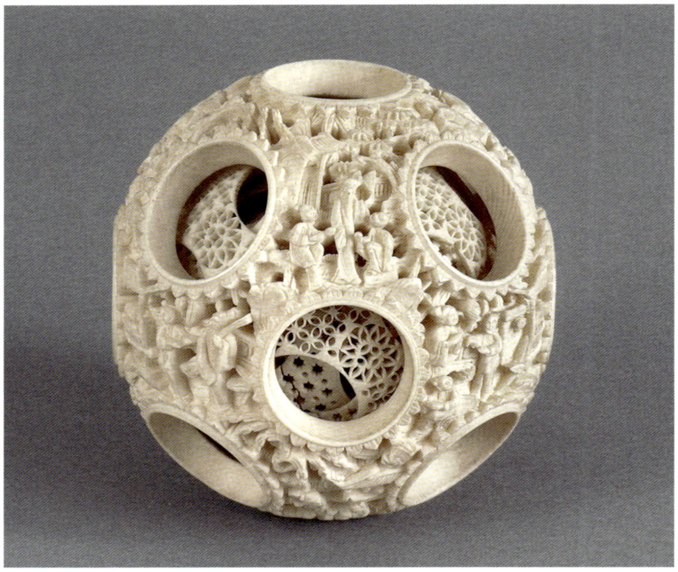

Fig. 5. Reticulated Ball. Qing dynasty (1644–1911), 19th century. Ivory, 3¾ inches (9.5 cm). Philadelphia Museum of Art. Bequest of Bartholomew Shea, 1914-164

that glowed on velvety pith paper (fig. 6).[9] Many of these works were made specifically to appeal to a Western audience with a fascination for the East and an appreciation of fine workmanship. A particularly accomplished example of such "export art" is the lacquered tilt-top table made for the Philadelphian John A. Lewis—whose father was involved in the China trade—while he was in East Asia around 1839 (see no. 94). An exceptional earlier example is a late eighteenth-century bookcase combining a Western form with Chinese decorative motifs (see no. 86) that once belonged to a Dutch-American trader, Andreas Everardus van Braam Houckgeest, who made his fortune in Canton working for the East India Trading Company and distinguished himself as the first American to meet the emperor of China, in 1795.

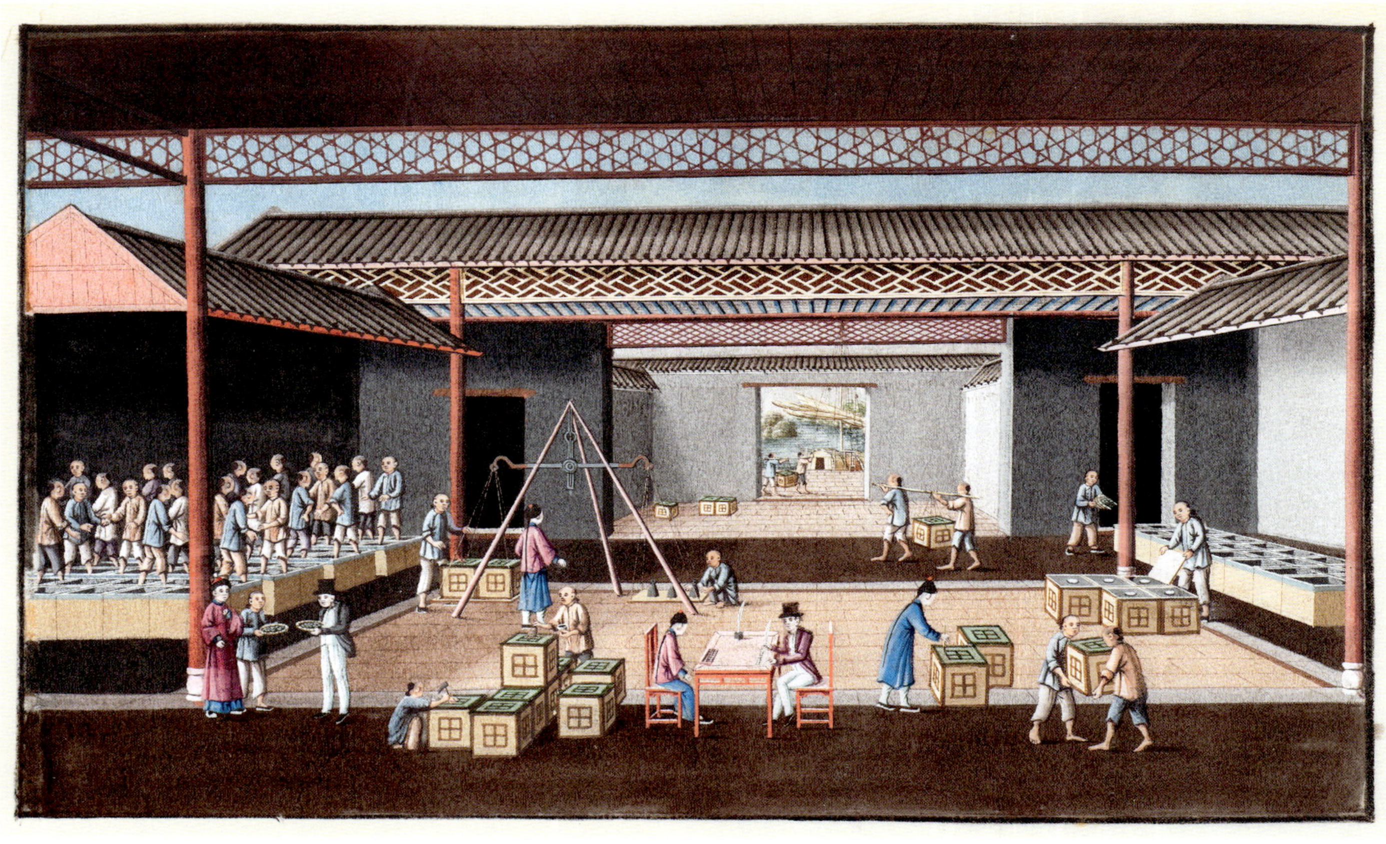

Fig. 6. Sun Qua (Chinese, act. 1830–70). *Book of Watercolors: Tea Cultivation*. Qing dynasty (1644–1911), c. 1843. Watercolor on pith paper, 6⅞ x 10½ inches (17.5 x 26.7 cm). Philadelphia Museum of Art. John G. Johnson Collection, 1917, inv. 174b

Beginnings, 1877–1910

Westerners became interested in Chinese porcelains early on, attracted by their superior quality, a result of both the local white clay and China's long tradition of firing ceramics. So it is no surprise that ceramics and porcelains make up the lion's share of the Philadelphia Museum of Art's Chinese collection and are one of its particular strengths. Among the earliest groups of porcelains to come to the museum were the hundred and fifty pieces donated in 1893 by Dr. Francis West Lewis (1852–1902), founder of the Children's Hospital of Philadelphia, America's first pediatric hospital. At the time, his gift was described as "one of the most important collections of the kind in this country."[10] The delicate, intricate openwork carving on a covered bowl in the collection (fig. 7) would have impressed nineteenth-century Americans, just as a similar bowl had earlier captured the attention of Father François Xavier d'Entrecolles (1664–1741), a French Jesuit missionary who traveled to China at the turn of the eighteenth century to discover the secret of Chinese porcelain manufacturing, already so admired in Europe; d'Entrecolles described the bowl as "full of Holes, as if it was pink'd [pierced]; in the middle is a Cup proper to contain Liquor, which is joined to that Part which is pink'd."[11] Dr. Lewis also collected Chinese cloisonné enamels, Western-influenced creations that gained popularity first in England and Europe and then in the United States thanks to their promotion at the Centennial Exhibition in Philadelphia.[12] Some of the museum's best cloisonné pieces, which range from a late Ming-dynasty basin (fig. 8) to Qing-dynasty objects bearing imperial marks from the reign of the Qianlong emperor (see no. 80), were donated by Lewis's sister, Mary Lewis.

A statement by the museum's then-director, Edward Atlee Barber (1907–16), in the *Bulletin of the Pennsylvania Museum* in 1909 conveys the direction of the institution's Chinese collecting in these early years:

> The Museum possesses several collections of Chinese porcelains which are exhibited in two rooms—the general collection, including the bequests of Dr. Francis W. Lewis, Edward S. Clarke and Miss Cornelia Thompson, with numerous rare pieces obtained from the Chinese Commission at the Centennial Exhibition, which are

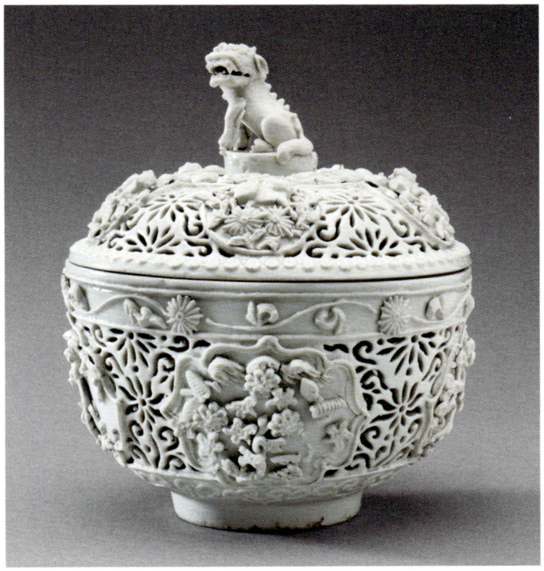

Fig. 7. Covered Bowl. Ming dynasty (1368–1644), early 17th century. Porcelain (Jingdezhen ware), 5 3/16 x 4 9/16 inches (13.2 x 11.6 cm). Philadelphia Museum of Art. Bequest of Dr. Francis W. Lewis, 1902-793a

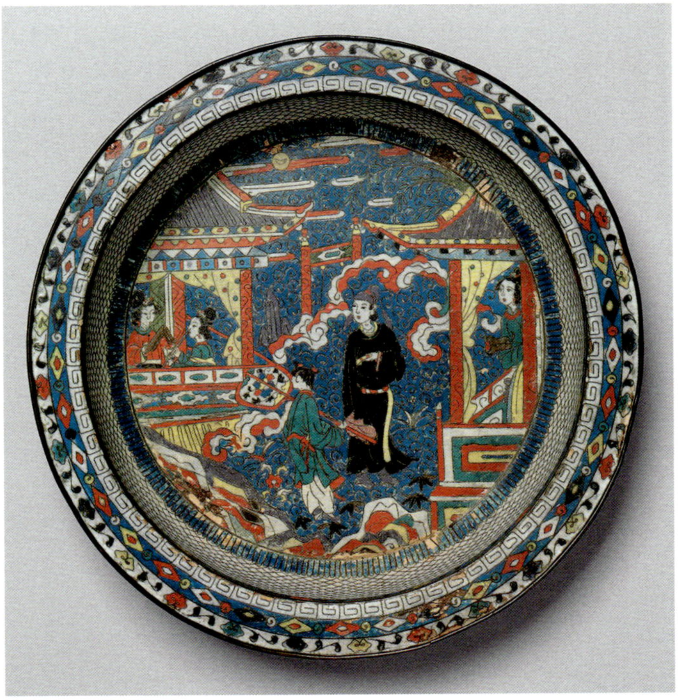

Fig. 8. Basin with Figural Scene. Ming dynasty (1368–1644), Wanli period (1573–1620). Cloisonné on copper, 2 3/8 x 14 1/4 inches (6 x 36.2 cm). Philadelphia Museum of Art. Bequest of Miss Mary Lewis, 1909-17

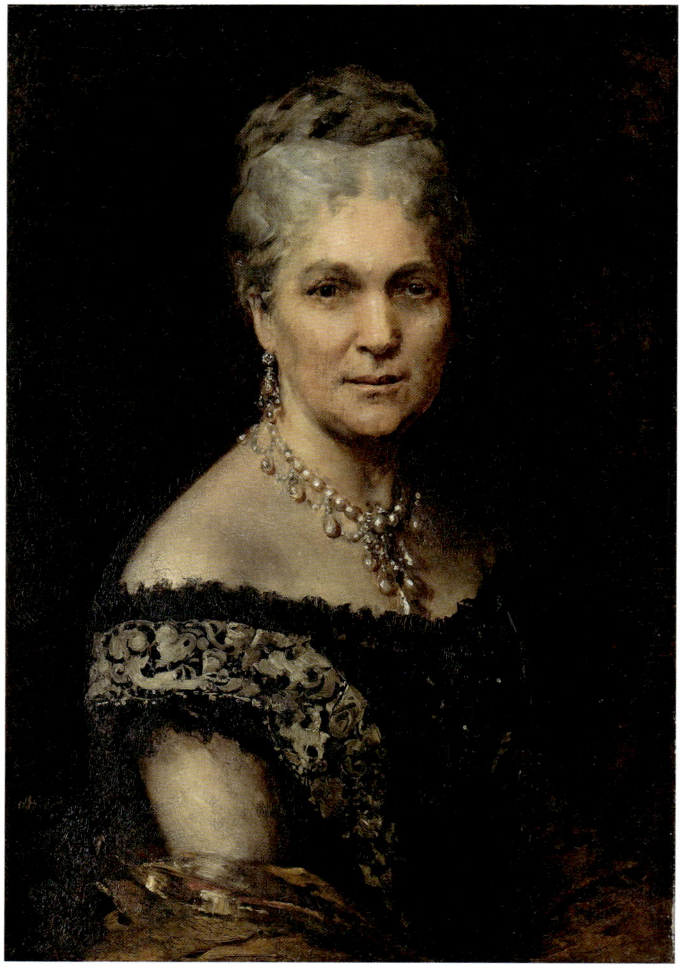

Fig. 9. Adolphe Weisz (French, b. Hungary, 1819–1878). *Portrait of Mrs. Bloomfield Moore*, 1877. Oil on canvas, 29 x 20¾ inches (73.7 x 52.7 cm). Philadelphia Museum of Art. The Bloomfield Moore Collection, 1899-1099

> arranged in the Southeast Pavilion, and the Bloomfield Moore collection, which is installed in the Northeast Pavilion. . . . The collections, taken in their entirety, are entitled to rank with the best public collections of Chinese porcelains in this country.[13]

The Bloomfield Moore collection cited by Barber consists of more than three hundred Chinese porcelains, donated to the museum in 1882 by Clara Jessup Bloomfield Moore (1824–1899; fig. 9) in memory of her late husband, Bloomfield H. Moore. Clara was the daughter of the distinguished scientist Augustus Edward Jessup, for many years an active member of the Academy of Natural Sciences in Philadelphia, as well as a participant in the Yellowstone Expedition, sent to explore the territory at the mouth of the Yellowstone River in 1819–20. Bloomfield Moore worked with his father-in-law to establish Jessup & Moore, a successful paper-manufacturing business that his wife later inherited. Clara was herself a prolific writer, publishing books on topics such as marriage, divorce, self-improvement, and university education for women. She spent her last years in London but bequeathed her estate to public scientific and art institutions in Philadelphia.[14] Many of the porcelains in the Bloomfield Moore collection are export wares, but a fair number of examples bear imperial marks, indicating that they were made for the Ming (1368–1644) and Qing (1644–1911) courts and thus reflect Chinese taste (see nos. 42, 43, 79).

Not mentioned in Barber's statement is Lydia Thompson Morris (1849–1932), a later benefactor whose Quaker roots had instilled in her a sense of community, charity, and stewardship. She gave the museum more than a thousand pieces of Chinese porcelain and donated her and her brother's summer home and garden to the University of Pennsylvania in Philadelphia (it is now the Morris Arboretum). While the majority of the porcelains from her collection are export pieces, outstanding examples made for imperial use include a Kangxi enameled porcelain bowl with incised dragon decoration (see no. 61), an enameled dragon and phoenix dish (fig. 10), and a Yongzheng bowl beautifully decorated in the *doucai* (contrasting) palette of underglaze blue outline filled in with brilliant enameling on a clear glaze that feels unctuous to the touch (see no. 72).

Systematic Collecting: The First Half of the Twentieth Century

In 1917 Langdon Warner (1881–1955) became director of the Pennsylvania Museum and soon afterward established a division of Eastern art (later renamed Far Eastern art), marking the museum's entry into more serious and systematic collecting of Chinese art.[15] Warner's success in acquiring art from Asia is lauded in Japan for helping to promote Japanese art throughout the world, but his endeavor "to arouse [China] to a sense of the grandeur of her own Buddhist antiquities and to aid her in saving them from neglect, theft, and oblivion" has made him a controversial figure in China today.[16] In the West he is generally recognized for his role as one of Monuments

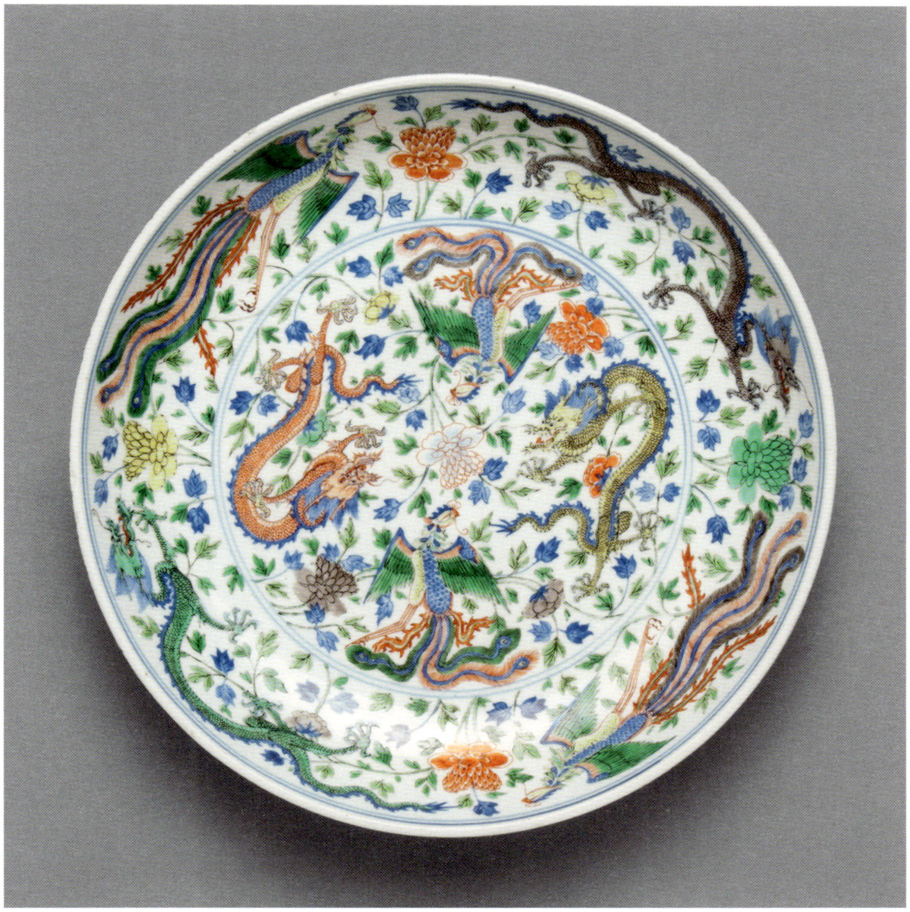

Fig. 10. Dish with Imperial Dragons, Phoenixes, and Peonies. Qing dynasty (1644–1911), Kangxi mark and period (1662–1722). Porcelain, underglaze blue and enamel (*wucai*) decoration (Jingdezhen ware); 2 7/16 x 12 3/4 inches (6.2 x 32.4 cm). Philadelphia Museum of Art. Bequest of Lydia Thompson Morris, 1932-45-20

Men, the more than three hundred curators, art historians, artists, architects, archivists, and educators tasked with protecting the cultural heritage of Europe during World War II, a duty that included locating stolen or missing works of art. Away from the museum for long stretches searching for Asian art treasures, the charismatic Warner is said to have inspired the intrepid film character Indiana Jones (fig. 11).[17] The Harvard-trained Warner had associations with many notable American cultural institutions, including the Freer Gallery of Art in Washington, DC, the Fogg Museum of Harvard University in Cambridge, Massachusetts, and the Nelson-Atkins Museum of Art in Kansas City, Missouri.[18] He was largely self-taught in the field of Asian art and archaeology, having gained his experience first by serving as associate curator of Asiatic art at the Museum of Fine Arts, Boston (1906–13), and then by helping the Smithsonian Institution

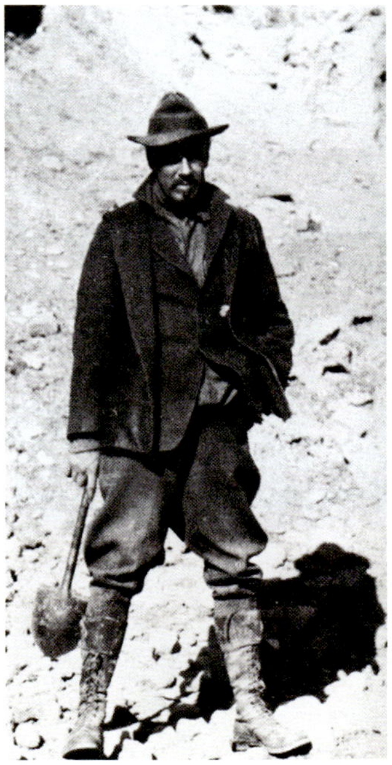

Fig. 11. Langdon Warner at Khara Khoto, Central Asia, 1923. Courtesy of the Monuments Men Foundation and the Warner Family

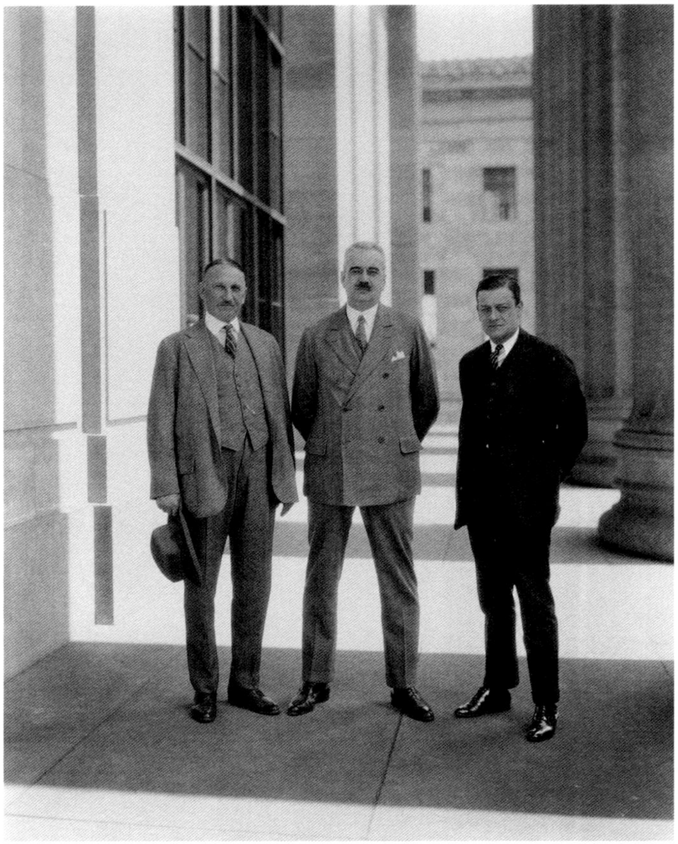

Fig. 12. J. Stogdell Stokes, Fiske Kimball, and Horace H. F. Jayne outside the east entrance of the Philadelphia Museum of Art building, still under construction, June 4, 1929. Philadelphia Museum of Art, Library and Archives

establish the American School of Archaeology in Peking.[19] During Warner's tenure as director of the Pennsylvania Museum, which lasted until 1923, significant examples of Chinese sculpture, architectural interiors, and archaeological objects were added to the collection. Warner also laid the foundation for the "period-room" idea that his successor, Fiske Kimball (1888–1955), built upon, introducing an installation technique that would become a defining feature of the Philadelphia Museum of Art experience.[20]

During his extensive travels in Asia, Warner's broad connections proved valuable in locating and acquiring important works for the museum. Through his acquaintance with George Crofts—an English fur merchant and antiquities dealer with offices in Tianjin, Peking, and London who was purchasing Chinese objects for the Royal Ontario Museum in Toronto—Warner was able to acquire ceramics and tomb sculptures from the Han (206 BCE–220 CE) through Tang (618–907) dynasties, now one of the strengths of the collection.[21] After an initial discussion with Crofts, in which he cited the mutual benefits of having a "first class collection in the United States that would supplement and emphasize the Toronto collection,"[22] Warner asked Charles T. Currelly (1876–1957), then director of the Royal Ontario Museum, about buying part of Crofts's collection for the Pennsylvania Museum.[23] It is no coincidence that the early tomb figures at the Philadelphia Museum of Art and the Royal Ontario Museum are similar in many ways (see nos. 6–8). A number of them reportedly came from Mangshan in Luoyang, Henan province, where they were excavated during the construction of railroads.

In 1923, with the financial support of board member Charles H. Ludington, the museum was also able to purchase 355 pieces of pottery, porcelain, and wood and stone sculpture with Crofts's assistance.[24] The choice to focus on early ceramic sculpture and vessels was strategic. Warner was initially interested in acquiring fine stone sculpture, but Crofts advised that funds would be better spent "building up a general collection of things Chinese that would not clash with the University [of Pennsylvania] Museum and in this way both Museums would be distinct yet at the same time have something in common."[25]

Warner also brought to the museum one of his Harvard students, a young Philadelphian by the name of Horace H. F. Jayne, nephew of the renowned Philadelphia architect Frank Furness (fig. 12). Jayne would serve as curator of Oriental art from 1921 to 1940,[26] seminal years for the Chinese collection, as a new museum building was being constructed on top of an old reservoir in the Fairmount neighborhood,[27] creating a vast new space that needed to be filled. After taking up his position at the museum, Jayne accompanied Warner on two expeditions to China and Central Asia with Harvard's Fogg Museum in 1923 and 1924.[28] He would later donate to the Pennsylvania Museum 175 rubbings acquired from the Forest of Stelae (Beilin Museum) in Xi'an, which he and Warner visited on their way to see Buddhist reliefs at the Dunhuang and Yungang cave temples.[29] A red clay head of a divinity that Jayne also gave to the museum, said to be from Turfan,

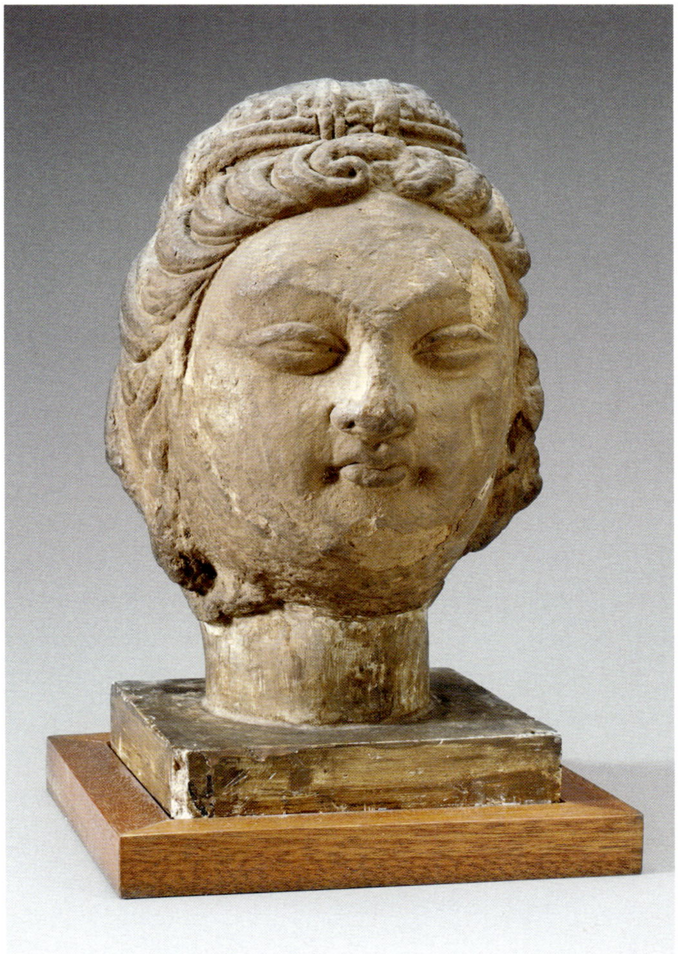

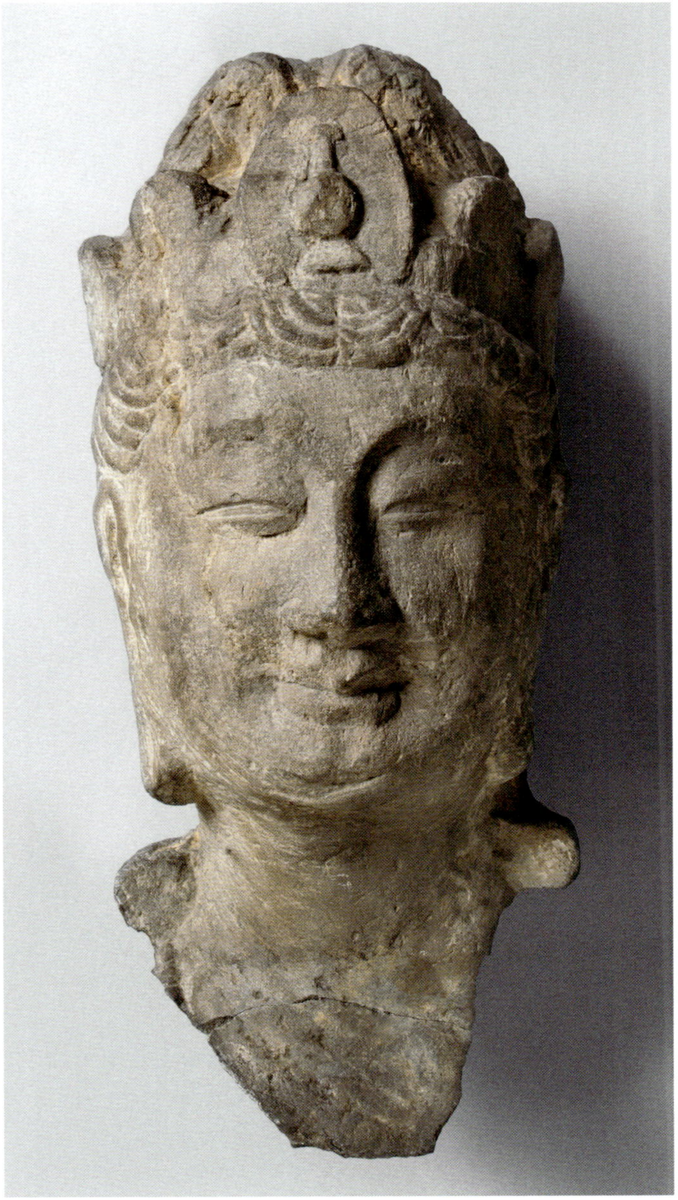

Fig. 13. Head of a Divinity (Tianshen) from Turfan, Xinjiang. Tang dynasty (618–907), 7th century. Stucco, 8¼ x 5½ x 6 inches (21 x 14 x 15.2 cm). Philadelphia Museum of Art. Gift of Horace H. F. Jayne, 1928-23-1

Fig. 14. Head of a Bodhisattva. Northern Wei dynasty (386–534), early 6th century. Gray limestone, 10¼ x 5 x 4½ inches (26 x 12.7 x 11.4 cm). Philadelphia Museum of Art. Purchased with Museum and Subscription funds, 1927-50-15

one of the cities along the Silk Road, was probably collected on the same journey (fig. 13). According to Fiske Kimball, who became the museum's director in 1925, Jayne was "of the greatest alertness and intelligence, of fine taste, personally amusing and delightful, with a charming irresponsibility which did not prevent him from getting results."[30] Jayne's archaeological training and his relationship with Warner would influence his own taste in Chinese art and shape the Philadelphia collection, with sculpture and architectural interiors being added in these years.

In 1927 Jayne acquired for the museum thirty-three works from the personal collection of one of the early Western scholars of Chinese sculpture and painting, Dr. Osvald Sirén (1879–1966), an art historian of Finnish descent who had trained in Italian art but later focused on Asian art. Among the objects in this group were a Northern Qi dynasty (550–77) white marble sculpture from Dingzhou in Hebei (see no. 3) and fragments from the cave temples of Longmen in Henan (fig. 14) and Tianlongshan in Shanxi. After his first trip to Asia in 1918, Sirén made multiple visits in the 1920s and 1930s to

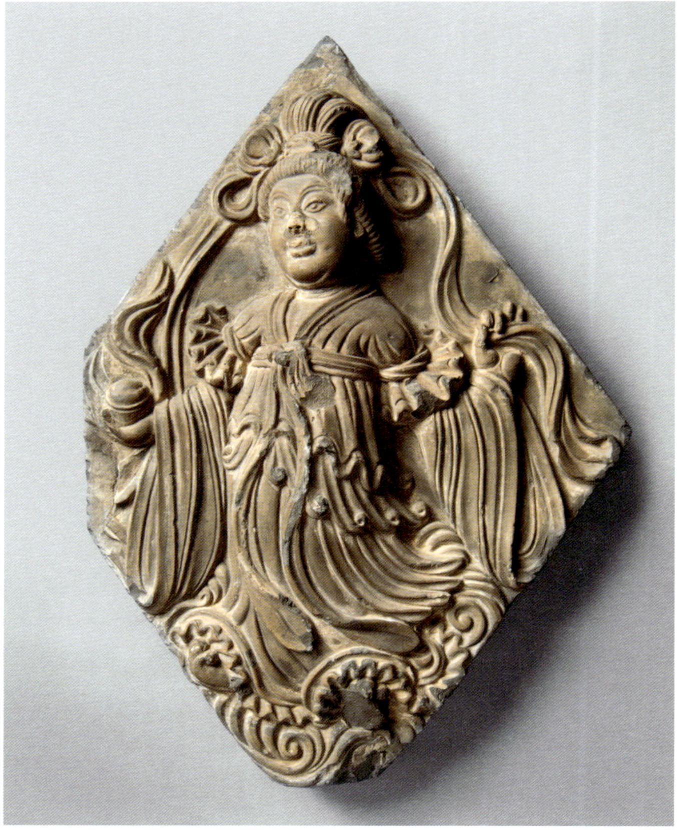

Fig. 15. Architectural Tile from Xiudingsi Pagoda, Anyang, Henan. Tang dynasty (618–907), 7th century. Earthenware, 24⅜ x 17⁵⁄₁₆ x 4½ inches (61.9 x 44 x 11.4 cm). Philadelphia Museum of Art. Gift of C. T. Loo, 1921-13-1

photograph and purchase works of art. In 1925, after studying the cave temples at Yungang and Longmen, he published *Chinese Sculpture from the Fifth to the Fourteenth Century*, illustrated with examples from his own collection. Sirén returned to Sweden in 1926 and sold most of his Chinese collection, including jades, bronzes, and ceramics, to the newly established Museum of Far Eastern Antiquities (Östasiatiska Samlingarna) in Stockholm,[31] and his personal collection of Chinese sculpture, described by the *Philadelphia Inquirer* as "the finest examples of early sculpture in marble ever brought out of China,"[32] to the Pennsylvania Museum.[33] Funds for the purchase were provided by John Story Jenks, a long-standing trustee who, with his wife, would later contribute to the museum's collection of Ming-dynasty blue-and-white porcelain through a gift of twenty examples (see no. 39), many of them acquired from the collector and dealer A. W. Bahr (1877–1959).[34] The museum's Chinese furniture collection also benefited from Jenks's largesse, through the gift of a pair of *zitan* hardwood stools carved with openwork designs of boys at play in a garden (see no. 87). The stools were once in the imperial collection of the Forbidden City, according to notes by Jenks, who first saw and admired them in Peking in 1930 at the home of a wealthy Manchu gentleman, who had collected them when "the Imperial Palace furniture was being disposed of in the early days of the Republic." Later that year, Jenks spotted the stools with the Japanese dealer Yamanaka in New York and acquired them for the museum.[35]

Adding to a growing collection of Buddhist sculpture, Jayne also purchased three Tang-dynasty architectural tiles from the Xiudingsi pagoda in Anyang (see no. 5), building on an earlier donation of a tile from the same site by the dealer C. T. Loo (fig. 15). These tiles remained in storage and for decades and were neither photographed nor displayed, perhaps because they needed conservation or because identification was difficult (the departmental cataloguing cards initially dated them to the thirteenth century). It was not until 1961, when the Xiudingsi pagoda and its unique decorative tiles were "rediscovered" by the Henan Cultural Relics Bureau, that the tiles were properly identified as seventh-century works.[36]

Jayne's foremost finds were three Chinese architectural interiors, all purchased in the late 1920s, that are today among the Philadelphia Museum of Art's most remarkable treasures. These acquisitions were the result of the vision of then-director Fiske Kimball (1925–55; see fig. 12), an architectural historian who saw value in presenting objects in their proper contexts. In 1927 and 1928, under his instructions, Jayne traveled to Peking, where he purchased an early Ming coffered ceiling from the Zhihua Temple (see no. 34),[37] a late Ming reception hall (no. 56), and a Qing-dynasty scholar's study with latticework and lacquered paneling (no. 88). After the dissembled architectural pieces arrived in Philadelphia, they lay in storage until they could gradually be integrated into the new museum building as it was completed. The reception hall was the first to be installed, in 1937,[38] when the museum was able to fund the work with help from the Works Progress Administration (WPA), a federal work-relief program introduced during the Depression (fig. 16). Assembling the different elements called for some improvisation; a descendent of one of the WPA

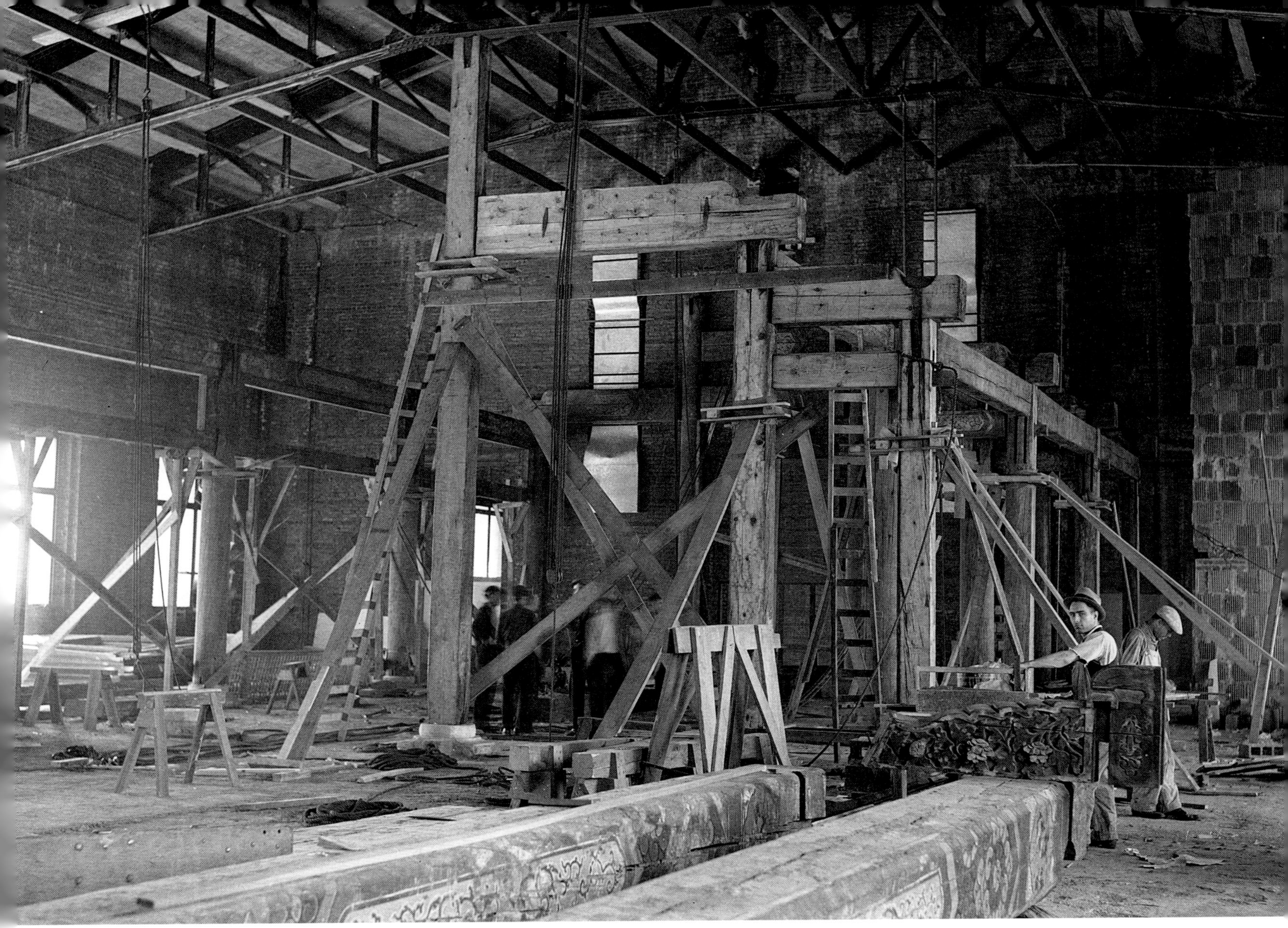

Fig. 16. Works Progress Administration (WPA) workers installing the Chinese Reception Hall interior in the Philadelphia Museum of Art, July 27, 1937. Philadelphia Museum of Art, Library and Archives

workers recounts that her father "had his Chinese laundryman interpret the Chinese symbols in fitting the pieces together."[39]

The reception hall is the only example of its type outside China. Believed to have belonged to the eunuch Wang Cheng'en, who served the last Ming emperor, Chongzhen (r. 1628–44), it was also the home of various noble families, including a grandson of the Kangxi emperor. Its soaring ceilings and the beautifully painted bracketing are indicative of the high status of the owners, as is its size, with its five-bay width conforming to the prescribed dimensions of an official's residence.[40]

The excitement around Jayne's purchases sparked the museum's ambition to develop one of the most important Chinese collections in the country, as recorded in the minutes of the Museum Committee of 1928:

> Following the mediaeval department will probably come the installation of the Oriental wing, wherein the museum's opportunity for a distinct advance over other Oriental departments in American museums is unique. Through a generous contribution from Mr. Joseph Wasserman and a pledge from Mr. Wright S. Ludington, two interiors for the Chinese section are assured. It has never before been attempted in this country or abroad to set up suitable interiors of this character which reproduce for the Oriental collections the period-style installation already achieved in the English and American wing.[41]

While Jayne was tasked with locating prime examples of architecture and works of art in China, it took the deep pockets of civic-minded businessmen such as Joseph Wasserman of the Art Loom Company, Charles H. Ludington of Curtis Publishing, and his son, Wright S. Ludington, to acquire these spectacular finds—through the provision of funds for the temple ceiling, the Crofts collection, and the scholar's study, respectively. Another generous supporter, Edward B. Robinette, funded the acquisition of the reception hall, and in 1929 also put up money for the purchase of 330 Chinese paintings from the collection of Vladimir G. Simkhovitch (1874–1959), intended to be installed in the hall. A native of Russia, Simkhovitch was a distinguished professor of economic history at Columbia University in New York, but also a collector and trader in ancient art from all cultures.[42] Simkhovitch likely purchased his Chinese paintings—which he attributed to the Tang through Qing dynasties—mainly in New York from such well-known dealers as the American Art Association, John Fergusson, Knoedler & Company, C. T. Loo, and Yamanaka & Company.[43]

The competitiveness of American museums racing to assemble the best Chinese collection in the country comes through palpably in an account published in the *Boston Messenger* on August 10, 1929: "Remarkable Gift of 300 Paintings and Chinese Palace Hall to Pennsylvania Museum. . . . Boston Collection Out-Done. . . . With this combined gift . . . the Pennsylvania Museum not only acquires a group of pictures . . . , but it acquires the unique opportunity of showing these paintings for the first time in such a setting as they were designed to be shown in." The collection was described, somewhat overly optimistically, as "all of extraordinarily high artistic quality, which neither needs weeding nor strengthening,"[44] though after careful review it can be said to include some fine Song and Yuan album leaves (see nos. 19–22) and Qing-dynasty paintings (nos. 58, 74).

The force behind these acquisitions would soon move across the Schuylkill to the University of Pennsylvania, where Jayne took up the position of director of the Museum of Archaeology and Anthropology from late 1929 to 1940/41, when he left to become vice director of the Metropolitan Museum of Art in New York (he continued in the role of curator of Asian art at the newly renamed Philadelphia Museum of Art through 1940). From 1935 to 1947, Carl Schuster (1904–1969), a Harvard-trained art historian and gifted Chinese linguist, held the honorary position of assistant curator of Chinese art at the Philadelphia Museum of Art.[45] Schuster traveled to China in 1935 for an eventual stay of three years, making several collecting trips to the southwestern part of the country while studying symbolism in folk art.[46] The majority of the regional textiles he collected are in the Field Museum of Natural History in Chicago, but in 1940 the Philadelphia Museum of Art purchased nearly eight hundred textiles from his collection, including court robes, rank badges (see no. 57), and a group of five hundred rare sutra covers that provide important information on textile production in the Ming dynasty (fig. 17).[47] Today the museum's Chinese collection includes more than two thousand

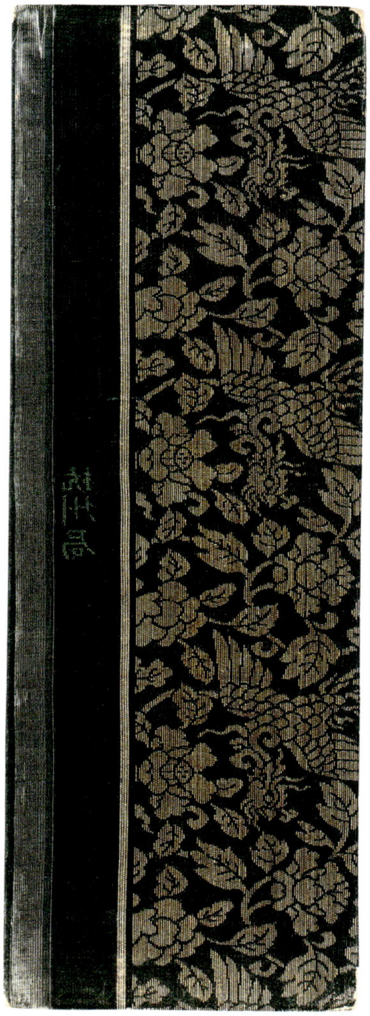

Fig. 17. Sutra cover with mark of the official Ming weaving department, Hangzhou ju (characters written as shown). Ming dynasty (1368–1644), 16th–early 17th century. Complex gauze with supplementary gold strips; 14¼ x 5 inches (36.2 x 12.7 cm). Philadelphia Museum of Art. Purchased with the John T. Morris Fund from the Carl Schuster Collection, 1940-4-339

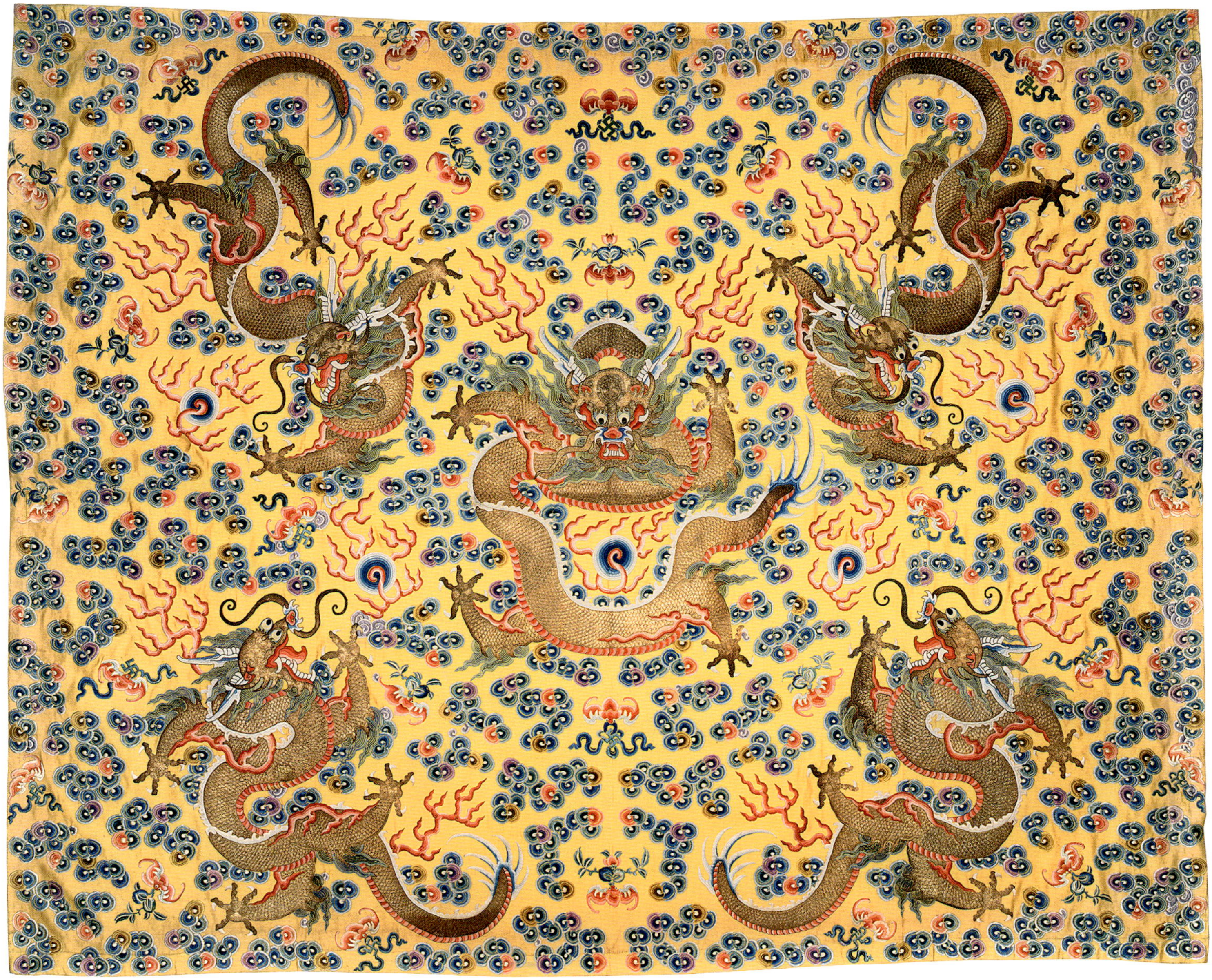

Fig. 18. Textile with Five-Dragon Design. Qing dynasty (1644–1911), 19th century. Silk satin embroidered with floss silk satin, long and short, and outline stitches; couched gold leaf on paper wrapped thread; 52¾ x 65 inches (134 x 165.1 cm). Philadelphia Museum of Art. Gift of Mrs. Henry W. Breyer, Sr., 1961-148-1

clothing and textile objects ranging in date from the Han dynasty—represented by fragments of cloth excavated by Russian archaeologists at Noin Ula in northern Mongolia (see no. 2)—to both formal and informal Qing-dynasty dress and 133 embroidery designs for court robes and hangings from a late Qing imperial embroidery workshop, the latter given to the museum by the Dutch collector Dr. Robert van Gulik in 1955.[48] Local donors have been the source of some notable holdings, including an imperial hanging with five dragons (fig. 18) and a group of Chinese opera costumes (see no. 91) donated by Mrs. Henry W. Breyer, Sr., heiress to the Philadelphia ice cream company.

Another noteworthy gift came from Major General William Crozier (1855–1942) and Mrs. Mary Hoyt Williams Crozier (1865–1955). General Crozier was Chief Ordinance Officer of the U.S. Army in Peking during the Boxer Rebellion (1899–1901), an uprising fueled by anti-imperial

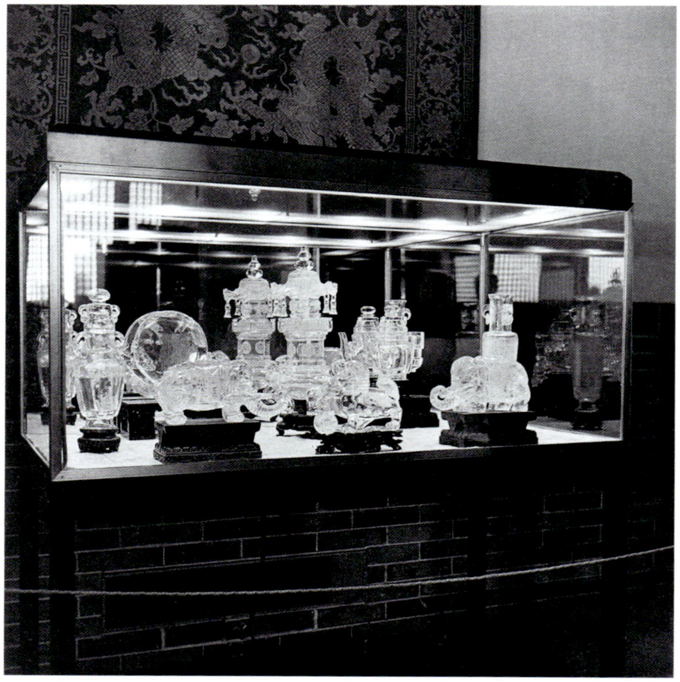

Fig. 19. A case of Mrs. Crozier's rock crystals displayed in the Chinese Reception Hall for the opening of the new Asian wing of the Philadelphia Museum of Art, spring 1940. Photography by Alfred Eisenstaedt/The LIFE Picture Collection

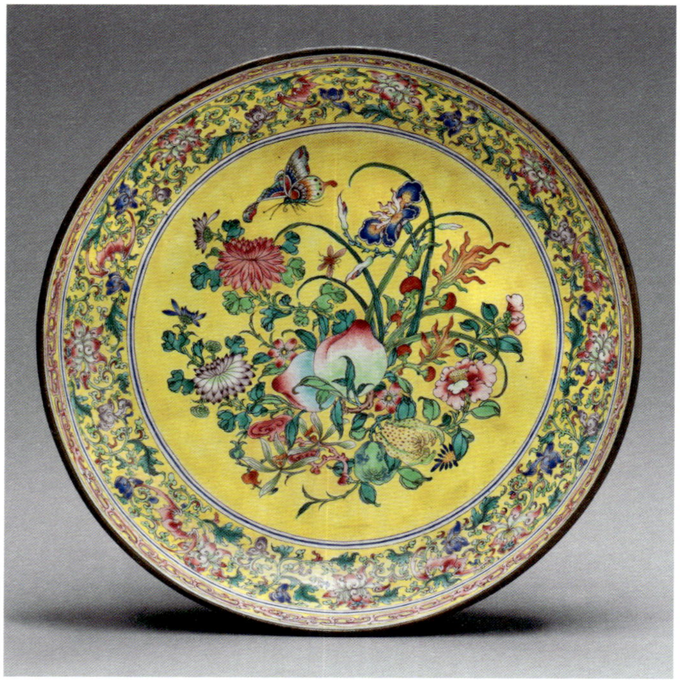

Fig. 20. Dish with Peach, Pomegranate, and Buddha's Hand Citron (Three Plenties). Qing dynasty (1644–1911), Qianlong period (1736–95). Copper alloy with enamel decoration; 1⅝ x 8¼ inches (4.1 x 21 cm). Philadelphia Museum of Art. Gift of Major General and Mrs. William Crozier, 1944-20-527a,b

sentiment against Western colonization and Christian activities that sought to revive an ailing Qing dynasty. After his retirement in 1919, the general and his wife traveled extensively, making almost annual visits to Peking until the Japanese invasion and occupation of that city in the 1930s. It was when they were residing at the Grand Hôtel de Pékin, now the Grand Beijing Hotel, that Jayne met the Croziers in 1926.[49] The couple called Peking one of the best places in the world to live; both lovers of Chinese art and culture, they even gave money to repair one of the towers of the imperial palace in the Forbidden City.[50] Mary Crozier purchased directly from Chinese dealers in Peking and was especially enamored of works from the Qianlong period (1736–95), though later research has shown that not all the items she acquired are in fact what she believed them to be, reflecting the difficulties of collecting in China at that time.

Although the Croziers eventually returned to the United States and settled in Washington, DC, where the Freer Gallery of Art hoped to be the beneficiary of their thousand-piece collection, Mrs. Crozier ultimately gave it to the Philadelphia Museum of Art, thanks to her acquaintance with trustee John Story Jenks. Jenks invited Mrs. Crozier to the museum to tour the newly installed Chinese reception hall with Fiske Kimball, and she was so impressed that she agreed to lend her porcelains and rock-crystal carvings for the 1940 opening of the museum's new Oriental wing.[51] Mrs. Crozier had firm ideas about the display of her collection. For the opening of the new wing she advised that her rock crystals be arranged in two cases hung with red-velvet-and-gold dragon panels (fig. 19), and her porcelains exhibited in four lacquer wardrobes within the reception hall.[52] When she offered her Ru-ware brush washer to the museum (see no. 14), Kimball replied, "We shall indeed be most delighted to have the Ju-Yao and will immediately place it in the cases whenever it comes," wryly adding, "trusting to you to help us arrange or re-arrange it when you are here."[53]

Mrs. Crozier's rapport with Kimball, Jenks, and Jayne was surely among the reasons she chose the Philadelphia Museum of Art as the recipient of the entire Crozier collection in 1944 (see nos. 1, 24, 37, 44, 45, 47, 54, 66, 67, 70, 89). Strengths of the collection include textiles, Song ceramics, Ming and Qing porcelains (including a rare pair of gilded and silvered blue-and-white saucers from the Yongzheng period; no. 71), and imperial enameled porcelain and glass snuff bottles from the Qianlong period (no. 68).

Another strength of the Philadelphia Museum of Art's Chinese collection is its holding of Qing-dynasty enameled works on copper made in Canton, many of them also dating to the Qianlong period. These came to the museum not only through the Crozier gift—which included such gems as an enameled copper dish decorated with flowers and peaches, pomegranates and Buddha's Hand citrons, conveying wishes of longevity, blessings, and many sons (fig. 20)—but also through the three hundred plus works donated in 1899 by Mrs. Bloomfield Moore (see p. 18; no. 76) and the fifty works given in 1988 by the local collector Constance Andrew Jones, whose family was in the steel business (fig. 21).

Along with the prominent Philadelphian George D. Widener, Jr., chair of the museum's board of trustees, Mrs. Crozier was also helpful in securing the gift of the Gow collection of more than four hundred Qing porcelains from Alfred and Margaret Caspary in 1955.[54] This impressive group of mainly Kangxi-period (1662–1722) porcelains was initially compiled by Leonard Gow (1859–1936), son of a Glaswegian shipping magnate, who became a senior partner in the shipping company Gow, Harrison & Company and later director of the Burmah Oil Company. Gow was inspired to collect Chinese porcelains after admiring "the grace, the beauty of . . . color and design and wonderful sense of rhythm" of examples in the Salting Collection, bequeathed to the Victoria and Albert Museum, London, in 1909, although he acknowledged that the true collector must also understand the meaning of the designs to truly appreciate porcelains.[55] Ranging from blue-and-white wares to enameled porcelains, the collection includes some pieces with impressive provenances. Two vases (see nos. 62, 63) once belonged to Augustus the Strong (1670–1733), king of Poland and elector of Saxony, whose fascination with porcelain and determination to find the secret of its manufacture saw the establishment of the Meissen porcelain factory in 1710. Many other pieces in the collection were among those included in the prestigious 1935–36 International Exhibition of Chinese Art at the Royal Academy in London (fig. 22), which displayed treasures from the Palace Museum in China never before seen in the West[56]—a turning point in the perception and study of Chinese art. After Gow's death, the collection was purchased by Alfred H. Caspary (1877–1955), a successful New York stockbroker. Why Caspary, a renowned stamp collector, chose to buy a group of Chinese porcelains that he never displayed nor expressed much interest in is a mystery, but he may have been influenced by John D. Rockefeller, Jr., his New York neighbor, who was an avid collector of Chinese porcelains.[57] Asked why he had bought the porcelains, Caspary said simply that he could always make more money, but he could not guarantee that the opportunity to acquire a collection such as Gow's would ever present itself again.[58]

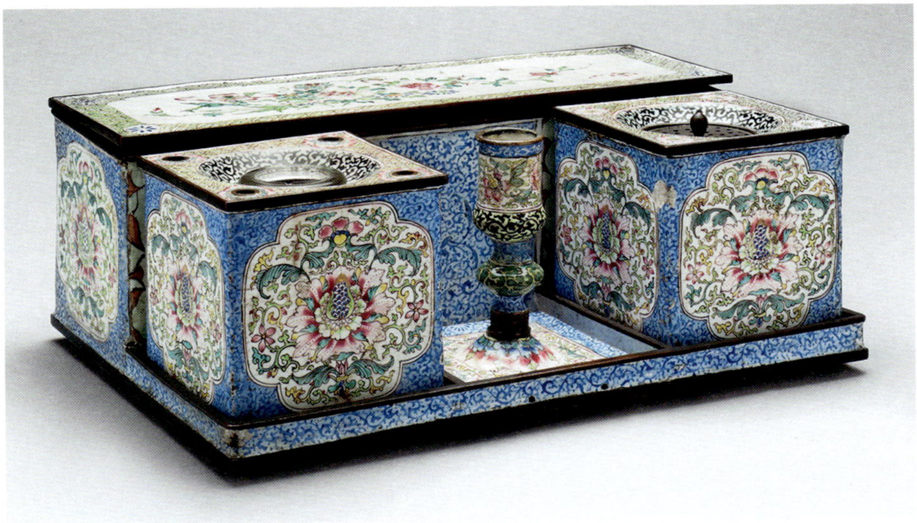

Fig. 21. Inkstand with Floral Cartouches. Qing dynasty (1644–1911), Yongzheng period (1723–35), early 18th century. Copper alloy with enamel decoration; 3¼ x 8¹³⁄₁₆ x 5⅞ inches (8.3 x 22.4 x 15 cm). Philadelphia Museum of Art. Bequest of Constance A. Jones, 1988-27-107a–d

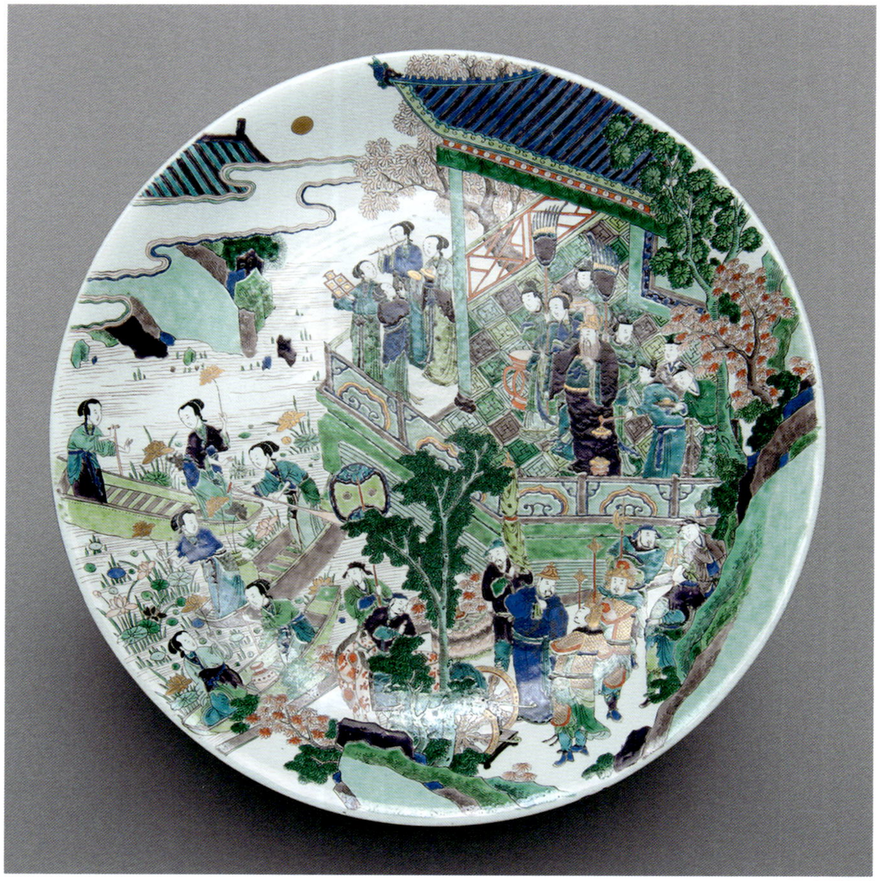

Fig. 22. Large Dish Depicting Picking Lotus in the Palace. Qing dynasty (1644–1911), Kangxi mark and period (1662–1722). Porcelain with enamel decoration (*famille verte*); 3 x 20⅝ inches (7.6 x 52.4 cm). Philadelphia Museum of Art. The Alfred and Margaret Caspary Memorial Gift, 1955-50-78

In 1955, the year of the Caspary gifts, Jean Gordon Lee (1919–1997) was promoted to curator of Far Eastern art, a position she held until 1986.[59] Lee's expertise in Chinese ceramics had helped to secure the Crozier and Caspary gifts, as well as the acquisition of Ming porcelains and other works of art (see nos. 27, 30–32). A Philadelphian through and through, she had an abiding interest in the China trade, in 1984 combining her two loves to produce the seminal catalogue and research on this topic, titled *Philadelphia and the China Trade, 1784–1844*. She also expanded the Chinese furniture collection, which today comprises some sixty works, including traditional forms of furniture made for the Chinese market, such as Ming-dynasty *huanghuali* rosewood tables and chairs (see no. 49). Lee acquired works from the well-known dealer Alice Boney (a gaming table, for example, as well as the rare Tang-dynasty Buddhist text *Admonitions to the Monks*; nos. 55, 4),[60] and from Boney's student, the larger-than-life connoisseur, collector, and dealer Robert Ellsworth, who sold Asian art in New York in the 1950s and 1960s under the name Ellsworth and Goldie (the source of a sixteenth-century *huanghuali* canopied bed; fig. 23).

Over more than a century of collecting the art of China, through gifts from supporters, close relationships with dealers, and the vision and expertise of directors and peripatetic curators, the museum has seen its Chinese collection grow to more than seven thousand objects. The addition in recent years of works by Chinese contemporary artists (see nos. 96–98), along with promised gifts (no. 29), has ensured that the Chinese collection continues to bring wonder and beauty, exquisite workmanship and historical significance, to the Philadelphia Museum of Art's visitors, offering a unique window into China's past and present.

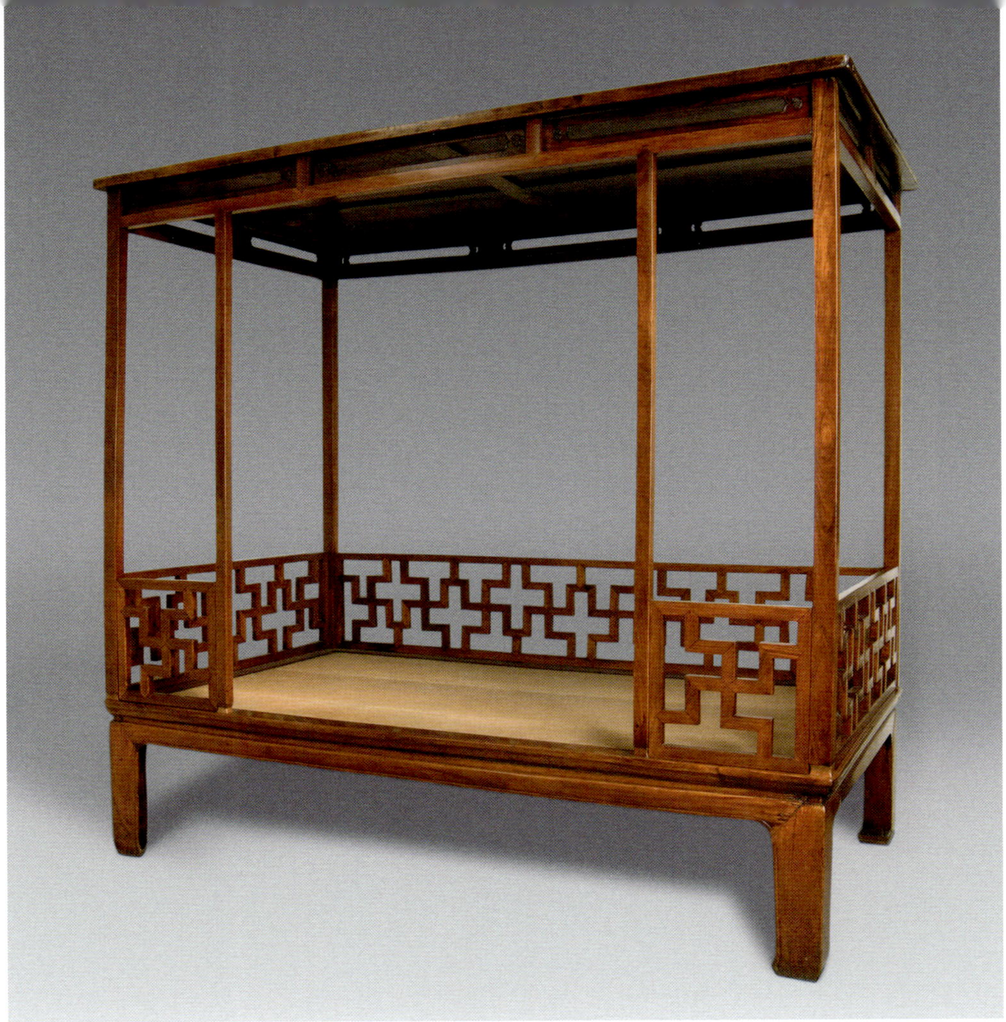

Fig. 23. Six-Post Canopy Bed. Ming dynasty (1368–1644), 16th century. Wood (*huanghuali*, with red pine); 6 feet 5¼ inches x 6 feet 9½ inches x 47½ inches (196.2 x 207 x 120.7 cm). Philadelphia Museum of Art. Purchased with Museum funds, 1961-89-1

Notes

1. Located at Ninth and Sansom Streets, Dunn's museum, called the "richest Chinese collection in the world," included a "large pavilion, a silk draper's shop, and a Chinese street, nearly filled up by a palanquin and its bearers"; yet not all his collection fit within, "such is the extent . . . of curiosities gathered by Mr. Dunn, during his nine years residence in China, that a large redisuum remains in the store-rooms." See E. C. Wines, *A Peep at China in Mr. Dunn's Chinese Collection; with Miscellaneous Notices Relating to the Institutions and Customs of the Chinese and Our Commercial Intercourse with Them* (Philadelphia: Printed for Nathan Dunn, 1839), 11–12. Dunn, whose ambition was to reproduce China through his museum and let the objects stand for the culture, claimed to have real access to Chinese people and their objects, since he was not involved in the opium trade. See Steven Conn, "Where Is the East? Asian Objects in American Museums, from Nathan Dunn to Charles Freer," *Winterthur Portfolio* 35, nos. 2–3 (2000): 160. For more on Dunn, see Aaron H. Caplan, "Nathan Dunn's Chinese Museum," August 15, 2011, SSRN [Social Science Research Nework], accessed April 2018, SSRN: https://ssrn.com /abstract=2038655 or http://dx.doi.org/10.2139 /ssrn.2038655.

2. Other institutions collecting Chinese art at this time included the Brooklyn Museum and the Metropolitan Museum of Art in New York, and the Museum of Fine Arts in Boston.

3. Jennifer Pitman, "China's Presence at the Centennial Exhibition, Philadelphia, 1876," *Studies in the Decorative Arts* 10, no. 1 (Fall–Winter 2002–3): 49–52.

4. Hu was the chief purchasing agent and financier for the campaigns of General Zuo Zongtang (Tso Tsung-t'ang), a military leader and statesman during the late Qing dynasty. Over a period of twenty-five years, Hu is said to have amassed a fortune of twenty million taels ($33.4 million), but he lost it all in 1883 by speculating in the silk market. See Charles John Stanley, *Late Ch'ing Finance: Hu Kwang-Yung as an Innovator*, Harvard East Asian Monographs 12 (Cambridge, MA: East Asian Research Center, Harvard University, 1961), 1–18, 73. Hu's connections with the Chinese Maritime Customs Service, the Chinese government agency that collected tax on trade, and the local elite probably allowed him access to Chinese works of art.

5. Large quantities of Chinese ceramics were exhibited in the Centennial Exhibition, including monochromes, polychromes, underglaze blue-and-white wares, crackled wares, celadons, *pâte sur pâte*, and Canton *famille rose*, mostly of modern manufacture but some antique. See Pitman, "China's Presence at the Centennial Exhibition," 55.

6. The emperor's dragon boat is shown being pulled along by the most beautiful women in the empire. The enormous project to build a canal linking the populous north with the fertile south entailed the conscription of more than two million people; Yangdi's rule ended in revolution.

7. See Béatrice Quette, ed., *Cloisonné: Chinese Enamels from the Yuan, Ming, and Qing Dynasties*, exh. cat. (New York: Bard Graduate Center, 2011), 324.

8. These were the criteria of the father and son collectors William and Henry Walters, who assembled sixty-five hundred objects, including porcelains, lacquers, metalwork, bronzes, and ivories. Other collectors at the end of the nineteenth century were also captivated by Chinese porcelains, their taste influenced by travels in Europe. See C. Griffith Mann, "Exporting China: The Collecting Taste of William and Henry Walters," in *Collecting China: The World, China, and a History of Collecting*, ed. Vimalin Rujivacharakul (Newark: University of Delaware Press, 2011), 100, 102.

9. Incorrectly called rice paper, pith paper is made from the core of the pith tree (*Tetrapanax papyrifer*), which is thinly sliced into sheets and dried; see "Pith Paper: Rice Has Nothing to Do with It," *Harvard Magazine*, March–April 2009, accessed April 2018, https://harvardmagazine.com/2009/03/pith-paper. Using gouache (opaque watercolor) on pith paper, artists such as Sunqua, whose studio was located on China Street in Canton, produced pith paintings for Westerners in the nineteenth century. He may have opened a business in Hong Kong in the 1840s; see Li Shizhuang, *Zhongguo waixiao hua 1750s–1880s* [China trade painting, 1750s–1880s] (Guangzhou: Zhongshan daxue chubanshe, 2014). Depictions tended toward the didactic and informational, ranging from albums of the various flowers of China to tradesmen activities, porcelain production, and tea cultivation (see Philadelphia Museum of Art, inv. 174b).

10. Edwin Atlee Barber, "The Lewis Bequest," *Bulletin of the Pennsylvania Museum* 7, no. 26 (April 1909): 21.

11. J[ean]-B[aptiste] Du Halde, *The General History of China: Containing a Geographical, Historical, Chronological, Political, and Physical Description of the Empire of China*, trans. Richard Brookes (London: printed by John Watts, 1736), vol. 2, 334; quoted in William R. Sargent, *Treasures of Chinese Export Ceramics from the Peabody Essex Museum* (Salem, MA: Peabody Essex Museum, 2012), 75.

12. Dealers such as Hu Kwang-yung promoted cloisonné at the Centennial Exhibition. See Susan Weber, "The Reception of Chinese Cloisonné Enamels in Europe and America," in Quette, *Cloisonné*, 204. Regarding the development of this technique, see also Béatrice Quette, "The Emergence of Cloisonné Enamels in China," in ibid., 3–17.

13. Edwin Atlee Barber, "Chinese Porcelains," *Bulletin of the Pennsylvania Museum* 7, no. 28 (October 1909): 61, 67.

14. See Bertha Adams, "Clara Sophia Jessup Bloomfield-Moore (1824–1899)," in *An Enduring Legacy: The Philadelphia Museum of Art and Its Benefactors*, comp. Adams (February 2013), an electronic resource available on the Philadelphia Museum of Art Library's online catalogue.

15. Americans initially considered Asian art to be of ethnographical and anthropological interest; it was not until around the first quarter of the twentieth century that they were able to cultivate an appreciation for Asian art on a par with their appreciation for Western art. See Conn, "Where Is the East?," 159.

16. Langdon Warner, *Langdon Warner through His Letters*, ed. Theodore R. Bowie (Bloomington: Indiana University Press, 1966), v.

17. See Karl E. Meyer and Shareen Blair Brysac, *The China Collectors: America's Century-Long Hunt for Asian Art Treasures* (New York: Palgrave Macmillan, 2015), 63.

18. Warner had a prolific career as a museum curator, director, art advisor, and university professor. See Benjamin Rowland, Jr., "Langdon Warner, 1881–1955," *Harvard Journal of Asiatic Studies* 18, nos. 3–4 (December 1955): 449.

19. See *Warner through His Letters*, 38–39.

20. Horace Jayne credits the period-room idea to Warner; see *Warner through His Letters*, 104–5. Warner also acquired for the museum the sixteenth-century South Indian stone pillared hall from the Madana Gopala Swamy Temple (acc. no. 1919-714), an important feature of the South Asian galleries.

21. Hsiao-Yen Shih, "Introduction," in *Homage to Heaven, Homage to Earth: Chinese Treasures of the Royal Ontario Museum* (Toronto: University of Toronto Press, 1992), 2.

22. Warner to Crofts, May 16, 1922, Fiske Kimball Records, Box 165, File 14, Philadelphia Museum of Art, Library and Archives.

23. Warner to Currelly, May 17, 1922, Langdon Warner Records, 1918–1923, File R, Philadelphia Museum of Art, Library and Archives.

24. Warner to Ludington, February 14, 1923, Langdon Warner Records, 1918–1923, Philadelphia Museum of Art, Library and Archives; Langdon Warner, "The Crofts Collection," *Pennsylvania Museum Bulletin* 19, no. 80 (November 1923): 23–25. Charles H. Ludington, a lawyer practicing in Manhattan, was vice-president and treasurer of the Curtis Publishing Company in Philadelphia, which produced the *Ladies Home Journal* and *The Saturday Evening Post*, among other publications.

25. Warner to Crofts, August 8, 1922, and Crofts to Warner, December 19, 1922, Fiske Kimball Records, Box 165, File 14, Philadelphia Museum of Art, Library and Archives.

26. Jayne started out as assistant curator under Langdon Warner's directorship from 1921 to 1923 before becoming curator of Oriental art from 1924 to 1926 and then chief curator of the Division of Eastern Art from 1927 to 1940. Jayne would concurrently serve as director of the University of Pennsylvania Museum of Archaeology and Anthropology in West Philadelphia, across the Schuylkill from the Pennsylvania Museum, from 1929 to 1940/41. See Dilys Pegler Winegrad, *Through Time, Across Continents: A Hundred Years of Archaeology and Anthropology at the University Museum* (Philadelphia: University Museum, University of Pennsylvania, 1993), 98. It was during this time that the two institutions reached an agreement on how each would concentrate its collecting efforts, with the University Museum focusing on archaeological material and the art of ancient peoples and the Pennsylvania Museum (soon to be Philadelphia Museum of Art) thereafter covering the later periods. Board of Trustees Records, Series I, Minutes, June 1941, Philadelphia Museum of Art, Library and Archives.

27. See David B. Brownlee "The Museum of Art: 'A Philadelphia Acropolis,'" chap. 3 in *Building the City Beautiful: The Benjamin Franklin Parkway and the Philadelphia Museum of Art*, 2nd ed. (Philadelphia: Philadelphia Museum of Art, 2017), 41–72, esp. 46.

28. Jayne was given leaves of absence to join Warner in China; *Warner through His Letters*, 103. For Jayne's other appointments, including vice director of the Metropolitan Museum of Art in New York (1941–49), see "Horace H. F. Jayne (1898–1975)," *Archives of Asian Art* 29 (1975–76): 96.

29. *Warner through His Letters*, 108.

30. Kimball also wrote of Jayne: "He had come from Harvard into the Museum as a volunteer . . . and had been drawn by Langdon Warner into the field of Chinese art, where he had already distinguished himself on expeditions to the interior of China." Quoted in George Roberts and Mary Howland Roberts, *Triumph on Fairmount: Fiske Kimball and the Philadelphia Museum of Art* (Philadelphia: Lippincott, 1959), 64.

31. Minna Törmä, *Enchanted by Lohans: Osvald Sirén's Journey into Chinese Art* (Hong Kong: Hong Kong University Press, 2013), 97–100.

32. "Just Acquired by Pennsylvania Museum: Siren Collection in Memorial Hall," *Philadelphia Inquirer*, September 25, 1927.

33. Sirén was friends with Jayne and Warner and traveled with Warner in Japan. See Törmä, *Enchanted by Lohans*, 40.

34. Bahr, who was born in Shanghai to a German father and a Chinese mother, held art exhibitions in China, London, and Canada; at his death, parts of his collection were donated to the Metropolitan Museum of Art, New York; the Royal Ontario Museum, Toronto; and the British Museum, London. His papers from 1919 to 1957 are in the Freer Gallery of Art and Arthur M. Sackler Gallery Archives, Smithsonian Institution, Washington, DC.

35. See a note written by Jenks, November 9, 1931, and the invoice for the pair of stools, dated October 29, 1931; object record file, East Asian Art, Philadelphia Museum of Art. The Manchu gentleman, formerly a banker, was looking to sell his collection following the loss of his fortune. The stools remained with Jenks after his death, when they were gifted to the museum by his wife.

36. Other tiles from this site are in a number of different museum collections in North America and Europe, including the University of Pennsylvania Museum of Archaeology and Anthropology, Philadelphia; the Metropolitan Museum of Art, New York; the Cleveland Museum of Art; the Art Institute of Chicago; the Asian Art Museum, San Francisco; the Royal Ontario Museum, Toronto; the British Museum, London; and the Ferenc Hopp Museum of Eastern Asiatic Arts, Budapest.

37. The ceiling—an eight-sided caisson made of wood painted with reddish-brown lacquer and then gilded—came from the Hall of Transforming Wisdom (Zhihuadian) from the Zhihua Temple in Beijing, which was built by the Ming eunuch Wang Zhen in 1444 as a private residence; it was converted to an ancestral hall after Wang's death. Although purchased by Jayne in 1928, the ceiling would not be installed in its present gallery until 1954, when the funds to build the last part of the Asian galleries were raised.

38. In 1928, when the museum opened to the public, there were only ten galleries of British and American art installed. In 1931 the medieval galleries opened, and in 1932, when the effects of the Depression took hold, work on other galleries, including the Asian, was halted due to lack of funds. In 1935 work resumed with funds from the Works Progress Administration (WPA); see http://www.philamuseum.org/information/45-227-23.html. The new Asian wing, which included Chinese, Japanese, Indian, and Persian galleries, opened to the public on April 5, 1940.

39. Catherine Quinn Tome to Adriana Proser, July 24, 2001, describing her father, Albert Martin Quinn. Reception Hall object file, East Asian Art, Philadelphia Museum of Art. The symbols were most likely Chinese characters, which are sometimes written discreetly on Chinese wood constructions such as furniture and architecture to help match up pieces.

40. This was dictated by sumptuary laws; see Adriana G. Proser, Sally Malenka, and Beth A. Price, *Painted Splendor: The Context and Conservation of a Chinese Reception Hall in the Philadelphia Museum of Art* (Philadelphia: Philadelphia Museum of Art, 2004), 18.

41. Minutes of the Museum Committee, May 1928, p. 72, Philadelphia Museum of Art, Library and Archives.

42. Simkhovitch sold Islamic, Byzantine, and Chinese art from his collection to the Rhode Island School of Design in Providence in order to buy Chinese paintings. Deborah Del Gais, "The Early Formation of the Rhode Island School of Design Museum's Chinese Collection," in *Collectors, Collections, and Collecting the Arts of China: Histories and Challenges*, ed. Jason Steuber and Lai Guolong (Gainesville: University Press of Florida, 2014), 53.

43. On Simkhovitch and the paintings in his collection, see Diandian Li, "Provenance of Prominence: The Simkhovitch Collection of Chinese Paintings at the Philadelphia Museum of Art," *Orientations* 47, no. 3 (April 2016): 2–9.

44. "A Great Collection of Chinese Paintings," *Boston Messenger*, August 10, 1929, book section.

45. Kimball saw great potential in Schuster and offered him this unpaid position. See Dilys Blum's essay on Carl Schuster and his collection, in Xu Zheng, *Meiguo Feicheng yishu bowuguan cang sichou jingmian yanjiu* [A study of the collection of sutra covers at the Philadelphia Museum of Art] (Shanghai: Donghua daxue chubanshe for Zhongguo sichou bowuguan, 2018); hereafter Blum 2018.

46. See Schuyler van Rensselaer Cammann, "In Memoriam: Carl Schuster, Ph.D. (1904–1969)," *Textile Museum Journal* 3, no. 3 (December 1972): 2.

47. Schuster's study of Buddhist scriptures while he was a graduate student at Harvard and at Yenching University in Beijing likely inspired him to collect sutra covers. See Blum 2018.

48. Dilys Blum, *The Fine Art of Textiles: The Collections of the Philadelphia Museum of Art* (Philadelphia: Philadelphia Museum of Art, 1997), 163.

49. Roberts and Roberts, *Triumph on Fairmount*, 220.

50. As recounted by their friend Dr. Hu Shih, the former Chinese ambassador, who recalled that "the General was looked upon as a sage and philanthropist." See "William Crozier 1876," memorial article published by the West Point Association of Graduates, accessed April 2018, https://www.westpointaog.org/memorial-article?id=247cdd01-88aa-4423-8e98-32ad109dc516.

51. Bertha Adams, "Mary Crozier (1865–1955), in *An Enduring Legacy* (see note 14 above).

52. Crozier to Jayne, March 23, 1940, Fiske Kimball Records, Box 165, File 6, Philadelphia Museum of Art, Library and Archives.

53. Kimball to Crozier, April 29, 1943, Fiske Kimball Records, Box 165, File 6, Philadelphia Museum of Art, Library and Archives.

54. Widener knew Caspary "intimately"—both owned property nearby in South Carolina—and offered to speak to him about the museum borrowing something. Kimball to Crozier, October 4, 1943, Fiske Kimball Records, Box 165, File 6, Philadelphia Museum of Art, Library and Archives. Caspary also frequently referred to their common interest in art, as stated in a letter to the museum from George Murnane, Executor of the Will of Alfred H. Caspary, dated May 24, 1955, Caspary file, East Asian Art, Philadelphia Museum of Art. Widener's uncle Joseph Widener, whose collection of important Western paintings was called "the finest private collection in the world" by the head of the British Museum in London, gave his paintings and Qing porcelains to the National Gallery of Art in Washington, DC, much to the disappointment of Fiske Kimball. See Roberts and Roberts, *Triumph on Fairmount*, 176.

55. Leonard Gow, "Foreword," in *Catalogue of the Leonard Gow Collection of Chinese Porcelain*, by R. L. Hobson (London: George W. Jones, 1931).

56. The International Exhibition of Chinese Art was the largest exhibition of Chinese art ever mounted, displaying more than 3,000 objects from some 240 lenders, including museums, collectors, and dealers from all over the world. See Jason Steuber, "The Exhibition of Chinese Art at Burlington House, London, 1935–1936," *Burlington Magazine* 148 (August 2006): 528.

57. Notes from a telephone conversation between Caspary's niece Dorothy Davis and Jean Gordon Lee, April 30, 1970, Caspary file, East Asian Art, Philadelphia Museum of Art.

58. This is recorded in notes about the Gow collection written by Roger A. Van Der Straeten, a New York dealer who sold the collection to Caspary, sight unseen, from the catalogue of the Gow estate. Caspary file, East Asian Art, Philadelphia Museum of Art.

59. Lee's promotion coincided with Horace Jayne's elevation to vice director following his return to the museum in 1953. Lee was associated with the museum for nearly half a century. She first worked for Fiske Kimball's office after graduating from the University of Michigan in 1938 with a degree in Far Eastern art history, and then was appointed assistant curator in 1940 under Jayne, remaining as curator until her retirement. Thomas Lawton, "Jean Gordon Lee, January 20, 1919–June 5, 1997," *Artibus Asiae* 57, nos. 3–4 (1997): 369.

60. Boney's authority in Chinese art earned her the title "doyenne of Oriental art dealers." Her clients included the Metropolitan Museum of Art in New York, the Freer Gallery of Art in Washington, DC, and President Herbert Hoover; see "Alice Boney, 1901–1988, Dealer in Chinese Art," Freer/Sackler, Smithsonian Institutions, Washington, DC, accessed April 2018, https://archive.asia.si.edu/collections/downloads/Boney-Alice.pdf.

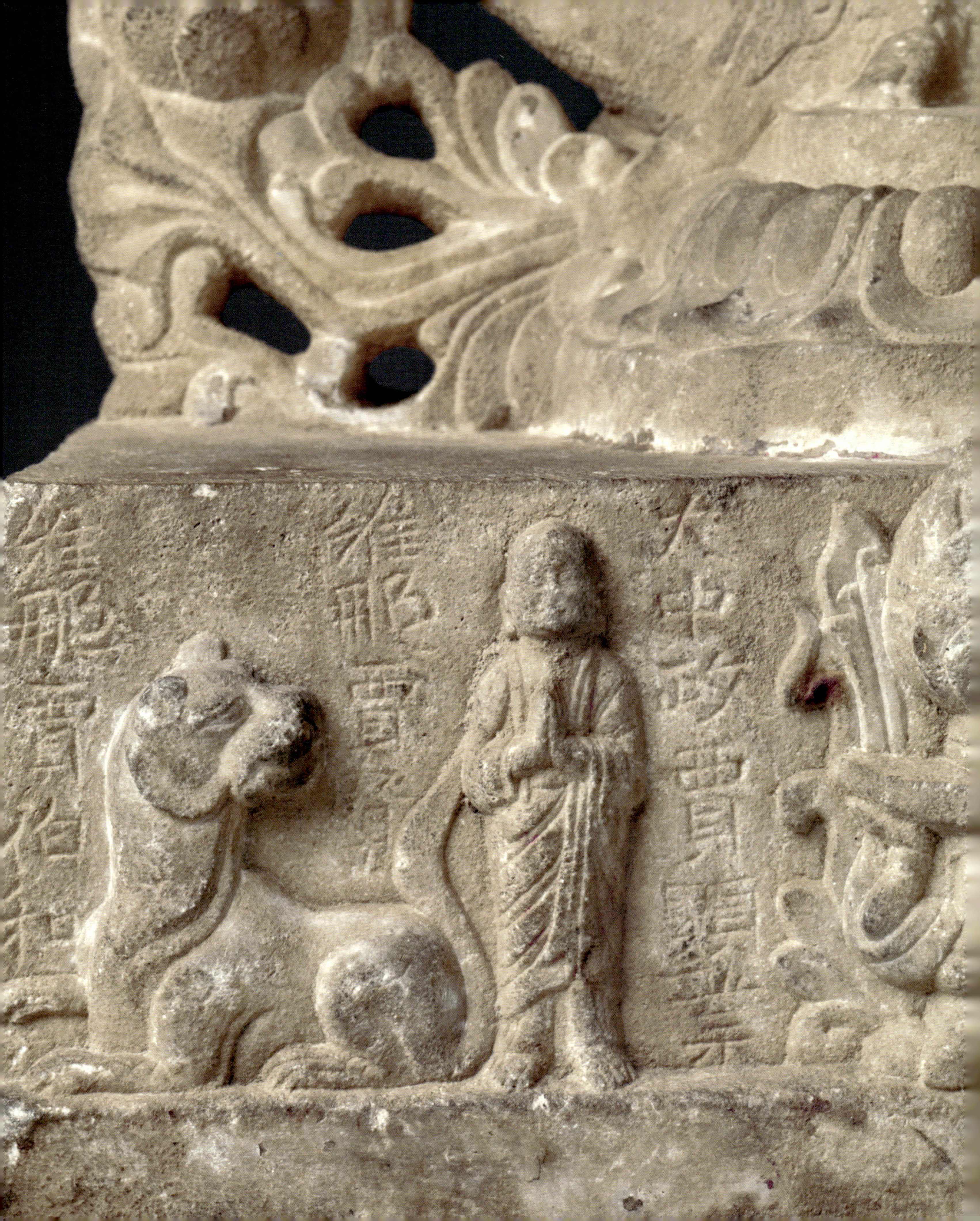

HIGHLIGHTS FROM THE COLLECTION

Huang Xiaofeng, Hiromi Kinoshita, Diandian Li, and John Vollmer

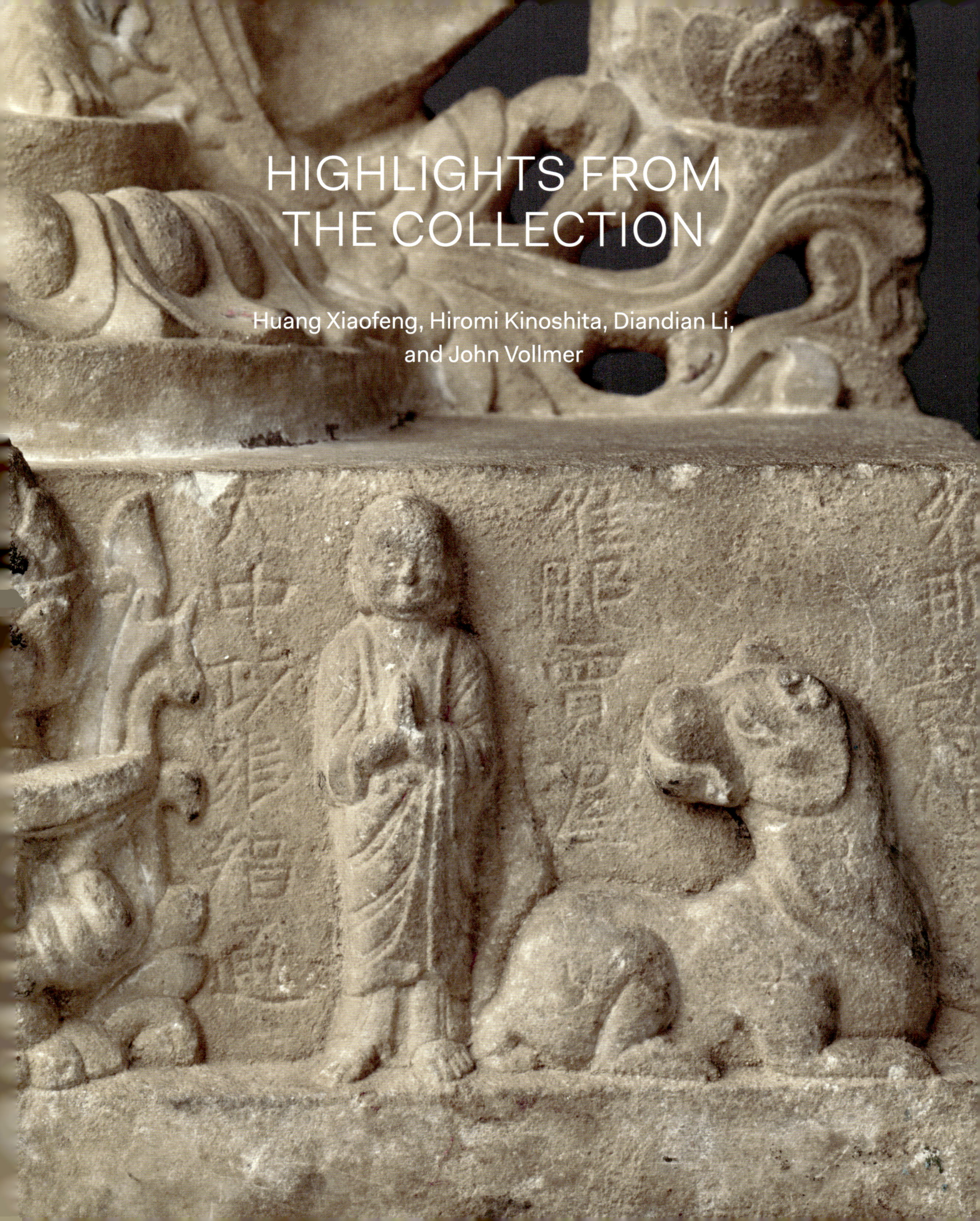

1

Ritual Disc (*Bi*)

Neolithic period, Liangzhu culture (c. 3400–2250 BCE), c. 2250 BCE
Jade; wood stand
Disc 6¹¹⁄₁₆ x ⅜ inches (17 x 1 cm); h. of stand 7⁵⁄₁₆ inches (18.5 cm)
Gift of Major General and Mrs. William Crozier, 1944-20-497a,b

The jade disc, or *bi* (pronounced "bee"), is one of the most recognized forms of Chinese jade carving.[1] This example, created more than four thousand years ago in southern China, is an astonishing accomplishment considering that jade is a very hard mineral to work and that metal tools had not yet been invented.[2] It was most likely fashioned using a hand drill, bamboo tools embedded with grit for grinding, and sand for polishing.[3] The not-entirely-circular form and the central hole drilled from both sides, as indicated by a low ridge where the two holes meet, is characteristic of *bi* from the Liangzhu culture.[4]

Finely worked *bi* appear to have been placed in Liangzhu graves as part of a ritual ceremony and to indicate high status.[5] While their specific function is unknown, the *Zhouli* (Rites of Zhou), an ancient text that records the rituals performed by the Zhou court (c. 1100–256 BCE), describes them as objects held by fourth- and fifth-rank nobles at gatherings.[6] It was through this association that *bi* were sought after and collected, especially by later rulers, who wished to demonstrate their mandate to rule.[7] Owning such a *bi* was particularly meaningful for an emperor, the "Son of Heaven," as it referred not only to antiquity but also to rulership. The toughness of the material, which could be polished to a soft sheen, contributed to its association with immortality and Confucian gentlemanly virtues.[8] HK

1. *Bi* discs have proportionally small holes, while *huan* discs have holes that are larger in relation to the area of the jade body.
2. Use of the term *jade* here refers to nephrite, which was used in antiquity. Jadeite from Burma was introduced in the eighteenth century. See Cambridge 2009, 8.
3. Rawson 1995, 21.
4. See Rawson 1995, 130–32, no. 4:1.
5. Archaeological evidence shows that finely worked *bi* were placed around the stomach area of the deceased, whereas coarse ones were piled in larger numbers by the feet; Wilson 2004, 13.
6. Wilson 2004, 14.
7. An example of such a collector is the eighteenth-century Qianlong emperor (r. 1736–95), who sought to emulate the legendary rulers of Chinese antiquity and highly educated Chinese scholars in order to create an ideal empire; see Holzwarth 2005.
8. Jade *bi* discs were integrated into the jade burial suits believed to protect and preserve the bodies of Han aristocrats of the second century BCE. See Cambridge 2012, 49–57, 196–204; New York 2017, no. 101.

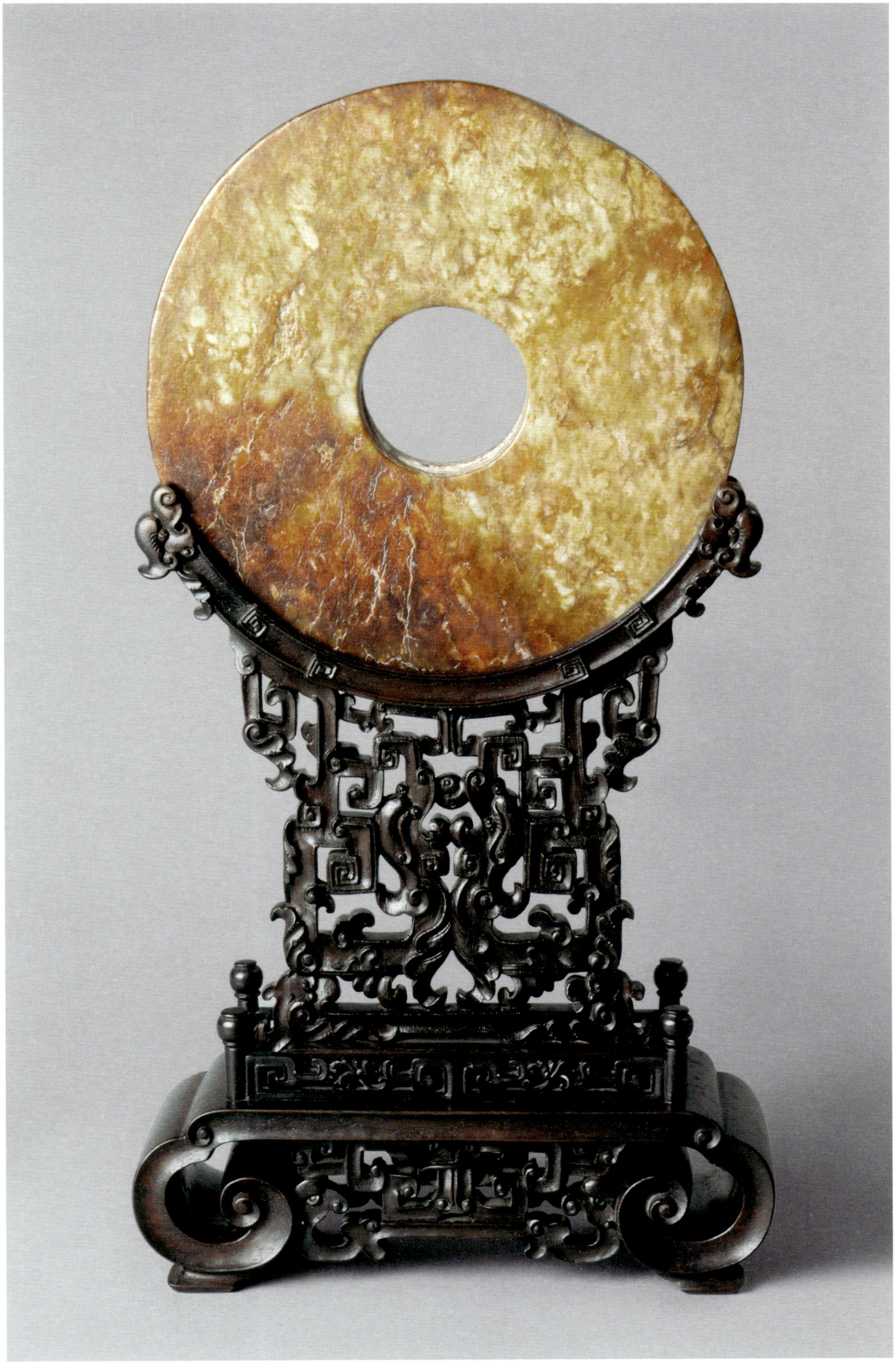

2

Silk Fragments from Noin Ula, Mongolia

Han dynasty (206 BCE–220 CE), 1st century CE
Warp-faced compound silk plain weave; silk complex gauze
3¾ x 2½ inches (9.5 x 6.4 cm); 3⅜ x 1¾ inches (8.6 x 4.5 cm)
Purchased with the Bloomfield Moore Fund, 1934-2-2, 1934-2-6

The nine textile fragments from the site of Noin Ula (of a total of thirteen fragments) acquired by the Philadelphia Museum of Art in 1934 were for many years the only examples of Chinese luxury weaving from the Han dynasty preserved in North America. These two fragments represent the highest technical achievements of the imperial weaving workshops that supplied the Han court with its celebrated silks for clothing and furnishings.

The four-end complex gauze (*si jingjiao lou*), with its intricate triple-lozenge pattern (right), is a type of fabric frequently used for gossamer garments. In contrast, the heavy warp-faced tabby (*jin*) textile, with its design of cranes and clouds (left), represents the epitome of a complex weaving technology unique to East Asia that was capable of producing polychrome pictorial patterns. The pattern seen here includes the character for 10,000 (*wan*),

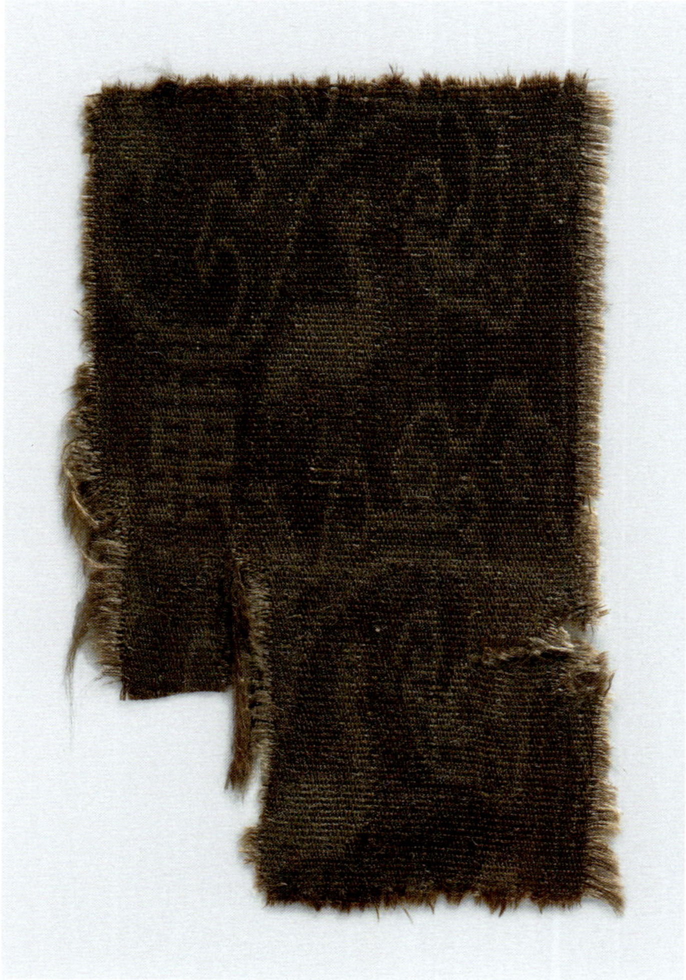

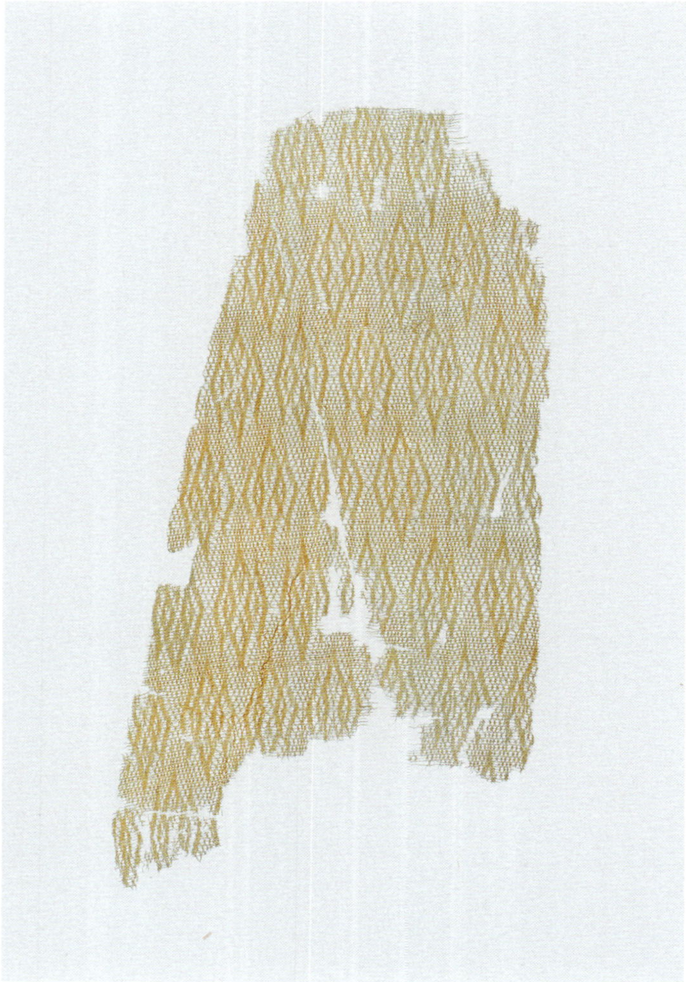

which undoubtedly formed part of a longer inscription reflecting Chinese concerns about life after death and wishes for the well-being of progeny.[1]

These fragments are a testament to two developments that ensured China's primacy in East Asia: the discovery that silk could be cultivated by domesticating the silk-producing moth, and the monopolization of silk production by the state. From the second millennium BCE, silk enriched the state treasury domestically when the government accepted thread and cloth as payments for taxes, and then used them as entitlements and compensation for government and military service. Internationally, silk became a much-coveted luxury, both in commerce and diplomacy, generating income and ameliorating aggression. The crucial overland trade routes would become known as the Silk Road.

Noin Ula, located in Mongolia, north of the capital of Ulan Bator (Ulaanbaatar), was the burial site of the tribal Xiongnu aristocracy from the first century BCE to the first century CE, when China reached a détente with the Xiongnu, a confederation of nomadic peoples from the eastern Eurasian Steppe who had often been in conflict with the Chinese states to the south. Chinese sources record that twenty-two to thirty-three thousand pounds of silk thread and twenty to thirty thousand bolts of silk cloth were sent to the Xiongnu annually.[2] The Mongol-Tibetan Russian Geographical Society expedition led by the explorer P. K. Kozlov excavated eight elite tombs at Noin Ula between 1924 and 1925, recovering more than a thousand textiles, including 250 pieces of silk.[3] JV

1. Sheng, 2017, 108–9.
2. Yu 1967, 41–42, 47.
3. Pankova 2016, 59–61.

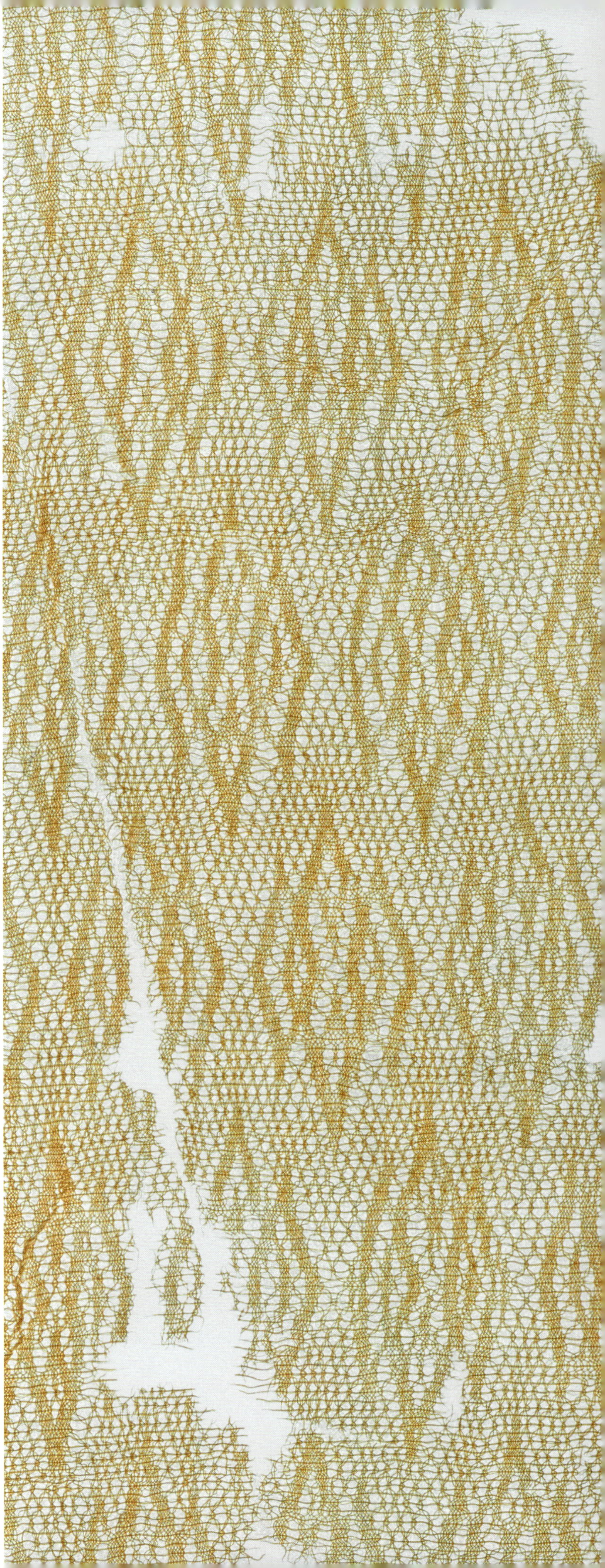

3

Votive Stele

Northern Qi dynasty (550–77), mid-6th century
Marble with traces of paint
22 1/16 x 10 7/8 x 5 7/8 inches (56 x 27.6 x 15 cm)
Gift of Stanley Griswold Flagg, Jr., 1927-20-2

This stele depicts a benevolent manifestation of the Buddha,[1] his right hand raised in a gesture of fearlessness and his left hand reaching forward in a motion of wish-granting. The downcast eyes and serene expression convey an introspective calm and spiritual bliss. Two smaller crowned bodhisattvas (beings who have chosen to delay their enlightenment to save all beings from suffering) flank the Buddha, each holding a lotus bud and standing on a lotus pedestal supported by leafy tendrils. A large mandorla frames the figures, with four female celestial divinities (*apsaras*) with fluttering scarves carved in low relief in its upper part, two of them carrying stupas (structures containing Buddhist relics). The rectangular base, carved on the front with an incense burner supported by a caryatid figure and flanked by a pair of monks and recumbent lions, is inscribed on all four sides with the names of donors, many of them from the Jia clan, which commissioned this devotional image, most likely for worship at a private shrine or as an offering.[2]

This stele is one of a group of ten white marble sculptures collected by the noted art historian Osvald Sirén (see pp. 21–22) and acquired by the museum through a gift in 1927 (see also fig. 24). The distinctive fine white marble, once painted and gilded, exhibits a simplified style of carving that recalls Buddhist statuary from Quyang (Dingzhou) in Hebei province, where Buddhist sculpture in a range of different styles was produced in the Northern Wei (386–534), Eastern Wei (534–50), Northern Qi, Sui (581–618), and Tang (618–907) periods.[3] The modeling of this particular stele and the figures on it suggest that it may have come from the western pit of Xiude Temple in Quyang, Hebei province. More than two thousand mostly fragmentary Buddhist figures and steles, ranging in size from twenty to fifty centimeters in height, were unearthed there,[4] all made of fine white marble said to have come from the Yellow Mountains in Quyang, and embellished with vermilion, sapphire blue, ocher, malachite, and black pigments, with some gilding.[5] HK

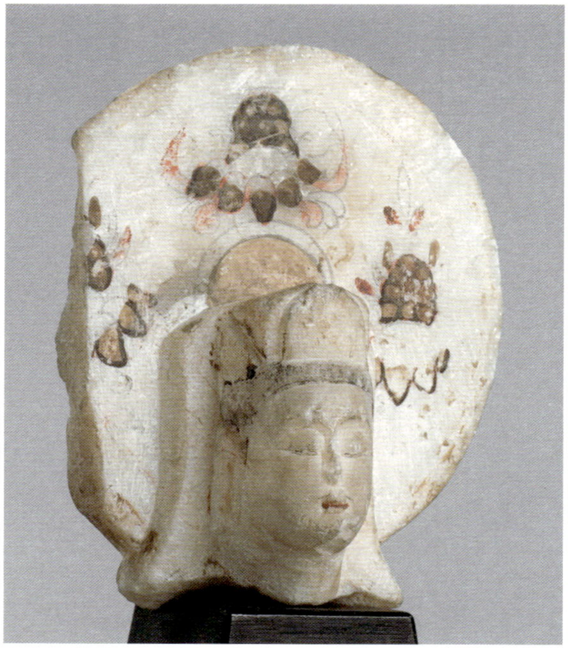

Fig. 24. Head of a Bodhisattva. Northern Qi dynasty. Marble with traces of painted decoration, h. 4 1/2 inches (11.5 cm). Philadelphia Museum of Art. Purchased with Museum and Subscription Funds, 1927-50-11

1. Without an inscription it is difficult to determine whether this is Shakyamuni, the historical Buddha, or Maitreya, the Future Buddha, who at this early period had not yet developed distinctive iconographic traits.
2. Sirén 1940, 487.
3. Attribution to these periods is confirmed by inscriptions that range in date from 520 to 750. The inscriptions indicate that most examples of small statuary were dedicated by local residents and commoners; Yang 2004, vol. 2, no. 107.
4. It is unclear when and why these pieces were buried there, but the suggestion that they were hidden for protection at times of Buddhist persecution is reasonable.
5. Yang 2004, vol. 2, 343. An Eastern Wei stele of Guanyin with some of its colorful painted decoration still remaining is illustrated in Wan and Wang 2011, 64. Other similar steles are illustrated in Gugong 2009, no. 129, which depicts just the two bodhisattvas, and no. 46, with the Buddha flanked by two bodhisattvas.

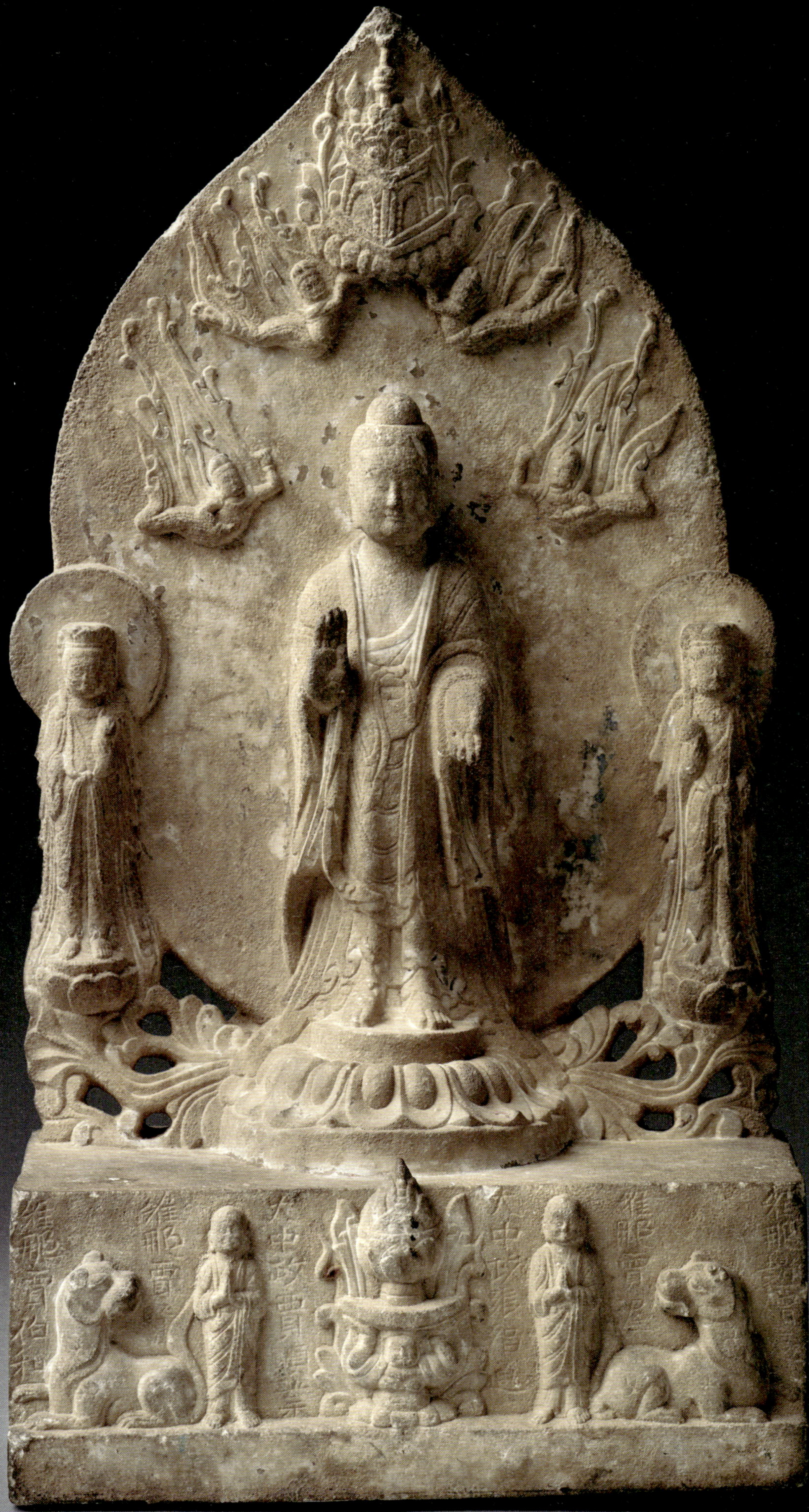

4

Admonitions to the Monks (Subcommentary on the "Quadripartite Prātimokṣa" by Śramaṇa Hui)

Tang dynasty (618–907), mid-9th century
Ink on paper
11¾ inches x 34 feet 7¾ inches (29.8 x 1056 cm)
Gift of Alice Boney, 1968-227-1

The translation and copying of Buddhist texts (or sutras) has long been a ritual practice to convey devotion and advance one's religious standing. In the Tang dynasty there were generally three types of scribes—monks and nuns, Buddhist laymen, and professionals who copied sutras for a living.[1] Textual evidence has revealed that, as early as the fourth century, scribes paid special attention to the quality of their calligraphy in such sacred writings.[2]

Expanding on the *Quadripartite Prātimokṣa*, which prescribes extensive rules for the moral and ascetic conduct of monastic members, the *Subcommentary* was compiled by Śramaṇa Hui in the mid-Tang dynasty.[3] The fourth and final "volume" of the set, it is written in a combination of standard and running scripts, possibly influenced by the notable development in cursive styles during the eighth century. At the same time, many of the characters, with their slightly squat composition and the emphasis on ending strokes that generate a sense of rhythm and strength, have an archaic flavor inherited from the earlier, clerical script. The red insertions throughout the text are proofreading marks made by an editor, who also noted at the end of the scroll that this copy was made at Qianyuan Temple in Shazhou (or Dunhuang) in the year *hai*.[4]

This scroll was likely once stored in the Library Cave at the Mogao grottoes of Dunhuang in Gansu province. This oasis town was a crucial stop on the Silk Road, the trade route that had fostered communication, commerce, and the transmission of various religions since the Han dynasty (206 BCE–220 CE). Uncovered by a Daoist priest in 1900, the sacred cache in the Library Cave, also referred to as Cave 17, contained an astonishing number of cultural relics, including paintings, artifacts, and religious texts in multiple languages and spanning more than seven centuries.[5] DL

1. Mao 2014, 125.
2. Mao 2014, 81–85.
3. Hui and Mair 1984, 328.
4. Mair suggests that this *hai* year is probably *yihai*, or 855, based on the text's association with Chos-grub (Facheng), an influential teacher active in Dunhuang in the mid-ninth century; Hui and Mair 1984, 328–29. During the era of Guiyijun (Returning-to-Righteousness Army) rule, beginning in 848, the Qianyuan Temple was an important male monastery and the location of the official sutra production bureau; Zheng 2006, 4.
5. Rong 1999, 247–48. As a result of the multiple foreign expeditions to Chinese Central Asia in the early twentieth century, materials from Dunhuang are dispersed in different collections around the world. The website of the International Dunhuang Project offers substantial information on Dunhuang manuscripts along with many photographic images; http://idp.bl.uk/.

遠

故別緣有五一是畜生二畜生想三有煞心四起

初略制以次隨開後乃廣結初因迦留陀夷不喜

次因比丘坐起誤煞小虫畏犯提罪仏隨便開不知

生命者波逸提　此滿足戒本文有四句一犯人二知

并相三中初句可知二言故煞者律云若自手斷若

安坑陷煞若安刀著常行住處及已毒藥如是

言畜生者律云不能變化者是所害境界四言波逸提者是犯罪句故律云若作如上

方便欲煞畜生若煞者犯波逸提方便欲煞而不煞者吉羅律云不犯者若不故煞或

以瓦石及餘刀杖欲擲異處而誤斷命若營房舍失手墮石而誤煞者若扶土塹林木

之屬失捉不禁誤墮而煞乃至餘事但无害心縱有死者悉皆无犯　飲虫水戒六十二

制意同上前戒約限分中制要待斷命然後方犯此戒為護物命深防中制但使知水有

虫飲用結罪不待命斷故分二戒又於此戒就飲得提虫无別論別緣有五一是虫水

二虫水想三不作濾法四飲用五隨咽犯若虫命斷則屬前戒若就俱是虫水无殊應

為一戒但以性悪故為重物命内外兩用分為二戒壞生種中若約内外亦應兩分以遮

軽故且就生種无別生罪以因緣同故但合為一戒已下正明戒本文如前三一略二隨三廣

初因六群取雜虫水而共飲用居士譏嫌仏略制戒次因比丘不知故飲畏犯提罪仏開不

知有虫雖飲无犯言廣制者　若比丘知水有虫飲用波逸提　此滿足戒本文有三

句一者犯人二所飲水三結罪　并相者可知律中初明犯罪軽重次解境想四句初輕重者彼

知是雜虫水飲用者犯提除水已若雜虫漿苦酒清酪漿清麦汁飲用同犯次境想四

句者虫水想有虫作无虫想吉无虫有虫想亦吉无虫无虫想不犯疑亦四句濾水之法外

用中以說故祇云比丘受具要畜漉囊應法澡罐伽論云畜使清淨聽畜物覆瓶口此律半

由旬行不得无漉囊五分聽半由旬内无水囊行十律不持漉囊行廿里犯若清流

大河泉水從此寺至彼寺者得祇云漉水不得甚遠眼闇人看若有可信令漉若无可信者自應

漉若无漉囊用袈裟角漉若知水有虫不得持器繩借人若知漉用應与若人問此水有虫

不應答長老自得意視厚語言此中有虫當漉水用律中不犯者先不知有虫若作无虫想

若有麁虫觸水使去漉水飲一切不犯　疑惱比丘戒六十三　制意者凡出家所期標心受遠

盡形畢命專意崇道令以生年等六令他疑惱内心懷惑廢其正脩事惱殊深是故聖制

別緣有五一是大比丘二作疑惱意三於六事一一說之四言詞了了五前人聞知不聞惱不惱但使

聞便得罪下戒本言少時不樂者此就能惱之意非謂妄待前人少時不樂方始結罪

此戒總有三段初因六群惱十七群故略制次因餘比丘共集論法有一比丘退去心疑諸比

此一偈半引七仏說偈同讃及略教為證七仏說偈同讃戒勸諸弟子護三業令彼凡

聖俱得道諸縛永盡證涅槃　尊行大仙說　聖賢稱譽戒　弟子之所行

入寂滅涅槃　此偈勸尊釋迦教文引七仏證若能同彼七仏諸弟子尊重師教不違

犯亦能入於寂涅槃一切賢聖共稱誉持戒之行慧業故仏密意偏為傳說令彼速

解脫　世尊涅槃時　興起於大悲　集諸比丘衆　与如是教誡　莫謂我涅槃

淨行者无護　我今說戒經　亦善說毗尼　我雖般涅槃　當視如世尊　此兩偈半文

引仏遺教勸持禁戒故経說言仏垂滅度世間无師阿難啓請仏言若能奉戒是汝大

師若我在世无異此世乃至仏言我不滅度半月一來又言仏有二身應身雖去法身

在世若敬戒法即見法身若能護戒便為護仏如飲水煞虫喩又大乘経亦同此說

當知持戒行者諸聖共護　此経久住世　仏法得熾盛　以是熾盛故　得入於涅槃

此偈明勸傳戒経故善見云仏語阿難我滅度後有五種法令正法久住一者毗尼是

汝大師二者下至五人持律在世三者中国十人邊地五人如法受戒四者於清衆必法出

罪五者比丘守護禁戒因此五法而令仏法住世五千年故知持戒因緣仏法熾盛故

得入涅槃　若不持此戒　如所應布薩　喩如日沒時　世界皆闇暝　此偈明毀戒之損故

十誦云比丘廢學戒因此仏呵責乃由戒法故仏法久住世智度論云破戒之人人所不敬

其受如塚人所不近如大病人雖披袈裟次第捉籌實非比丘常懷怖懼我為仏賊四分律

云破戒比丘有五過種一常自害二智者所訶三惡名流布四臨終生悔五死墮悪道

當護持是戒　如猫牛愛尾　和合一處坐　如仏之所說　此偈勸持戒如智論說若求

大利益當堅持禁戒是諸德本出家之所要護如惜重寶如護身命財若人无脚

足遠涉无能趍无翅不能飛若護持禁戒能渉涅槃路又云戒如明日月亦如

瓔珞珠戒日若沒時僧衆皆迷闇是故應護戒如仏廣遺囑

我已說戒経　衆僧布薩竟　我今說戒経　所說諸功德　施一切衆生　皆共成仏道

此偈明律主迴向功德法護尊者說戒已了因此即發大乘願從雖同彼二乘之

根性即是菩薩種所作功德廣迴施令彼法界共成仏

四分戒本疏卷第四

庚年十月八日於沙州乾元寺寫及勘了故記之

5

Architectural Tile from Xiudingsi Pagoda

Tang dynasty (618–907), 7th century
Earthenware
23⅝ x 18½ x 3⅜ inches (60 x 47 x 8.6 cm)
Purchased with Museum funds, 1929-17-3

Captured in high relief at the moment of executing an exuberant movement, this dynamic figure of a Central or West Asian dancer with prominent features and a thick beard is a reminder of the cosmopolitan nature of the early Tang dynasty. The "foreign" dancer's upper body is shown in three-quarter view to the right, with one arm raised and the other behind his back, while his lower body and crossed legs twist in the opposite direction, as if he is in mid-twirl; his face bears an expression of intense concentration. The fluid lines delineating his flowing garments, which ripple around his legs and arms, recall depictions of dancing foreigners in other mediums from the sixth century (fig. 25) to the Tang dynasty.[1]

Modeled from dense clay, this heavy architectural tile is just one of several thousand that were made to decorate the exterior of the Xiudingsi pagoda located in Anyang in Henan province.[2] Part of a larger Buddhist complex established sometime in the early sixth century, the Xiuding Temple was destroyed several times as a result of anti-Buddhist persecutions but was rebuilt each time. The pagoda is thought to have been constructed in the seventh century, during the reign of emperor Taizong (r. 626–49).[3]

From the seventh to ninth century, beginning with Taizong's rule, China was one of the most powerful empires in the world. Foreign ideas and aesthetics were arriving from the West via the Silk Road, as shown by the interplay of Buddhist and foreign-style motifs decorating the predominantly diamond- and square-shaped tiles and ornamental borders that decorated the pagoda. An intricate system of mortise-and-tenon joinery was used to attach the tiles securely to the brick facing.[4] Tile designs on the exterior include other dancing figures,[5] flying deities (*apsaras*),[6] elephants carrying the Sacred Jewel of Buddhism on their backs, lions, muscular figures wrestling with a snake,[7] kneeling figures holding a flaming jewel, female court attendants, and military figures. The Xiudingsi pagoda is so far unique in its decorative program. HK

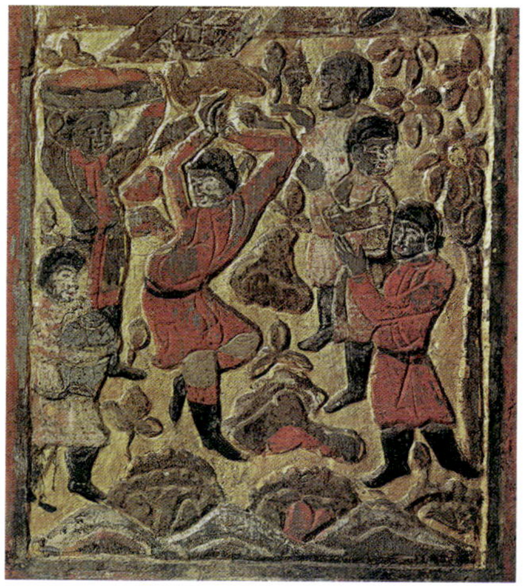

Fig. 25. Detail of a foreign dancer depicted on the stone funerary couch of a Sogdian official, An Qie (d. 579), excavated from Xi'an, Shaanxi

1. Similarly dressed Central Asian dancers decorate the base of a marble funerary couch in the Freer Gallery of Art, Smithsonian Institution, Washington, DC (F1915.110), dated to the Northern Qi dynasty (550–77), and on the stone funerary couch of a Sogdian official found in Xi'an, Shaanxi (Shaanxi 2003, col. pl. 63). Other foreign dancers are depicted on jade belt plaques excavated in Shaanxi (from the Zhaoling tomb complex of the emperor Taizong in Xi'an) and Anhui provinces (found in Hefei); see Gu and Liu 2005, 185; Gu and Yang 2005, 168, respectively.
2. See Henan and Anyang 1983.
3. Royal Ontario Museum 1992, 166.
4. Swart and Till 1990, 67–69.
5. Another dancer, captured in a different pose, is in the Cleveland Museum of Art (1921.263).
6. Two examples of tiles decorated with flying deities are in the Metropolitan Museum of Art, New York (65.178.1, 65.178.2)
7. Examples of the latter three designs can be found in the Asian Art Museum of San Francisco (B60S119+, B62S8+, B73S12).

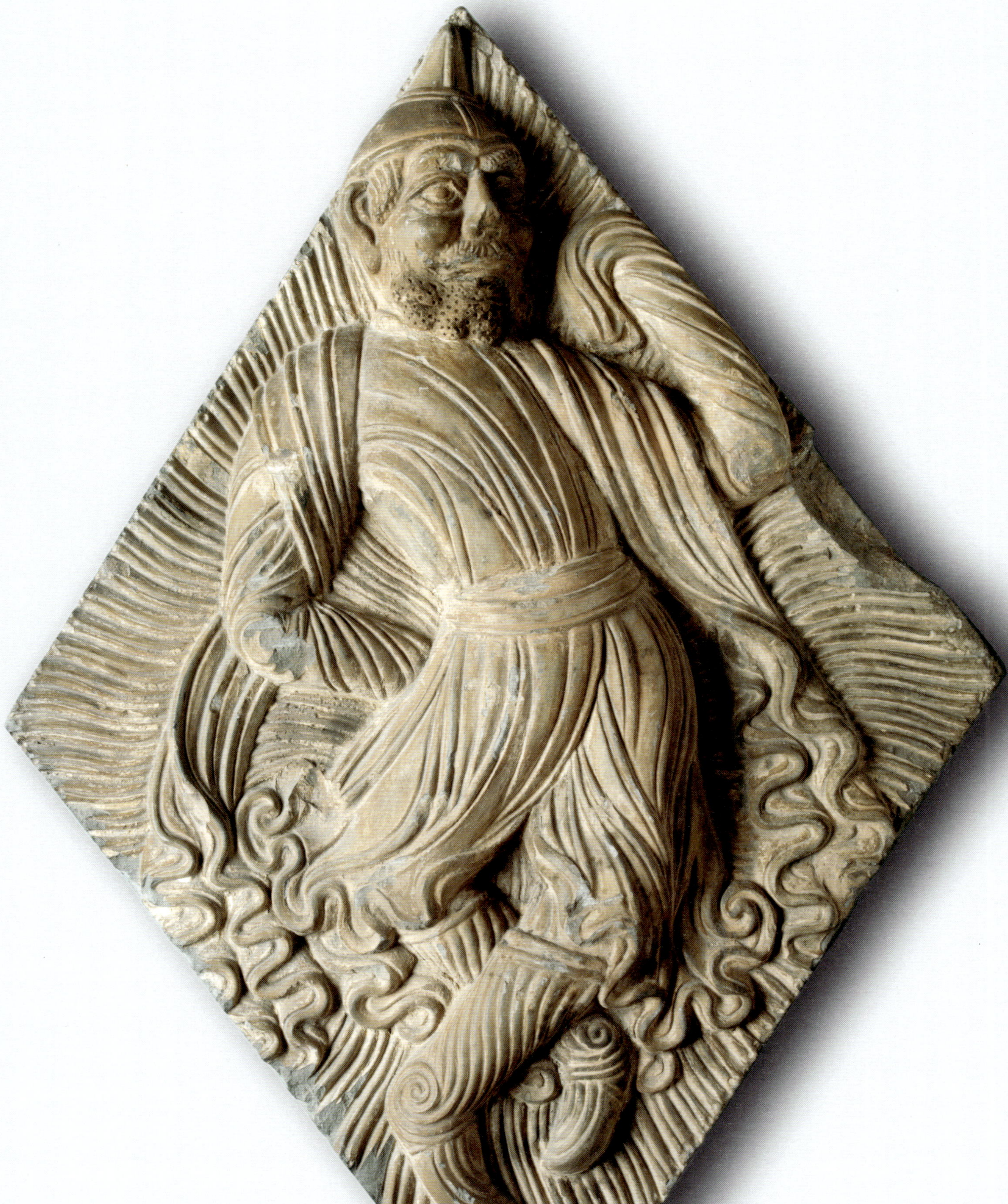

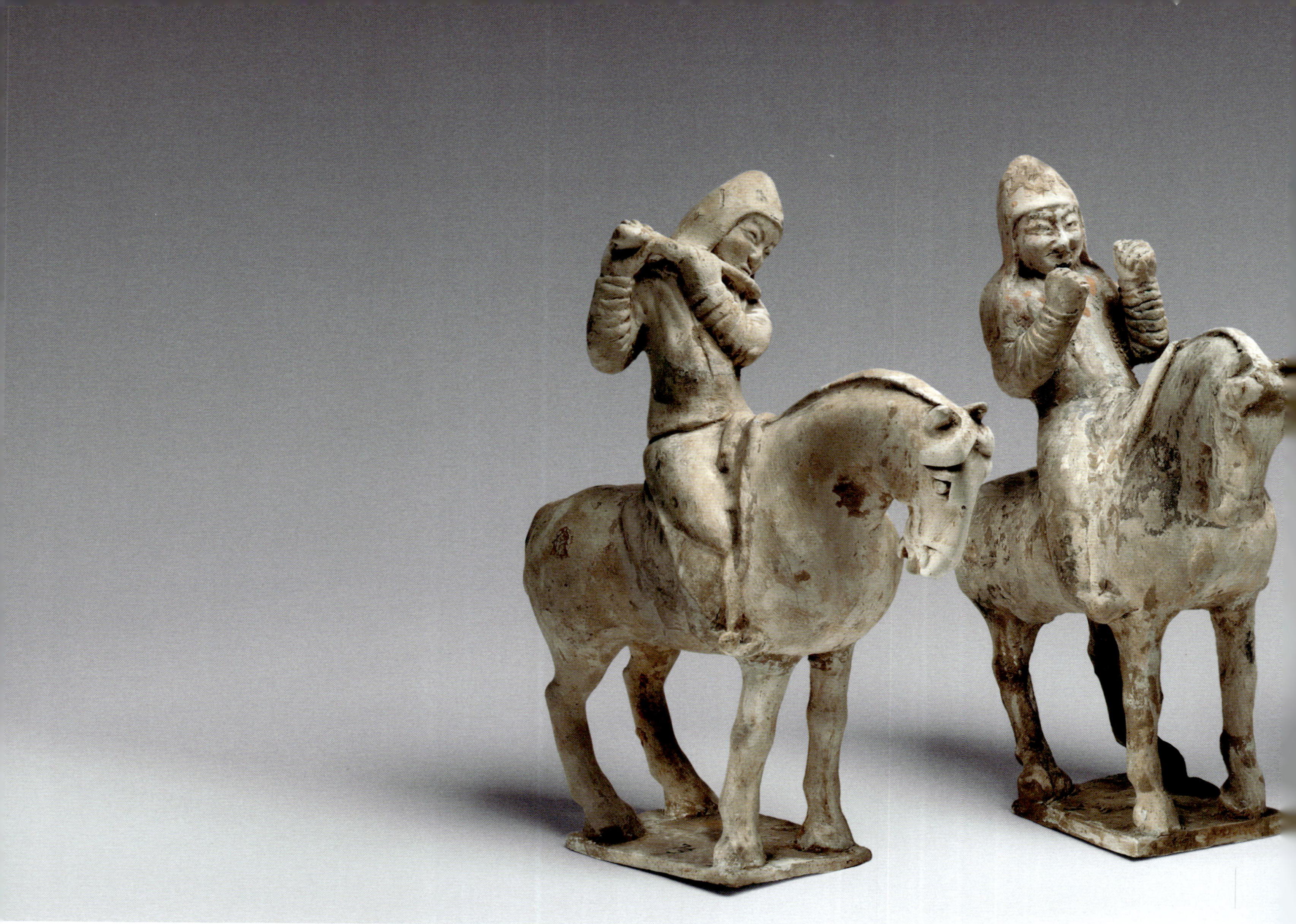

6

Musicians on Horseback

Tang dynasty (618–907), mid-7th century
Earthenware with traces of paint
H. 10¾–12⁵⁄₁₆ inches (27.3–31.3 cm); w. 8¹¹⁄₁₆–9⁷⁄₁₆ inches (22.1–24 cm)
Gift of Charles H. Ludington from the George Crofts Collection, 1923-21-146–50

Each of these five male musicians on horseback wears a long-sleeved tunic, boots, and a distinctive *fengmao* (a hat that protects from the wind) that covers the ears and back of the neck. The instruments they animatedly play (some now missing) include the horizontal flute, the vertical flute, and the pan pipes. Groups of similarly modeled mounted musicians have been found in the tombs of wealthy officials,[1] and indicate that the group originally included a drummer, modeled with a small, flat drum resting horizontally on the upper thigh. The two musicians missing their instruments may have been playing a long horn (middle figure) and a type of percussion instrument held between clenched fists (second figure from left).

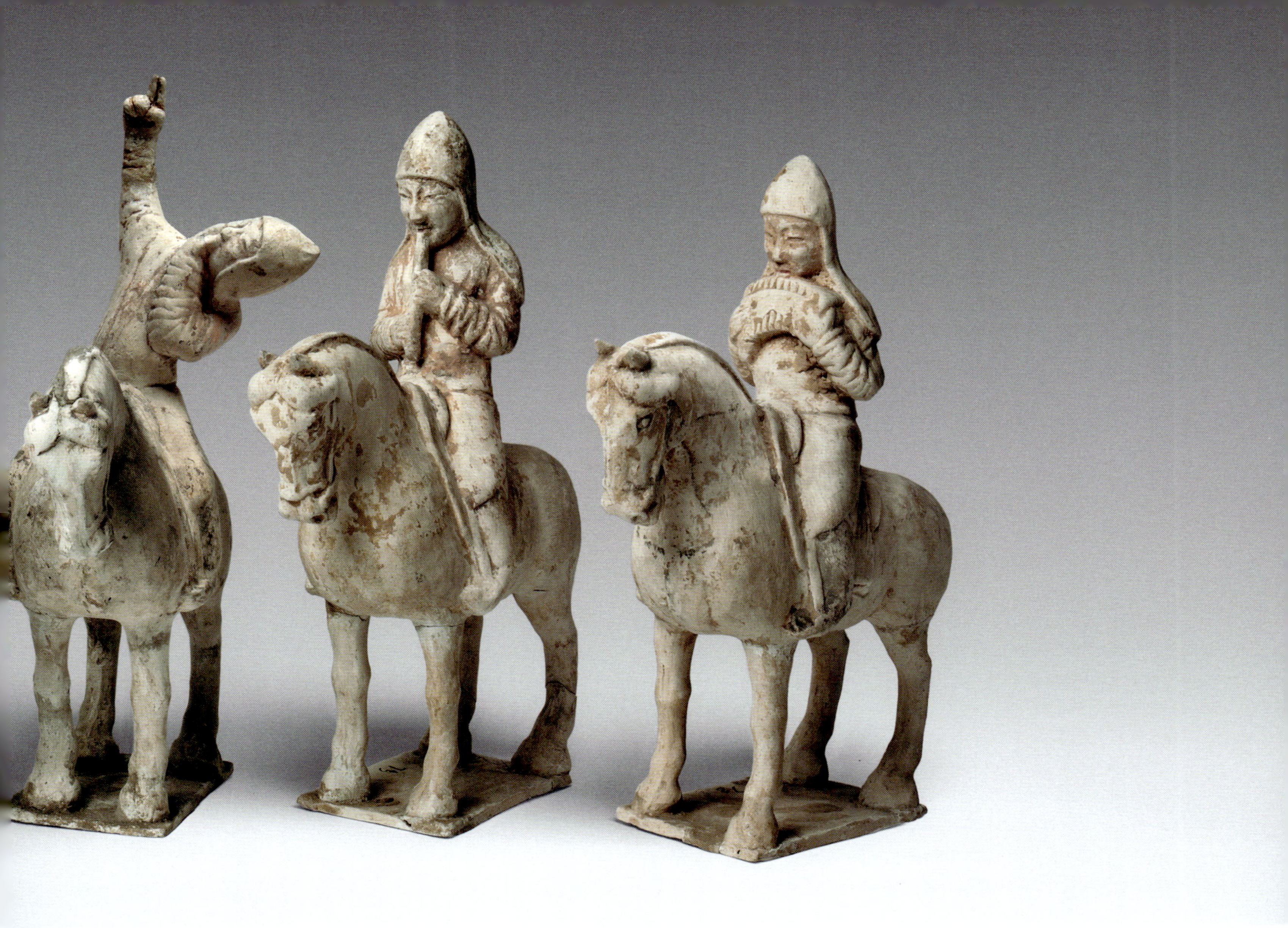

Musicians on horseback, both male and female, were interred with the deceased at least as early as the fourth century, a practice that continued into the high Tang period (mid-8th century).[2] In the Tang tomb belonging to the palace attendant Zheng Rentai (d. 664), buried in the mausoleum complex of Taizong, the second Tang emperor, thirty-eight earthenware male mounted musicians were placed in two different parts of the tomb, suggesting that they were fulfilling different purposes.[3] Mounted musicians served in the army to signal battle orders, and they may also have accompanied funeral processions.[4]

Similar forms of these types of mounted musicians can be attributed to how they were made—formed in molds but differentiated by the application of painted decoration or glaze. This group is molded from buff earthenware, with the pigments applied after firing (only an orange-red pigment remains). Other excavated examples of mounted musicians were glazed in a clear straw color with pigment applied on top of the glaze, as seen in the thirty-eight mounted musicians from Zheng Rentai's tomb.[5] HK

1. Eleven very similarly modeled, painted earthenware mounted musicians were excavated from the tomb of Liu Kai, a country magistrate who died in 626, and his wife at Yanshi, Luoyang, Henan province; see Li 1992, 27–28, col. pls. 6, 7.
2. Florence 2007–8, no. 131, illustrates two three-color (*sancai*) glazed mounted musicians.
3. Shaanxi 1972, 37, 43 (illus.). The two groups are distinguished by their different hats and robes. Musicians with cowl hats similar to those worn by the figures in the Philadelphia grouping were found in the third and fourth "heavenly well" niches within the sloping tomb passage.
4. Florence 2007–8, no. 131.
5. Eight similarly molded Tang-dynasty mounted musicians decorated in straw-colored glaze, and including a vertical flute, horizontal flute, trumpet, and drum player, are in the National Museum of History, Taipei.

7

Pair of Tomb Guardian Creatures (*Zhenmushou*)

Tang dynasty (618–907), early to mid-8th century
Earthenware with three-color (*sancai*) glaze and paint
38⁵⁄₁₆ x 13¹⁵⁄₁₆ x 9¹¹⁄₁₆ inches (97.3 x 35.4 x 24.6 cm); 38¹⁄₁₆ x 15¹⁄₁₆ x 9⅜ inches (96.7 x 38.2 x 23.8 cm)
Gift of Charles H. Ludington from the George Crofts Collection, 1923-21-5, 1923-21-6

Finely worked from clay using molds and freehand modeling, and then glazed, with some facial features picked out in pigments after firing, these fantastic guardian creatures were created with a ferocious lion head, grotesque human face, and spikes and horns specifically to ward off evil spirits. Their large size, fine details, and intricate glazing indicate that they were made for the tomb of a member of the Tang elite, such as a high-ranking official or prince.[1] Part of a larger retinue that included guardian figures and officials, the pair of horned guardian beasts would have been placed nearest to the tomb entrance.

The tradition of guarding a tomb with frightening creatures is a practice that began centuries earlier in tombs of the Warring States period (453–221 BCE).[2] Figures with animal heads and human faces first appeared in fifth-century BCE tombs and underwent various transformations over time. By the early Tang dynasty, as this pair illustrates, non-native influences had been integrated into their modeling and glazing. The use of lions as guardian creatures was itself a foreign idea, since lions were not native to East Asia but originated in West Asia (in today's Iran and Iraq), appearing in China as tomb guardians sometime during the Han dynasty (206 BCE–220 CE). They also entered the culture through Buddhism and Buddhist art, where they are depicted as protectors of the dharma (Buddhist law; see no. 4).[3]

The figures are covered in a distinctive lead glaze called *sancai*. The term *sancai* (three colors) describes the triad of colors most commonly seen with this technique—straw, amber, and green—but yellow, brown, and, in rarer cases, blue and black were also used. The chests of the figures are decorated with an attractive dotted design that appears to have been created using a resist material applied before the glaze, much as in the technique of tie-dying fabric, which has led to suggestions of possible influence from contemporary textiles,[4] or of contact with the Middle East.[5] HK

1. The status of a tomb's occupant is reflected in the size and modeling of the tomb figures. A pair of similarly sized and decorated guardian figures in the British Museum, London (1936,1012.224, 225), are said to be from the tomb of General Liu Tingxun (d. 728) of the Zhongwu army, lieutenant of Henan and Huaiyan districts and Imperial Privy Councilor. See Harrison-Hall 2017, 92.
2. Zhang 2004, 2–3. After the mid-eighth century (mid to late Tang), as burial practices changed, such figures were no longer placed in the tomb; Zhang 2004, 42.
3. Fong 1991, 189.
4. Kerr and Wood 2004, 501.
5. It is a matter of debate whether the use of multi-colored (*sancai*) glaze was influenced by contact with the Middle East or was a Chinese development; Jiang 2010, 1.

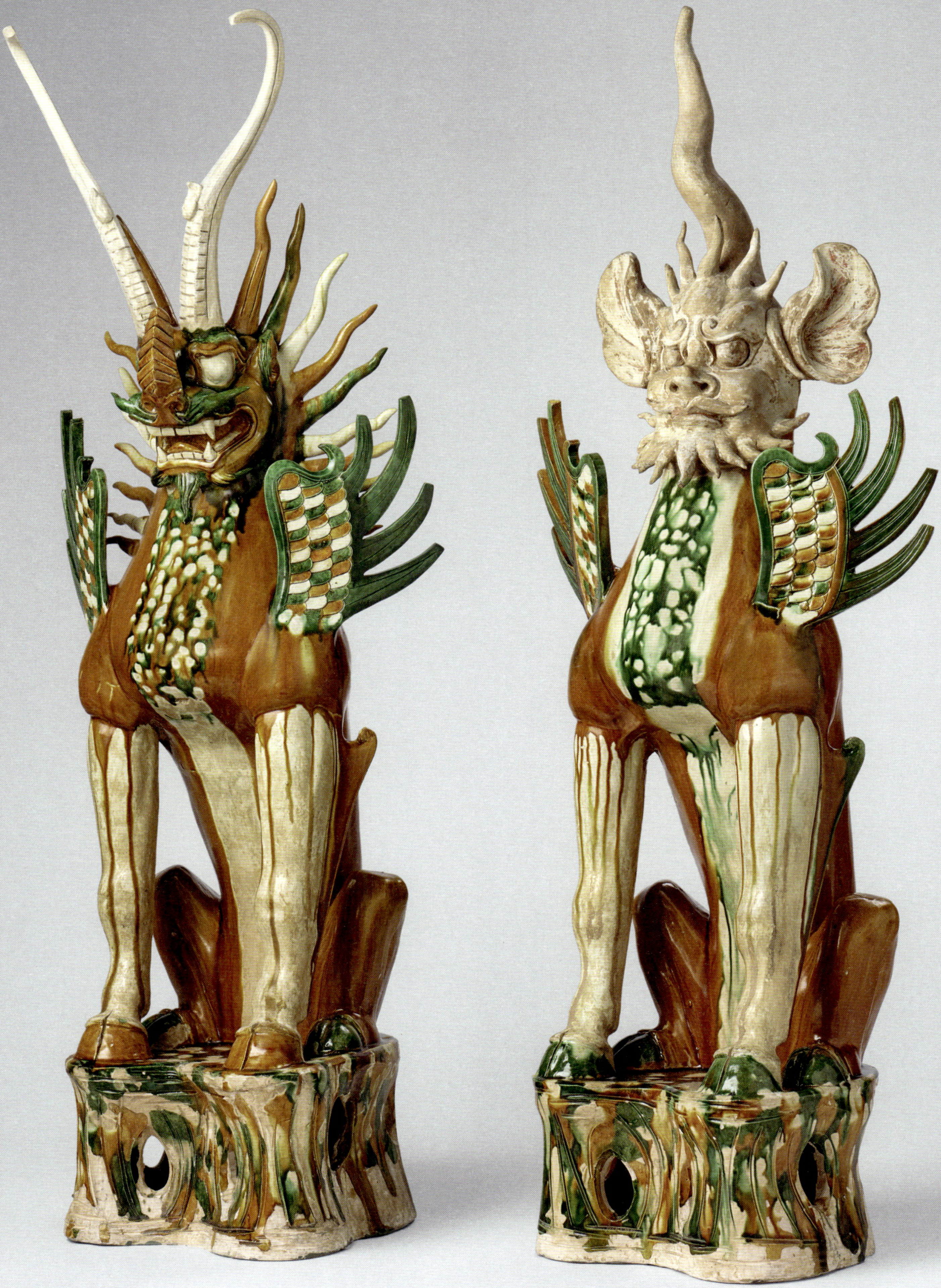

8

Tomb Guardian Warrior

Tang dynasty (618–907), early to mid-8th century
Earthenware with three-color (*sancai*) glaze and paint
39⅛ x 15¾ x 5⅛ inches (99.3 x 40 x 13 cm)
Gift of Charles H. Ludington from the George Crofts Collection, 1923-21-24

This ferocious warrior with bulging eyes and open mouth standing triumphantly on a recumbent bull once brandished a weapon in his raised left hand. He wears elaborate armor featuring epaulettes in the form of *makaras* (mythical sea creatures), breastplates embellished with animal heads, and rivet-decorated shin guards. While pairs of armed warriors had been placed in elite Chinese tombs since early times, this particular model appears to have been inspired by *lokapala*, heavenly guardian figures from the Buddhist pantheon, beginning in the early Tang dynasty. His headdress decorated with a bird (in this case a phoenix), however, is typically Chinese; a *heguan*, or pheasant hat, was often seen on high-ranking officials in the Tang military and was associated with courage.[1]

Sculptures such as this one were made in separate parts—in molds that formed the head, torso, arms, legs, and base—which were then luted together and covered in a three-color (*sancai*) lead glaze. The head and hands were left unglazed and were originally painted in flesh colors, with the details picked out in darker-colored pigments, possibly with the addition of gilded decoration. The size, fine workmanship, and quality of the glazed decoration indicate that this figure protected the tomb of a high-ranking official or other member of the elite.[2] Originally part of a larger retinue of figures that included a pair of seated guardian creatures (*zhenmushou*; see no. 7) and a pair of civil officials,[3] this warrior and his companion replaced the pair of military officials that guarded the tomb dressed in armor, often armed with a shield as well. Both the military and civil branches of government were represented in tombs.[4] HK

1. Sydney 2016, 147, no. 90.
2. An even larger glazed tomb guardian (h. 162 cm) was buried in the tomb of General Anpu, who died in 709; Xie 2013, 62–63.
3. Philadelphia Museum of Art, acc. nos 1923-21-21, 1923-21-22.
4. Fong 1991, 191.

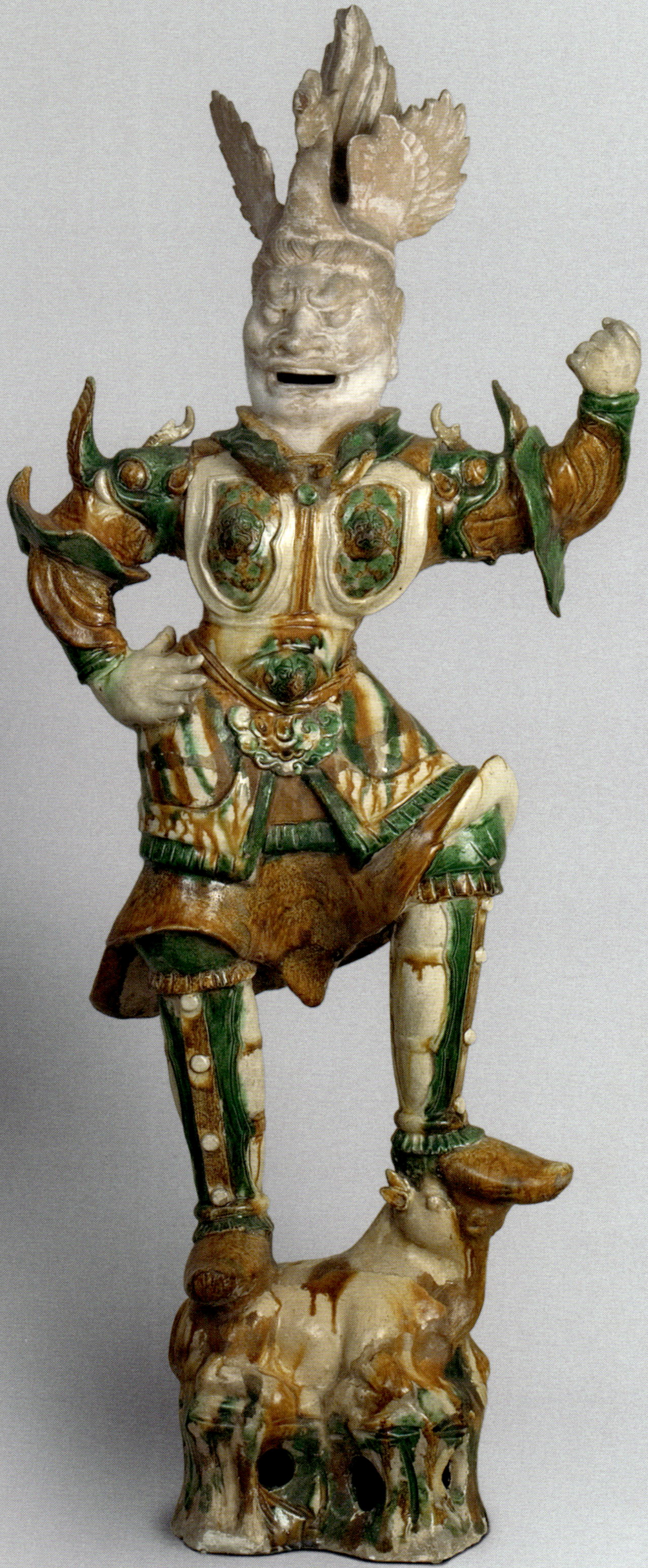

9

Tomb Figure of a Bactrian Camel

Tang dynasty (618–907), first half of the 8th century
Earthenware with three-color (*sancai*) glaze
32 x 10 x 25 inches (81.3 x 25.4 x 63.5 cm)
Gift of Mrs. John Wintersteen, 1964-9-1

Modeled from buff earthenware and constructed in separate molds, with the two halves then luted together, this impressively large, finely modeled earthenware camel once graced the tomb of a high-ranking individual, possibly a court official or a member of the imperial family.[1] The attractive *sancai* (three-color) glaze of cream, amber, and yellow was applied judiciously and allowed to drip in places to create what looks like a deliberate decorative effect. *Sancai* wares were made in the two Tang capitals of Luoyang, in Henan province, and Xi'an, in Shaanxi province, and were used only for burial and ritual offerings, as the lead-based glaze was not suitable for eating and drinking.[2]

It was believed that burying earthenware figures and utensils with the deceased would allow them to continue to enjoy in death what they had experienced in life. Along with figures of officials, servants, and entertainers, saddle horses and Bactrian pack camels (whose two humps distinguish them from their one-humped African cousins) led by foreign grooms give a sense of the exotic trading activities carried out between China and countries to the west. Called "ships of the dessert," camels were hardy animals highly valued for their dependability in traveling long distances under harsh, arid conditions.[3] This rather ferocious-looking, braying specimen carries a full pack in addition to food and drink, including a rack of ribs and an amphora and two rounded flasks, likely used for wine. HK

1. The size and the quality of figurines buried in tombs were directly related to the status of the tomb occupant. This camel is similar in size and fineness to one from the tomb of Li Xian, Prince of Yong, the sixth son of the Tang emperor Gaozong. See Eckfeld 2005, 47.
2. Li, Bower, and He 2010, 251.
3. See Knauer 1998.

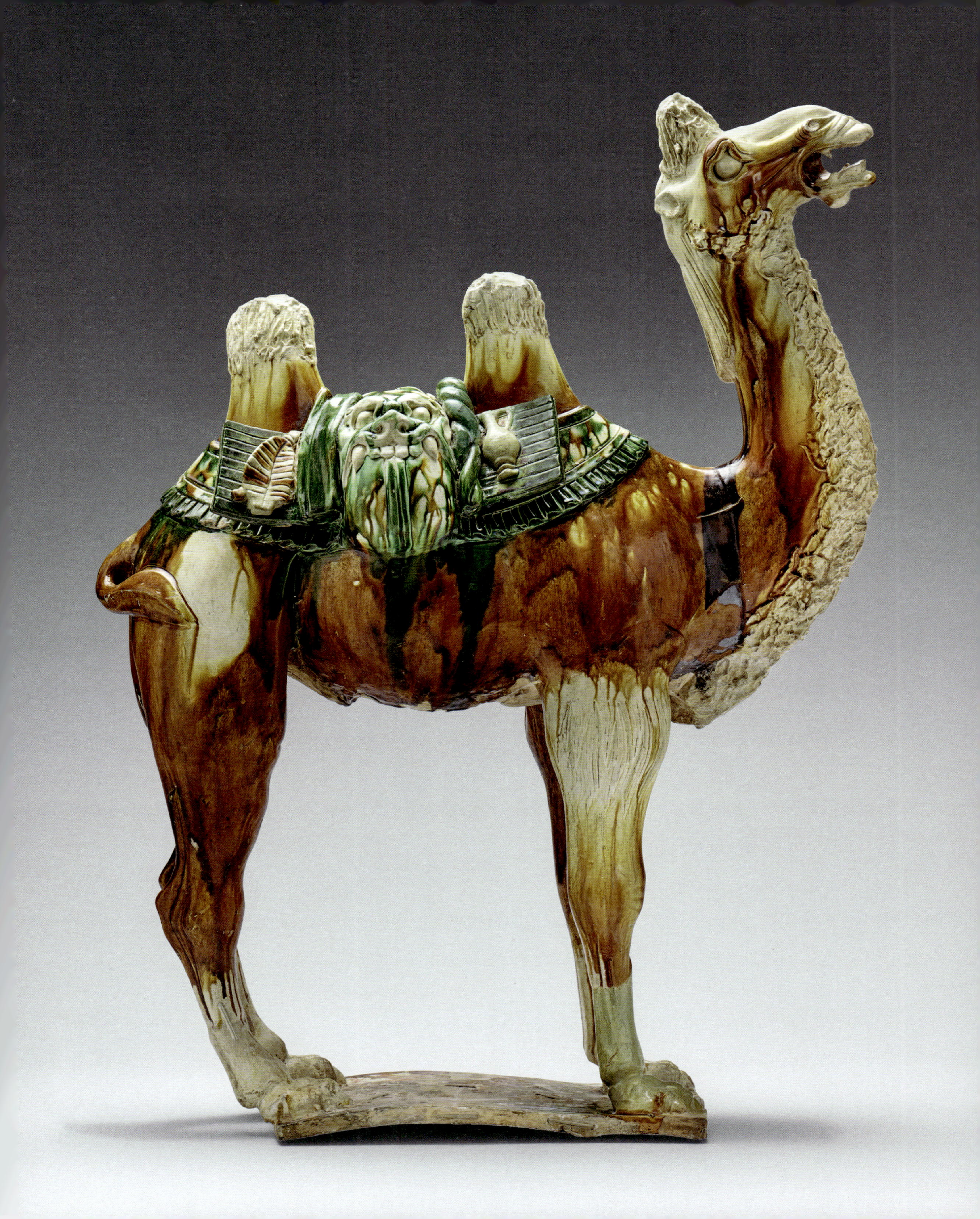

10

Panel and Posts from a House-shaped Sarcophagus

Tang dynasty (618–907), first half of the 8th century
Limestone
a) $41\frac{5}{16}$ x $22\frac{13}{16}$ x $3\frac{9}{16}$ inches (105 x 58 x 9.1 cm); b) $41\frac{5}{16}$ x $11\frac{7}{16}$ x $8\frac{1}{16}$ inches (105 x 29 x 20.5 cm);
c) $41\frac{5}{16}$ x $11\frac{7}{16}$ x $6\frac{15}{16}$ inches (105 x 29 x 17.7 cm)
Purchased with Museum funds, 1931-50-11, 1931-50-3, 1931-50-5

These richly carved and incised limestone panels and posts comprised part of an immersive environment created for the deceased within the setting of an elite tomb.[1] Made in the early eighth century, during what is considered the height of the Tang dynasty, they once formed the sides of an elaborate house-shaped sarcophagus for a high-ranking member of the Tang aristocracy (fig. 26).[2] The exteriors of the three slabs, from a group of fifteen panels and posts, are carved in shallow relief. The widest panel (a) shows a pair of male attendants in robes and boots surrounded by rich floral scrolling decoration and (above) phoenix-type birds, leaping winged leonine creatures, and flying horses. A corner post (b) depicts a female attendant dressed in male garb considered fashionable at the time, with a pouch hanging at her belted waist and deferentially presenting a rounded object with both hands. A middle post (c) is decorated with a lion chasing a goose or swan (at the bottom), cavorting lions, birds, and other winged hybrid feline creatures, set against densely scrolling peony blossoms. All three panels are lightly incised on the reverse, with two robed female attendants in a garden with rocks, plants, and a butterfly (a), a flowering plant (b), and a male attendant pointing to a butterfly and bird overhead (c).

The walls of Tang aristocratic tombs were often decorated with mural paintings, while the deceased was placed in an elaborately decorated stone sarcophagus[3] and accompanied by ceramic figures to ensure that he or she was well provided for in the afterlife. Mural paintings in some tombs depict scenes similar to those on the sarcophagus panels shown here, with male and female attendants in a garden and a reception hall, representing the different types of activities that the deceased's spirit could enjoy.

The panel and posts of the sarcophagus are of equal height but vary in thickness and width, as the posts have channels on either side to hold the panels securely in place, mimicking the walls and columns in a room. The resemblance of the sarcophagus to a building, complete with a roof and a doorway guarded by attendants, suggests that it was intended to re-create a reception hall setting.[4] HK

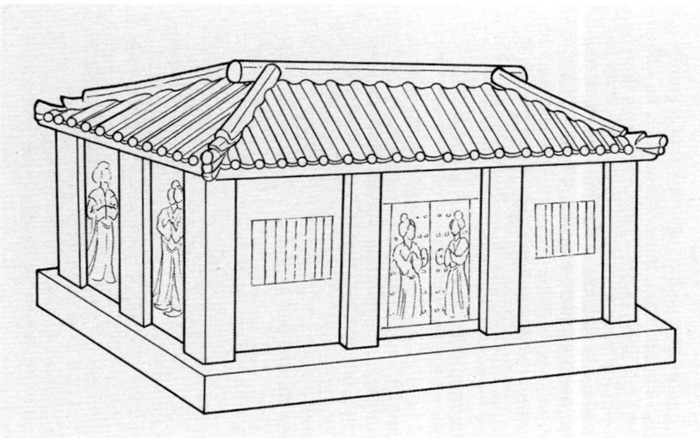

Fig. 26. Line drawing of the stone sarcophagus of Xue Jing (d. 720), found in Yuncheng region, Shanxi province. After Shanxi 2000, fig. 5

1. Tombs of the Tang dynasty were designed and conceived as a dwelling of the type that the deceased experienced while alive and were furnished for the afterlife. An important consideration of the tomb was to ensure that it was properly aligned with the correct cosmic forces to ensure the best possible outcome for the deceased and his or her descendants, while also providing the comforts of everyday life.
2. The motifs found on the Philadelphia panels, including the lions, flying horses, and figures, are similar to decoration found on the house-shaped sarcophagus belonging to Xue Jing (d. 720), a member of the Tang imperial family (nephew to the son-in-law of Tang Taizong), who was buried in southern Shanxi province; see Shanxi 2000, 109–11. Only certain nobles closely related to the emperor were allowed such elaborately decorated sarcophagi. For other examples, see Yang 2004, vol. 1, 354–55.
3. Similar carved stone panels from a sarcophagus in the Cleveland Museum of Art are illustrated by Pearlstein 1984, 309–11.
4. Hay 2010, 31. For a discussion of the similarities between line-engraved stone carvings and mural paintings, see Fong 1987.

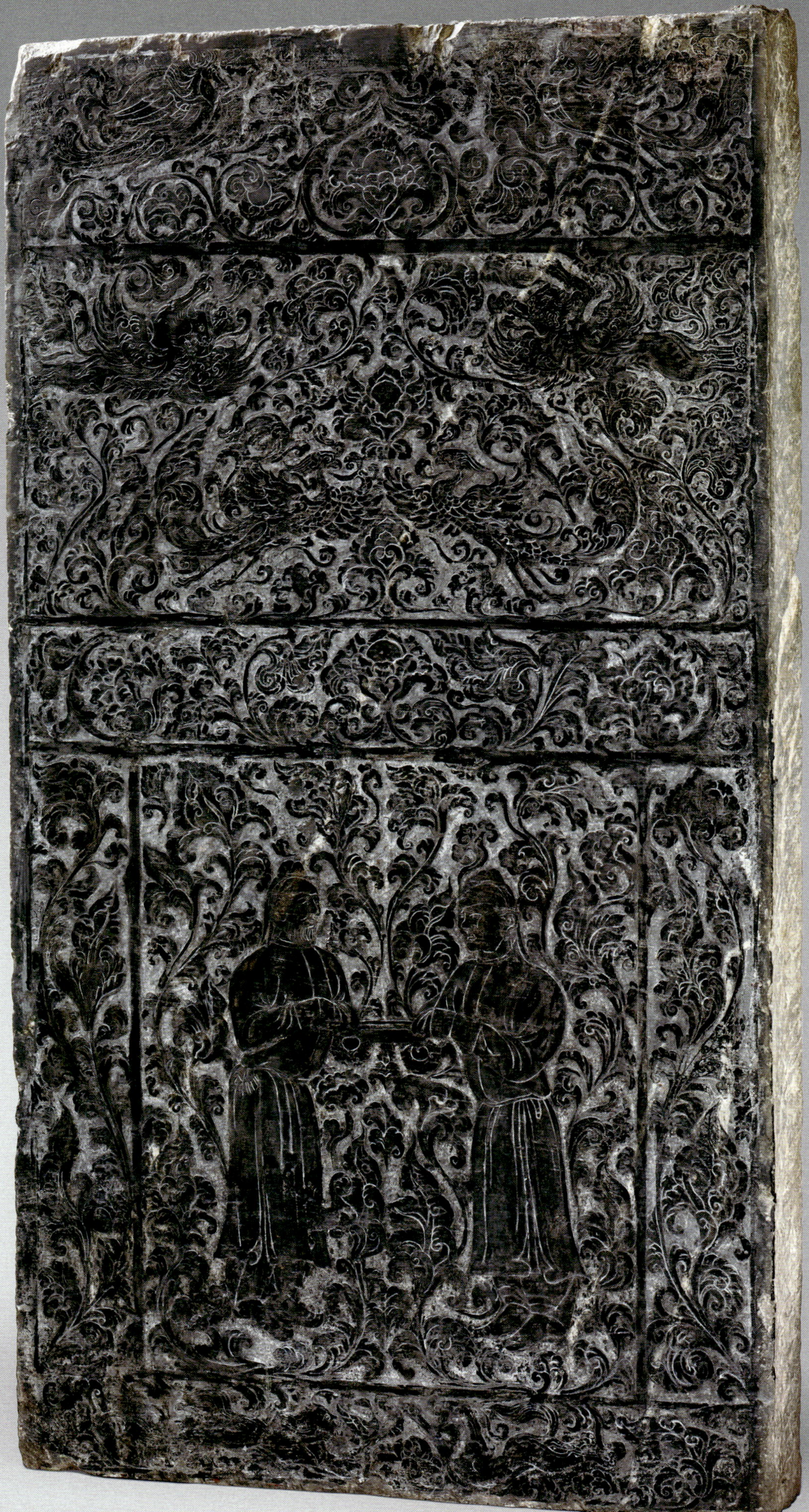

a

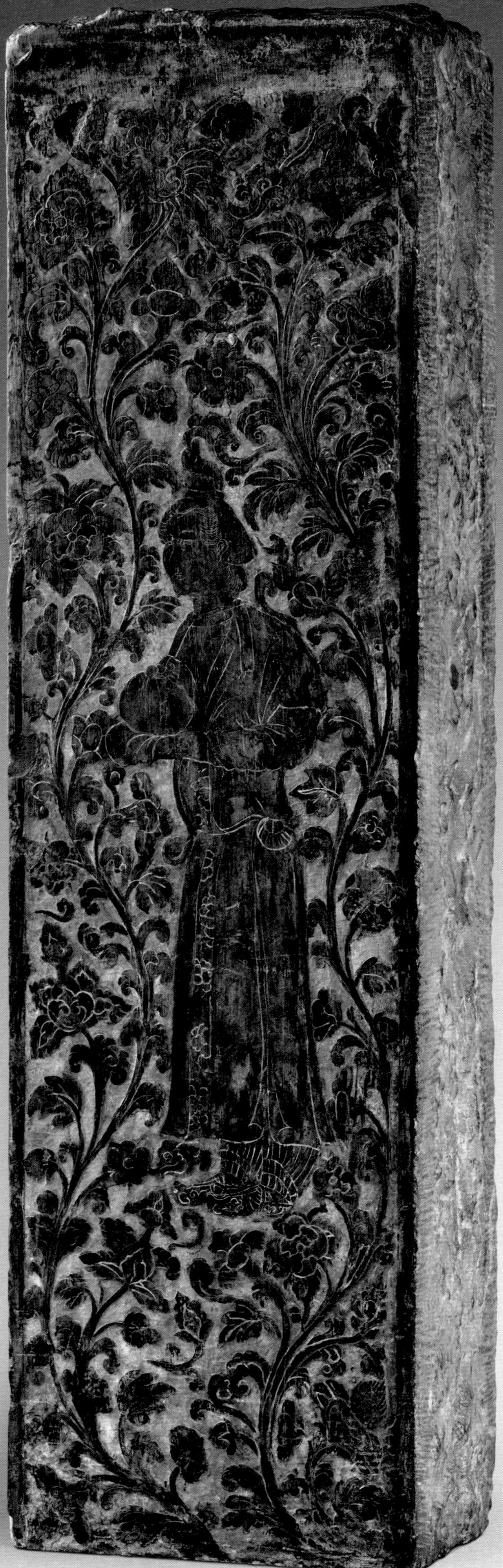

b

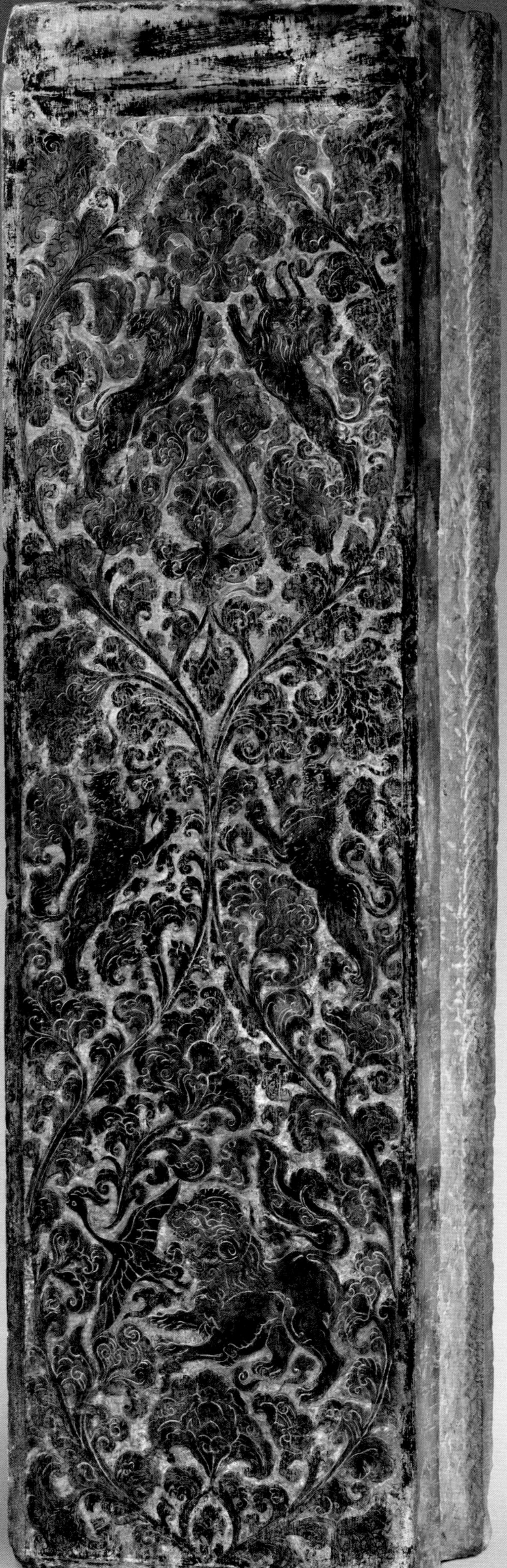

c

11

Funerary Mask

Liao dynasty (907–1125), late 10th–early 12th century
Silver alloy
8¾ x 8½ x 13/16 inches (22.3 x 21.6 x 2 cm)
Purchased with funds contributed by Marguerite and Gerry Lenfest, 2012-53-1

This striking mask depicts the serene face of a male member of the seminomadic Khitan, who established the Liao dynasty in northern China. The silver sheet was carefully hammered and modeled to form the closed eyes, elongated nose, and thin lips, while the eyebrows, moustache, and small beard were delicately incised on the surface. The ears are pierced and were probably once adorned with earrings, the wearing of which was a custom practiced by both male and female Khitan.

Among Chinese burial traditions, placing a metal mask over the face of the deceased was distinctive to the Khitan, who interred their high-ranking men and women with various amounts of metal body attire, including a suit "woven" from wire to cover the body and sometimes metal shoe soles or boots. It was believed that this burial practice may have helped to preserve the body and protect it from decay.[1] Masks were highly personalized and were fashioned in a variety of shapes and sizes, while the type of metal used depended on the status of the wearer. The simplest were made of thinly hammered bronze sheets, while those fashioned of more precious metals—silver and, in rare cases, gold (fig. 27)[2]—were reserved for the elite.

Funerary masks are well documented in many ancient cultures, including in Egypt and Greece, and are related to religious ideas of life after death.[3] In central China, jade masks and shrouds were used to cover the faces of members of the imperial family in the Eastern Zhou period (770–256 BCE). The Liao Khitan use of metal funerary masks is not related to this earlier jade mask tradition, however, but appears to be more closely aligned with customs practiced by the tribal cultures of southern Siberia and to the west of China.[4] HK

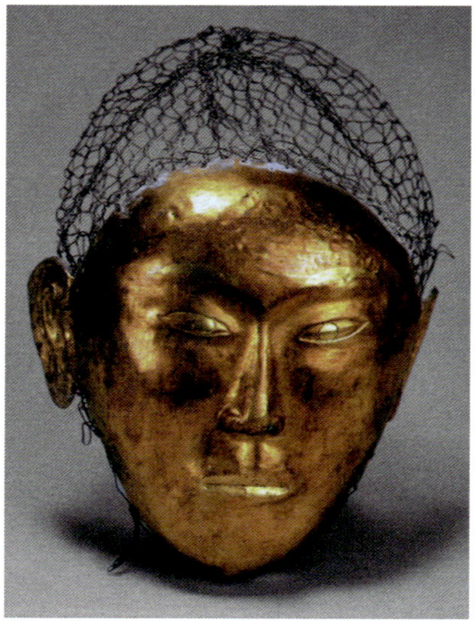

Fig. 27. Funerary Mask. Liao dynasty, 1018. Gold with silver netting, 8½ x 7⅜ inches (21.7 x 18.8 cm). Excavated from the tomb of the princess of the state of Chen (d. 1018), Tongliao City, Inner Mongolia

1. New York, Cologne, and Zurich 2006–7, 98; the metal body attire was worn over clothing. The Khitan appropriated the Tang Chinese tradition of "encoffining" the deceased in burial; see Kinoshita 2006, 74. For more on Liao tombs, see Steinhardt 1997, 241–351; Kuhn 1998.
2. This gold example, one of only two known, is illustrated in New York, Cologne, and Zurich 2006–7, 108. The type of material and the quality of workmanship were directly related to the status of the wearer. Both gold and silver were treated as precious materials and given as tribute to the Liao. See Kinoshita 2006, 110–12.
3. Kinoshita 2006, 119.
4. Kinoshita 2004, 135–43.

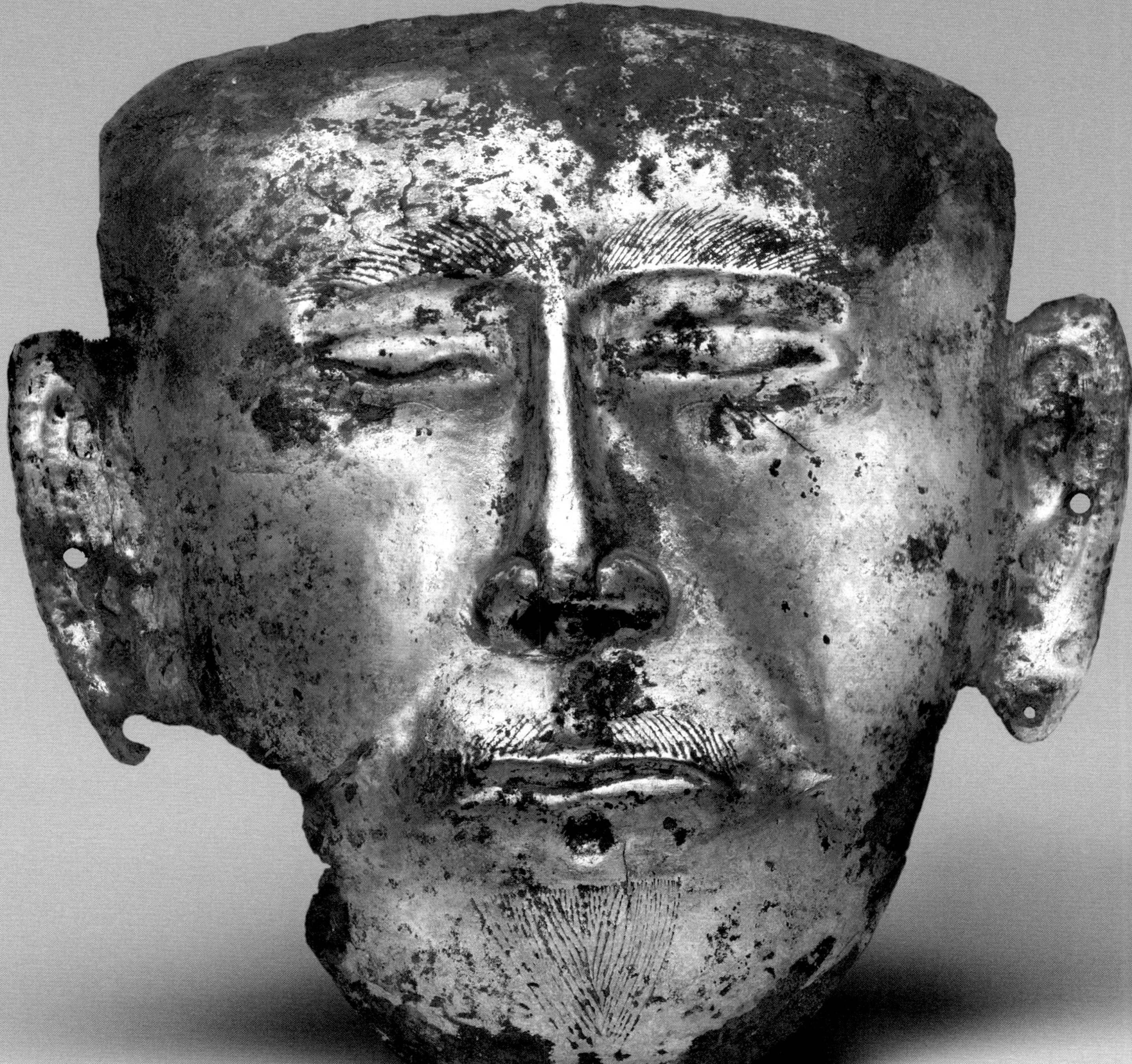

12

Bodhisattva

Northern Song (960–1127) or Liao (907–1125) dynasty, 11th century
Wood (willow, *Salix* sp.) with traces of paint, stone
60 x 16⅛ x 10¼ inches (152.4 x 41 x 26 cm)
Gift of Charles H. Ludington from the George Crofts Collection, 1925-53-10

Solemn in expression, this Buddhist deity likely flanked a larger figure of a Buddha in a northern Chinese temple. Carved in deep relief and originally brightly painted and gilded, the standing bodhisattva wears armlets, an elaborate necklace, and a thin shawl. A sarong-like garment draped over one shoulder and cinched at the waist partially covers an ankle-length skirt that falls in folds alongside long scarves that form two deep swags in front. Around the figure's hips is a belt made of rectangular plaques over a sash whose long ties, weighted by an elaborate knot in front, cascade down to rest in a neat heap between the fleshy feet. The plump rendering of the figure and the Indian style of clothing relate closely to painted clay figures of attendant bodhisattvas flanking a seated Buddha in the Liao-dynasty Buddhist temple of Huayansi,[1] located in the northern province of Shanxi (fig. 28). A painted marble bodhisattva (missing its head) in the Metropolitan Museum of Art, New York, dated to the Jin dynasty (1115–1234), shows a similar rendering of scarves and garment but carved in shallower relief.[2] The Philadelphia figure's downcast eyes, with pupils made of a dark stone to provide a realistic touch, have a peculiar intensity.

Microscopic analysis has revealed that the figure is fashioned from willow,[3] one of the wood types used most frequently in Chinese Buddhist statuary. Its softness, light color, and fine grain make it an easy material to carve, although it is not particularly durable.[4] Carved from a single piece of wood—with the forearms (now missing) possibly separately attached—the figure has been hollowed out at the back into three rectangular openings, which originally would have held offerings such as prayers, colored stones, or other relics, placed within the sculpture to ensure the efficacy of this benevolent figure. HK

1. For a description of the Huayan temple and an illustration of the clay figures found inside the Sutra Repository, see Steinhardt 1997, 124–25, fig. 119. The date 1038 was written on the underside of a beam in the repository.
2. An illustration of the piece in the Metropolitan Museum of Art, New York (acc. no. 34.56a,b), can be found in Leidy and Strahan 2010, 181, no. A48, or on the Met's website.
3. Wood identification is based on analysis of a sample taken from inside a hollow at the back of the lower torso. The sample was prepared as thin sections in the cross (transverse), radial, and tangential directions and viewed under an optical microscope. See Dr. Mechtild Mertz, Prof. Tazuru Suyako, Prof. Itoh Takao, and Prof. Sugiyama Junji, "Final Wood Identification Report for the Philadelphia Museum of Arts [*sic*]: Micrographic Expertise," unpublished report, May 2018, Kyoto. Copies of the report are available in the Philadelphia Museum of Art conservation and curatorial files.
4. Mertz and Itoh 2010, 216.

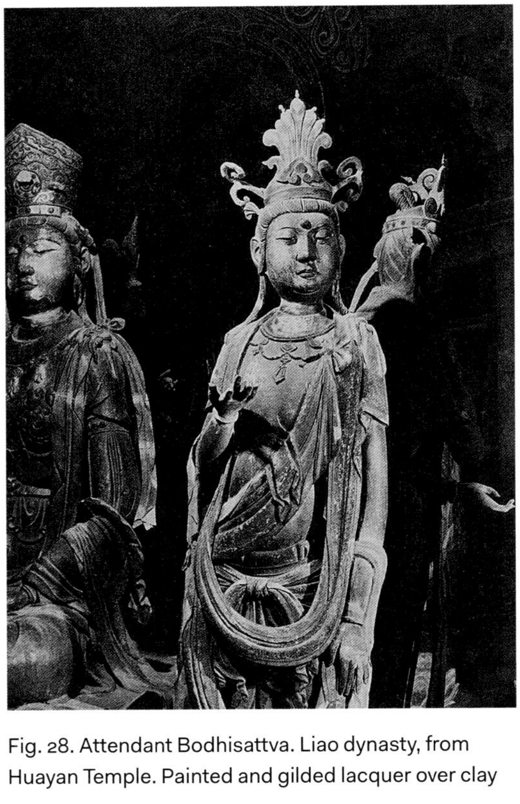

Fig. 28. Attendant Bodhisattva. Liao dynasty, from Huayan Temple. Painted and gilded lacquer over clay

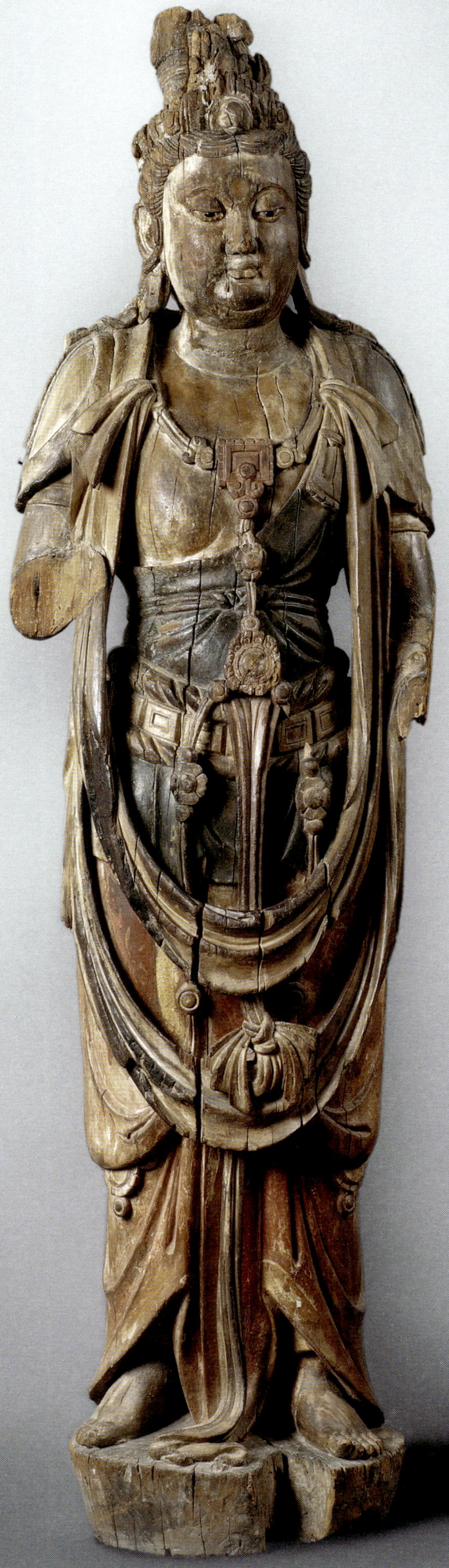

13

Wine Bottle

Northern Song dynasty (960–1127), 11th century
Porcelain with russet glaze (Ding ware)
14¾ x 9 inches (37.5 x 22.9 cm)
Gift of Charles H. Ludington from the George Crofts Collection, 1923-21-272

This elegantly potted, ovoid bottle with widely swelling shoulders is surprisingly lightweight and delicately potted for a vessel of its size. It is covered in an even, russet-colored glaze that stops just short of the base. When the bottle is turned over, the fine, unglazed white porcelain and neatly cut foot reveal that it is Ding ware, produced in the Ding kilns in Hebei province in northern China.

Ding ware, considered by collectors and connoisseurs to be one of the five great wares of the Song dynasty,[1] was renowned for its fine white porcelain covered in warm, ivory-toned clear glazes. The ware enjoyed such high status that the Ding site was one of the few kilns obliged to supply the early Song imperial court with tribute wares.[2] While known mainly for carved and incised (as well as molded and impressed) wares covered in a clear ivory glaze, and made for everyday use, the Ding kilns also produced dark-colored glazes—such as the russet-colored glaze on this bottle, called "purple Ding"—through the addition of iron pigment.[3] These darker glazes were more highly prized by collectors than the white Ding pieces, as noted by an early Ming collector, Cao Zhao, who explained in his treatise on assessing antiquities—*Essential Criteria of Antiquities* (1388)—that although ancient Ding-ware pieces with fine bodies and white lustrous glazes were valuable, purple and inky Ding wares were more expensive.[4] This upright form is also rarer, as the majority of the Ding wares produced were bowls and dishes. HK

1. The four other wares are Ru, Guan, Ge, and Jun. Ding ware was exalted by both Song-dynasty and Ming-dynasty scholars; see Kerr and Wood 2004, 160. So famous were Ding wares that other kilns attempted to copy them.
2. They were also obliged to supply wealthy Buddhist monasteries; Kerr and Wood 2004, 157–59.
3. Pierson and McCausland 2003, 14. There was also black Ding; the difference between the russet and black glaze was dependent on the firing, with russet glaze fired at a higher temperature. In the early part of the Northern Song dynasty, the glaze colors for purple Ding ranged from russet brown to a brownish yellow or a reddish to purplish brown. A somewhat smaller bottle with a glaze similar to the Philadelphia example was excavated from the tomb of Zhang Min (d. 1071) in Zhenhong, Jiangsu province. See Mu 2002, 154–55, fig. 204.
4. See David 1971, 141.

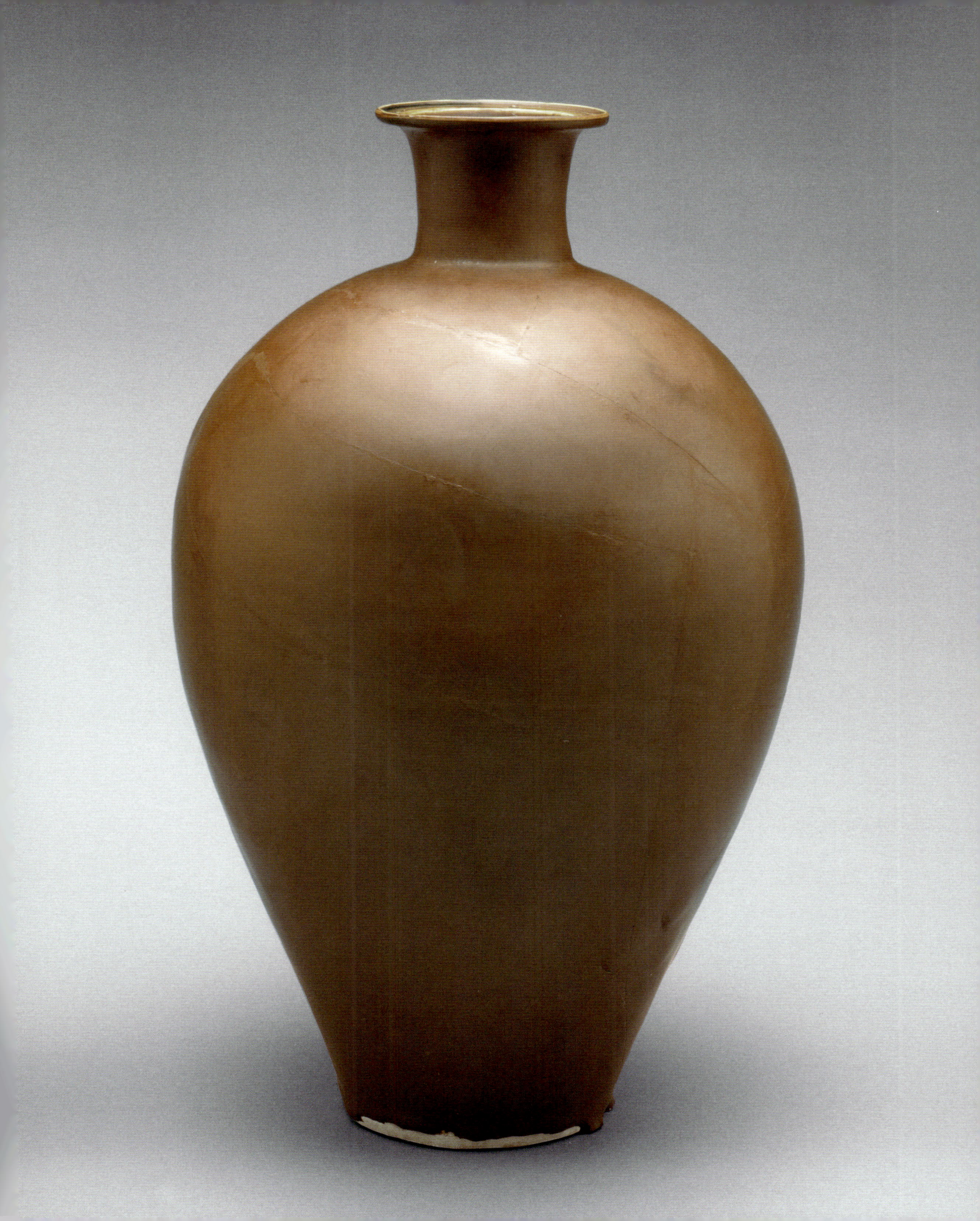

14

Brush Washer

Northern Song dynasty (960–1127), late 11th–early 12th century
Stoneware with pale blue glaze (Ru ware)
1 5/16 x 5 1/8 inches (3.4 x 13 cm)
Gift of Major General and Mrs. William Crozier, 1944-20-95a,b

Free of any decoration save its opaque glaze, this brush washer epitomizes the quiet elegance of Ru ware. Known for its simple naturalistic forms, which include vases, flower pots, bowls, dishes, saucers, and brush washers,[1] Ru ware is primarily characterized by the distinctive thick, pale glaze—poetically described as the "color of the sky after rain"[2]—that covers the body of the vessel, ranging in hue from green to gray-blue.[3] The base of this example (fig. 29) also exhibits the sesame seed–shaped spurs (unglazed marks left by the stand that supported the vessel during firing to prevent the glazed foot rim from fusing to the kiln furniture) that are typical of the ware.

Ru ware is considered to be one of the finest Song-dynasty ceramics.[4] Made exclusively for the Northern Song imperial court, it was produced for only a brief period from about 1086 to 1106,[5] when the kilns were abandoned following attacks by the Jurchen that forced the court to flee south; the Jurchen subsequently established the Jin dynasty (1115–1234) in the north. As Ru ware was manufactured for just twenty years, fewer than eighty complete examples survive, which makes it one of the rarest and most sought after wares among collectors.[6]

The inscription on the base of this brush washer demonstrates China's deep reverence for its past. Archaism, or the veneration of antiquity, has been a guiding principle of Chinese art since the Song dynasty. Paintings, calligraphy, bronzes, jades, and ceramics from revered earlier periods have been appreciated by connoisseurs and collectors, including emperors. The renowned and prestigious imperial Ru, Guan, and Ge wares of the Song dynasty were especially valued by the Qianlong emperor (r. 1736–95), who collected scores of examples, often inscribing them with his own poetic musings.[7] The inscription on the base of this piece reads:

> The Song imperial kiln for making celadons was established at Ruzhou. It is said that powdered agate was used to make the glaze. Nowadays, however, this method is not used at Jingdezhen. It also produced a precious blue color on the surface. Composed by the Qianlong emperor in the cyclical year of Yihai [1755].[8]

HK

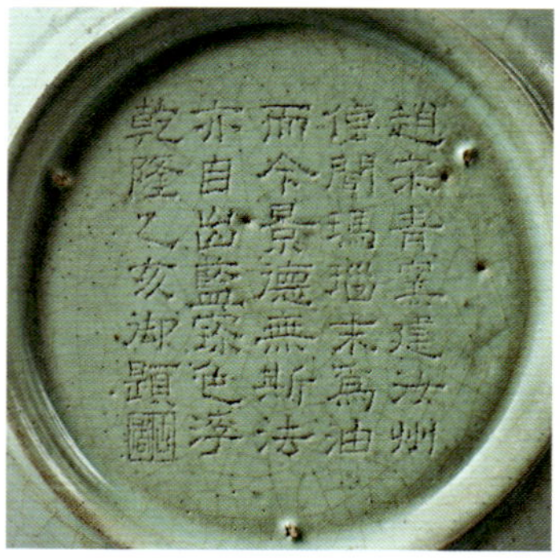

Fig. 29. The base of the brush washer, inscribed with a poem by the Qianlong emperor

1. Examples of these different forms can be found in the Taiwan Palace Museum and the Percival David Collection, British Museum, London. See also the Ru-ware kiln site at Qingliangsi, Baofeng, in Henan province, discovered in 1950; Henan 2008, 80.
2. This description was originally used by early Ming writers to describe the glaze of Chai wares (of which no examples have yet been identified) and then was extended to Ru; Wood 1999, 128.
3. See Taipei 2012, nos. 10–22, for the wide range of colors in Ru glazes, with and without crackle.
4. Along with Ding, Jun, Guan, and Ge wares, Ru ware was considered in the Ming and Qing dynasties to be one of the five great wares of the Song dynasty.
5. Taipei 2006–7, 22.
6. The appreciation for and high status of Ru ware took hold as a fashion statement from the mid-fifteenth century onward, after Ming collectors and connoisseurs sang its praises; Taipei 2006–7, 23–24.
7. The quality of the calligraphy on the Philadelphia brush washer differs somewhat from the more formal, clerical script found on most Qianlong inscribed wares. However, an inscription on another Ru-ware round brush washer in the National Palace Museum, Taipei, is closer in style to the inscription on the Philadelphia example and is notably written in the same square format; see Taipei 2006–7, no. 6.
8. I thank Diandian Li for the translation. The same inscription is on the base of another Ru brush washer, now in the National Palace Museum collection in Taipei; illustrated in Taipei 2006–7, no. 35.

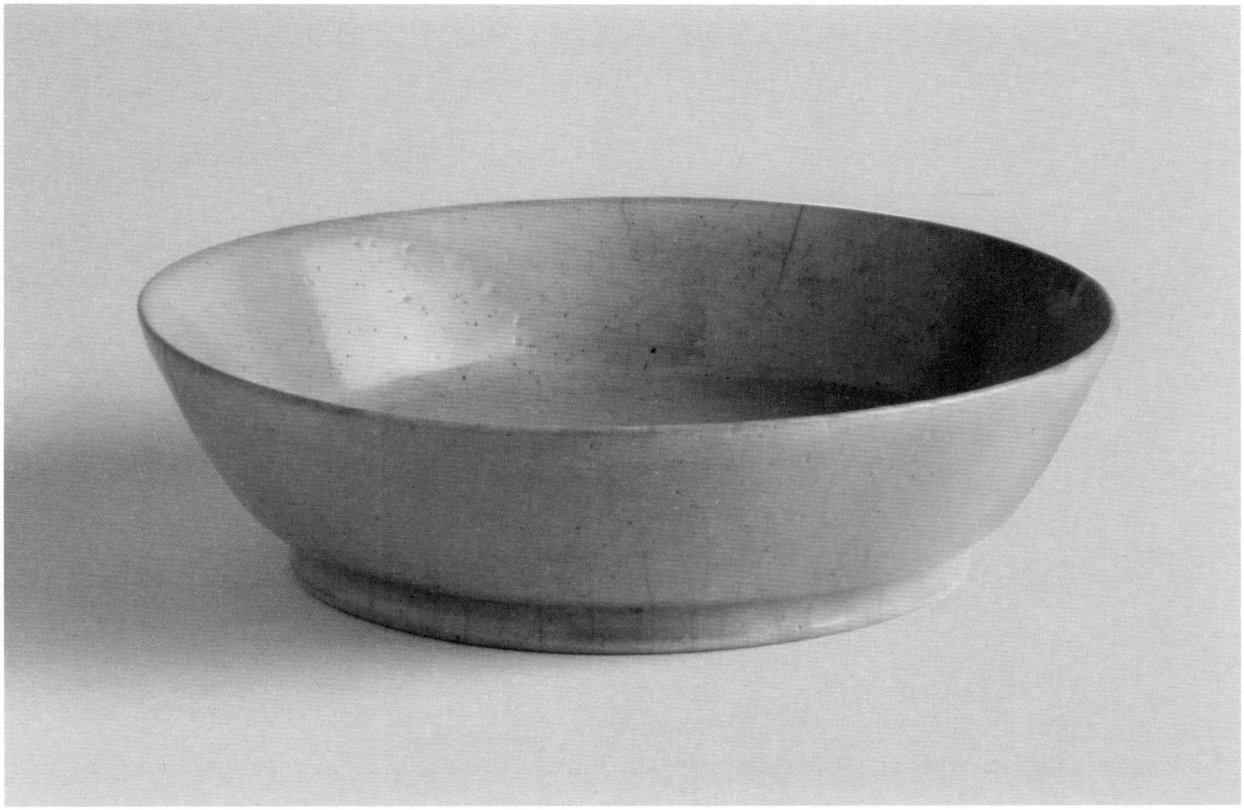

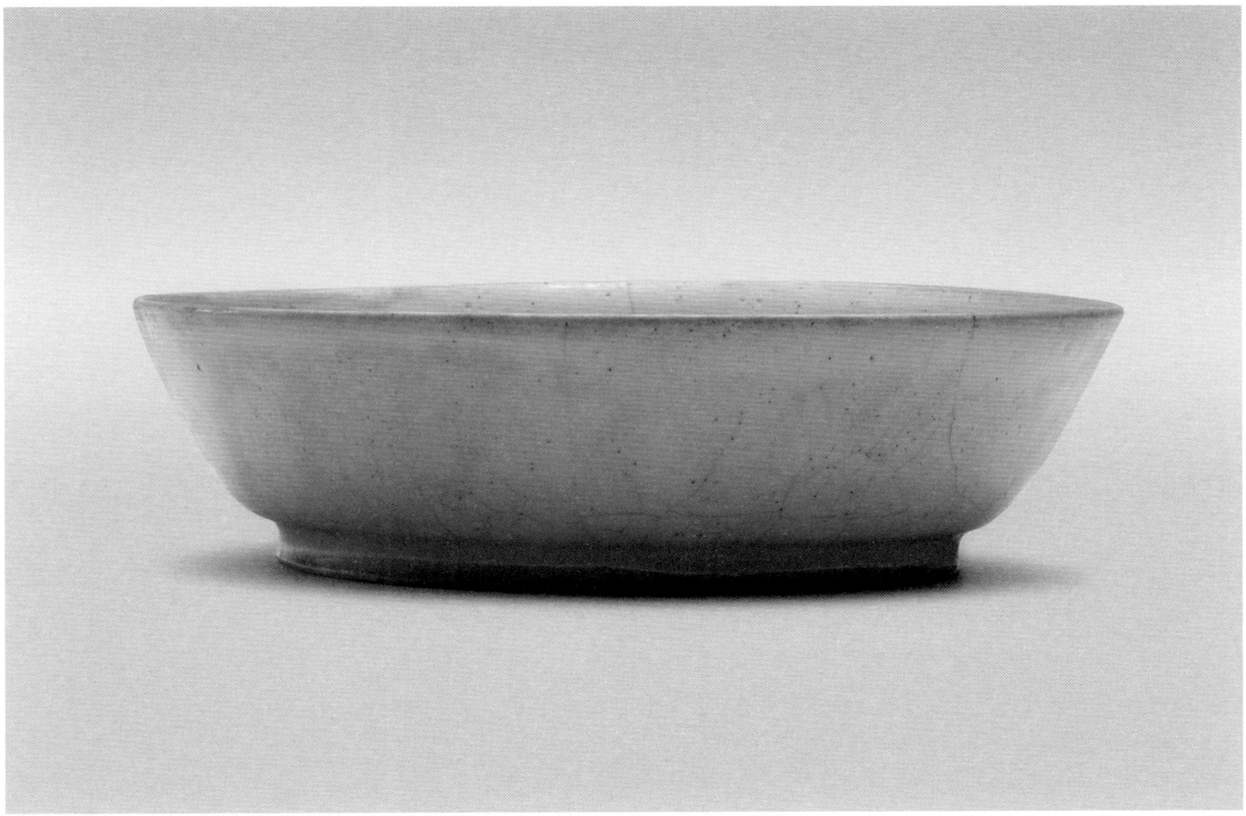

15

Pillow with Phoenix and Peony Blossoms

Northern Song (960–1127) to Jin dynasty (1115–1234), 11th–12th century
Porcelain with underglaze slip decoration (Ding ware)
5 9/16 x 9 7/16 x 6 11/16 inches (14.2 x 24 x 17 cm)
Gift of Mrs. Carroll S. Tyson, 1957-26-3

This tall, bean-shaped pillow was to be used in life and the afterlife to support the head or neck. Intricately scrolling floral tendrils decorate the sides, while the slightly concave resting surface is embellished with three full peony blossoms amid scrolling foliage. Entwined in the foliage at the center is a phoenix, wings outstretched and long tail feathers streaming behind. Peonies were grown by Yangdi, the emperor of the Sui dynasty (r. 605–18), as well as by the Tang emperors, and thus the flower became associated with royalty. Known as the king of flowers, the peony together with the phoenix, the king of birds, conveys wishes of wealth and high status.[1]

The technique used to make the low relief design required a steady hand and a good deal of time. The form was first built up from slabs of white clay that were luted together, after which a thin layer of pale, khaki-colored

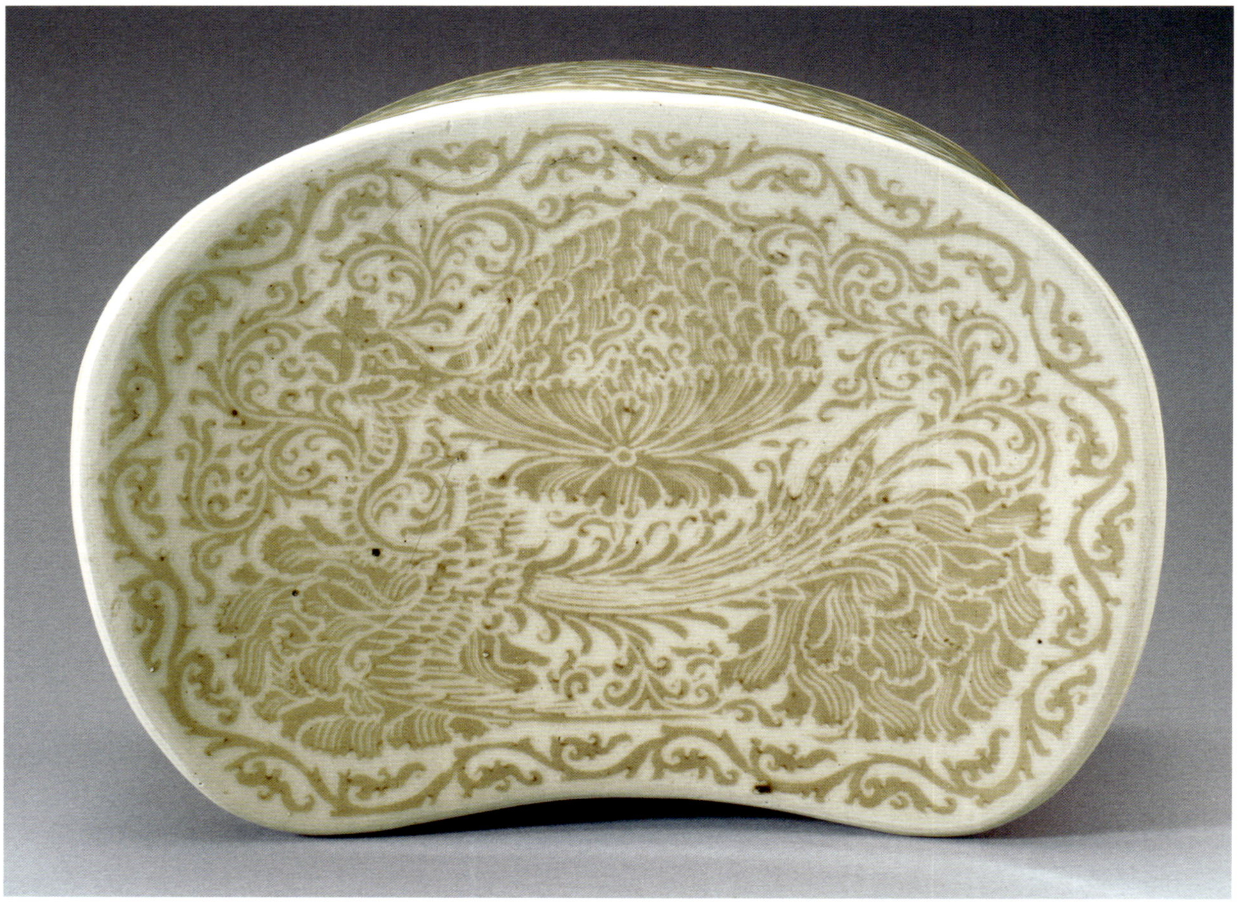

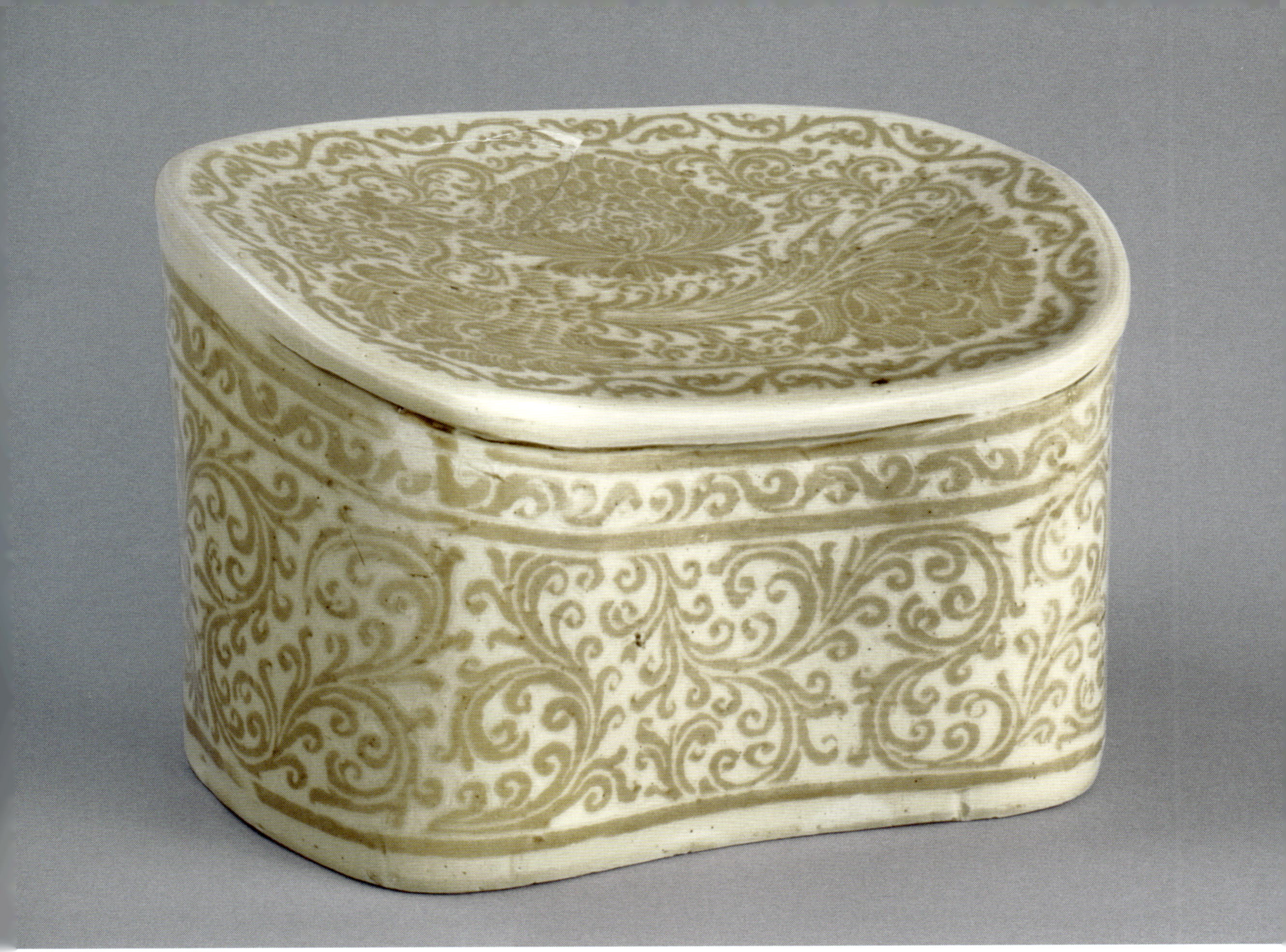

glaze tinted with iron pigment was applied over the sides and top; the glaze was then skillfully carved away to reveal the white clay underneath, creating the design through a process focusing on the negative spaces. Smaller details, such as the combed effect on the peony petals, were then incised and a clear glaze applied overtop before the piece was fired. This technique, known as *sgraffito*, was popular in the Cizhou kilns located throughout northern China and first appeared in the Northern Song period.[2] Ding craftsmen borrowed what originally was a Cizhou technique, while Cizhou craftsmen then tried to imitate the appearance of the more expensive and highly regarded Ding ware, showing how kilns influenced and copied each other.

The design may have been inspired by precious metalwork, such as gold and silver, or by fine silk textiles. During the Northern Song dynasty a special type of silk tapestry textile called *kesi* (pronounced "ke se"), with bird and flower designs, was produced in Dingzhou, where the Ding kilns were located.[3] HK

1. San Francisco 2006, 155, 160.
2. Mu 2002, 148. There are two types of Ding bodies with *sgraffito* designs, one in which the body was covered in a white slip before application of the glaze, and one with a white clay body that did not require a white slip.
3. See Cleveland and New York 1997–98, 59, figs. 12, 16, for such examples.

16

Pillow with Confucian Scholar, Buddhist Monk, and Daoist Priest

Jin dynasty (1115–1234), 1178 (eighteenth year of the Dading period, 1161–89)
Stoneware with underglaze slip decoration (Cizhou ware)
3⅞ x 10¹⁵⁄₁₆ x 7¹¹⁄₁₆ inches (9.8 x 27.8 x 19.5 cm)
Gift of Mrs. Carroll S. Tyson, 1957-26-1

Ceramic pillows were made for everyday use in China in a variety of shapes, sizes, and glazes.[1] Built up from slabs of clay, the hollow body was pierced to form a hole at the top back edge, so that when fired, hot air expanding inside could escape, preventing cracking. The design in dark brown slip over a cream-colored-slip background covered in a clear glaze identifies this piece as Cizhou ware from northern China.[2] According to a partially preserved, dated inscription brushed in ink on the base, the pillow was made in the year 1178 of the Jin dynasty, when the Cizhou kilns reached peak production.

The Cizhou kilns produced many different wares for the popular market and were known for some of the liveliest and most carefree designs of the period, including birds and flowers and designs based on contemporaneous paintings, dramas, and stories. The scene on this example of a Confucian scholar, a Buddhist monk, and a Daoist priest playing Chinese chess is unique among known examples of Cizhou pillows. The figures represent the three important belief systems of Chinese civilization—Confucianism, Buddhism, and Daoism—which before the tenth century were viewed as distinct yet complementary, representing a single tradition. The so-called Three Teachings (*sanjiao*)[3] comprised a popular theme in tenth- to thirteenth-century paintings and also appeared in tomb decorations (fig. 30),[4] demonstrating the relevance of this theme in both life and the afterlife. HK

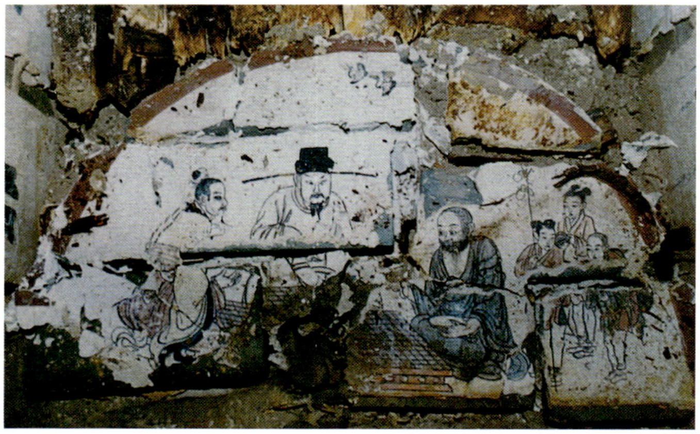

Fig. 30. *Three Old Men Playing Weiqi Chess*. Liao dynasty (907–1125), 1093. Mural painting in the tomb of Zhang Wenzao (d. 1093), Xuanhua, Hebei province

1. Pillows made from ceramic and other hard materials such as jade, stone, and wood were used not only by the dead, but also by the living. Plentiful pillow shards have been found at the Cizhou kiln site at Guantai, Hebei province, showing that they were mass produced in the Song dynasty; however, archival records state that the pillow was purportedly from the Dangyangyu kiln in Henan.
2. The ware takes its name from Ci county in Hebei province, where the main kilns were located at Guantai. Produced from the early Northern Song (960–1127) to the Ming (1369–1644) dynasty, Cizhou wares were also produced in Henan, Shaanxi, Shanxi, and Shandong.
3. Confucianism, Buddhism, and Daoism were described by a prominent sixth-century scholar as separate yet coexisting indispensable phenomena of the natural world; see Teiser 1999, 3.
4. See Hebei 1996, 26, fig. 8.

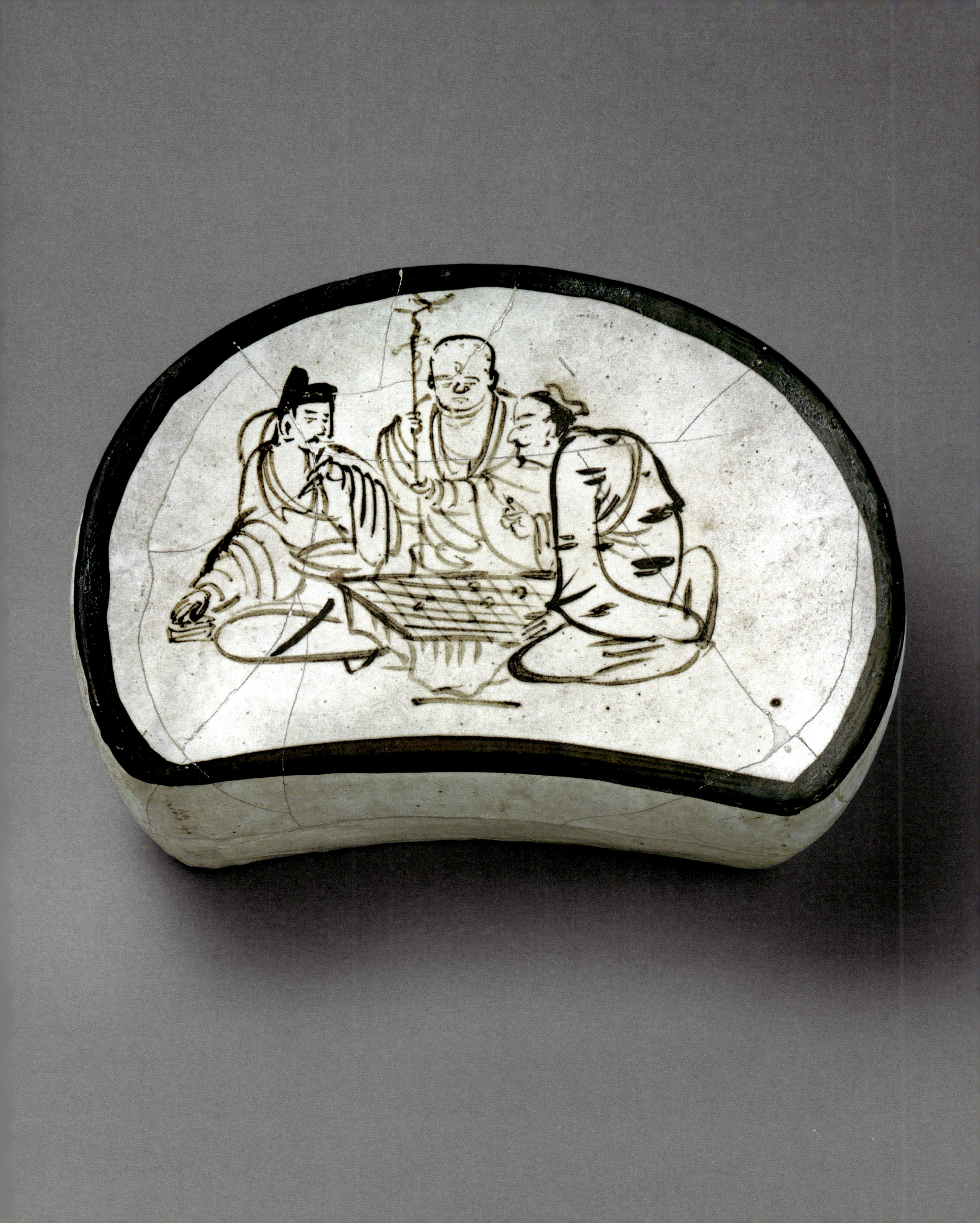

17

Flower-form Cup

Song dynasty (960–1279), 12th century
Jade
2 x 2½ inches (5.1 x 6.4 cm)
Gift of the Far Eastern Art Committee in honor of Henry B. Keep, 1978-41-1

The elegant form of this foliate cup—carved to mimic a six-petal flower blossom and with a raised, slightly flared foot—is in keeping with the aesthetics of the Song dynasty. Ruled in the Confucian tradition by the educated elite, the Song dynasty followed the doctrines of Confucianism in its pursuit of the "right" or "correct" way, aiming to revive an idealized, utopian antiquity in the pursuit of a better state.[1] The Song elite were known for their sophisticated and refined taste, showing a preference for subtle, understated monochromatic forms over the garish and opulent. This jade cup perfectly epitomizes the cultured aesthetic of the Song elite, not only in its form inspired by nature, but in the material itself. Jade was considered to be the embodiment of virtue, since Confucius (551–479 BCE) praised its smoothness, solidity, and translucency as qualities that the gentleman should cultivate.[2]

Jade examples of this foliate form are rare,[3] but the shape is often seen in other mediums, such as lacquerware (fig. 31) and ceramics. Monochrome lacquerware in black and cinnabar red was produced in large quantities during the Song dynasty, its plain forms free of surface decoration and simulating naturalistic floral shapes,[4] similar to imperial Ding ware. Floral bowls were also produced in pale blue glazed Ru ware,[5] which, like Ding ware, appears to mimic silver objects (see no. 14). HK

1. Kuhn 2008, 12.
2. Wilson 2004, 6.
3. A plain green jade cup with flared mouth now in the Anhui Provincial Museum was excavated from the Southern Song tomb of Zhu Xiyan and his wife at Chengguan, Xiuning, Anhui province; illustrated in Gu and Song 2005, 174.
4. See Münster 2008, 106, pl. 15.
5. For an example, see the ten-petal bowl resembling an open lotus blossom, and used to warm a pot of liquor, in the National Palace Museum, Taipei; illustrated in Taipei 2006–7, 126, no. 26.

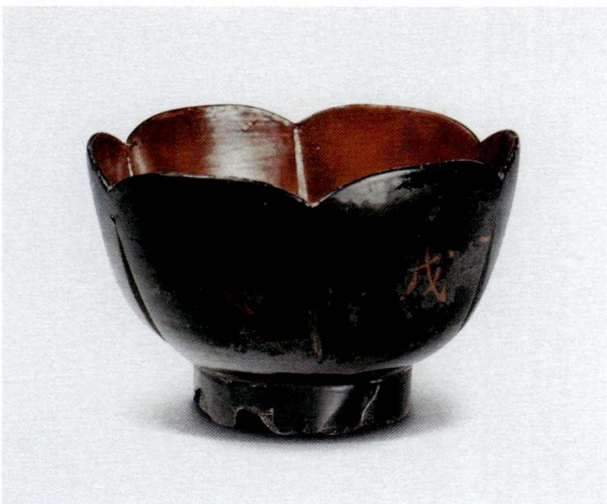

Fig. 31. Bowl in the Form of a Lotus Flower. Northern Song dynasty (960–1127), excavated in Changzhou, Jiangsu province. Black and red lacquer, 3¹⁵⁄₁₆ x 6¼ inches (10 x 15.8 cm). Changzhou Museum

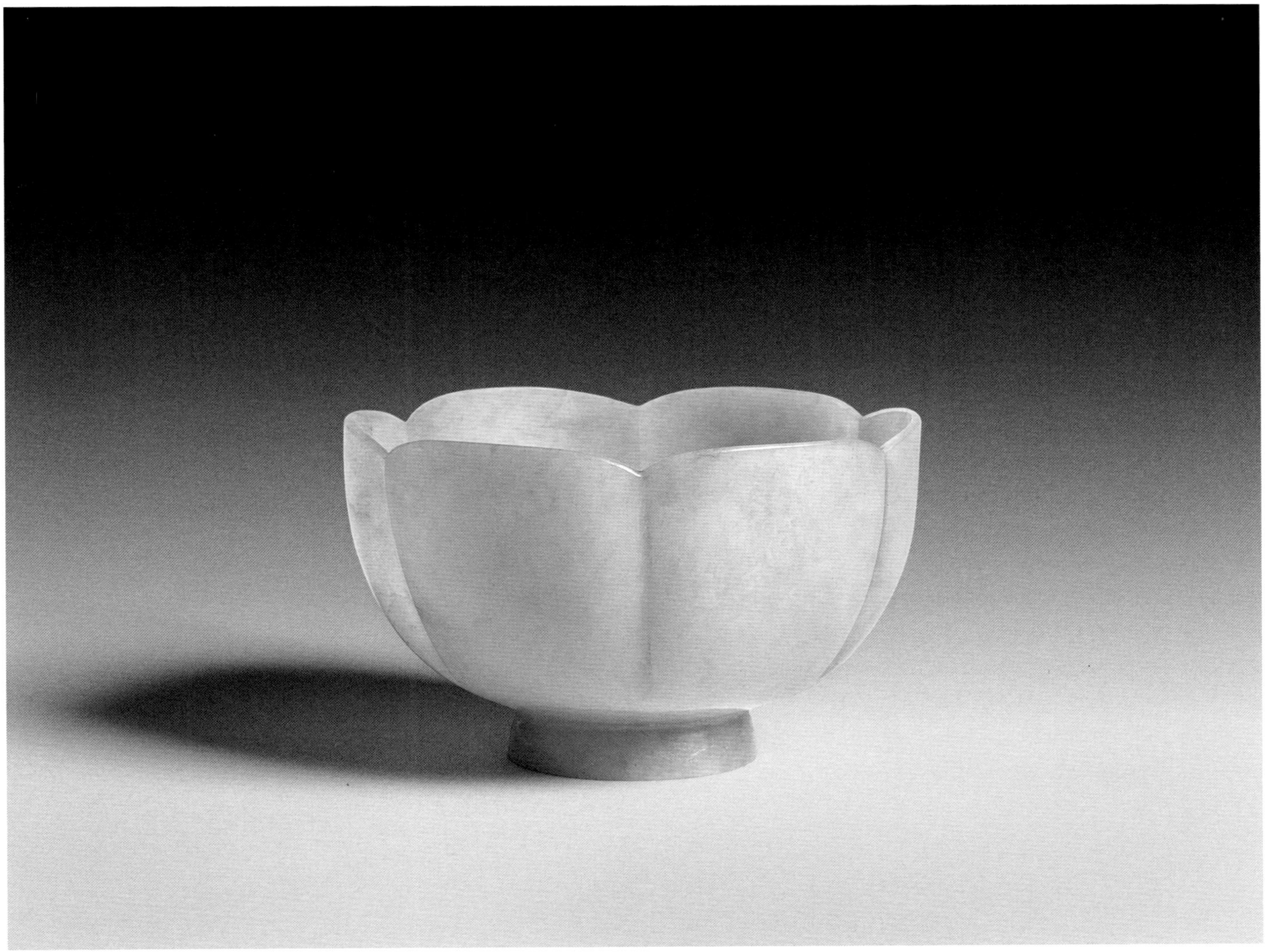

18

Flower-form Dish

Southern Song dynasty (1127–1279)
Wood with fabric under lacquer; metal on rim
1 1/16 x 6 3/8 inches (2.7 x 16.2 cm)
Purchased with the John T. Morris Fund and the Elizabeth Wandell Smith Fund, 1974-29-1

This lobed dish emphasizing a simple, naturalistic form over surface decoration is in keeping with the understated aesthetics espoused by the Song elite. Plain, lobed, monochrome lacquer dishes like this one—as well as other lacquer tableware, tea utensils, cosmetic boxes, trays, tables, and luxury items such as cosmetic sets—were produced in small workshops in southern China, where the lacquer tree *Rhus verniciflua* flourished.[1] Lacquerwares are light and durable but expensive and time-consuming to make, and so were enjoyed by only the privileged few.

Chinese lacquer's glossiness was achieved using a complex formula, described by an early Ming author, that involved boiling the lacquer tree's raw sap, mixing part of it with egg white, exposing this combination to the midday sun while stirring until a glossy chestnut color was achieved, adding the mixture back to the boiled lacquer, and finally adding a paste of iron filings (black colorant) mixed with rice vinegar.[2] The final mixture was applied over a substrate, usually a soft wood that was treated to prevent warping, after which the wood was covered with fabric that was itself covered with a ground layer of lacquer mixed with glue and ground-up ceramics. The lacquer was then applied to this ground in layers, with each layer allowed to cure before it was sanded and the next layer applied.

On the base of this dish is a red seal mark (see p. 244).[3] Marks are not commonly found on lacquerwares, and since no examples with seal marks have been excavated in controlled contexts, it is hard to say what the mark might indicate, though the name of a workshop or owner is among the possibilities. HK

1. Vainker 2012, 22.
2. Frick 2008, 24–26.
3. A similar lobed dish, also with a red seal mark, is in the National Palace Museum, Taipei (Chen 2008, no. 1), while one with a brushed mark is illustrated in Hong Kong 1993, no. 18. The metal on the rim of the Philadelphia example may be a later addition.

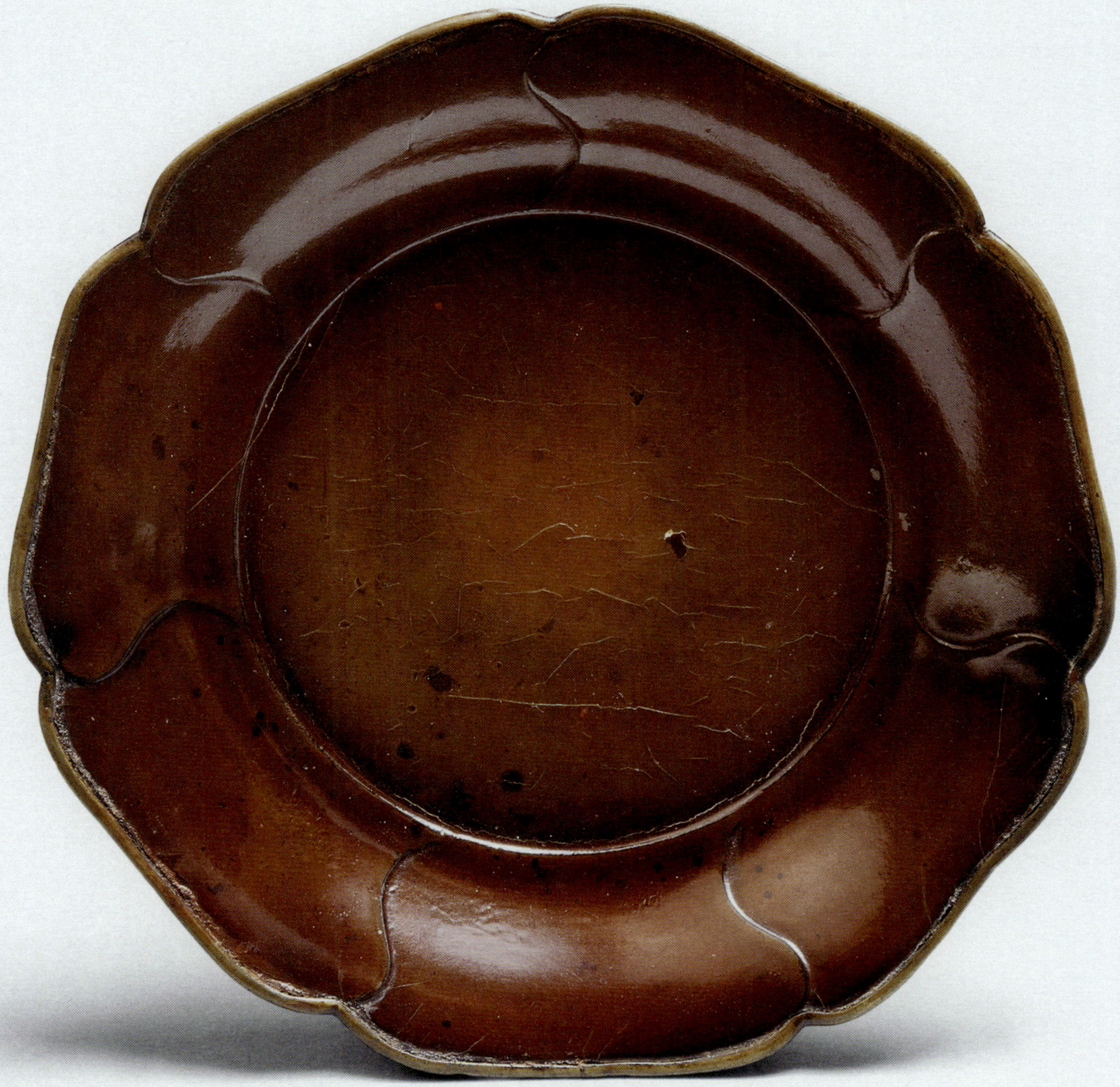

19

Lady beneath Tall Bamboo

Southern Song dynasty (1127–1279), 13th century
Ink and color on silk; fan mounted as an album leaf
9⅜ x 9⅛ inches (23.8 x 23.2 cm)
Purchased with Museum funds from the Simkhovitch Collection, 1929-40-29a,b

The subject of this painted fan is poetic in origin, the image of the solitary lady drawn from the final couplet of the poem *Jiaren* (Fair Lady), composed by the celebrated Tang poet Du Fu (712–770):

> The weather is cold, her azure sleeves are thin,
> At twilight she rests by tall bamboo.[1]

The four poetic images—cold air, azure sleeves, twilight, and bamboo—are vividly visualized in the painting. The lady wears the typical Tang-style blue-green half-sleeves, ending at the elbows. The pale ink washes that make up the background indicate the approach of dusk, and the four tall, thin bamboo branches connecting the upper and lower edges of the painting provide the rest of the poem's setting. In between a pierced Taihu rock[2] and the tall bamboo is a plum tree with a profusion of white blossoms. Together with the camellias at the lower right, they indicate that the cold winter night is coming. The grouping of plum blossom, bamboo, and rock is called the Three Purities (*san qing*), echoing the character of the lady who is the embodiment of surpassing beauty.

Du Fu's poem was composed against the backdrop of the An-Shi Rebellion (755–63), led by the powerful general An Lushan (703–757). In the poem, a lady from a good family has lost her brothers and been forsaken by her dissolute husband. She has retreated from the capital city to the remote mountains, living a simple and austere life. In the early years of the Southern Song dynasty, immediately following the horrific wars, painters were inspired by such beautiful, poetic imagery. The painting can probably be dated to the late Southern Song period.[3] A similar fan painting is in the Palace Museum in Beijing.[4] HX

1. The translation is by Stephen Owen; Owen 2016, vol. 2, book 7, 115.
2. The Taihu rock is an ornamental garden rock from Lake Tai in Jiangsu province collected and sought after for its distinctive craggy appearance.
3. The painting was catalogued by Li Zuoxian (1807–1876) in Li 1871 (1997), vol. 12, pp. 16–17, and by Pang Yuanji (1864–1949) in Pang 1909, vol. 11, p. 23.
4. Yu 2005, 248. This painting is dated to the Southern Song period.

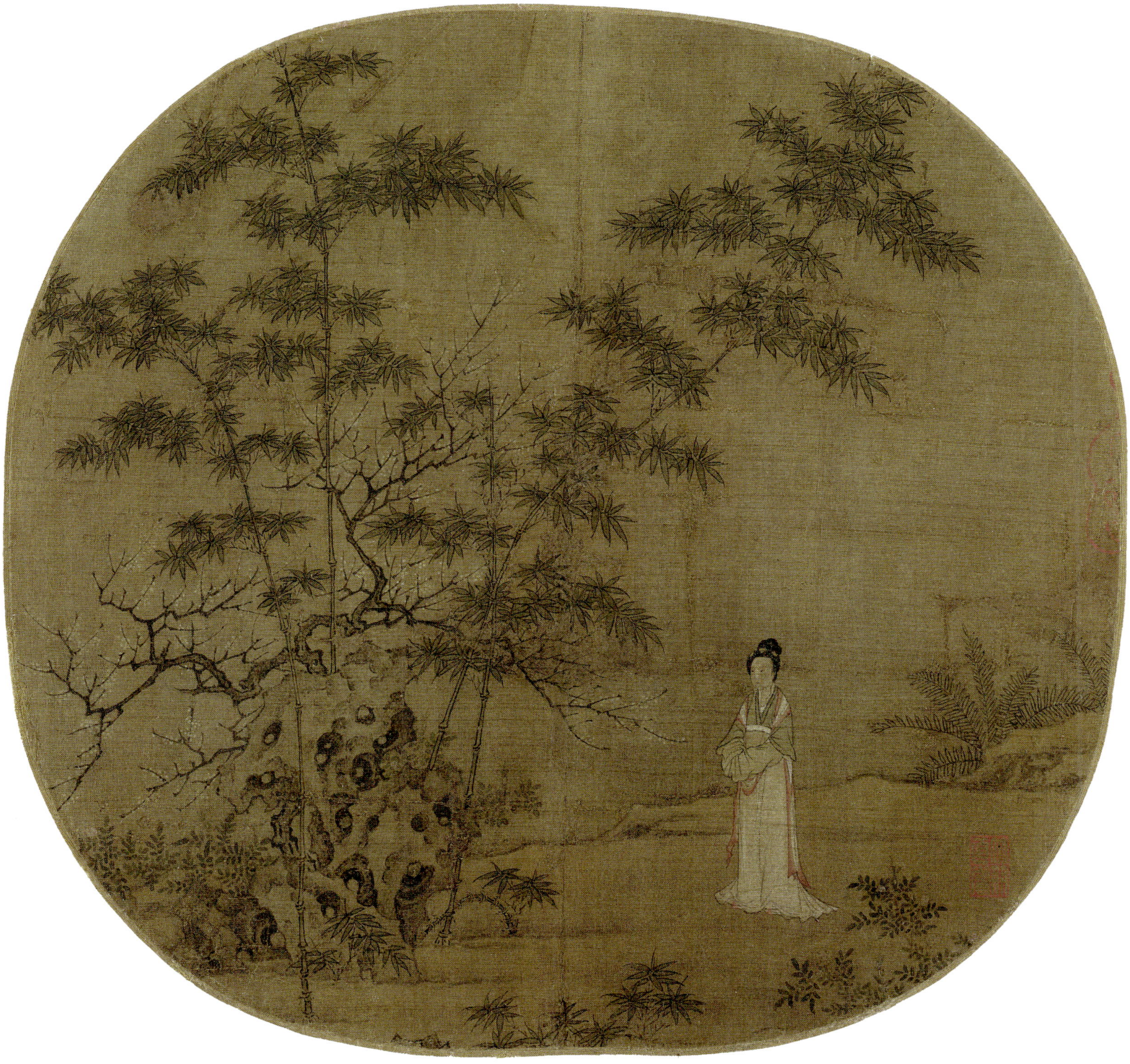

20

Palace beneath Lofty Pines

Southern Song dynasty (1127–1279)
Ink and color on silk; fan mounted as an album leaf
9¾ x 9¼ inches (24.8 x 23.5 cm)
Purchased with Museum funds from the Simkhovitch Collection, 1929-40-35

A classic moment in the leisurely life of the Southern Song court in Hangzhou is represented on this round silk fan, which was later mounted as an album leaf.[1] On a late spring evening, members of the imperial family have gathered on one of the highest terraces at the back of the palace to take in the grand view and enjoy a delicious repast. The curtains of the building have been let down, concealing the figures inside, leaving only a group of female attendants visible outside, standing at the ready with utensils. The invisible protagonists are signified by a pair of lofty pine trees at the left edge of the painting, their joined roots and branches indicating intertwining trees (*lian li mu*), an auspicious spectacle at court. Images of intertwining trees can be traced back to the Eastern Han dynasty (25–220) and symbolized the good reign of a sage king, a Confucian "gentleman," or a loving couple. In the context of a court fan painting, the intertwining pine trees function as a visualization of the imperial couple, most likely the emperor and empress sitting behind the lowered curtains.

Although the artist did not sign his work, it displays qualities typical of landscape painting at the Southern Song court, such as the one-corner composition and the large ax-chop brushstroke (*fu pi cun*) used to render the giant stone in the foreground. It was common practice for the Southern Song court to prepare large numbers of painted fans for distribution among the imperial clan and high-ranking officials as gifts celebrating holidays and other special occasions.[2] HX

1. The painting came from the collection of Pang Yuanji (1864–1949) but was not catalogued in either his *Xuzhai minghua lu* (Record of Famous Paintings from Xuzhai's Collection; 1909) or *Xuzhai minghua xulu* (Supplement of the Record of Famous Paintings from Xuzhai's Collection; 1924). Two seal marks of an earlier collector, Xu Zan (1473–1548), a high-ranking official of the Ming dynasty, are found on the painting.
2. For a discussion of fan painting in the Southern Song court, see Weitz 2011, 39–48.

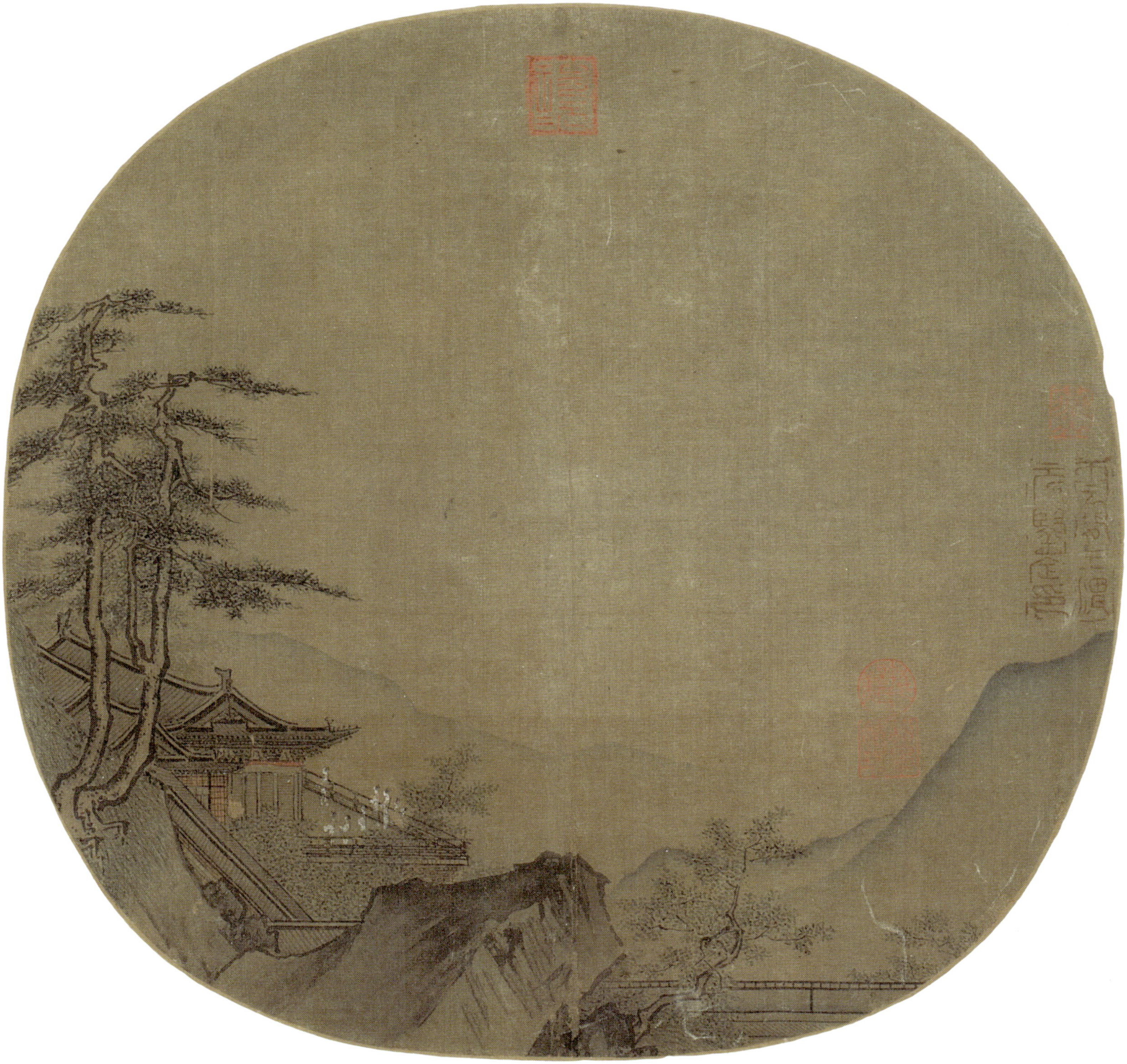

21

Three Fish

Southern Song dynasty (1127–1279), 13th century
Ink and color on silk, mounted as an album leaf
8¾ x 9 inches (22.2 x 22.9 cm)
Purchased with Museum funds from the Simkhovitch Collection, 1929-40-2

Three fish play in a pond, the silk on which they are painted transformed into water.[1] They dart around a cluster of water plants, ephemerally rendered in pale ink washes, swimming head to tail to form a rhythmic motion. Dots of green duckweed indicate the surface of the water, together with the underwater elements creating an illusion of depth. This type of depiction was first seen in the Northern Song dynasty (960–1127) in paintings of carefree fish by the famous artist Liu Cai (act. 1080–1120), to whom this painting was once attributed. The Philadelphia example shares similar motifs, format, and style with two other paintings, one in the Metropolitan Museum of Art,[2] and the other in the Palace Museum, Beijing (fig. 32),[3] both dated to the thirteenth century.

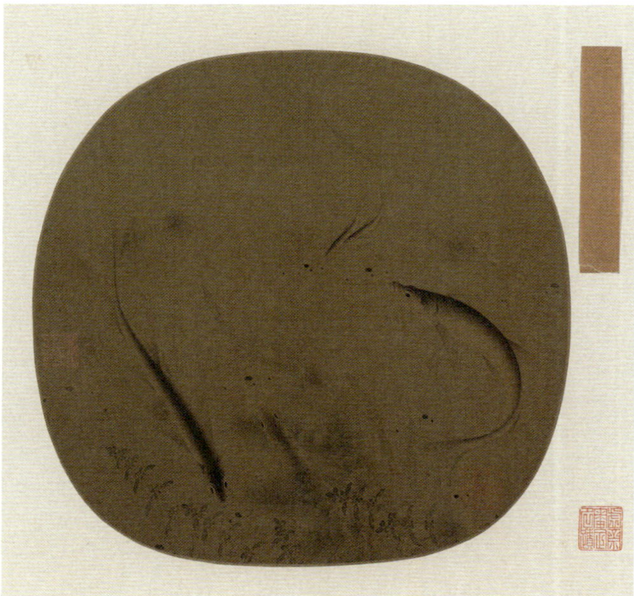

Fig. 32. *Fish Playing among Weeds.* Southern Song dynasty, 13th century. Ink and color on silk, mounted as an album leaf; 9⅝ x 10 inches (24.5 x 25.5 cm). Palace Museum, Beijing

In addition to these examples depicting similar fish, two other examples place different types of fish together in the same painting: *Fish Swimming amid Falling Flowers*, in the Saint Louis Art Museum,[4] and *The Pleasures of Fishes*, also in the Metropolitan Museum, painted by Zhou Dongqing (act. late 13th century) in 1291.[5] In his inscription on the Met painting, Zhou refers to both the famous fish story in the Daoist classic *Zhuangzi*[6] and the Confucian classic *Doctrine of the Mean* (*Zhongyong*) to explain the motif. As stated in the *Zhongyong,* "It is only he who is possessed of the most complete sincerity that can exist under heaven, who can give its full development to his nature. Able to give its full development to his own nature, he can do the same to the nature of other men. . . . Able to give their full development to the natures of creatures and things, he can assist the transforming and nourishing powers of Heaven and Earth."[7] In this light, the painted image functions to reveal the nature of creatures and things, and the person engaged in its making or its viewing will share the same sensibilities as a cultivated sage like Zhuangzi. HX

1. Pang Yuanji (1864–1949), one of the former owners of the painting, catalogued it in Pang 1924, vol. 1, 45.
2. Fong 1992, 184–85.
3. Nie 2004, 116.
4. Barnhart et al. 1997, 118–19.
5. Fong 1992, 380–83.
6. Zhuangzi (c. 369–286 BCE), a Daoist philosopher, declared that he was able to feel what fish feel.
7. See the translation by James Legge (1815–1897); Legge 1991, 416.

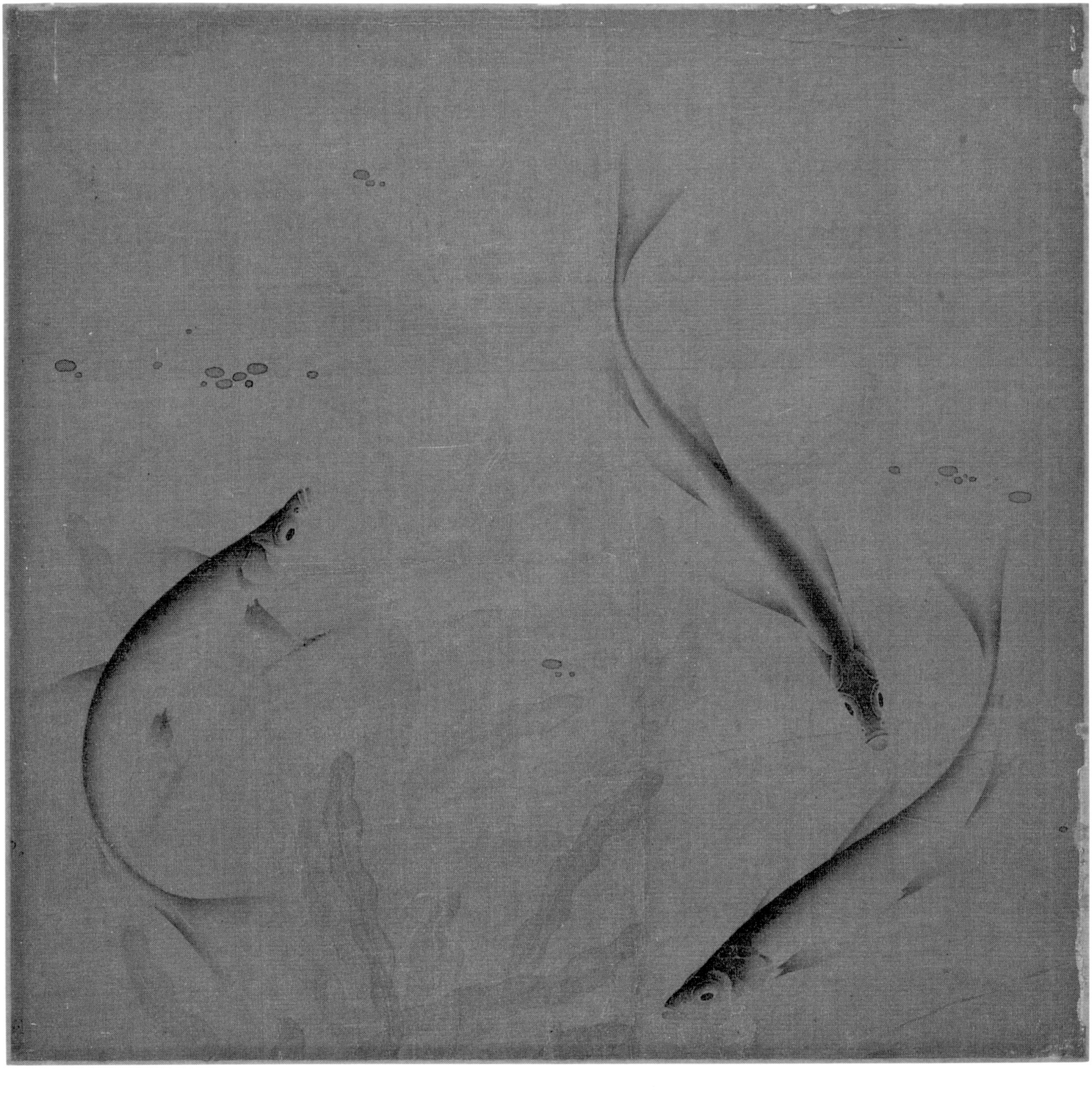

22

Possibly Sun Jue (act. c. 1225–27)
Female Immortals

Southern Song dynasty (1127–1279), 13th century
Ink and color on silk; fan mounted as an album leaf
9⅞ x 9¼ inches (25.1 x 23.5 cm)
Purchased with Museum funds from the Simkhovitch Collection, 1929-40-48a,b

The three female immortals painted on this fan wear cloaks and skirts made of grasses and leaves. Their hairy bodies, indicated by light ink washes on their bare feet, legs, and arms, identify them as the Feathered Women (*mao nü*) of Daoist lore, who live deep in the mountains searching for herbs.[1] This motif can be traced back to an eleventh-century painting found in the timber pagoda of Fogong Temple in Shanxi province (fig. 33). The rendering here captures the moment when the immortals are showing each other what they have gathered. Although the figure at the far left holds a *lingzhi* fungus (thought to bestow longevity if ingested) and a basket of plants draped over her arm, the focus of the painting is on a large health-benefiting ginseng root displayed in the hand of the central immortal. Other herbs include leaves of banana and palm tree carried in the baskets on their backs.

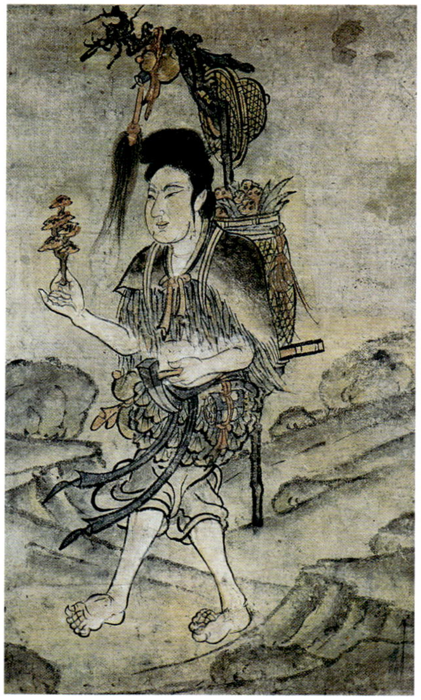

Fig. 33. *Gathering Herbs*. Liao dynasty (907–1125), 11th century. Ink on paper, 27½ x 15¼ inches (70 x 38.6 cm). From the wooden pagoda at Fogongsi in Yingxian, Shanxi province

The most surprising object is a small skull hanging beneath the canopy carried by the immortal on the left, along with the longevity fungus, a fan, and a small gourd. It most likely belonged to a macaque monkey. Skulls of humans and animals were believed to be restorative, with magical powers able to cure the most terrible illnesses.[2] The representation of a group of Feathered Women exhibiting precious medicinal items functions as a special talisman, protecting the owner from illness.

The inscription at the right edge reads "in the year of *gengyin*, Sun Jue painted this."[3] Sun Jue is possibly an artist mentioned by Xia Wenyan (act. c. 1365) in his *Precious Mirror of Painting* (*Tuhui baojian*), which states that Sun Jue was a court painter active in the Baoqing period (1225–27) of the Southern Song dynasty and known for depicting *mao nü* figures, although here his first name is recorded with a different character (also pronounced "jue").[4] HX

1. For a discussion of images of *mao nü*, see Yang 2016, 41–50.
2. For a discussion of skull images in Chinese painting, see Huang 2012, 72–74.
3. The painting was once in the collection of Luo Tianchi (1805–1866), and was catalogued by Li Zuoxian (1807–1876) in Li 1871 (1997), vol. 10, 590, and Pang Yuanji (1864–1949) in Pang 1909, vol. 11, 735.
4. See Kondō and He 1997, 53.

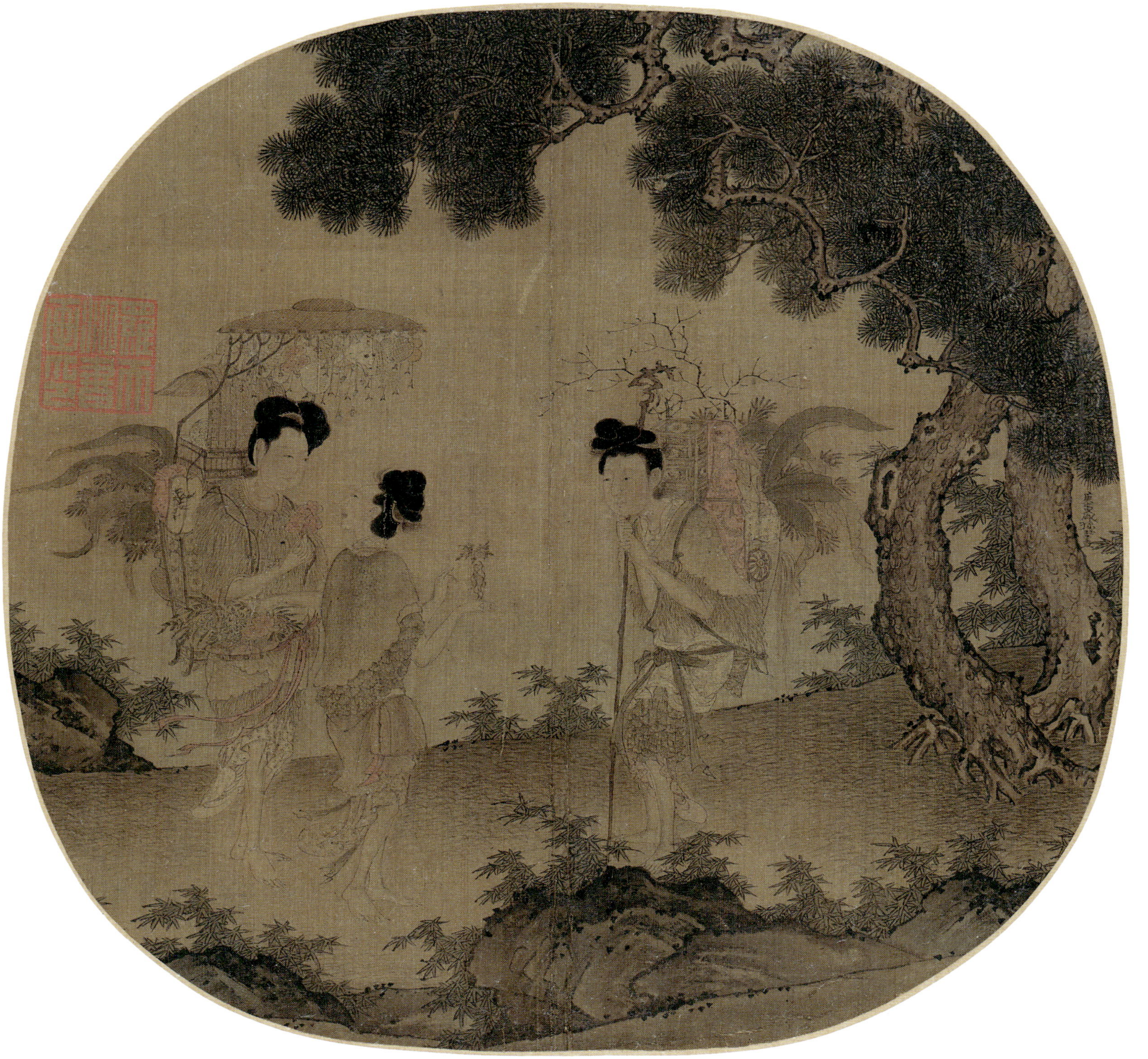

23

Octagonal Jar with the Eight Immortals

Yuan dynasty (1271–1368), mid-14th century
Porcelaneous stoneware with celadon glaze (Longquan ware)
10 x 7 inches (25.4 x 17.8 cm)
Gift of Mrs. S. Emlen Stokes, 1964-58-1

The eight Daoist immortals represented in the unglazed panels on this stoneware jar, each holding a distinguishing attribute, were popularly depicted on Yuan-dynasty celadons and later on Ming (1368–1644) blue-and-white porcelains. As early as the Eastern Han dynasty (25–220) there were differing opinions as to which eight immortals made up the group.[1] Those depicted on this Yuan jar include Lan Caihe, shown with a hoe and a bamboo basket of herbs (left); Cao Guojiu, with a bamboo strainer over his shoulder (center); Li Tieguai ("iron-crutch Li"), with an iron crutch and a medicine gourd (right); and Zhongli Quan (fig. 34), with a palm-leaf fan that has the power to extinguish wind and wipe out evil. The other four may be Xu Shenweng, dressed as an official (fig. 34); Zhang Guolao, carrying a folded object that transforms into a mule; Lü Dongbin, with a sword; and Han Xiangzi, holding a flute.

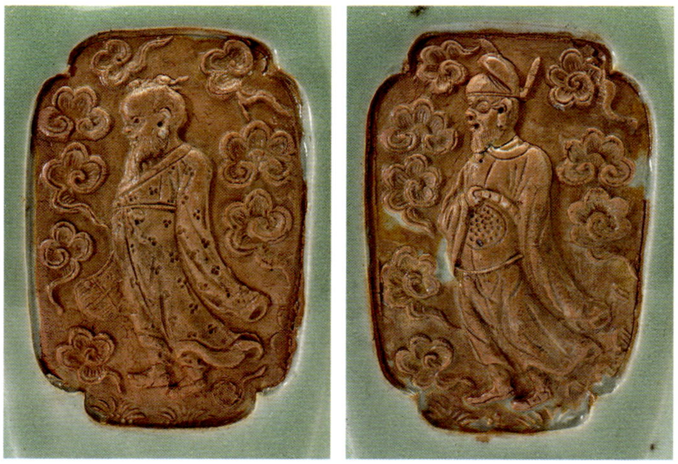

Fig. 34. Details of panels depicting Zhongli Quan holding a palm-leaf fan (left) and possibly Xu Shenweng dressed as an official (right)

This group of immortals originated in northern Daoism during the first half of the thirteenth century. The figures then became widespread, appearing in Yuan drama[2] and throughout the arts, including on bronze mirrors, in mural paintings, and even in tombs. The popularity of the eight immortals, who held supernatural and transformative powers, spread not only among Daoist practitioners but also among the general population, which believed they would bring good luck and aid in the search for immortality.[3]

This jar's unglazed decoration, set off against an ideal bluish-green glaze, exemplifies an unusual technique employed by potters working at the Longquan kilns in Zhejiang province in southern China from the Yuan to Ming dynasty. After the jar was formed, the floral decorations on the shoulder and above the base, as well as the figural designs in each of the eight recessed panels around the body, were formed using molds. The central panels were then painted with wax and the jar covered in a celadon glaze. When fired, the wax melted off, revealing the unglazed gray clay, which would fire a reddish-brown color due to the atmosphere in the kiln. HK

1. New York 2012, 143.
2. See New York 2010–11, 269.
3. Jing 1996, 213.

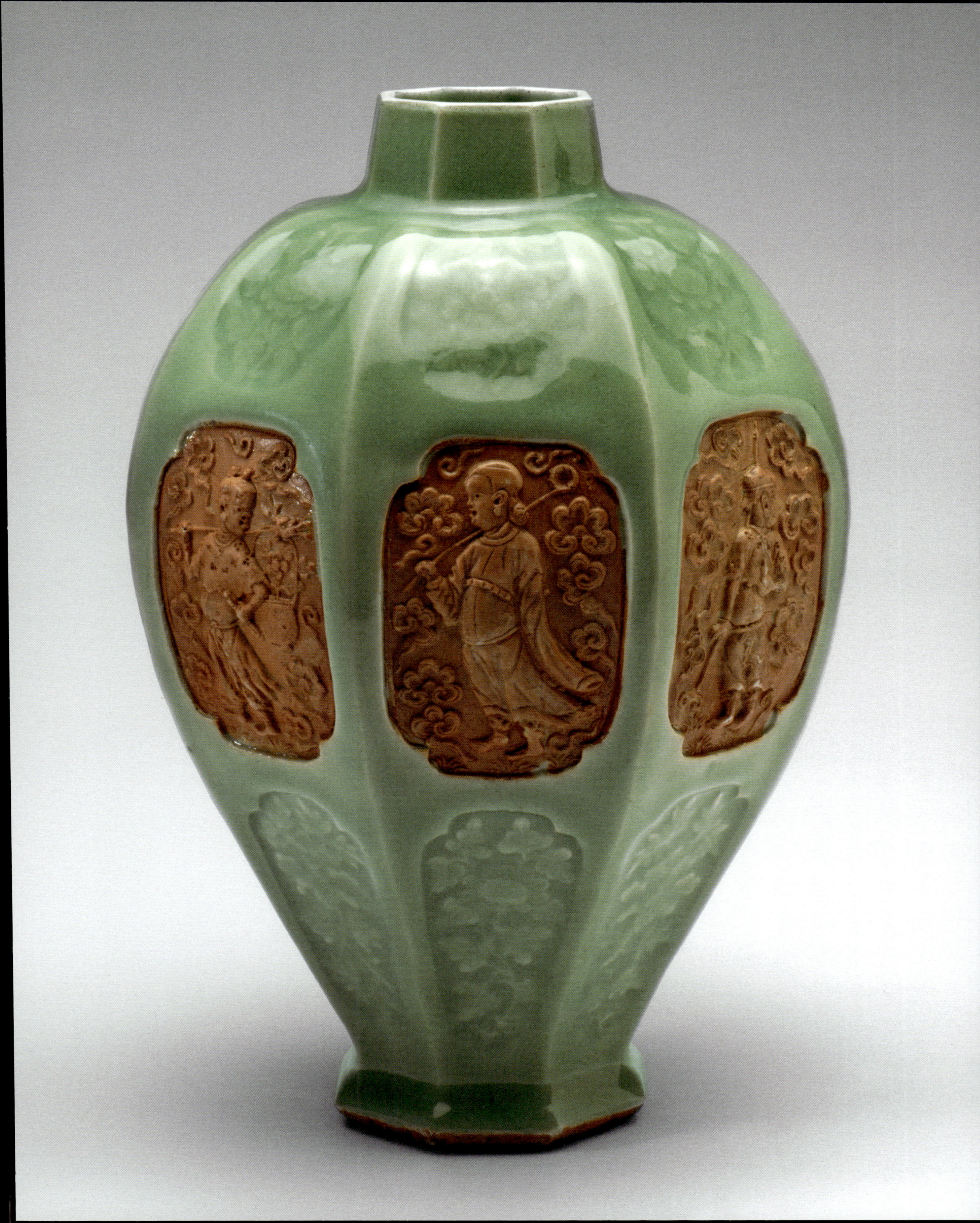

24

Pouring Vessel with *Lingzhi* Fungus

Yuan dynasty (1271–1368), 14th century
Porcelain with underglaze red decoration (Jingdezhen ware)
1¾ x 6¾ inches (4.4 x 17.1 cm)
Gift of Major General and Mrs. William Crozier, 1944-20-145a,b

This unusual spouted vessel is a form that appeared in both metal and ceramics in the Yuan dynasty, ruled by the Mongols.[1] Used for transferring and probably also drinking liquids such as wine and water, the original form seems to have been of metal (fig. 35), as indicated by the flat base, squared pouring spout, and small loop beneath the spout, which may have been used to hang the bowl from a belt. The horsemen of the early steppe cultures were known for suspending weapons and other necessities from their waists, a tradition popularly identified with the types of leather belts used by Turkic and Mongolian tribes from the sixth century onward.[2]

With their conquest of China, the Mongols inherited a flourishing ceramic tradition at the kilns at Jingdezhen in the south, and it was under their rule that large numbers of blue-and-white porcelains were produced, many of which were exported to Southeast Asia, India, and the Middle East. In addition to the well-known blue-and-white ware, underglaze-red-decorated porcelains like this one were also made. On the interior of the bowl is a freely brushed *lingzhi* fungus—a hard, woody plant with medicinal properties that was believed to confer longevity—surrounded by leafy foliate scrolls and enclosed within a thick band incised with undulating lines in copper red. Although derived from locally mined ore and thus easier to obtain than cobalt blue, which was largely imported from Persia, the copper used in underglaze red was notoriously unstable and difficult to control in the firing, with a tendency to blur and turn a dull gray, making these wares difficult to produce and rare in the archaeological record.

Aside from underglaze red and blue pouring vessels,[3] examples with celadon and monochrome blue glaze with applied gold decoration have also been excavated,[4] illustrating the popularity of this form. HK

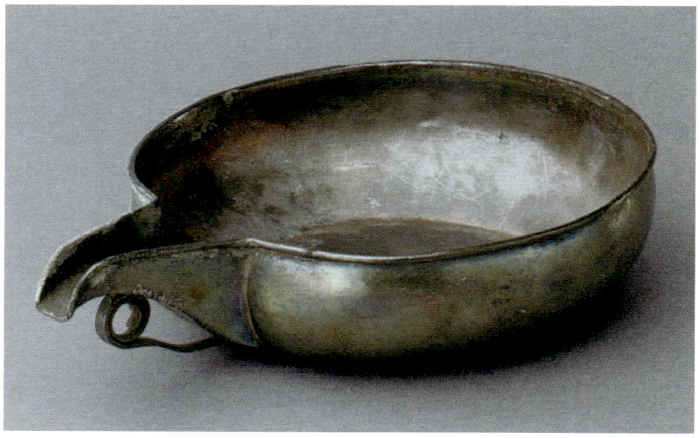

Fig. 35. Spouted Bowl. Late Yuan dynasty, 1333. Silver, diam. at rim 7⅛ inches (18.1 cm). Found in a hoard, inscribed with the year 1333 and the name of the maker, Zhang Zhongying. Anhui Provincial Museum

1. A blue-and-white pouring vessel in the British Museum, London, is illustrated in Harrison-Hall 2001, no. 1:22.
2. Hong Kong 1999, 30, 267.
3. A successfully fired vessel with bright copper-red decoration of a wild goose was excavated in Gao'an, Jiangxi; illustrated in Zhu 2010, 295–97.
4. A celadon example was excavated from a Yuan tomb belonging to the Wang Shixian clan in Gansu province; Beijing 2016, 104. A dark blue-glazed vessel with a vine-like sprig and *ruyi*-shaped clouds applied in gold on top of the glaze was excavated in Baoding, Hebei province; Yang 1999, 68–69, no. 62.

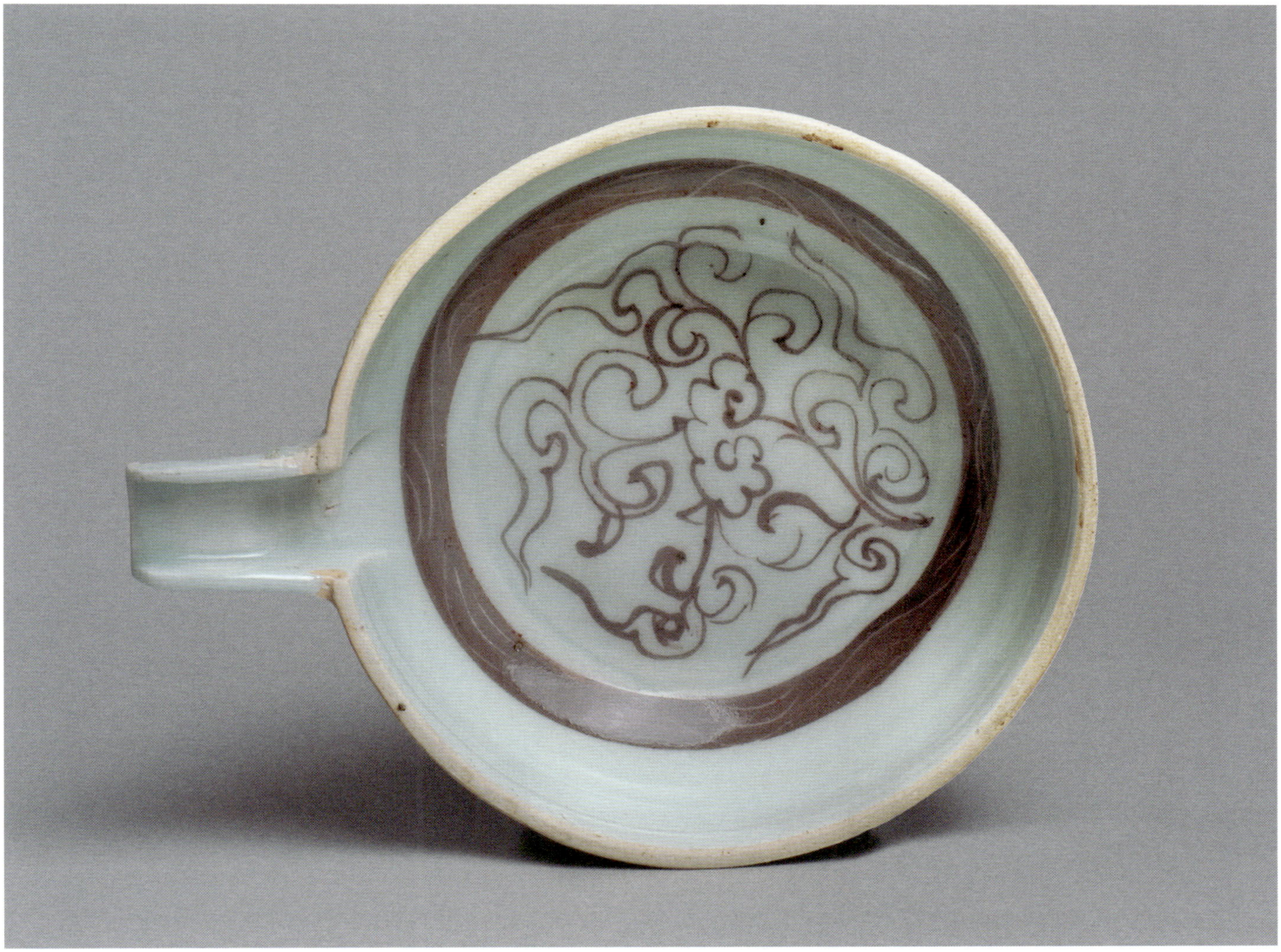

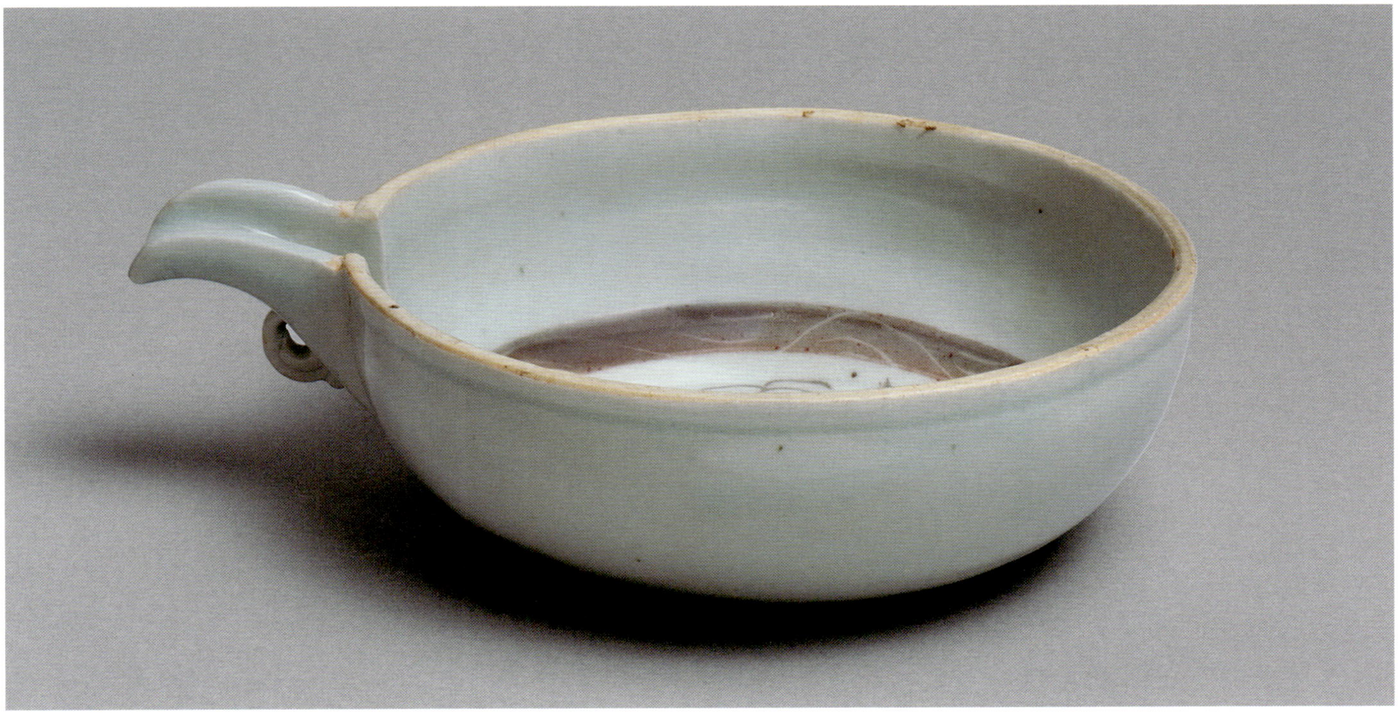

25

Gourd-shaped Vase with Scrolling Peonies

Yuan dynasty (1271–1368), late 13th–early 14th century
Porcelaneous stoneware with celadon glaze (Longquan ware)
13⅝ x 7¾ inches (34.6 x 19.7 cm)
Gift of Dr. Brian M. Salzberg, 2016-55-1

The attractive semiopaque green glaze covering this elegant vase, stopping just short of the foot to reveal the exposed body fired to a brownish red, identifies it as Longquan ware. Sometimes called celadon in the West,[1] the ware was produced in long, wood-fired "dragon" kilns (narrow brick kilns that reach up to 200 feet in length) in Zhejiang in southern China from the time of the Northern Song dynasty (960–1127), mainly in the form of bowls, plates, and other utilitarian vessels. It was not until the late Southern Song (1127–1279) to early Yuan dynasties that new shapes, such as ceremonial vessels, archaistic forms, and gourd-shaped vases like this one, were produced.[2] Appliqué decoration was also used alongside incised and carved decoration during this time.[3] The scrolling tendrils of peony blossoms on this example were made from liquid clay piped onto the vessel; the glaze has pooled in some low areas and thinned in the raised areas, revealing the pale gray clay used for the relief decoration.

The sumptuous jade-like glazes and durable porcelaneous bodies of Longquan ware made it extremely popular both in China and abroad. Compared to the numerous bowls and dishes in this ware, only a limited number of Longquan gourd vases have been excavated, one of them found in a Yuan-dynasty elite tomb,[4] and another recovered from a hoard,[5] suggesting that these were treasured items. Other gourd vases with applied scrolling decoration are in collections outside China, including two examples with more slender proportions in the Topkapi Palace in Istanbul that are fitted with Ottoman gilt mounts,[6] and one of very similar form that was once in the Tokugawa family collection in Japan.[7] HK

1. Celadon can describe a range of green-glazed ceramics, including those made at the Yue and Yaozhou kilns. The name is thought to have come from a reference to a character in pastoral sixteenth-century French romance who wore green ribbons, or to have derived from a corruption of the name Saladin, a twelfth-century Middle Eastern ruler who sent Chinese "celadons" to his Syrian counterpart; see Leidy 2015, 44.
2. Li 1994, 91.
3. Appliqué scrolling-lotus and peony-blossom designs are also seen on another type of vase with a flared trumpet neck. See Li 1996, no. 362, for an example in the Asian Art Museum of San Francisco.
4. An undecorated green-glazed gourd vase was excavated from a Zhang Hongfan family tomb in Henei, Dingxing, Hebei province; Beijing 2016, 63. Zhang Hongfan (1238–1280) was a Han Chinese general who led the Mongols in defeating the Southern Song army in 1279, thus establishing the Yuan dynasty. He and his clan are buried together in the family tomb.
5. A celadon gourd vase was excavated in 1984 from a hoard in Hecheng, Qingtian, Zhejiang province; Zhu 1998, no. 154.
6. Krahl 1986, vol. 1, nos. 202, 203. Another with French gilded bronze mounts is in the Huntington Library, San Marino, CA (no. 11.14).
7. It is now in the Hatakeyama Memorial Museum, Tokyo; illustrated in New York et al. 1977, no. 26.

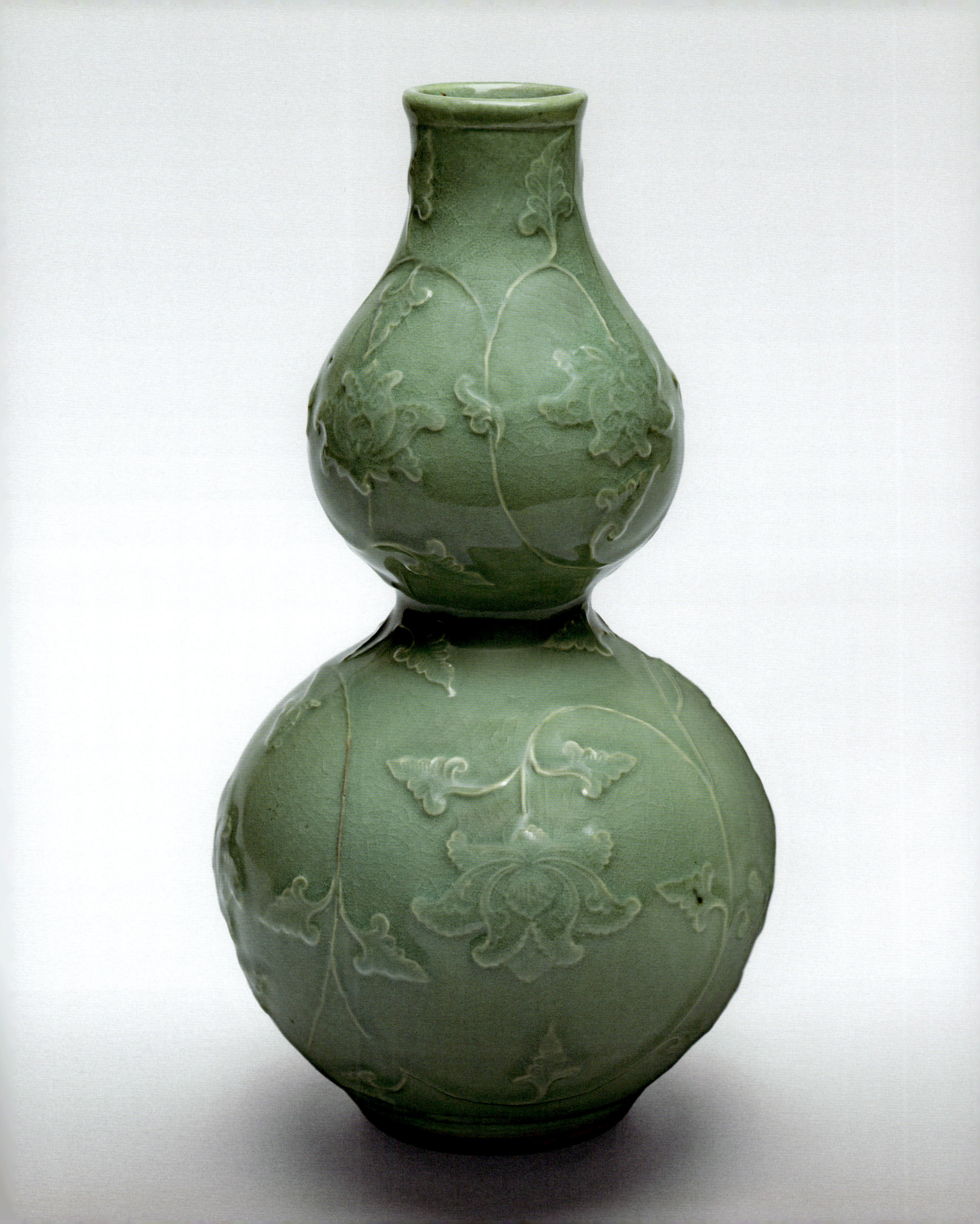

26

Guanyin Seated in Royal Ease

Yuan dynasty (1271–1368) or possibly Ming dynasty (1368–1644)
Wood (yellowwood, *Cladrastis* sp.) with traces of paint and gilded decoration
49 x 32 x 20 inches (124.5 x 81.3 x 50.8 cm)
Gift of Charles H. Ludington from the George Crofts Collection, 1925-53-11

With her relaxed pose of "royal ease" and serene expression, Guanyin, the Bodhisattva of Compassion, has been and continues to be one of the most popular and widely worshipped Buddhist deities in China. Guanyin was known for delaying enlightenment in order to help others, as was also true of other bodhisattvas of the Mahayana school of Buddhism.

It was after the Southern Song dynasty (1127–1279) that this particular representation, called Water-Moon Guanyin or Guanyin of the Southern Seas, appeared. The names refer to a chapter of the Buddhist text—the *Avatamsaka* (Flower Garland) Sutra—in which Guanyin is found seated in a rocky grotto on Mount Potalaka in the Southern Seas, meditating on the moon's reflection on the water. The moon on the water is a metaphor reminding Buddhist practitioners of the illusory nature of existence, the realization of which is a necessary step on the path to enlightenment. "Awakening," or enlightenment, is the goal of the believer, so that one may transcend the cycle of rebirth, be released from the suffering caused by attachments to worldly things, and reach a state of bliss (nirvana). In the eighth century numerous sutras discussed the concept of the emptiness of all things, an idea perhaps best conveyed by representations of Water-Moon Guanyin.[1]

The deity, here modeled from yellowwood that was once painted and gilded, would have been seated on a wood pedestal carved as a rocky outcrop to resemble Mount Potalaka. The slim figure is unusual, as it is simply clothed in a thin dhoti, adorned with a chunky necklace and a scarf around the shoulders; the seated Amitabha Buddha in the topknot that identifies this figure as Guanyin is also unusually large. Archival records state that the figure came from a temple in Guanyintang, Henan province, through George Crofts, who sold his collection of Chinese ceramics, many of them from Henan, to the Philadelphia Museum of Art in the early 1920s (see p. 20). HK

1. Rösch 2007, 32–33.

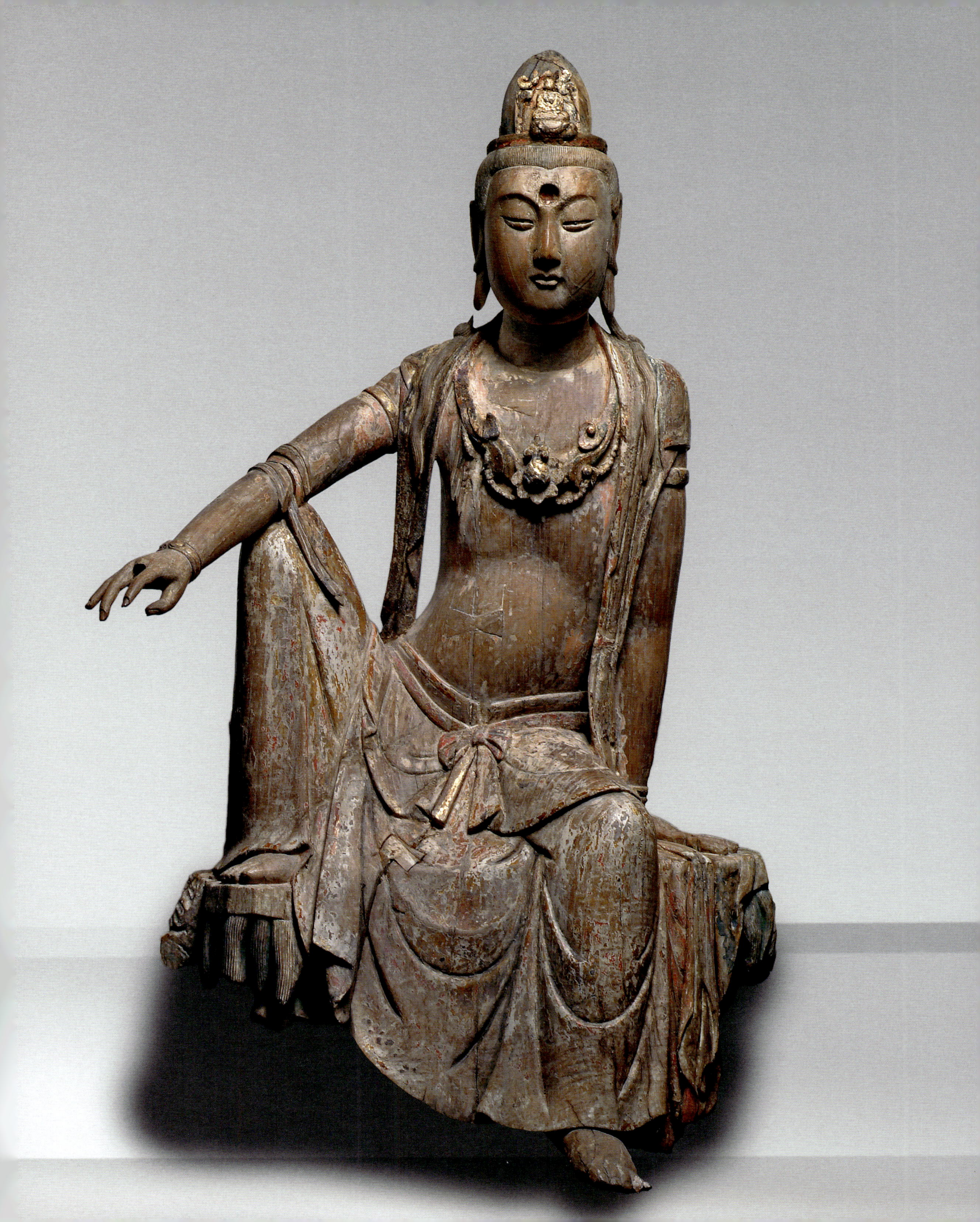

27

Bottle with Flowers of the Four Seasons

Ming dynasty (1368–1644), Hongwu period (1368–98)
Porcelain with underglaze blue decoration (Jingdezhen ware)
12⅝ x 8⅛ inches (32.1 x 20.7 cm)
Purchased with the John T. Morris Fund, 1952-30-1

This elegant form, with a widely swelling globular body narrowing to a slender neck and flared lip, is characteristic of blue-and-white wine bottles made during the reign of the first Ming emperor, Hongwu. In the previous Yuan dynasty (1271–1368), ruled by the Mongols, who openly welcomed foreign trade, the imperial kilns used cobalt imported from Persia and the Middle East, producing porcelains with a strong blue color. This changed during the reign of the Hongwu emperor, who was suspicious of foreigners. Instead, locally mined cobalt may have been used, producing the muted blue typical of this period.[1] The decoration of this bottle includes lotus-petal lappets above scrolling tendrils around the foot, overlapping plantain leaves above a narrower band of key fret on the neck, and a band of scrolling tendrils of *ruyi*-fungus inside the lip.[2] The design on the body of four seasonal flowers centered around a jagged ornamental garden rock includes camellia with bamboo (pictured), peony, pomegranate, and chrysanthemum.[3]

It is unusual to find seasonal flowers decorating this vase form, as the motif is more commonly found on wine ewers, which are often embellished with a scrolling floral spray such as peony.[4] However, excavations at the imperial kilns at Dongmentou, Zhushan, have revealed plates with floral decoration of the same seasonal flowers in the Hongwu strata.[5]

Although the previous Yuan dynasty had produced many blue-and-white wares in the porcelain workshops at Jingdezhen, the war that erupted toward the end of the dynasty disrupted production, and it was not until the second year of the reign of the Hongwu emperor that the kilns at Jingdezhen were revived and an imperial factory established. Although produced at the imperial kilns, this bottle and all Hongwu porcelains carry no reign marks, but rather have plain, unmarked bases.[6] HK

1. The paler, dull blue typical of blue-and-white wares made during this time may have been due to the use of smaller quantities of imported cobalt or the watering down of the foreign product with locally mined pigment, which contains higher amounts of manganese rather than iron. See Harrison-Hall 2001, 84.
2. *Ruyi*, meaning "as-you-wish," is an auspicious motif often seen in porcelain decoration. The structuring of the design to fill different sections of the object began in the Yuan dynasty under the influence of Islamic works of art.
3. Camellia and bamboo represent winter (the flower blooms around the time of the Chinese New Year, and bamboo remains green throughout the cold months), peony represents spring, the pomegranate flower signifies summer, and the chrysanthemum indicates autumn.
4. For a bottle decorated with the more typical single peony scroll and a ewer with similar depictions of floral sprays and decorative bands around the neck and foot, both in the Qing court (Imperial Palace) collections, Beijing, see Geng 2000, vol. 1, nos. 14, 15.
5. Beijing (Chen) 2015, 39, 44, 45.
6. Imperial reign marks incorporating the emperor's reign title were not used until the Yongle emperor's rule (1403–24; see Harrison-Hall 2001, 82), while the traditional four- and six-character reign marks in underglaze blue came into use in the Xuande period (1426–35).

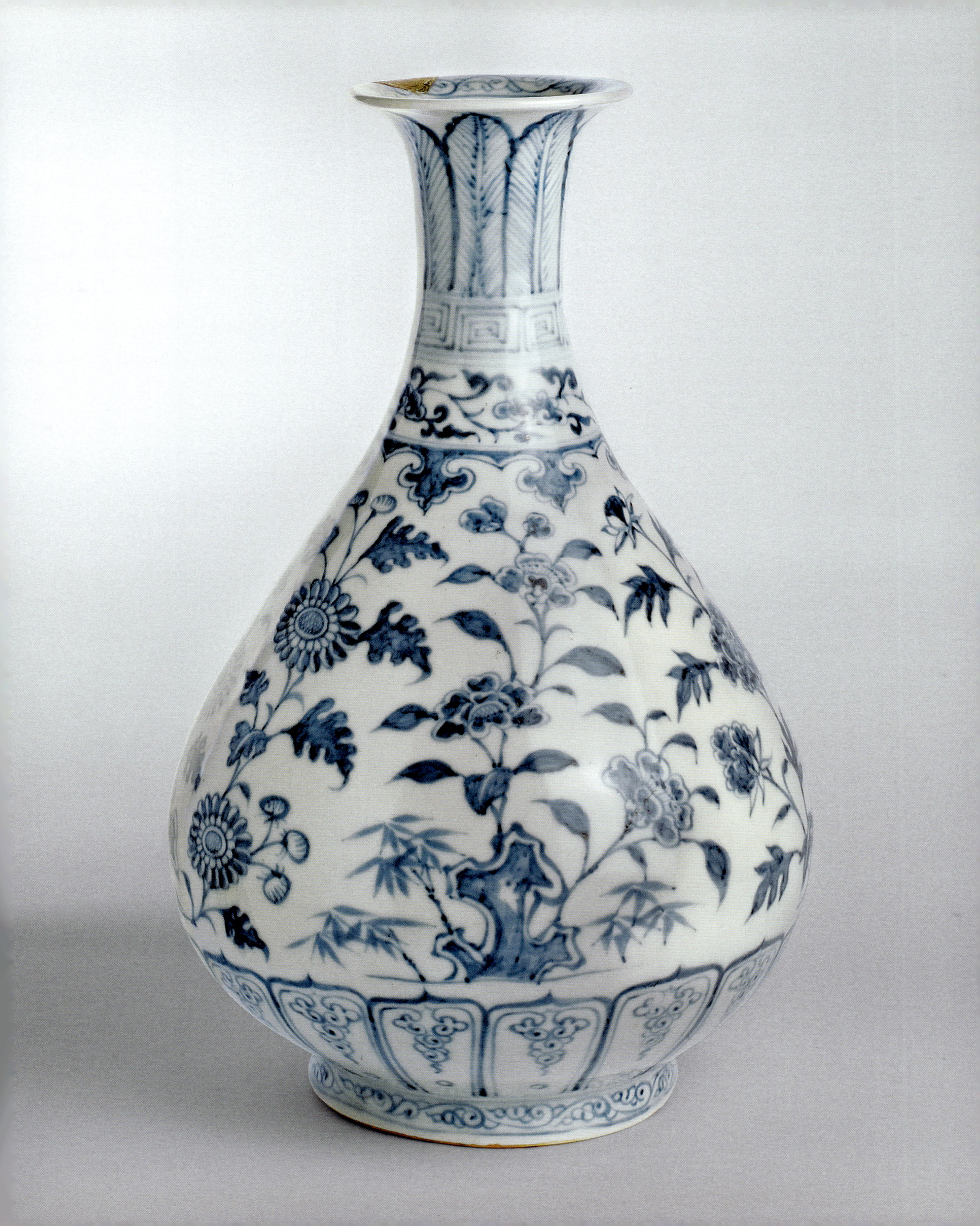

28

Covered Box with the Three Friends of Winter

Ming dynasty (1368–1644), Yongle period (1403–24)
Wood with carved red lacquer decoration
4¹⁄₁₆ x 10¾ inches (10.3 x 27.3 cm)
Gift of Mr. and Mrs. Morton Jenks, 1953-1-1a,b

Lacquer carving reached its peak in China during the early Ming dynasty, when this intricately decorated box was made. Carved through the red lacquer layers of the cover to reveal the yellow lacquer ground are plum blossoms, bamboo, and stylized pine, complexly arranged and intertwined on different planes to convey a sense of depth. This trio of plants, each able to flourish through the winter, was dubbed the Three Friends of Winter and came to convey integrity and fortitude, virtues associated with a scholar-gentleman (see no. 30).

A lightly incised mark on the side of the base reads "Da Ming Yongle nian zhi" (Made during the Yongle era of the great Ming). In the early fifteenth century, carved red lacquer was favored at the Chinese court, and many such boxes, especially examples with peony designs, were produced during this time.[1] Lacquers were also popular gifts; records indicate that during the reign of the Yongle emperor, fifty-eight lacquer items were sent from the Chinese court to the Japanese Shogunate in 1403, 1406, and 1407.[2] This particular type of container may have been used to store belts, necessary elements of official court formal attire that indicated one's rank.

Lacquer, a "natural plastic" first used more than three thousand years ago, was applied to everything from coffins to furniture and everyday objects, as it was not only decorative but also practical, being impervious to water as well as heat. Creating carved lacquer was a time-consuming process that involved first building up multiple coatings of lacquer on a wood surface. Each layer of lacquer had to cure fully in a humid environment and then be polished before the next layer could be applied; when the layers were completed, the design was carved. The complete process could take years, no doubt adding to the prestige of the object. HK

1. Chen 2008, nos. 8, 9, 10, and 11 have marks of the Yongle emperor, and nos. 12 and 13 have marks of the Xuande emperor (r. 1426–35). Some Xuande marks have been found on top of the lightly incised Yongle marks.
2. Garner 1971, 97–100.

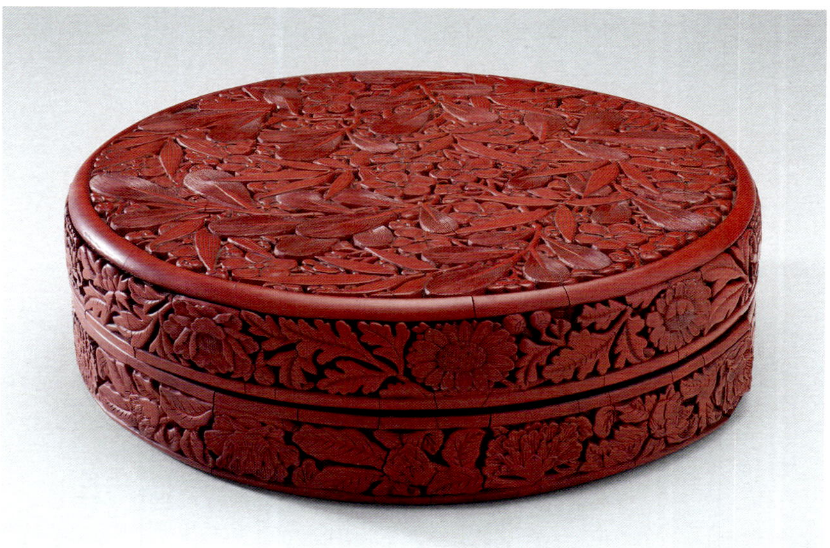

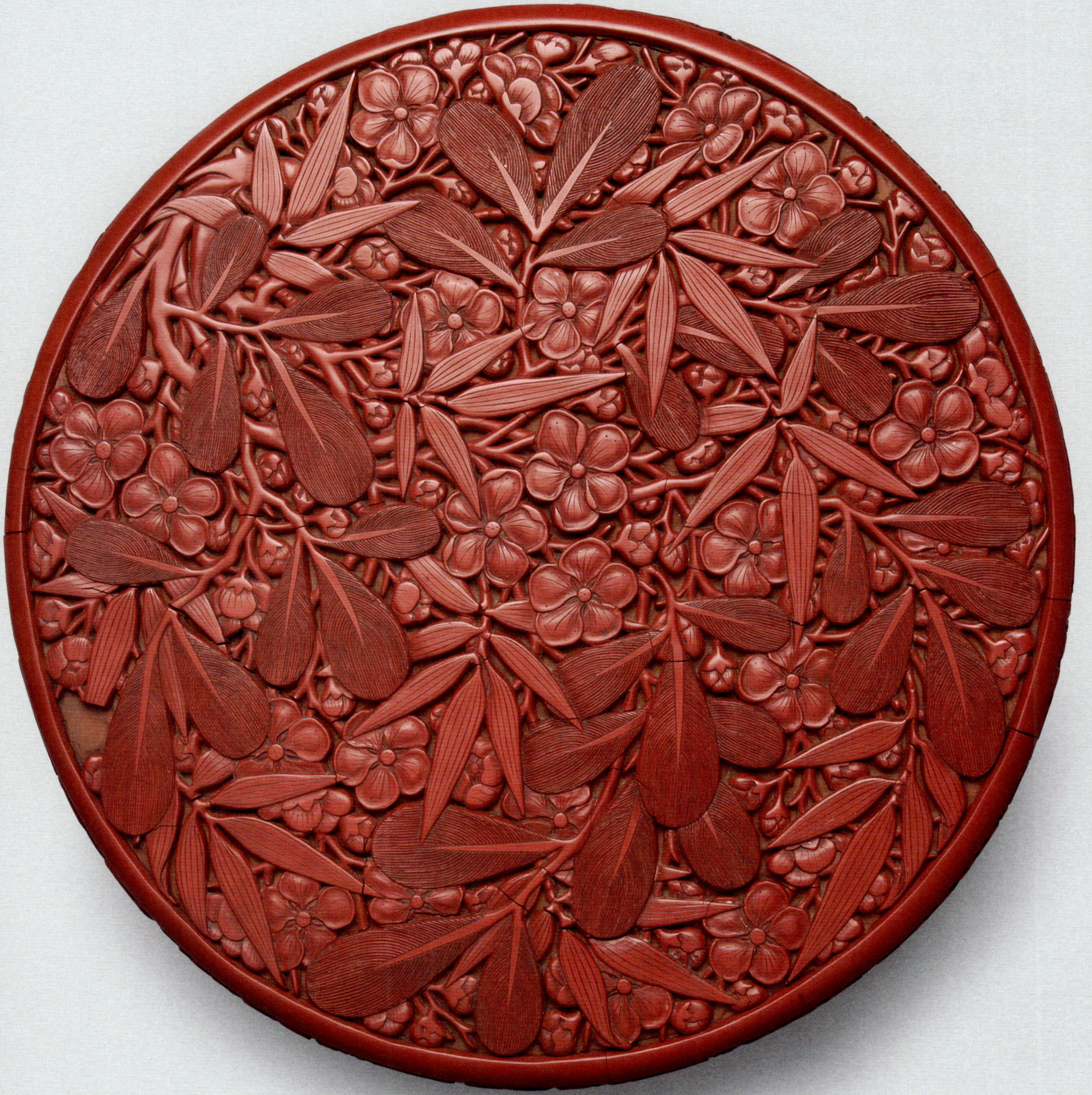

29

Dish with Beribboned Bouquet

Ming dynasty (1368–1644), Yongle (1403–24) to Xuande period (1426–35)
Porcelain with underglaze blue decoration (Jingdezhen ware)
Diam. 13 9/16 inches (34.4 cm)
Promised gift of Marguerite and Gerry Lenfest

This dish with cobalt decoration under a clear glaze was made in the early fifteenth century, a period that saw the production of some of China's finest blue-and-white porcelains.[1] The plate's interior, freely painted in a rich cobalt blue of varying tones, is decorated at the center with a beribboned lotus bouquet depicting different parts of the plant, including the seed pods and leaves, as well as a stalk of grain and a triangular-leaf arrowroot plant, which together convey auspicious wishes for harmony and prosperity. Pairs of scrolling blossoms of lotus, chrysanthemum, peony, gardenia, and camellia around the sides of the dish, bordered by a narrow band of scrollwork at the rim, are repeated on the exterior, enclosed by a scrollwork band at the rim and a keyfret border above the base.

The unglazed base reveals the white porcelain body and is free of any imperial marks. The underglaze blue-and-white four- and six-character marks found on many Ming and Qing imperial wares were first introduced during the Xuande period. This particular type of dish with an unmarked base appears to indicate a transition between the earlier Yongle- and Xuande-period blue-and-white wares.[2]

This dish and others with a similar lotus-bouquet design were created in the kilns at Jingdezhen in southern China, which were famous from the time of the Yuan dynasty (1271–1368) for producing large numbers of high-quality blue-and-white wares in many different sizes. Examples found in the Imperial Palace collections in both Taiwan and Beijing,[3] and in foreign collections such as the Ardebil shrine in Iran,[4] illustrate the popularity of this ware within as well as outside China. HK

1. Wang Shixing (1546–1598), a Ming scholar who traveled throughout China, observed in *Further Elucidations on My Extensive Record of Travels* (*Guang zhi yi*) that the best blue-and-white wares were made during the Xuande period; Liao 2000, 27. Later, in the Qing dynasty, emperors made porcelains modeled on early fifteenth-century Ming examples. A Kangxi version of this same design is illustrated in Liao 2000, 54.
2. Liao Baoxiu discusses the research that allows for differentiating between Yongle and Xuande unmarked pieces; Liao 2000, 30.
3. Two examples dated to the Xuande and the Yongle-Xuande period are in the National Palace Museum, Taipei; Liao 2000, nos. 26, 27. A Yongle-period dish is in the Palace Museum, Beijing; Gugong and Jingdezhen 2015, no. 57.
4. Seventeen examples were collected by the Persian ruler Shah Abbas and donated to the shrine in 1611. The dishes range in size from eleven to seventeen inches in diameter and have slight variations in the lotus design and borders; Pope 1956, pls. 30–31.

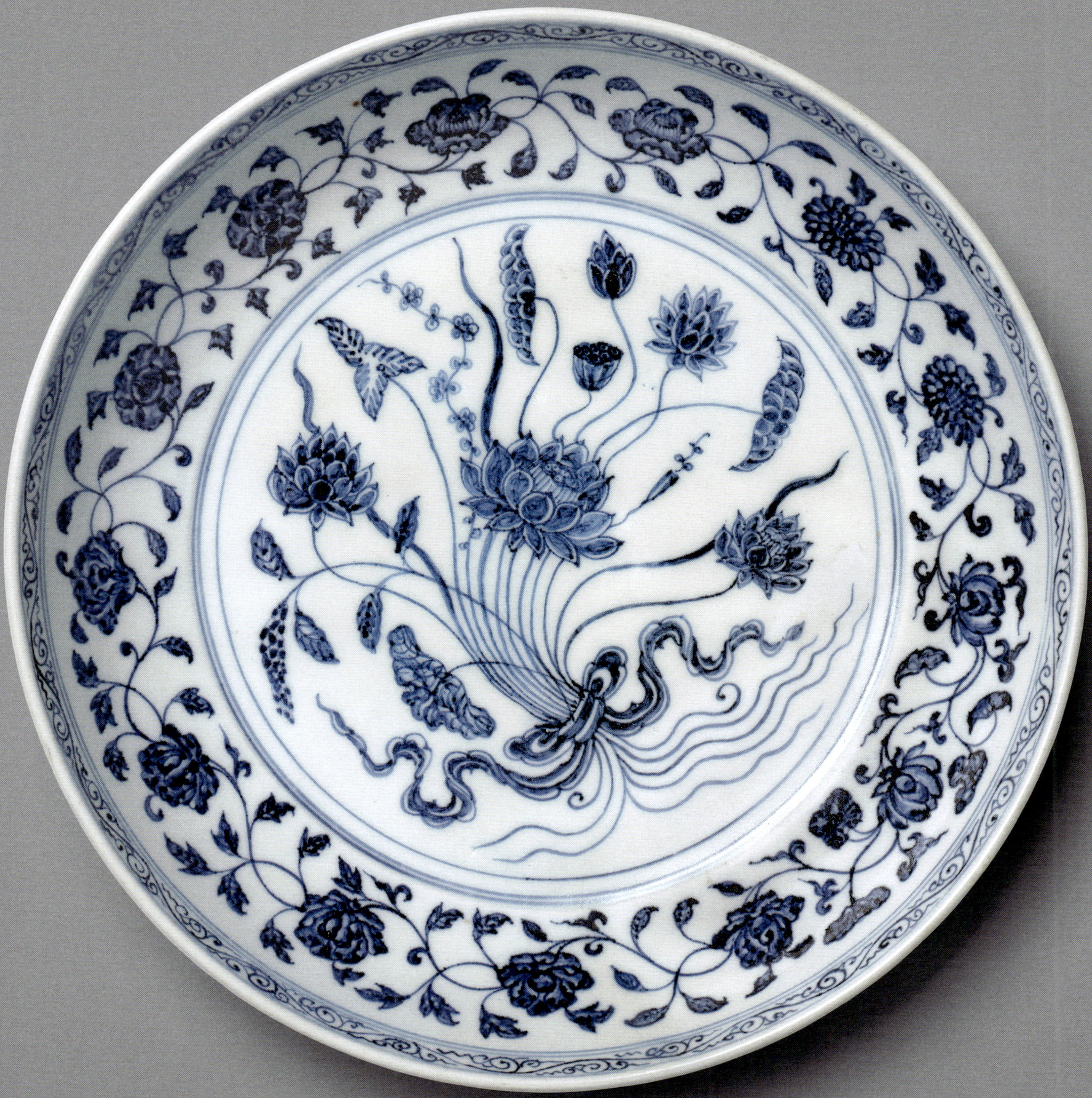

30

Conical Bowl with the Three Friends of Winter

Ming dynasty (1368–1644), probably Xuande period (1426–35)
Porcelain with underglaze blue decoration (Jingdezhen ware)
$3\frac{5}{16}$ x $8\frac{3}{4}$ inches (8.4 x 22.2 cm)
Purchased with the Henry B. Keep Fund, the Joseph E. Temple Fund, the Bloomfield Moore Fund, the John T. Morris Fund, and with funds contributed by Mrs. Walter H. Annenberg, The Beneficia Foundation, Mr. and Mrs. J. Welles Henderson, Mrs. Howard H. Lewis, Mrs. William F. Machold, Mrs. Donald Petrie, Meyer P. Potamkin, Hugh Scott, and Mrs. William L. Van Alen, 1984-116-1

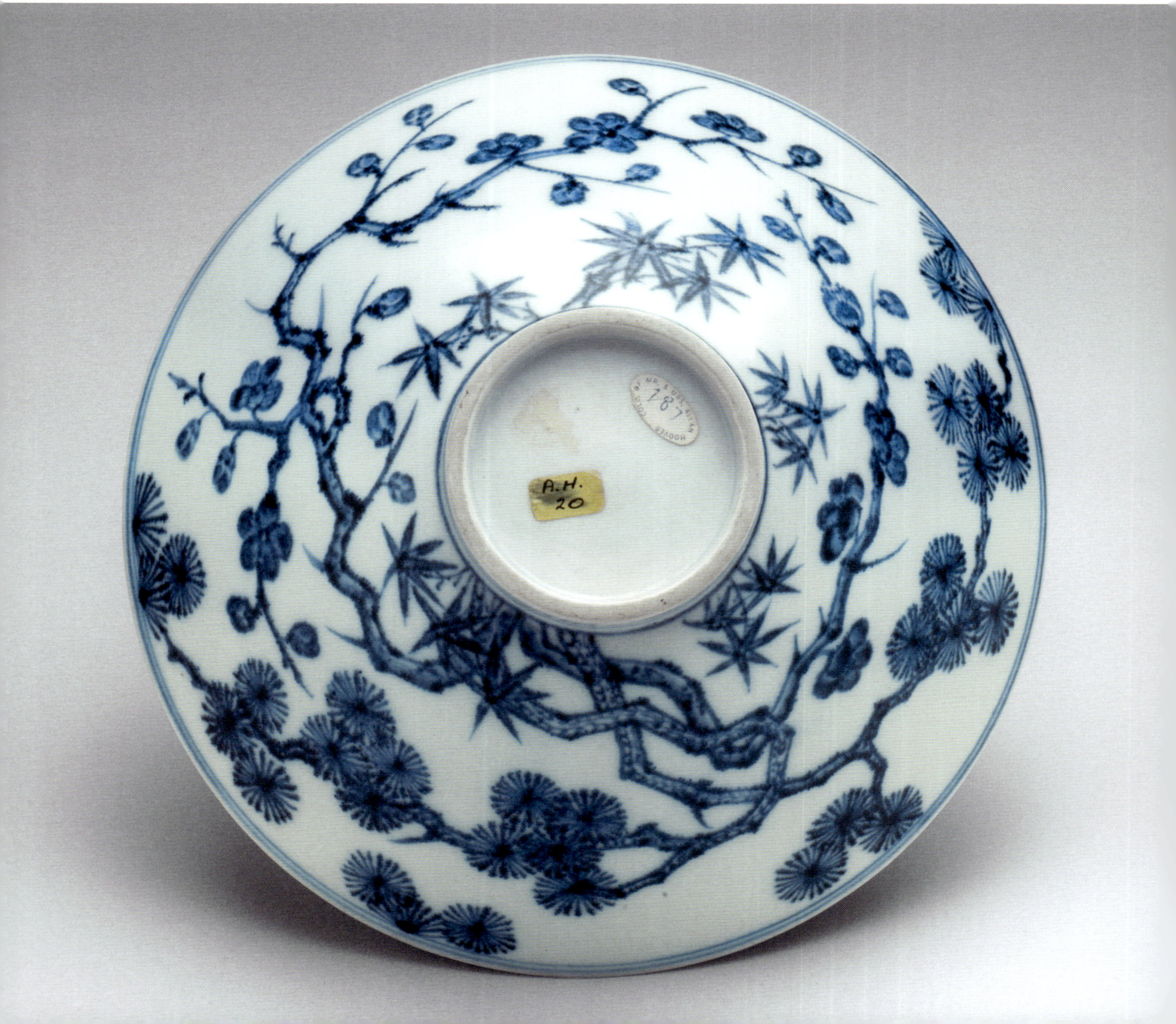

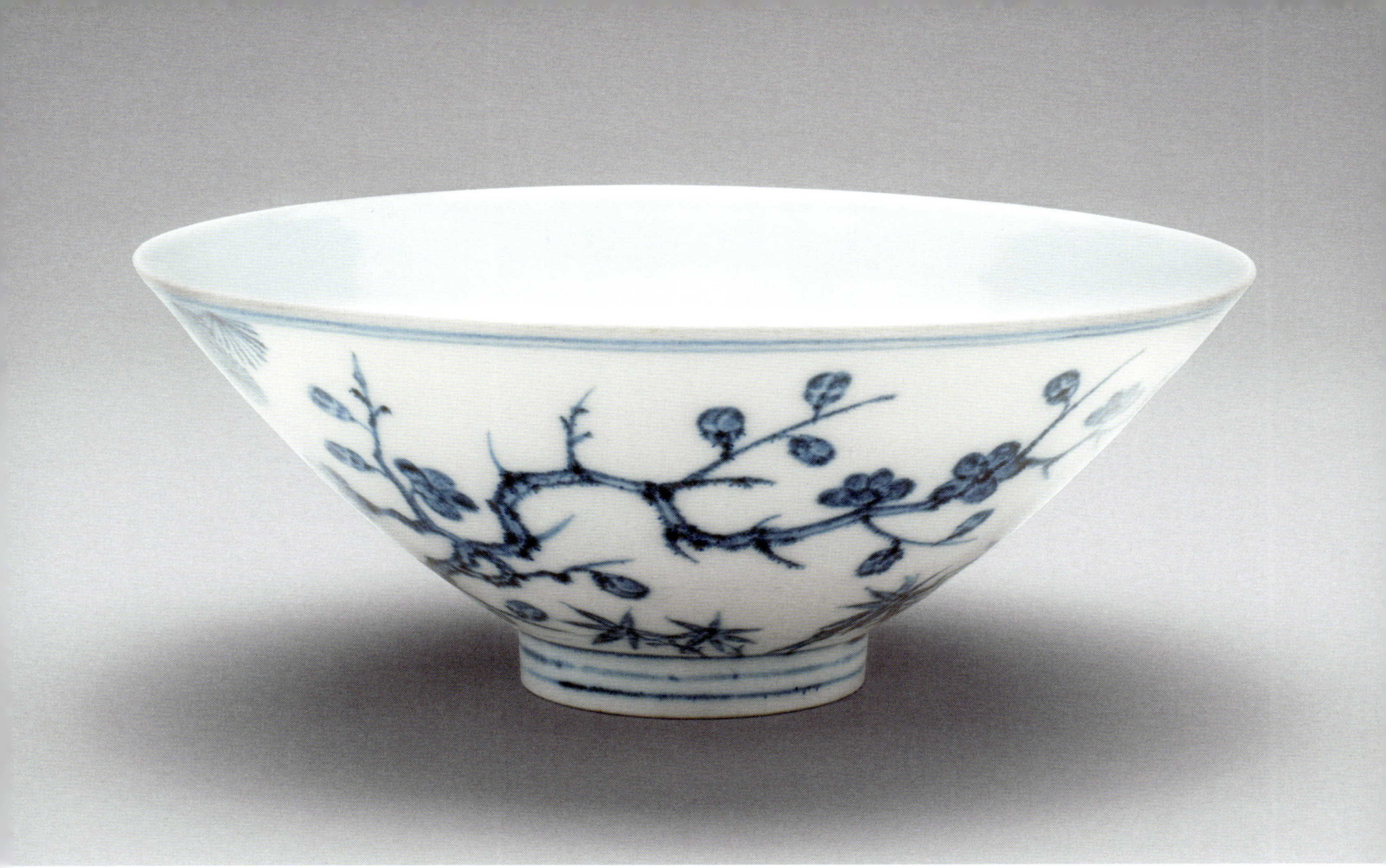

With its freely brushed design, painted in modulated tones of deep, inky blue against a glossy white ground, this bowl illustrates why "Ming blue and white" gained such currency in the West as well as in China. This example was made in the early fifteenth century, when the imperial kilns of Jingdezhen had developed new techniques to produce finer porcelains, with thinner, lighter clay bodies and shinier glazes.[1] Though locally mined cobalt for the blue was available, the kilns used cobalt imported from Persia (present-day Iran), which produced a stronger blue that could mimic the modulated ink tones of Chinese brush painting. So renowned were blue-and-white porcelains produced during the Yongle and Xuande periods that they were collected by later emperors and also given away as gifts.[2]

The painterly design of pine, bamboo, and plum represents a popular Confucian theme: the Three Friends of Winter, so named for their shared quality of remaining green during the cold winter months. The hardy pine flourishes in harsh environments and is a symbol of longevity; the tall hollow-jointed bamboo shows strength and resilience in its uprightness yet bends and conforms when in adverse conditions; and the plum is the first flower to bloom in late winter, representing perseverance. Together the Three Friends came to epitomize the moral characteristics the scholar-gentleman was to learn and live by. HK

1. London 2014–15, 88.
2. Imperially sponsored maritime trade and diplomatic missions to the Middle East in the early fifteenth century saw many blue-and-white wares end up in well-known collections, such as those at the Topkapi Palace in Turkey and the Ardebil Shrine in Iran. For two examples similar to the Philadelphia bowl, see Krahl 1986, vol. 2, no. 610; Pope 1981, 320–30, no. 29, pl. 47.

31

Ewer with Five-clawed Dragons

Ming dynasty (1368–1644), Xuande period (1426–35)
Gold alloy and semiprecious stones
8⁹⁄₁₆ x 8³⁄₁₆ x 5 inches (21.7 x 20.8 x 12.7 cm)
Purchased with the John T. Morris Fund, 1950-118-1

A product of the imperial workshops, this covered ewer is made from hammered gold sheet and elaborately decorated with chased designs and colorful semiprecious stones.[1] On each side is a rampant five-clawed dragon with powerful body, bulbous claws, and thick upright mane, depicted in profile amid flame-like clouds within a raised, teardrop-shaped cartouche. The squared spout, its base incised with the head of a fanged *makara* (mythical sea creature) with mouth agape, is set opposite an arched handle. The dragon and the *makara* head are stylistically similar to representations seen on porcelains of the Xuande reign,[2] suggesting an early fifteenth-century date for the ewer.

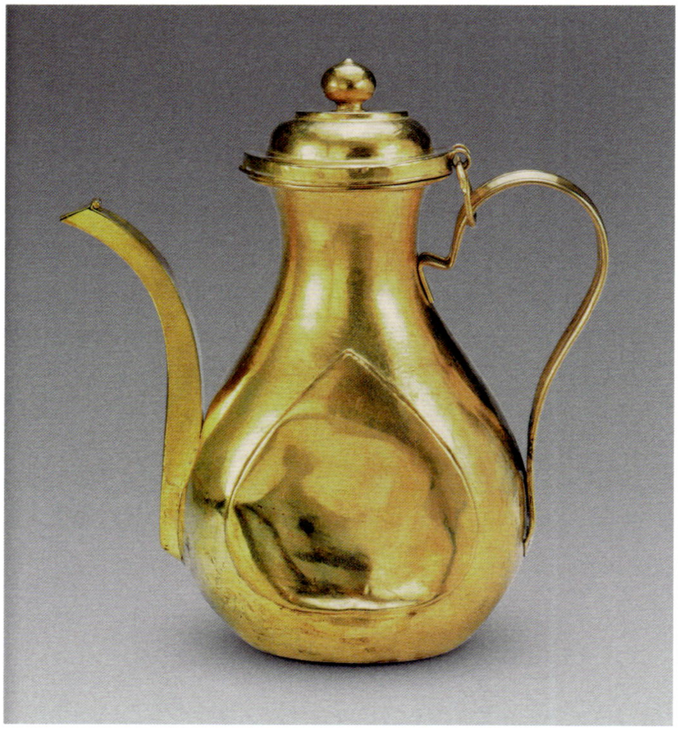

Fig. 36. Gold ewer from the tomb of Prince Zhuang of Liang (1411–1441), Zhongxiang, Hubei. Hubei Provincial Museum

Gold vessels from the Ming dynasty are rare, as laws restricted the use of this precious metal to the imperial family. A gold ewer with a similar squat form and squared spout was recently excavated from the tomb of Prince Zhuang of Liang, the brother of the Xuande emperor.[3] That ewer is undecorated (fig. 36), suggesting that the museum's more elaborate and bejeweled vessel likely belonged to a higher-ranking member of the imperial family.[4]

The use of semiprecious stones on gold is seen especially during the first half of the fifteenth century, a time when the Ming emperors were looking outward to the wider world. Admiral Zheng He's seven voyages across the "Western Ocean" from the South China Sea to the east coast of Africa marked the beginning of international commerce and diplomacy for the Ming dynasty (the first set out in 1405, the last in 1421). Through trade and tribute, Chinese goods were exported to the West, while foreign goods and gifts arrived in China from abroad. Gems from Southeast Asia, India, and Sri Lanka were among the precious items imported to China, along with gold, exotic animals, and spices.[5] HK

1. The term *chased* refers to a technique in which a metal object is worked from the front with a hammer and tools that raise, depress, or push aside the metal without removing any from the surface.
2. Geng 1993, 45, fig. 72, illustrates a ewer of similar form with an animal head at the base of the spout. For similar Xuande dragons, see Taipei 1998, 128–29, no. 37.
3. Liang 2007, vol. 1, 34 (for a line drawing of the ewer), vol. 2, col. pl. 21. More than 120 gold objects, including belts and jewelry inlaid with precious gems, were excavated from the tomb Prince Zhuang shared with his consort, Lady Wei, in Hubei province. See also London 2014–15, 67–68, 74–77.
4. A gold ewer was found in the tomb of a Ming-dynasty imperial concubine; see Hu 1954, 68.
5. Brook 2014, 280.

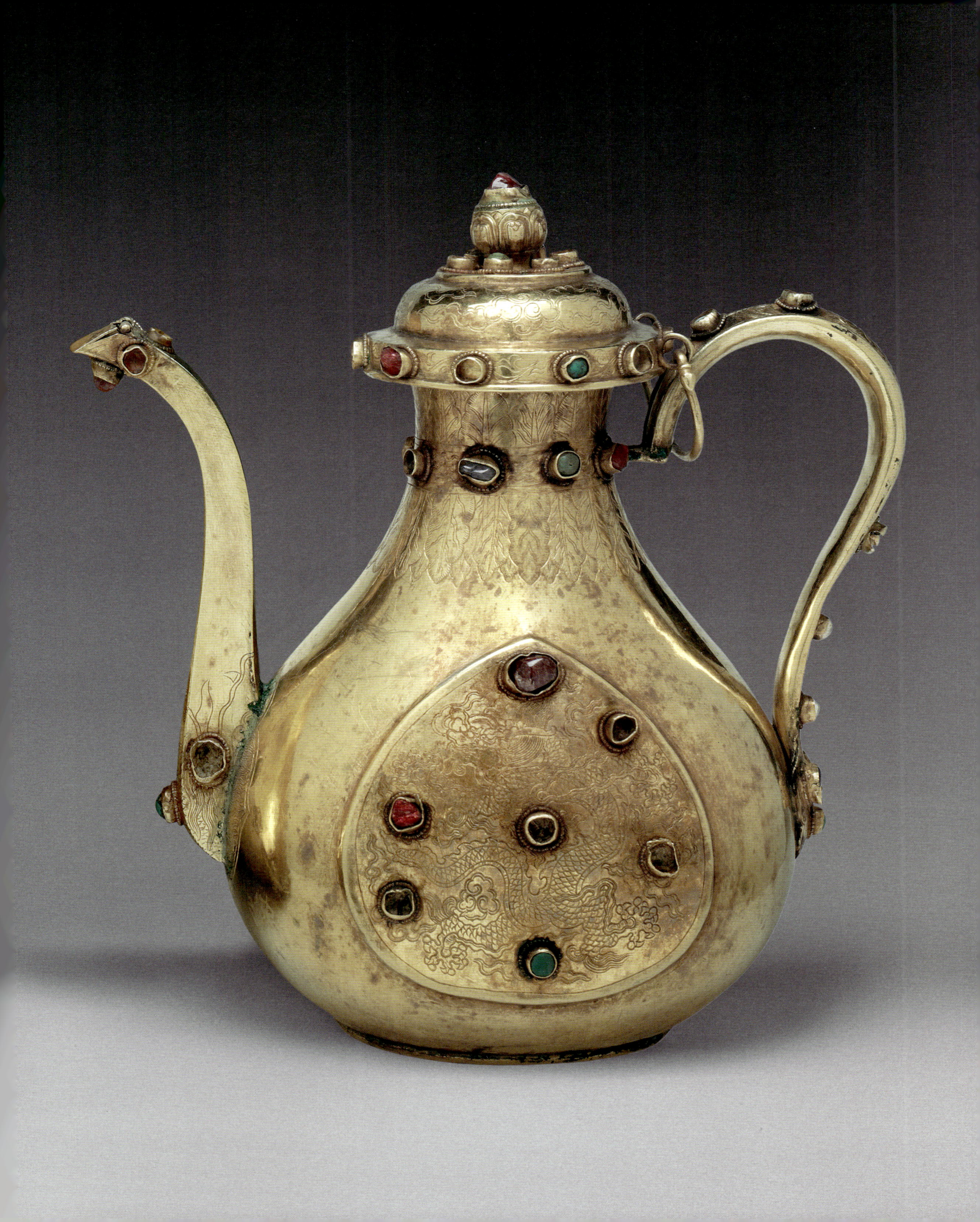

32

Basin with Five-clawed Dragons

Ming dynasty (1368–1644), Xuande period (1426–35)
Gold alloy and semiprecious stones
2 13/16 x 10 3/16 inches (7.1 x 25.9 cm)
Purchased with Museum funds, 1950-74-1

Made from a hammered gold sheet and formed with a rounded base, this elaborately chased basin is decorated with five powerful five-clawed dragons—two on the interior and three striding around the exterior walls—pursuing a flaming jewel amid clouds. The flat rim of the basin is engraved with a scrolling vine and set with twenty-four bezels with beaded edges, each to hold a semiprecious stone.

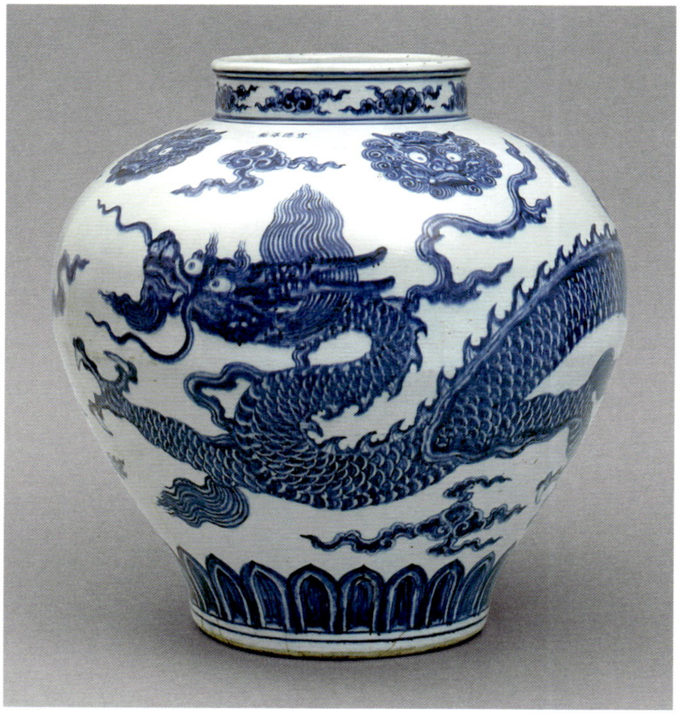

Fig. 37. Jar with Dragon. Ming dynasty, Xuande mark and period. Porcelain painted with cobalt blue under transparent glaze (Jingdezhen ware); 19 x 19 inches (48.3 x 48.3 cm). The Metropolitan Museum of Art, New York. Gift of Robert E. Tod, 1937 (37.191.1)

This basin, along with the ewer just illustrated (no. 31), is part of a known group of four gold vessels, all with chased dragon designs and inlaid with semiprecious stones.[1] The group can be dated stylistically to the Xuande period, as the chased decoration of the dragon and distinctive flaming "auspicious" clouds, shaped like *ruyi* fungus, are similar to decoration on blue-and-white Xuande porcelains (fig. 37). This dating has been confirmed by the gold discovered in 2001 in the tomb of Prince Zhuang of Liang (1411–1441) and his consort, Lady Wei, in Hebei, where more than 120 gold objects were found, among them two plain gold basins and two gold ewers (see fig. 36). They were found along with two gold ingots on the coffin platform and were perhaps once placed within the coffin, where the prince's body was laid, signaling their importance.[2] The ewer and basin may have been used for washing before ritual offerings were made,[3] as tombs have been found with ritual altars in the rear chamber.[4]

The inscriptions on the two gold ingots found in Prince Zhuang of Liang's tomb reveal that gold objects were made by the imperial workshops located in the capital of Nanjing, and that the material was also sourced from places outside China.[5] HK

1. A covered jar of gold with inlaid gems is in the Freer Gallery of Art (F1952.29a–b), Smithsonian Institution, Washington, DC.
2. Liang 2007, vol. 1, 24–25, shows a line drawing of the coffin and the placement of the associated objects. For a description of the gold vessels in the tomb, see Clunas 2005–6, 7–8.
3. London 2014–15, 85, fig. 67.
4. An example is the tomb of Zhu Zhen, the sixth son of the founding Ming emperor Taizu; see Clunas 2005–6, 3–7.
5. The inscription on one ingot reads, "Bought in the Western Ocean and other places"; see Clunas 2005–6, p. 8.

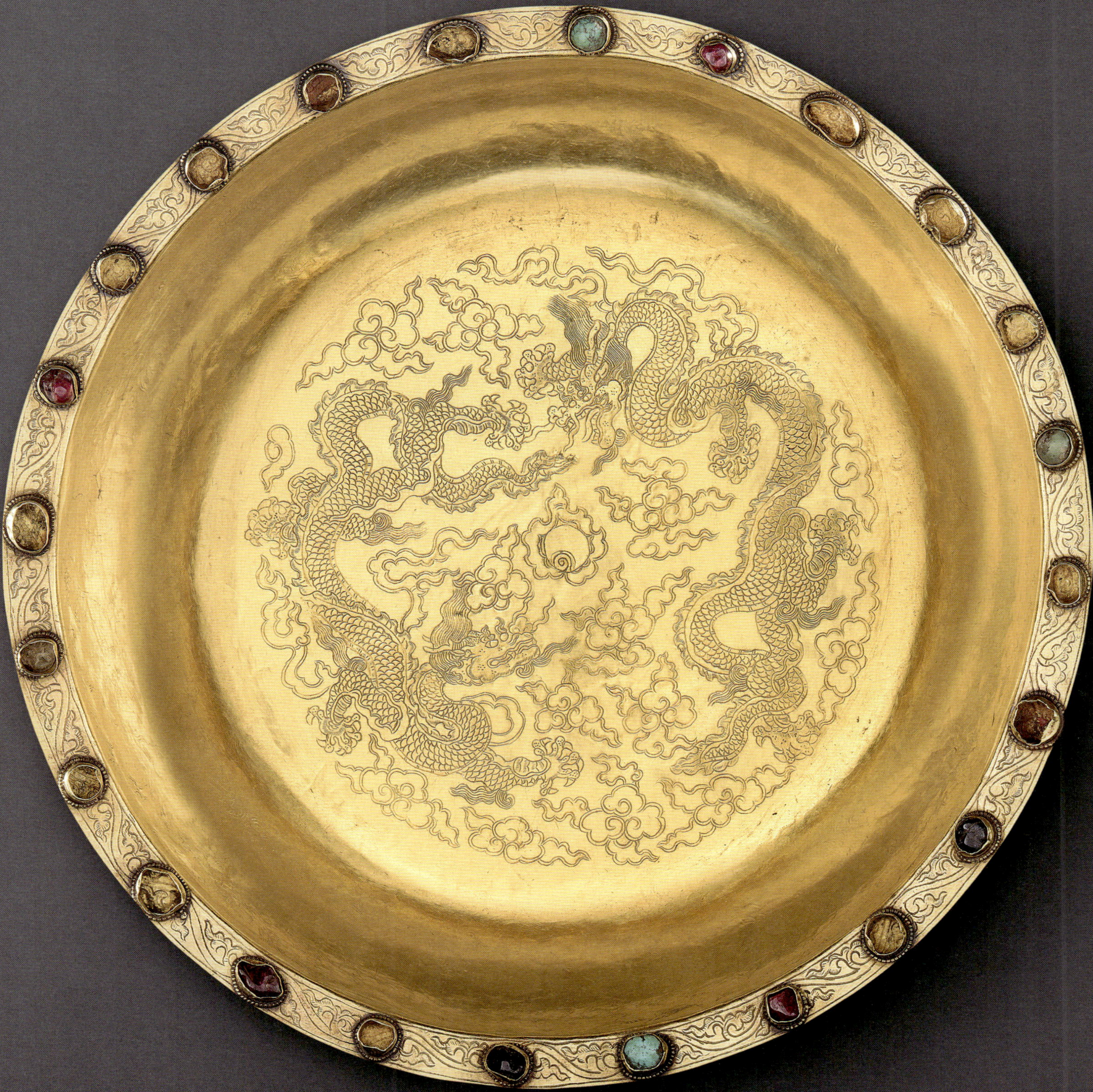

33

Set of Ten Volumes of the Sutra *The Great Perfection of Reason*

Ming dynasty (1368–1644), Zhengtong period (1436–49), dated by inscription to the 11th month, 11th day, 5th year of the Zhengtong reign (1440)
Wrapper: silk plain weave with silk supplementary weft over paper board; volume covers (top row): silk plain weave embroidered with silk floss over paper board; (bottom row): silk satin with supplementary wefts of gold leaf on paper strips over paper board; silk plain weave embroidered with silk floss over paper board; silk satin with supplementary wefts of gold leaf on paper strips over paper board; text: ink on paper
Wrapper $13\frac{7}{8}$ x $22\frac{9}{16}$ inches (35.2 x 57.3 cm); sutra volumes, $13\frac{7}{8}$ x 5 x ½ inches (35.2 x 12.7 x 1.3 cm)
Purchased with funds contributed by Peter A. Benoliel, 1974-200-1a–k

These ten volumes (*juan*)—numbered 111 to 120—and their wrapper (*shu han*) comprise one unit of the six-hundred-volume sutra (or scripture) *The Great Perfection of Reason* (*Mahāprajñāpāramitā sutra*; *Da bore boluomiduo jing*).[1] The volumes are part of a monumental imperial-sponsored publishing project known as the Yongle Northern Tripitaka (*Beizang*).[2]

In 1420 the Yongle emperor (r. 1403–24) moved the capital from Nanjing to Beijing. A year later he ordered the printing of the Buddhist canon (*tripitaka*), which required carving six thousand individual wood blocks and took nineteen years to complete.[3] Its distribution by imperial bestowal was extremely selective and required a separate building to house the canon, as well as the erection of a stone stele identifying the gift. The unit shown here would have occupied one of six hundred compartments in such a special monastery or temple library. The survival of a complete unit of the *Beizang* is very rare. Today, most evidence of this famed imperial commission consists of detached fabric-covered end boards (or covers); the Philadelphia Museum of Art has five hundred sutra covers in its collection (see p. 24).

The printing and binding of the Yongle *Beizang* was not completed until 1445, and for the next century few were distributed. By the time of the accession of the Wanli emperor (r. 1573–1620) only a dozen complete sets had been bestowed. The Wanli emperor and his mother, the Empress Dowager Cisheng (1545–1614), became the major benefactors for the distribution of the *Beizang* beginning in the 1580s. Over the next three decades more than a hundred sets of the Buddhist canon were bestowed on temples and monasteries across the empire.[4]

Each accordion-folded chapter (fig. 38) was protected by boards covered with recycled mid-Ming-dynasty silks made for the imperial court, indicating that this set was part of the renewed distribution of the Yongle *Beizang* during the later sixteenth century. Similar silks covered the board "wrapper." Only the rainbow-striped ribbon used as the tie seems to have been custom-made for the project. JV

1. The first title in parentheses is in Sanskrit, the second in Chinese.
2. See Pressreader 2017, accessed August 3, 2017.
3. Naquin 2000, 94–95.
4. Zhang 2016, 487–508.

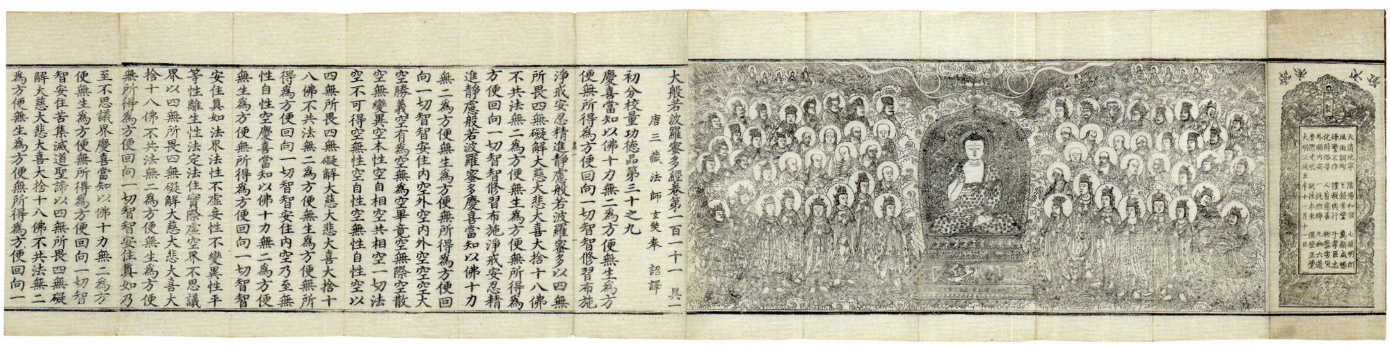

Fig. 38. The first volume in the set, unfolded

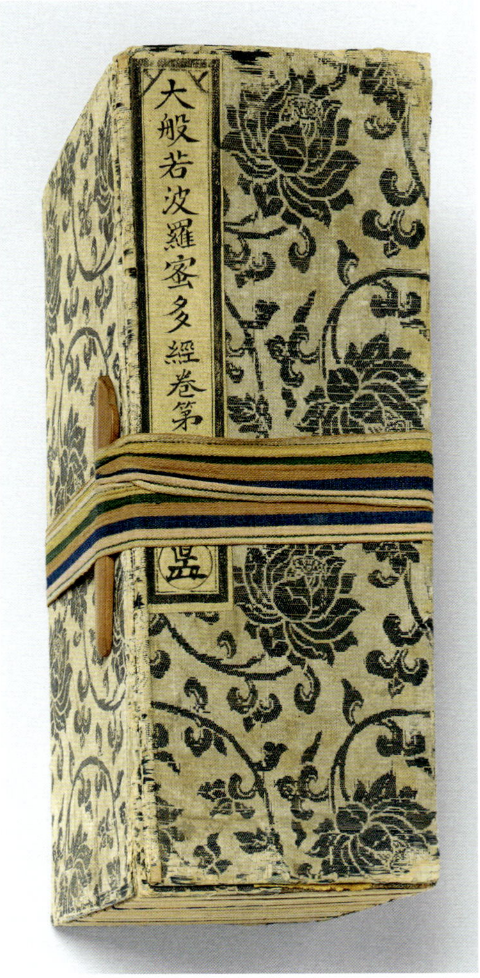
大般若波羅蜜多經卷第
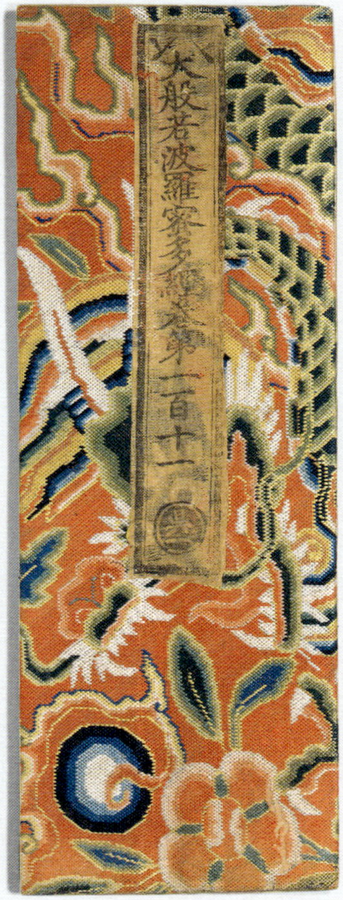
大般若波羅蜜多經卷第一百十一
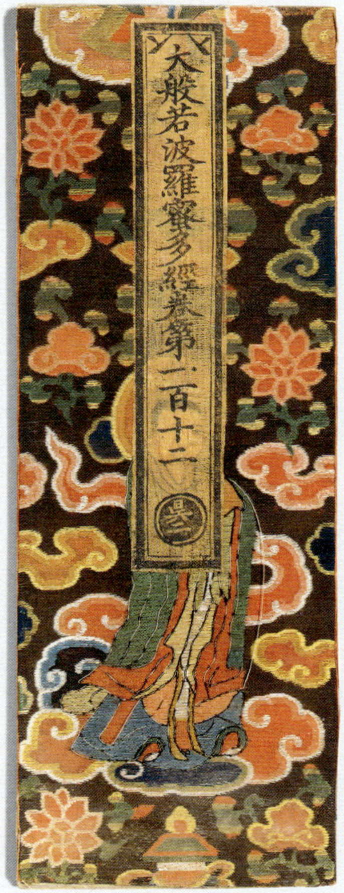
大般若波羅蜜多經卷第一百十二
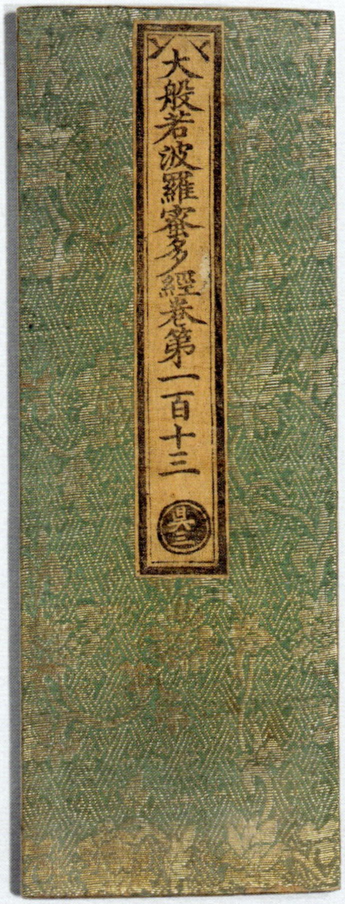
大般若波羅蜜多經卷第一百十三
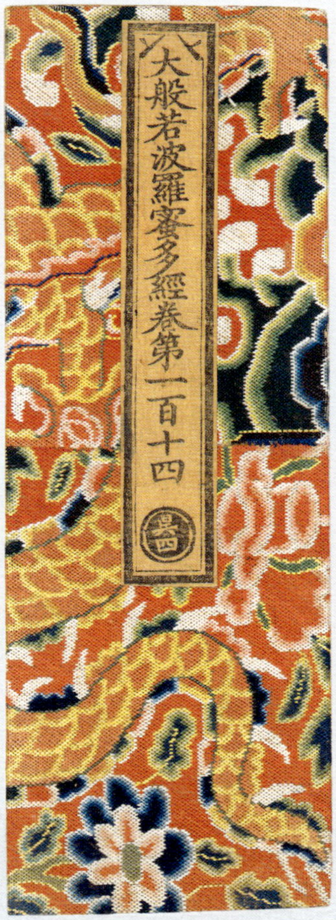
大般若波羅蜜多經卷第一百十四
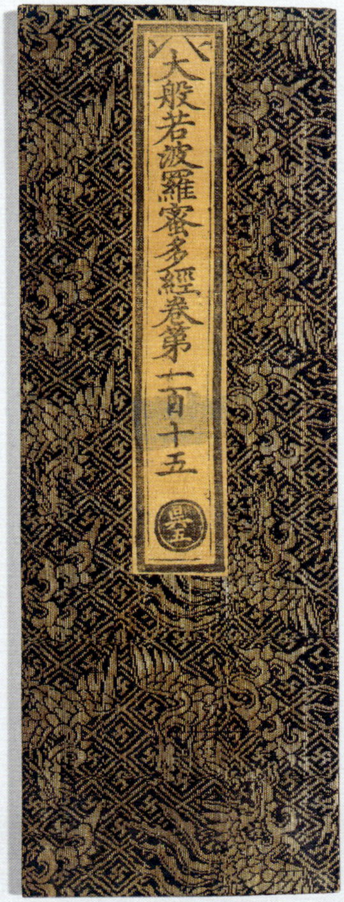
大般若波羅蜜多經卷第一百十五

34

Coffered Ceiling from Zhihuasi (Temple of Transforming Wisdom)

Ming dynasty (1368–1644), Zhengtong period (1436–49), c. 1444
Wood with lacquer, paint, and gilded decoration
16 feet 8 inches x 16 feet 8 inches (508 x 508 cm)
Gift of Mr. and Mrs. Joseph Wasserman, 1930-38-1a–n

This coffered ceiling, installed in the museum's East Asian galleries, is one of the best preserved examples of imperial monastic architecture from the early 1400s. The structure it belonged to was built by an infamous Ming eunuch as his private residence, but it was later converted to a temple, with imperial support.[1] Constructed without nails, using traditional interlocking mortise-and-tenon joinery, such elaborately decorated ceilings—called *zaojing* (water-plant well) or *tianjing* (heavenly well)—were thought to protect against fire and defined important spaces.[2] In the Zhihua Temple, the ceiling was located in the Hall of Transforming Wisdom (the second hall within the temple) above a Buddhist altar,[3] its intricately carved imperial and Buddhist-inspired designs appropriate to its function and status. In the center medallion a large, writhing dragon descends from cloud-filled heavens. Emblematic of imperial power since the fourteenth century, the dragon is a mythical creature associated with the cosmic male force. Here its potency is amplified by the eight smaller dragons in the octagon that immediately surrounds it.[4] Within the diamond-shaped panels in the corners of the outer octagon are eight heavenly beings (*devas*), each holding an auspicious symbol representing the Buddhist blessings (a); in the triangular panels between these are lotus blossoms, symbols of purity and a metaphor for the rebirth of souls from this earthly world to an enlightened state. A pair of male and female phoenixes (*fenghuang*), differentiated by their tail feathers—rounded feathers for the male (*feng*) and ribbon-like feathers for the female (*huang*)—occupy the four corners of the ceiling (b), further expressing imperial power.

Surrounding the ceiling and supported on dense scrolling clouds are multistoried heavenly pavilions (*tiangong louge*) that replicate imperially commissioned temple buildings (c), down to the miniature processional

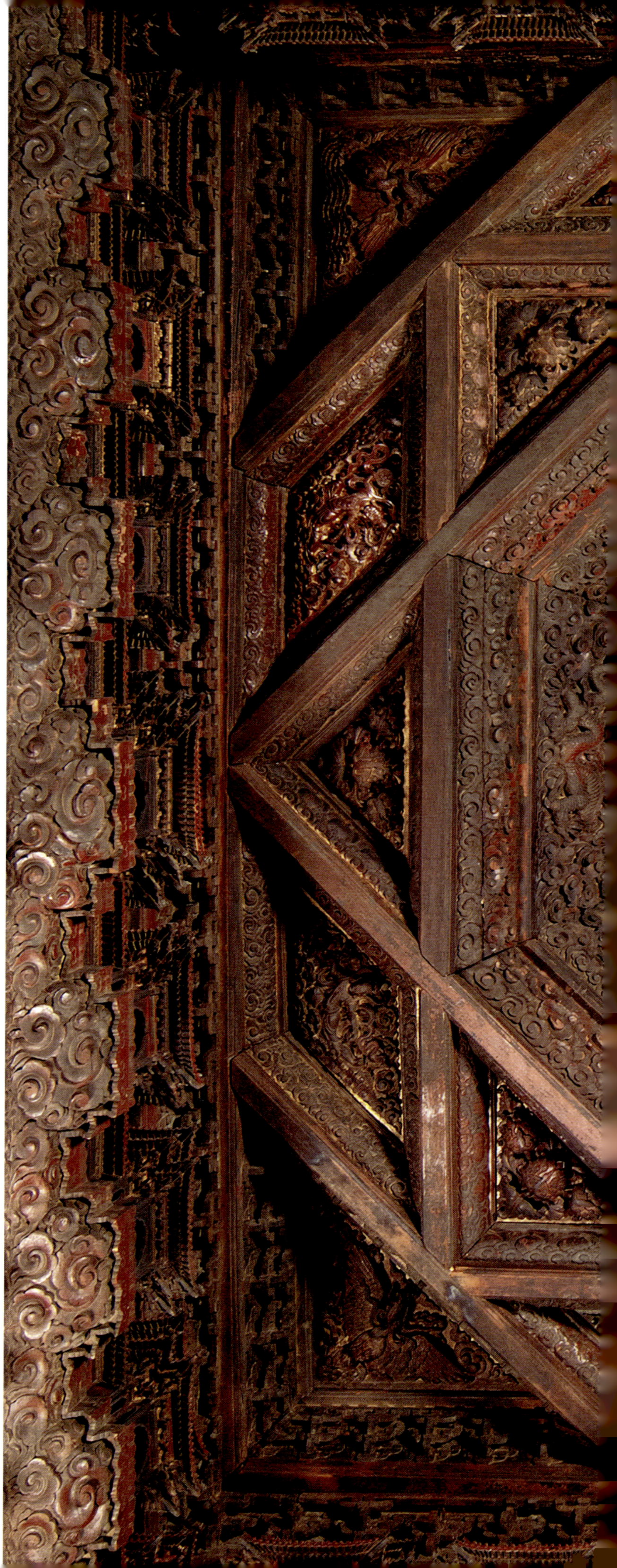

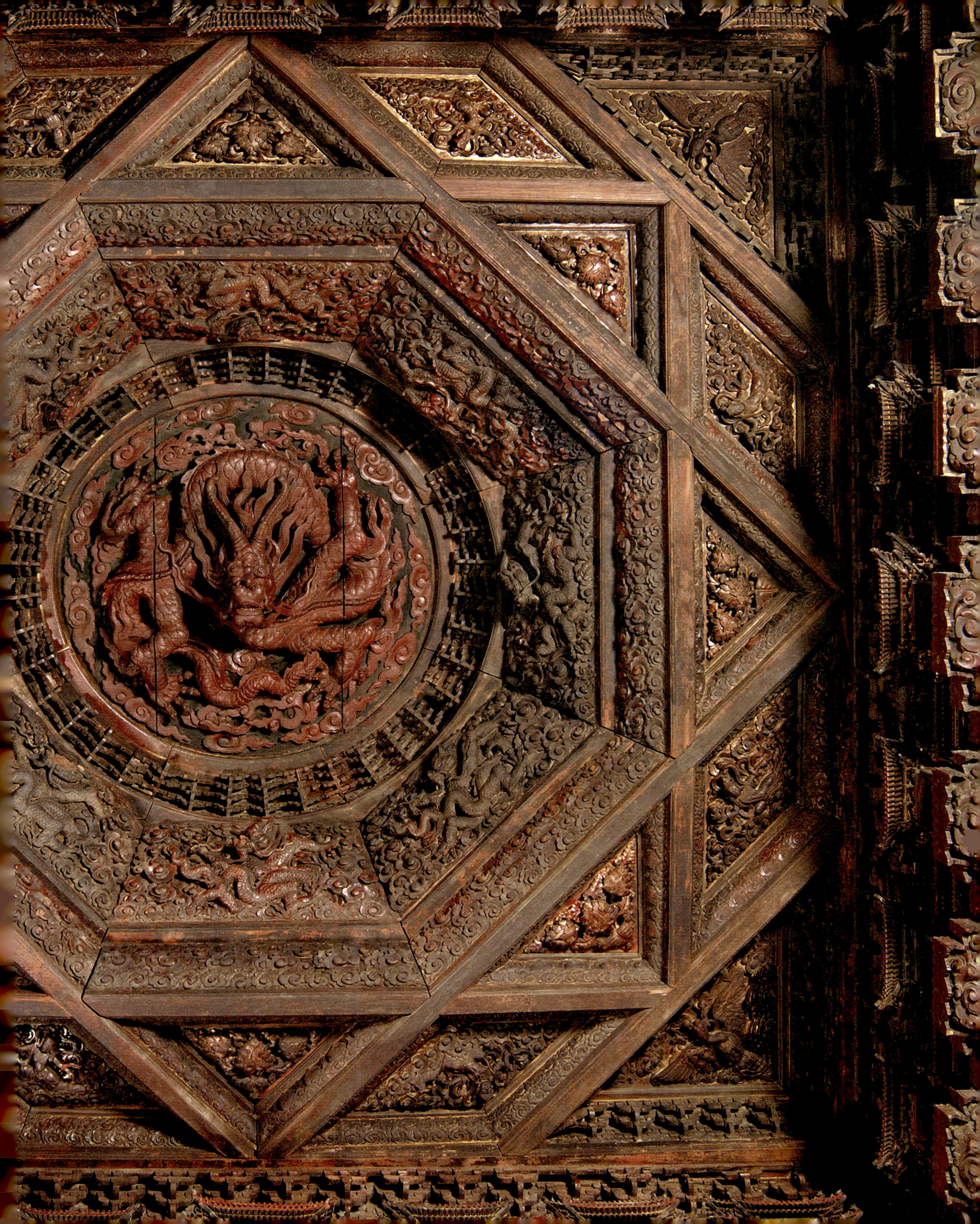

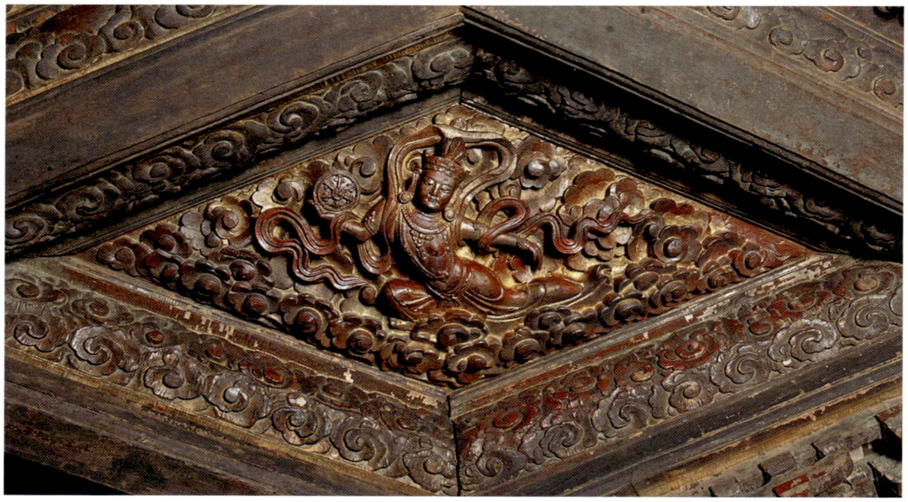
a

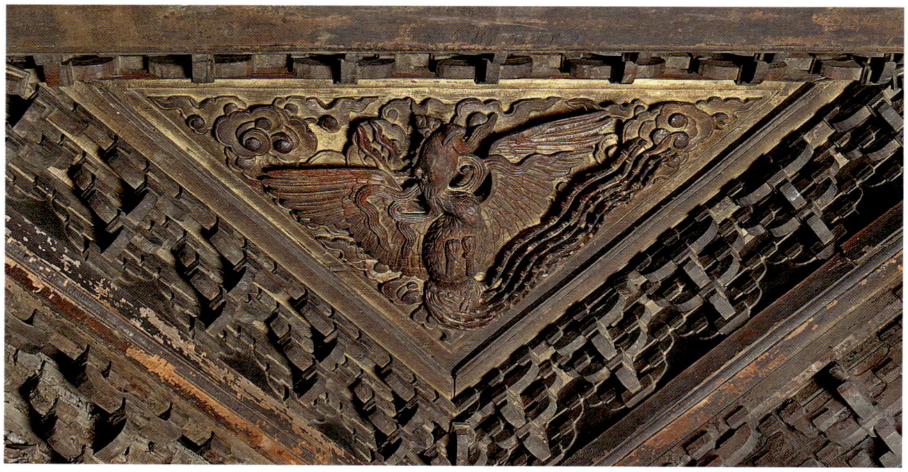
b

beasts, cast from metal, that are inserted on the roof ridges to protect and bring good fortune to the building (fig. 39).[5] Within the pavilions are crowned Buddhas seated on raised daises in the lotus position, their hands posed in various gestures, or *mudras*, and framed by elaborate openwork mandorlas (fig. 40). Their elaborate jewelry, five-pointed crowns, and the elegant draping of their robes are typical princely features found on Tibetan-influenced Chinese Buddhist statuary commissioned by the early Ming imperial court, possibly because of the close religious and political ties with Tibet at that time.[6] Creating a coffered ceiling with such intricate details, which would never have been perceived by human eyes other than those of the artisans who executed the design, illustrates the devotion of the craftsmen and the donor, who no doubt gained Buddhist merit from their work. The ceiling also demonstrates the inordinate power and wealth that certain eunuchs of the Ming dynasty possessed. HK

1. Wang Zhen served as chief consul to the Zhengtong emperor (r. 1436–49), becoming his close advisor after his accession at age eight. His mismanagement and malpractice are said to have caused the emperor to ride into battle against the Mongol enemy, causing the capture of the ruler, an offence for which Wang Zhen was killed. After the emperor was released, he erected a shrine at the temple to honor Wang Zhen for his loyalty. The temple received imperial patronage until the eighteenth century. For more on the history of the temple and the coffered ceiling, see Kinoshita 2018.
2. Steinhardt 2002, 8. A similar coffered ceiling can be found in the Yinghuadian, where empresses and consorts paid their respects to the Buddha. See Gugong bowuyuan gu jianzhu guanli bu 2007, 67, no. 66.
3. Sources cite differing numbers of statues in the hall at different times, from one Buddha and ten *luohan* (enlightened monks) (Liu 1932, 24) to three gilded and lacquered Buddhas (Amitabha, Shakyamuni, and Medicine Buddha) and eighteen *luohan* (Beijing wenbo jiaoliu guan 2005, 28).
4. Nine dragons are especially powerful, as in Chinese cosmology nine is the largest single-digit odd, or male (*yang*), number.
5. San Francisco, Indianapolis, and Saint Louis 2008–9, no. 91.
6. Haufler 2014, 247.

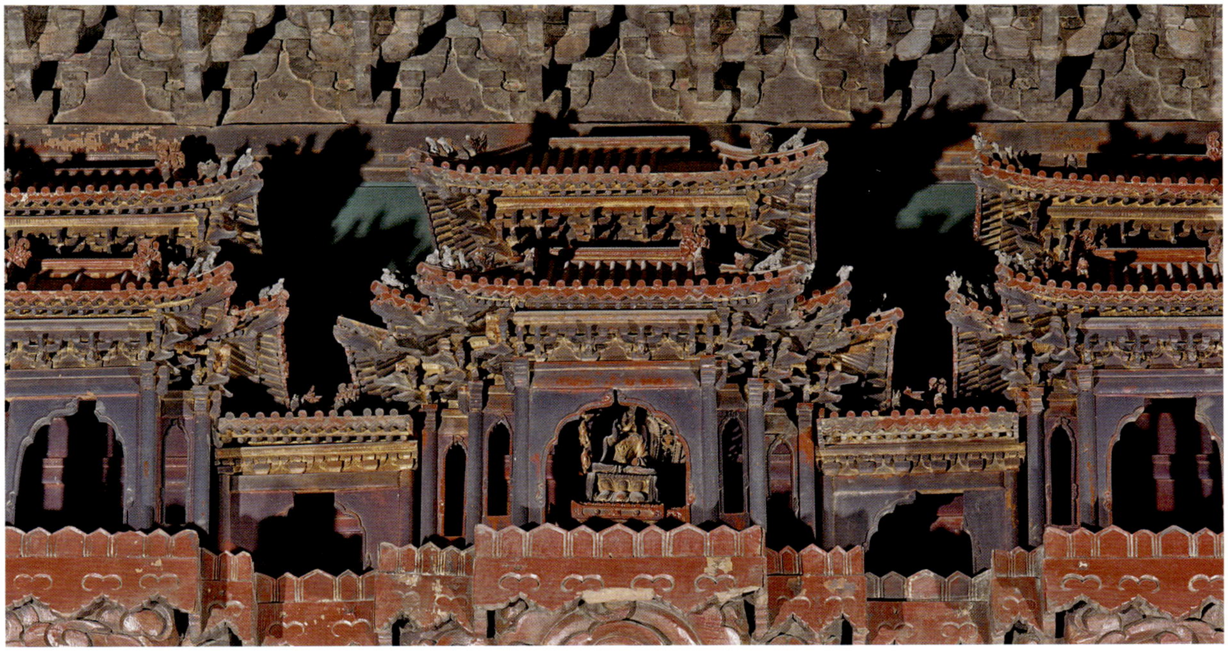

c

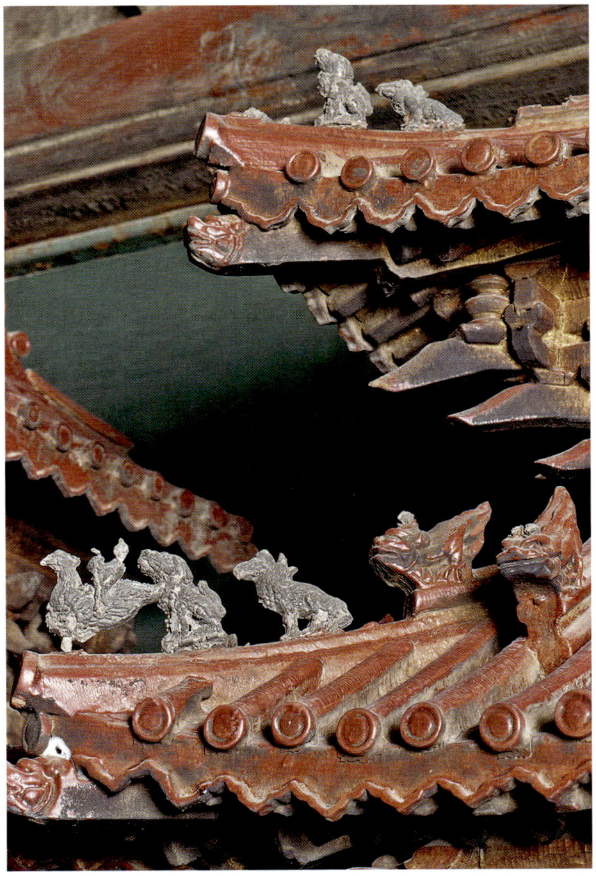

Fig. 39. Detail of miniature processional animals and mythological beasts (*zou shou*) cast from metal inserted into the wooden roof ridges

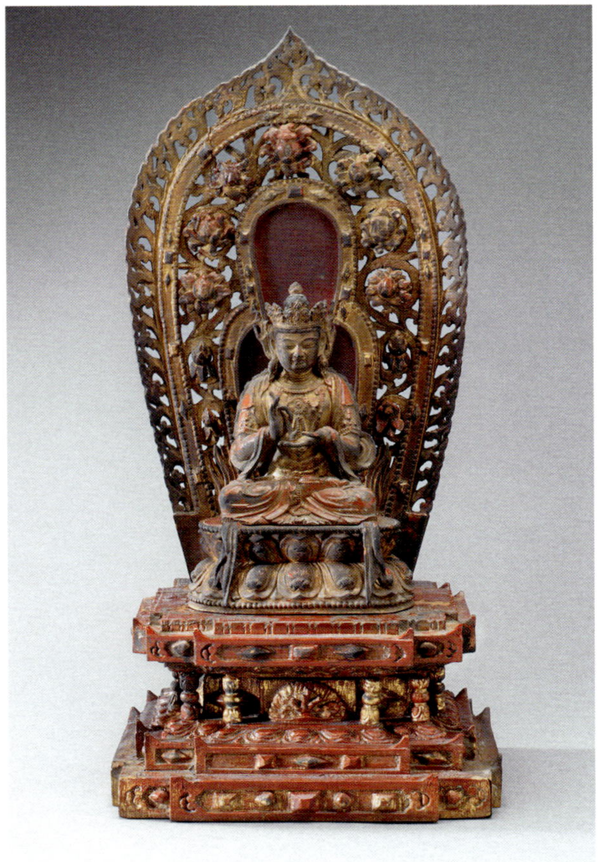

Fig. 40. Detail of one of the crowned Buddhas from the heavenly pavilions (*tiangong louge*) around the coffered ceiling

35

Mural Fragment of *Deva* from a Buddhist Assembly

Ming dynasty (1368–1644), probably 15th century
Clay substrate with glue-bound paint
9 feet 2 inches x 14 feet 7 inches (279.4 x 444.5 cm) (framed)
Purchased with the Special Oriental Fund, 1925-98-1

Various guardian deities or celestial protectors (*deva*) are depicted on this fragment from the outer part of a much larger mural that once decorated the hall of a Buddhist temple. On the far left is Weituo (Skanda in Sanskrit), the guardian of Buddhist temples and protector of the faith, who is recognizable by his winged helmet and the diamond sword resting on his arms (lower left), which was thought to destroy demons and other enemies of Buddhism. To his left is Yuetian (Candra), the youthful emperor or chief minister, wearing long robes. Two of four major guardians known as the Defenders of the Faith are at the center of the fragment: Virupaksa, the bearded Heavenly King of the West, brandishes a snake, while Vaisravana, the Heavenly King of the North, holds a parasol and a stupa (a structure holding Buddhist relics) or pagoda; next to him is the bodhisattva Mārīcī, a protective goddess, with three faces and multiple arms.[1]

Figures such as these—mostly Indian Hindu deities with a Chinese appearance—along with their costumes and rich jewelry, are typical of the iconography of northern Chinese temples built from the late Yuan (1271–1368) to the early Ming dynasty, when a mix of Chinese and Tibetan Buddhism was embraced by the ruling elite. Early Ming emperors showed great enthusiasm for Tibetan Buddhism and regularly met with Tibetan clerics. The Yongle emperor's (r. 1403–24) renewal of the priest-patron relationship with Tibetan patriarchs in particular sparked large-scale court patronage of art in the Tibetan manner, which continued through the mid-fifteenth century.

This mural fragment was purportedly found in a partially destroyed temple at Weihui near Xinxiang, in Henan province, where it was removed in eighty pieces and conserved at the Fogg Museum at Harvard University before being installed at the Philadelphia Museum of Art.[2] The mural was built up with mud and chopped straw and surfaced with a smoother coating of fine clay before the designs were outlined and then filled in with paint, a technique consistent with other wall paintings from Shanxi province, where numerous Buddhist temples flourished. The iconography is similar to mural paintings of *deva* from temples in the Western Hills of Beijing: the Dabei Temple, the Biyun Temple,[3] and the Fahai Temple,[4] the latter completed around 1443. HK

1. Stevens 1998–99: 63, 69, 73, 79.
2. Malenka and Price 1997, 127–31.
3. See Stevens 1998–99.
4. Yang 2001.

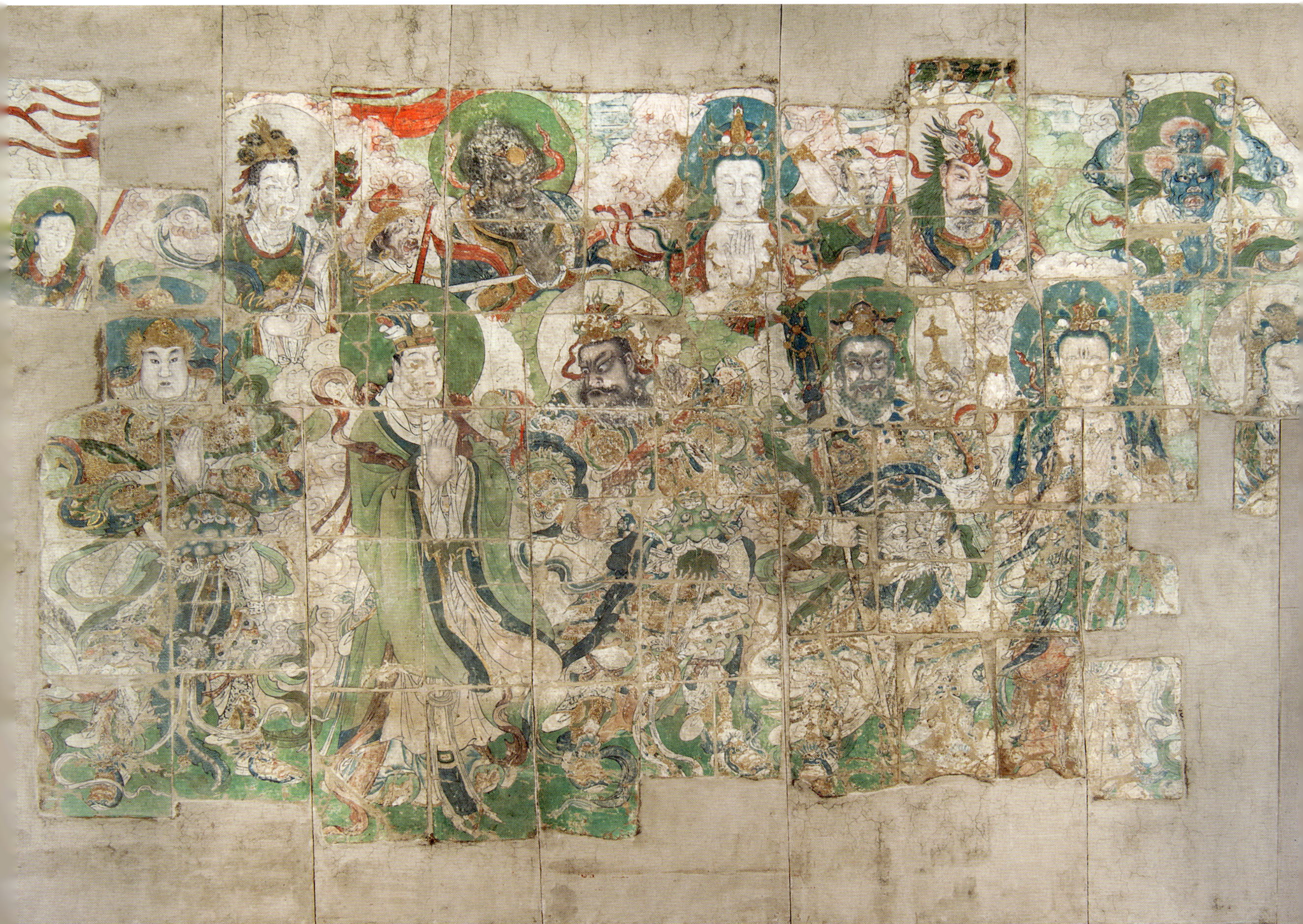

36

Roundel for an Empress

Ming dynasty (1368–1644), 15th century
Tapestry-woven silk and gold leaf on paper-wrapped thread (*kesi*)
Diam. 14⅛ inches (35.9 cm)
Purchased with the John T. Morris Fund from the Carl Schuster Collection, 1940-4-749

The phoenix (*fenghuang*) was one of four mythical beasts—together with the dragon, *qilin* (see no. 48), and tortoise—that were celebrated in China. The phoenix is among the most ancient symbols to evolve in East Asia. Its specific association with the Chinese empress, as seen in this roundel, appears with increasing frequency from the thirteenth century onward. Historically, there was a distinction between the male and the female phoenix, but the pairing of the phoenix with the dragon, symbol of the emperor, at this time resulted in the amalgamation of the word for each gender into the single name (see no. 34). Thereafter, dragon and phoenix conveyed the harmonious balance of male and female that was central to the Confucian ideals that related the position of the emperor of the nation with that of the father in the family.

Interestingly, on this roundel the ancient gender distinction of male phoenix (*feng*), with serrated tail feathers, usually five in number, and female (*huang*), with a pair of curly tail feathers, is present. The pair of birds displayed against a cloud background with rock and waves below and the auspicious coupling with a trio of large peony blossoms reflect early fifteenth-century design conventions for rank badges (*buzi*), as does the use of gold-wrapped thread for the background.[1]

The tapestry-weaving technique requires great skill to manipulate the colored wefts in the plain weave but uses extremely simple equipment. Each color area of the design requires a separate bobbin and must be built up precisely to overlap with other areas so that there are no disruptions in the overall image. The presence of a band of cloud heads butted up against a colored "jeweled" outer border, as well as evidence of infill cotton weft along the edges of the silk and metallic roundel, suggest that this example may not have been intended for a court garment, but possibly was made for use as the top face of a mirror case. JV

1. Vollmer and Simcox 2009, 80–81.

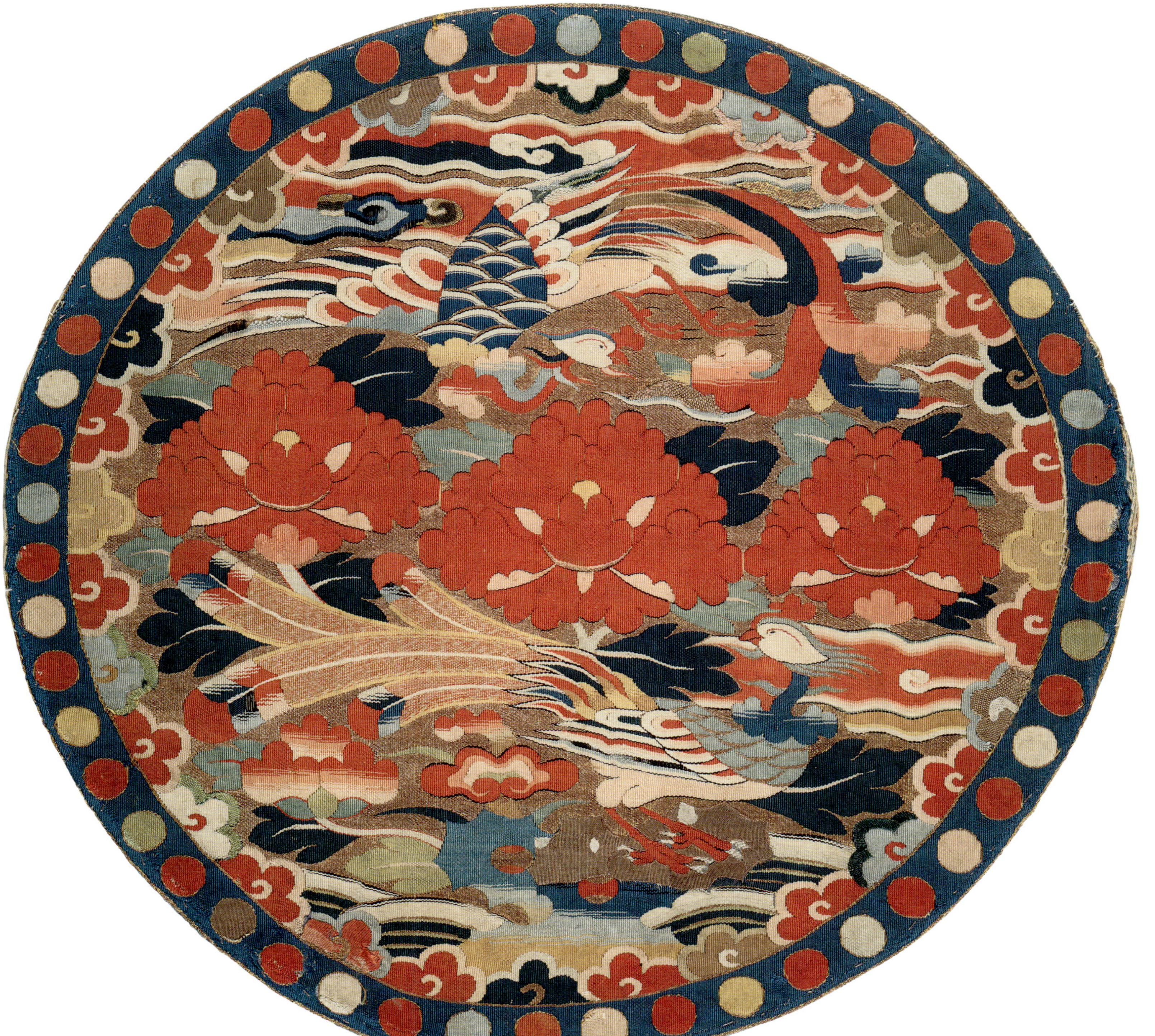

37

Dish with Gardenias

Ming dynasty (1368–1644), Hongzhi period (1488–1505)
Porcelain with underglaze blue and yellow enamel decoration (Jingdezhen ware)
1⅝ x 10¼ inches (4.2 x 26 cm)
Gift of Major General and Mrs. William Crozier, 1944-20-347

Painted in a soft underglaze blue of varying tones, this dish has a central design of a leafy branch of gardenia shown with two fully opened blooms and two buds. Encircling the interior wall around the central motif are branches of pomegranate, persimmon, grape, and a spray of lotus tied with a ribbon. The exterior is decorated with a continuous floral scroll of large blooms. Two firings were required to produce this decoration. The design and mark were first painted in cobalt blue that was covered in a colorless glaze, and the dish was fired. Yellow enamel was then applied to the white spaces around the blue-painted areas, and the piece was fired again, this time at a lower temperature.[1]

This attractive design with the pleasing use of contrasting colors first appeared in the early fifteenth century during the reign of the Ming-dynasty emperor Xuande (r. 1426–35). It was copied and continued to be made by subsequent Ming emperors for the next hundred years,[2] with the blue-and-yellow palette later revived in the Qing dynasty (1644–1911). The yellow enamel varies in hue and tone depending on the period when it was produced; the yellow of the Hongzhi reign is considered to be one of the best, noted for its delicate, soft, lustrous quality. Variations in the design, depicting other types of floral sprays, were made in blue and white as well,[3] and also in the rarer underglaze-brown palette,[4] of which there is an example (also Hongzhi in date) in the museum's collection (fig. 41). HK

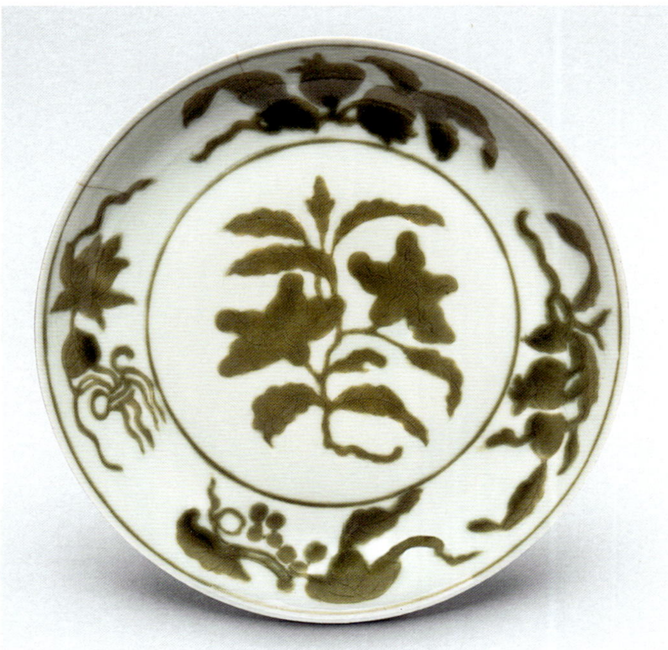

Fig. 41. Dish with Gardenias. Ming dynasty, Hongzhi period. Porcelain with underglaze brown decoration, 1¾ x 10¼ inches (4.4 x 26 cm). Philadelphia Museum of Art. Gift of Major General and Mrs. William Crozier, 1944-20-346

1. The second firing was at a lower temperature than the first in order to ensure that the enamel fused to the colorless glaze.
2. Examples made during the Xuande (1426–35), Chenghua (1465–87), and Zhengde (1506–21) reigns are in the British Museum (OA 1945. 10-16.3 and 2; 1929.7-22.11). Other examples with a Hongzhi mark are in the Metropolitan Museum of Art, New York (acc. no. 19.28.10), the Victoria and Albert Museum, London (C.320-1921), and the Palace Museum, Beijing (see Geng 2000, no. 231).
3. A Xuande blue-and-white dish with pomegranate spray is illustrated in Taipei 1998, no. 15. The base of the Xuande dish is unglazed, so the mark is written across the exterior rim.
4. The brown is from iron oxide and appears lighter, like a pale, milky coffee color (café au lait), on earlier Xuande examples. Another Hongzhi example is illustrated in Geng 1993, col. pl. 49.

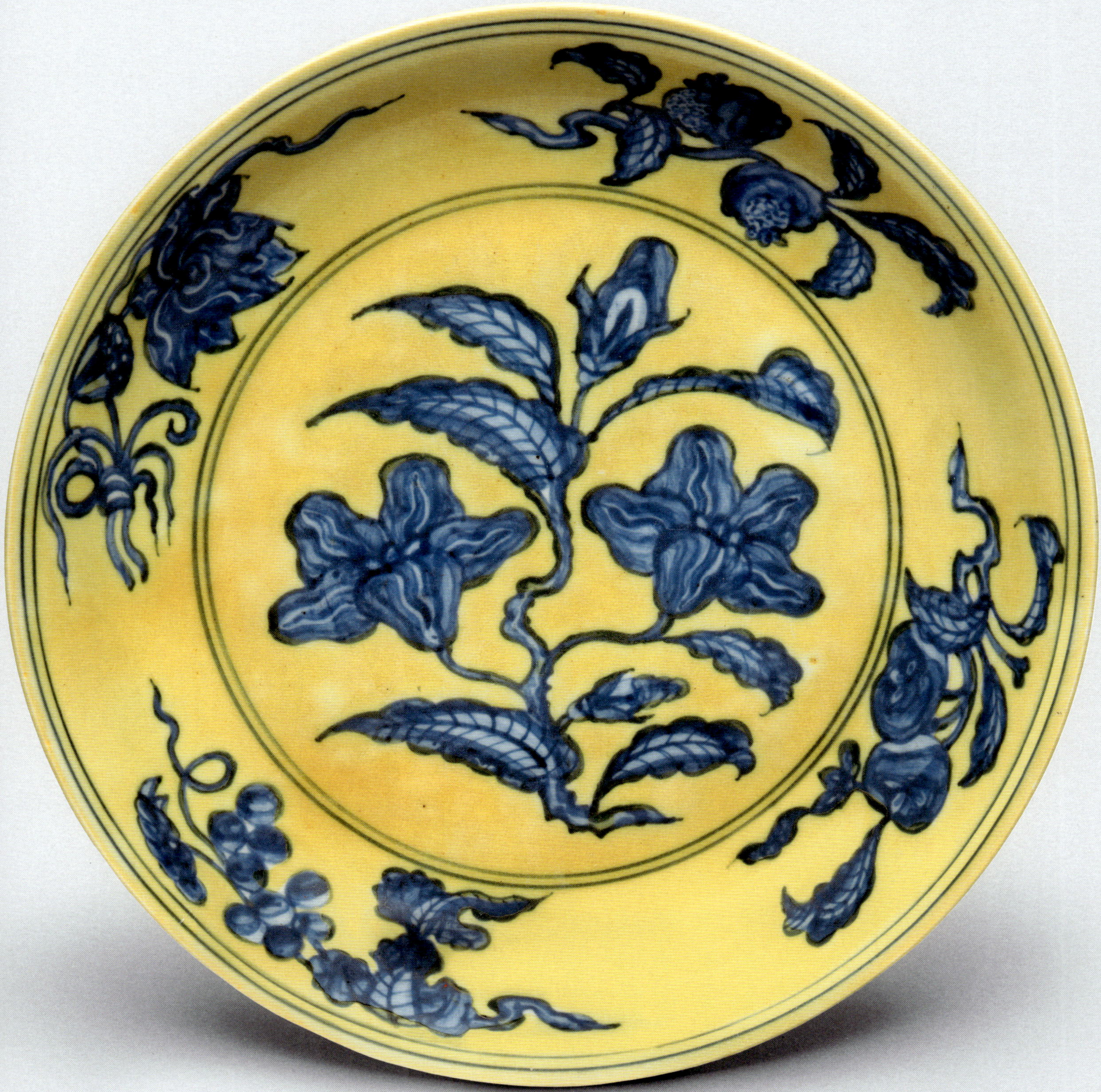

38

Insignia Badge for an Imperial Censor

Ming dynasty (1368–1644), possibly Hongzhi period (1488–1505)
Tapestry-woven silk (*kesi*)
14 x 14¼ inches (35.6 x 36.2 cm)
Purchased with the John T. Morris Fund from the Carl Schuster Collection, 1940-4-745

Rank badges such as this one, worn on the front and back of robes, signified members of the nobility and civil and military bureaucrats, and also designated a number of ancillary departments, or agencies, of the imperial government. The mythical beast seen here, called *xiezhi*, identified members of the imperial censorate (*duchayuan*). This supervisory agency had been part of the central government since the founding of the empire. Censors were directly responsible to the emperor, inspecting all levels of the administration to prevent corruption and wrongdoing.[1] The ancient one-horned beast *xiezhi* symbolized justice and was thought to distinguish the innocent from the guilty instinctively, butting the latter with its horn.

Court rank remained the key determinant of social status, economic stability, and prestige in imperial China.[2] The privileges of rank had first accrued to the aristocratic families of military origin that supported the court until the tenth century. Yet almost from the outset the imperial court relied on a professional civil service educated in the Confucian classics to enforce order. By the Ming dynasty, the privileges once reserved for the older order had shifted to the ranks of civil and military bureaucracies. JV

1. Hucker 1958, 49.
2. Meskill 1963, 17–28.

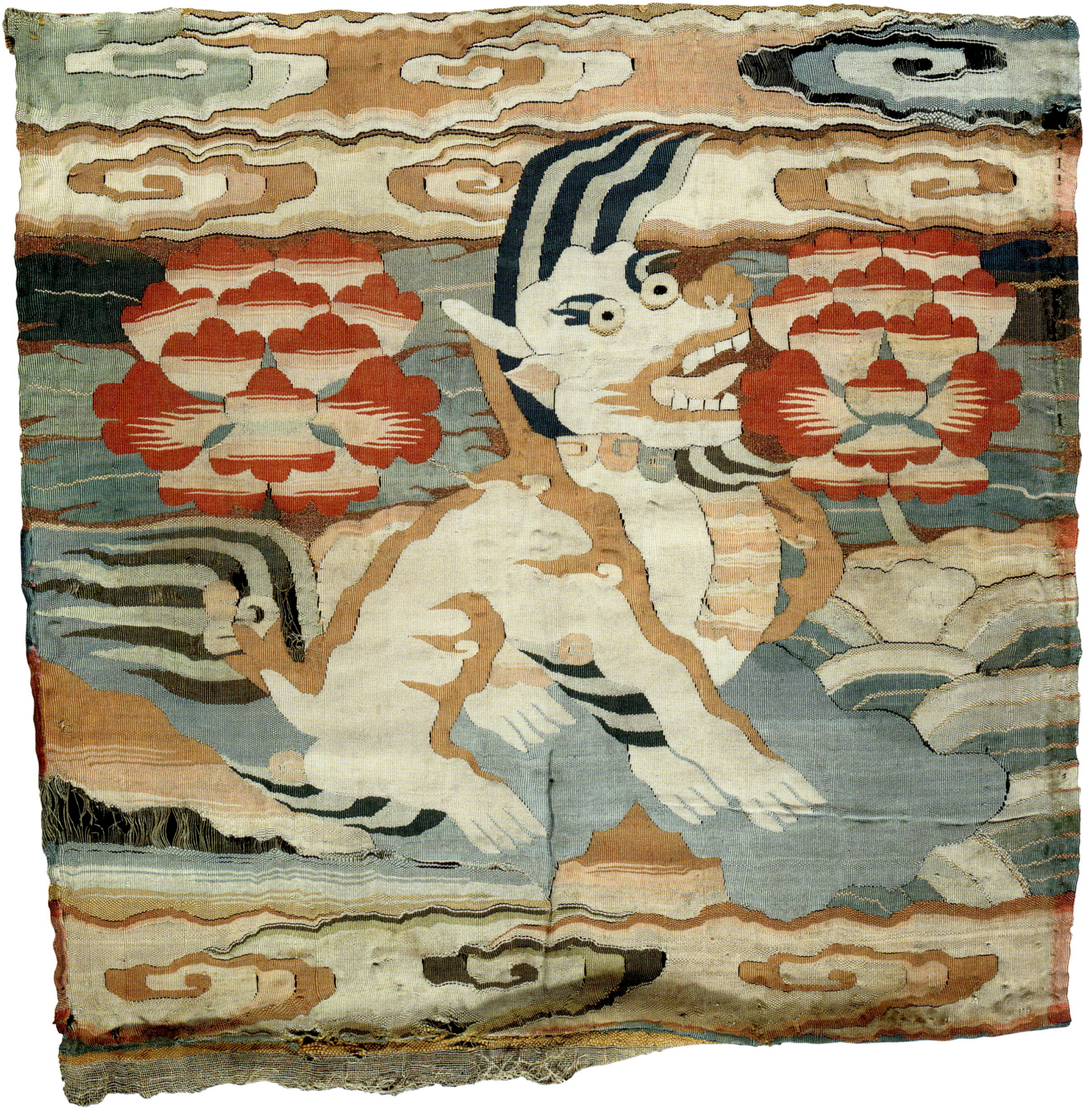

39

Hexagonal Candleholder with Persian Script

Ming dynasty (1368–1644), Zhengde period (1506–21)
Porcelain with underglaze blue decoration (Jingdezhen ware)
5 15/16 x 5 3/8 inches (15.1 x 13.7 cm)
Gift of Mr. and Mrs. John Story Jenks, 1944-38-1

Decorated in cobalt blue under a clear glaze, this candleholder integrates Islamic and Chinese stylistic elements. The hexagonal form appears to have been inspired by Persian metalwork,[1] while the lotus lappets that encircle the shoulder and base (see no. 27), along with the *ruyi*-cloud motifs of the feet (see nos. 32, 45), are typical Chinese motifs. Candles were used in rooms throughout the imperial palace, for lighting and likely also as a way to perfume the air, together with incense. Many incense burners with Tibetan, Islamic, Daoist, and Mongolian inscriptions were made during the Zhengde emperor's reign, in both porcelain and metal,[2] but candleholders appear to be rarer.[3] Most distinctive is the Sufi verse written in Persian script in the quatrefoil cartouches on the six sides of this example : "I am willing to follow him [God/Allah]; entering into an intoxicated state of cultivation, there is still [hope] to suddenly [with grace] obtain the Treasure."[4]

Historical documents demonstrate the Zhengde emperor's interest in and reverence for the Muslim faith, in particular Persian Sufism.[5] This is also evident in the number of Persian inscriptions found on porcelains produced during his reign, ranging from incense burners to brush rests, and including a group of red-enameled porcelain dishes inscribed "Made by King Suliman of the Zhengde reign of the Great Ming dynasty."[6]

Enthroned at the age of fifteen, the Zhengde emperor was not one of the more politically successful rulers; he was better known for his interest in material luxury, beautiful women, and opulent displays. Chinese sources seem to suggest that his interest in Islam may have been closely related to his pursuit of exoticism and eroticism.[7] HK

1. See, for example, a Saljuq silver-inlaid brass candlestick dating to the thirteenth century in the Freer Gallery of Art, Washington, DC (F1954.128).
2. A copper or bronze incense burner with Arabic script is illustrated in San Francisco, Indianapolis, and Saint Louis 2008–9, 178–79, no. 110.
3. Two other similar blue-and-white candleholders with Persian inscriptions are known, one in the Musée Guimet, Paris, and the other in the Tianjin Museum. One of circular section, in a private collection, is illustrated in Garner 1970, pl. 45B.
4. Author's translation after Weng 2012, 18. Weng transcribes the verse from a very similar candleholder in the Musée Guimet, Paris, which has the same inscription as this candleholder. This is a slightly different interpretation of the inscription than that published by Sir Harry Garner on this piece: "I was loitering in a deserted place when suddenly I found a treasure"; Garner 1970, 29. Weng notes (p. 24) that of the three sects of Islam—Sunni, Shīah, and Sufi—the Sufi is characterized by mysticism and asceticism.
5. Toh 2000, 3. The emperor's conversion to Islam has been disputed.
6. Weng 2012, 25.
7. Toh 2000, 13.

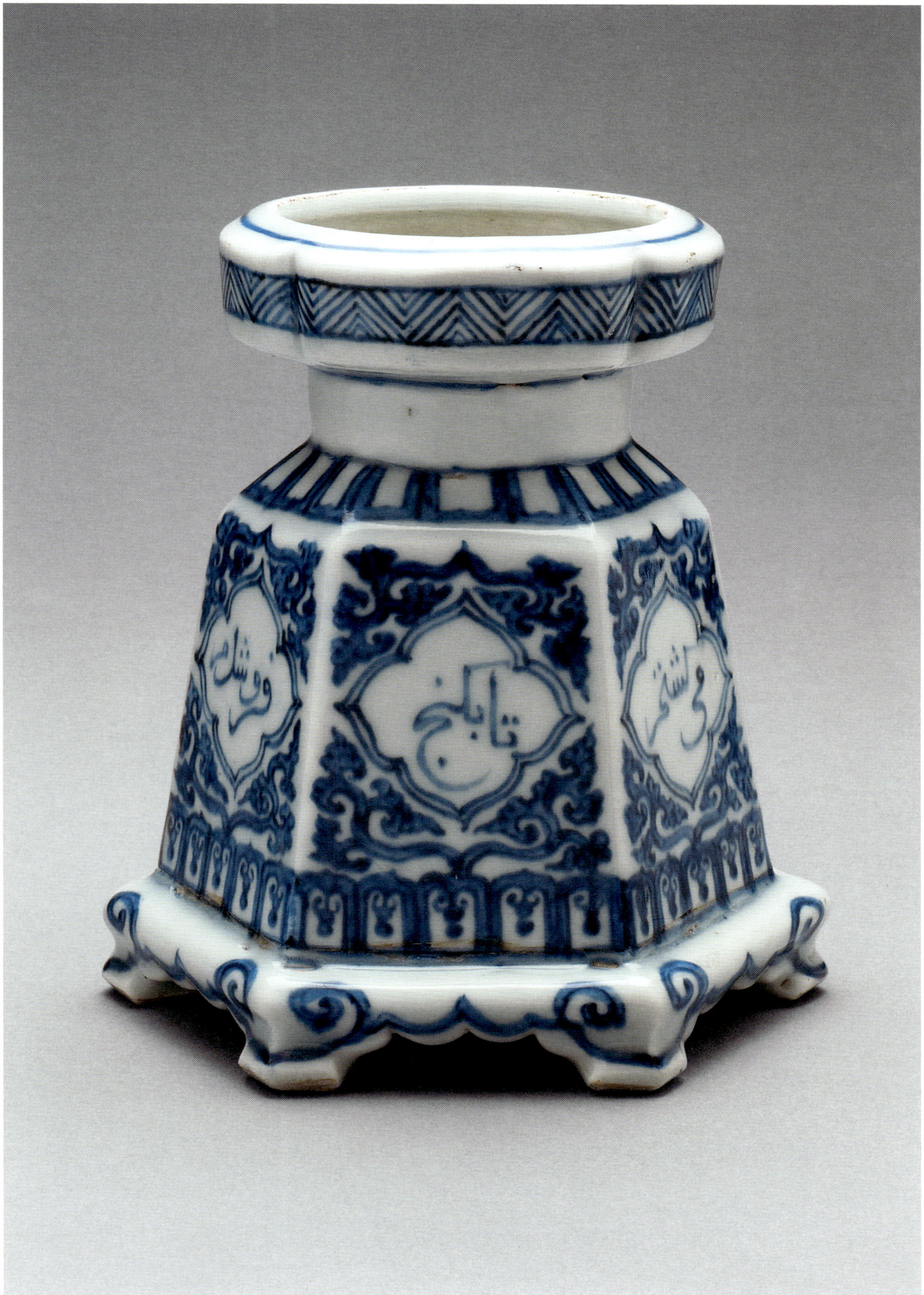

40

Imperial Yellow Dish

Ming dynasty (1368–1644), Zhengde period (1506–21)
Porcelain with yellow glaze (Jingdezhen ware)
1 9/16 x 7 7/8 inches (4 x 20 cm)
Gift of J. Mitchell Elliot in memory of his wife, Annie Yerkes Elliot, 1946-49-1

Plain monochrome yellow glazes were applied to utilitarian porcelains, such as dishes and bowls of various sizes, produced by the imperial kilns in the Ming and Qing (1644–1911) dynasties.[1] This dish, with a slight dip in its sunken center, is covered in a rich, warm yellow glaze that would be described by the Chinese as "chicken fat" (*jiyou huang*) yellow. The name by which it is known in the West, "imperial yellow," indicates its importance at the Chinese court: yellow was the color of wares used exclusively by members of the imperial family for daily use, display, and rituals. Imperial monochrome yellow porcelains may also have been given away as gifts by the court, as sixteen yellow monochrome dishes and bowls with Ming imperial marks were collected by Shāh ʻAbbās, the Safavid ruler of Persia (present-day Iran), before 1611.[2]

The yellow color was produced by adding to the glaze just a small amount of iron, sourced from iron oxide in clays found in plentiful supply all over China.[3] During the Ming dynasty potters experimented with different types of glazes fired at lower and higher temperatures to create a range of yellow hues. The luminosity of the yellow on this dish was produced by first firing the white porcelain, which was covered with a clear glaze, at a high temperature, after which a yellow "enamel" glaze was applied to the surfaces. The dish was then fired at a lower temperature to fuse the glazes. The porcelain glaze underneath gives luminosity and brilliance to the yellow enamel. HK

1. A slightly smaller Zhengde yellow dish, 17.8 cm wide, is in the Qing court collection (Yang 1999, no. 41), while the British Museum in London has three Zhengde dishes, 12.8 cm (acc. no. PDF.557), 15.4 cm (1943,0215.17), and 21 cm (PDF.597) wide.
2. Pope 1956, 151. The yellow-glazed dishes and bowls with Hongzhi, Zhengde, Jiajing, and Wanli marks were collected by Shāh ʻAbbās and donated in 1611 to the Ardebil shrine in what is today northwest Iran in memory of the founder of his lineage.
3. Oxford 1988, 9–10.

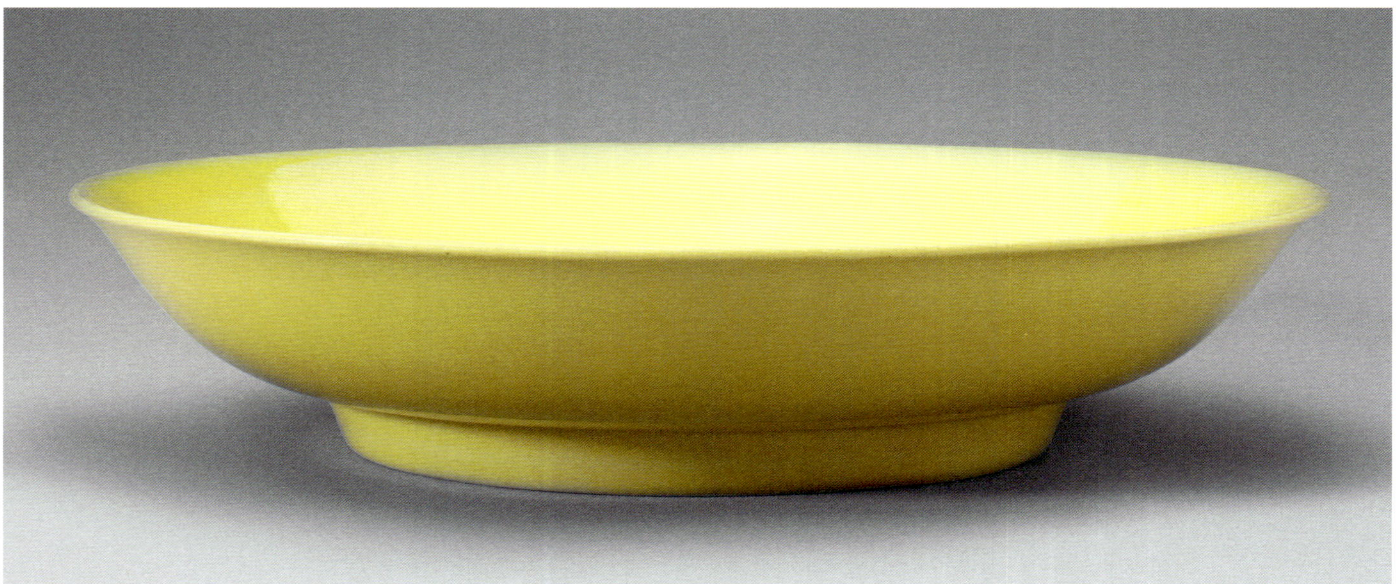

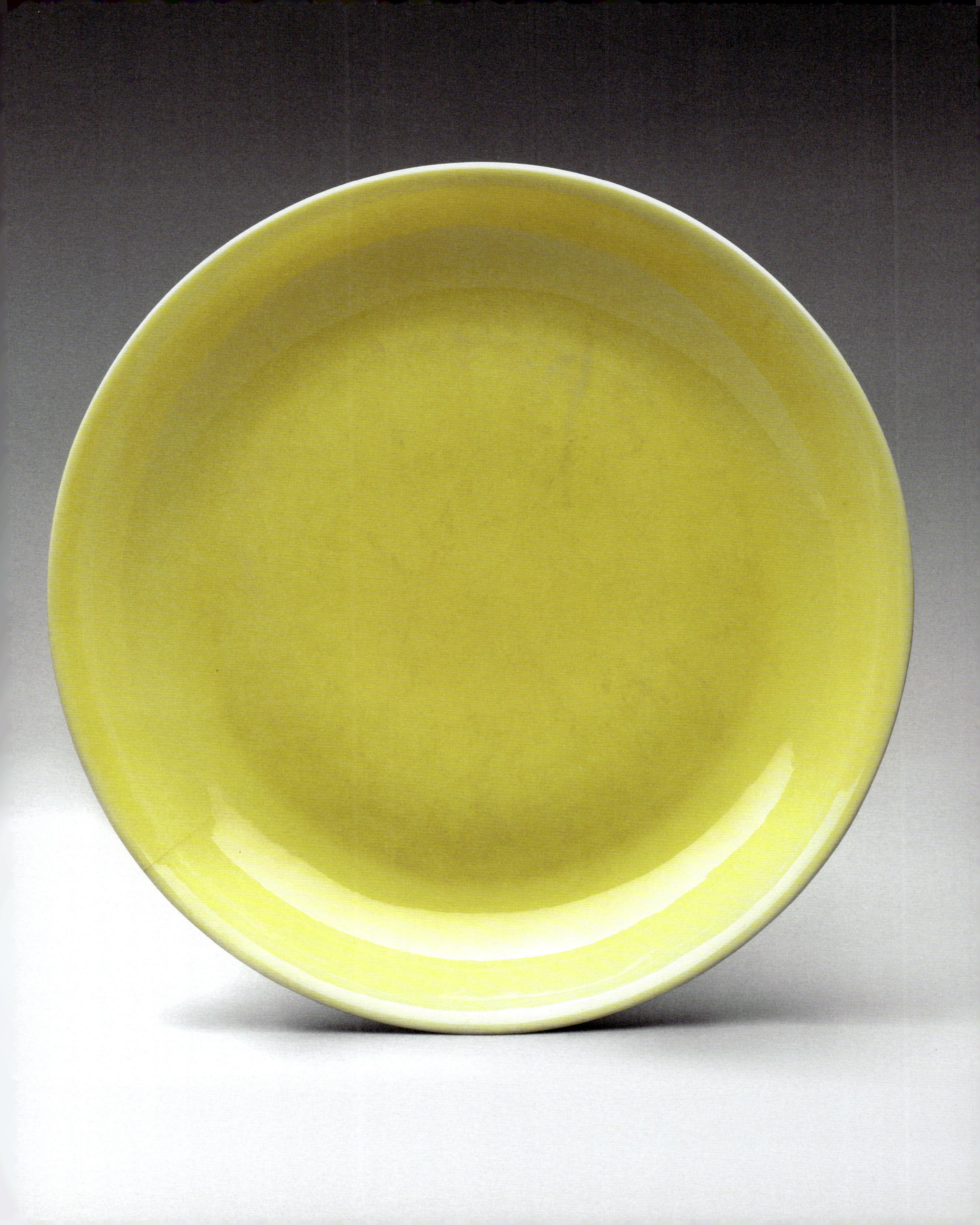

41

Qiao Bin (act. 1481–after 1500)
Guanyin, Bodhisattva of Compassion

Ming dynasty (1368–1644), 1507
Stoneware with polychrome glaze
$36\frac{7}{8} \times 19\frac{13}{16} \times 9\frac{3}{4}$ inches (93.6 x 50.3 x 24.7 cm)
Gift of Charles H. Ludington from the George Crofts Collection, 1923-21-441

Guanyin, the Bodhisattva of Compassion, is one of the most popular Buddhist deities in China. Here Guanyin is shown in feminine form and identified by the seated Buddha in her crown. Modeled in clay glazed in a predominantly three-color palette of green, amber, and cream, she is seated in royal ease on a rocky outcropping. Her left foot rests on an open lotus blossom between a twisting dragon grasping a jewel in one claw and a hybrid creature, the feline *hou*, whose presence may identify the figure as Guanyin of the South Sea.[1]

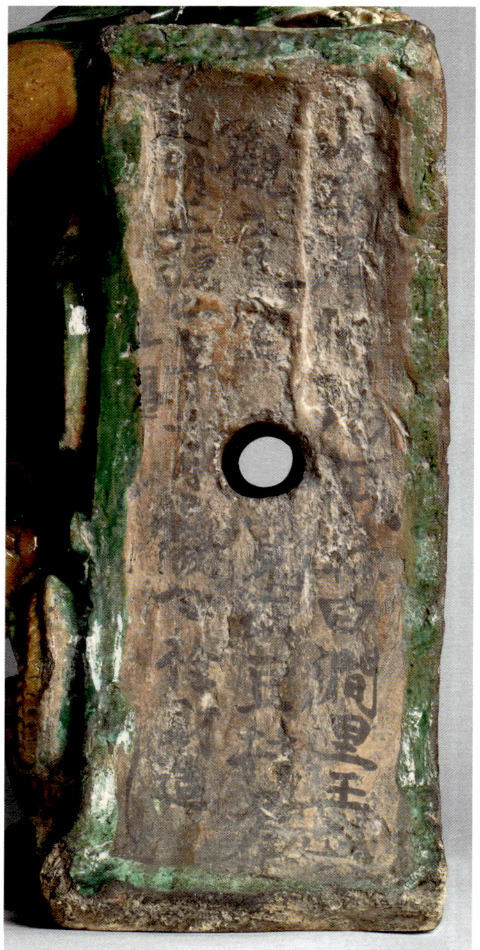

Fig. 42. Inscription inked on the side of the base (see p. 246)

The figure's most remarkable aspect are the inscriptions inked by the donor on the two short, unglazed sides of the rocky base, which provide valuable information about the work's creation (fig. 42; p. 246). To the figure's proper left, above the firing hole, is written "Guanyin Hall, Tongji Temple," while the right side records that Wang Xing of Yangcheng, in Shanxi province, donated the sculpture in 1507, and that it was made by Qiao Bin.[2]

Wang Xing, most likely a wealthy donor who benefited from the robust economic growth of the middle Ming period, commissioned Qiao Bin to make this sculpture as a way to accrue merit in Buddhism.[3] The Qiao family workshop in Yangcheng in Shanxi province was the most famous maker of glazed architectural ceramics from at least as early as the late fifteenth century, reaching peak production in the late sixteenth century.[4] HK

1. The hybrid *hou*, a cross between a tiger and lion, became associated with the animal mount of Guanyin of the South Sea, a feminized form of Guanyin that arose with the establishment of a new pilgrimage center of Guanyin on Putuo Island off the coast of Zhejiang in southern China from the sixteenth century; Yü 2001, 25, 438–48. The dragon, associated with control over water, may also suggest that this is the South Sea Guanyin. A related glazed stoneware figure of Guanyin with a *hou*, dated 1500 and made by the same family workshop in Shanxi, is in the Princeton Art Museum, New Jersey; illustrated in Hsu 2012–13, 36.
2. The full inscription names Wang Xing of Baijian community, Yangcheng, Zezhou, in Shanxi as currently residing in Doucun village in the twenty-second year of Zhengde of the Great Ming. For the Chinese, see Lü et al. 2017, 358.
3. Buddhist sutras state that donating images of the Buddha and bodhisattvas to temples is a way to accrue merit; Hsu 2012–13, 41.
4. The earlier palette tended to be more basic, as on the Philadelphia and Princeton examples, while later Qiao-family works incorporated more colors, including light green, peacock blue, and aubergine as a result of improved technology and changes in aesthetics. See Hsu 2012–13, 40–41, for more about the Qiao family workshop. A Qiao-family inscribed sculpture of Guanyin dated 1573 is in the British Museum, London (1988,0728.1), and a Buddhist group depicting the Western Paradise, dated 1615, is in the Asian Art Museum of San Francisco (B60P142+).

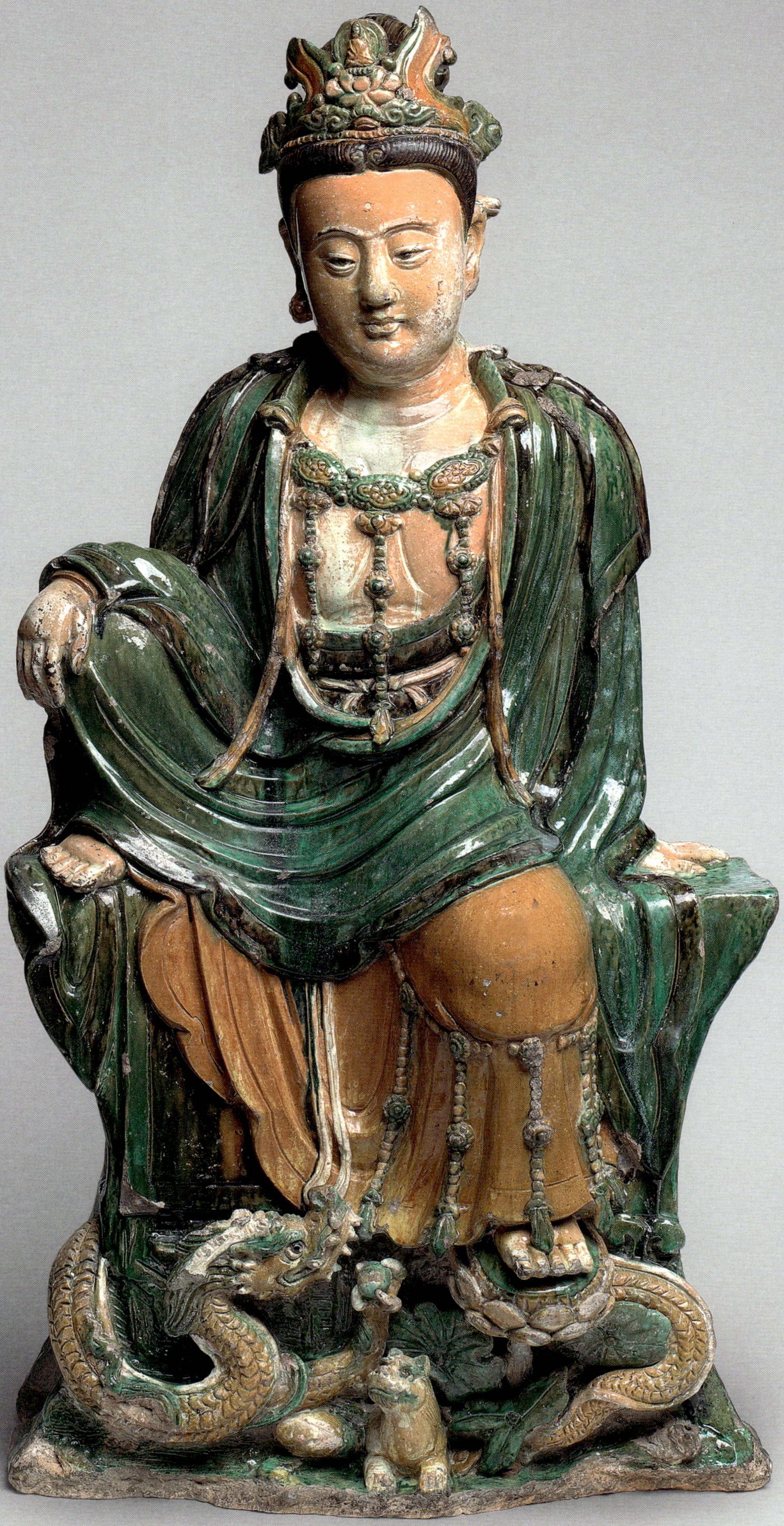

42

Gourd-shaped Vase with Dragons, Phoenixes, and Cranes

Ming dynasty (1368–1644), Jiajing period (1522–66)
Porcelain with underglaze blue decoration (Jingdezhen ware)
18⅝ x 10½ inches (47.3 x 26.7 cm)
The Bloomfield Moore Collection, 1882-727

This large, distinctively shaped vase in the form of a gourd is just one of many types of porcelains made for use by the Jiajing emperor, a devout Daoist dedicated to the pursuit of immortality. In 1542 he retreated to West Park,[1] outside the Forbidden City but within the Imperial City in Beijing, beautifully landscaping it with mountains, lakes, and pavilions to mirror the land of the immortals. He had palaces constructed within the park for carrying out Daoist activities and rituals, and he commissioned great numbers of porcelains by imperial command in order to furnish these buildings for the performance of Daoist rituals and feasting and for display.[2]

Covering the surface of this vase are imperial and auspicious motifs: five-clawed dragons, cranes, and phoenixes (both *feng* and *huang*, or male and female, identified by their distinctive tail feathers) within round medallions separated by floral sprays supporting longevity fungus (*lingzhi*) and the Eight Treasures (a silver ingot and an ancient coin separate the top two medallions). Other examples of this form are also decorated with longevity symbols, such as the Eight Daoist Immortals, deer, pine trees, bamboo, and cranes, as well as auspicious characters.[3]

The word for gourd, *hulu*, sounds like *fulu*, meaning wealth and prosperity—hence its popularity as a motif. Within a Daoist context, the double gourd was regarded as a microcosm of the universe, its form symbolizing the unity between heaven and earth. Gourd-shaped vessels, with their reference to the caves where immortals dwell, were therefore eminently appropriate for storing Daoist elixirs of longevity. HK

1. For more about the Jiajing emperor's West Park, see Wan 2009.
2. Wan 2012, 53–55.
3. An example with similar motifs is in the Ashmolean Museum, Oxford (EA1978.938), while other gourd vases with different decoration can be found in the British Museum, London (Harrison-Hall 2001, 230–31); the Baur Collection, Geneva (Ayers 1999, 129, pl. 75); and the Topkapi Saray Museum, Istanbul (Krahl 1986, vol. 2, pls. 656, 870, 871, 925, 1040).

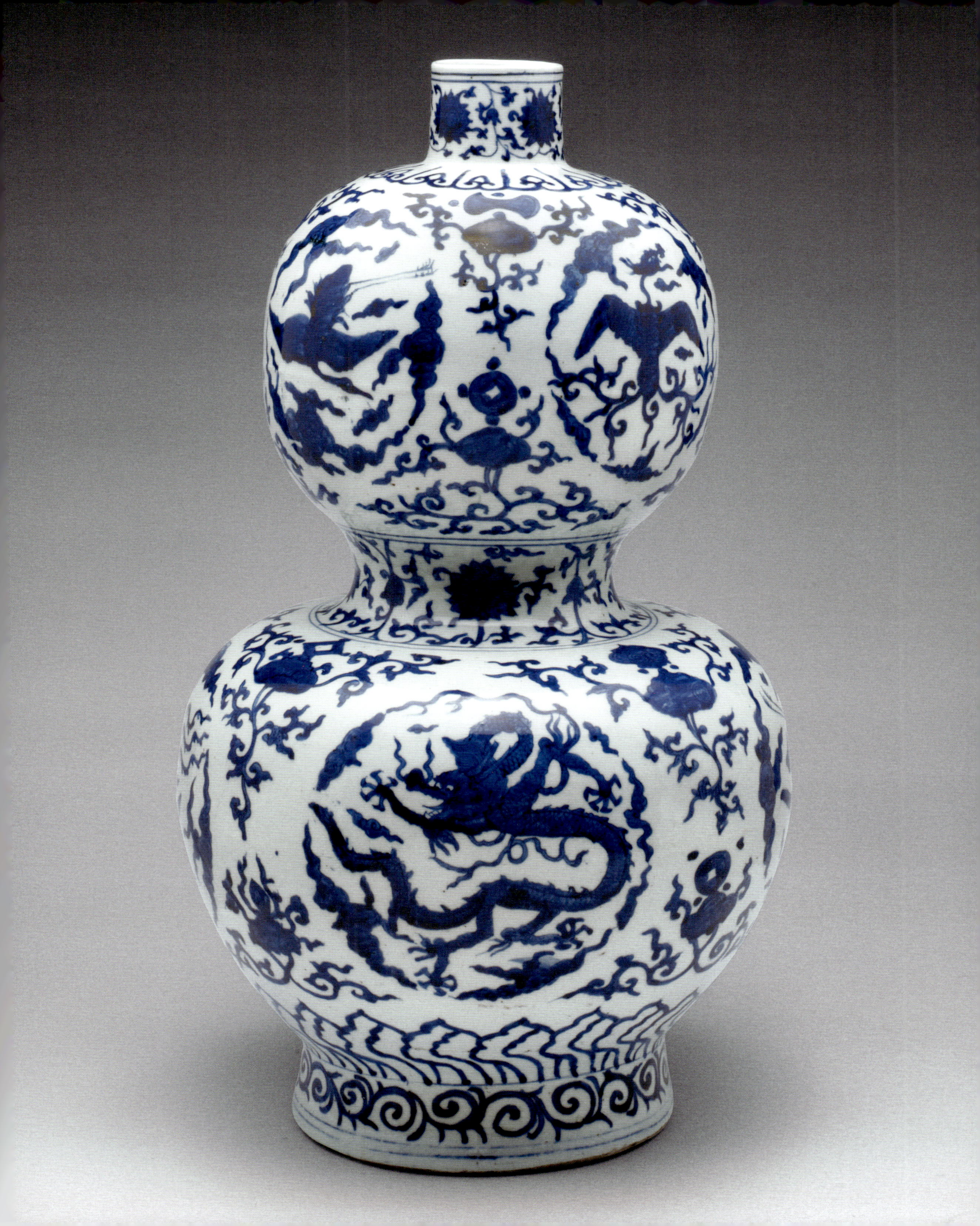

43

Square Dish with Peonies and Chrysanthemum

Ming dynasty (1368–1644), Jiajing period (1522–66)
Porcelain with underglaze blue and yellow and red enamel decoration (Jingdezhen ware)
1 9/16 x 7 3/8 x 7 3/8 inches (4 x 18.8 x 18.8 cm)
The Bloomfield Moore Collection, 1882-1313

This heavy, square dish is decorated in yellow and red enamel on both the interior and exterior with blossoming peonies and chrysanthemums growing to either side of a craggy pierced rock, from which two *lingzhi* plants emerge. The base of the dish, free of any enameling, has a six-character Jiajing mark painted in deep blue (see p. 246).

Rocks together with *lingzhi* fungus comprise a well-known mid-sixteenth-century motif that was often depicted with the *shou*, or longevity, character (see nos. 44, 45). The combination conveys the wish for immortality, a preoccupation of the Jiajing emperor, who ordered large quantities of porcelains for use and display at West Park, the "immortal" realm he built within the imperial city (see no. 42).[1] The peony and chrysanthemum are flowers often associated with the four seasons, representing spring and fall, respectively. The existence of square dishes integrating *lingzhi* and rocks with the Three Friends of Winter (bamboo, plum, and pine tree)[2] prompts the question whether the function of these dishes might be related to the seasons.

Unusual forms and color combinations are characteristic of porcelains made during the reign of the Jiajing emperor. The square dish with flaring sides was an innovation of the era, as was the distinctive yellow and reddish-brown color combination.[3] Several firings were required to create the glaze: first the blue mark on the

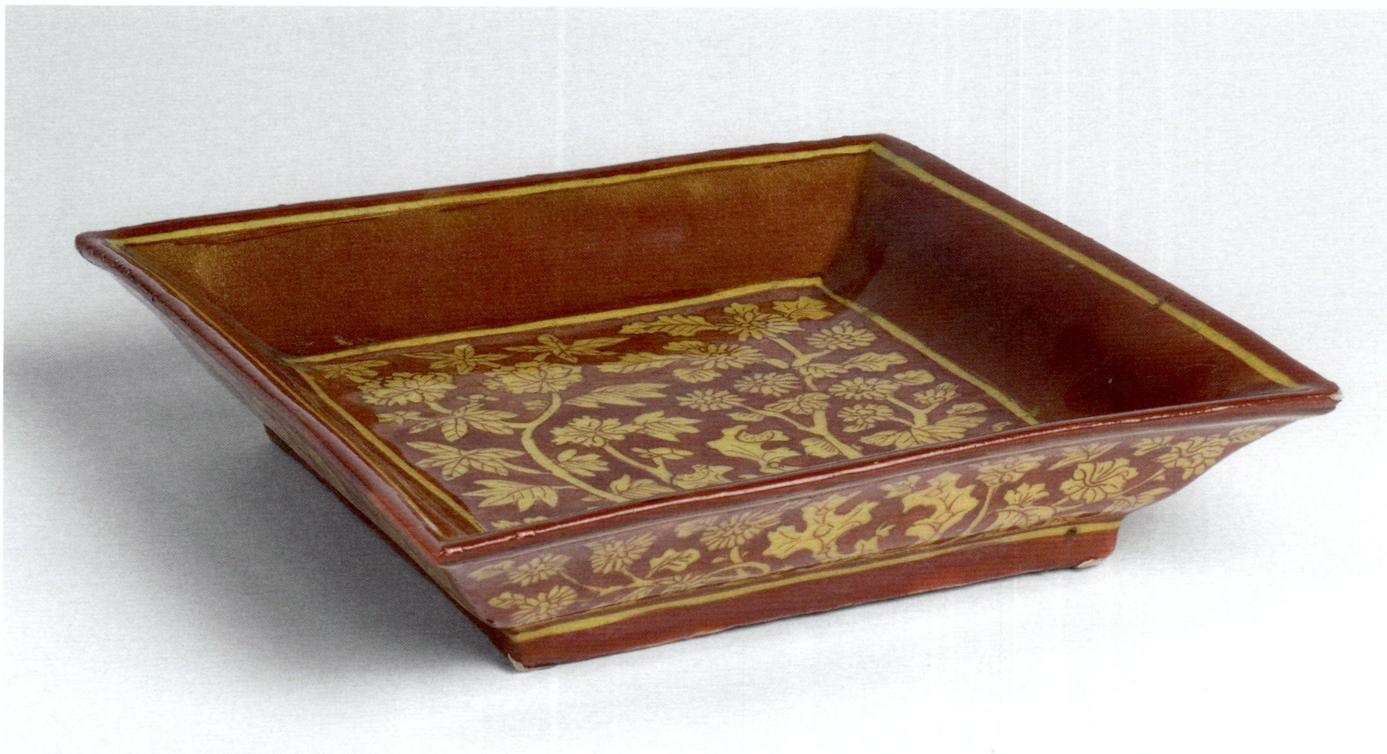

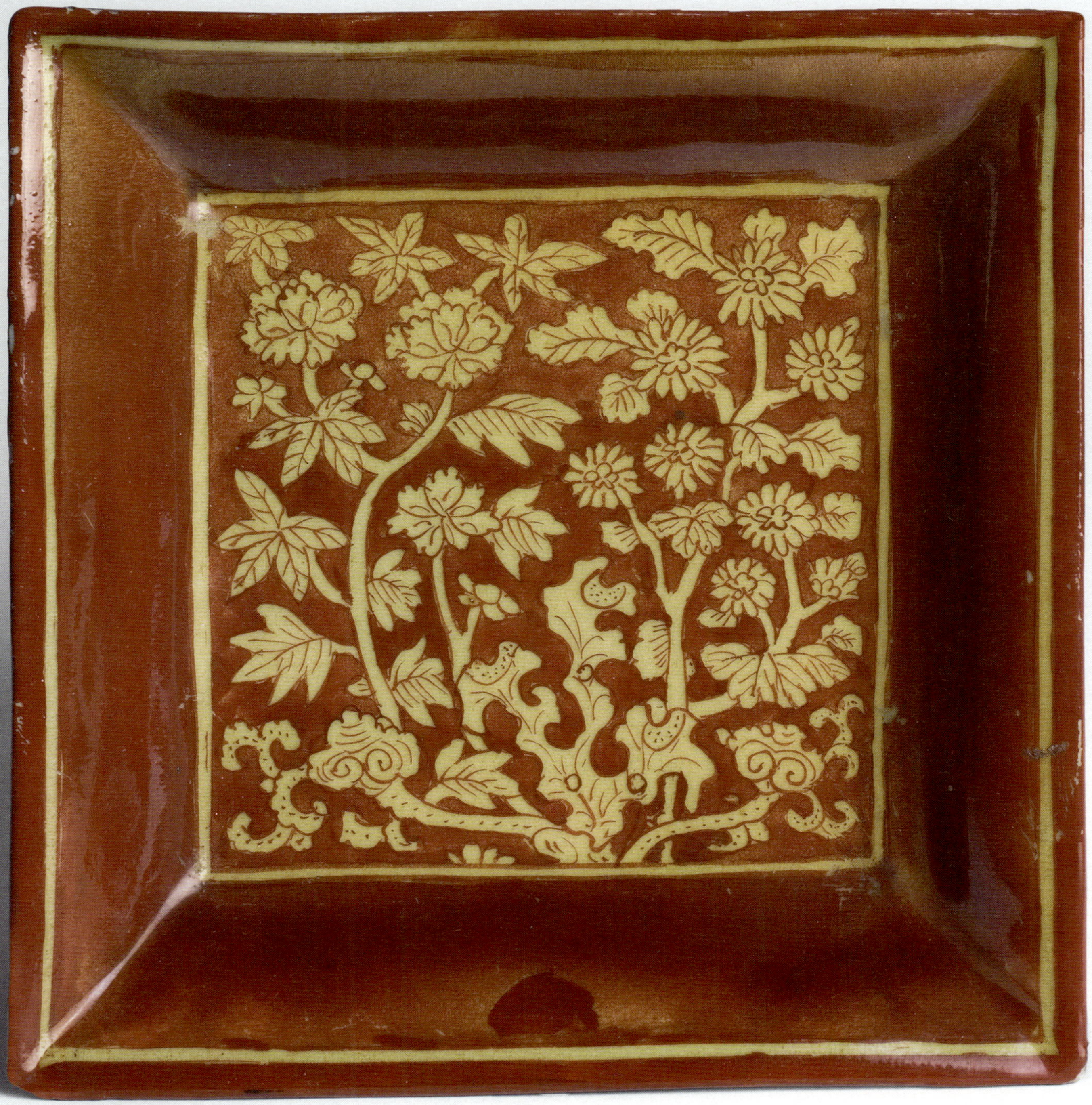

base was fired under a clear glaze at a high temperature; then the yellow enamel was applied and fired; and finally the iron-red enamel was painted on and fired. Despite the labor-intensive technique, the low-fired enamels, applied over a shiny glaze, tend to rub off quite easily. HK

1. Wan 2012, 42, 53.
2. The two examples of this combination, decorated in underglaze blue and yellow enamel of varying tone, are in the British Museum, London (1937,0716.86; PDF.716); the former is illustrated in Harrison-Hall 2001, 253.
3. Two similar red-and-yellow enameled dishes are in the Metropolitan Museum of Art, New York (19.137), and the Victoria and Albert Museum, London (C.110-1929). Other color combinations include underglaze blue with overglaze red on a dish in the British Museum; however, the design incorporates dragons and lions (PDF,A.732).

44

Jar with Dragons and *Shou* Characters

Ming dynasty (1368–1644), Jiajing period (1522–66)
Porcelain with underglaze blue decoration (Jingdezhen ware)
20½ x 20¼ inches (52.1 x 51.4 cm)
Gift of Major General and Mrs. William Crozier, 1944-20-78a,b

Two dragons painted in inky blue on this large, heavily potted jar cavort amid clouds above rocks and waves. Between the dragons on each side is a loosely written *shou* (longevity) character, while a six-character inscription across the jar's short neck indicates that it was produced in the imperial kilns, most likely for use by the Jiajing emperor in his imperial residence, *Xiyuan* (West Park), designed to evoke the immortal lands. Large quantities of porcelains were made for West Park, and large vessels such as this one may have been used to store wine or grain for Daoist rituals, feasting, or display.[1]

The five-clawed dragons symbolize imperial power, while the *shou* character, composed of a wisp of *qi* (or *chi*) emanating from a fungus growing from a three-peaked rock that points heavenward, has Daoist overtones. *Qi,* or life energy, is the basic substance of all things, according to ancient texts, and maintains the working of the cosmos.[2] The emanation of *qi* from a rock and a *lingzhi* fungus—a hard, woody medicinal plant that was believed to grant longevity—would have been understood in the late Ming period as an auspicious omen. Such an omen was taken as a sign that the rule of the emperor was in line with the Will of Heaven,[3] thus sanctioning his reign.

The Jiajing emperor was an enthusiastic practitioner of Daoism and a great believer in immortality. One of his favorite activities was communicating with immortals or spirits through "automatic" or "passive" writing, in which a T- or Y-shaped wooden implement allowed gods and spirits to write answers to diviners' questions through tracings in sand. The *shou* characters on this jar are each written in one continuous stroke resembling spirit writing, suggesting that the motif may have served as a reminder to the Jiajing emperor of the heavenly blessings bestowed upon him, bolstering his own ardent hope of everlasting life.[4] HK

1. Wan 2012, 53–55.
2. This explanation of the cosmos can be found in the *Huainanzi*, written in the second century CE; see Wan 2007, 104.
3. Wan 2007, 106.
4. Wan 2012, 61.

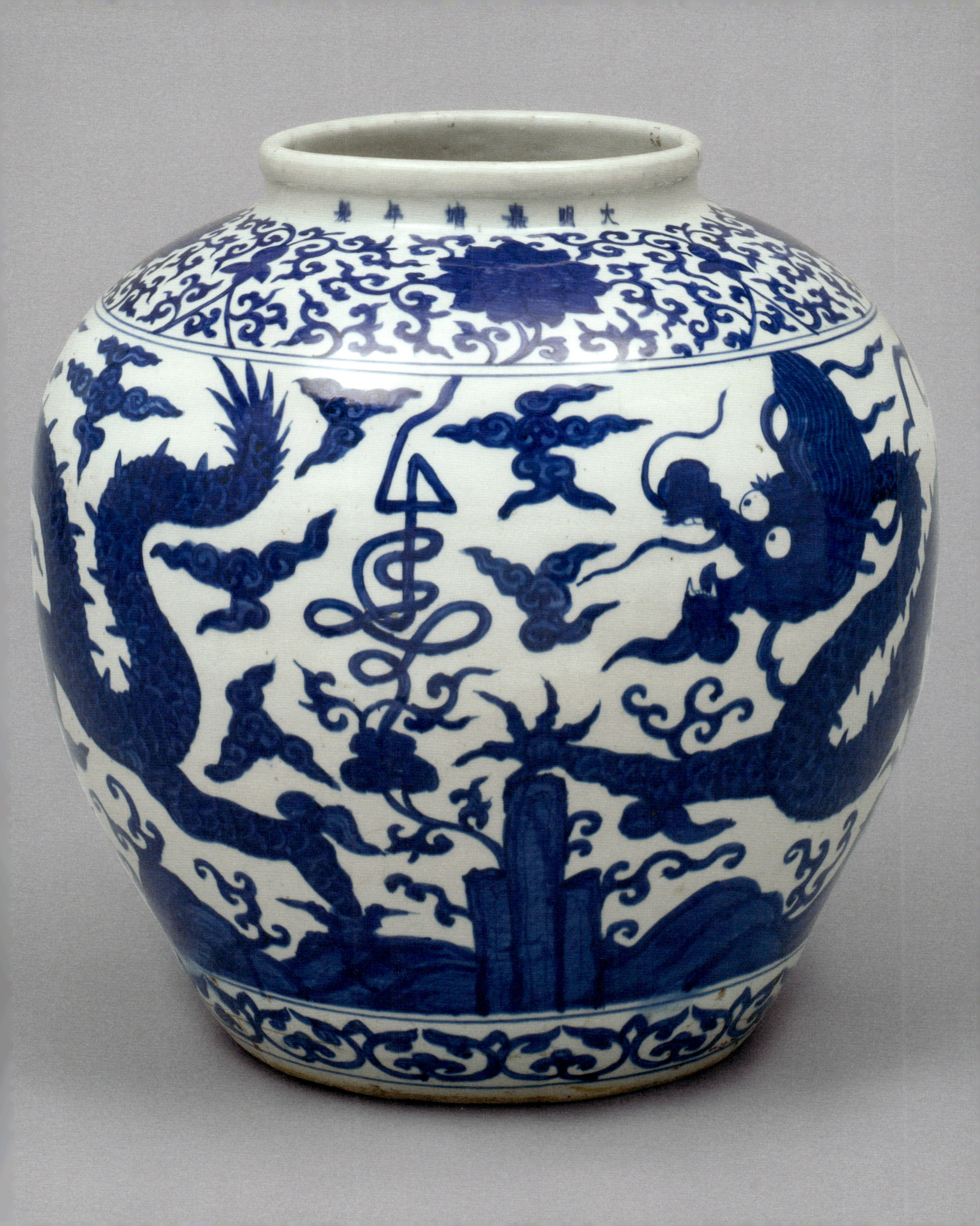
大明嘉靖年製

45

Jar with *Shou* Characters

Ming dynasty (1368–1644), Jiajing period (1522–66)
Porcelain with underglaze blue decoration (Jingdezhen ware)
17¼ x 19 inches (43.8 x 48.3 cm)
Gift of Major General and Mrs. William Crozier, 1944-20-83a,b

Elegantly proportioned, this heavily potted jar with wide, swelling shoulders is decorated with a hundred-*shou*-characters design (*bai shou zi*) in cobalt blue under a clear, lustrous glaze. The entire body is covered with roundels enclosing *shou* (longevity) characters supported on lotus blossoms against a background of densely spaced scrolling tendrils. Different styles of *shou* characters appear on Jiajing porcelains, some written in cursive, as on the Jiajing jar decorated with dragons just illustrated (see no. 44), and others, as on this vessel, modeled after a loose form of Chinese seal script. An unusual scroll band ornaments the short neck, while a linked *ruyi*-cloud motif encircles the base. The unglazed base itself has a six-character Jiajing mark in underglaze blue within a recessed roundel (see p. 246).

Records of the household department of the imperial palace indicate that blue-and-white jars with scrolling lotuses and a hundred *shou* characters were produced in the twenty-fourth year of the Jiajing reign, or 1545.[1] Such jars originally had covers, as seen on one example in the imperial collection of the Forbidden City.[2] This type of well-proportioned jar must have been popular, as it was also produced with only slight changes in form and design in the following Wanli period (1573–1620), when the body became more rotund, the *shou* characters expanded in size to fill the entire roundel, and the enlarged cover knop (decorative knob) was encircled by a dragon.[3]

The blue of this vase is softer than that on the other Jiajing blue-and-white ceramics included here (see nos. 42, 44). The difference may be due to the cobalt pigment. Beginning in the Zhengde period (1506–21), cobalt was imported to China and mixed with local ore.[4] The imported cobalt, called *sulaiman* or *sumali* (presumably after Suleiman, the Ottoman sultan) and *huiqing* (Muslim blue),[5] suggesting its source, fired to a more purplish hue than the locally mined product. HK

1. Wang 2012, 66–67, fig. 12, 73–74.
2. In the Palace Museum, Beijing; see Geng 2000, 115, no. 105.
3. A Wanli example with a cover was excavated in 1971 in Beijing (Guang 1971, 64, fig. 3), and another is in the Tianjin Museum (on display in the galleries).
4. The imported cobalt came from Burma, via Yunnan, Central Asia, or "ancient Arabia"; Kerr and Wood 2004, 684. It may have been traded via sea by the Portuguese; Wang 2012, 71.
5. Kerr and Wood 2004, 685.

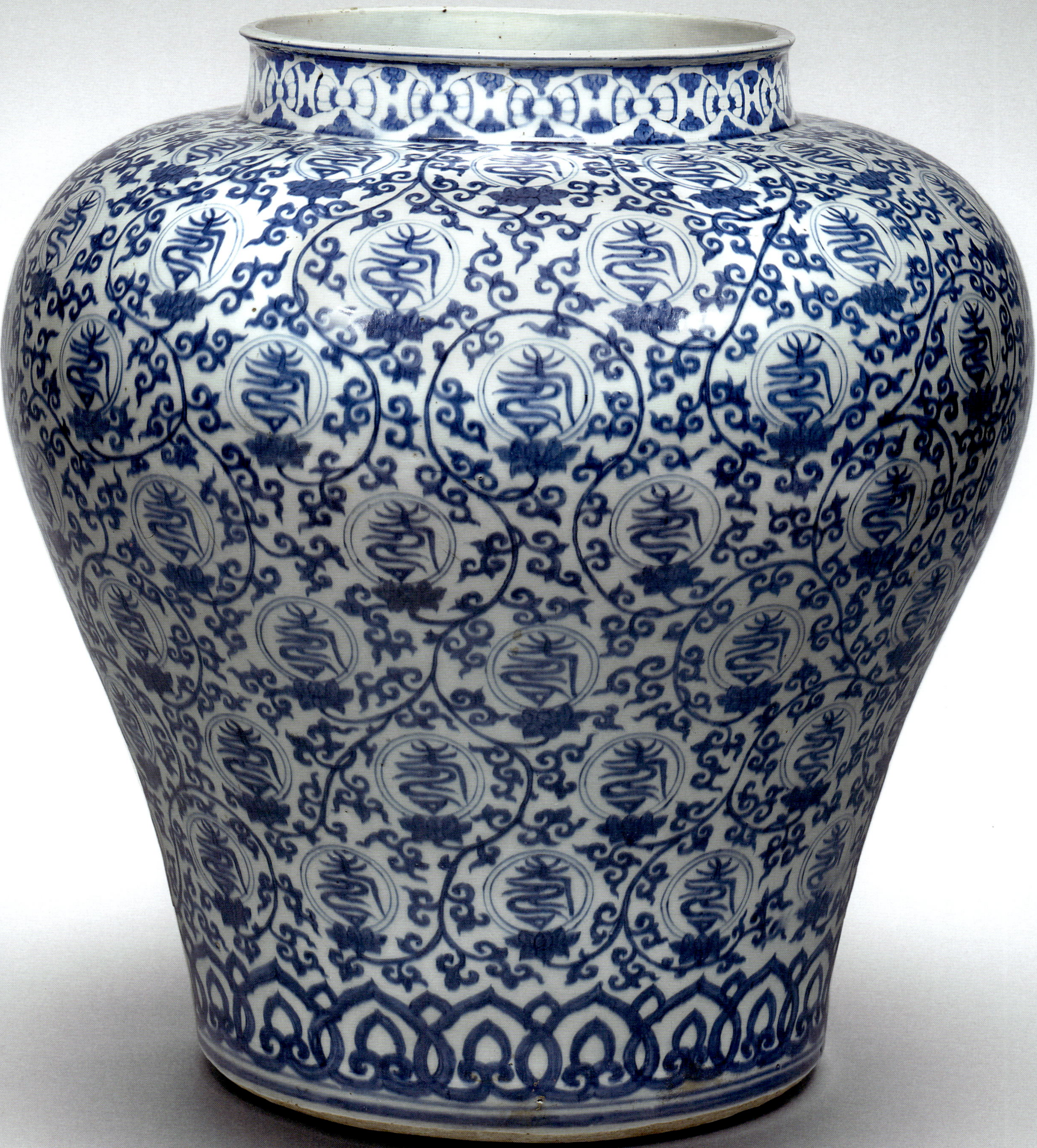

46

Lobed Dish with Cloud Scrolls

Ming dynasty (1368–1644), mid-16th century
Wood with carved lacquer (*tixi*)
2 1/16 x 21 5/8 inches (5.3 x 55 cm)
Gift of J. T. Tai, 1979-55-2

This impressively large nine-lobed lacquer dish, inspired by the form of a hollyhock or mallow flower, is decorated with three concentric rows of *ruyi*-cloud scrolls around a central four-petal floral motif; the border is embellished with scrolling vines on both the interior and exterior. Similar looking *ruyi*-cloud scrolls and vines were also used to decorate the borders and background of Jiajing porcelains, which are often covered with auspicious Daoist motifs related to the emperor's wish to attain immortality (see nos. 42, 44).[1] A round lacquer dish in the Asian Art Museum of San Francisco has similar designs and an inscription dating the piece to the *renyin* year of Jiajing (1542).[2]

After the artisan had built up alternating layers of dark brown and red lacquer, he cut the cloud scrolls into the lacquer at an angle to reveal three layers of red. Cloud-scroll designs first appeared in the Song dynasty (960–1279) and continued to be widely used in the Yuan (1271–1368) and Ming dynasties, though the style of the carving changed over time. The earlier Song examples are characterized by sharply cut sides, and Yuan examples are carved with deeply curved sides, creating an almost a sculptural quality. The carving of this Ming dish has a less dramatic profile, with more gently curving cloud scrolls creating an attractive overall surface design.[3]

This type of Chinese lacquer technique, called *tixi* (*tee hsi*),[4] is sometimes referred to by its Japanese name, *guri*, meaning "crook ring," after the shape of the pommel ring on ancient Chinese swords. *Tixi* lacquerwares were brought to Japan in the thirteenth century by a Chinese monk who became the first abbot at a temple in Kamakura,[5] but it appears that the technique was not copied there until the eighteenth century.[6] HK

1. The *ruyi*-cloud motif is also often likened in form to the *lingzhi* fungus, a woody plant that was believed to confer longevity (see no. 44).
2. The inscription painted on the base reads: "in the *renyin* year of Jiajing [1542], Yiquan made six examples of this type"; Shangraw 1986, 38.
3. Guan 2012, 62–63.
4. For a summary of the origins and history of this technique, see Lee and Hu 1993.
5. At the end of the Southern Song dynasty (1127–1279), the monk Xu Ziyuan went to Engaku-ji, bringing with him forty-three pieces of lacquerware, among which were *tixi* examples; see Hong Kong 1993, 19–20.
6. Hutt 1987, 209.

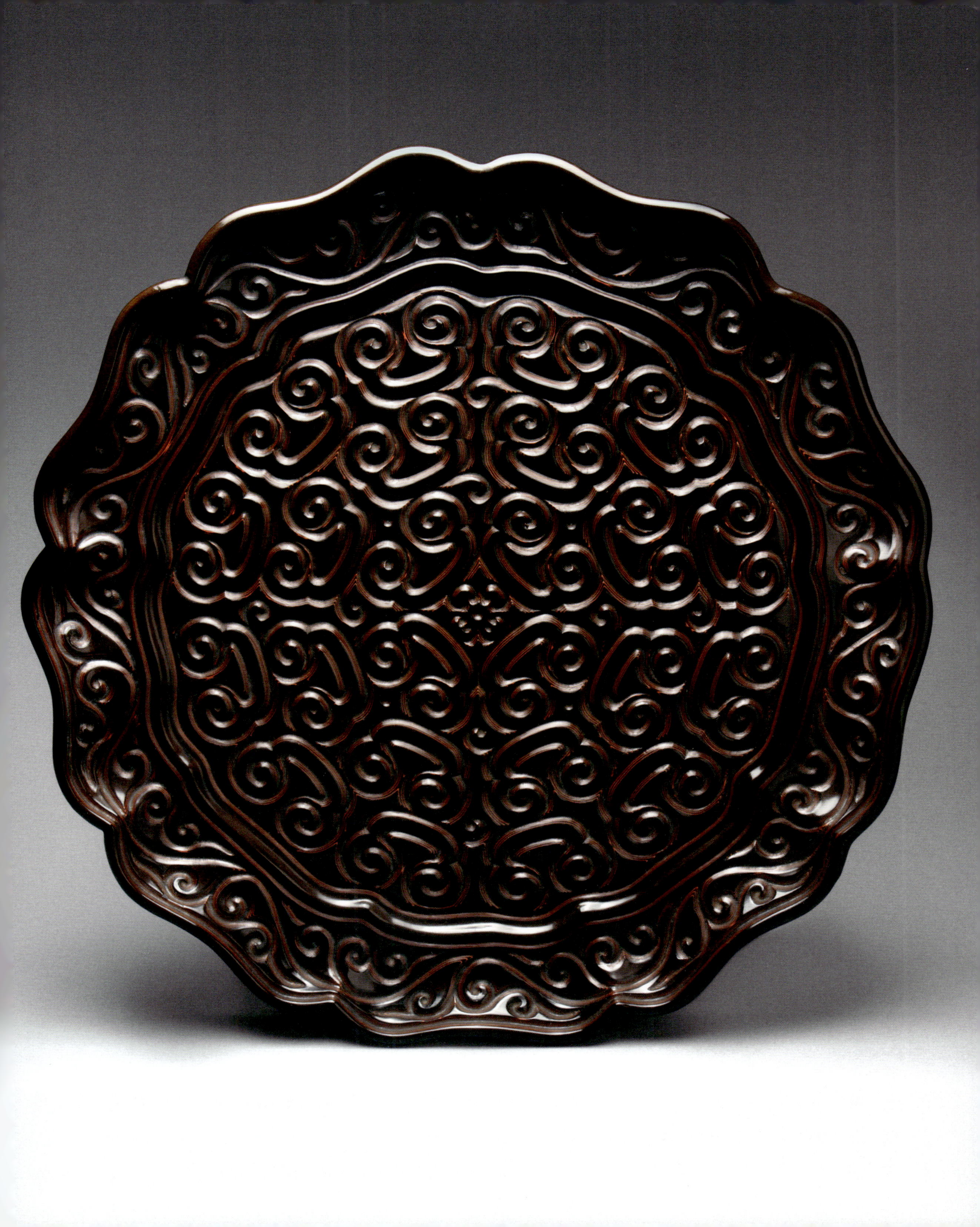

47

Faceted Vase with Morning Glories

Ming dynasty (1368–1644), 16th century
Porcelain with underglaze blue decoration (Jingdezhen ware)
5⁹⁄₁₆ x 3¹⁄₁₆ inches (14.2 x 7.8 cm)
Gift of Major General and Mrs. William Crozier, 1944-20-292a,b

Harking back to an early Ming example, this vase illustrates one of the foundational principles of Chinese art: the veneration of ancient traditions. Since early times, emperors collected and treasured paintings, bronzes, jades, and ceramics from the revered dynasties of the past. The reign of the Xuande emperor (1426–35) was especially celebrated for producing the finest blue-and-white porcelains, and later Ming and Qing emperors frequently commissioned copies, distinguishable from the originals by differences in raw materials and technology.[1]

The painted decoration on this vase is of morning-glory blossoms on a continuous scroll, while the faceted, angular body and the monster masks at the base of the handles show the influence of Middle Eastern metalwork, popular in the early fifteenth century, when the Ming empire was at its most outward looking. An apocryphal Xuande mark (see p. 247) is written on the base. What distinguishes this vase from those made during the Xuande reign, however, is the underglaze blue pigment and the clear "white" glaze. Xuande examples are decorated in a deep cobalt blue, high in iron, that was imported from Persia (see no. 30). Where the painting was more saturated than in other places, the iron and other impurities in the blue separated in the firing, causing some areas to appear much darker, sometimes accumulating to form matt brown or black spots described as "heaped and piled."[2] Later, in the sixteenth century, a local cobalt that contained more manganese than iron was used, resulting in a paler, less intense blue, as seen on the surface of this vase, which lacks the typical early fifteenth-century "heaped and piled" effect. Moreover, what should have been a clear "white" glaze applied over the underglaze blue has fired to a bubble-infused slightly greenish tint more commonly seen on sixteenth-century blue-and-white wares, such as the Zhengde blue-and-white candleholder illustrated earlier (see no. 39). HK

1. The Yongzheng (r. 1723–35) and Qianlong (r. 1736–95) emperors of the early Qing dynasty made porcelains inspired by the Xuande originals both in blue and white and in blue and overglaze yellow. A larger Yongzheng marked, faceted vase is illustrated as no. 70 in this volume.
2. See the painting on the Xuande vase in the British Museum, London, with a Xuande mark (PDF A633) and on a vase in the National Palace Museum, Taipei, without a mark (Taipei 1998, no. 15). It is interesting to see the variations in the form, painting, and glazes of these vases, eight of which are in the National Palace Museum in Taipei and illustrated together in Taipei 2015, 52, no. 1-13.

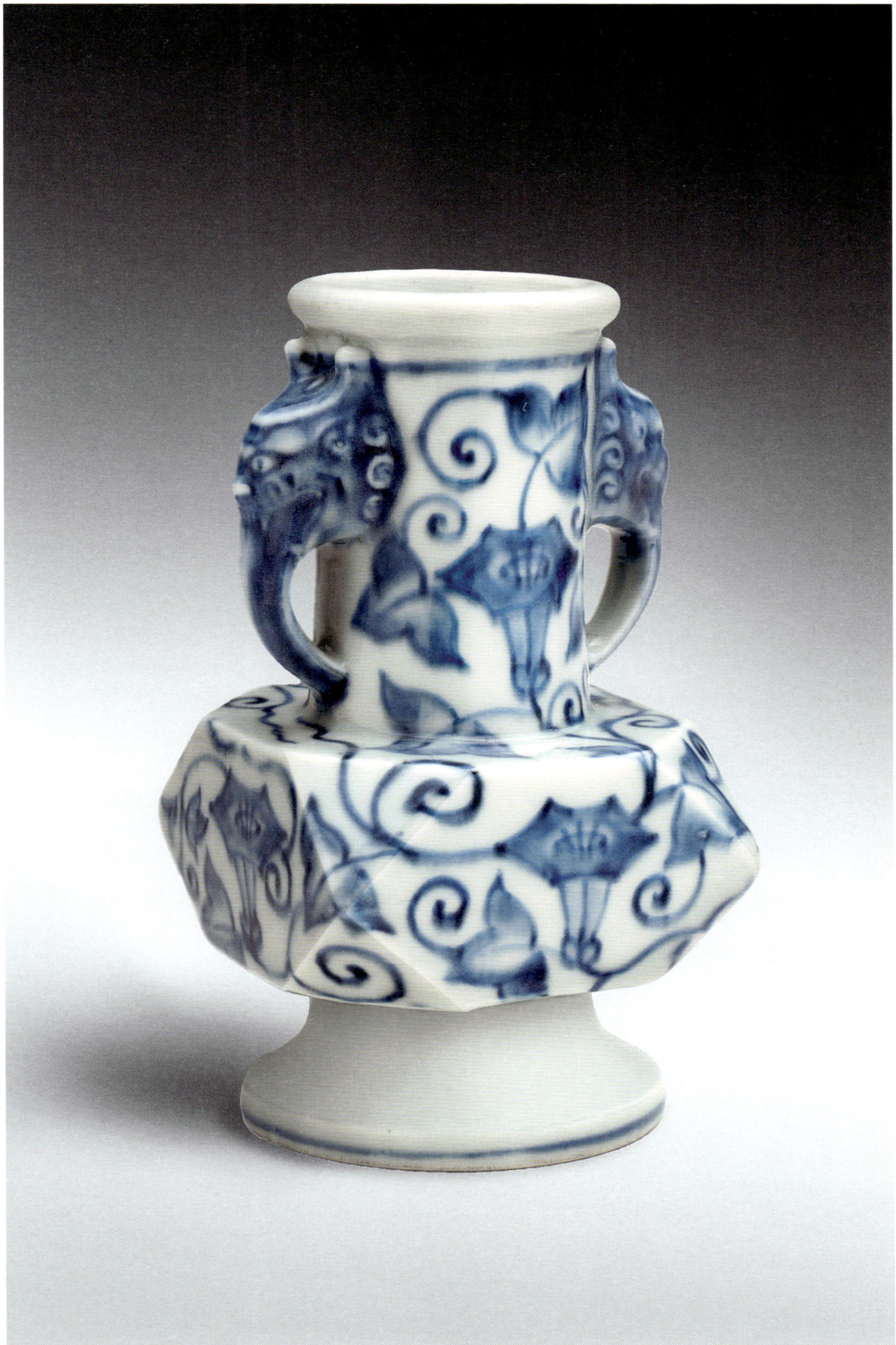

48

Tribute Giraffe with Attendant

Ming dynasty (1368–1644), 16th century
Ink and color on silk, mounted as a hanging scroll
31½ x 16 inches (80 x 40.6 cm)
Gift of John T. Dorrance, 1977-42-1

Foreign to China, giraffes were brought to Asia as rare specimens from their homeland in Africa in the early 1400s, becoming unique witnesses to the age of maritime explorations. To secure tributary and trade relations with regions in South Asia and beyond,[1] the Yongle emperor (r. 1403–24) sent imperial fleets sailing across the Indian Ocean, reaching as far as East Africa.[2] In the autumn of 1414, the noted eunuch-commander Zheng He (1371–1433) brought back from Bengal (now Bangladesh) various tribute gifts, including a giraffe, marking the first among a series of efforts to introduce this African mammal and other exotic species to China.[3]

When the giraffe debuted at the Ming court, it was immediately described as a *qilin*, a fantastic creature of Chinese mythology whose presence is considered a good omen brought about by a righteous ruler.[4] Thus the arrival of the *qilin* was met with enthusiasm and lauded by court officials and artists, much to the emperor's delight. The inscription above this painting consists of an ode and a preface composed for the occasion by Shen Du (1357–1434), the most esteemed scholar-calligrapher at the court of the Yongle emperor. Shen's brilliant verses praised the emperor's sagacious governance and confirmed the giraffe's *qilin* identification in an authoritative manner. These verses were copied on several similar paintings to spread the auspicious message, leading to the frequent misidentification of Shen as the painter of these works.[5]

The simple composition of a giraffe in profile led by a Central Asian attendant against a blank background has an archaic flavor in keeping with traditional Chinese tribute paintings,[6] though the imagery was most likely inspired by earlier works produced in the Middle East, where giraffes were domesticated and typically portrayed wearing a harness and accompanied by a groom.[7] In the Philadelphia scroll the giraffe appears with a light layer of hair over its patterned body, suggesting an effort to adapt the imagery to the description of the mythical *qilin* (fig. 43).[8] DL

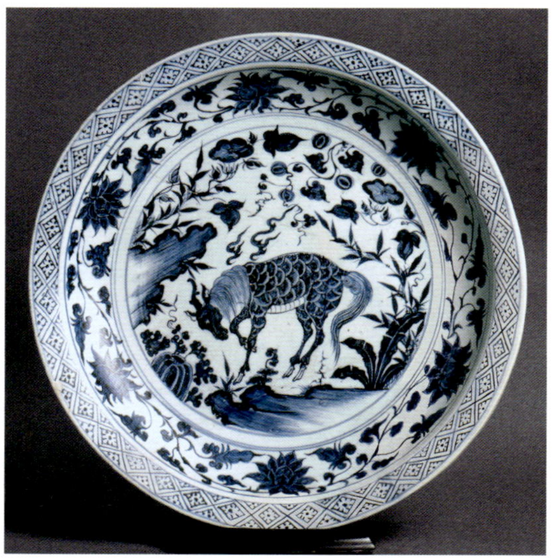

Fig. 43. Dish with a *Qilin*. 2nd half of the 14th century. Porcelain with cobalt blue underglaze, 3¹⁄₁₆ x 18 inches (7.7 x 45.7 cm). Ashmolean Museum, Oxford University. Bequeathed by Professor A. H. Sayce, 1933

1. The centuries-old tributary system is a series of diplomatic protocols that regulated trade and other exchanges between China and its neighbors, based on the belief that the Chinese emperor ruled "all under heaven" and that "vassals" must pay tribute to gain imperial favors.
2. Li and Yang 1991, 950–1014.
3. Duyvendak 1939, 399–400. For further information on these exotic gifts and the imperial menagerie, see Robinson 2013, 279–85.
4. In the Confucian classic *Mengzi* (late 4th–early 3rd century BCE), the *qilin* is said to be the king of all wild beasts and is likened to a sage ruler. See Lau 2004, 35.
5. Other paintings bearing Shen Du's composition include a similar hanging scroll (c. 1414) at the National Palace Museum, Taipei, and a few versions made in the Qing dynasty (1644–1911). Many later copies of Shen's verses added his name next to the painted images, mistakenly attributing the pictorial work to the scholar.
6. The earliest example is a handscroll with tribute bearers by Xiao Yi (508–554).
7. Liscomb 2016, 353.
8. In traditional Chinese literature, the *qilin* is typically described as a composite beast with a dragon's head, a deer's body, horse hooves, and a bull's tail. One of the Confucian classics, *Da Dai Liji*, mentions *qilin* as the foremost animal of the furred category. See Dai and Lu 1987, vol. 13, 21–22.

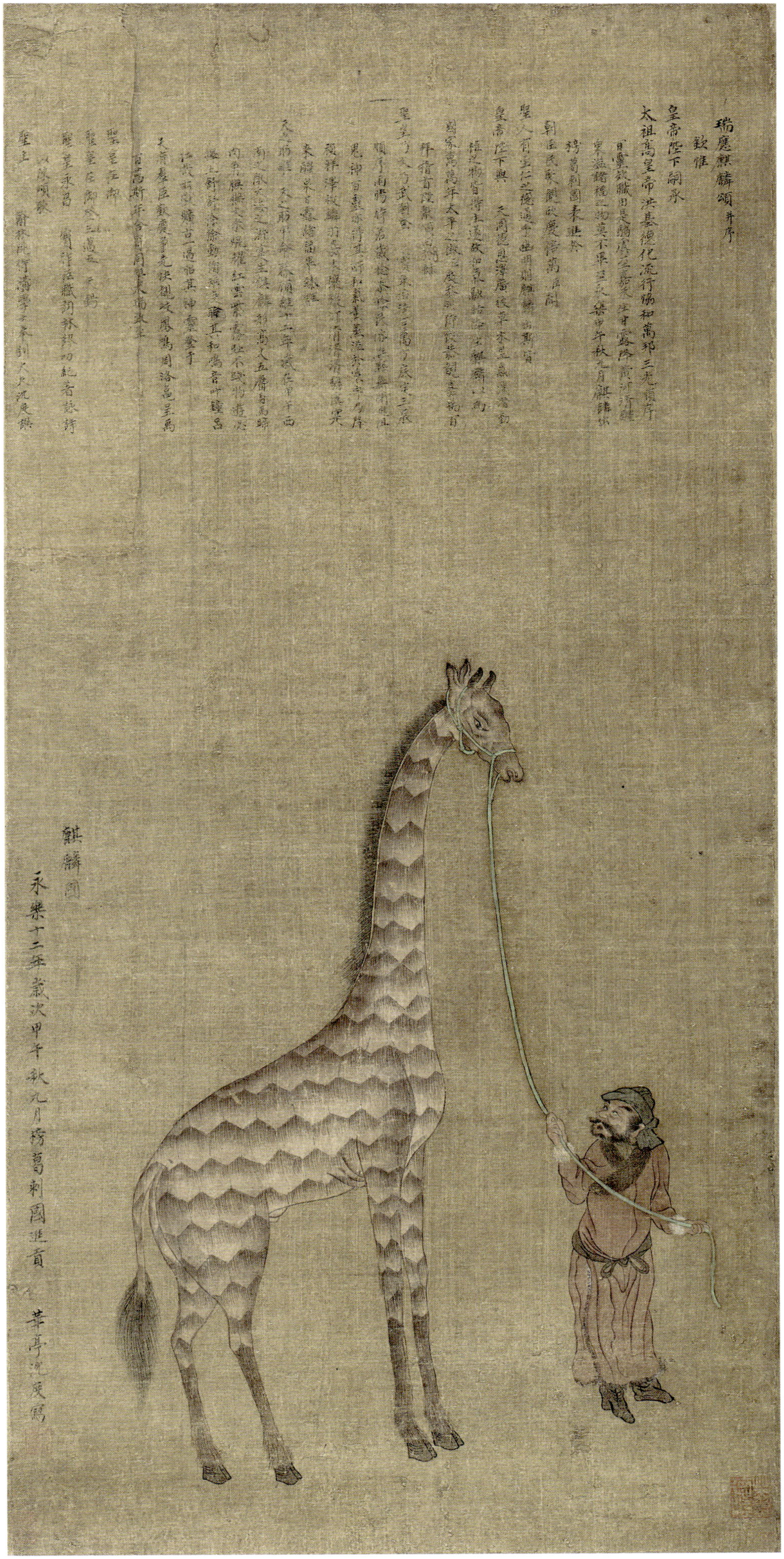
瑞應麒麟頌 并序
麒麟圖
永樂十二年歲次甲午秋九月榜葛剌國進貢
華亭沈度寫

49

Round-back Armchairs (*Quanyi*)

Ming dynasty (1368–1644), 16th century
Wood (*huanghuali*), woven fiber
36 x 26 x 29 inches (91.4 x 66 x 73.7 cm)
Purchased with the J. Stogdell Stokes Fund, the John T. Morris Fund, the Thomas Skelton Harrison Fund, the George W. B. Taylor Fund, and with funds contributed by Mr. and Mrs. Howard Lewis and Henry B. Keep, 1971-12-1, 1971-12-2

Each of these elegantly proportioned round-back armchairs has a curved top rail with a continuous arm post, a much rarer construction than yokeback chairs with squared armrests that protrude and flare outward.[1] The chair's undecorated surfaces and simple lines show off the rich color and varied grain of the *huanghuali* wood, especially on the curved back splat. Whereas the top rail of most round-back chairs is constructed of five pieces of wood, the top rails of these examples are each made from only three pieces, connected by highly developed joinery. The gracefully flowing lines are further emphasized in the construction, with the vertical rails made from a single piece of wood mortised and tenoned into the arm rail and continuing through the seat frame to form the legs.

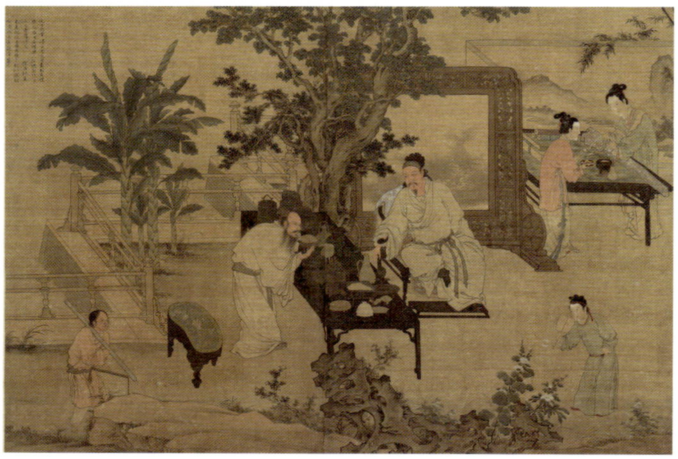

Fig. 44. Du Jin (act. c. 1465–1505). *Enjoying Antiquities*. Ming dynasty, c. 1400–1500. Ink and color on silk, 49⅝ x 73⅝ inches (126.1 x 187 cm). National Palace Museum, Taipei

Round-back armchairs could serve various functions in a home: as ceremonial seating in a reception area, as dining chairs, as work chairs positioned by a painting table in a studio, or as rest spots in a garden (fig. 44). Though commonly used in sets of two or four, pairs are difficult to find because of the fragility of the rounded arms rests, which required strong joinery and skillful use of the wood grain in order to maintain the structural soundness of the curved arm rail.[2]

Chairs in China were not designed for comfort in the Western sense, as individuals were expected to sit upright with their feet resting on the chair's front runner or on a footstool. The round-back armchair was more comfortable than most, however, as the curved top rail offered support for the upper arm and elbow.[3] On formal or ceremonial occasions, the chair would have been draped with a cloth or runner.[4] The placement of chairs within a room conveyed a person's social position, following Confucian rules of propriety. An individual's importance was determined by his or her official rank or age. Within a room, the eastern part (that to the left of the place of honor) had greater status than the western.[5] HK

1. The yokeback chair is the most popular form of chair in China. For examples, and for the chair's history, see Handler 2001, 43–59.
2. For an illustration of such joinery, see Wang and Evarts 1995, 62.
3. Wang 1986, 24.
4. Handler 2005, 112.
5. Handler 2005, 110.

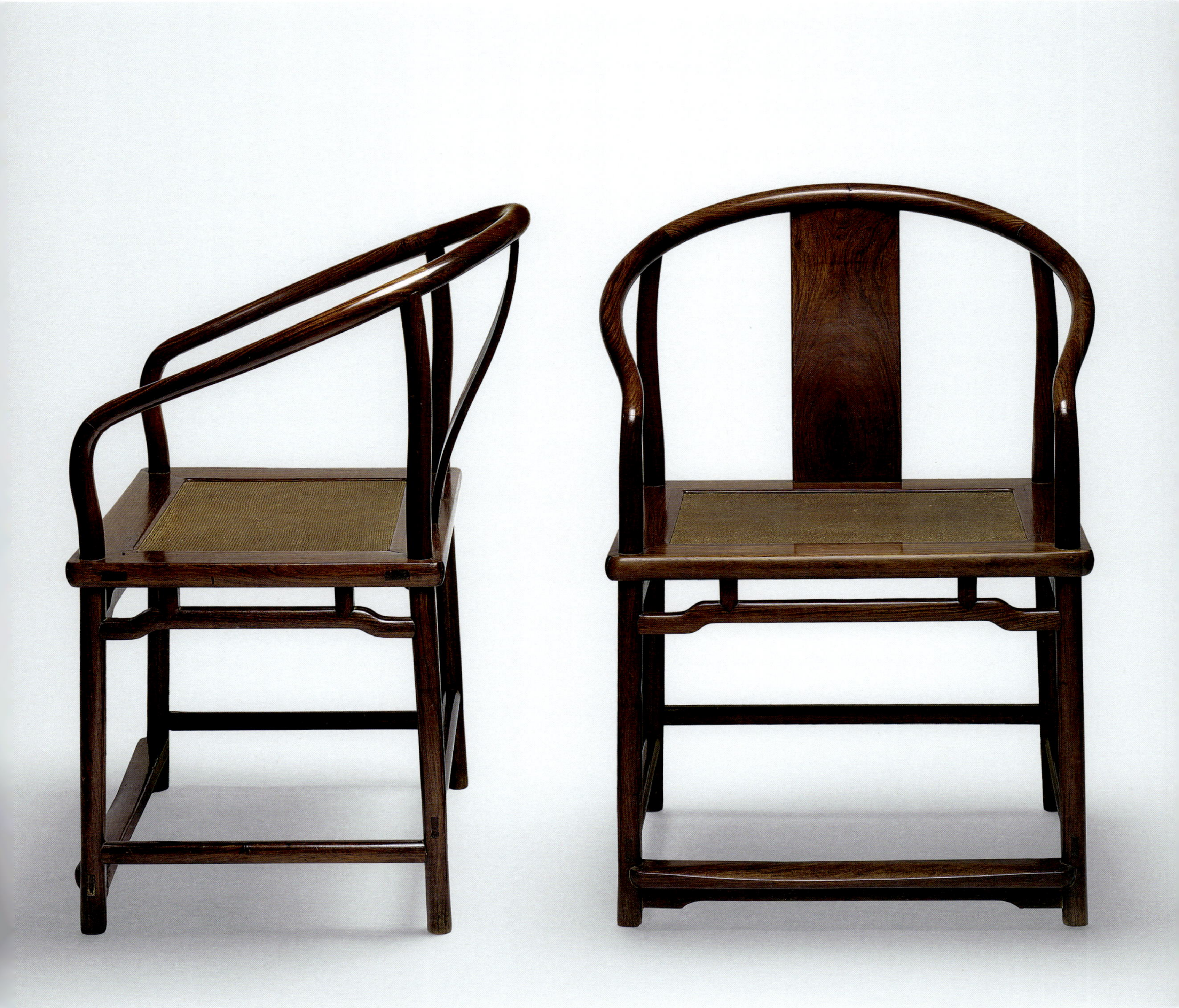

50

Xu Wei (1521–1593)
Sixteen Flowers

Ming dynasty (1368–1644), 16th century
Ink on paper, mounted as a hanging scroll
10 feet 11 inches x 39 inches (332.7 x 99.1 cm)
Purchased with the Fiske Kimball Fund and the Marie Kimball Fund, 1968-29-1

A native of Shaoxing in Zhejiang province, Xu Wei was famous for his expressive ink abstractions of flowers and plants, as well as for his literary talent and eccentric personality. The name *Sixteen Flowers* comes from the title of Xu Wei's long poem on this painting. Although he singles out the peony in his verse, he illustrates many other species—sixteen in all. Xu Wei enjoyed depicting flowers representative of each of the four seasons together in one space. Spring is represented here by the peony and hydrangea; summer by the daylily, pomegranate flower, lotus flower, and plantain lily; autumn by the chrysanthemum, gumbo, and hibiscus; and winter by the plum blossom, narcissus, and camellia. Of the remaining four plants, the banana tree and bamboo are without apparent seasonal associations, and two additional flowers are unrecognizable. Surrounding a beautiful Taihu rock (also called a scholar's rock), these flowers and plants of different seasons are united to create a corner of a garden that transcends time.

In the sixteenth century it was common to use the handscroll format to reveal the unfolding of the seasons through different flowers, but combining all the flowers into a single circumscribed space on a hanging scroll is unusual. It is impossible to encounter this scene in reality, but as Xu Wei has written in his poem, "[Flowers of] Twelve months are blooming on the surface of the paper." The illusionary painting to some extent becomes reality.

In his poem, Xu Wei imagines the flowers becoming beautiful ladies. Viewing the painting is like watching a dance unfold. But where the illusion is fleeting, the painting remains as a finely executed work of art.[1] HX

1. *Flowers and Bamboo* in the National Palace Museum, Taipei, shares a similar motif, composition, and inscription with *Sixteen Flowers*. See *Gugong shuhua tulu* 8, 1991, 145.

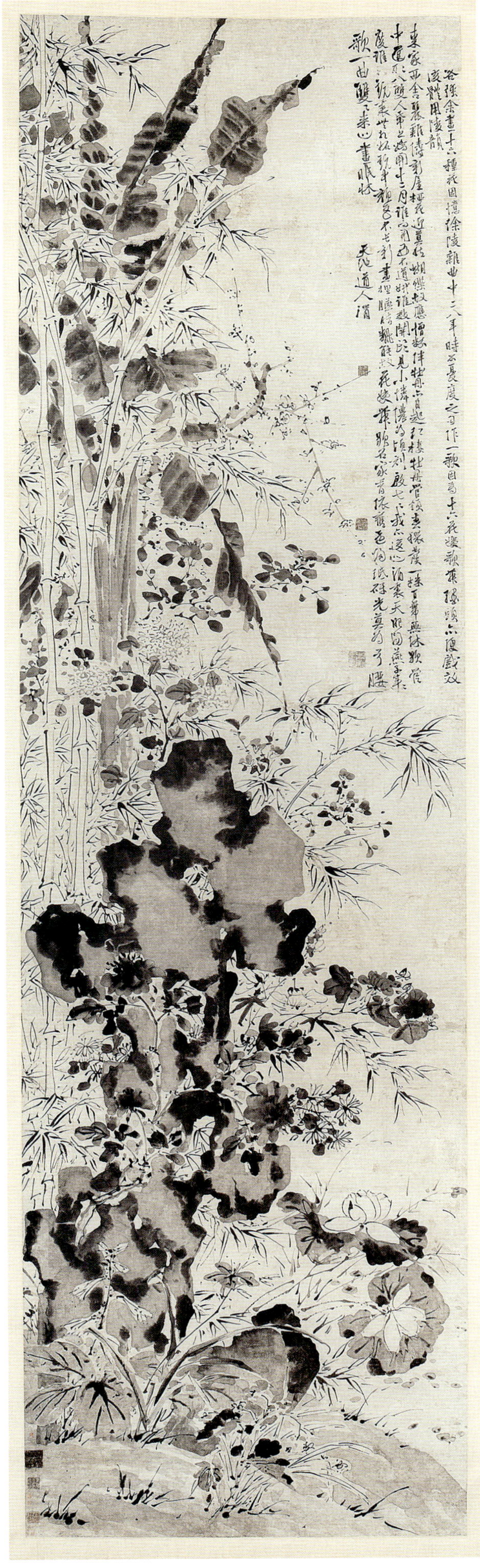

51

Seated Luohan

Ming dynasty (1368–1644), 16th–17th century
Figure: wood (linden; *Tilia* sp.) with fabric and paint, glass eyes; base: wood (magnolia) with traces of paint
55½ x 38 x 27 inches (141 x 96.5 x 68.6 cm)
Purchased with funds contributed by the Wyncote Foundation, 2013-74-1

This serene figure of a Chinese monk (*luohan* in Chinese, *arhat* in Sanskrit), seated on a base carved to resemble a rocky outcrop, represents an enlightened being tasked with protecting the dharma—the spiritual interests of Buddhism and its believers, or Buddhist law—until the coming of the future Buddha, Maitreya.[1] It most likely accompanied seventeen other *luohans* placed along the sides of a Buddhist temple hall flanking centrally placed Buddha figures.

Luohans were first worshipped in groups of sixteen beginning in the seventh century, but after the eleventh century groups of eighteen and sometimes five hundred were also depicted.[2] Although the sixteen *luohans* were named and discussed in detail in a Chinese text,[3] craftsmen and artists took liberties with their depictions, so that identifying specific *luohans* is often challenging. This figure with arms outstretched may once have held a scarf or a sutra (Buddhist text) and bears some resemblance to a Ming painted-clay *luohan* at Lingyan Temple near Ji'nan, Shandong.[4] Carved from linden, the Philadelphia sculpture was originally brightly painted and gilded. Over the centuries, the decorations were refreshed and repainted several times over, as cross-section analysis has shown.

X-rays of the body have revealed what appears to be a metal disc or mirror decorated with two of the "eight precious" motifs—the lozenge, a pun for victory and a demon-dispelling emblem, and the rhinoceros horn, a symbol of longevity and good fortune—attached to a double rhomboid, an auspicious symbol, inside a cavity in the chest area (fig. 45).[5] Relics or relic-like objects were frequently placed within a cavity in a sculpture's torso in order to "activate" and make it real. Only through worshipping a consecrated figure would believers gain fortune, such as health, wealth, and many sons.[6] HK

1. The *luohan* was purchased by Reverend Theodore Pitcairn (1893–1973) on a trip around the world in 1922. Pitcairn was a minister of the New Church in Bryn Athyn, Pennsylvania, a new Christian community based on the revelations of the eighteenth-century philosopher and scientist Emanuel Swedenborg. The community was established by his father, John Pitcairn, a wealthy industrialist who made his fortune as cofounder of the Pittsburg Plate Glass factory and through investments in oil, coal, gas, and the Pennsylvania Railroad.
2. Little 1992, p. 255.
3. *Da aluohan nantimiduoluo suoshuo Fazhuji* (Record on the Duration of the Dharma as Explained by the Great Arhat Nandimitra [Fazhuji]), translated into Chinese by Xuanzang in 652. See Shih 2002, p. 1.
4. Zhongguo 1988, no. 113.
5. A Liao amber container in this form, inscribed with two characters implying double happiness, is illustrated in Hong Kong 1999, p. 158.
6. Bieberly 2013, p. 154.

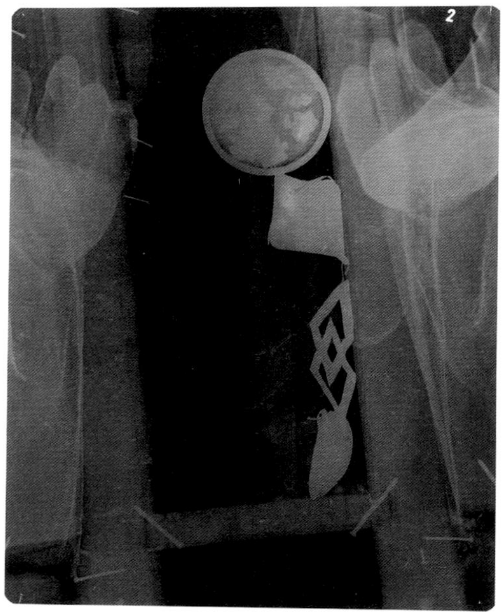

Fig. 45. X-ray of the cavity in the figure's chest showing enshrined objects

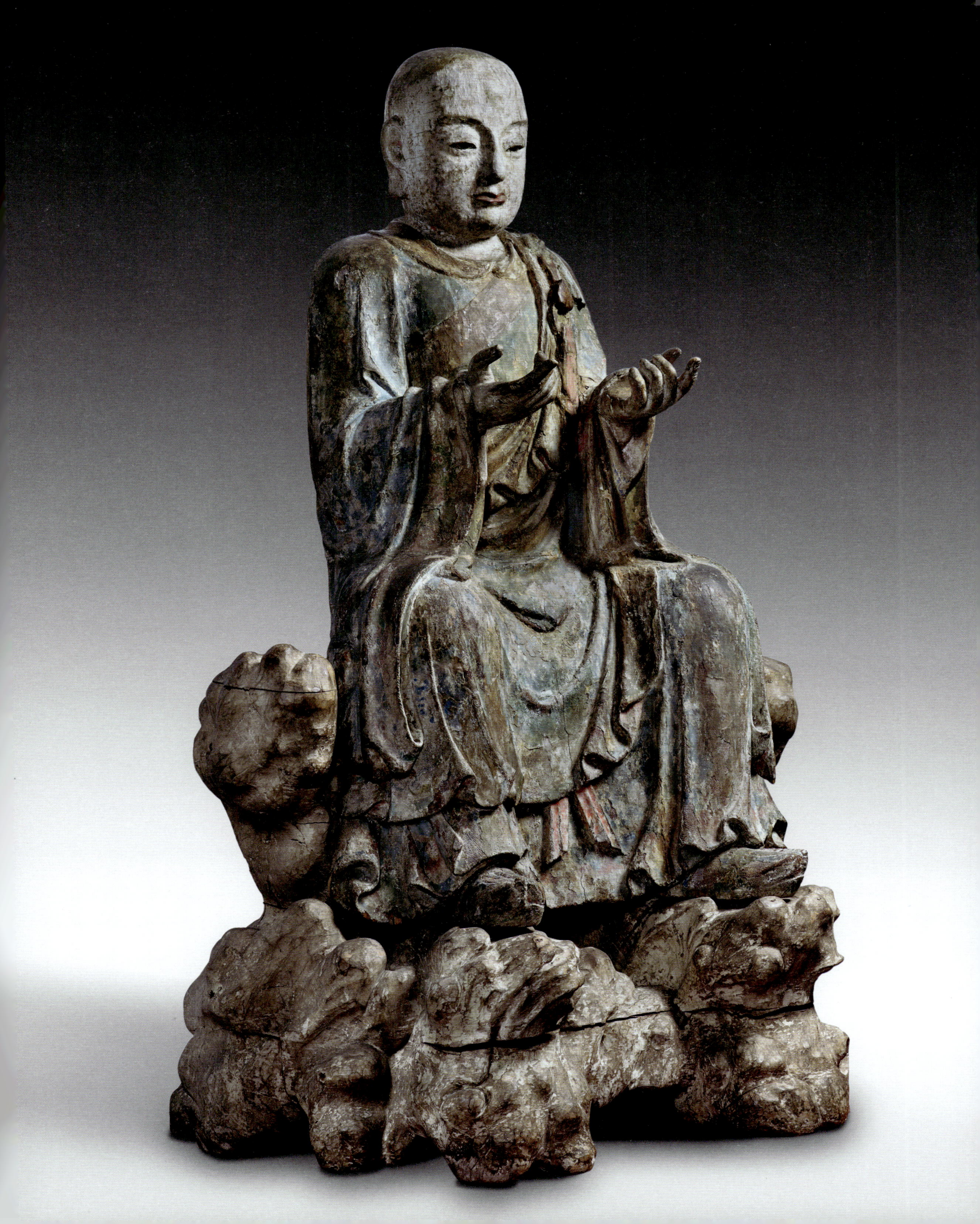

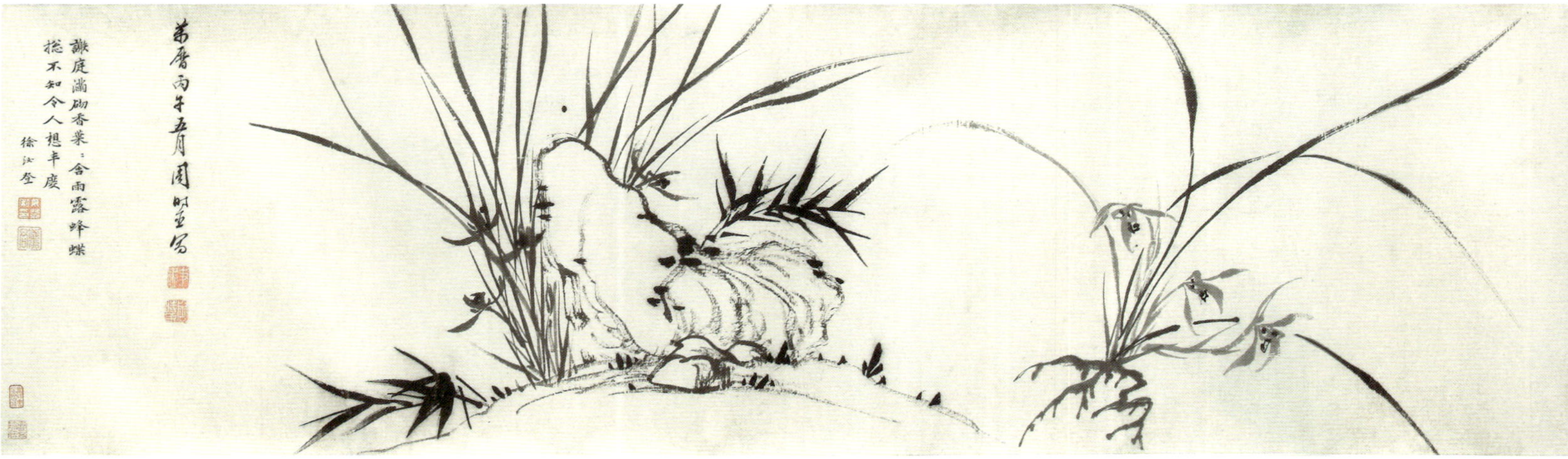

52

Chen Dao, Cao Xi, and Zhou Shichen (act. late 16th–early 17th century)
Orchids and Rocks

Ming dynasty (1368–1644), Wanli period (1573–1620), 1606
Ink on paper, mounted as a handscroll
12⅛ inches x 7 feet 3¼ inches (30.8 x 221.6 cm)
Purchased with the J. Stogdell Stokes Fund, 1968-9-1

In this quietly lyrical painting, orchids and rocks are rendered with swift, dry brushwork that accentuates their pale, unassuming beauty, while darker ink, used for moss and bamboo leaves, punctuates the composition throughout. The orchid, regarded as a symbol of purity, resilience, and loyalty, has been a beloved floral motif in Chinese culture since antiquity. The eminent poet and statesman Qu Yuan (c. 343–c. 277 BCE) was known for his fondness for the orchid,[1] and his unwavering loyalty to his country came to be associated with the flower's virtuous qualities. Similarly, the simple depiction of an orchid by the scholar-artist Zheng Sixiao (fig. 46)—emulated in the present painting—became canonical in Chinese art,[2] partly owing to Zheng's resistance to the Mongol rule that supplanted the Song dynasty (960–1279), to which he was deeply devoted.

Two of the five signed inscriptions on the scroll make subtle references to Qu Yuan and mention the Xiang River in his home country, the state of Chu. Since the Mongol era, the act of painting orchids was likened to the writing or copying of *Li sao* (Departing Sorrow), one of Qu Yuan's best-known literary works.[3] The present painting, created three centuries after Zheng Sixiao's rendering of a single orchid, was likely intended to evoke the same sentiment at a time when the Chinese gentry class was deeply concerned about the fate of the ailing Ming dynasty.[4] Toward the end of the scroll a cluster of orchids appears to be uprooted (center left), clearly reminding us of the "groundless" plant by Zheng.

Though three different artists created the three clusters of orchids on the scroll, the work has a coherence reflecting influence from the Wu school, a literati painting style that developed in the fifteenth to mid-sixteenth century around the Suzhou region in southern China.[5] Indeed, most of the painters and inscription writers who contributed to this work were natives of Suzhou

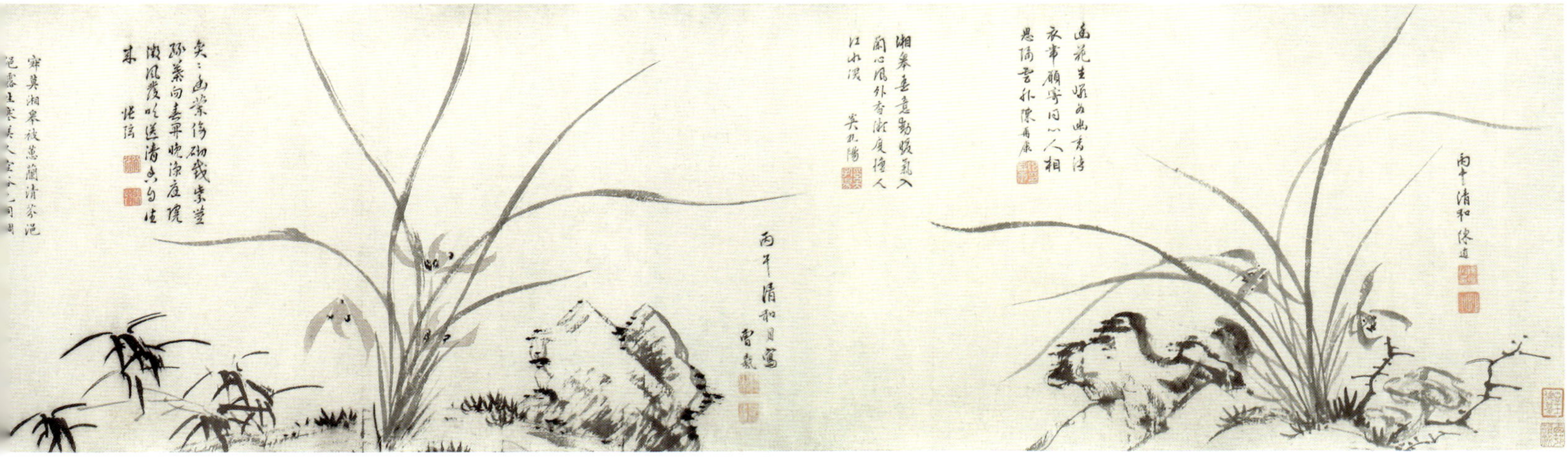

(see p. 247), and Zhou Shichen and Xu Zhideng were followers of Wen Zhengming (1470–1559), a celebrated scholar-artist from this region. DL

1. Qu Yuan's fondness for orchids is evident in his frequent mention of them in his verses, such as the *Li sao* (Departing Sorrow) and *Jiu ge* (Nine Songs), in which he praises the orchid's fragrance and serene beauty.
2. This single extant painting by Zheng Sixiao inspired much admiration among Chinese scholar-artists, many of whom, including such renowned artists as Ni Zan (1306–1374) and Wen Zhengming (1470–1559), composed poems about it.
3. For instance, Ni Zan, in his poem composed for Zheng's orchid painting, laments that Suonan (Zheng's sobriquet) combined his tears with ink to paint the *Li sao*; Gu 1987, 21–26.
4. The Wanli emperor was generally known as an incapable ruler, and his distrust of scholar-bureaucrats caused deep grievances among the gentry; Miller 2009, 78–79.
5. Artists of the Wu school were mainly amateur painters who practiced painting and calligraphy for scholarly self-cultivation. They took delight in applying their calligraphic skills in painting, striving to express their lofty ideals rather than creating formal likenesses. For discussion of the Wu school and late Ming painting, see Cahill 1982, 31–62.

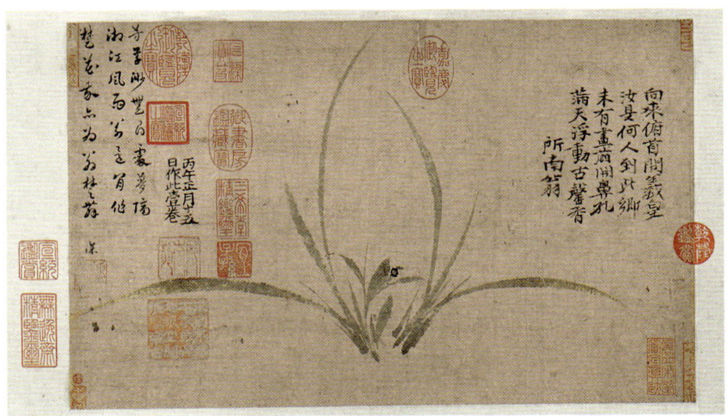

Fig. 46. Zheng Sixiao (1241–1318). *Orchid*. Yuan dynasty (1271–1368), 1306. Ink on paper, 10⅛ x 16¹¹⁄₁₆ inches (25.7 x 42.4 cm). Abe Collection, Osaka City Museum of Fine Arts

53

Lobed Cup Stand

Ming dynasty (1368–1644), first half of the 17th century
Silver alloy with gilding
⅜ x 6⅛ inches (1 x 15.6 cm)
Purchased with the John T. Morris Fund, 1969-260-1a

Designed to hold a small wine cup (fig. 47), this seven-lobed silver cup stand has detailed scenes incised on its surface, which is enhanced with gilding.[1] The combined tableaus express multiple good wishes to the user: On the right, a monkey climbs a peach tree to poke at a hive with a stick, home to a large wasp or bee hovering nearby, while a magpie swoops down at the far left and a spotted deer emerges from behind rocks below. The magpie (*que*), deer (*lu*), wasp or bee (*feng*), and monkey (*hou*) together convey the phrase *juelu fenghou* (may you receive high rank and salary).[2] Many Chinese words have similar sounds yet different meanings, and artists of the Ming and Qing dynasties in particular exploited this characteristic by creating visual puns that could be "read" to express auspicious messages.

On the left, one of the two conversing scholar-officials points to the sun, above the peach tree branch; the word for pointing to the sun sounds like *soon*, thus creating the rebus "may you soon rise in rank."[3] The peach tree in fruit symbolizes longevity, referring to the legend in which the Daoist deity the Queen Mother of the West grew peaches in her garden that were thought to provide eternal life. The last rebus is the *lingzhi*, or woody fungus, growing next to the peach tree and also appearing in the shape of the clouds above (as well as giving form to the handles of the wine cup; fig. 47). The fungus, believed to bestow eternal life if ingested, is also called *ruyi*, or "as you wish," and so together with the other auspicious designs creates a complex and meaningful design.

The late Ming dynasty, when this cup stand was made, was a time of great economic expansion and wealth. Contemporary Ming paintings and woodblock prints illustrate banqueting scenes that depict such utensils along with other types of wine vessels in use at elaborate gatherings. Gilded silver cup stands, while rare, have been found in both northern and southern China: one six-lobed example was excavated from the tomb of Du Mao, a high-ranking eunuch in Beijing, dated to 1620,[4] while two seven-lobed examples were found in Hunan province among a group of silver wine utensils belonging to an official of the Southern Ming dynasty who died in 1647.[5] HK

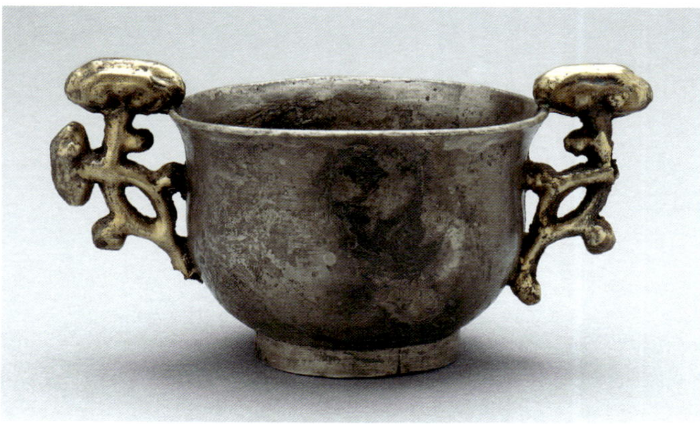

Fig. 47. Wine Cup with *Lingzhi*-shaped Handles. Ming dynasty, first half of the 17th century. Silver alloy with gilding, 1¾ x 3½ x 2⅛ inches (4.5 x 8.9 x 5.4 cm). Philadelphia Museum or Art. Purchased with the John T. Morris Fund, 1969-260-1b

1. This is one of two in the museum's collection; the other (acc. no. 1969-260-2a) is of similar design but lacks the *lingzhi* fungus plant by the peach tree.
2. San Francisco 2006, 130, no. 5.35.3.
3. San Francisco 2006, 129, no. 5.33.3.
4. Yang 2011, 136–37. The cup stand is slightly larger and has six lobes rather than seven, but the design appears to be very similar. Du Mao had the title of Managing Grand Eunuch of the Ceremonial Directorate (*Sili bingbi taijian*), one of a group of eunuchs who took turns running this directorate, the most powerful eunuch agency inside the imperial city.
5. The silver vessels, which included peach-shaped cups, a rectangular Ding vessel, a pouring vessel (*yi*), and other cup stands, belonged to Dang Zhe, an official of Jingzhou who died in 1647. See Huaihua and Tongdao 1984, 92.

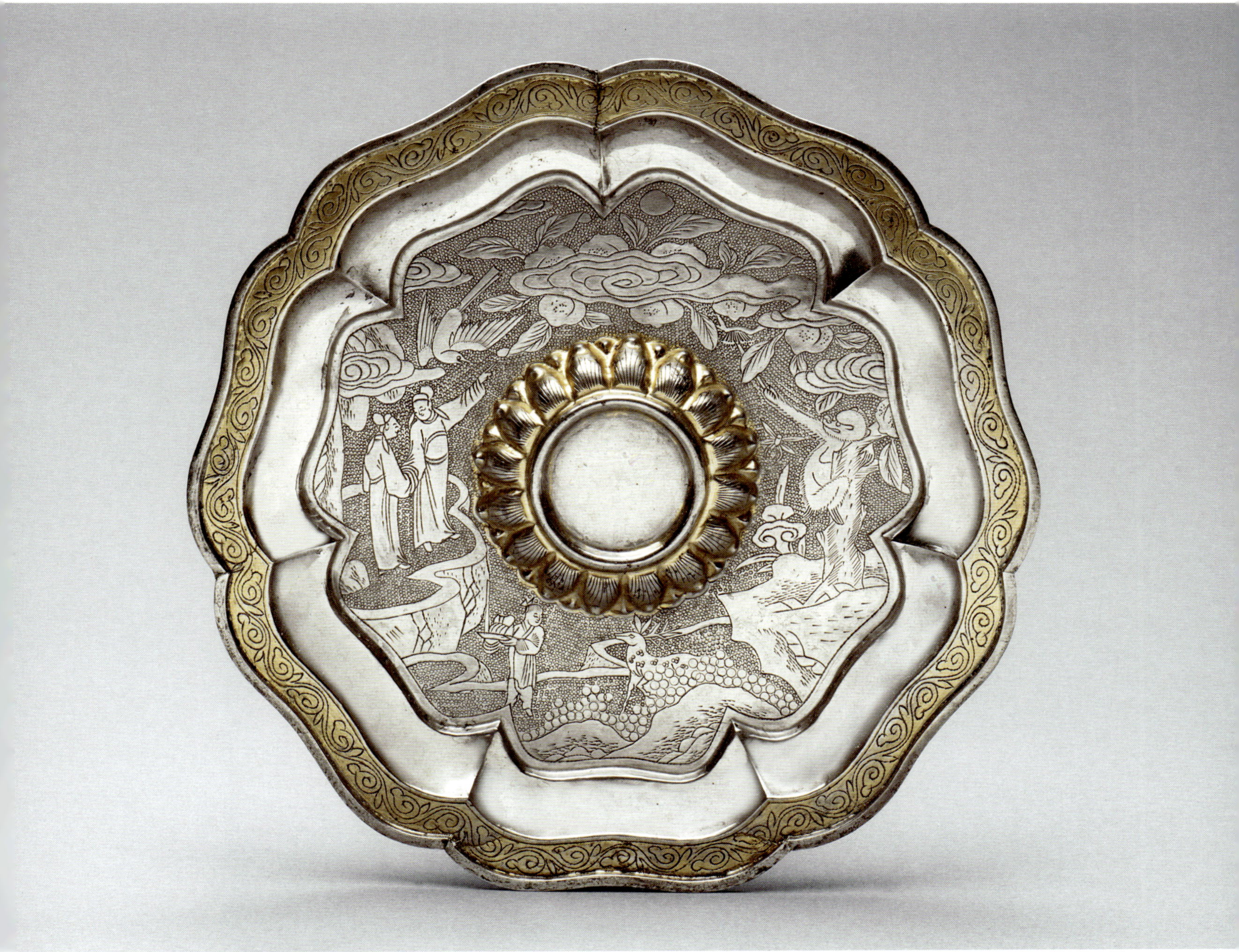

54

Seated Twins of Union and Harmony, Hanshan and Shide

Late Ming–early Qing dynasty, 17th century
Porcelain with ivory glaze (Dehua ware)
4½ x 6⁵⁄₁₆ x 3⁹⁄₁₆ inches (11.4 x 16 x 9 cm)
Gift of Major General and Mrs. William Crozier, 1944-20-324a–c

Rarely in Chinese clay sculpture does one come across the humor and playfulness of these delightful figures representing the eighth-century Chan Buddhist monks Hanshan and Shide, made at the Dehua kilns in Fujian province in eastern China in the seventeenth century. Chan Buddhism was enjoying a revival at this time, which may have prompted the depiction of these two historical figures,[1] along with other Buddhist deities.

The "He He Twins," as they were popularly known, sit laughing together, one barefoot, the other holding a covered basket from which a bat—a symbol of happiness and good fortune—is emerging. This detail, coupled with the union and harmony that the twins embody, would have made the sculpture an auspicious gift, especially appropriate for a wedding.[2]

Impressed on the figures' backs are two seals of the potter Zhang Shoushan (act. 17th century), one square and the other a double gourd in form (see p. 247).[3] The artist's attention to detail in the carving, seen in the graceful curve of the fingers and the texturing of

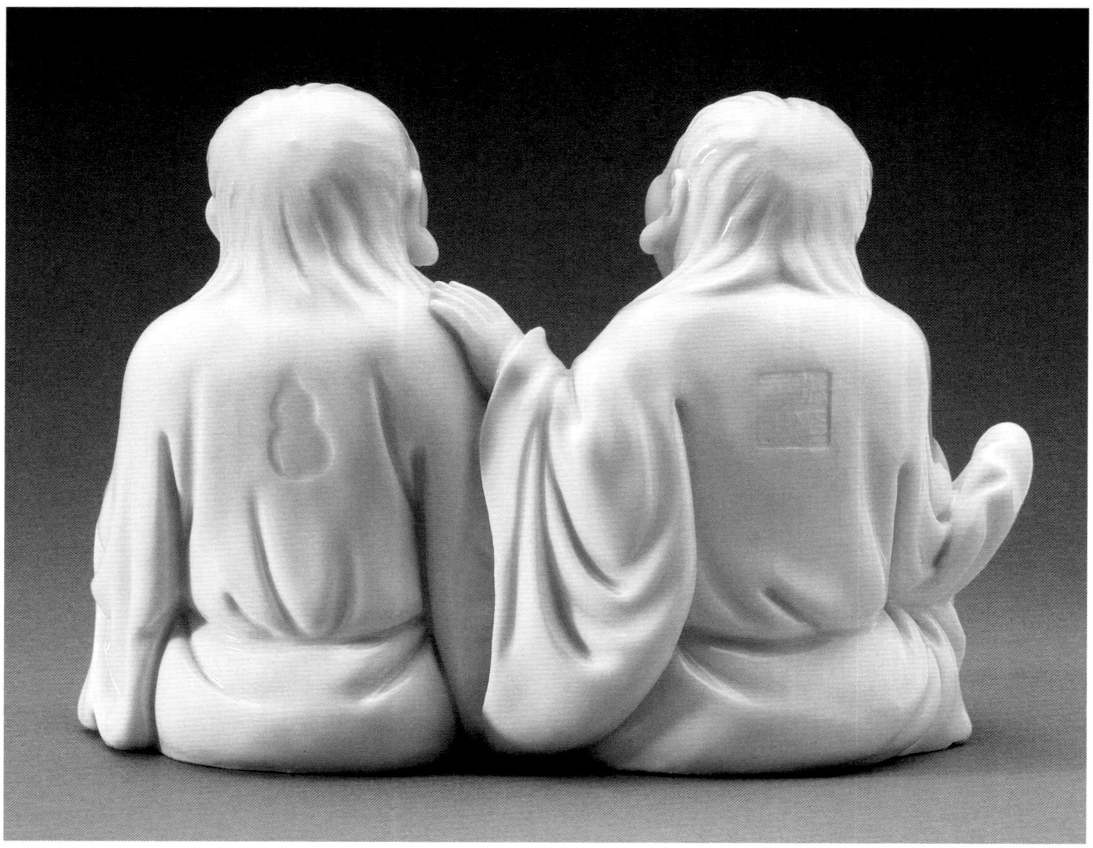

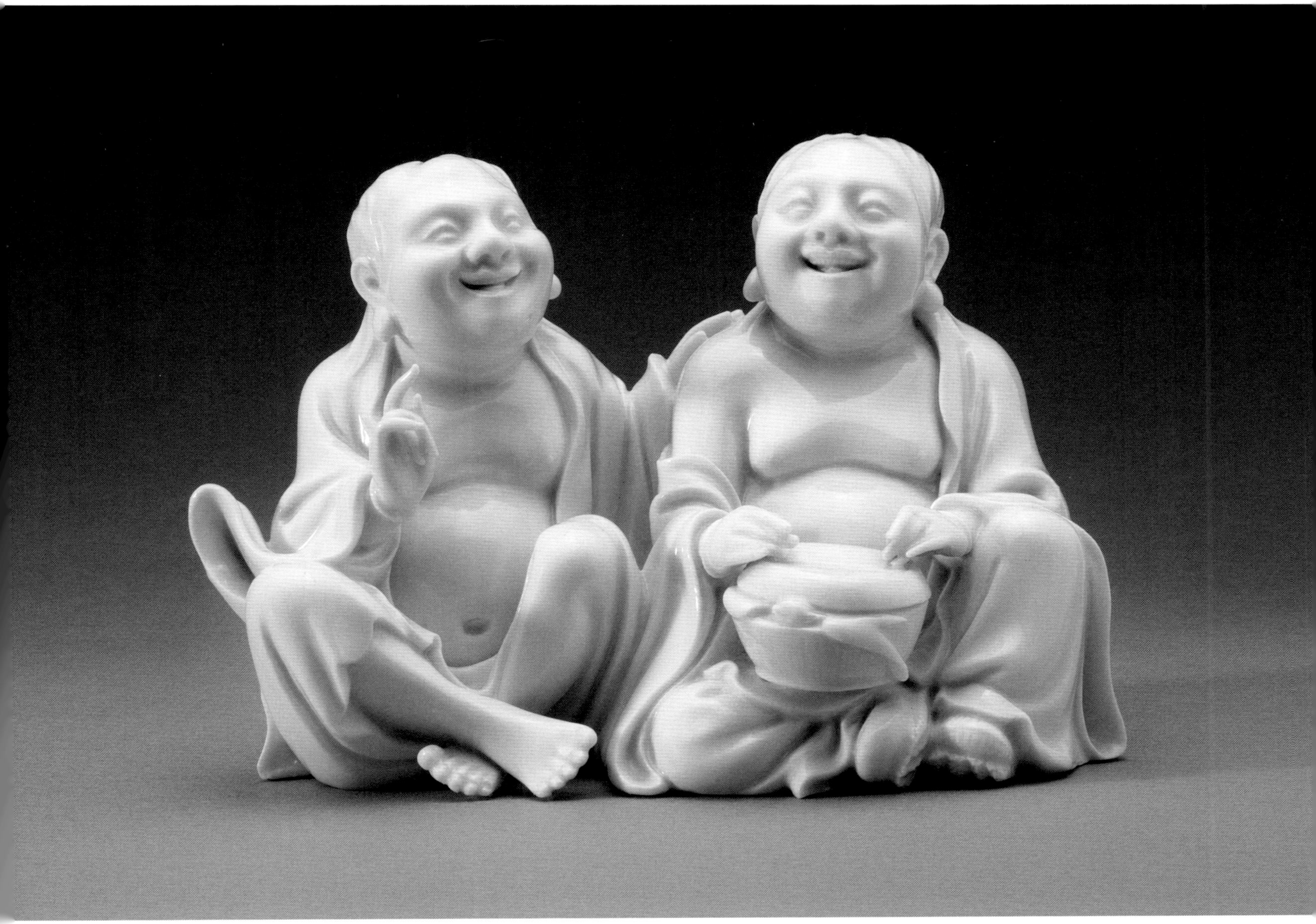

the woven basket and shoe soles, confirms that he was just as skilled as his better-known contemporary He Chaozong (c. 1522–1612).[4] But while He Chaozong was relatively prolific, Zhang Shoushan's identified works number fewer than ten.[5]

The Dehua kilns primarily made utilitarian wares and figures such as this one for local use in the home and at temples, but a limited number of Dehua products were imported to Europe, where they were admired for their exoticism and quality of porcelain. Dehua figures would later inspire European kilns—such as those at Saint-Cloud, west of Paris—to make their own porcelain versions. HK

1. Kerr and Ayers 2002, no. 23.
2. Fong 1990, 48.
3. See Donnelly 1969, 357, for a drawing of the seals.
4. Two sculptures of the twins with He Chaozong's marks are in the British Museum, London (1936.10.12.191, PDF. A447).
5. Blumenfield 2002, 138. Another Dehua figure of the seated twins is illustrated in New York 2002, 91, no. 42.

55

Games Table

Ming dynasty (1368–1644), 17th century
Wood (*huanghuali*; *Dalbergia* sp.), with inlaid ivory or bone
33¼ x 27½ x 38½ inches (84.5 x 69.9 x 97.8 cm)
Purchased with Museum funds, 1958-158-1

Plain and minimalistic in style but fashioned from expensive, precious *huanghuali* hardwood, this flush-sided, corner-leg table with "giant's arm" braces and hoof feet appears at first glance to be a standard rectangular table used for dining or other everyday activities. The top lifts off, however, to reveal a recessed tray inlaid with bone or ivory for the game of double sixes (*shuang lu*). Two long, rectangular hinged compartments flanking the tray have peach-shaped perforations used as finger holds to open the covers of the compartments where the game pieces were stored. The tray and compartments would have been covered by a removable, square, double-sided game board (now lost) for playing two types of Chinese chess, *xiangqi* and *weiqi*, the latter also known by its Japanese name, *go*. Along the short sides of the table are two removable square containers, possibly for holding the pieces and the dice.

Double sixes, in which the two players moved their fifteen game pieces around the board when dice were rolled, is similar to backgammon. The game was played in China from the fifth century to the early nineteenth century and is thought to have originated in India.[1] The shape of the game pieces differed depending on region: bottle- or mallet-shaped pieces were used in the north, while flat, rounded pieces were used in the south and outside China (in Southeast Asia and Japan).[2] The arrangement of this double-sixes board, with rows of six circular markers—"paths" or "roads"—flanking a crescent-shaped "gate" on each long side, indicates a northern style.[3]

Double sixes was a game that had an element of luck in addition to requiring intellect, and was taken up across all levels of society, becoming one of the most popular games in the Song dynasty (906–1279; fig. 48), remaining in fashion through the late Ming dynasty, when this table was made. HK

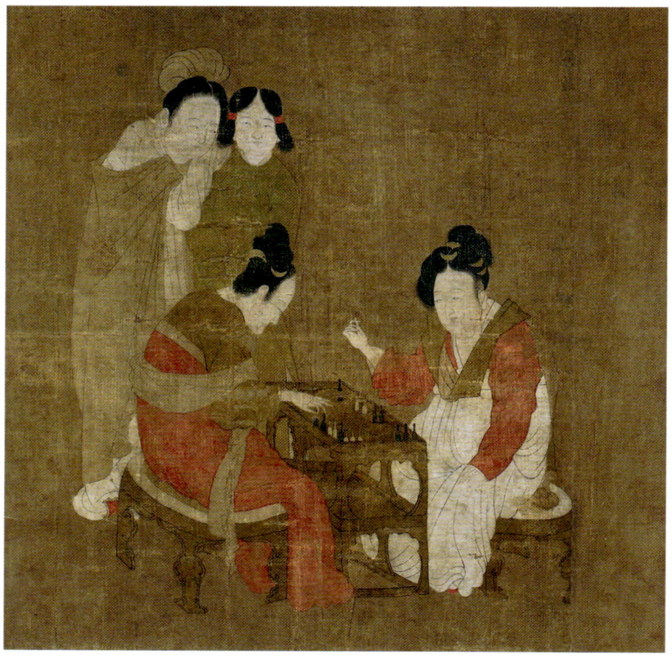

Fig. 48. Traditionally attributed to Zhou Fang (c. 730–c. 800). Detail of *Palace Ladies Playing Double Sixes*. Southern Song dynasty (1127–1279), late 12th to mid-13th century. Ink and color on silk, 12 x 27³⁄₁₆ inches (30.5 x 69.1 cm). Freer Gallery of Art and Arthur M. Sackler Gallery, Smithsonian Institution, Washington, DC. Gift of Jean-Pierre Dubosc, Lugano, Switzerland, F1960.4

1. Lo 2004, 100.
2. Illustrated in Hong Zun's Song dynasty games manual, *Pu shuang*; see Lo 2004, 102.
3. It is similar to the earliest recorded complete double sixes board found with playing pieces and dice in a Liao (10th century) tomb at Yemaotai, Liaoning; illustrated in Xu and Sun 1995, 218, nos. 216-17, where it is suggested that the earliest double sixes game came from West Asia five thousand years ago.

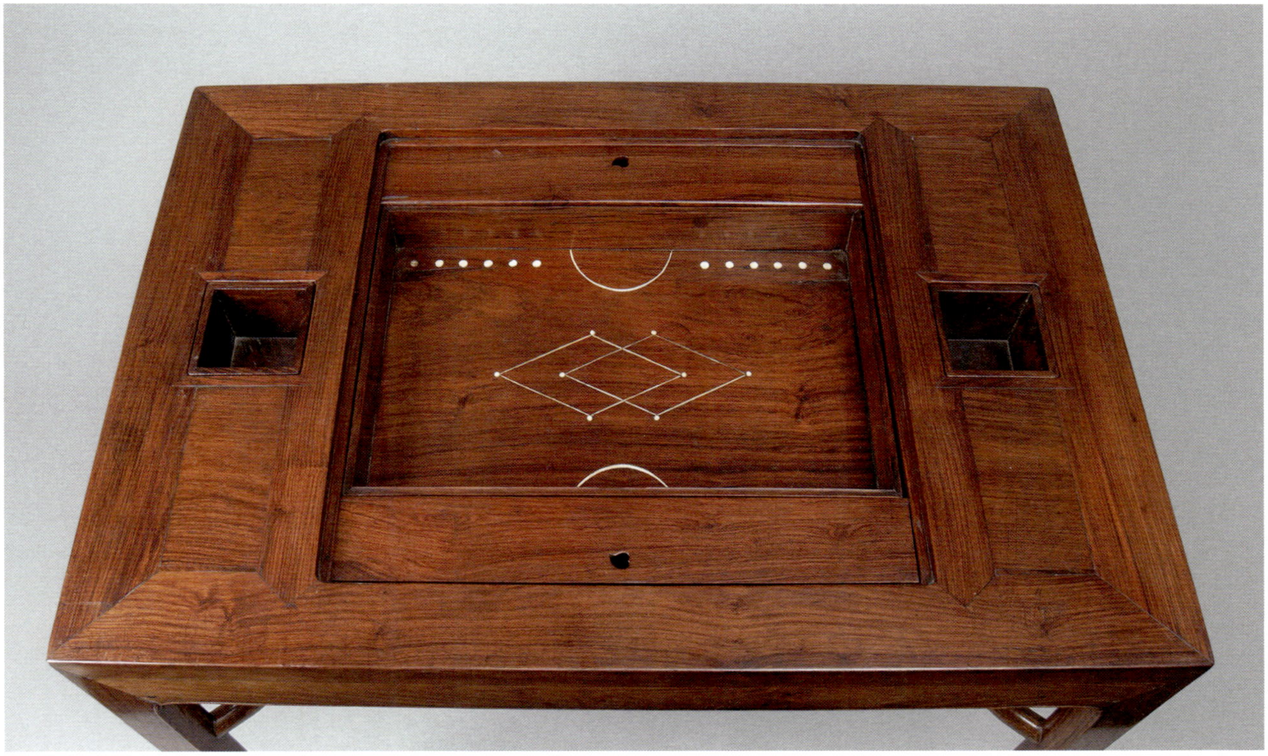

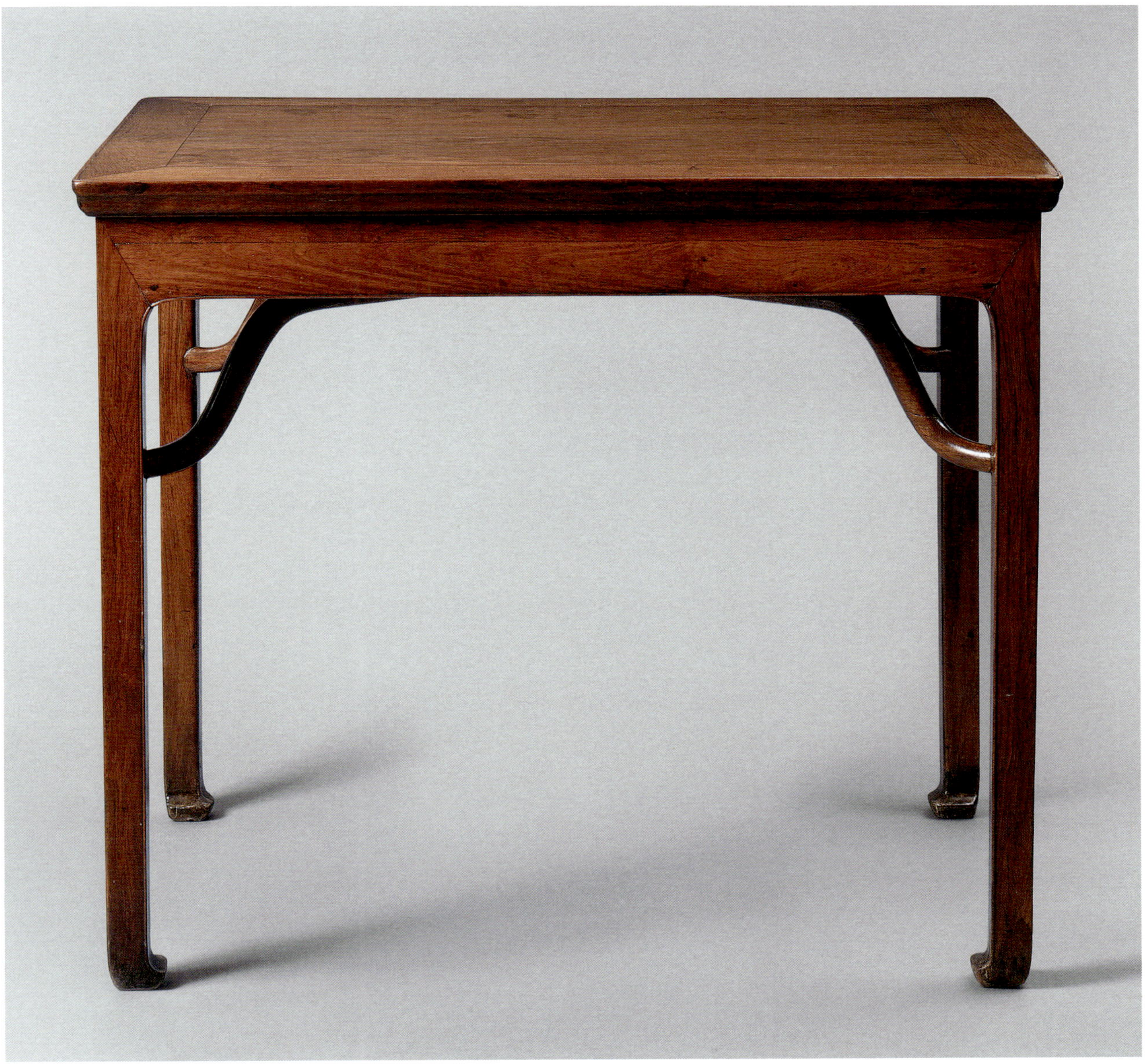

56

Reception Hall from the Palace of Duke Zhao (Zhaogongfu)

Ming dynasty (1368–1644), first half of the 17th century
Wood (red pine group, possibly *Pinus massoniana*) with glue-bound paint
18 feet x 46 feet 4¼ inches x 35 feet 2½ inches (548.6 x 1412.9 x 1073.2 cm)
Gift of Edward B. Robinette, 1929-163-1

The Chinese reception hall installed in the Philadelphia Museum of Art, the sole example of its kind outside of China, was the first main hall of a three-courtyard home of a high official, where guests were greeted and formal activities carried out. In China, the tradition of decorating roof beams with painted designs, as here, has been in practice for over two thousand years.[1]

The soaring ceilings and the brackets of this hall are elaborately decorated with flowers, fruit, and animals, conveying good wishes and prosperity. Among the flowers representing the four seasons is the peony (fig. 49), which blooms in spring and expresses wishes of wealth and rank through its association with Tang-dynasty (618–907) rulers who cultivated the costly flowers and started a peony craze that infiltrated all levels of society. Chrysanthemums and peaches (pp. 150–51, center of main tie beam) symbolize longevity, the latter through their association with the legend of the peach tree that grew in the garden of the mythical Queen Mother of the West, whose fruit was said to grant one eternal life. The black lacquer hanging plaque decorated with five repeating gilded *fu* characters (opposite),[2] meaning happiness or blessings, also conveys good wishes—for wealth, long life, health, love of virtue, and a peaceful death.

This reception hall was part of a larger mansion or palatial complex built in the early 1640s by the wealthy eunuch-official Wang Cheng'en,[3] and was located in the northeast corner of the Inner City, an exclusive enclave reserved for the ruling Manchus.[4] During the Ming dynasty, the size of a residence was based on the rank of the owner. This hall was originally five bays wide (a bay is the space between two columns), the standard size of an official's residence. The hall originally consisted of a stone platform paved with gray stone floor tiles, above which the brick and timber structure was raised (fig. 50), with columns supporting the weight of a tiled roof and with lattice doors and windows to let in light. After Wang Cheng'en's death, his palace was passed down through various noble families, including that of Prince Li, a grandson of the Kangxi emperor. Its current name comes from its last resident and owner, during the Xuantong period (1909–11).

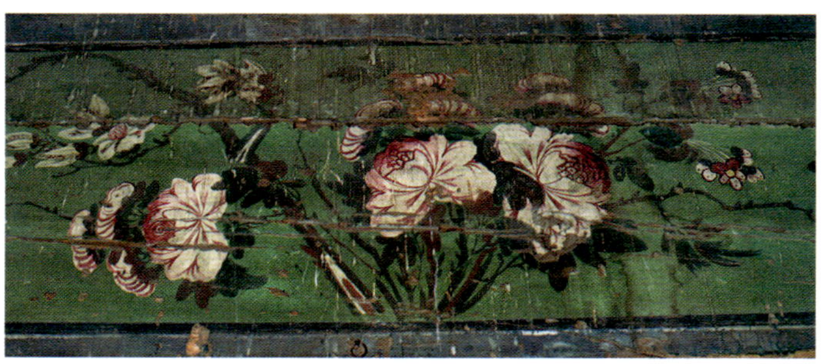

Fig. 49. Detail of peonies painted on the side of the main tie beam to the left of the main entrance

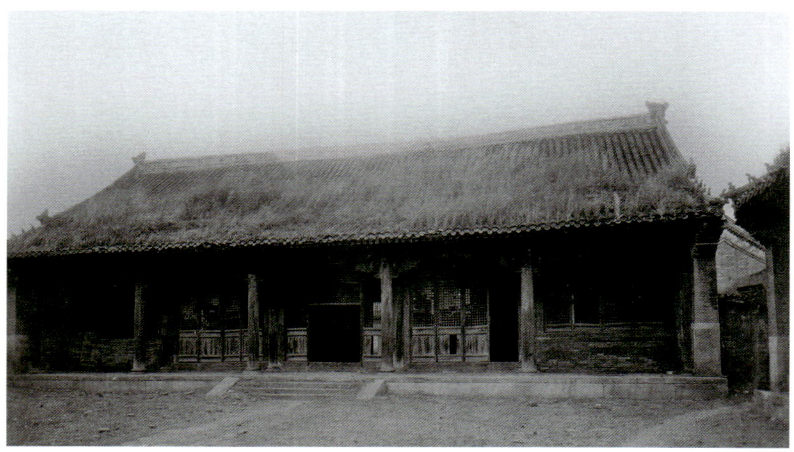

Fig. 50. The main entrance to the Reception Hall in Beijing before it was dismantled, 1928. Philadelphia Museum of Art, Library and Archives

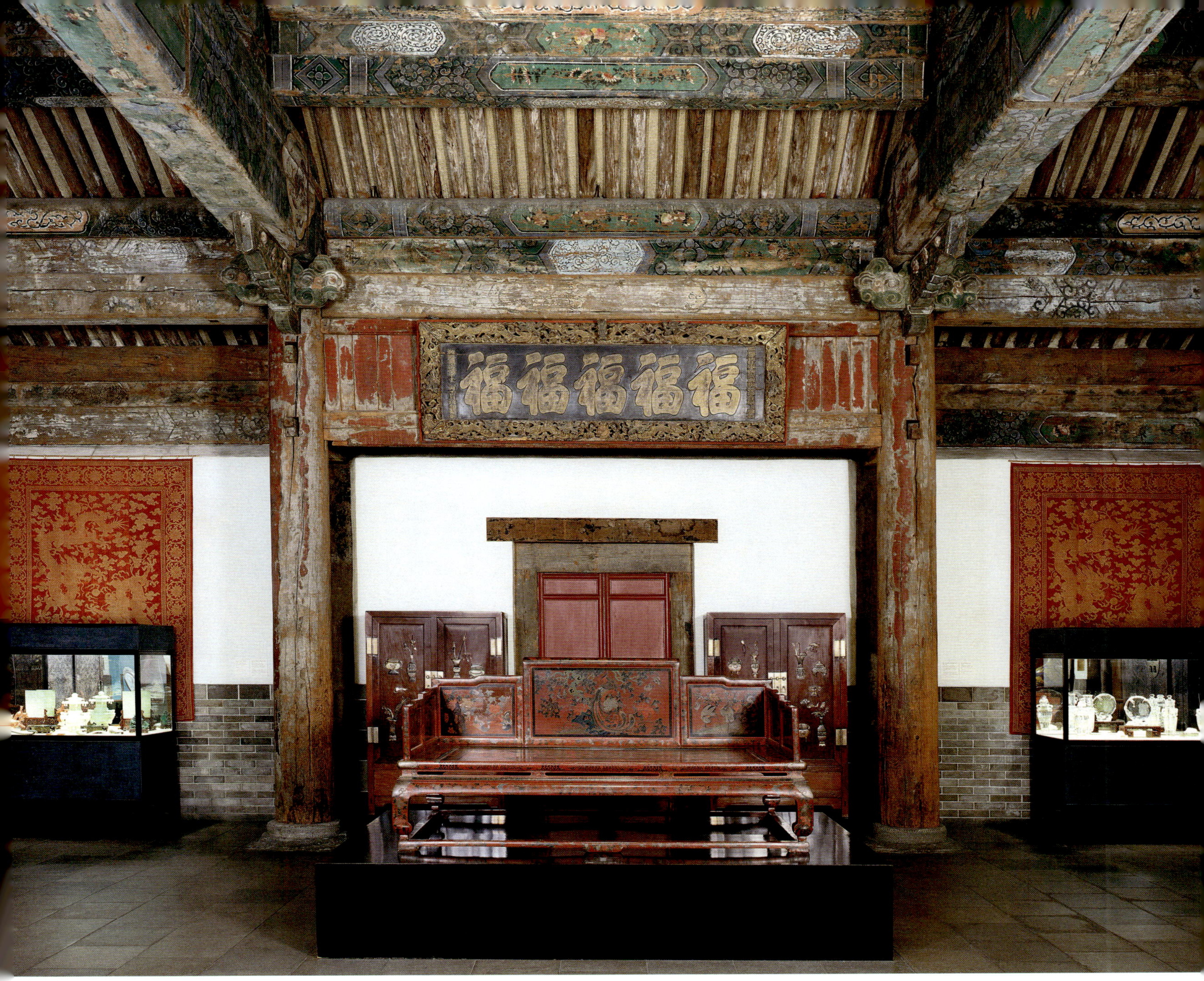

In 1928 the museum's curator of oriental art, Horace H. F. Jayne, traveled to China with the express aim of acquiring Chinese interiors for the museum. Through the dealer Edith A. Punnett, he found this hall in a state of disrepair and purchased it from the family that owned it. Eight years later, the beams, purlins, and posts were reassembled by American craftsmen in the museum's gallery (see pp. 22–23),[5] with some modifications made to the structure to accommodate the smaller space. HK

1. As is typical with Chinese wooden architecture, the painted decoration was touched up over time. Two to three layers of decoration were detected through cross-sectioning of the paint layers. See Sally Malenka and Beth A. Price's essay on the conservation of the painted decoration in Proser, Malenka, and Price 2004, 36–37.
2. The plaque (acc. no. 1929-88-38) may not be original to the reception hall. It commemorates General Rong Bao, who served the Qianlong emperor (r. 1736–95).
3. Wang Cheng'en served the Chongzhen emperor (r. 1628–44) in the Ceremonial Directorate, transcribing and writing imperial memoranda and other communications. He was made supervisor of the capital barracks in 1643, and it was around this time that he built his palatial complex. He famously hanged himself when the last Ming emperor committed suicide at the fall of the dynasty to prevent capture by rebels. See Proser, Malenka, and Price 2004, 15.
4. The Inner City surrounded the Forbidden City, where the emperor and his family resided and held court. See Proser, Malenka, and Price 2004, 16, fig. 7.
5. The work was paid for through the Works Progress Administration (WPA), a federal work-relief program to engage workers during the Depression on projects of public usefulness. Chinese characters had been written in ink on the wood elements in order to assist in the assembly.

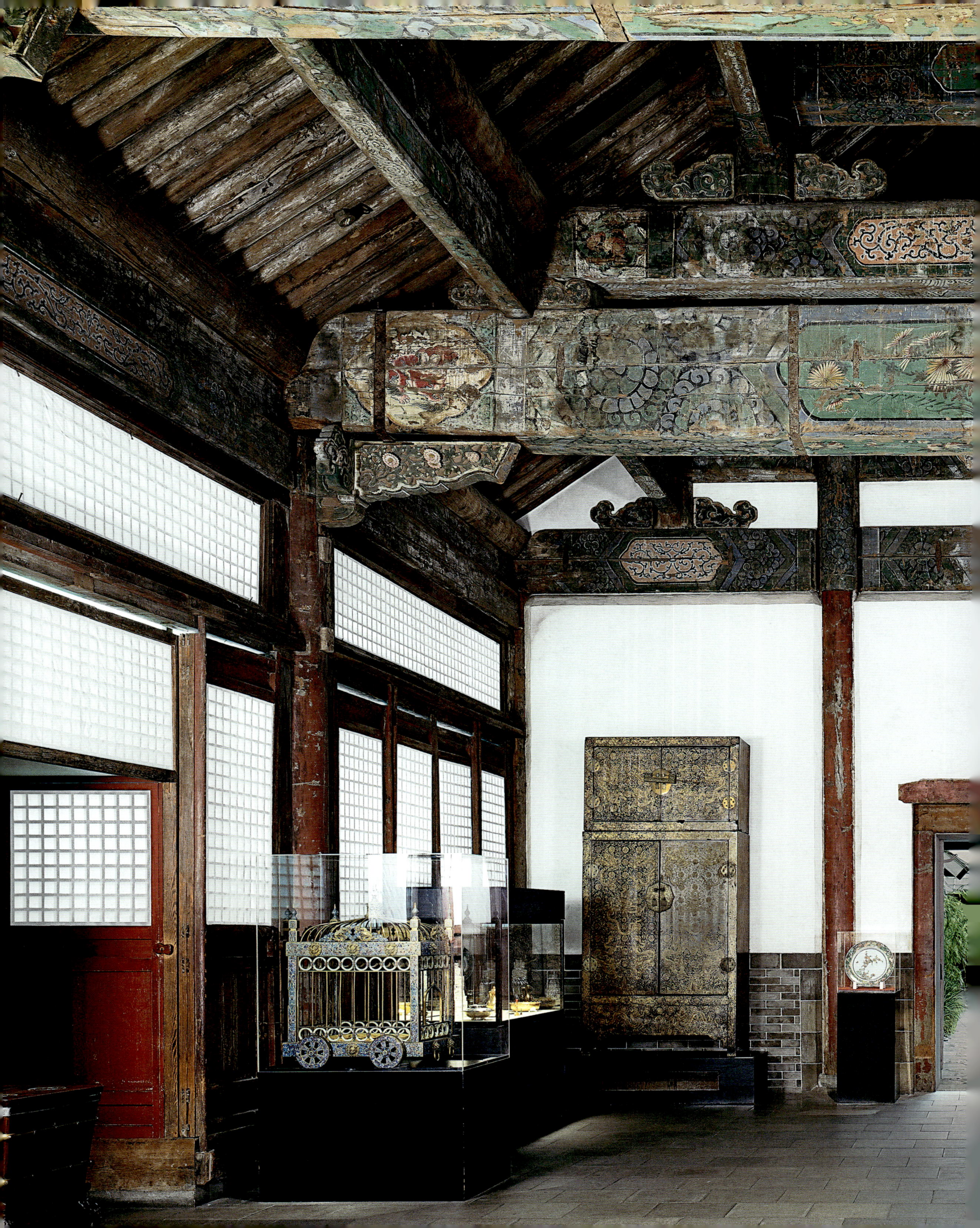

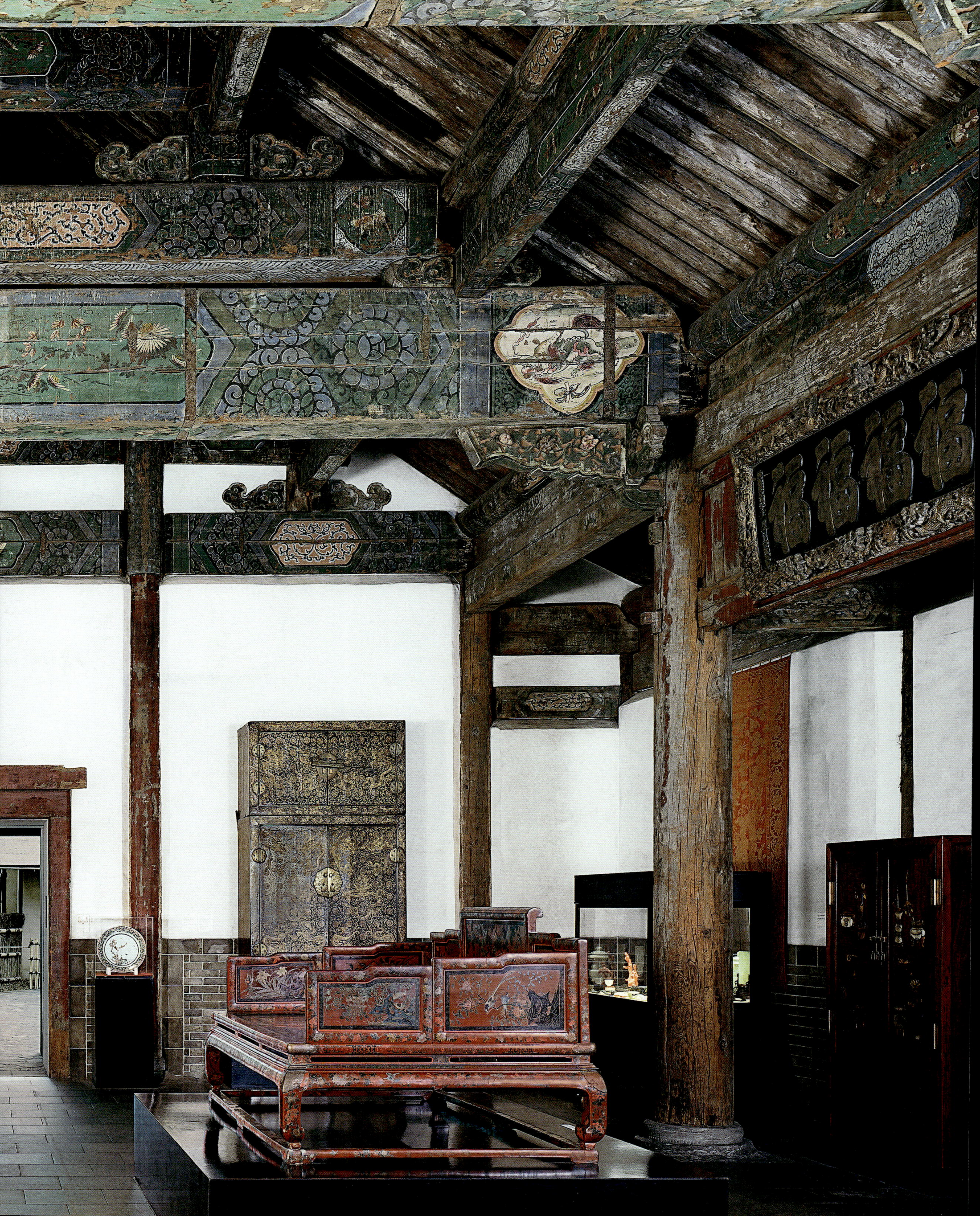
福福福福

57

Insignia Badge for an Imperial Noble or Military Officer

Qing dynasty (1644–1911), Kangxi period (1662–1722)
Silk gauze embroidered with floss silk in satin stitch; couched gold leaf on paper-wrapped thread and peacock-feather-wrapped thread
14¾ x 13¾ inches (37.5 x 34.9 cm)
Purchased with the John T. Morris Fund from the Carl Schuster Collection, 1940-4-731

Boldly patterned pictorial badges (*buzi*) prominently displayed on the chest and back of official robes were among the most overt displays of rank and status in late imperial China.[1] Although a variety of symbols had been used since antiquity to indicate rank, an all-inclusive court ranking system was instituted in 1391 and continued in force with small adjustments until 1911. Different categories of beasts distinguished the aristocracy from the gentry, while other types differentiated status within the nine grades of the military and civil bureaucracies.[2] Various dragons identified members of the imperial family and princes of the first to eighth ranks.

This badge is decorated with a *qilin*, one of the four benevolent mythical beasts (see no. 48). The *qilin* identified nobles of the ninth rank, as well as military officers of the first rank. (Nobles of the tenth through twelfth ranks were assigned other animals; see no. 36). *Buzi* were made in pairs. This badge was designed for the back of a robe; its pair for the front of a robe is now in the collection of the Metropolitan Museum of Art, New York (36.65.6) JV

1. Ebrey 1981, 126, 177–9.
2. Cammann 1942, 2–28; Cammann 1944, 71–130; Vollmer and Simcox 2009, 62–63, 74.

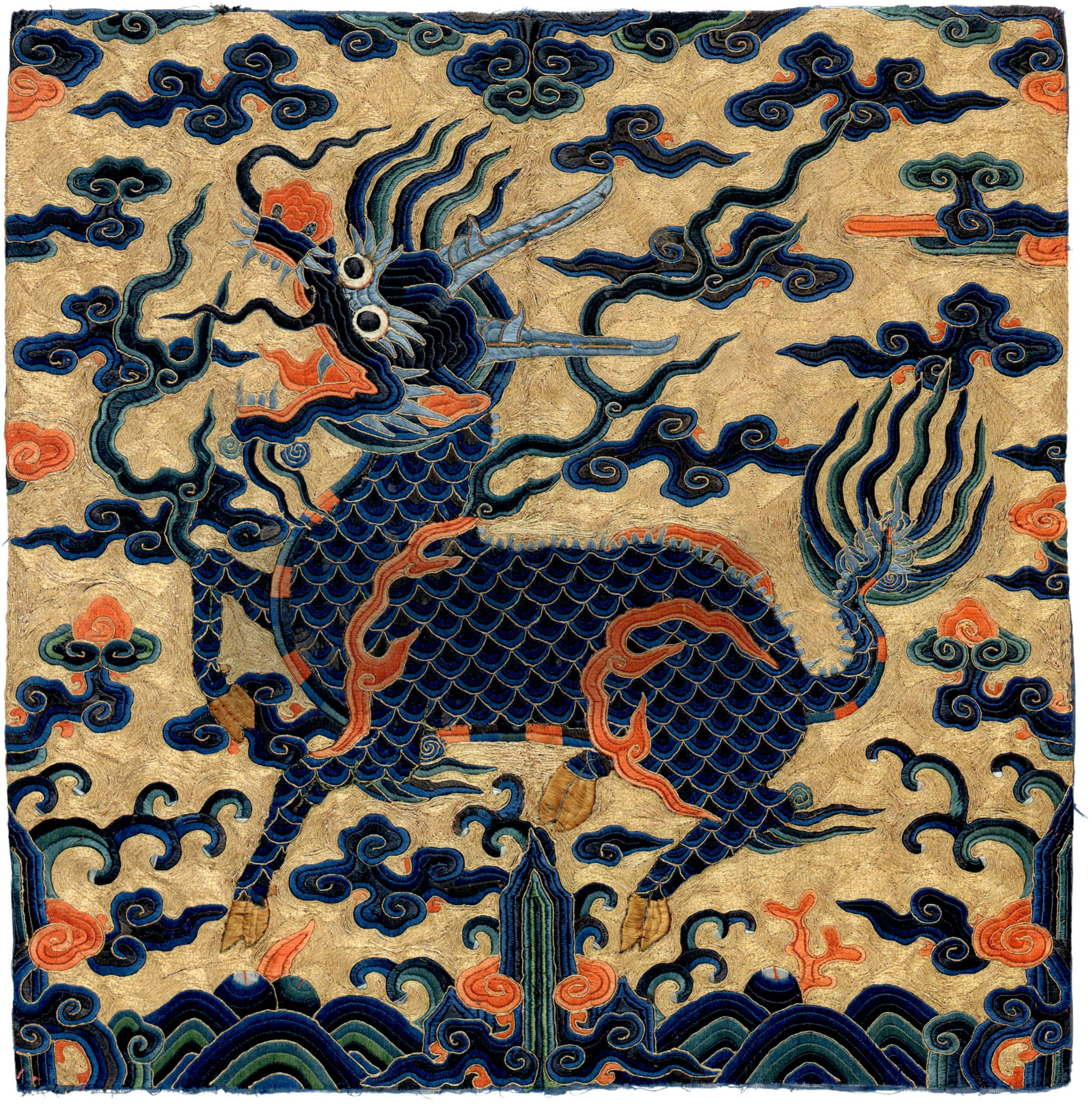

58

Liu Du (act. c. 1628–75)
Landscapes

Qing dynasty (1644–1911), 1670
Ink and color on silk, mounted as album leafs
Each 12⅝ x 14¼ inches (32.1 x 36.2 cm)
Purchased with Museum funds from the Simkhovitch Collection, 1929-40-82a–e

These scenes of tranquil riverside villages offer a glimpse into the versatile style of Liu Du, known primarily for his monumental landscapes rendered in vivid colors.[1] Liu was a student of Lan Ying (1585–1664), a professional painter with a reputation for producing conventional works derived from the landscape traditions of the court of the Song dynasty (960–1279).[2] Liu had a good command of the varied techniques and trademarks of earlier land-scapists in the canon of Chinese art.[3] His well-rounded skills and art-historical knowledge, when applied in large-scale compositions emulating the styles of the old masters, can seem restrictive. But in smaller landscape scenes he was able to escape the mannerism associated with the Lan school and focus on expressing his own vision and demonstrating his grasp of a wide array of brushwork techniques.[4] Liu's sensitive handling of ink tonality in the rhythmic compositions found on these five leaves is reminiscent of the scholarly expression first exemplified by masters of the Yuan dynasty (1271–1368).[5]

As noted in his inscription on the last leaf, Liu was a native of Qiantang, part of modern-day Hangzhou in Zhejiang province, which has been a cultural center of China since it served as the capital of the Southern Song dynasty (1127–1279). The Qiantang River that courses through Hangzhou is known for its attractive scenery, inspiring poetic compositions as early as the Tang dynasty (618–907). The local sights may have inspired Liu to create these lyrical landscapes,[6] which appear to have survived from an original set of twelve leaves.[7] DL

1. These are largely hanging scrolls, such as the paintings *Villa in Spring Mountains* at the National Palace Museum in Taipei, dated to 1636, and *The Peach Blossom Spring* at the Cleveland Museum of Art, dated to 1650.
2. Lan Ying and his followers are traditionally categorized as the last remnants of the Zhe school, although this designation has been challenged by some modern scholars; see, for example, Chou and Chung 2015, 321. Emerging in the early Ming dynasty with the pioneering artist Dai Jin (1388–1462), the Zhe school (Zhejiang province; 15th–early 17th century) revived the artistic traditions of the Southern Song painting academy; Zhe-school painting is characterized by powerful brushwork and an untrammeled quality.
3. Liu Du's extant paintings reveal indebtedness to Li Cheng (919–967) and Zhao Mengfu (1254–1322), known, respectively, for monochrome landscapes done with dry, dense brushwork, and for evoking an archaic impression through the use of color.
4. Liu's biography in the *Tuhui baojian xubian* (Additional Compilation of the *Precious Mirror of Painting*) mentions that "the smallest of his paintings are especially excellent"; see Yu 1974, vol. 2, 877. Translations are my own unless otherwise noted.
5. The discrepancy between Liu's large scrolls and small album leaves may be attributed to the different functions and audiences of these works, as hanging scrolls often served a decorative purpose, while album leaves were meant for private appreciation. For a discussion on "the uses of paintings" in late Ming, see Cahill 1994, 33–35.
6. Although later Chinese painters, such as Lan Ying and Liu Du, honed their skills primarily through copying earlier archetypes, they also made paintings by directly observing nature. Lan was noted for being an avid traveler and painted at least two sets of albums titled *Cheng guan shanshui* (Landscape from Pure Observation); see Liu 1997, 410, 413.
7. This supposition is based on information recorded on the title slip that came with these paintings (written by the previous owner). Liu also made a set of twelve landscape leaves in 1659, which he described as "copying natural sceneries" in his inscription. See Christie's Hong Kong, *Fine Classical Chinese Paintings and Calligraphy*, May 30, 2005, lot 980.

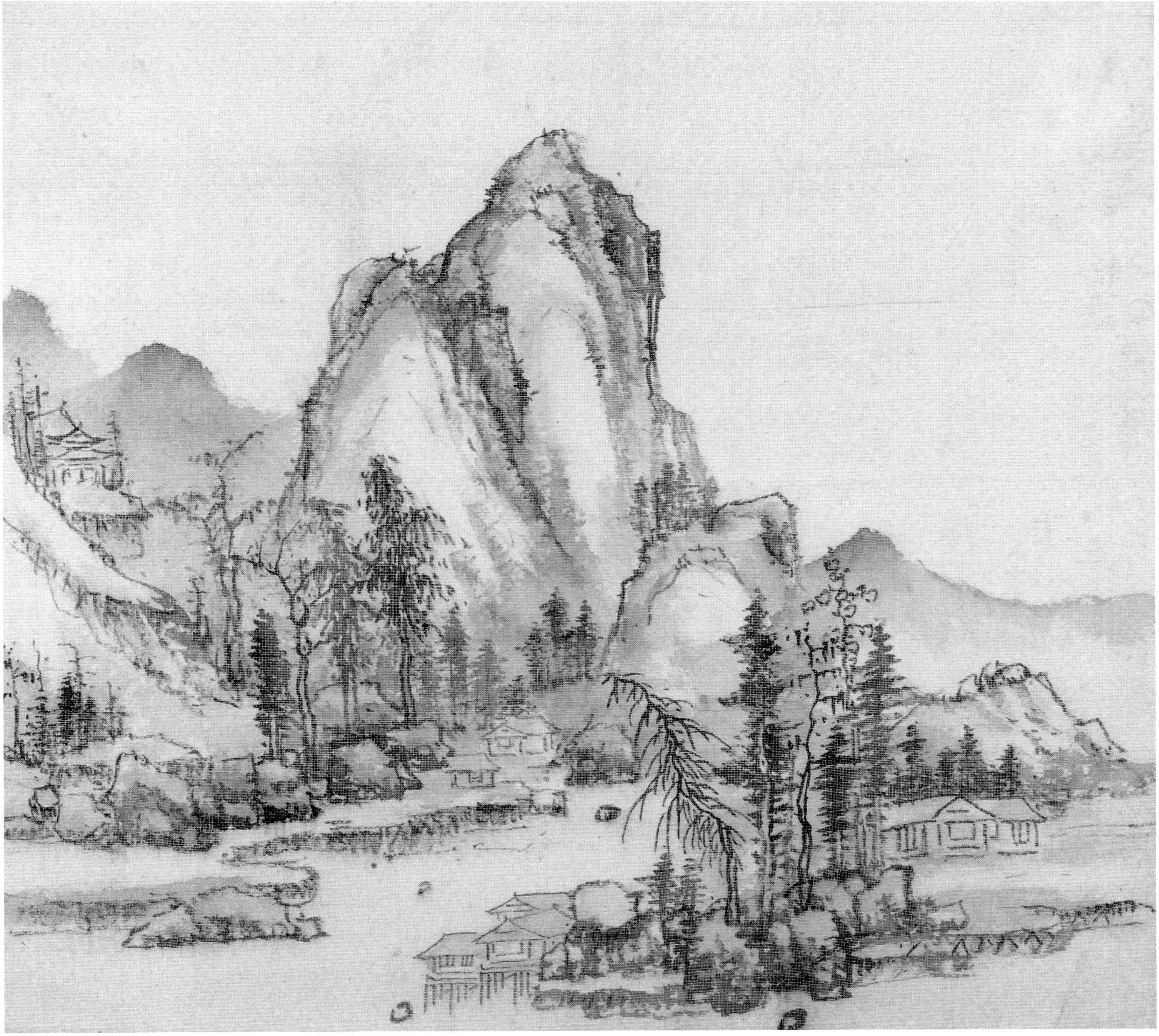

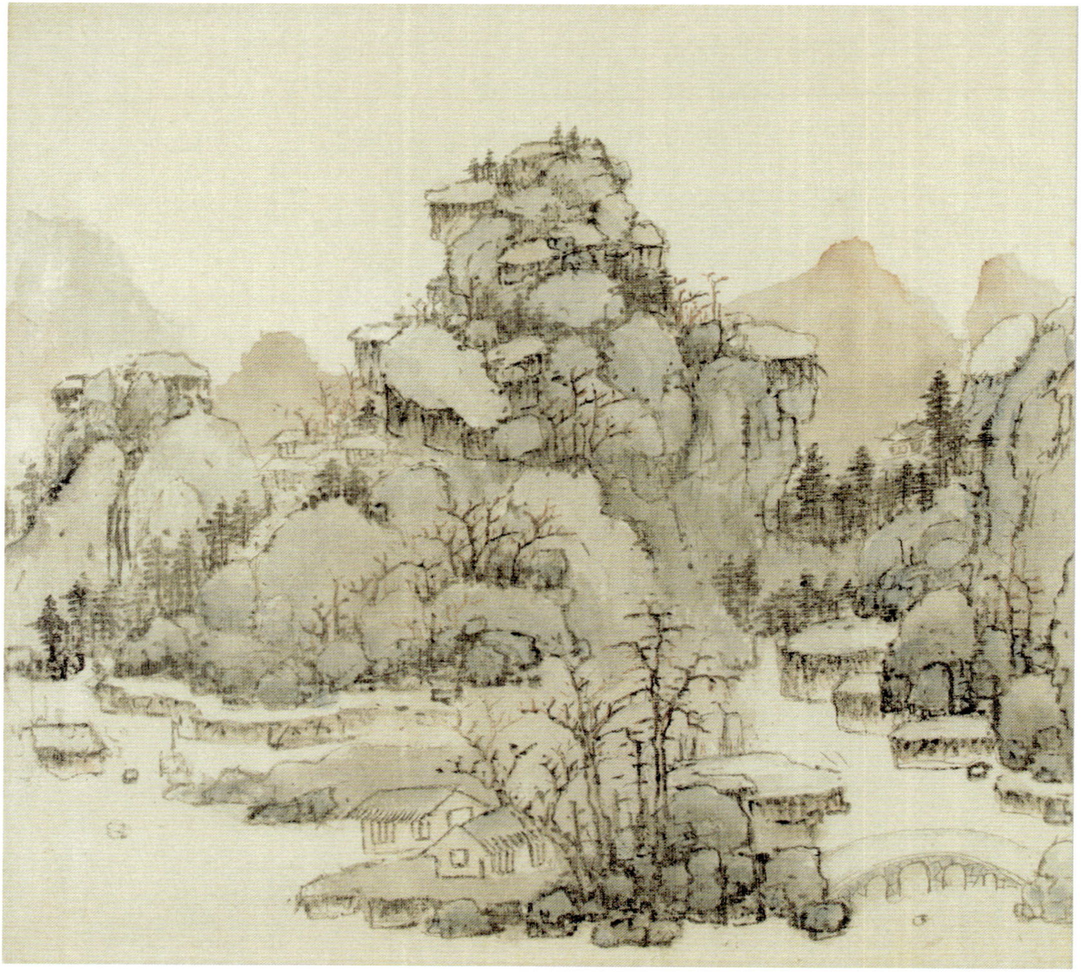

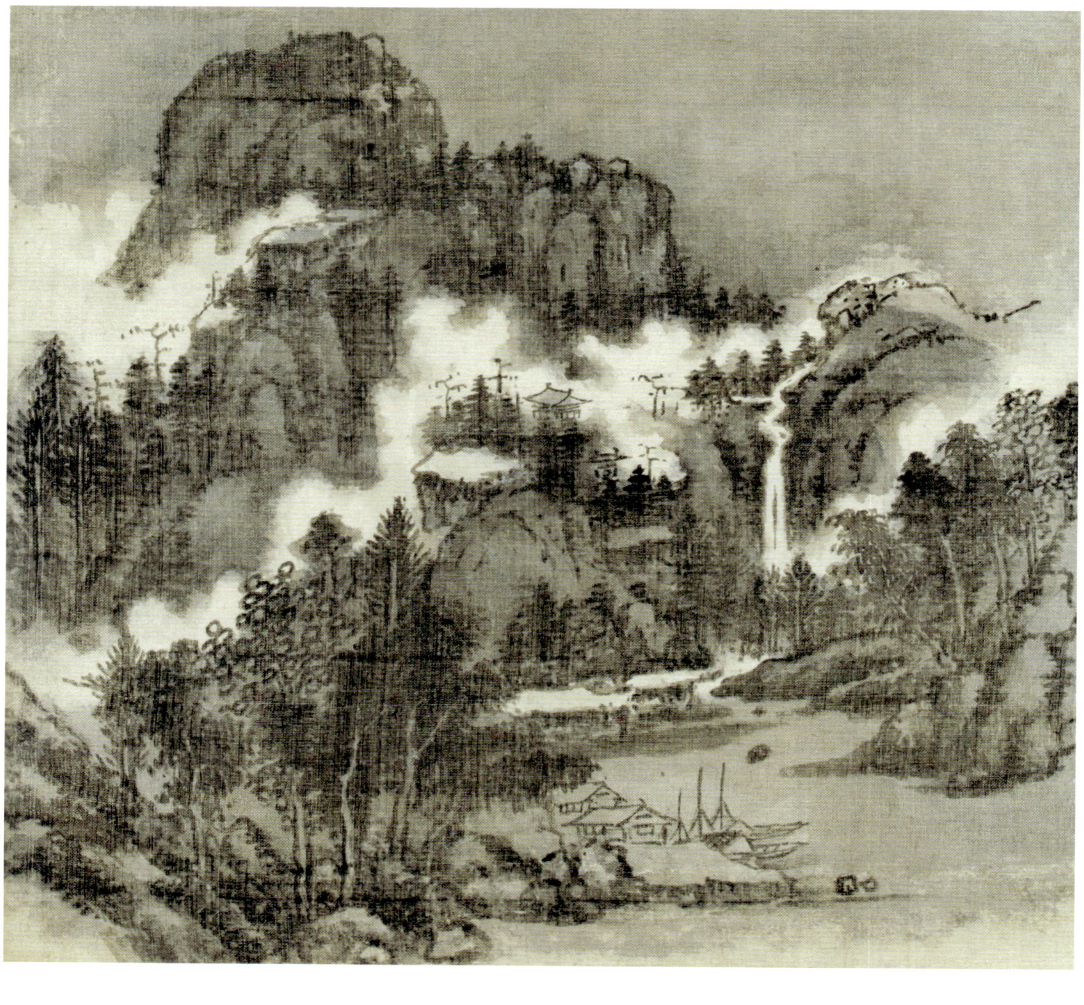

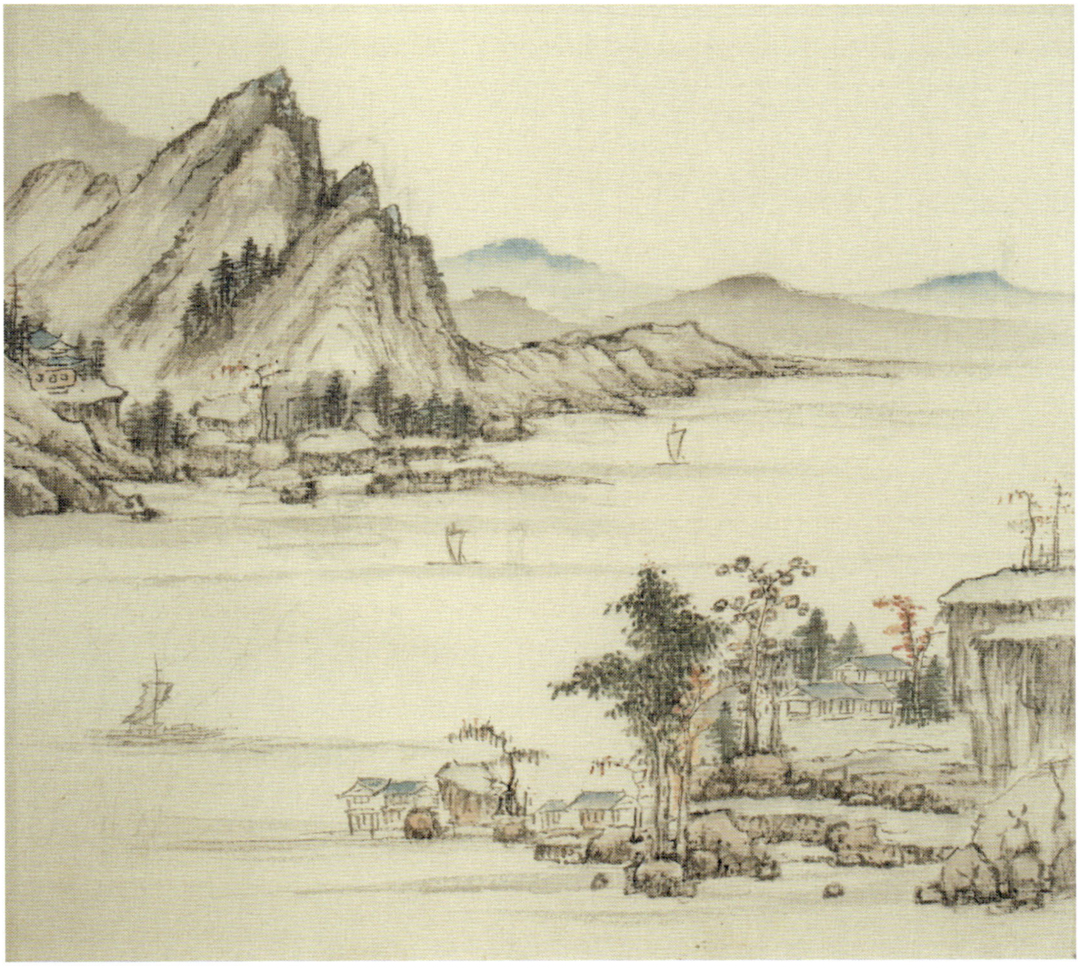

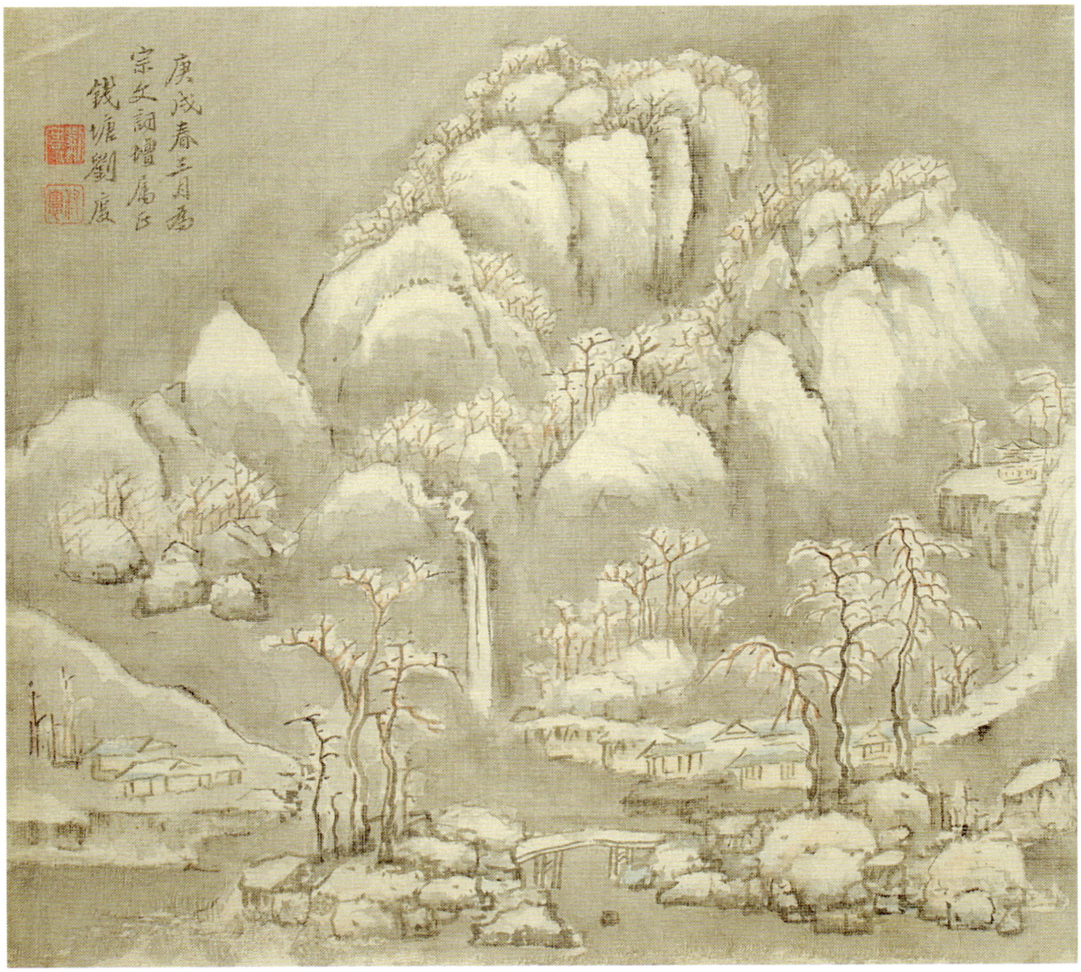
庚戌春三月為
宗文詞壇屬正
錢塘劉度

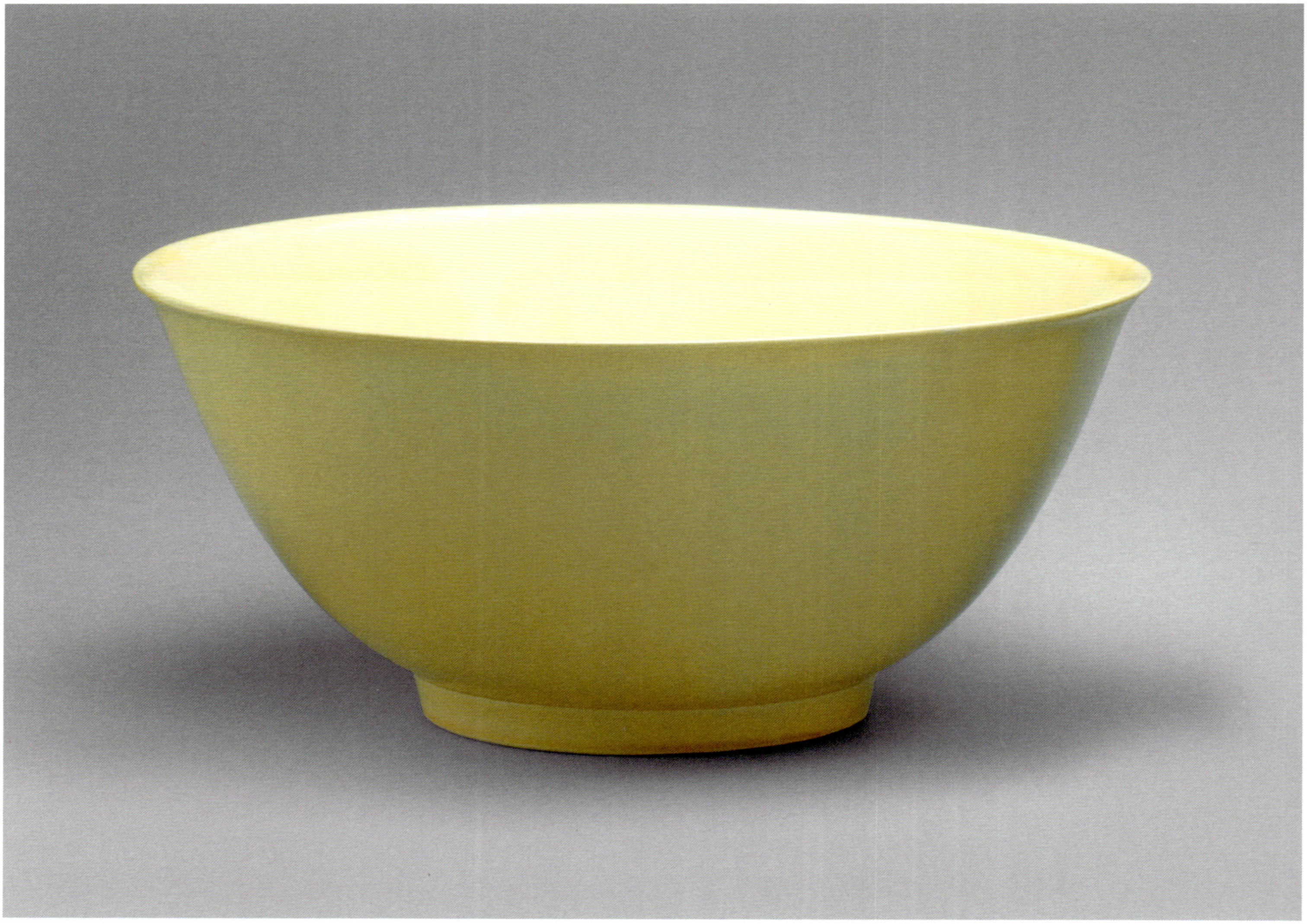

59

Large Imperial Yellow Bowls

Qing dynasty (1644–1911), Kangxi period (1662–1722)
Porcelain with yellow glaze (Jingdezhen ware)
6⅞ x 14¾ inches (17.5 x 37.5 cm)
Purchased with the Henry P. McIlhenny Fund in memory of Frances P. McIlhenny and the Henry B. Keep Fund, and with gifts (by exchange) of Mrs. Henry W. Breyer, Sr., Mrs. William B. Hackenburg in memory of her husband, Mrs. D. B. Kase, the Dr. Robert H. Lamborn Collection, Richard M. Samson, the Simon A. Stern Collection, and Mrs. David Townsend in memory of her husband, and with bequests (by exchange) of Morris R. Bockius, Mary H. Griffith, and Helen E. Hayday, 1989-75-1, 1989-75-2

These large, heavy bowls are covered in a bright egg-yolk yellow enamel glaze, while their white-glazed bases carry a six-character Kangxi mark fired to a matt blue (see p. 247). Yellow porcelains were restricted to members of the imperial family, used for utilitarian purposes such as eating and drinking as well as in ritual ceremonies. The yellow enamel was typically produced using a small amount of iron, the main colorant that yielded the various tones of yellow on porcelains with imperial marks produced in the Ming (1368–1644) and Qing dynasties (see

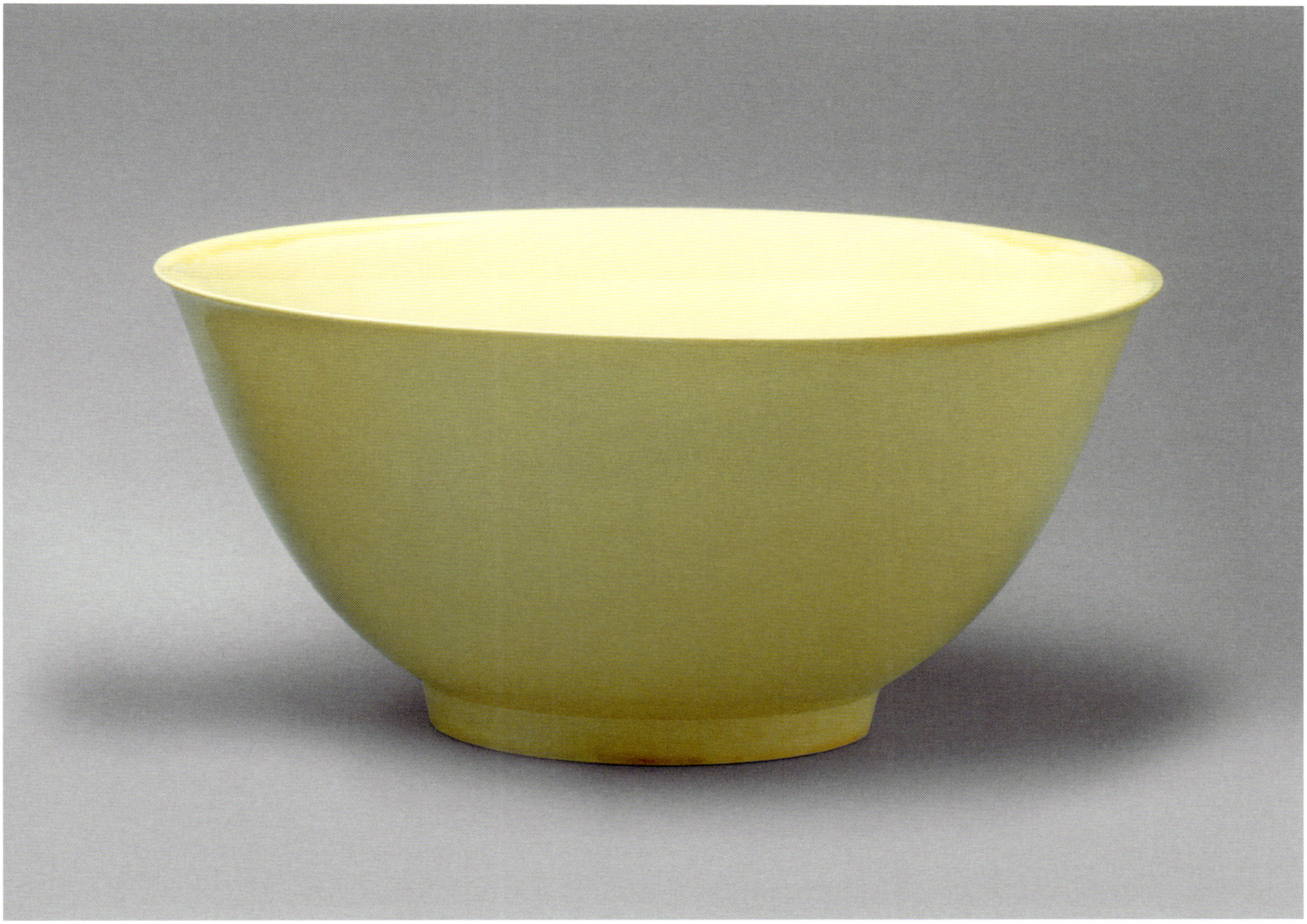

no. 40). During the Kangxi period, a light yellow opaque glaze was introduced that used antimony as its colorant, though it was the earlier glaze that came to be known as "imperial yellow."

Beginning in 1530, the emperor and his officials would make regular state sacrifices at the Altars to Heaven, Earth, Sun, and Moon. Symbolically laid out within the imperial city oriented to the cardinal directions, each altar was assigned a color.[1] At the Altar to Earth, located in the north, yellow robes were worn by those officiating, and yellow-glazed ritual vessels containing food and wine were offered to appease the earth spirits every summer solstice. These large, deep bowls may have been used to hold wine in such ritual ceremonies.[2]

In the Qing dynasty, palace regulations outlined strict rules for the use of yellow porcelains: those that were completely glazed in yellow both inside and out, like these bowls, were for use by the emperor, empress, and the dowager empress (the emperor's mother);[3] those glazed yellow on the outside but white on the inside were for imperial concubines. HK

1. The Altars to Heaven, Earth, Sun, and Moon used ritual vessels coated in blue, yellow, red, and "moon white" glazes, respectively; London 2005–6, 396–97, no. 37.
2. Xu and Nanjing 2003, 119, illustrates a similar-sized yellow-glazed Kangxi bowl in the Nanjing Museum. Other ritual ceremonies that had to be regularly performed included sacrificing to agriculture, to sericulture, and to the imperial ancestors. See Berger and Yuan 2005.
3. Chapter 17 in *History of the Palace* (*Guochao gongshi*) by E'ertai and others was completed in 1742 and rewritten in 1769. It outlines palace regulations, rituals, and expenses. See Hong Kong 1995, no. 5.

60

Scholar's Desk Implements: Vase, Brush Washer, and Water Coupe

Qing dynasty (1644–1911), Kangxi period (1662–1722), late 17th century
Porcelain with peach-bloom glaze (Jingdezhen ware)
8½ x 3½ inches (21.6 x 8.9 cm); 1½ x 5 inches (3.8 x 12.7 cm); 3½ x 5 inches (8.9 x 12.7 cm)
The Alfred and Margaret Caspary Memorial Gift, 1955-50-51 (left), and 1955-50-52 (lower right); Gift of Mrs. Herbert C. Morris, 1977-255-1a (upper right)

This small vase, brush washer, and water coupe are decorated with a peach-bloom glaze, one of the innovative glazes produced during the reign of the Kangxi emperor.[1] Copper red is notoriously difficult to control in firing, so producing a glaze using this pigment required great skill. The challenge is illustrated by the variety of colors found in peach-bloom glazes, which range from a kidney-bean[2] or apple red to dusty or pale pink with mottled patches of green. The technique involved first applying a clear glaze to the surface of the pot, with the copper pigment layered on top, possibly blown on, and another clear glaze applied over the pigment. When fired, the different concentrations of copper in the glaze transformed into various shades of pinkish red or mottled green, creating an effect much like the variegated skin of a ripening peach.

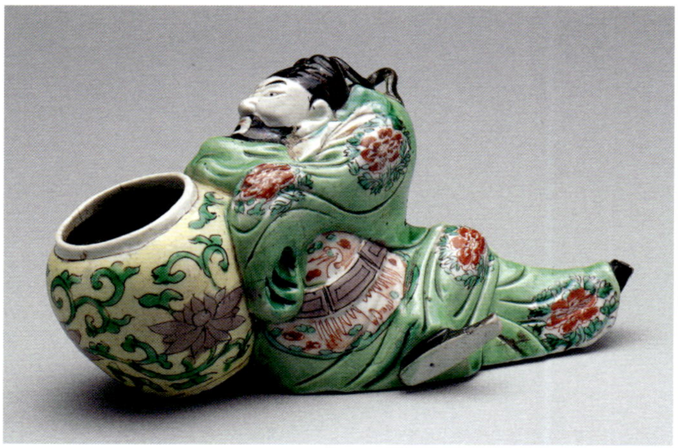

Fig. 51. Water Pot in the Form of Li Taibo. Qing dynasty, Kangxi period. Porcelain with enamel decoration on the biscuit (*famille verte*), 3⅞ x 7¼ x 3⅜ inches (9.8 x 18.4 x 8.6 cm). Philadelphia Museum of Art. The Alfred and Margaret Caspary Memorial Gift, 1955-50-200

This glaze was used on a limited number of forms, all intended for the scholar's table.[3] The vase, with its delicately incised band of chrysanthemum petals around the base, was probably used to hold flowers, while the water coupe and the brush washer would have been used as writing implements. The water-coupe form is called "Taibo's wine jar" in Chinese, after the celebrated eighth-century poet Li Taibo or Li Bai, who famously composed poetry while inebriated and thus is often shown leaning against a large rounded wine jar similar in form (fig. 51).

Two of these implements once belonged to the noted collector of Chinese art Leonard Gow (1859–1936); in 1938 Gow sold the greater part of his collection to Alfred H. Caspary of New York (1877–1955), who bequeathed more than four hundred pieces to the Philadelphia Museum of Art (see p. 27). HK

1. The peach-bloom glaze is thought to have been produced for a short period of time by Liu Yuan, who worked in the imperial kilns in the late seventeenth century; see Lam 2005–6, 53–57.
2. While Westerners call this glaze "peach-bloom," the Chinese describe it as "kidney-bean red," among other names; see Yang 1999, nos. 18, 19.
3. See Ayers 1999–2000, p. 49.

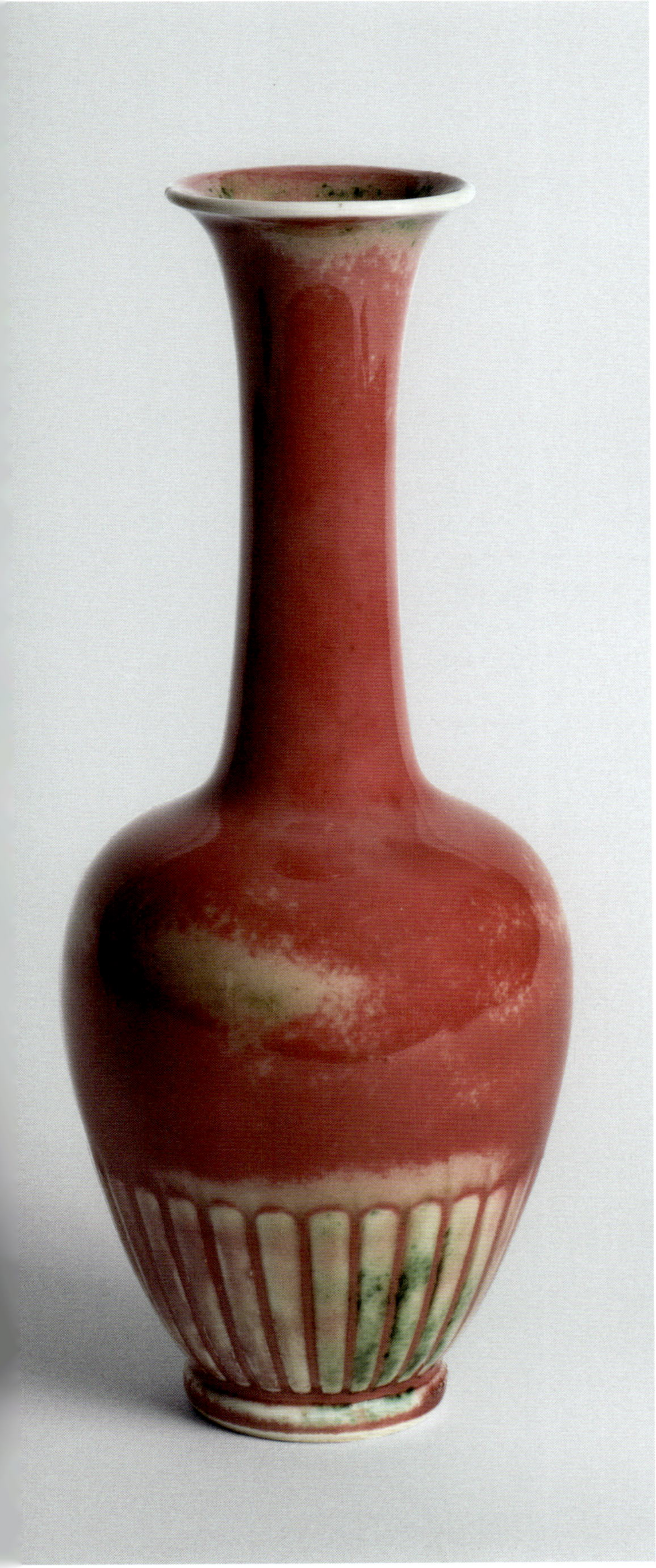
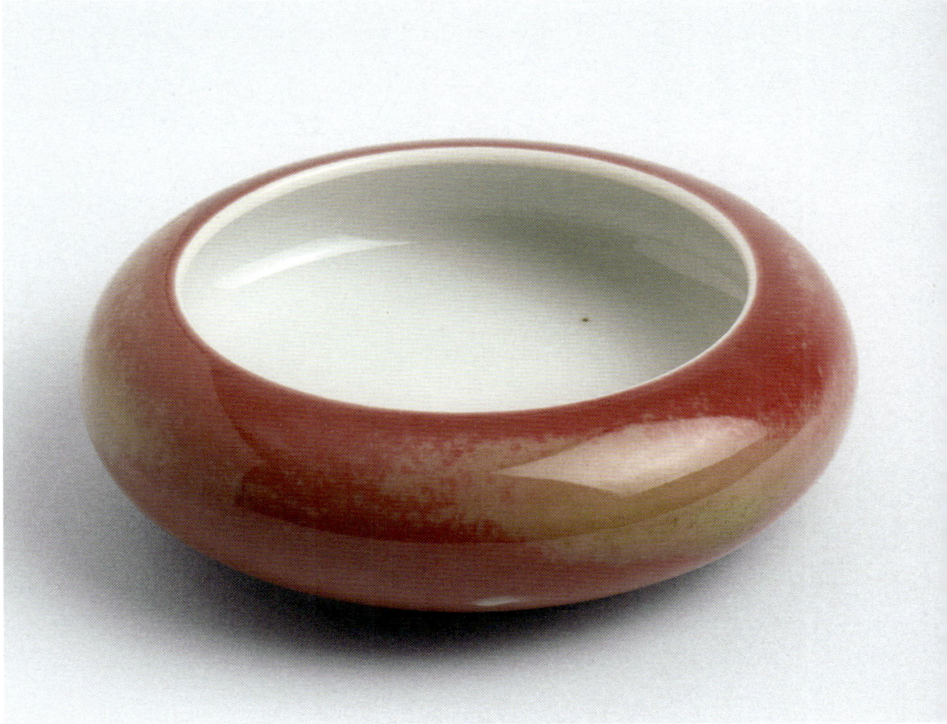
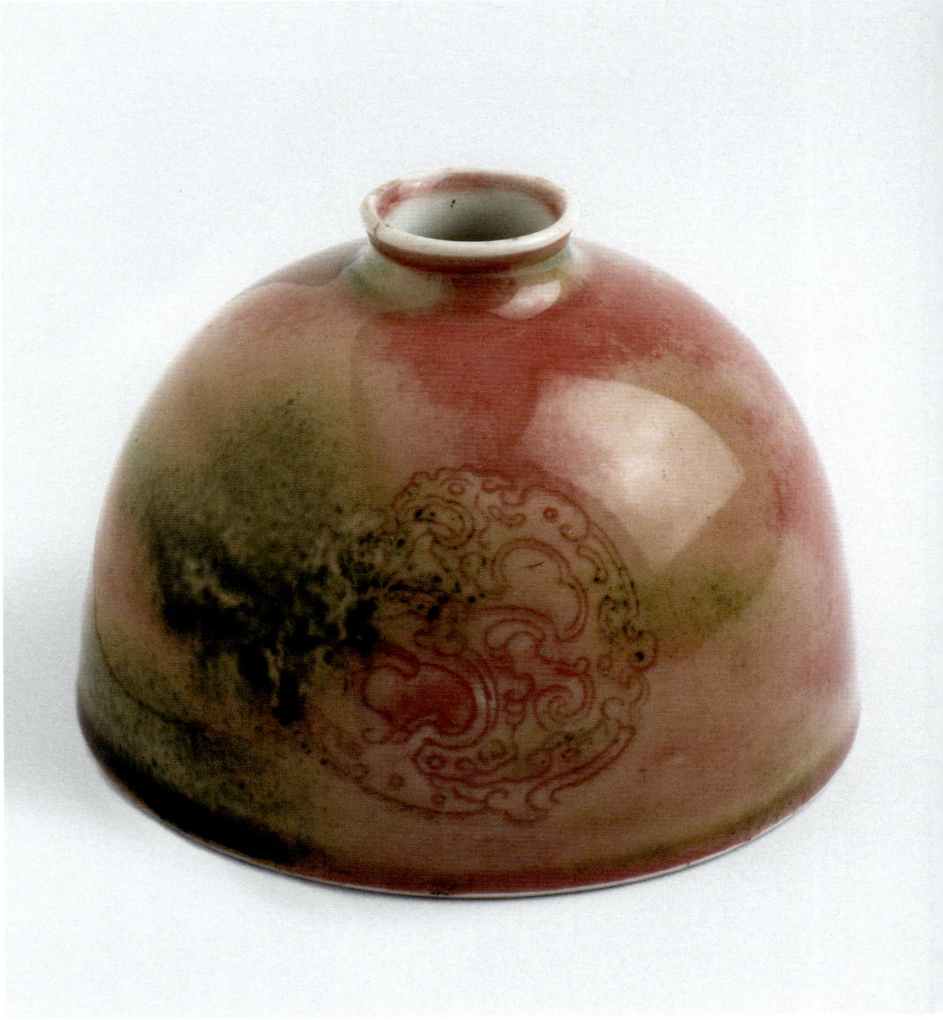

61

Bowl with Incised Dragons and Enameled Flowers

Qing dynasty (1644–1911), Kangxi period (1662–1722)
Porcelain with incised design, underglaze blue, and three-color enamel decoration (*susancai*) (Jingdezhen ware)
2 11/16 x 5 7/8 inches (6.9 x 14.9 cm)
Gift of Lydia Thompson Morris, 1925-27-37

The Kangxi period saw the production of a great many porcelains decorated in polychrome enamels. This bowl, with a six-character mark in underglaze blue on the base indicating its use by the imperial court (see p. 248), demonstrates a new technique of this time, however, which makes use of both enameling and incising to unusual effect. Incised around the bowl's exterior are two striding five-clawed dragons, each chasing a flaming pearl amid clouds, over which are painted two bunches of flowering branches separated by a butterfly. The imperial dragon design was first incised in the unglazed porcelain body, and then the enamel decoration (an ivory ground with yellow, green, purple, and turquoise outlined in black) was applied. Although incising and enameling were employed together in porcelains of the fifteenth to sixteenth centuries,[1] painting a different design over an incised imperial dragon motif instead of enhancing the incised design with enamels appears to be specific to the Kangxi period.[2]

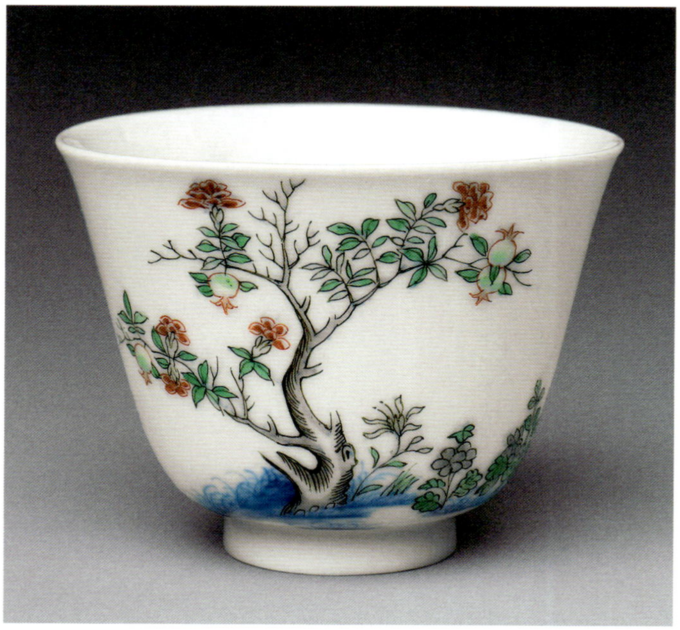

Fig. 52. Wine Cup with Flower of the Fifth Month (Pomegranate). Qing dynasty, Kangxi period. Porcelain painted with colored enamels over a transparent glaze (Jingdezhen ware); 1 15/16 x 2½ inches (4.9 x 6.4 cm). The Metropolitan Museum of Art, New York. Bequest of Mary Stillman Harkness, 1950 (50.145.271)

Plates in this same technique and palette, with fruit and flowering branches depicted on their interiors, were also produced.[3] One of the fruits represented is the pomegranate. The flowering branches on the exterior of the Philadelphia bowl and others have been variously described as peony, hibiscus, and carnation,[4] but pomegranate should be considered, since the fruit is shown on plates, and bowls and plates were likely made as sets. Other Kangxi porcelains depict pomegranate blossoms along with the fruit (fig. 52). HK

1. Geng 1993, 218.
2. Produced by the designer Lin Yuan in the late seventeenth century; see Lam 2005–6, 54.
3. One is in the Asian Art Museum of San Francisco (B60P1754), illustrated in Li 1996, 296, no. 613.
4. They have been variously described as peony (Geng 1993, col. pl. 91; Geng and Lü 2009, 272, no. 221), for a bowl in the Palace Museum, Beijing, collections and one in the Victoria and Albert Museum, London (C.1051-1917); hibiscus, for a bowl in the Asian Art Museum of San Francisco (B60P2099); and carnations, for one in the Musée Guimet, Paris (Grandidier Collection, G 1346).

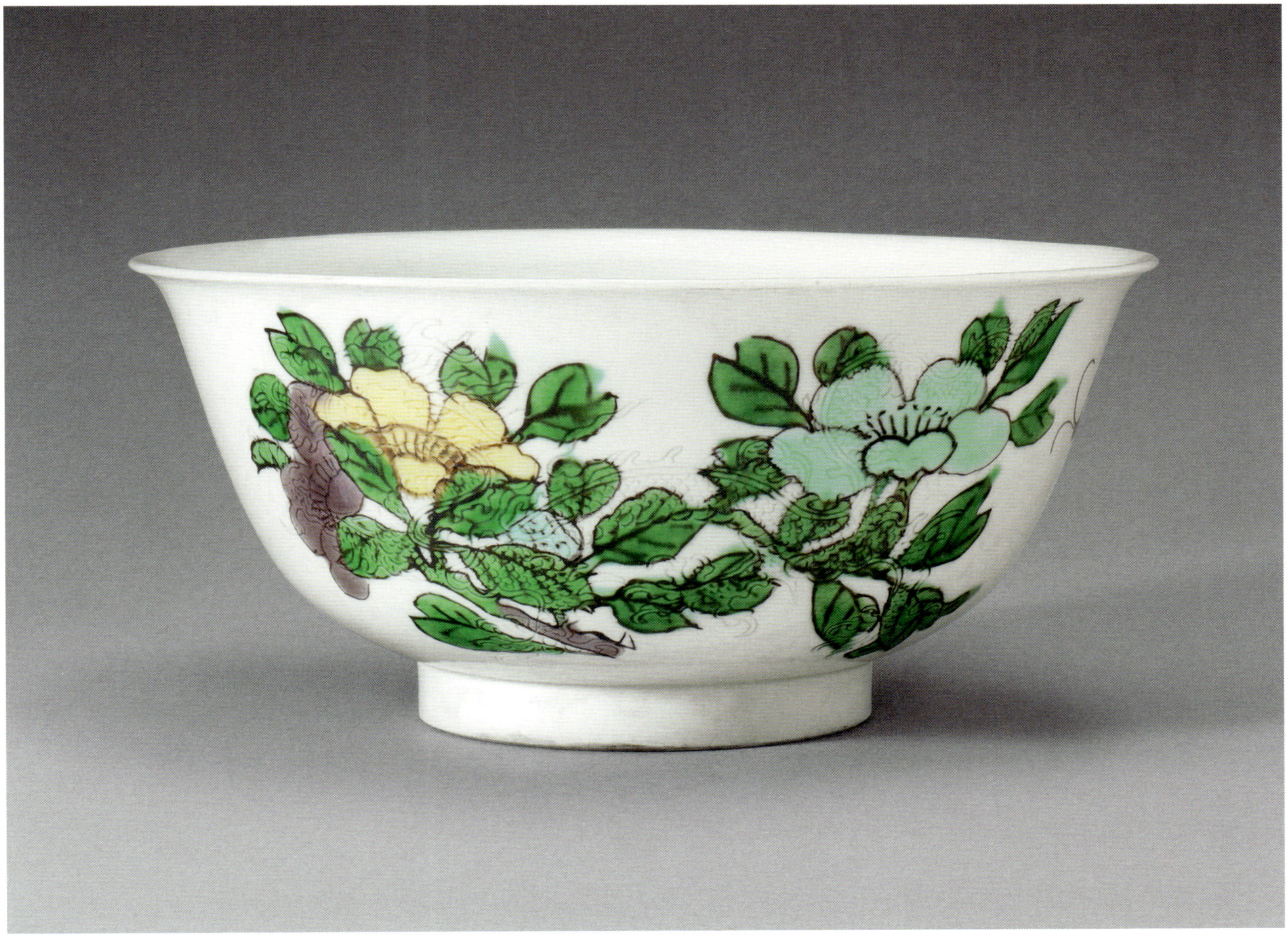

62

Phoenix-tail Vase

Qing dynasty (1644–1911), Kangxi period (1662–1722), late 17th century
Porcelain with underglaze blue, polychrome enamel, and gilded decoration (Jingdezhen ware)
28⅛ x 11⅛ inches (71.4 x 28.3 cm)
The Alfred and Margaret Caspary Memorial Gift, 1955-50-99

Porcelains decorated predominantly with brilliant, transparent green enameling were produced during the Kangxi period for both domestic and export markets. This vase is one of two pieces in the Philadelphia Museum of Art that were once in the collection of Augustus the Strong, king of Poland and elector of Saxony, in Dresden (see no. 63).[1] Augustus amassed the largest collection of Chinese and Japanese porcelains in the West, some twenty-nine thousand pieces, in the hopes of discovering the formula for making porcelain, then known only in China and Japan. He opened the first porcelain factory in Europe in 1710 at Meissen.

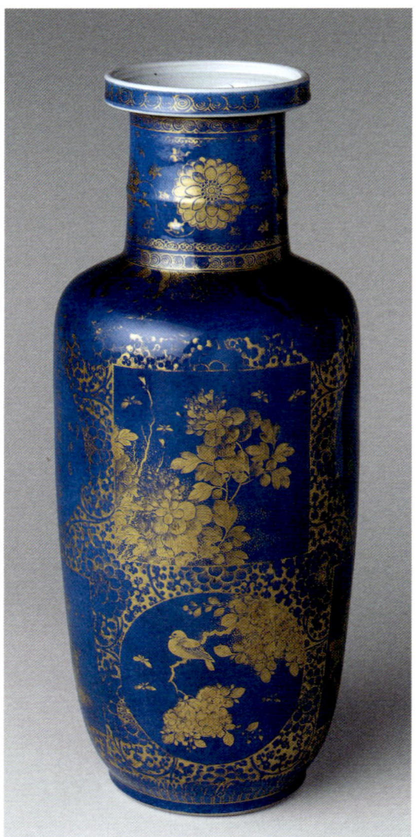

Fig. 53. Vase with Flowers, Birds, and Poems. Qing dynasty, Kangxi period, 1709. Porcelain with powder blue glaze and gilding (Jingdezhen ware); 17½ x 4⅝ (at rim) inches (44.5 x 11.7 cm). The Metropolitan Museum of Art, New York. Purchase by subscription, 1879 (79.2.153)

The vase's elegantly curving sides are divided into rectangular panels embellished with landscapes, birds and flowers, and the "hundred antiques" design (lower right panel), all images associated with erudition. The "hundred antiques"—a decorative pattern that includes antique bronzes, objects for the scholar's desk, and the Eight Treasures—became popular in China beginning in the seventeenth century and was used in all types of mediums to convey auspicious wishes; floral subjects seem to have been popular from around 1700 (fig. 53).[2] These images most likely were taken from Chinese woodblock prints, which were prevalent from the late Ming onward.

The overall palette of this vase, called *famille verte* (literally, "green family") by Westerners, is unusual in its restrained use of the green enameling. Instead, a pinkish tone predominates, an optical effect created by the underglaze blue-trellis diaper pattern filled with red-enamel rosettes dotted with gilding in the background.[3]

Around the base of the neck in cartouches are four of the Eight Treasures (*ba bao*)—an Artemisia leaf, the double cash (coin), the double lozenge, and a musical stone (chime)—which were popular for their association with wealth.[4] The vase was once part of a three-piece garniture set that included two other vases like it.[5] HK

1. The vase was acquired by Augustus the Strong before 1721 (author's correspondence with Karolin Randhahn). The collection was dispersed beginning in the nineteenth century and continuing into the 1920s; see Kerr 2001.
2. The version in the Metropolitan Museum of Art illustrated here (fig. 53) is decorated with cartouches of bird and flower designs and carries a poetic inscription that gives a date of 1709, while a brush pot with birds on branches and an inscription dated to 1709 is in the Grandidier collection, Musée national des arts asiatiques—Guimet, Paris (G4217).
3. This decoration is reminiscent of diaper-pattern grounds found on carved cinnabar lacquer wares from the sixteenth to eighteenth centuries; see Hong Kong 1993, nos. 73, 75, 76, 77.
4. Eight, or *ba*, rhymes with *fa*, to grow or expand, which usually refers to wealth. See San Francisco 2006, 141, no. 6.10.
5. The other two vases are in the Porzellansammlung in Dresden (inv. nos. PO 6255, PO 6256).

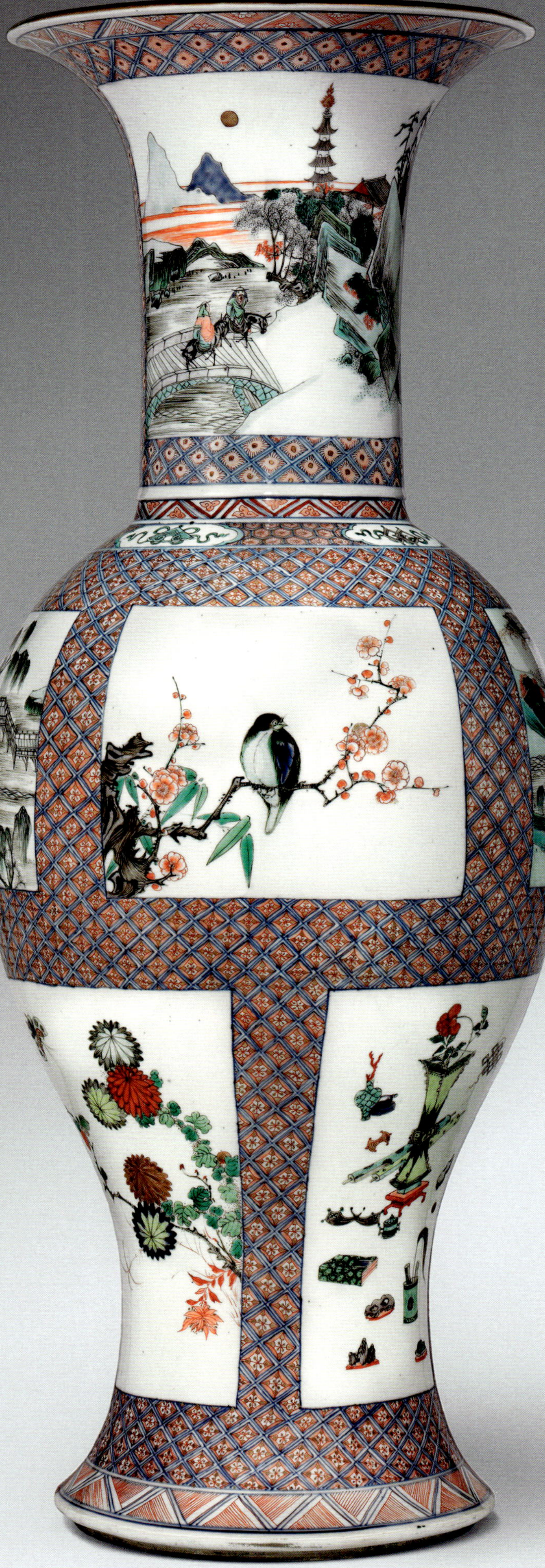

63

Covered Jar with *Qilin*, Lion, and Elephant

Qing dynasty (1644–1911), Kangxi period (1662–1722), late 17th century
Porcelain with underglaze blue, polychrome enamel, and gilded decoration (Jingdezhen ware)
22⅛ x 12⅜ inches (56.2 x 31.4 cm)
The Alfred and Margaret Caspary Memorial Gift, 1955-50-75a,b

Painted in brilliant enamels with touches of gilding, this large, ovoid covered jar is unusual for its impressive size and exceptional decoration,[1] depicted in the *famille verte* palette introduced in the seventeenth century, during the Kangxi period. As its name implies, green enamel dominates over the blue, red, yellow, and black enamels. Represented on the jar's swelling sides, within rectangular cartouches that each contain a different landscape, are a lion, its head turned back to toss a beribboned brocade ball into the air, an elephant, and a galloping *qilin*, all set against a green brocade pattern inset with red lotus blossoms. On the shoulder is a cloud-collar design with further lotus blossoms interspersed with a cash (coin) design[2] against a stippled fish-roe patterned ground. The cover knop is modeled as a seated lion in mid-roar, its head turned to one side.

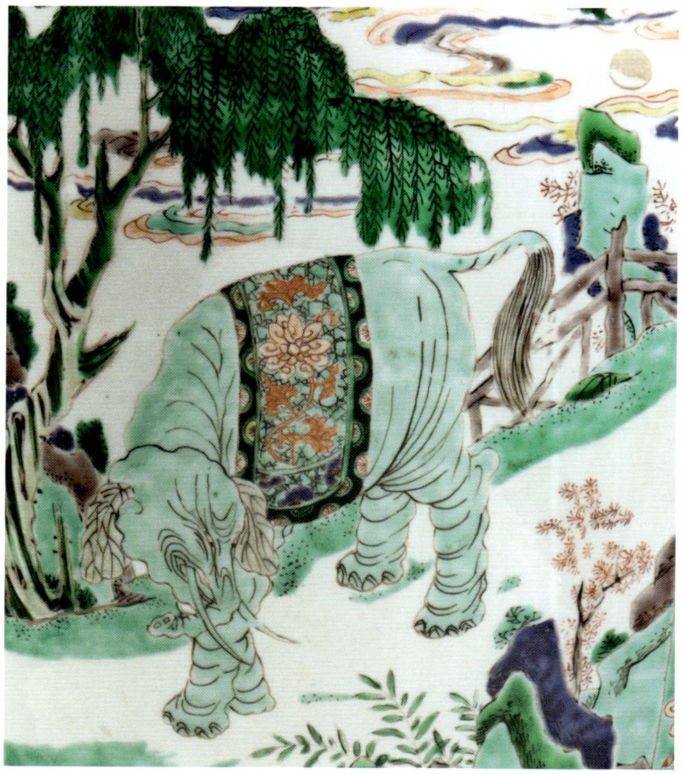

Fig. 54. Detail of the elephant represented in one of the three cartouches on the jar

Together the three animals can be seen as auspicious creatures, with the *qilin* and elephant (fig. 54) conveying wishes for peace. The mythical *qilin*—identified by its dragon head, scaly body, and deer hooves (with the unusual addition here of a pair of wings not present in most Kangxi depictions; see no. 57)—is associated with the bringing of peace, as its appearance is connected with the birth of a sagacious ruler; the elephant's association with peace is through a rebus.[3] An alternative reading of the animals within a Buddhist context could also be considered, if interpreted along with the lotus blossoms, a symbol of rebirth, in the background: the lion is the traditional mount of Manjusri, the elephant is the mount of Samantabhadra, while Shakyamuni rides a *qilin*.[4]

The quality of the enameling is extremely high on this unusually large jar, and it comes as no surprise that it was once in the collection of Augustus the Strong in Dresden.[5] HK

1. A powder-blue *famille verte* enameled covered jar only three-fifths the size of this example, and described as rare for its size and quality, is in the collection of Rijksmuseum, Amsterdam, illustrated in Groningen 2011–12, 104, no. 95.
2. The cash or coin motif, one of the Eight Treasures, often conveys wishes for wealth.
3. In Fang Yulu's 1589 compilation, *Fangshi mopu* (The Fang Family Chart of Ink Illustrations) is an illustration of an ink-cake design by Fang (vol. 1, 9) depicting a similar type of elephant and the four characters *taiping you xiang*, "may there be peace" or "where there is peace there are signs," since "elephant" (*xiang*) sounds like "signs" (also *xiang*). See Li 1871 (2002), vol. 1114.
4. For an example of this grouping, see the three ivory carvings in the Metropolitan Museum of Art, New York, illustrated in Leidy and Strahan 2010, 132–33, no. 30.
5. The jar was part of a five-piece garniture set that included two identical covered jars (inv. nos. PO 3027, PO 6323) and a pair of beaker vases (PO 6318, PO 6319) now in the Porzellansammlung, Dresden. The inventory mark $^{\text{N4}}_{\text{I}}$ on the base and inside the cover (now both partially worn away) indicates that it was in the collection before 1721 (author's correspondence with Karolin Randhahn).

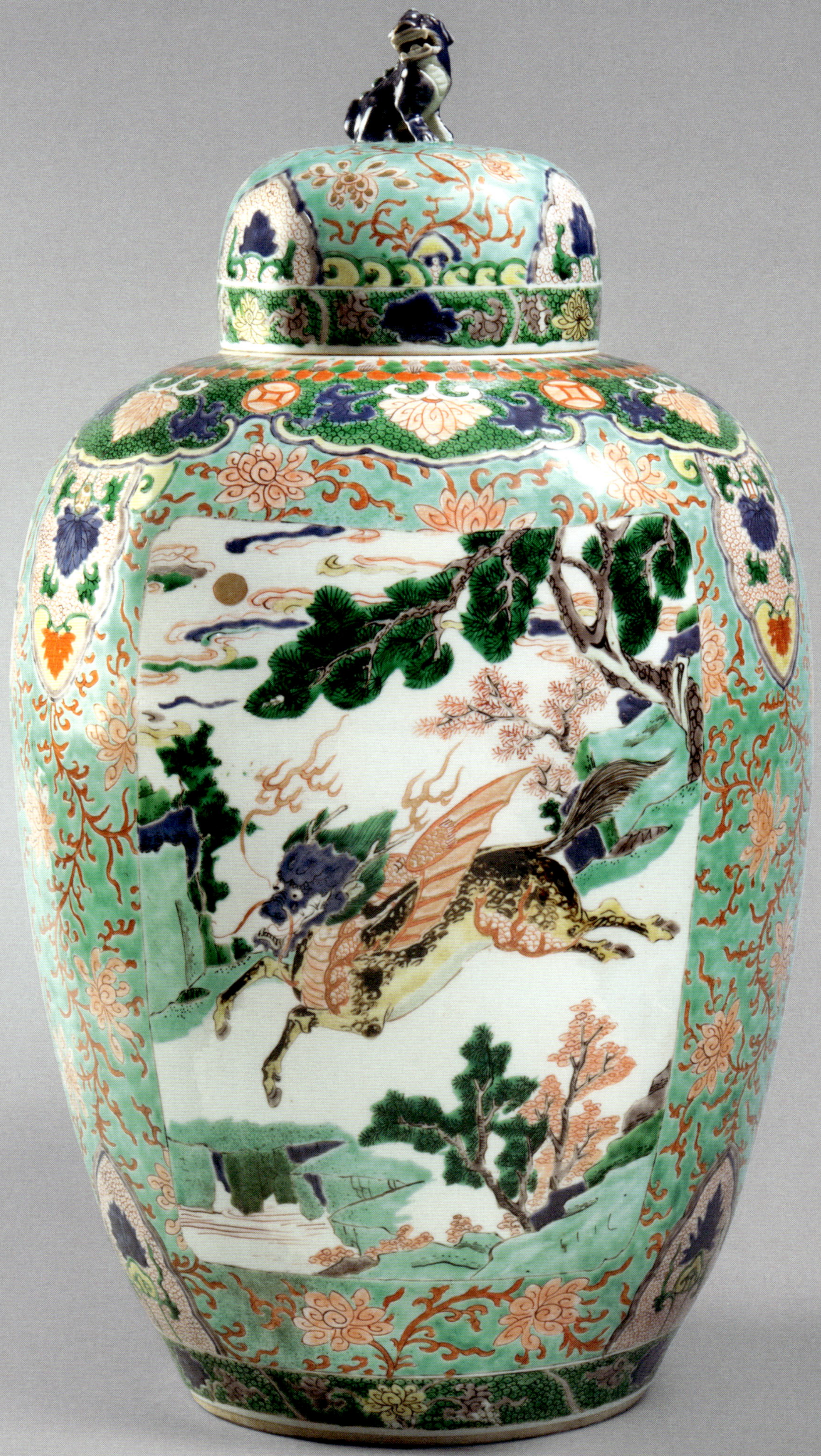

64

Phoenix-tail Vase with the Battle of Sishui Pass

Qing dynasty (1644–1911), Kangxi period (1662–1722)
Porcelain with underglaze blue, polychrome enamel, and gilded decoration (Jingdezhen ware)
29⅞ x 10⅝ inches (75.9 x 27 cm)
The Alfred and Margaret Caspary Memorial Gift, 1955-50-84

Painted around the body of this large phoenix-tail vase (so called because the flaring neck mimics the form of a phoenix tail) is an elaborate battle scene. A plaque above the gatehouse of the fortress indicates that this is the Battle of Sishui Pass, a fictional encounter described in the sixteenth-century novel *Investiture of the Gods* (*Fengshen yanyi*). This popular and highly entertaining novel, part fact and part fantasy, was based on the historical events of the wars between the Shang (c. 1600–1050 BCE) and Zhou (c. 1100–256 BCE) dynastic royal houses.[1]

Wishes of auspicious blessings are conveyed on the vase's neck by the depiction of the *San Xing*, or "Three Stars": Shou Xing, the god of longevity, shown as an old man with a tall forehead; Fu Xing, the god of happiness, dressed as a retired scholar-official in robes and a plain head cloth and surrounded by young boys, the smallest of whom he holds in his arms (happiness is having many sons); and Lu Xing, the god of wealth and the tallest figure, shown as a high-ranking official wearing embroidered robes and a winged hat. Reinforcing the blessings expressed by these figures are motifs such as red bats, symbolizing happiness,[2] and a pine tree, an emblem of long life, as is the *ruyi* ("as you wish") fungus growing from a rock. The boys holding lotus blossoms and seed pods to the right of the fungus, one of them playing the mouth organ, are a visual pun conveying the wish for the continual advancement of many sons within the ranks of officialdom (fig. 55).[3]

The depiction and arrangement of the figures in the battle scene, like the representation of the star gods on the neck, recall contemporary woodblock prints. The woodblock printing of popular novels such as *Investiture of the Gods*, *The Romance of the Three Kingdoms* (*Sanguo yanyi*), and *Water Margin* (*Shuihu zhuan*) was a flourishing industry in Anhui and Fujian provinces and influenced the designs on porcelains produced in nearby Jingdezhen.[4] The small, gilded square seal written in iron-red on the neck of this example reads *Zhuju* (Bamboo Studio; fig. 55), which, like the more commonly seen seal *Mushiju* (Wood and Stone Studio), indicates a private workshop in Jingdezhen.[5] Within the growing and affluent merchant class, such literary depictions on porcelains would have been instantly recognizable. Many of these porcelains made their way to the West, however, where the non-Chinese audience would have enjoyed them purely for their exotic and beautifully executed decoration. HK

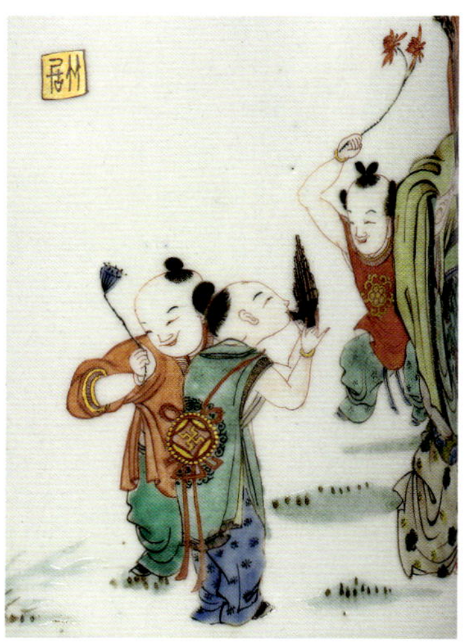

Fig. 55. Detail of the neck of the vase showing boys playing near the Three Stars; the seal of the Bamboo Studio (*Zhuju*) is at the upper left

1. The novel also includes fantastic tales of gods and demons that interact with human characters and fight in large-scale battles with their magic weapons. Depictions of the *Investiture of the Gods* are rare on this vase form. A mallet-shaped vase with a scene from the novel is in the Asian Art Museum of San Francisco (Li 1996, no. 646), and battle scenes from other popular novels are depicted on mallet vases in the Taft Museum of Art in Cincinnati (Du Boulay 1995, 639–40, 642–45).
2. *Fu*, meaning bats, sounds similar to (but is a different character from) *fu*, meaning happiness.
3. "Lotus" sounds like "continual" (*lian*), while "mouth organ" sounds like "to rise" or "to give birth" (*sheng*); San Francisco 2006, 74, no. 3.20.
4. Seattle 2000, 117.
5. Li 1996, no. 648. A powder-blue vase dated to 1709 with the Wood and Stone Studio seal mark is in the Metropolitan Museum of Art, New York (79.2.153).

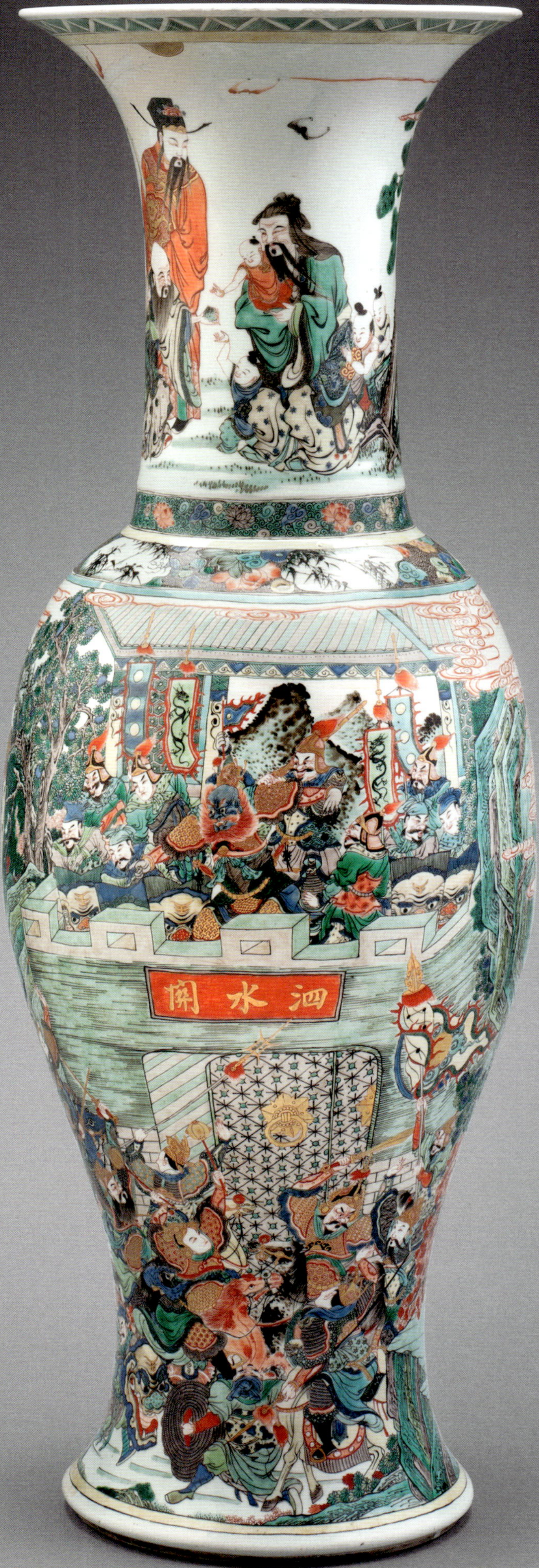
泗水關

65

Large Bowl with Illustrations of Tilling and Weaving

Qing dynasty (1644–1911), Kangxi period (1662–1722), early 18th century
Porcelain with underglaze blue, polychrome enamel, and gilded decoration (Jingdezhen ware)
6½ x 13⅝ inches (16.5 x 34.6 cm)
The Alfred and Margaret Caspary Memorial Gift, 1955-50-170

Wrapped around the exterior of this large bowl are scenes representing two of imperial China's most important industries, rice cultivation and silk production. One scene shows two men sifting rice into baskets, and the other three women tending to trays filled with silkworms and their fodder of mulberry leaves.[1] Both scenes are taken from the Kangxi edition of *Pictures of Tilling and Weaving* (*Yuzhi gengzhi tu*), created by the court artist Jiao Bingzhen (act. 1680–1720), who in turn based his paintings on an earlier series designed by the Southern Song artist Lou Shu (1090–1162). The Kangxi emperor revived the depictions during his long sixty-year reign as a form of political propaganda, to show that he knew the wealth of the empire depended on the hard work of farmers and laborers.[2]

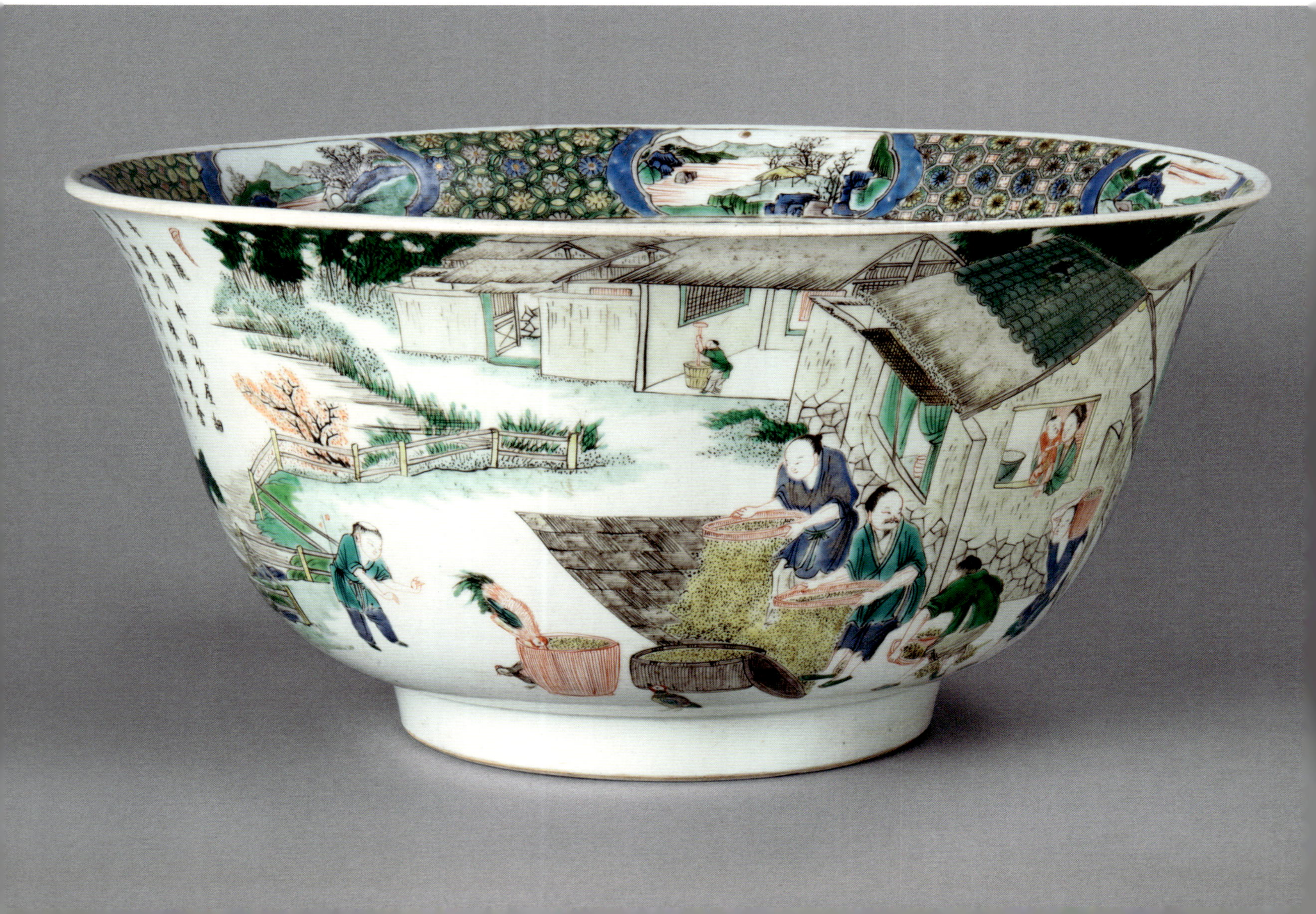

The original *Pictures of Tilling and Weaving* designed by Lou Shu is now lost. It most likely consisted of two scrolls of pictures accompanied by poems, one depicting rural women manufacturing silk fabric, and the other showing farmers cultivating grain.[3] Jiao Bingzhen created forty-six scenes, half of them illustrating rice planting, including preparation of the seeds, planting, ploughing, weeding, harvesting, and, finally, a sacrificial offering of rice at an altar, and the other half portraying the care of the silkworms, from egg to cocoon, as well as the preparation of silk, from the boiling of the cocoons to the tailoring of silk garments. Lou Shu's original verses were included within the illustrations.

The Western feel of the scenes in the edition by Jiao Bingzhen, which employ one-point perspective and shadowing not usually found in Chinese painting, may have resulted from Jiao's contact with Jesuit painters residing at Kangxi's imperial court. Jiao's paintings were published as a series of woodblock illustrations, from which craftsmen working in the imperial kilns probably copied. The square seal found at the end of each inscription reads *Mushiju* (Wood and Stone Studio), the name of a well-known private workshop that produced high-quality enameled porcelains with literary themes.[4] These Chinese scenes would have appealed to a local clientele, although porcelains carrying images from *Pictures of Tilling and Weaving*, such as this example, also found their way into collections abroad. HK

1. For translations of the stanzas represented on the bowl, see Hammers 2011, 186, 195.
2. Groningen 2011–12, 73.
3. Hammers 2011, 1.
4. See Shanghai Museum 1998, no. 108, for an enameled plate with a scene of weaving and a *Mushiju* mark at the end of the inscription, also with a similar "ding" mark as on this example. Wang Qingzheng discusses private workshops on pp. xxiii–xxv.

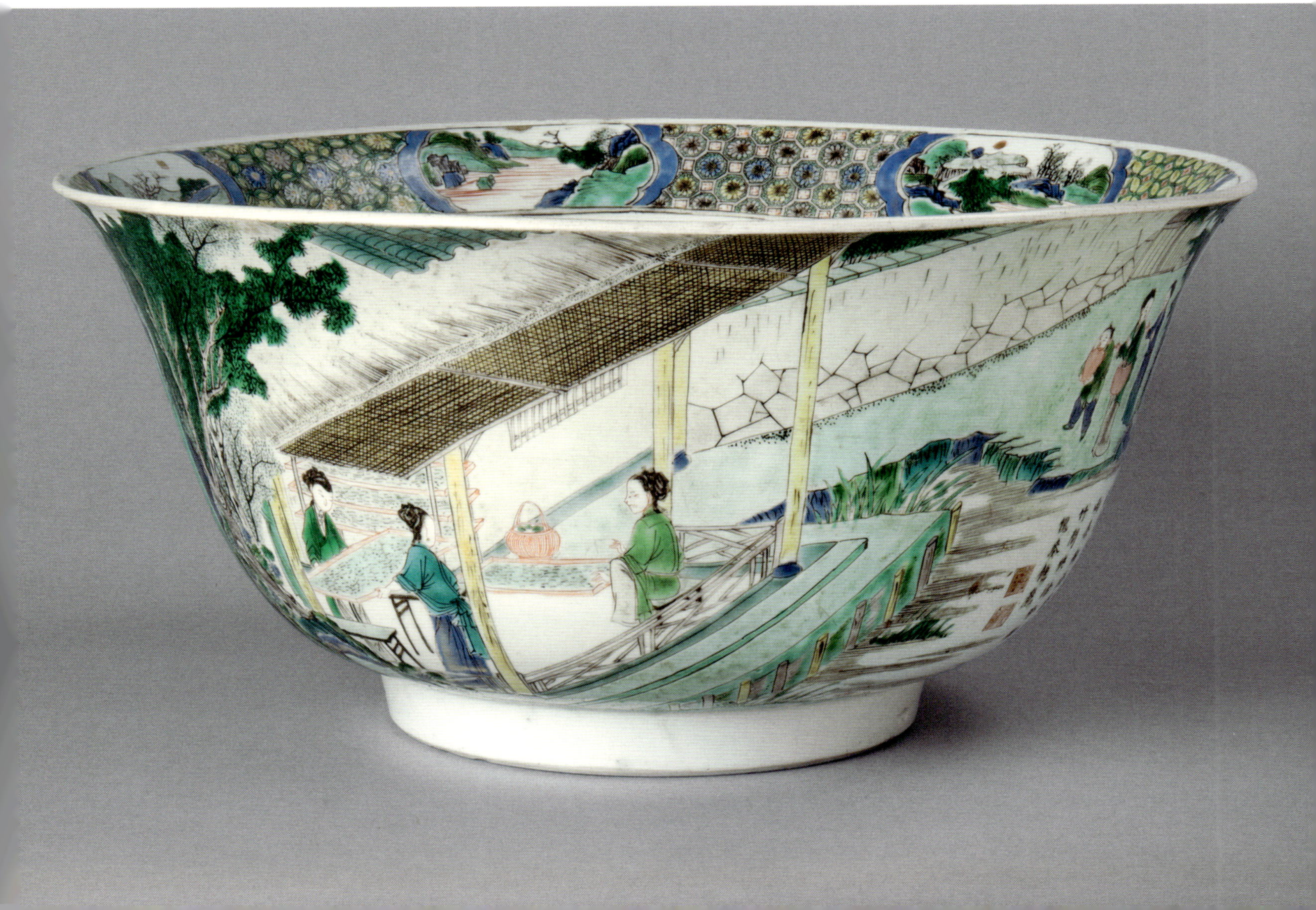

66

Wine Cups with Roosters, Hens, and Chicks

Qing dynasty (1644–1911), Kangxi period (1662–1722), early 18th century
Porcelain with underglaze blue and polychrome enamel decoration (Jingdezhen ware)
1½ x 3¼ inches (3.8 x 8.3 cm)
Gift of Major General and Mrs. William Crozier, 1944-20-463, 1944-20-464

These delicately formed wine cups are each decorated with the same charming scene of a rooster and his brood in a garden setting. The technique involved first applying cobalt blue to the unfired white porcelain, used to outline the forms and to create the thin lines bordering the scenes at the base and rim, the rockwork, and the square mark on the base (see p. 248). The porcelain was then fired, after which other colors were added in bright polychrome enamels, creating a detailed scene of a crowing cockerel leading a foraging hen and three young chicks between flowering yellow lilies and red roses or pomegranate plants issuing from rockwork. So-called chicken cups were first made during the reign of the Chenghua emperor (1465–87). They were greatly treasured for their fine porcelain, freely painted designs,[1] and refined, soft color schemes.

The Ming and Qing courts so admired these cups that some emperors commissioned the imperial kilns to make copies of renowned earlier pieces. Of the chicken cups produced during the Qing dynasty, those made during the Kangxi emperor's reign most closely resemble the original Ming Chenghua versions[2]—in their soft underglaze blue, luminous enamel palette, and the silky feel of the glaze.[3] The design was no doubt also attractive for its auspicious associations, as the word for rooster or chicken (*ji*) sounds similar to *ji*, meaning good luck. HK

1. The motif of chickens with chicks may have been related to the Chenghua emperor seeing a Song dynasty (960–1279) painting of hens with chicks foraging for food, which elicited a commentary in 1486. See Krahl and Harrison-Hall 2009, 74.
2. His son, the Yongzheng emperor (r. 1723–35), changed the chicken design somewhat, while Kangxi's grandson, the Qianlong emperor (r. 1736–95), created a whole new upright form and design and included a poem in praise of the Chenghua version. A Qianlong chicken cup is in the Museum of Fine Arts, Boston (54.103).
3. The straight sides of the cup rather than flared lip, the slight difference in painting style, and the square reign mark on the countersunk base are the main differences. Other Kangxi examples are in the Museum of East Asian Art in Bath, England (BATEA: 189), and the Shanghai Museum (both with apocryphal Chenghua mark); the Percival David Collection at the British Museum, London (PDF A749); and the Palace Museum, Beijing (Beijing 2015, 158–59).

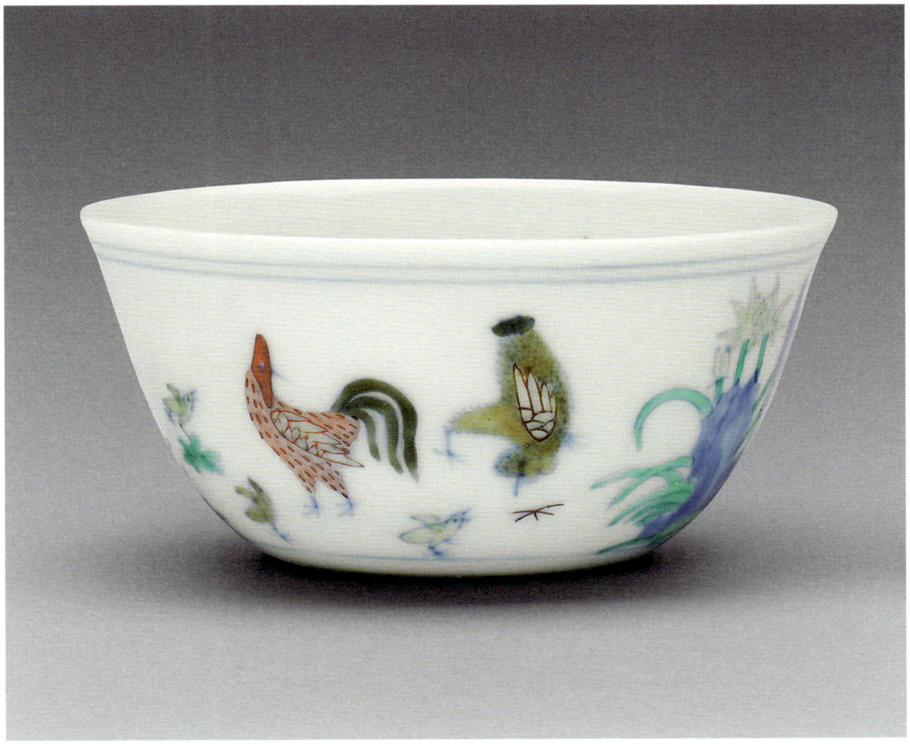

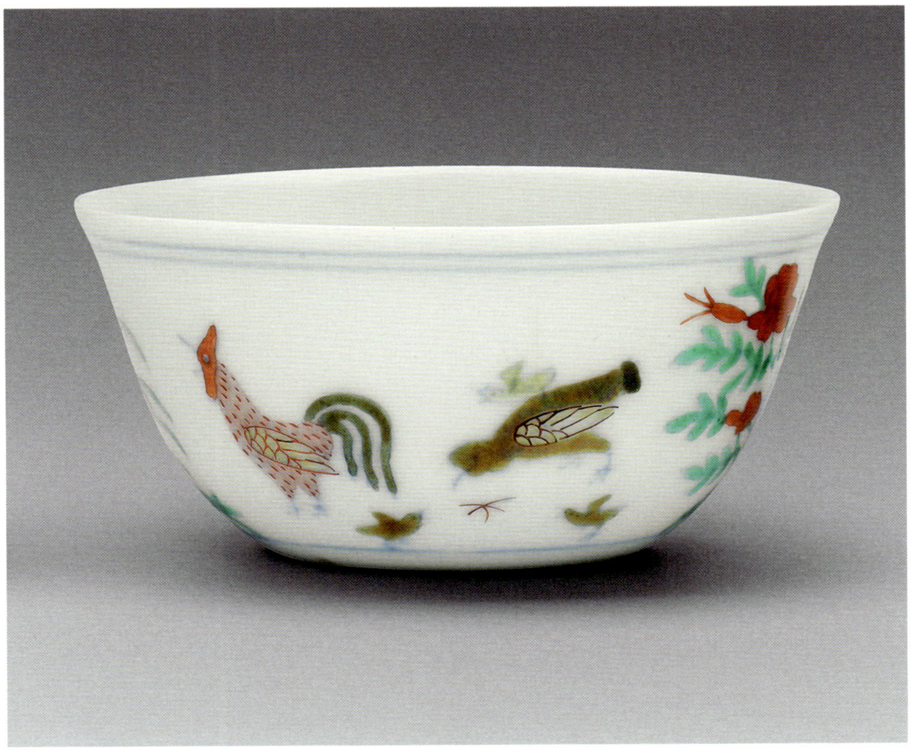

67

Oxblood Glazed Bowl

Qing dynasty (1644–1911), Kangxi period (1662–1722), first quarter of the 18th century
Porcelain with red glaze (*Langyao*, or oxblood ware); ivory stand
2 15/16 x 7 15/16 inches (7.4 x 20.2 cm)
Gift of Major General and Mrs. William Crozier, 1944-20-39a,b

Porcelains for use by the court and members of the imperial family were produced at the imperial porcelain factory in Jingdezhen, Jiangxi province, in southern China. They filled a variety of uses, including as vessels for eating and drinking or for ritual use, and as curios for the appreciation and enjoyment of the imperial family or gifts to court officials.[1]

During the Kangxi period at least three different types of red glazes were produced: a "sacrificial" red for wares used in ritual ceremonies that revived a fifteenth-century red glaze employed during the Ming Xuande emperor's reign (1426–35); a "peach-bloom" glaze, known in Chinese as "bean red" or "apple red" (see no. 60); and, the most highly treasured of the red glazes, "oxblood" (*sang de boeuf*), so called in the West for its resemblance to freshly congealed blood. The latter is known in China as *Langyao*, and for many years it was thought that "Lang" referred to Lang Tingji (1663–1715), the governor of Jiangxi province and supervisor of the imperial kilns at Jingdezhen from 1705 to 1712. However, it seems that this association first appeared among Beijing dealers in the second half of the nineteenth century.[2]

The appeal of the *Langyao* glaze lies in its characteristic rich red color and glassy viscous quality, which makes the glaze transparent or pale green where thinly applied, such as around the rim, as a result of the copper oxide evaporating during firing. Where the glaze thickens from the pull of gravity and stops, usually in a well-controlled roll just above the neatly cut foot, the color deepens to a dark bruised-strawberry red. HK

1. See Lai Suk Yee, "Qing Imperial Vase Forms and Handles," in Hong Kong 2007–8, 67.
2. For a discussion of Lang Tingji and his role in porcelain production during the Kangxi period, see Lam 2003–4.

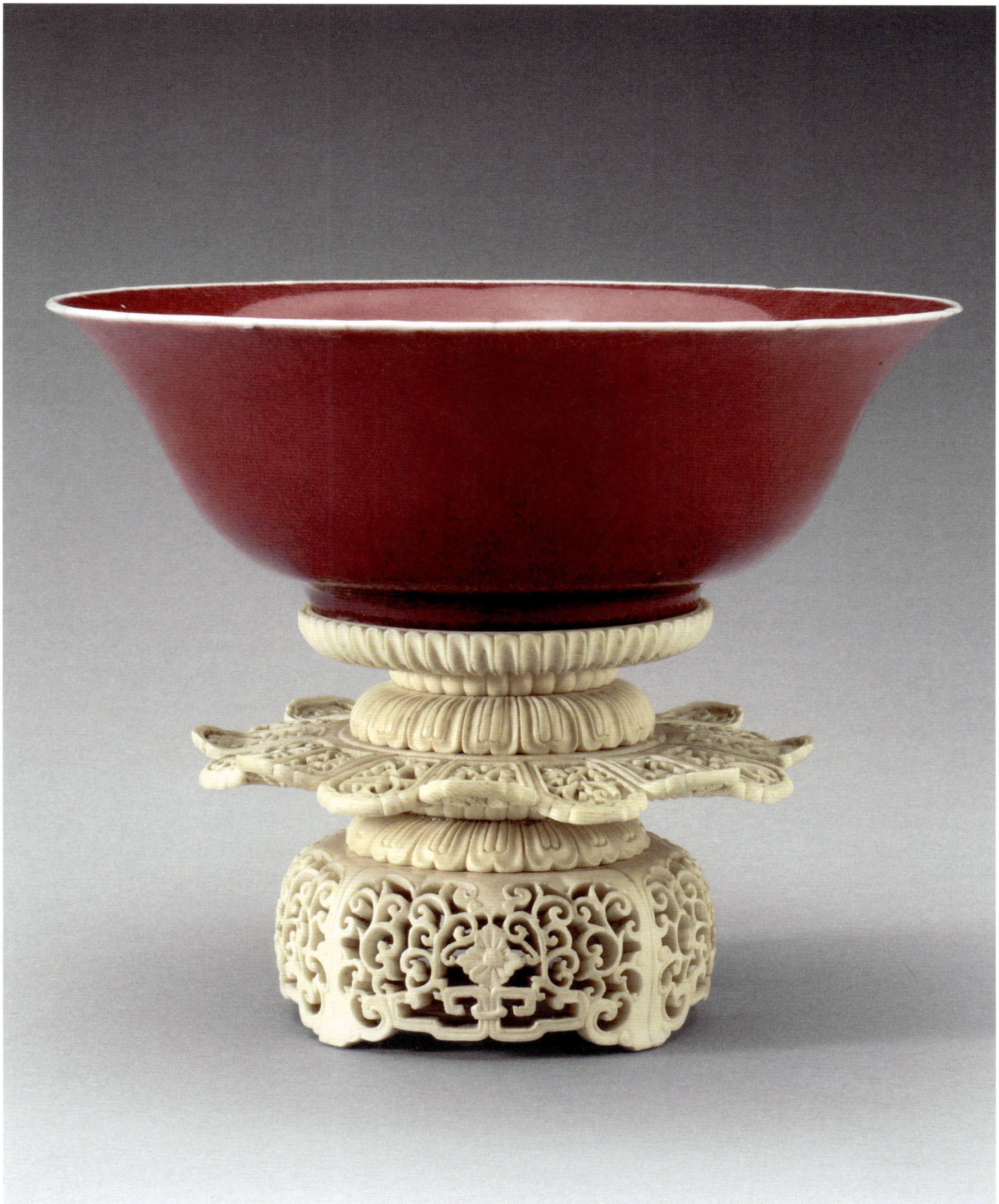

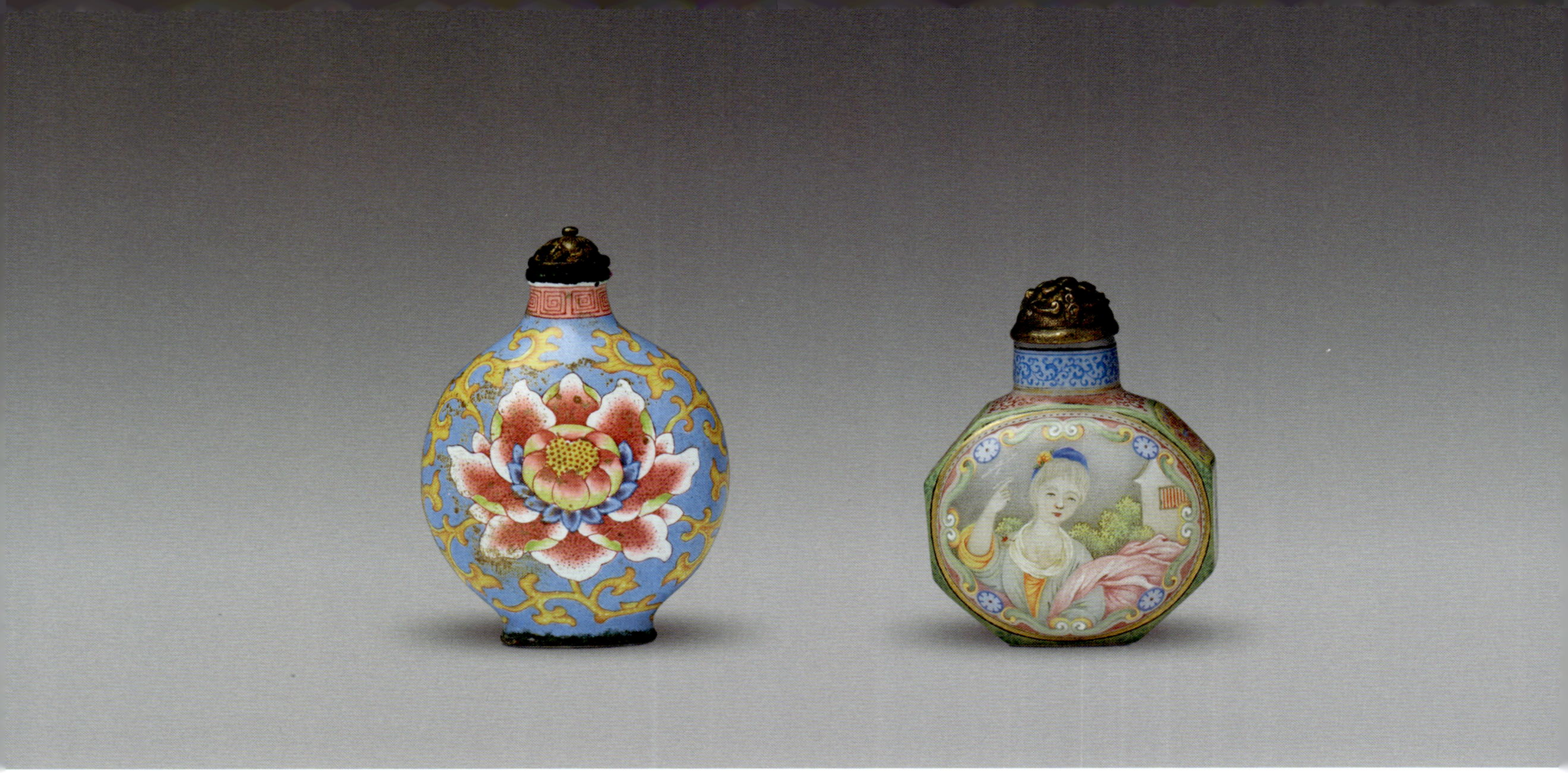

68

Snuff Bottles

Qing dynasty (1644–1911)

a) Kangxi period (1662–1722)
Copper with enamel decoration; stopper and spoon: copper alloy with traces of gilding; ivory
$2\frac{1}{8}$ x $1\frac{9}{16}$ x 1 inches (5.4 x 4 x 2.5 cm)

b) Qianlong period (1736–95)
White glass with enamel; stopper and spoon: gilded copper alloy, jade
$1\frac{13}{16}$ x $1\frac{7}{16}$ x $\frac{7}{8}$ inches (4.6 x 3.6 x 2.3 cm)

c) Qianlong period
White glass with enamel; stopper and spoon: gilded copper alloy, ivory
$2\frac{3}{8}$ x $1\frac{3}{16}$ x $\frac{3}{4}$ inches (6 x 3 x 1.9 cm)

d) Qianlong period
White glass with enamel; stopper and spoon: gilded copper alloy, ivory
$2\frac{11}{16}$ x $1\frac{1}{4}$ inches (6.8 x 3.1 cm)

e) Qianlong period
White glass with enamel; stopper and spoon: jade, ivory
$2\frac{5}{16}$ x $1\frac{5}{8}$ x 1 inches (5.9 x 4.2 x 2.5 cm)

Gift of Major General and Mrs. William Crozier, 1944-20-586, -551, -550, -553, -558

Snuff bottles—used to hold a mixture of finely ground tobacco and aromatics—emerged as an entirely new genre of decorative art in the early Qing dynasty, attesting to the Manchu rulers' eclectic taste, which propelled the widespread popularity of these charming miniature vessels in the eighteenth century.[1] The Kangxi emperor's interest in snuff bottles and enameling techniques spurred the foundation of imperial workshops for both enameling and glass making,[2] led by Jesuit missionaries with specialized knowledge in the arts and sciences.[3] The high achievement of these newly established workshops can be seen in a delicate enamel-on-copper specimen in the museum's collection (a), which once had a four-character Kangxi reign mark on its base (now only partially preserved).[4] The floral decorations on this bottle are characteristic of enameled metalwork of the Kangxi period, when an effort was made to create a wide spectrum of enamel colors, especially shades of blue, red, and pink (fig. 56). The mid-eighteenth century saw the zenith of snuff-bottle production, as the technique of painting enamel on glass improved and the decorative repertoire expanded substantially. This development can be seen in the octagonal bottle with a European flair shown here (b), which demonstrates an interest in foreigners, architectural surroundings, and the use of shading and perspective.

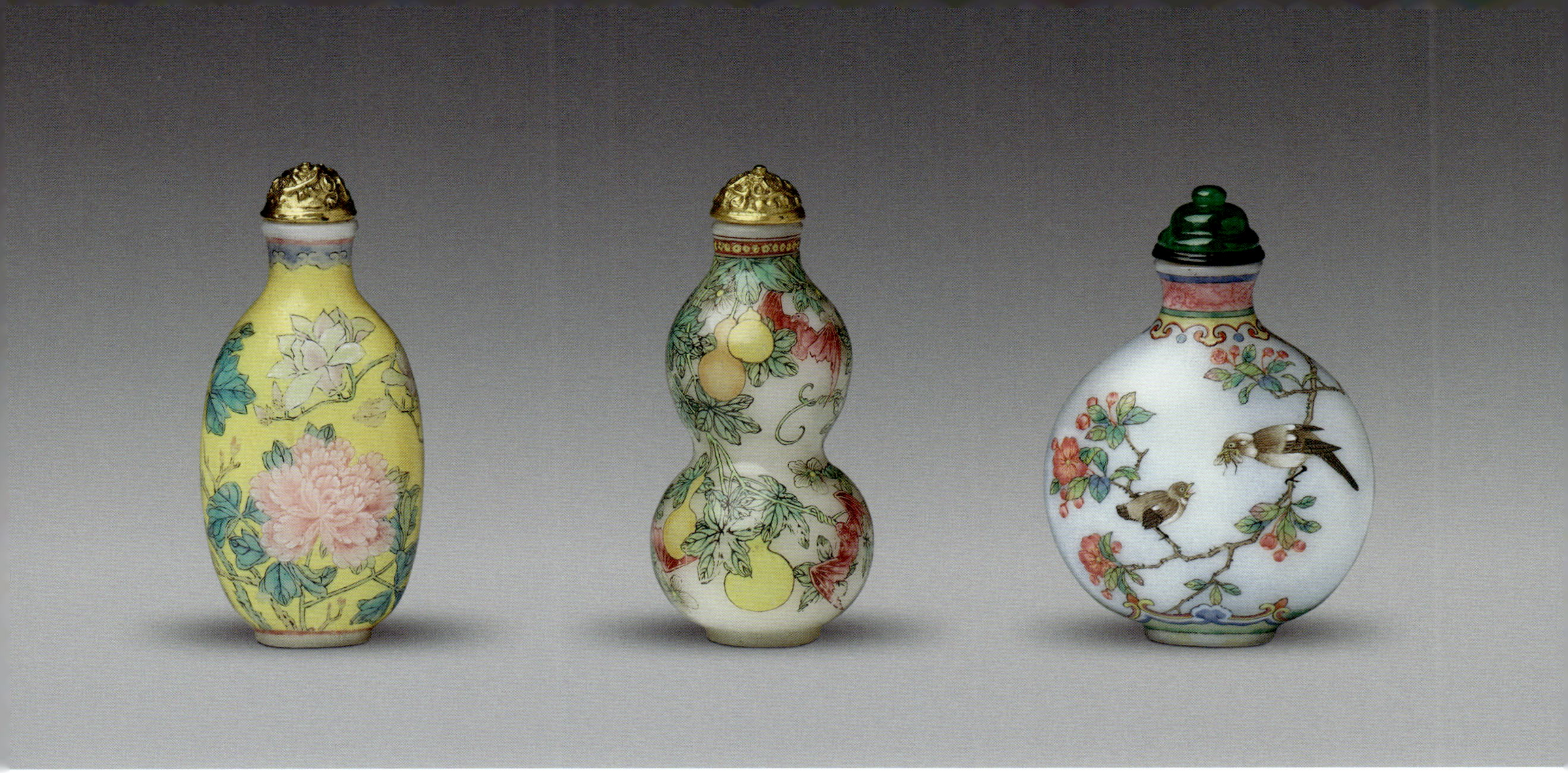

a–e

The taste for these finely crafted vessels spread beyond the court through the practice of gift giving, with emperors presenting snuff bottles to favored officials and foreign envoys. Their importance as gifts explains why the majority of Qing snuff bottles display traditional Chinese motifs, many of which convey auspicious tidings. On the third bottle in this group (c), for example, naturalistic depictions of peonies and magnolias—composing a rebus for wealth and nobility—are painted against a background of brilliant yellow, a color reserved for the imperial family.[5] The gourd-shaped snuff bottle (d) conveys a wish for the happiness and prosperity of many generations, with the red bats (*hong fu*) expressing good fortune, and the gourds on scrolling vines symbolizing endless offspring. The final example (e), its bird pairings combined with auspicious plants, would have made an ideal marriage gift; the peach blossom is a symbol of spring and romance, together with the grain stalks (*he*) representing peace and harmony and signifying happy, united couples.[6] DL

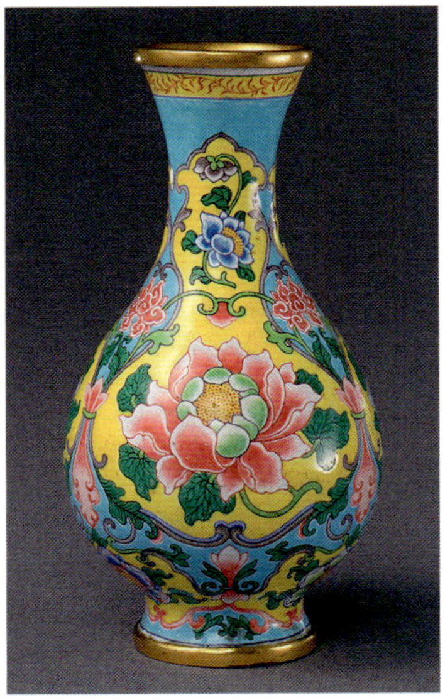

Fig. 56. Vase with Peony Design. Qing dynasty, Kangxi period. Copper with enamel decoration, h. 5⁵⁄₁₆ inches (13.5 cm). Palace Museum, Beijing

1. Unknown in Chinese culture prior to the seventeenth century, the consumption of snuff, primarily for medicinal purposes, was most likely an imported habit resulting from the expansion of global trade networks in the early modern era.
2. Snuff bottles were commonly made of glass, though there are also examples of metal, porcelain, precious stones, and even organic materials, such as gourd and coconut shells.
3. The manufacturing of snuff bottles began shortly after the establishment, in 1696, of the first glass workshop for the imperial court, which was led by the Jesuit priest Father Kilian Stumpf (1655–1720), who also experimented with painted enamels. Requests for enamel experts were repeatedly sent to France and Italy from the Qing court. For detailed records, see Xu 2015.
4. Snuff bottles with reign marks are often considered to be "made by imperial command." Indeed, production of these playful accoutrements was a serious matter that often entailed the emperor's supervision and judgment. The designs for snuff bottles were drafted by skilled court painters, and then presented to the emperor for review before the bottles were fabricated. See Lo 2009, 140.
5. San Francisco 2006, 137.
6. The grain stalk, pronounced "he," is a homophone for harmony (*he*). It is also considered a symbol of peace, brought about by a good harvest and the ruler's righteous governance. See San Francisco 2006, 55.

69

Manggūri (Mang Huli; Mongolian-Manchu, 1672–1736)
Portrait of a Manchu Lady

Qing dynasty (1644–1911), probably Yongzheng period (1723–35)
Ink, color, and gold on silk, mounted as a single panel
66½ x 43¾ inches (168.9 x 111.1 cm)
Gift of Mrs. W. James Anderson, Mrs. Samuel Bell, Jr., Mrs. Richard Drayton, and Charles T. Ludington, Jr., in memory of their parents, Mr. and Mrs. Charles Townsend Ludington, 1970-259-2

The Manchu ethnicity of the aristocratic lady painted on this hanging scroll (mounted as a single panel) is revealed by the three gold hoops in her left earlobe, a traditional element of dress for women of this ethnic group.[1] Striking an elegant pose next to a stack of books that indicates her literary aptitude, she holds a delicate silk fan painted with bamboo leaves, the air around her perfumed by a Buddha's Hand citron resting on the couch next to her and the incense and sprigs of roses and orchids on the table. Her elite status is indicated by the phoenix roundels adorning her silk dress and the four-clawed dragon on the nearby porcelain stool, both designs permitted only to royals. The Ming-style hardwood table, couch bed (*luohan chuang*), and lacquered incense stand with gilded decoration were highly desirable furnishings in the early eighteenth century, further attesting to the lady's refined taste and the luxurious lifestyle of the Yongzheng period (fig. 57).[2]

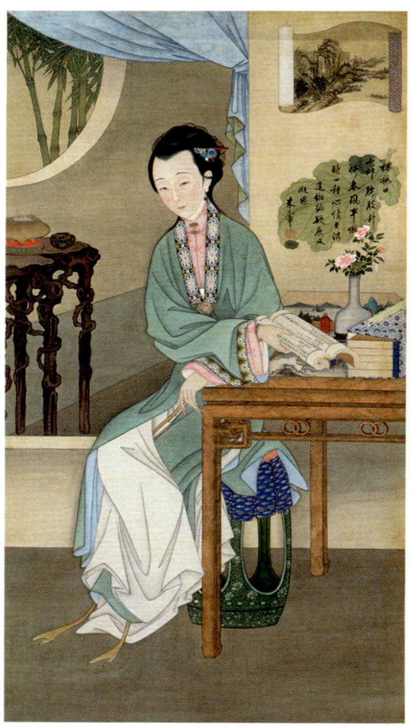

Fig. 57. *Prince Yong's Twelve Beauties*. Qing dynasty, early 18th century. Ink and color on silk, one of a set of twelve, previously mounted as a folding screen; 72 7/16 x 38½ inches (184 x 98 cm). Palace Museum, Beijing

The artist of this painting is Manggūri, a Manchu bannerman of Mongolian descent.[3] He had an extensive career in the Qing government, rising from a clerk in the Board of Tributary Affairs to the Manchu Commander-in-Chief of the Plain Blue Banner.[4] Noted for his skills in portraiture, he was directed by the Yongzheng emperor to paint a posthumous portrait of his father, the Kangxi emperor (r. 1662–1722).[5] The few extant works by Manggūri are all portraits of Manchu elites, among which this seated lady is the sole female portrayal.[6] DL

1. Xu 1984, vol. 13, 6146–47.
2. Similar interior settings can be seen in a few other paintings produced at the Yongzheng court or slightly earlier, for instance, the *Album of Ladies' Seasonal Activities of the Twelve Months* by Chen Mei (act. 1720–40) and *Prince Yong's Twelve Beauties* by an anonymous artist, both in the Palace Museum, Beijing.
3. Bannermen were members of the Eight Banners, a system established by the Manchus to organize and govern their military groups.
4. Zhao et al. 1976–77, vol. 291, 10286–87. While originally a member of the Mongolian Plain Blue Banner, he became affiliated with Manchu banners at the beginning of the Yongzheng period.
5. Zhao et al. 1976–77, vol. 85, 2567.
6. Manggūri's primary patron was Prince Guo (1697–1738), the seventeenth son of the Kangxi emperor. At least two extant portraits of this prince bear Manggūri's signature. The nineteenth-century connoisseur Li Yufen records seeing a portrait by Manggūri of a Manchu lady freeing a silver pheasant, already for sale at an antique shop in the late Qing period; Li 1897, vol. 2, 28.

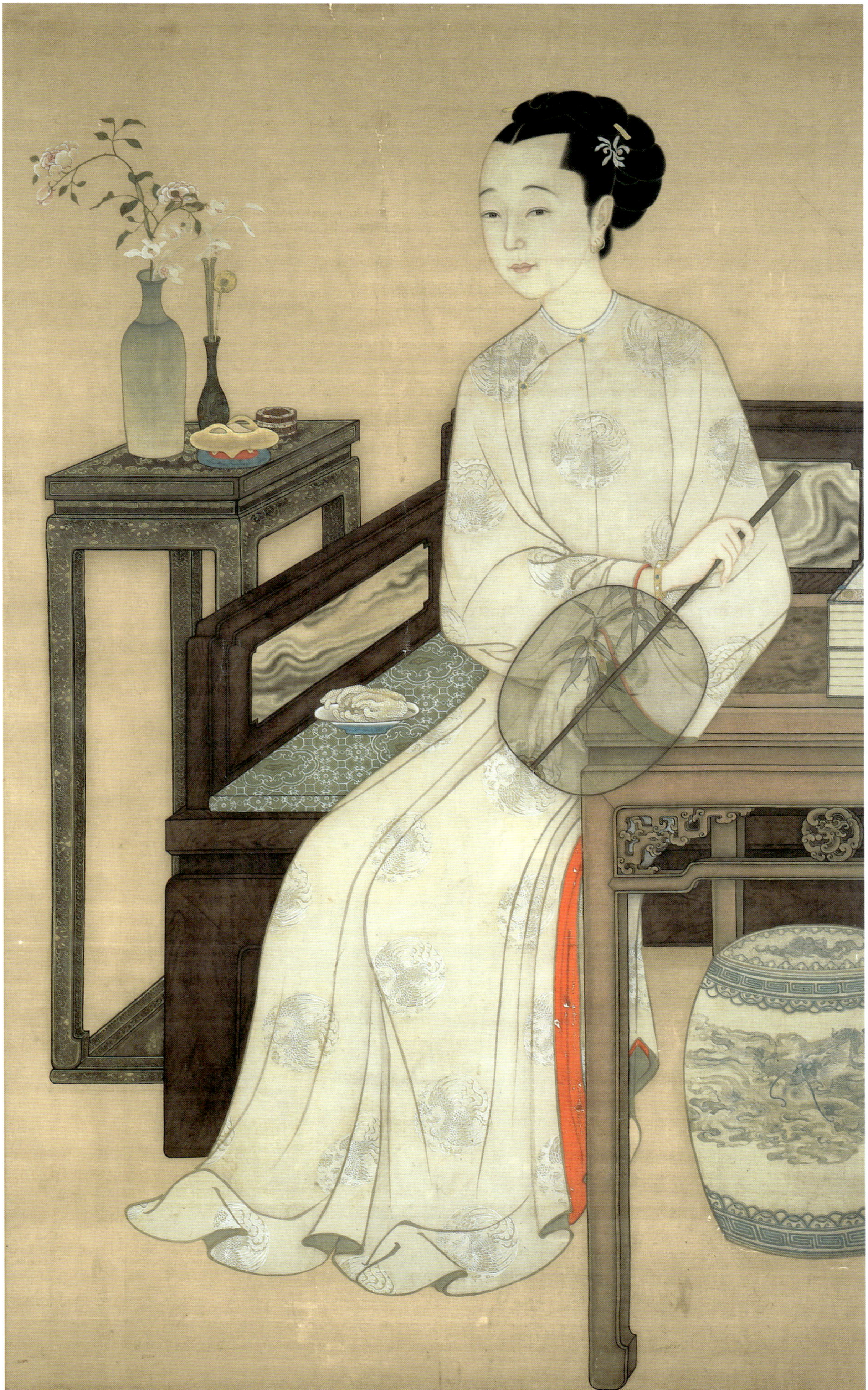

70

Faceted Vase with Morning Glories

Qing dynasty (1644–1911), Yongzheng period (1723–35)
Porcelain with underglaze blue decoration (Jingdezhen ware)
9 7/16 x 4 15/16 inches (24 x 12.5 cm)
Gift of Major General and Mrs. William Crozier, 1944-20-831

Scrolling morning glory vines in varying shades of underglaze blue cover the body and tall, cylindrical neck of this porcelain vase, which—with its faceted form and monster-mask handles—was probably modeled after Middle Eastern metalwork. The added decorative borders and the Yongzheng mark on the base (see p. 249) identify it as a Qing-dynasty reinterpretation of a Ming vase made during the reign of the Xuande emperor (1426–35).

Since early times, emperors collected and treasured works from the past. During the Ming and Qing dynasties, ancient paintings, calligraphy, bronzes, jades, and ceramics from China's most revered dynasties were collected not only as amusing curios, but as objects whose reflection of a glorious past served to legitimize one's own rule. Among porcelains, imperial blue and white from the Xuande and Chenghua (1465–87) periods was especially prestigious and treasured (see no. 47 for a 16th-century blue-and-white vase of this form). The Yongzheng and Qianlong (1736–95) emperors' reigns saw the creation of this faceted vase form in both the original smaller size in blue and white or blue on yellow ground,[1] and a larger version in blue and white[2] or decorated with such archaistic glazes as the crackled glaze of the celebrated thirteenth-century *Ge* ware.[3] Most unusual is a plain, white-glazed vase of the larger size in the Freer Gallery of Art in Washington, DC.[4] HK

1. A smaller-size vase decorated in underglaze blue on yellow enameled ground is in the collection of the Fondation Baur, Geneva; Ayers 1974, vol. 4, no. A577.
2. A Yongzheng blue-and-white vase of this larger size is illustrated in Xu and Nanjing 2003, 135; a Qianlong-marked version is in the Shanghai Museum, illustrated in Zhou 2014, 303, fig. 5-33.
3. An imitation *Ge*-ware faceted vase with a Yongzheng seal mark is illustrated in Taipei 2009, 204, no. II-30.
4. It is described by the Freer as "Vase made as sample, with date '4th year'" (F1956.32). The four-character mark on the base is poorly written, however, and the piece may well be a later copy; see the Freer's online collection for an illustration and further information.

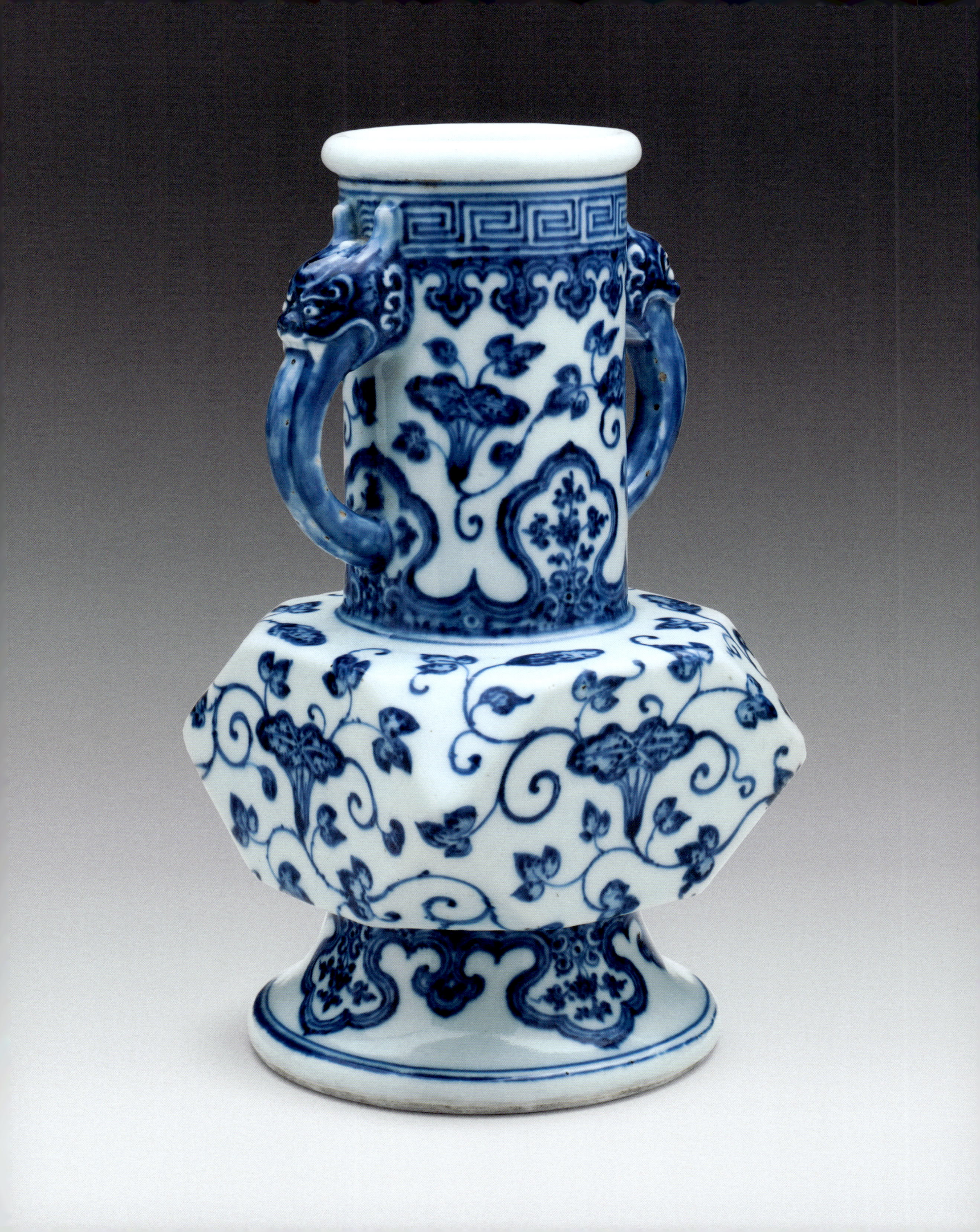

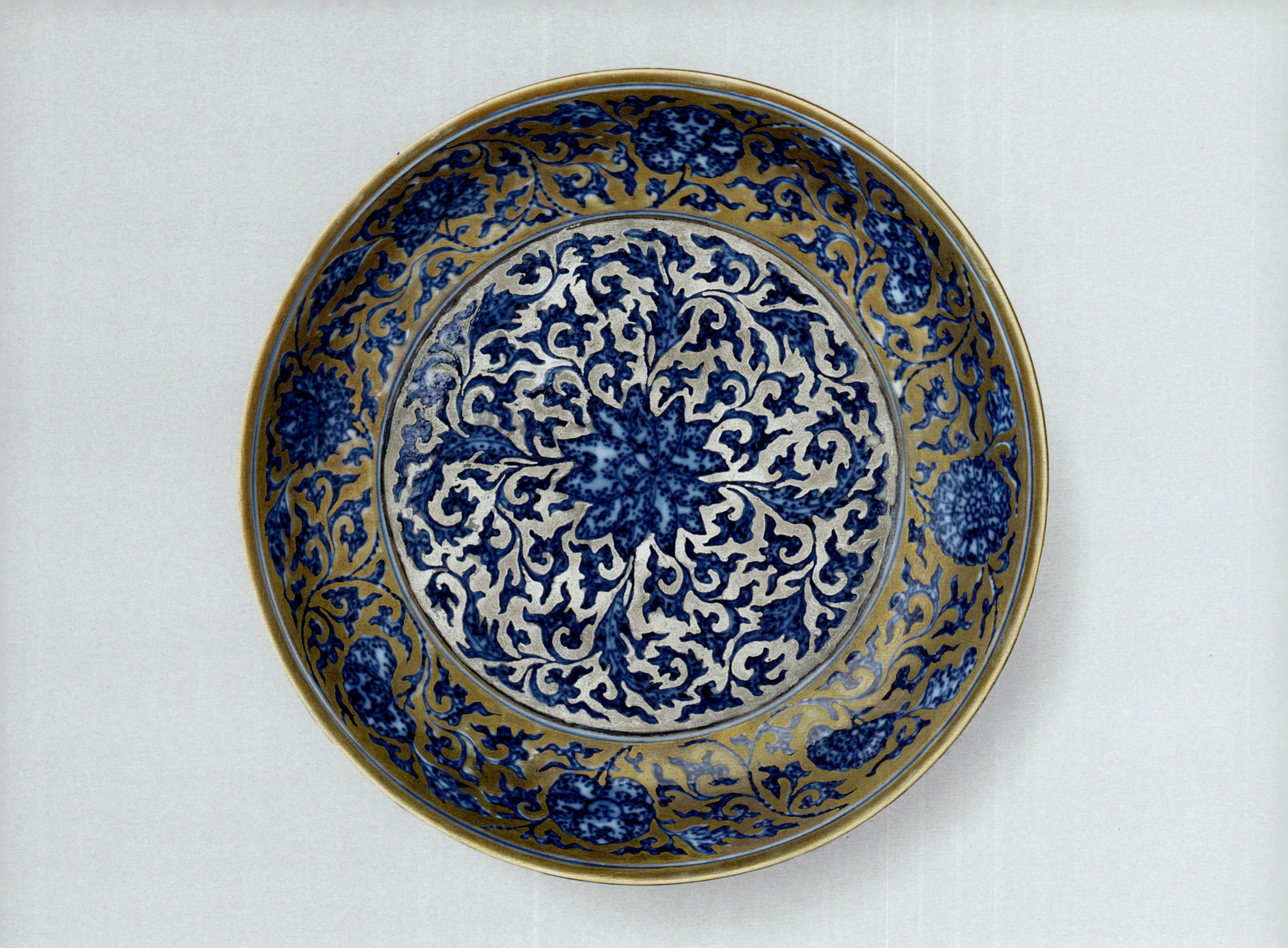

71

Saucers with Floral Blossoms

Qing dynasty (1644–1911), Yongzheng period (1723–35) or later
Porcelain with underglaze blue and gilded and silver decoration (Jingdezhen ware)
1³⁄₁₆ x 5⁷⁄₈ inches (3 x 15 cm)
Gift of Major General and Mrs. William Crozier, 1944-20-287a,b, 1944-20-288a,b

These rare saucers are decorated in an unusual technique that required two stages. The first entailed painting the white porcelain in underglaze cobalt blue with lotus and other floral blossoms on dense scrolling foliage before firing the dishes, which were then embellished with silver in the center and gold on the sides and fired a second time. The white glazed bases carry a six-character Yongzheng mark in cobalt blue (see p. 249).

Although gold and silver decoration appeared in the Song dynasty (960–1279) on Ding wares that were possibly created in imitation of lacquer vessels,[1] gilding was first tried experimentally at the imperial kilns in the Yongle

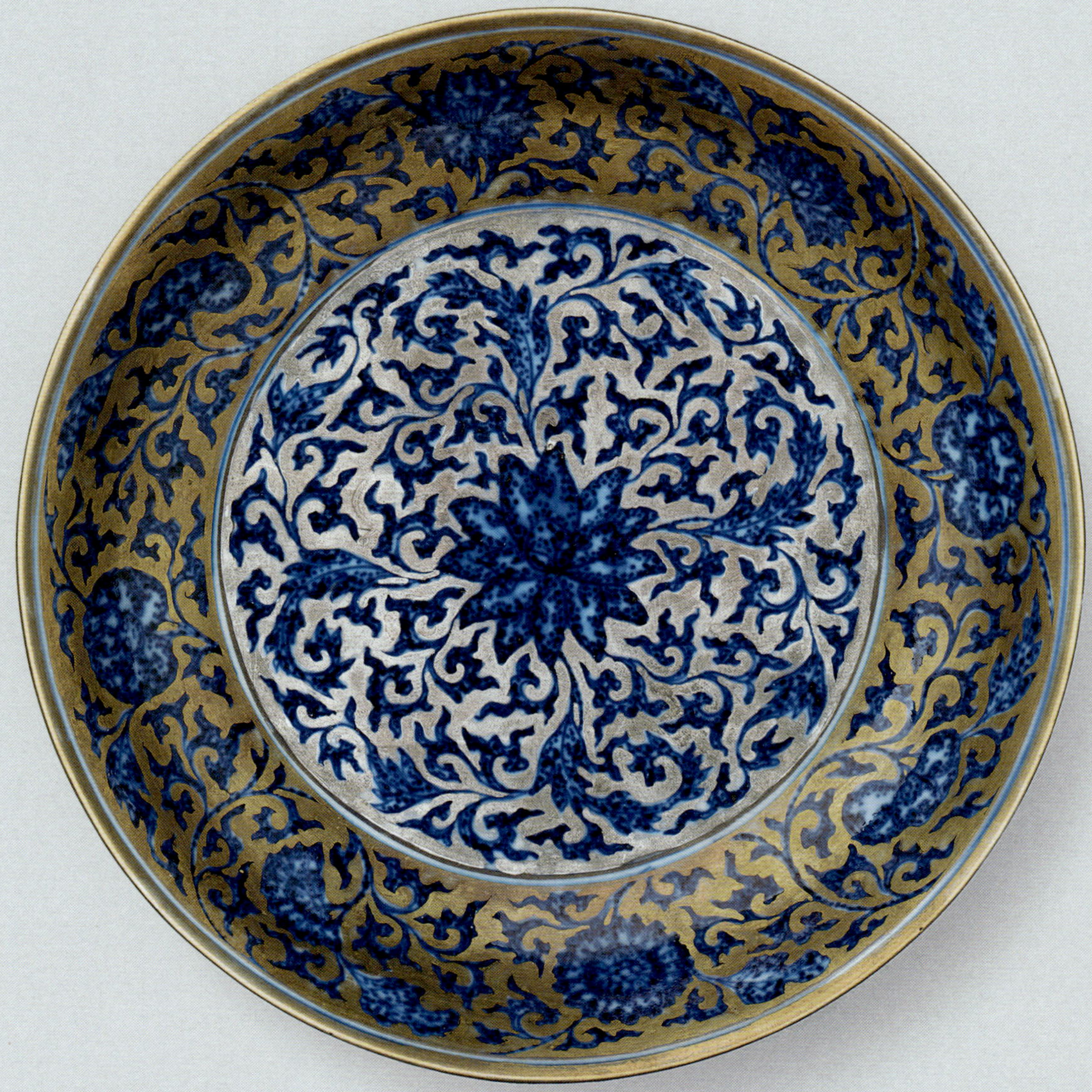

period (1403–24) of the Ming dynasty (1368–1644). During the Jiajing (1522–66) emperor's reign, gilded floral scrolling designs on white and coral-red enameled bowls were among the more elaborate examples produced, and were especially appreciated in West Asia and in Japan, where they were called *kinran-de* (gold brocade).[2] Whereas the Jiajing gilding technique utilized small pieces of gold foil cut and adhered to the surface of the porcelain, the gilding and silvering on these saucer dishes appears to have been painted on and then fired.

The Yongzheng emperor's reign saw the creation of some of the most unusual new ceramic forms and glazes. During this time the imperial kilns were run by Tang Ying (1682–1756), who had served the Kangxi emperor and had the experience of producing large amounts of porcelains of exacting quality. Yongzheng was one of the most cultured emperors of the Qing dynasty and took an intense personal interest in the arts. He would send antiques from the palace to the kilns in Jingdezhen as models for archaistic designs and inspiration for new designs.[3] The dark spots of cobalt and the scrolling lotus design on these saucers harked back to fourteenth- and fifteenth-century Ming-dynasty blue-and-white ceramics, but the application of gold and silver was a new technique only in use during Yongzheng's short reign.[4] HK

1. Kerr and Wood 2004, 703.
2. Kerr and Wood 2004, 704–6.
3. Krahl 2005, 245.
4. A similar pair of dishes in the Shanghai Museum is illustrated in Zhou 2014, fig. 3-3. A new type of decoration during the Yongzheng period was silver-decorated blue-and-white floral bowls and dishes; see Geng 1993, 289.

72

Conical Bowl with Floral Medallions

Qing dynasty (1644–1911), Yongzheng period (1723–35)
Porcelain with underglaze blue and polychrome enamel decoration (Jingdezhen ware)
2$\frac{7}{8}$ x 8$\frac{3}{4}$ inches (7.3 x 22.2 cm)
Gift of Lydia Thompson Morris, 1925-27-36

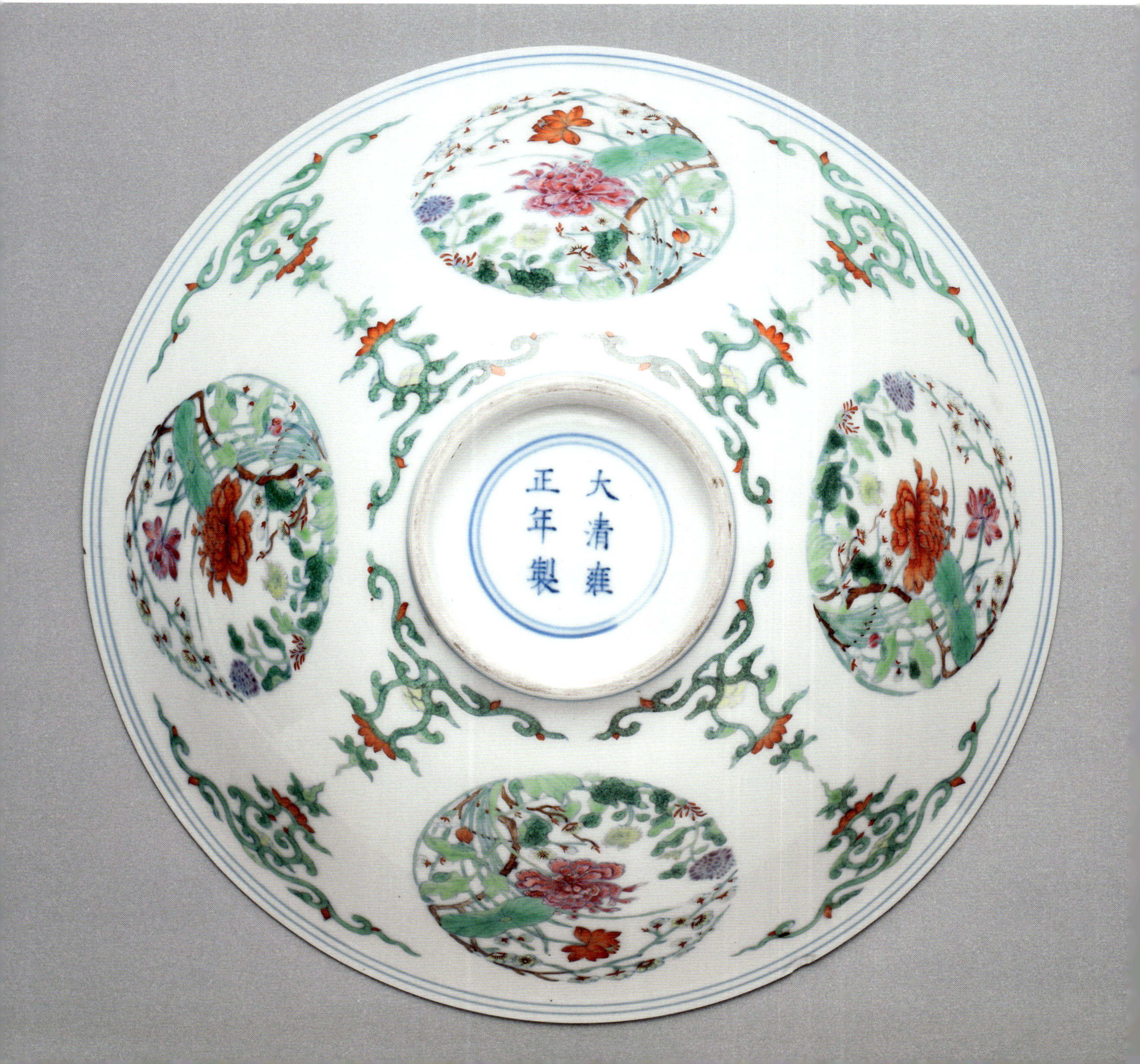

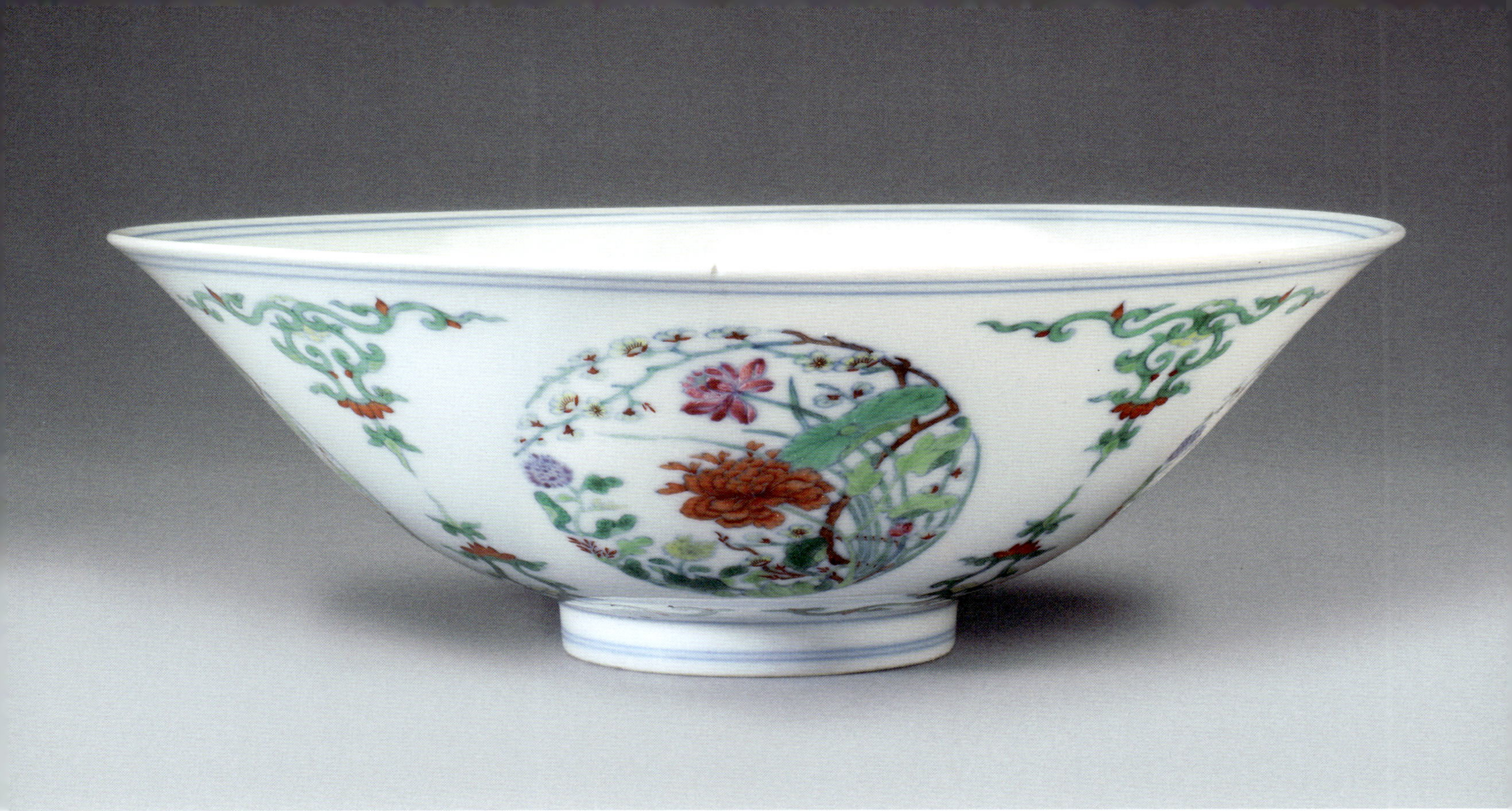

The high standards of porcelain production at the imperial kilns during the Yongzheng period are demonstrated in this conical bowl by the pleasing contrast of the underglaze blue outline with the luminous enamels of the design. Four floral medallions containing flowers of the four seasons—prunus, peony, lotus, and chrysanthemum—are picked out in yellow, purple, red, light green, dark green, and pink enamels, separated by light and dark green foliate scrolling ornaments that form auspicious pendant *ruyi* ("as you wish") heads around the rim and vase forms around the base. On the interior, a medallion encloses a pair of butterflies (fig. 58), one shown in bird's-eye view and the other in profile flitting between two flower sprays.

Most conspicuous among the wide range of colors used on this bowl is the bright pink palette, sometimes called *famille rose*, which first appeared in Chinese porcelains, glass, and metal enameling in the early eighteenth century.[1] During the reign of the Yongzheng emperor, opaque enamels were introduced to the imperial kilns, adding to the range of transparent enamels already being used and thus expanding the color palette.[2] Three new enamel colors were introduced: ruby pink, opaque white, and opaque yellow,[3] as seen on the peony and lotus blossoms on this bowl, where white was added to the ruby pink.[4] HK

1. See Kerr and Wood 2004, 638; also Kingery and Vandiver 1985.
2. New enameling pigments, primarily from Europe, were supplied to the imperial court workshops, allowing artisans to experiment with a wider range of designs. The court workshops in Beijing and the imperial kilns at Jingdezhen had a close relationship and would have influenced each other. For example, white (blank) porcelains were fired at Jingdezhen and sent to Beijing to be enameled (Shih 2005, 7), and the imperial workshops in Beijing included porcelain painters from Jiangxi, where Jingdezhen is located (Shih 2005, 9).
3. Kerr and Wood 2004, 634. Copper objects with enamel decoration also exhibit these new colors.
4. An imperially marked Yongzheng foliate dish with a similar design of butterflies amid flowers in the Palace Museum, Taipei, also uses this new opaque enamel palette; see Taipei 2009. For an example in the Palace Museum collections, Beijing, see Wang 1999, pl. 229.

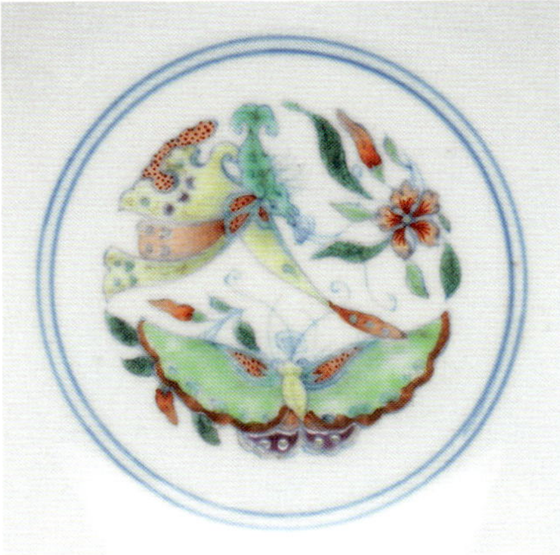

Fig. 58. Central medallion on the interior of the bowl

73

Pair of Hexagonal Lanterns

Qing dynasty (1644–1911), Yongzheng period (1723–35)
Porcelain with polychrome enamel decoration (Jingdezhen ware)
12⅞ x 8⅜ inches (32.7 x 21.3 cm)
The Alfred and Margaret Caspary Memorial Gift, 1955-50-105, 1955-50-106

These delicately formed, six-sided lanterns, so light in the hand as to feel almost weightless, are made of eggshell-thin porcelain decorated with enamels. The lattice design on each of the six sides required great skill on such fine clay walls, and was accomplished by letting the porcelain dry to a leather-hard stage before cutting the many separate openings that form the pattern. The lanterns were then glazed and fired, after which the different colored enamels were applied and the pieces fired a second time. Raised up on wood or metal stands, the lanterns would have glowed and flickered softly from the candles placed within (fig. 59).

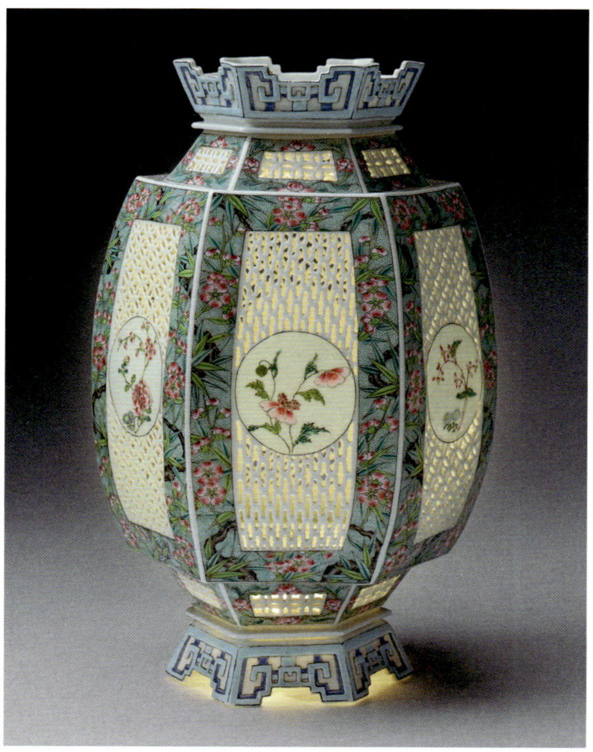

Fig. 59. The egg-shell thin, minutely pierced white porcelain walls of the lantern appear translucent when lit from within.

The borders of each of the six sides are decorated with pink and white plum blossoms against a ground of green bamboo leaves picked out in fine, translucent pink, white, green, aqua, and black enamels. The plum and bamboo are both associated with winter; along with the pine, they are known as the Three Friends of Winter because they flourish over the cold winter months. Flowers representative of other seasons—including camellia, rose, lily, and peony—are contained within the central medallions on each of the six sides, conveying auspicious wishes of peace, unity, and longevity.

The distinctive hexagonal form of these lanterns, with flared lip and base, first appeared in the Kangxi period (1662–1722). The Kangxi versions have a separate base and solid sides, however, and are decorated in polychrome (*wucai* or *famille verte*) enamels with figural scenes.[1] The later piercing of the sides allowed the release of more light from the burning candle within and appears to have begun in the Yongzheng period, as did the use of opaque white and bright ruby pink enameling, which is visible in the enamel palette used on this pair.[2] Judging by the soft, translucent colors of these examples, they likely were made during this period.[3] The form continued throughout the Qing dynasty, with later examples displaying somewhat thicker walls and more opaque enameling. HK

1. See an example in the Taft Museum of Art, Cincinnati; Du Boulay 1995, 633. Another, without its stand, is in the National Gallery of Art, Washington, DC (Widener Collection, 1942.9.586).
2. This type of palette, called *famille rose*, was being used on porcelains produced both for the court and for export; Kerr 2000.
3. The color palette is reminiscent of the Yongzheng enameled conical bowl depicting seasonal flowers illustrated above (no. 72). Lanterns with heavier and more opaque enameling appear to be mid-eighteenth century in date; see the example in the Victoria and Albert Museum, London; illustrated in Kerr 1991, no. 50.

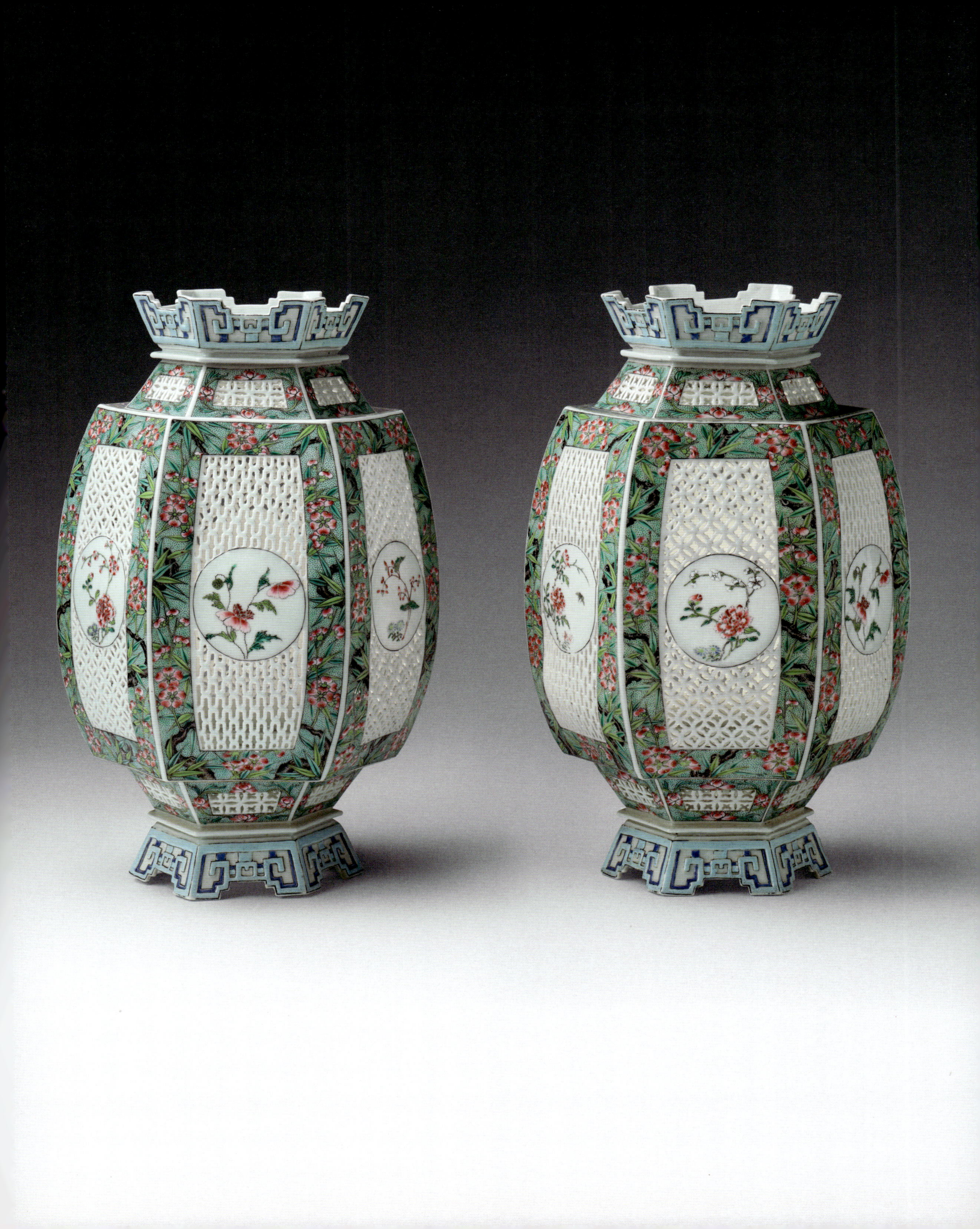

74

Huang Shen (1687–after 1768)
Lady Carrying a Zither

Qing dynasty (1644–1911), early 18th century
Ink on silk, mounted as a hanging scroll
57⅞ x 27 9/16 inches (147 x 70 cm)
Purchased with Museum funds from the Simkhovitch Collection, 1929-40-139

After immigrating from his hometown in Fujian province to the metropolis of Yangzhou, the artist Huang Shen developed a remarkable style for depicting figures that mimicked the writing of cursive scrip, and won him fame as one of the so-called Eight Eccentrics of Yangzhou. In the painting a girl holds a *qin*, or zither, in her arms. It appears that something has caught her attention, so she has stopped to look back, her body twisting in a graceful curve. Who is the girl? The answer lies in Huang Shen's poem in the upper right corner of the painting. The poem's narrator is a newlywed lady whose husband has left to travel to a remote place. Missing her lover very much, she is lonely and fearful. The words of the poem are also the lyrics of a song. The narrator of the poem is also the singer of the love song; she is the girl holding the *qin*, traditionally played to accompany singing. In his poem, Huang Shen mentions another ancient stringed instrument, the *se*. *Qin* accompanied by *se* is a metaphor for a harmonious couple, a much favored theme in Chinese painting.

Three almost identical depictions of the same scene, but painted on paper, can be found in the Shenyang Palace Museum,[1] the Huai'an Municipal Museum,[2] and the Taizhou Municipal Museum.[3] HX

1. Dated 1731; see Wu and Li 2006, 2.
2. Dated 1725; see *Huai'an* 2011, 28.
3. Dated 1724; see *Yangzhou* 1998, 3.

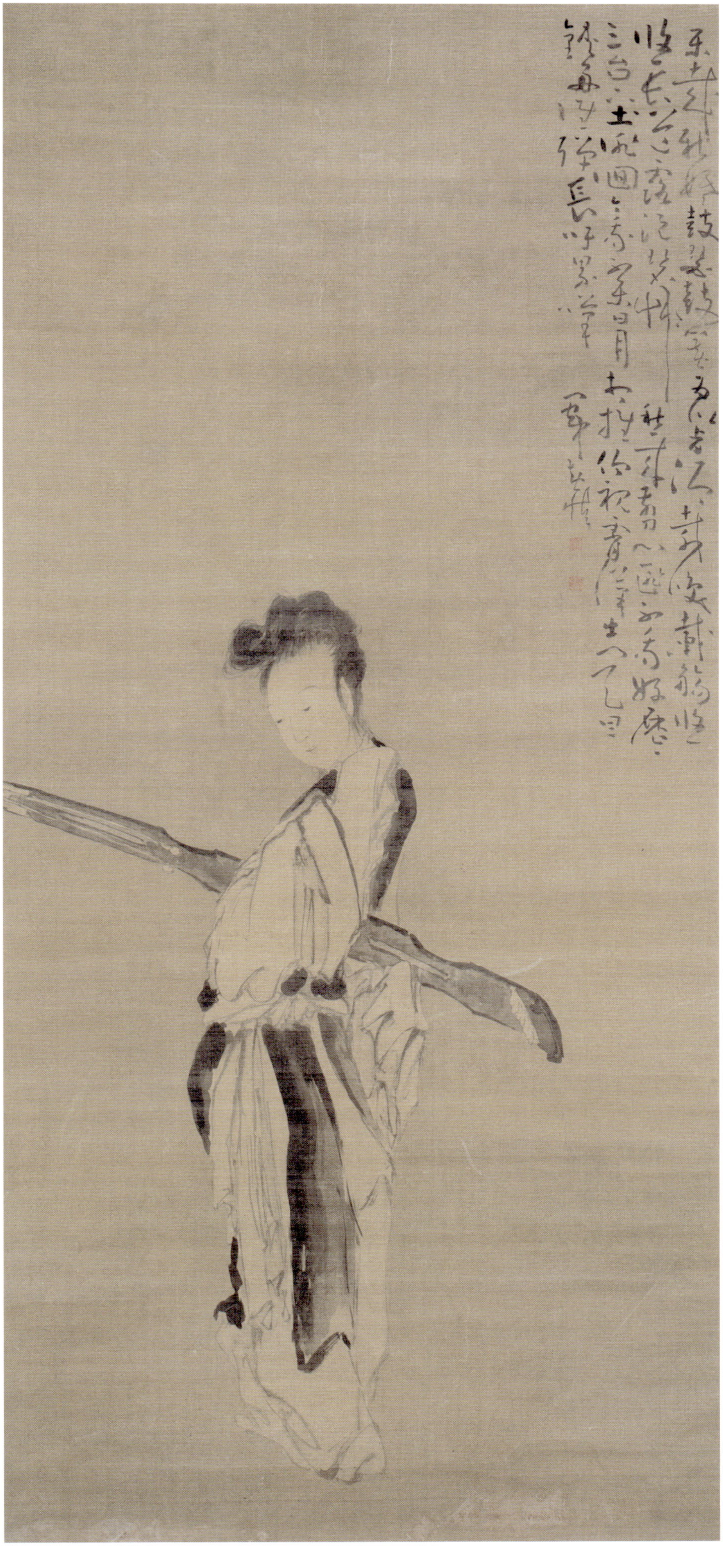

75

Cup in the Form of a Half Peach

Qing dynasty (1644–1911), 18th century
Stoneware (Yixing ware)
2¾ x 4⅞ x 3⅞ inches (7 x 12.4 x 9.9 cm)
The Dr. Francis W. Lewis Collection, 1905-201

The lustrous reddish clay of this cup is characteristic of wares made at the Yixing kilns in Jiangsu province in southern China from the Song dynasty (906–1279) to the present day. Known as *zisha* (purple sand),[1] the locally mined, dense clay produces colors ranging from red to purple to pale buff and even black, and has been renowned from the time of the late Ming dynasty (16th–17th century) for the making of teapots. Yixing teapots were praised in texts by tea connoisseurs for their ability to retain not only heat but also the taste and aroma of steeped tea leaves, as well as for the rich patina produced after years of handling, lending a natural gloss and appealing feel to the surfaces.

Yixing potters typically depicted natural forms, of which this sensitively modeled peach-shaped cup is an excellent example. Pointed on one side of the rim to mimic the shape of a peach bottom, the molded cup rests on a separately carved, twisted and gnarled branch that acts as a stand, not only elevating the cup but also enveloping the peach with separately modeled buds, blossoms, and furled leaves. Ancient legend recounts that peaches grown in the garden of the Daoist deity the Queen Mother of the West take three thousand years to flower and three thousand years to fruit, and bestow immortality when eaten;[2] the fruit thus came to be associated with longevity. Representing one of the most popular of the auspicious motifs, a cup such as this would have been an appropriate birthday gift.

Yixing wares became popular in Europe in the seventeenth century, and soon kilns in France and Germany were producing their own versions. Though they resemble Chinese Yixing wares, the European-made forms (or their seal marks) often give away their Western origin. HK

1. Kilns at Yixing have been producing ceramic wares for thousands of years, with sherds excavated that date back to 3000 BCE. Though the use of *zisha* clay may have started in the Song dynasty, it was not until the late Yuan (1271–1368) and Ming (1368–1644) periods that it became popular, after *zisha* teapots caught the attention of the scholar class, who sang their praises in poetry and paintings. See Lo, Lai, and Ip 1986, 13, 18.
2. San Francisco 2006, 204, no. 7.44.

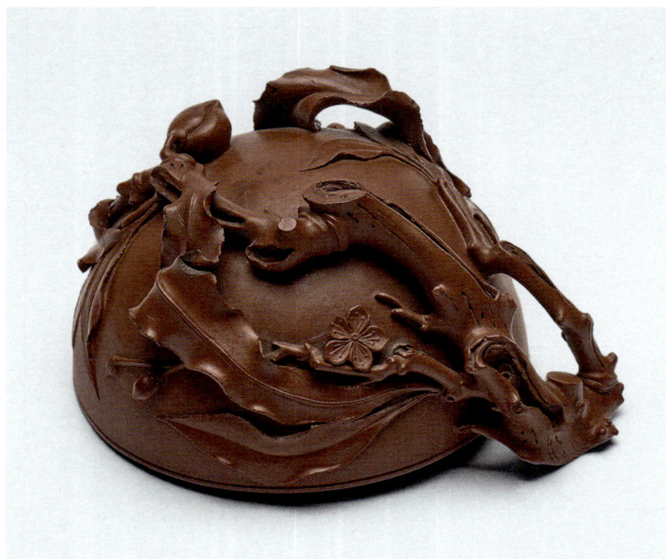

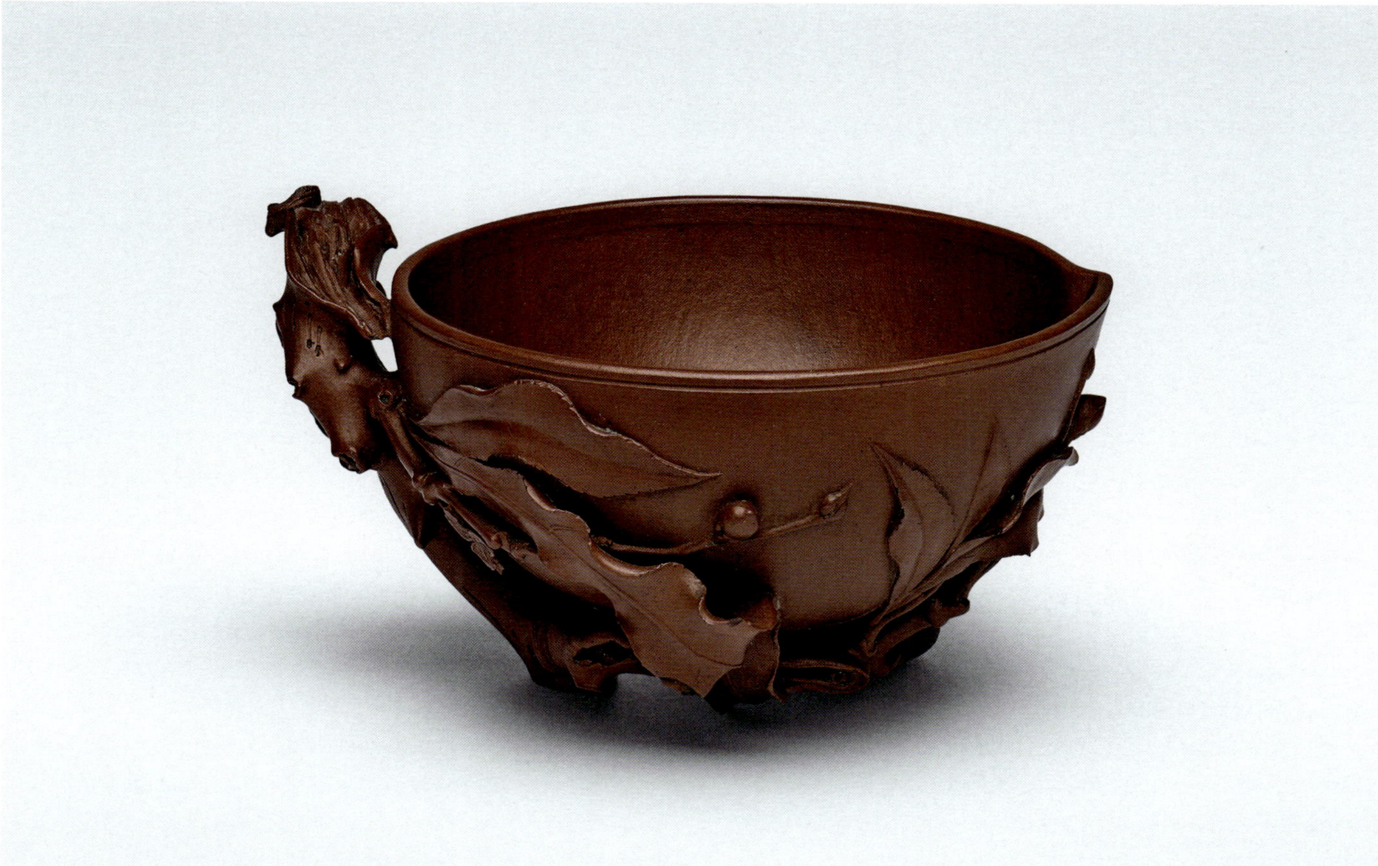
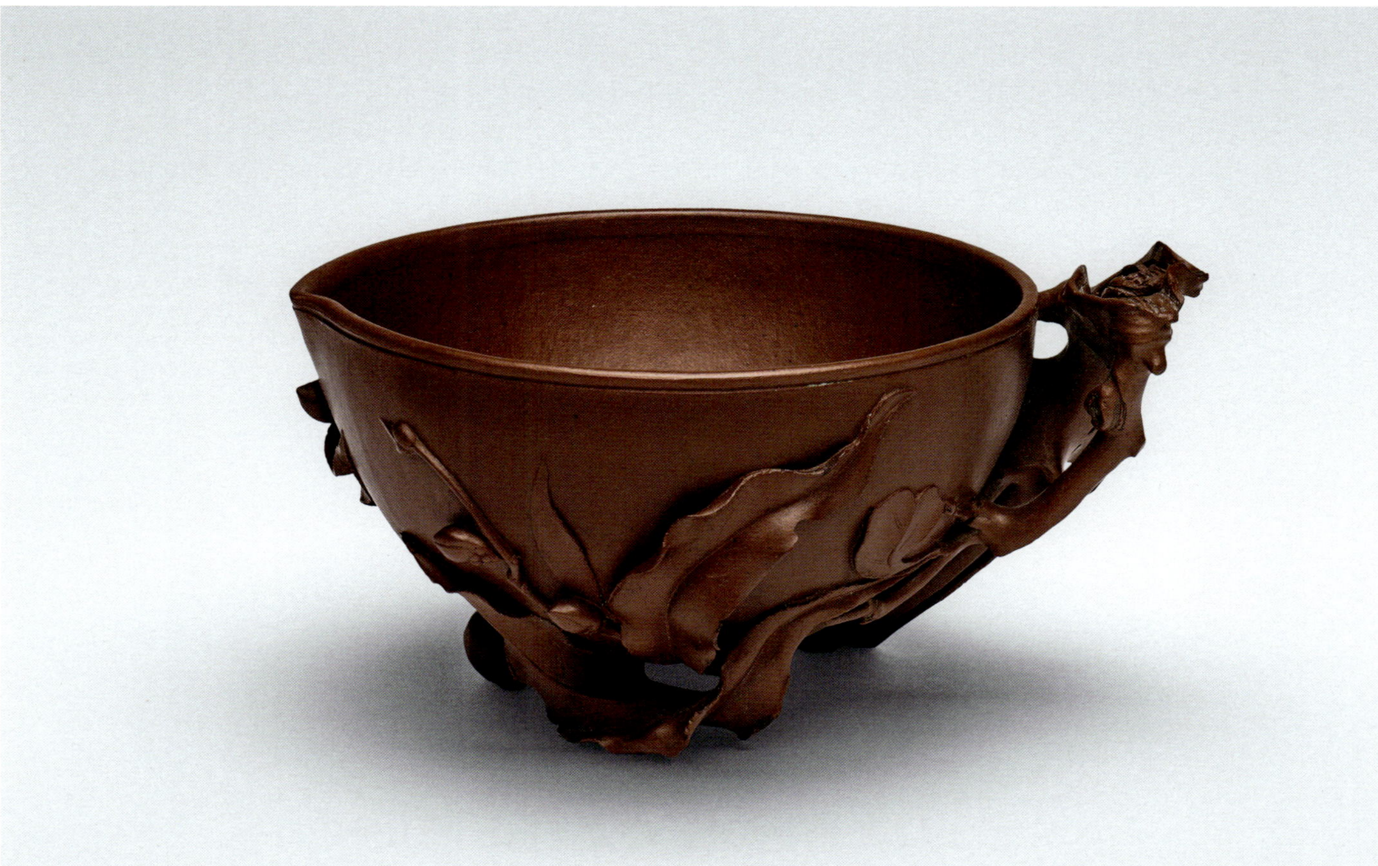

76

Cup and Saucer with Roman Mythological Figures

Qing dynasty (1644–1911), mid-18th century
Copper with painted enamel decoration
Cup $2\frac{3}{8}$ x $3\frac{15}{16}$ inches (6 x 10 cm); saucer $1\frac{3}{16}$ x $5\frac{9}{16}$ inches (3 x 14.2 cm)
The Bloomfield Moore Collection, 1899-804a,b

Chinese and Western techniques and motifs are displayed on this painted enamel cup and saucer depicting Roman mythological figures. Delicately painted on the interior of the saucer in soft, opaque enamels using washes and stippling is the goddess Proserpina, seen offering a wreath to the goddess Cybele, who is seated in a carriage drawn by two lions within a European landscape. The exterior of the cup is decorated with two vignettes; one depicts Pomona (goddess of fruit and orchards) with two dogs and her consort Vertumnus (god of the seasons), while the other (fig. 60) shows the goddesses Ceres (grain and harvest), Flora (flowers and spring), and Pomona.

The style of painting, subject matter, and decorative motifs, such as the strapwork borders, suggest the inspiration of Western porcelain or prints,[1] although the enameling was done in China. When enameled works of art were first introduced to the Chinese court by European envoys and Jesuit missionaries in the 1680s, the Kangxi emperor (r. 1662–1722) established imperial workshops in Beijing to produce glass and enamels for the court (see no. 68),[2] initially drawing upon European methods of enameling, especially those being used for enamel on metal at Limoges. Both the Kangxi emperor and his grandson, the Qianlong emperor (r. 1736–95), sought raw materials for coloring as well as European enamelers in order to improve the court workshop.[3] This cup and saucer were most likely produced in the mid-eighteenth century, when ruby pink and lead-arsenate white were added to the color palette.[4]

Enamels were produced not just in Beijing, but also at workshops in Guangzhou (Canton) in southern China. So highly skilled were the craftsmen in Guangzhou that its enamelers were sent to the imperial workshops in

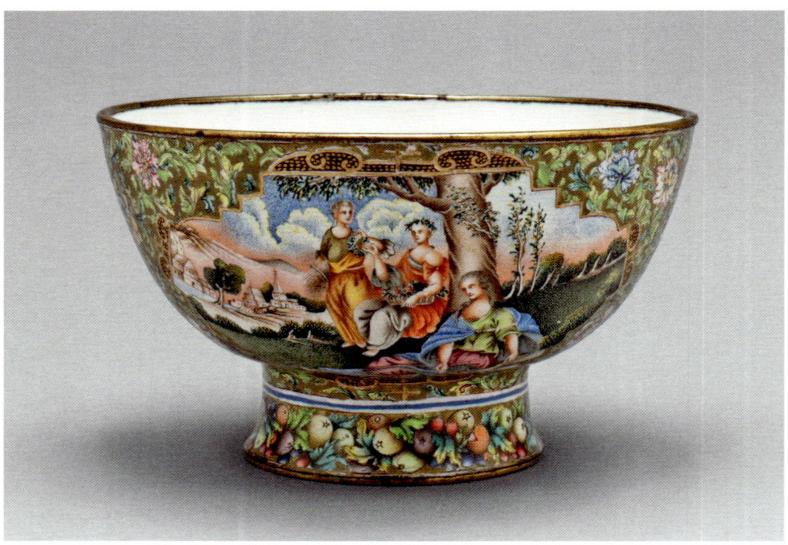

Fig. 60. The other side of the cup, showing the Roman goddesses Ceres, Flora, and Pomona

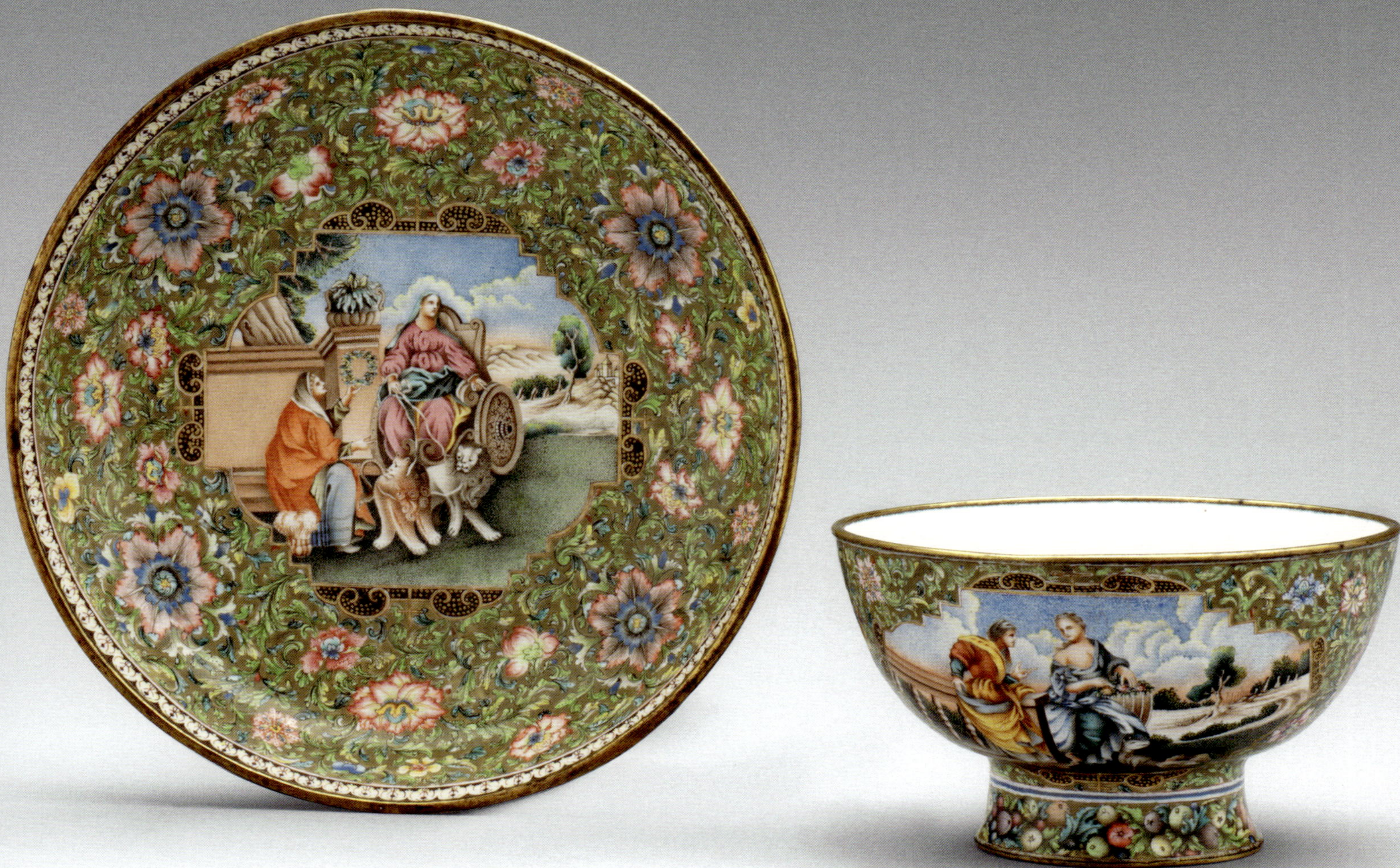

Beijing.[5] It is difficult to say for certain whether this cup and saucer were produced in Beijing or Guangzhou, nor is it known for whom they were made. Because they are lacking a mark, it seems unlikely that the pair was destined for the Chinese court,[6] though the enameling is clearly of high quality. Closely related examples in both enameled copper and porcelain can be found in collections outside China, suggesting that they may have been made for export.[7] HK

1. It has been suggested that the strapwork borders were derived from Meissen porcelain from Germany; Howard and Ayers 1978, no. 662.
2. The Kangxi emperor promoted painted enamels and set up his own glass and enameling workshops in the palace; Curtis 1993, 93.
3. Curtis 1993, 95–100.
4. New colors were introduced on both metal and porcelain during the Yongzheng emperor's reign (1723–35); Xu 2015, 98. This new set of colors, called *fencai* (powdery colors) or *yangcai* (foreign colors), reflects both the colors' foreign origin, imported from Europe by the Jesuits, as well as the soft opaque palette.
5. Xu 2015, 101–2. Beginning in 1687, after the withdrawal of a maritime prohibition, Guangzhou was open to foreign ships.
6. A painted-enamel squared vase with Western figures on a ground of scrolling blossoms, and with a six-character Qianlong mark, is in the National Palace Museum, Taipei; Guoli Gugong bowuyuan 1971, no. 47.
7. A similar cup and saucer, though by a different hand, is in the Victoria and Albert Museum, London (C.39-1962). An enameled porcelain version with three vignettes around the side of the cup can be found in the Peabody Essex Museum, Salem, MA (Sargent 2012, 242–43, no. 118), and a *grisaille* decorated plate is in the collection of Washington and Lee University, Lexington, VA (Litzenburg 2003, 189, no. 186). A Western audience would immediately have recognized the specific mythological reference.

77

Dragon Robe Opera Costume

Qing dynasty (1644–1911), Yongzheng (1723–35) or Qianlong (1736–95) period
Silk satin with discontinuous supplemental wefts in floss silk, gold leaf on paper strips and gold leaf on paper-wrapped thread; silk lampas binding; gilded brass buttons
L. 53½ inches (135.9 cm)
Purchased with Museum funds, 1951-29-6

Although styled like early eighteenth-century Qing-dynasty semiformal court attire, this dragon robe is a costume built for the imperial theater. Three virtually identical garments now in the collection of the Palace Museum, Beijing, are made of the differently colored discontinuous supplemental weft-patterned silk satins with the same bold designs of dragons in two sizes, and are identified as "light martial attire" for the court stage.[1] Nearly twenty other examples—mainly in the collections of the Metropolitan Museum of Art, New York; the Minneapolis Institute of Art; and the Museum of Fine Arts, Boston—can be linked to the robes in the Palace collection on technical and stylistic grounds. Yet for decades the designation of these garments has been incorrect. The problem can be traced to a catalogue published in 1945, in which they are identified as consorts' robes.[2] Despite the seemingly feminine and atypical Qing robe colors, however, nearly all the examples are tailored in the male style, with front and back skirt vents. Additionally, most are constructed without separate fabric sleeve extensions and contrasting cuffs, but instead have the same fabric for body, sleeve, and cuff.

Information accompanying the 1902 acquisition from Yamanaka & Company of five of these exquisitely woven robes by the Museum of Fine Arts, Boston, describes them as having been acquired in China from a source who claimed they came from the imperial chapel and were of the Qianlong period.[3] One of the Boston pieces[4] also bears identical chops on the linings at the back of the neck, matching the *daxi jiyong* mark in red and the *ruyi* mark in black on the robe in the Palace Museum collection.[5]

Most theatrical costumes for Chinese opera are based on fantastical, quasi-historical dress (see no. 91). These particular martial costumes evoke contemporary Qing official court dragon robes. They may have been designed to celebrate the military success of the Manchu conquest of the empire in 1644 and the Qing-dynasty emperors' complete transformation of the imperial wardrobe. Interestingly, by the nineteenth century dragon robes made for the opera had also reverted to historical models, with wide sleeves, sweeping skirts, and Ming-style hoop belts.[6] JV

1. Huang 2003, 166; Gugong 2008, 98, 99.
2. New York 1945, 8, fig. 17.
3. See Museum of Fine Arts, Boston, accession records 02.48, 02.50, 02.51, 02.52, and 02.53, examined September 22, 2005.
4. See Museum Fine Arts, Boston, accession record 02.48, examined September 30, 2017.
5. Gugong 2008, 99.
6. Bonds 2008, 50–68.

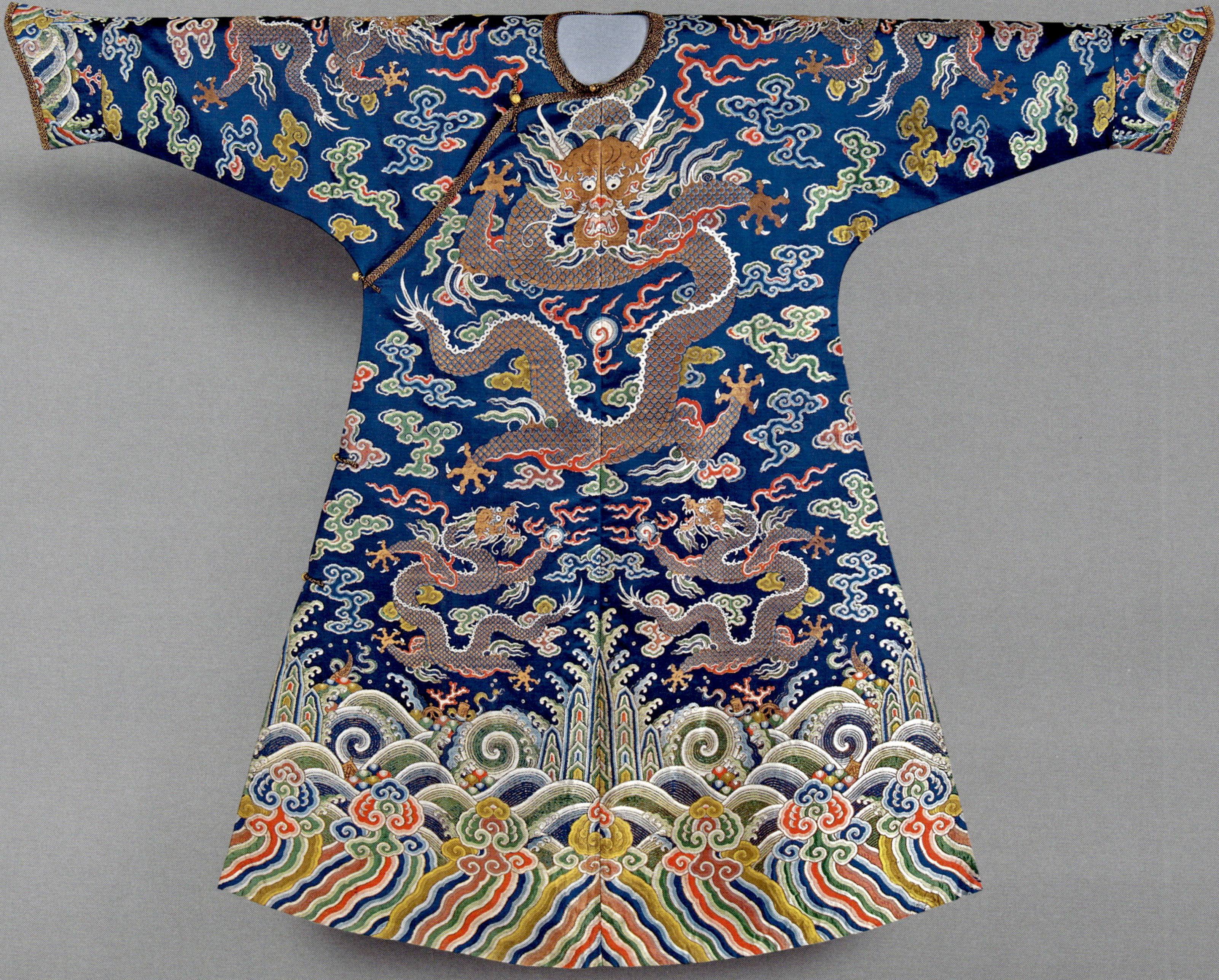

78

Pair of Compound Wardrobes

Qing dynasty (1644–1911), 18th century
Wood (softwood), lacquer with gilded decoration, brass hardware
Each 9 feet 6¼ inches x 56½ inches x 26⁵⁄₁₆ inches (290.2 x 143.5 x 66.8 cm)
Purchased with the Bloomfield Moore Fund, 1940-7-1a–c, 1940-7-2a–c

Standing more than nine feet tall and decorated with a dazzling design of gilded five-clawed dragons chasing flaming jewels amid scrolling lotuses over a black lacquer ground (fig. 61), this pair of compound wardrobes once graced the home of a member of the nobility or even the imperial family. Called *sijian gui* (four-part wardrobe), the form was used for storing fine garments such as silk robes, which were kept folded flat on shelves in the lower cabinet; the matching upper cabinet, accessed by ladder, held smaller items, such as hats, or less frequently used clothing.[1] Two large brass locks and keys, also impressive in their size and weight, and cast in high relief with a pair of five-clawed dragons confronting a flaming jewel, secure the upper cabinets (fig. 62). The six-character mark cast on the inner edge of each lock reads "made in the year of Qianlong of the Great Qing" (r. 1736–95; fig. 63), which matches the likely eighteenth-century date of these wardrobes.

The wardrobes' design is reminiscent of the decoration of a late sixteenth-century single wardrobe—now missing its upper cabinet—in the Musée Guimet, Paris, which has a mark dating it to the Wanli period (1573–1620).[2] Paying tribute to the past through re-creating earlier objects and styles—a trend called archaizing—was especially popular during the seventeenth and eighteenth centuries of the Qing dynasty and continued into the early years of the nineteenth century.

Lacquered as well as plain wood compound wardrobes were found in the mansions of the upper-class elite during the late Ming (16th–17th century) and the Qing dynasties, placed both in the private areas of a house and in the public spaces at the front. Based on the large size

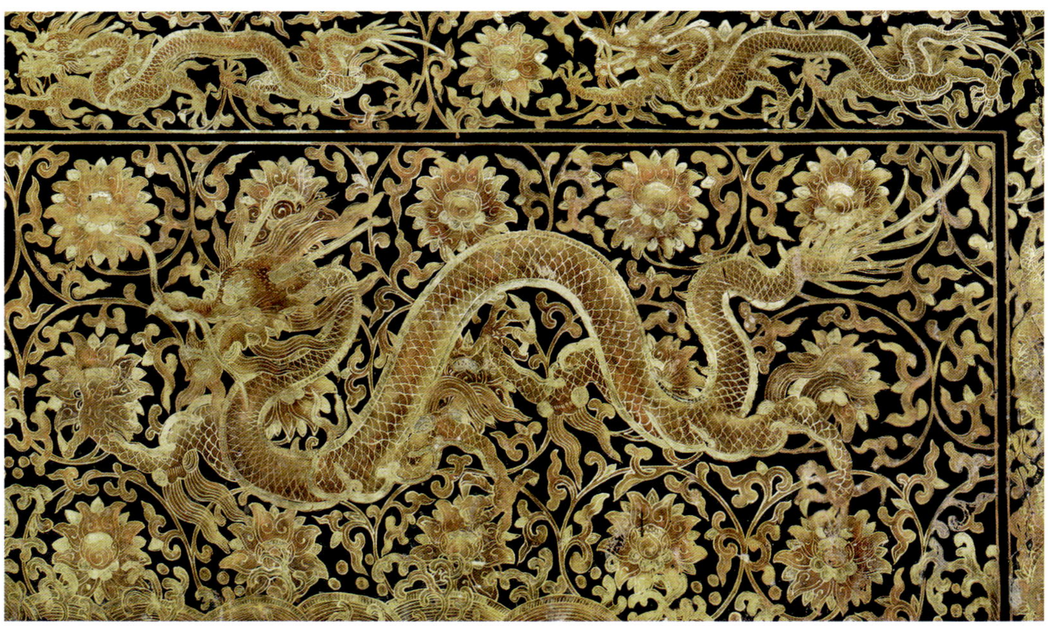

Fig. 61. Detail of a dragon on a bottom drawer

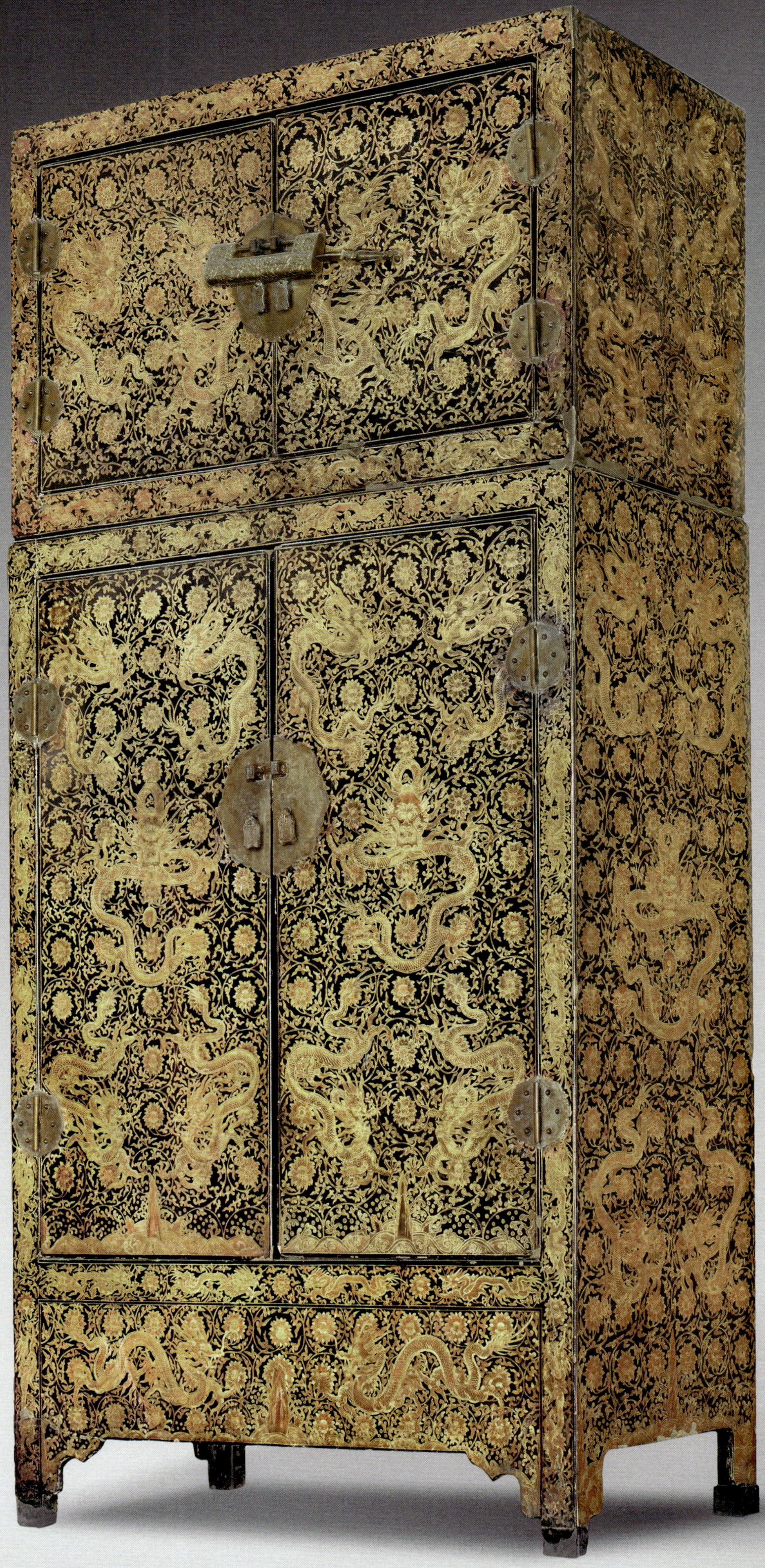

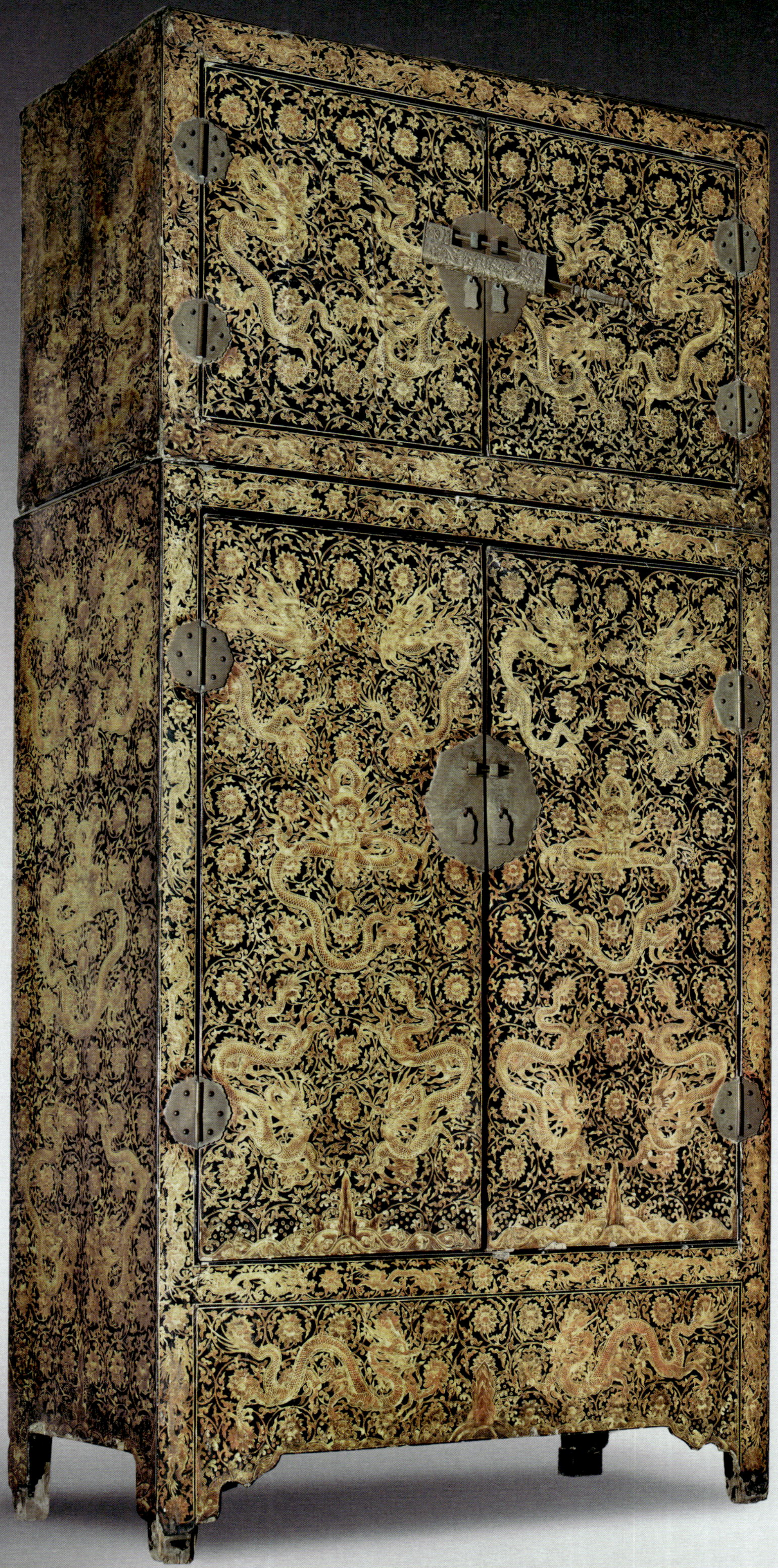

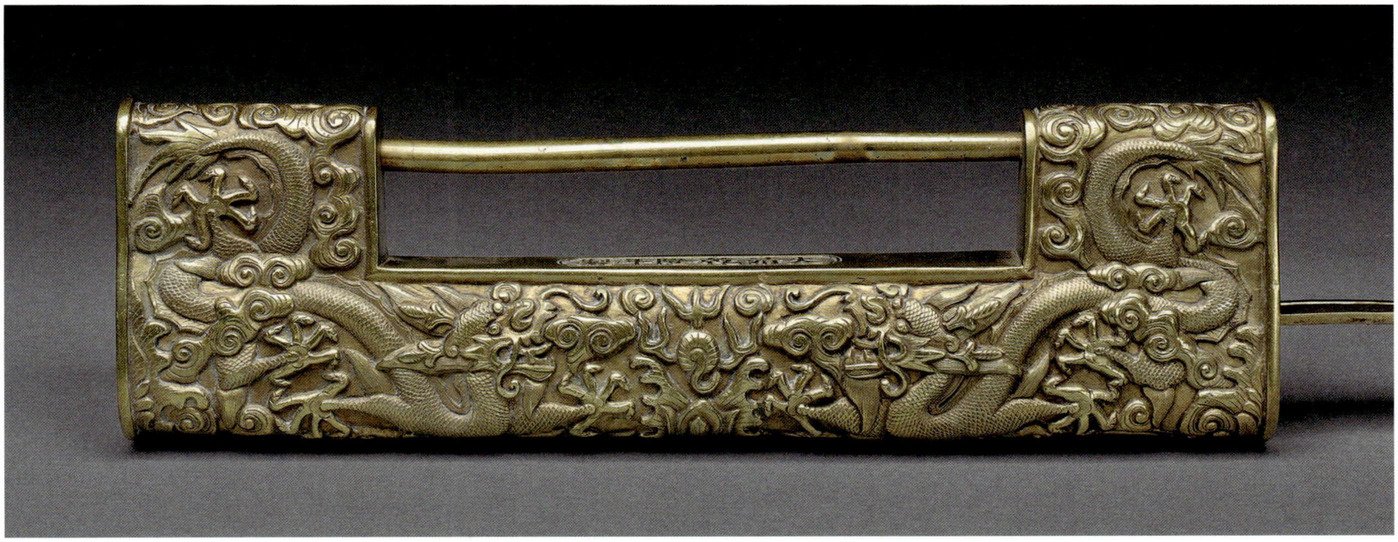

Fig. 62. Brass lock and key, the lock cast on both sides with five-clawed dragons in clouds chasing a flaming pearl

and the dragon design of these examples, the pair most likely stood in a public space, such as a reception hall, where they could be appreciated by visitors and guests. The dragon, a mythical creature that could bring rain, came to be associated with imperial power and authority in the fourteenth century.

Recent conservation and technical study of the wardrobes indicate that they had an interesting life.[3] When first purchased by the museum in 1940 their interiors were lined in fabric-covered Masonite and fitted with lighting in order to display Chinese porcelains.[4] Examination revealed that, in addition, the upper and lower cabinets were of different construction, and that the upper cabinets had two layers of decoration, while the lower cabinets had only one. These discrepancies indicate various restorations and redecorations over time, a common feature of historic Chinese furniture and architecture. HK

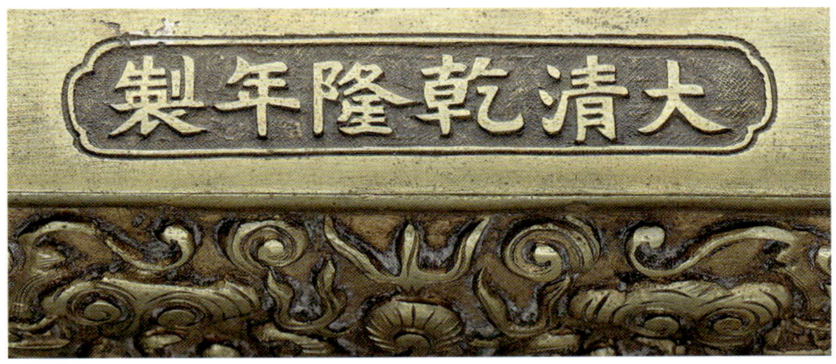

Fig. 63. Six-character mark in horizontal format, reading from right to left: *Da Qing Qianlong nian zhi* (Made in the reign of the Qianlong emperor of the Great Qing)

1. Handler 1993, 23.
2. Illustrated in Garner 1979, 196, nos. 144, 145.
3. Kao et al. 2017.
4. The Masonite has now been removed. While examining the interior of the cabinets, matching Chinese characters were discovered on some wood members and shelf edges, probably for use in matching up surfaces when assembling the piece.

79

Tea-dust Glazed Bottle

Qing dynasty (1644–1911), Qianlong period (1736–95)
Porcelain with tea-dust glaze (Jingdezhen ware)
7⅜ x 4⅝ inches (18.7 x 11.7 cm)
The Bloomfield Moore Collection, 1882-1577

This attractive example of a "tea dust" glaze was produced with the same colorant (iron oxide) used in imperial yellow glazes (see nos. 40, 59). Depending on the firing conditions, the glaze might fire a lighter yellowish brown, called eel yellow, or a greener hue, called snakeskin green.[1] The speckling effect also varied, ranging from a smooth soufflé (as if the glaze was blown out from a straw) to a more textured, mottled appearance. The tea-dust glaze is evenly applied over this bottle, except where a six-character seal mark of the Qianlong emperor is incised on the base (see p. 250), revealing how a thinner layer of the glaze fired to a transparent iron-ocher yellow, while incised areas of the reign mark, where the glaze is thicker, turned an opaque olive brown.

The monochrome glaze highlights the form of the porcelain—in this case, a well-proportioned bottle with a globular body rising to a slightly tapered neck with everted rim, and supported on a flared foot. The form appears to have been inspired by metalwork, especially archaic bronze forms, as other examples of tea-dust-glazed porcelains show.[2]

During the Qing dynasty, beginning in the early eighteenth century, the imperial kilns at Jingdezhen began to produce new and innovative glazes. Tea-dust-glazed porcelains were first created in the Yongzheng period (1723–35) and continued to be made into the nineteenth century. The highest quality examples were produced during the reigns of the Yongzheng and Qianlong emperors.[3] HK

1. Hong Kong 2005, 243.
2. See Hong Kong 2005, nos. 165–70, for examples ranging from the Yongzheng to the Xianfeng (1851–61) periods. The greenish-brown color of the glaze also matches the color of archaic bronzes.
3. Another Qianlong tea-dust-glazed bottle is illustrated in Hong Kong 2007–8, no. 64. This particular bottle form continued to be made into the reign of the Qianlong emperor's son, Jiaqing (r. 1796–1820). For an example in the Palace Museum, Beijing, see Yang 1999, 273, no. 250.

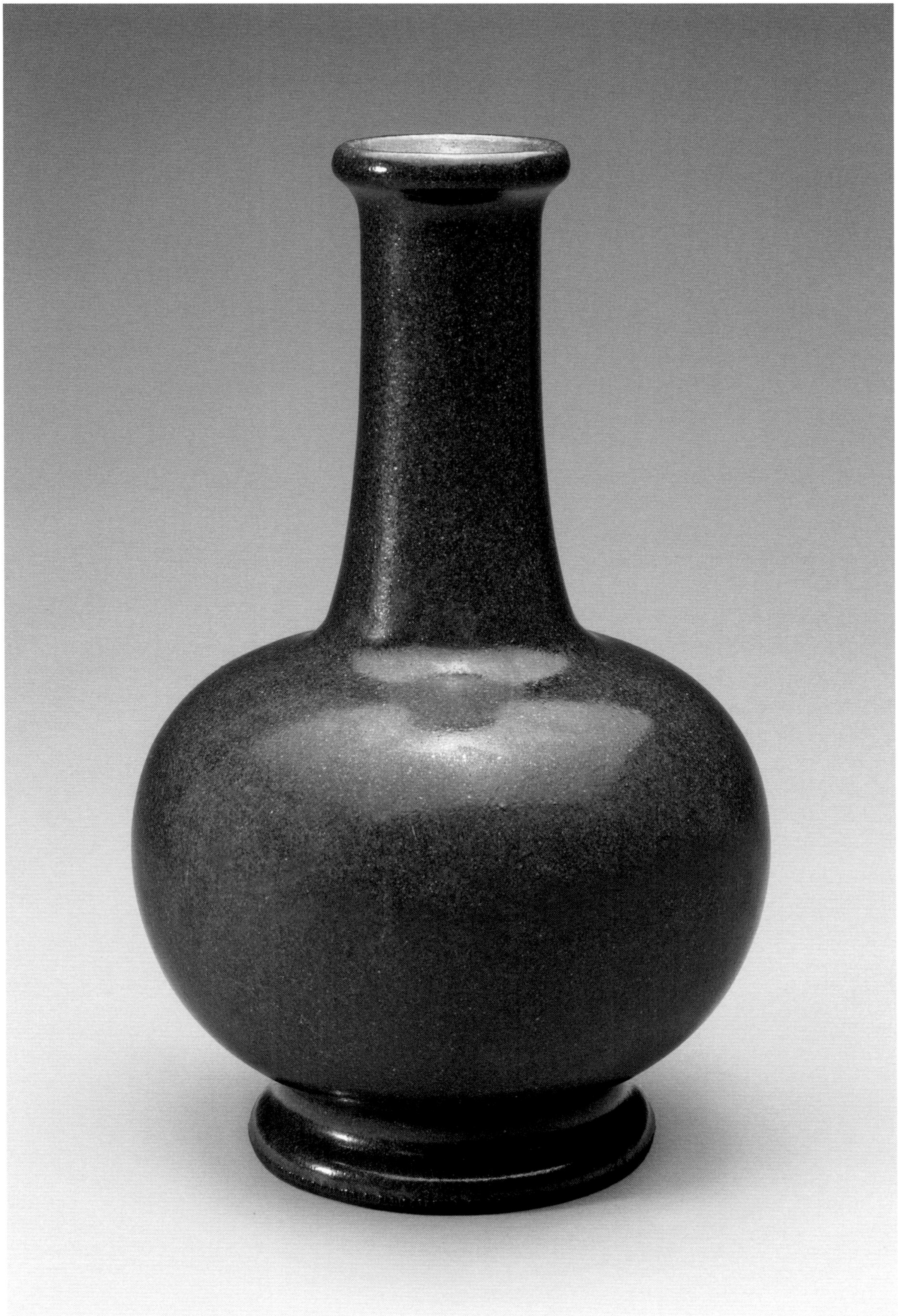

80

Vessel in the Form of a Bird on Wheels

Qing dynasty (1644–1911), Qianlong period (1736–95)
Gilded cast copper alloy with cloisonné enamels
7½ x 6¹¹⁄₁₆ x 3¾ inches (19 x 17 x 9.5 cm)
Bequest of Miss Mary Lewis, 1909-41

The fanciful bird at the center of this unusual vessel is modeled with a pigeon-like beak, leaf-shaped ears, swept-back wings, and a thick tail that curls downward to stabilize the body. With the neck of a *zun* wine vessel issuing from its back (similar to an archaic bronze animal-form *zun*),[1] and supported on two movable spoked wheels, it is a particularly creative example of the type of work commissioned by the Qianlong emperor, reflecting his interest in antiquity and collecting.[2] Made from cloisonné enamel, the heavily cast piece appears to be a reinterpretation of a Ming dynasty (1368–1644) bronze version in the imperial collection in Taipei (fig. 64).[3] That piece is illustrated in the *Xiqing gujian* (Mirror of the Antiquities of the Western Apartments, 1755), a catalogue of bronzes in the imperial collection with notes on their sizes and origins,[4] where it is described in a caption as a "Han dynasty pigeon/turtle dove on wheels *zun*."[5] While no other archaic bronze wheeled-bird *zun* vessels have yet been found, bronze bird toys on wheels have been excavated from both a Han dynasty (206 BCE–220 CE) tomb[6] and a Western Jin (265–317) tomb,[7] and may have been the inspiration for this composite *zun* vessel. It is not known why this *zun* form was so popular, nor what function it served within the palace, but as with other ancient bronzes, many versions were made during the Qianlong period, not only in cloisonné,[8] but also in jade. HK

1. A rare example of an archaic bronze animal-shaped wine vessel (*zun*) is the Shang dynasty (c. 1600–1050 BCE) double-ram *zun* in the British Museum, London (1936,1118.1).
2. Well versed in literature and the arts, the Qianlong emperor amassed a vast collection of paintings, calligraphy, bronzes, porcelains, and other types of objects, not only as a form of learning and enjoyment, but as a way to reinforce his legitimacy as ruler of China; Rawson 2005, 272.
3. See Taipei 2003, 174, no. III-42.
4. This is a four-part catalogue commissioned by the Qianlong emperor in 1755, and modeled on the catalogue of bronzes created for the Song emperor Huizong.
5. Kerr 2011, 80, fig. 5.15 (author's translation).
6. Taipei 2003, 252 n. 3.
7. Excavated in 1989 from a tomb in Yanshi, Luoyang, it is now on view at the Luoyang Museum.
8. The imperial collection in Beijing has two related pieces, one with wheels but dating to the mid-Qing dynasty (illus. in Zhang and Gugong 2011, vol. 4, 113, no. 65), and another that lacks wheels but is more similar in form and bears a Qianlong mark (Zhang and Gugong 2011, vol. 3, 44, no. 13).

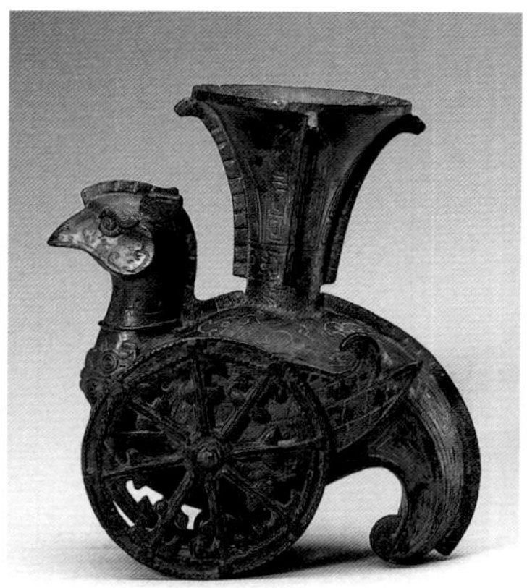

Fig. 64. Bird-form Vessel with Wheels. Ming dynasty (1368–1644), 16th–17th century. Bronze, 6½ x 6⅛ inches (16.5 x 15.5 cm). National Palace Museum, Taipei

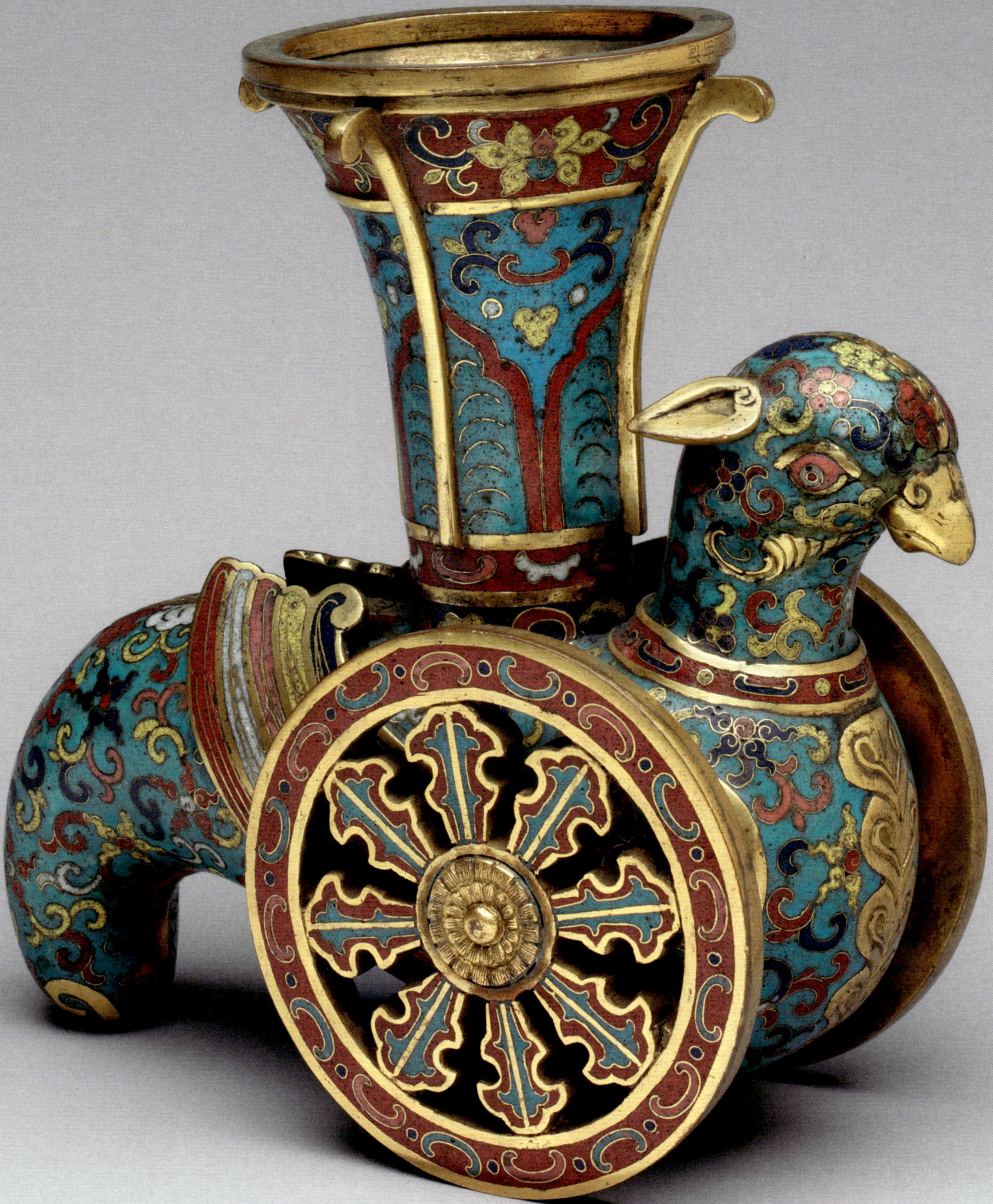

81

Devotional Hanging (*Thangka*)

Qing dynasty (1644–1911), Qianlong period (1736–95), dated by inscription to the third day of the second month of the twenty-sixth year of the Qianlong reign (1761)
Silk satin and damask applique, silk floss embroidery, boarders of silk lampas with gold leaf on paper strips and gold leaf on paper-wrapped thread
25 x 17½ inches (63.5 x 44.5 cm)
Gift of Natacha Rambova, 1960-131-5

This hanging depicts Amitayus, the Bodhisattva of Infinite Life (*wuliangshou*), a manifestation of Amitābha Buddha. In the bodhisattva (or peaceful) manifestation, the figure is portrayed in the bloom of youth, wearing silks and jewels and assuming a relaxed posture. The image here is rendered in applique technique using a variety of luxury secular silk fabrics. Such a transfer of goods from worldly society to Buddhist institutions was characterized as an act of piety. Metaphorically, secular cloth was "destroyed" by cutting it into pieces and "resurrected" when the pieces were given a new role in the service of devotional practices (see no. 33). The manufacture of objects such as this involved a myriad of mantra-like repetitions of shapes, their cut edges turned under and meticulously stitched to the fabric ground.

The bodhisattva is shown holding a jar containing the elixir of immortality (*amrita*) in his lap, sitting on a blue lotus rising from a lake of foaming waves. The idealized landscape, with offerings of multicolored jewels, elephant tusks, and a red coral branch under a sky in which the sun and crescent moon appear simultaneously, evokes Sukhāvatī, or the Western Paradise, created by Amitābha and often referred to as the Pure Land paradise.[1]

The cult of Amitayus was popular in the Vajrayana Buddhist traditions of Tibet, Mongolia, and the Qing court. Devotees believed that devotion to this Buddha could prolong life. An image such as this one may have aided visualization in the meditation practice called *phowa*, described as the "practice of conscious dying" or the "transference of consciousness at the time of death."[2] Among some devotees it was believed that by practicing *phowa* at the moment of death, one's consciousness would be transferred directly into paradise.

The inscription on the back of the *thangka*, written in Tibetan, Manchurian, Mongolian, and Chinese—the official languages of the Qing dynasty—states that it was made as the imperially commanded Changkya Rölpé Dorjé (1717–1786) directed in the year 1761. Rölpé Dorjé served as the principal Buddhist teacher to the Qing court.[3] JV

1. Coulter and Turner 1997, 529.
2. Ponlop 2006, 144–57.
3. See Benard 2004, 123–35.

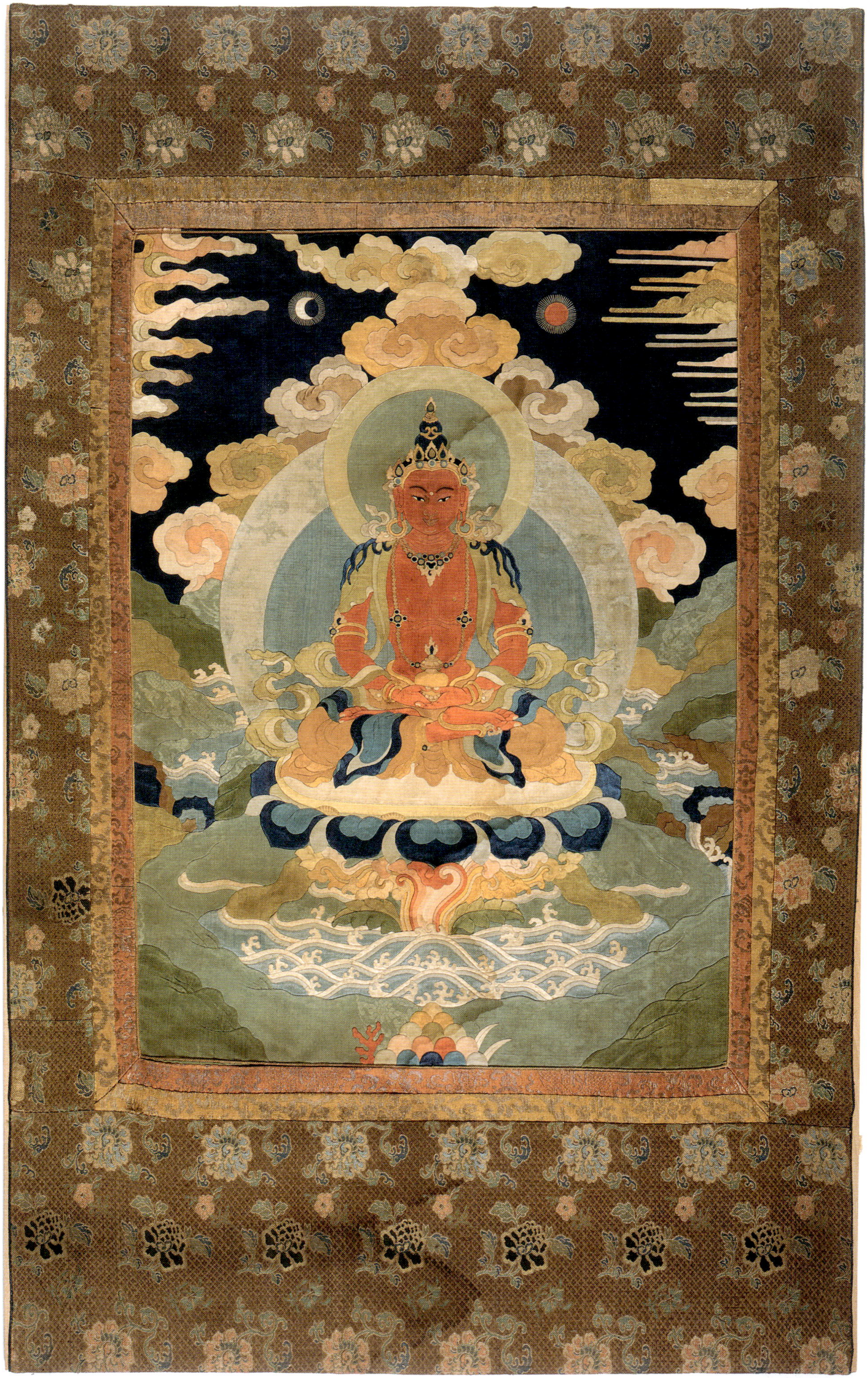

82

Yokeback Armchair for Guanyin

Qing dynasty (1644–1911), Qianlong period (1736–95), c. 1776
Wood (*huanghuali*) with lacquer and gilded decoration
27 x 17 x 11 inches (68.6 x 43.2 x 27.9 cm)
Bequest of Constance A. Jones, 1988-27-72

This well-proportioned yokeback armchair is ornately decorated with a trisectional carved and pierced splat and openwork key-fret aprons between the legs. Projecting dragon heads modeled with mouths open to reveal a pearl inside, and still showing remains of lacquer and gilding on the surfaces, embellish the ends of the arms and the humpback top rail. On the front rail is the original sliding footstool with curved legs.

Identified as a child's chair when it first came to the museum, based on its small size, this well-proportioned armchair was in fact made specifically for a temple statue of Guanyin, the Bodhisattva of Compassion, according to an inscription on the reverse of the back splat (see p. 250). The inscription also names the donor, the disciple Cheng Dianwen; the place, Xin'an; and the date of donation, the eighth month of the forty-first year of the Qianlong emperor (1776). Xin'an is the ancient name for Huizhou in present-day Anhui province.

Suzhou in nearby Jiangsu province was traditionally known for producing fine-quality furniture as well as jades and silks, but a chair of this quality, if made in Huizhou, would indicate that it too must have been a thriving center of carpentry. This should not be entirely surprising, as Huizhou had a history of producing hardwood furniture from the sixteenth century, as one observer noted:

> During the Longqing [1567–72] and Wanli [1573–1620] periods, even lower officials began to use fine wooden furniture, and cabinetmakers from Huizhou . . . opened shops in Yunjian where they made wedding furniture and other objects. At that time the wealthy families did not consider *ju* wood good enough and so it had become customary for them to have all their beds, cabinets, and tables made from *huali* wood, burl wood, blackwood, *xiangsi* wood [*jichi* wood], and boxwood. This furniture is very fine and exorbitant, each piece costing 10,000 cash, a most extravagant custom.[1]

This chair provides important information about carpentry in southeastern China, broadening our understanding of the various schools of furniture making in the Qing dynasty.[2] HK

1. From *Yunjian jumu chao* (Record of Things Seen in Yunjian) by Fan Li'an (b. 1540); quoted in Wang 1986, 14.
2. Tian 2001, 93.

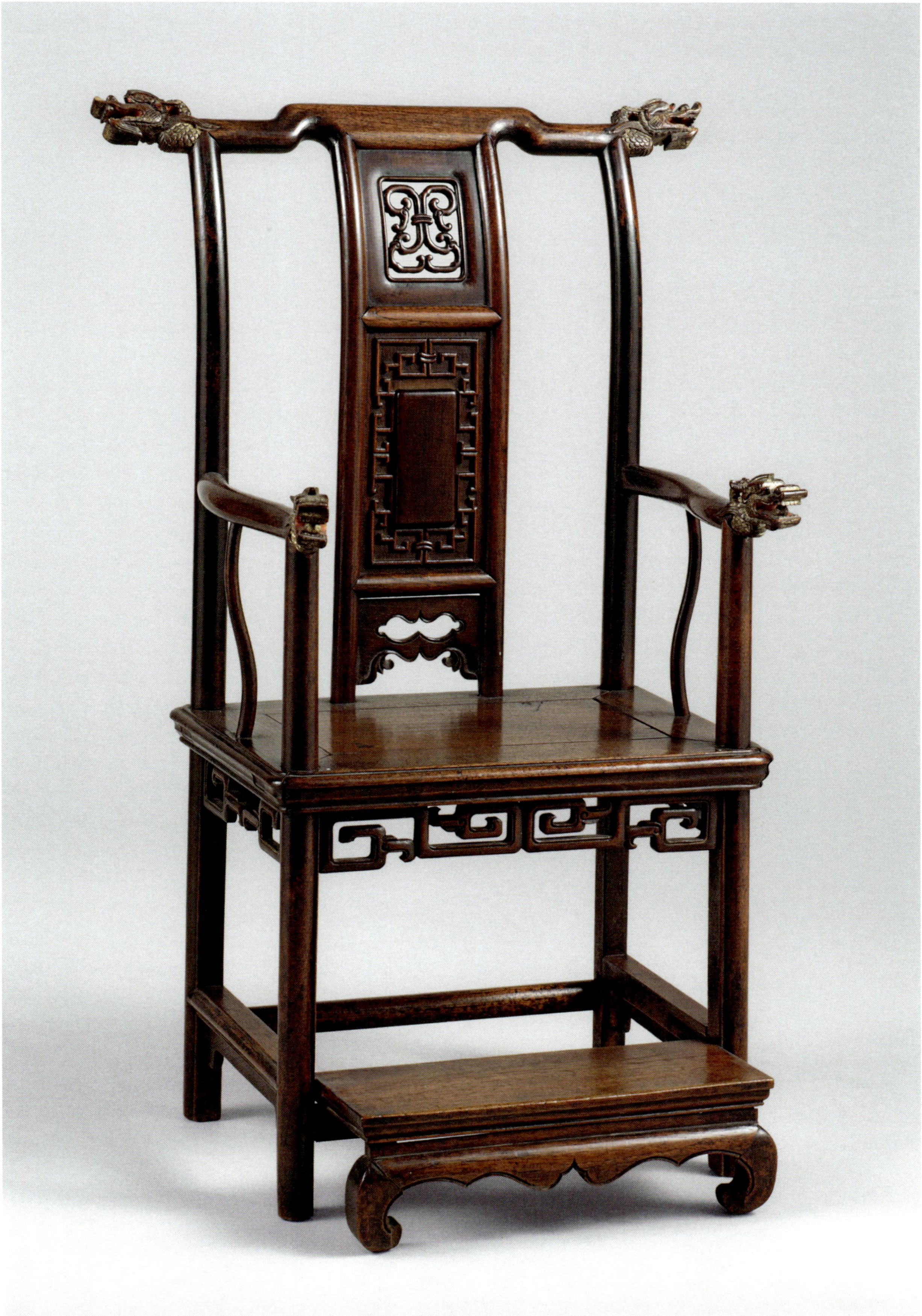

83

Semi-formal Court Robe

Qing dynasty (1644–1911), Qianlong period (1736–95) or Jiaqing period (1796–1820), c. 1790s
Silk gauze embroidered with floss silk in count stitch and couched gold leaf on paper-wrapped thread; bindings of silk satin with gold leaf on paper-wrapped-thread supplementary wefts; silk gauze sleeve extensions
56½ x 6 feet 6 inches (143.5 x 198.1 cm)
Gift of the Friends of the Philadelphia Museum of Art and purchased with funds contributed by Mr. and Mrs. Howard H. Lewis, 1983-15-1

The wearing of dragon-patterned garments (*jifu*, also called *long pao*) was an imperial prerogative in China as early as the tenth century. The Manchu, who established their dynasty (the Qing) in the 1630s, inherited the bold dragon-robe designs of the Ming court (1368–1644). But the Qing immediately initiated a process of rethinking dragon imagery for robes such as this one, which were primarily worn while performing the administrative functions relating to government. The modified decoration embodied a vision of the emperor's centrality within the cosmos and the purpose of imperial governance.[1]

From the early eighteenth century the number of dragons was set at the auspicious total of nine. Four of the dragons radiate from the neck of the robe onto the chest, back, and shoulders, pointing in the direction of the cardinal points on the compass when the wearer was aligned with the axial organization of the Forbidden City. Four additional dragons on the skirts—two at the front and two at the back—indicate the intermediate directions. A ninth dragon, unseen, is placed on the skirt's inner flap. Once donned, the robe and its wearer were joined in the cosmic enterprise of imperial rule.

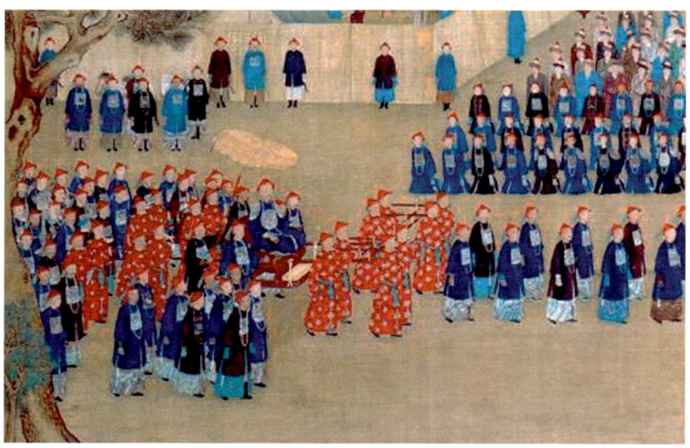

Fig. 65. Attributed to Giuseppe Castiglione, S.J. (Italian, 1688–1766; act. China, 1715–66). Detail of *Imperial Banquet in the Garden of Ten Thousand Trees*. Qing dynasty, Qianlong period, dated to 1755. Ink and colors on silk, mounted as a hanging scroll; 87¼ x 165 inches (221.5 x 419 cm). Palace Museum, Beijing (Gu6275)

The entire surface of this summer court robe for a male member of the imperial family, with skirt vents at front and back, is embroidered in brilliantly colored floss silk worked in counted stitch, using the threads of the ground fabric to determine stitch length and placement. An overall diagonal *wan* fret, the swastika—a semantic variant of the Chinese character for 10,000 (*wan*) and one of the auspicious signs recognized in Buddhism, most commonly associated with wishes for long life—makes up the background (see pp. 210–11). Against this are set symbolic representations of the terrestrial universe (waves, rocks, and clouds), dragons as emblems of imperial authority, and emblems of the Eight Daoist Immortals. Yet most of this exceptional workmanship would have remained unseen: in accordance with the imperial edict governing court attire, the *jifu* was most often worn under a plain, dark-colored surcoat that displayed the insignia badges (*buzi*) indicating rank (see nos. 38, 57), thus obscuring everything but the wave border at the robe's hem and cuffs (fig. 65). JV

1. Vollmer 2002, 103–8.

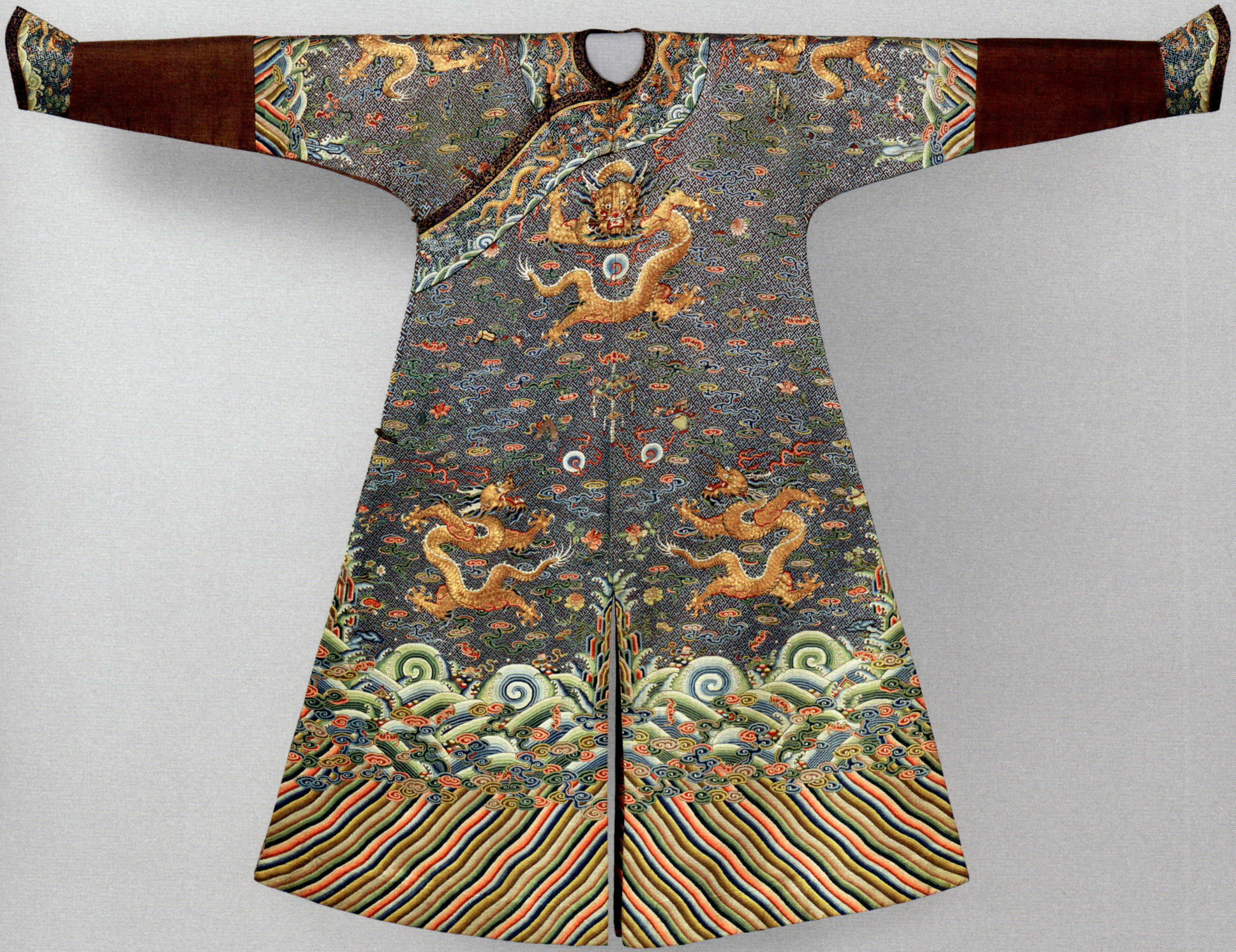

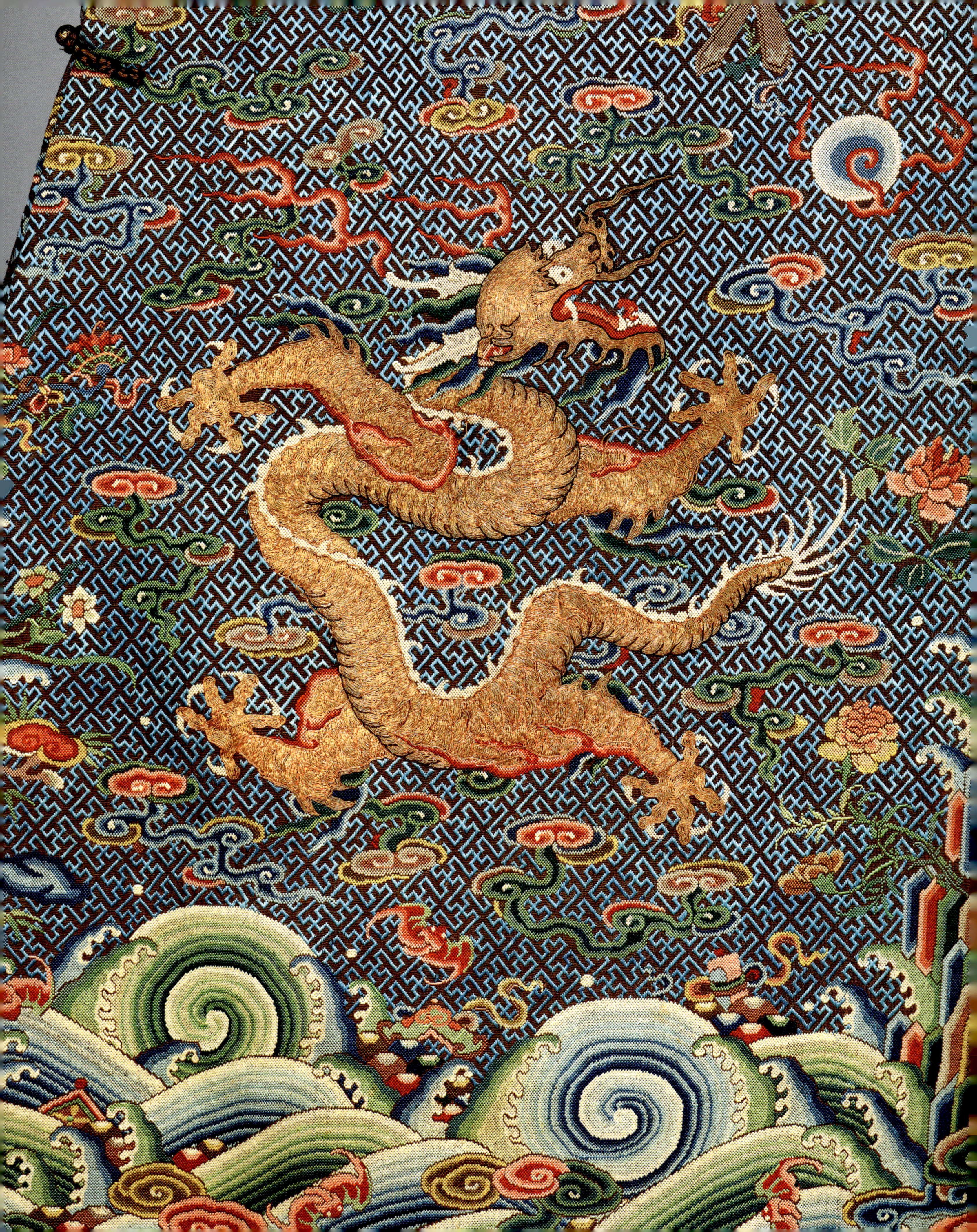

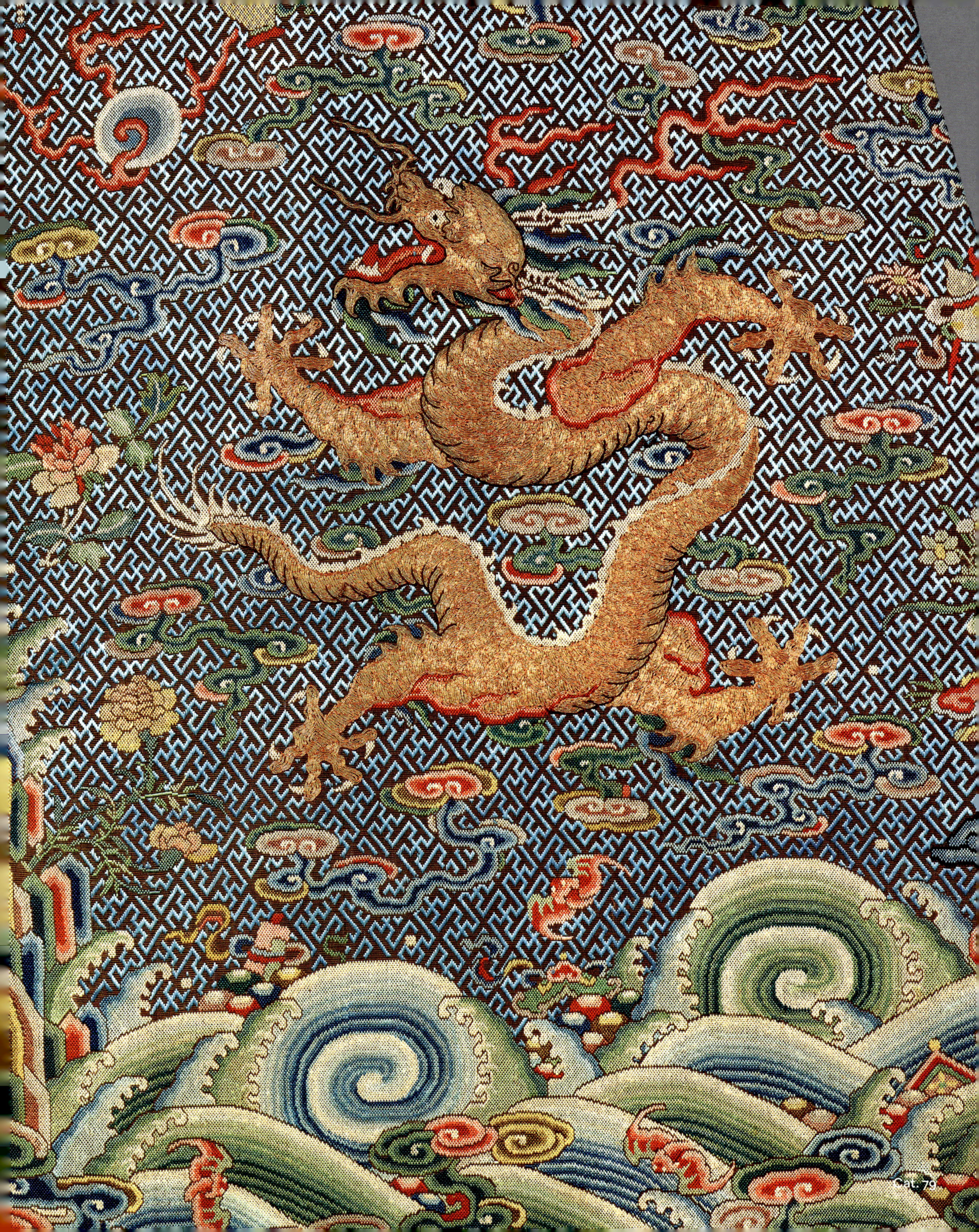

Cat. 79

84

Luo Ping (1733–1799)
Flowering Plum Branch

Qing dynasty (1644–1911), 1782
Ink on paper, mounted as a hanging scroll
55 x 13¾ inches (139.7 x 34.9 cm)
Purchased with the Edith H. Bell Fund, 1983-26-1

A flowering plum branch cascades down this narrow hanging scroll. The dangling branch separates the painting into two long, thin spaces, each bearing a lengthy inscription, one referencing the history of plum-blossom painting and the other describing the beauty of nature. The downward movement of the elongated branch from right to left juxtaposed with text written from left to right is unusual and indicates how history and nature are intricately intertwined.

The inscription on the left transcribes a poem by Wang Mian (1287–1359), one of China's greatest plum-blossom painters. His poem was originally written on a hanging scroll with inked plum blossoms now in the Shanghai Museum (fig. 66),[1] whose composition and hanging plum branch are very close to Luo Ping's, indicating that Luo may have known about and even learned from the earlier work. Created in the early spring of 1355, Wang Mian's painting circulated in the Suzhou area for hundreds of years.

Luo Ping's second inscription states that his painting was made in Suzhou in the spring of 1782, when he stayed for some time at the famous Tiger Hill (Huqiu). Nearby is another celebrated site in Suzhou, Dengwei Hill, nationally known for its plum-blossom viewing, a revered tradition among the Chinese. Unfortunately, Luo missed the peak time to watch the flowers bloom, so he created this painting to capture his feelings at that moment. XH

1. Zhongguo 1999, 69.

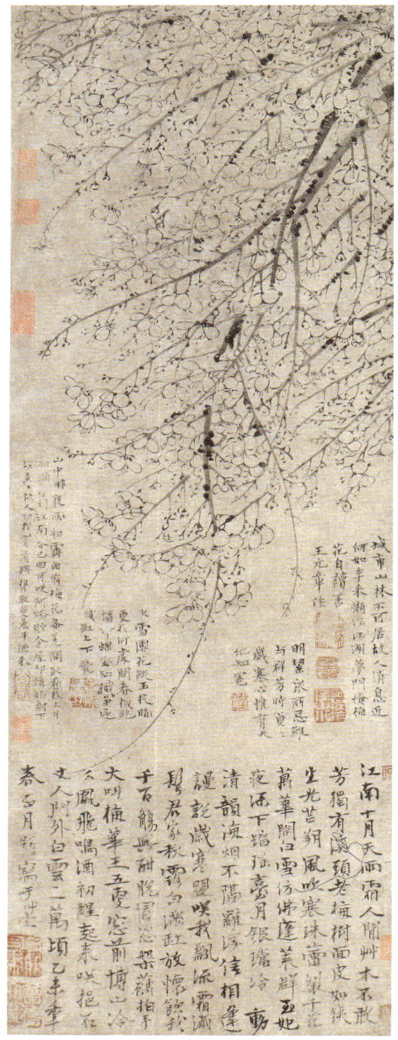

Fig. 66. Wang Mian (1287–1359). *Ink Plum*. Yuan dynasty (1271–1368), 1355. Ink on paper, mounted as a hanging scroll; 26⅝ x 10³⁄₁₆ inches (67.7 x 25.9 cm). Shanghai Museum

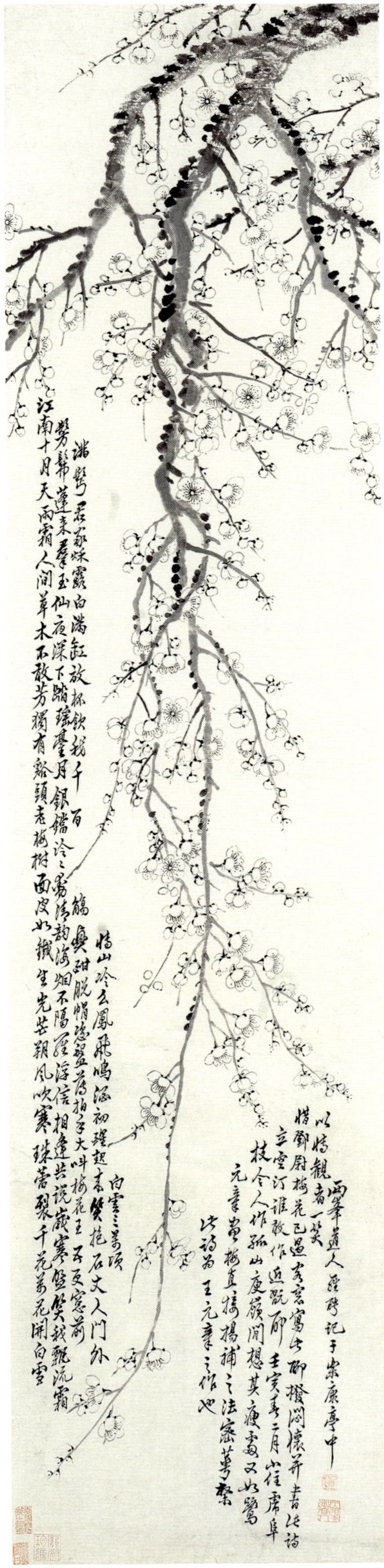

85

Hua Guan (1740–c. 1822)
Elegant Gathering Honoring the Studio of Inebriating Ink

Qing dynasty (1644–1911), Qianlong period (1736–95), 1792
Ink and color on paper, mounted as a handscroll
Image 13 x 40⅜ inches (33 x 102.6 cm)
Gift of Anne Rowland, 1967-173-1

Seated at an expansive table surrounded by attentive friends, Hongwu (1743–1811), a grandson of the Kangxi emperor (r. 1662–1722), is clearly the host of this scholarly gathering. The multiple colophons following the painting (partially illustrated) reveal a prestigious guest list that included Liu Yong (1719–1804), Yu Ji (1738–1823), and Ruan Yuan (1764–1849), some of the most renowned scholar-officials of the eighteenth century. Based on seniority and information provided in the colophons, Liu Yong, the eldest of the group, is most likely the figure to the right of the table holding a tea cup. Yu Ji, a close associate of Hongwu, is probably the man seated next to the host raising a brush washer in his hands, while Ruan Yuan, compiler of an imperial painting catalogue, stands across the table appreciating a scroll painting.

A Manchu princeling, Hongwu was well versed in the arts esteemed in Chinese literati culture—painting, calligraphy, and poetry—the latter evinced by the two poems he composed and inscribed following the painting (fig. 67).[1] As indicated in the colophons, the inspiration for naming his studio "inebriating ink" can be credited to the eleventh-century calligrapher Shi Cangshu and the preeminent scholar-official Su Shi (1037–1101), who once wrote in a playful tone that Shi Cangshu would become intoxicated from the fragrance of ink while writing calligraphy, discarding all his worries as if drunk on good wine.[2] Since the true artist attains inebriation through ink rather than alcohol, the only beverage served at this gathering is tea, freshly brewed by an attendant to the left of the scene.

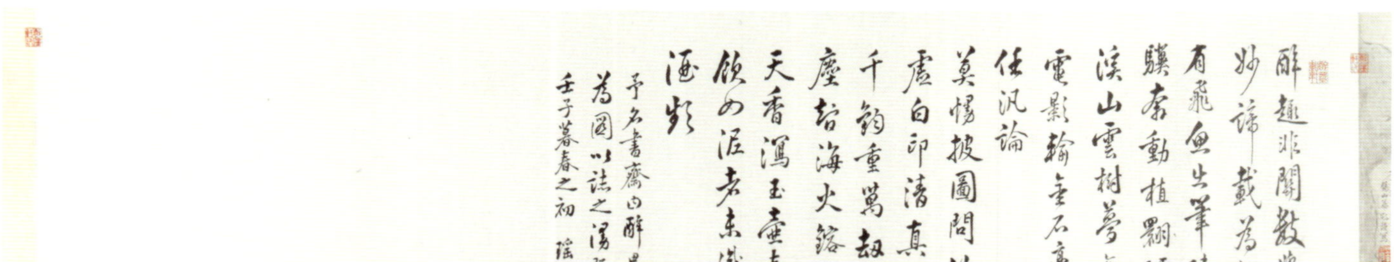

Fig. 67. Hongwu's inscription and seal marks following the painting (reading from right to left)

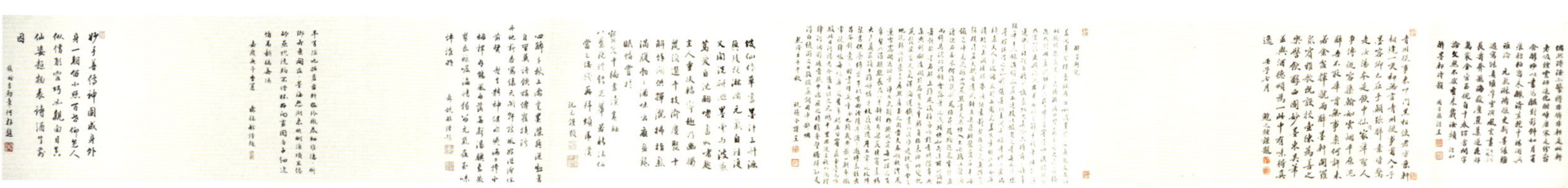

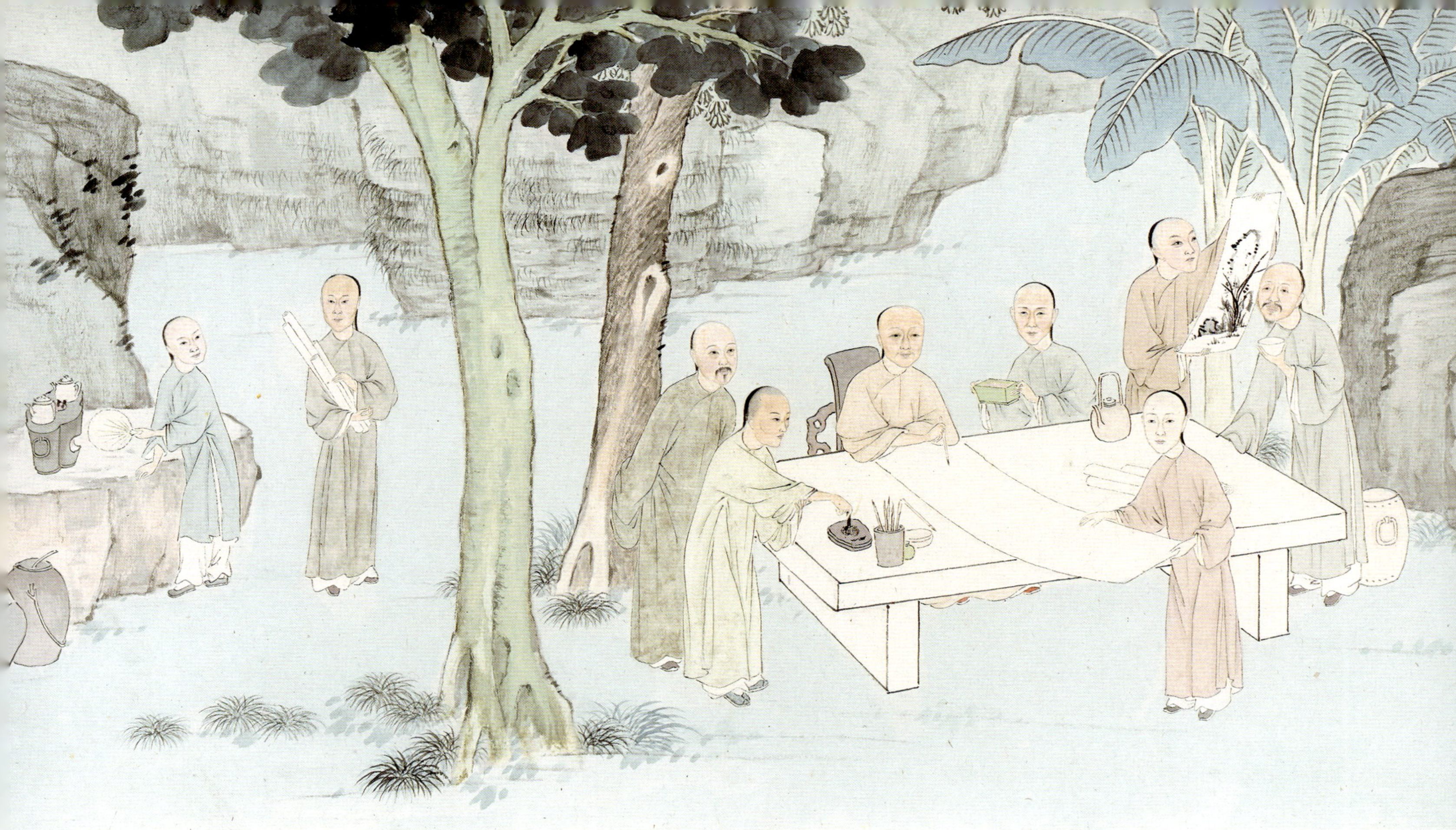

Hua Guan, the painter of the scroll, was a native of Wuxi in Jiangsu province and made a living as a professional painter in Beijing from the 1760s, primarily portraying Manchu noblemen and their distinguished associates.[3] Combining fine brush technique with subtle shading, Hua became known for his naturalistic depictions of physiognomy and was praised for his ability to capture not only his sitters' outer likenesses, but also their inner characters.[4] Such group portraits as this abound with indicators of social connections, while also satisfying the desire to preserve one's youthful appearance in the form of pictorial art, a sentiment expressed in Hongwu's inscription.[5] DL

1. Hongwu also took an interest in seal carving, as shown in the multiple seals he impressed on this scroll.
2. This is in the poem *Shi Cangshu Zuimotang* (Shi Cangshu's Inebriated Ink Hall), written by Su Shi in 1069. For more on the life and arts of Su Shi, see Egan 1994.
3. Hua Guan's major patron in Beijing was Yongrong, the sixth son of the Qianlong emperor; Yang 2010, 30–41.
4. Feng Jinbo (1738–after 1797), a noted art connoisseur and Hua's contemporary, remarked that Hua was able to represent the spirit and vitality of his sitters; see Lu et al. 1992, 736.
5. Richard Vinograd notes that such group portraits have a strong emblematic function, serving as "reaffirmation of group affiliation" or expressing "personal ambitions and aspirations"; Vinograd 1992, 14 (different types of Chinese portraiture are discussed on pp. 10–14). The effigy function, although typically associated with formal ancestral portraits, is mentioned in the last colophon, written by a relative of the host, who commented that the excellent portrayal of Hongwu would allow the next hundred generations of descendants to admire their forefather.

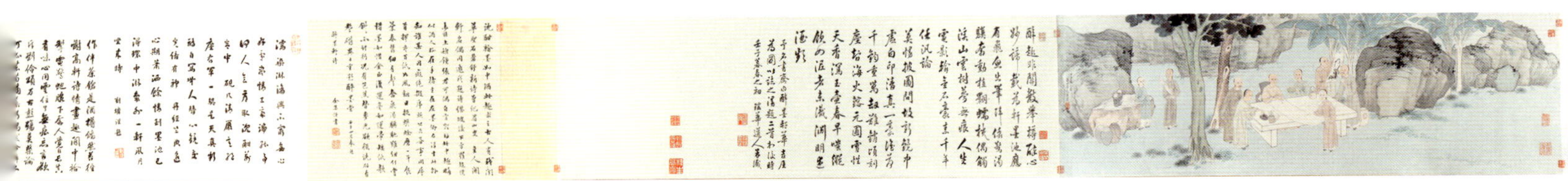

86

English-style Bookcase

Qing dynasty (1644–1911), late 18th century (c. 1798)
Wood (rosewood, mahogany) with lacquer and gilded decoration
73½ x 39¾ x 12⅝ inches (186.7 x 101 x 32.1 cm)
Purchased with the Thomas Skelton Harrison Fund, 1970-109-1

In this elegant bookcase, a Western form is adroitly combined with Chinese decorative elements to create a unique piece of Chinese export furniture. Standing on bracketed feet, the English-form bookcase has a cornice molding of dentils punctuated by rosettes, with a Greek-key fret below.[1] The latticework of the door is a Chinese "cracked-ice" pattern,[2] serving as background for three naturalistically carved wood panels in the form of (from top to bottom) a leaf, a gourd or melon enclosing a black-lacquer incised and gilded plaque with the initials of the owner (*vBH*), and a Buddha's Hand citron. For those adept at reading visual rebuses, the two fruit convey wishes for a long life, blessings, and many sons.[3] The solid panel at the bottom of the bookcase and the inner edges of the flanged feet are decorated with scrolling vines in low relief. The interior has adjustable shelves and a handwritten label adhered to the back that reads, "Purchased of M^{r}. Andrew Edvardus Van Braam Houckgest 8th. May. 1798."

The first American to be presented at the imperial court of the Qianlong emperor, in 1795, Andreas Everardus van Braam Houckgeest (1739–1801) began his career working as a merchant for the Dutch East India Company, the major importer of Chinese luxury goods to Europe. He worked in Macao and Canton from 1758, returning to his home country of the Netherlands in 1773 to "live the life of a country gentleman."[4] However, he became interested in the American Revolution and its cause, which brought him and his family to Charleston, South Carolina, where he became an American citizen in 1784. He returned to Canton in 1790 to become head of the factory for the Dutch East India Company, and it was during this time that he traveled to Beijing to congratulate the Qianlong emperor on his sixtieth birthday.[5] In 1796 he arrived in Philadelphia and purchased a farm in nearby Bristol, Pennsylvania, where he constructed a fifteen-room house with Chinese features, naming it China's Retreat, but he left two years later for London, where he sold his Chinese collection.[6] HK

1. Crossman 1991, 241.
2. This pattern is decorative but also serves to strengthen the framework. A seventeenth-century rosewood (*huanghuali*) clothes rack with a cracked-ice pattern on the central panel is in the Minneapolis Institute of Art; Jacobsen and Grindley 1999, 163, no. 56. The cracked-ice pattern was also used in wall and window latticework in upper-class households. See the seventeenth-century illustration for the erotic novel *The Plum in the Golden Vase* at the Nelson-Atkins Museum of Art, Kansas City (F80-10/1).
3. San Francisco 2006, 30–31.
4. Philadelphia 1984, 80.
5. His meeting with the emperor is recorded in Van Braam Houckgeest 1798, vol. 2.
6. He died in Amsterdam in 1801; see Philadelphia 1984, 81–82.

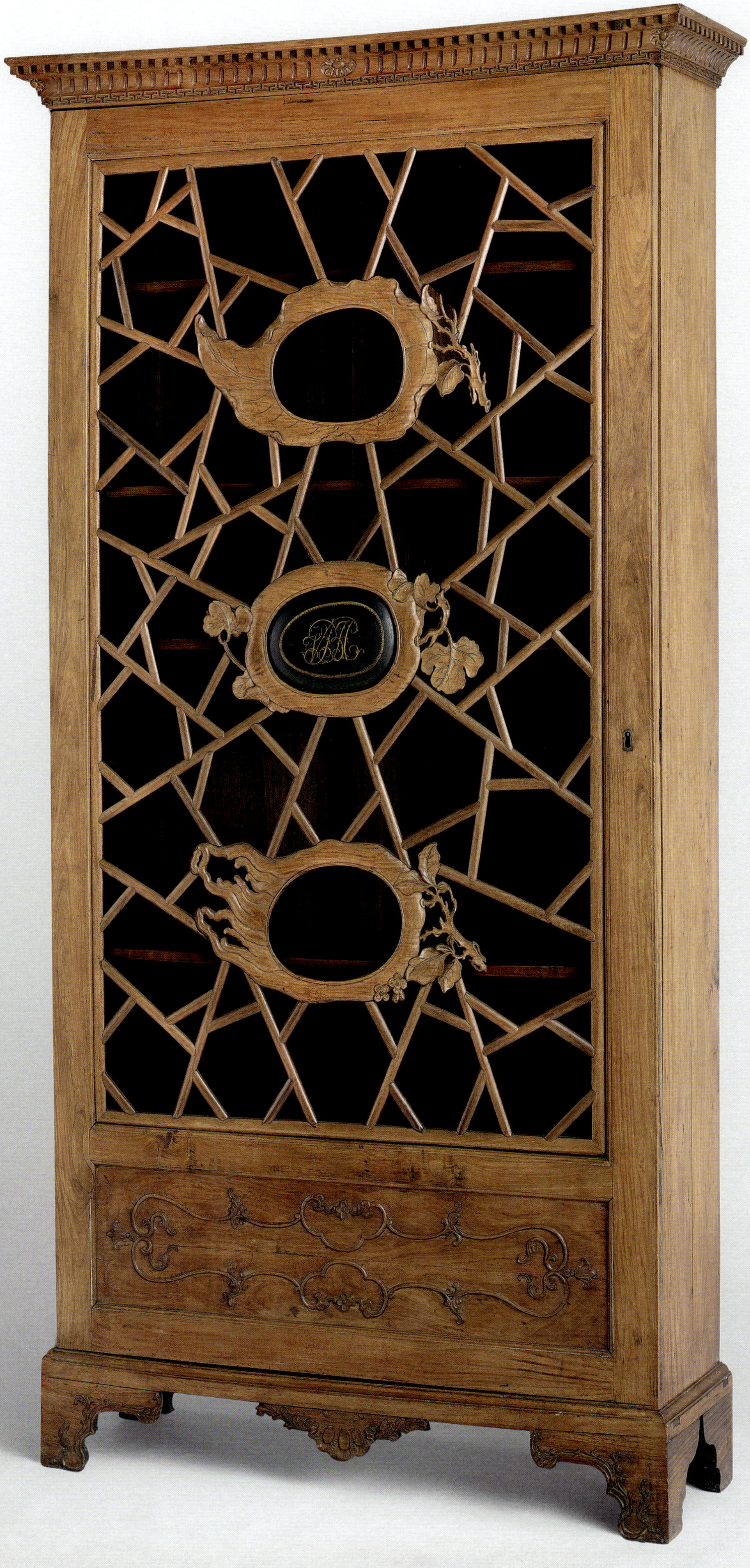

87

Pair of Hexagonal Stools

Qing dynasty (1644–1911), Qianlong period (1736–95)
Wood (*zitan*; *Pterocarpus* sp.)
20½ x 14½ inches (52.1 x 36.8 cm)
Gift of Mrs. John Story Jenks, 1946-85-1a,b, 1946-85-2a,b

These Qing-dynasty stools are unusual in the extent of their intricate carved openwork decoration. Each of the six sides has a quatrefoil panel showing a pair of young boys in belted tunics holding branches of fruit or flowers, their location outdoors signaled by small pierced rocks in the foreground (fig. 68). The types of fruit and flowers—pomegranate, Buddha's Hand citron, lychee, persimmon, peach, and lotus—were specifically chosen for their auspicious meanings. The pomegranate, with its numerous seeds, conveys wishes for many sons, as the word for sons (*zi*) is also the word for (and sounds like) seeds (*zi*). The Buddha's Hand citron (*fushou*), a fragrant citrus fruit often used to perfume the air, resembles the fleshy hand of the Buddha, thus expressing wishes for longevity and happiness; moreover, the word *fu* sounds like the word for Buddha and also like the word for happiness, and the word *shou*, or hand, sounds like the word for longevity. The lychee (*lizhi*), like the pomegranate, conveys wishes for many sons,[1] while the word for persimmon (*shizi*) sounds like "to serve" or "affairs," expressing the wish for a successful career.[2] Peaches signal wishes for long life because of their association with the Daoist immortal

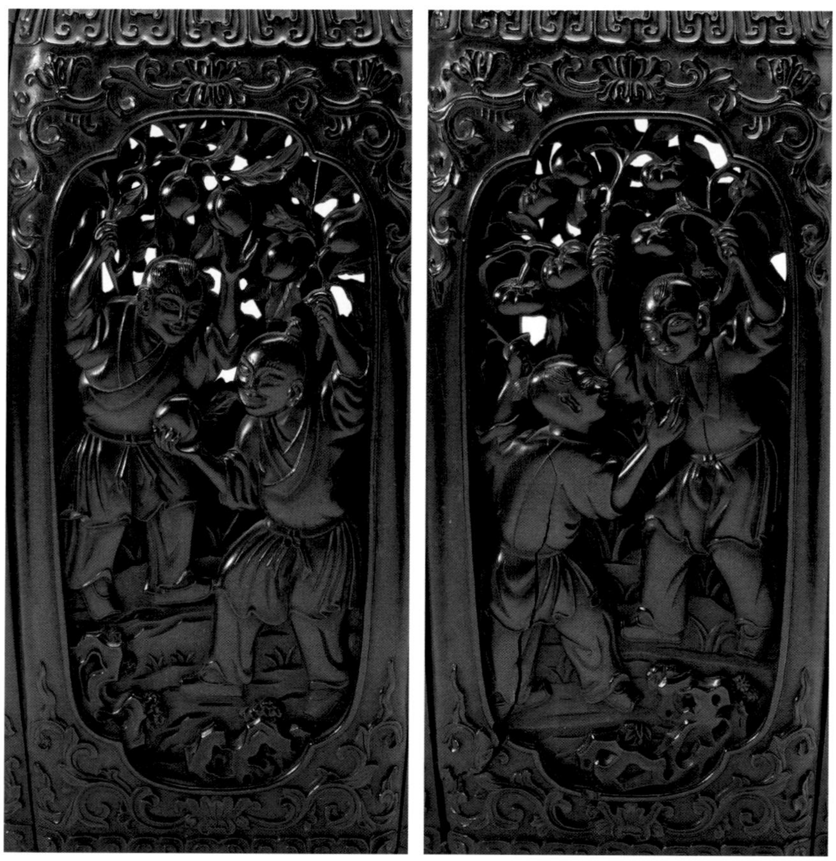

Fig. 68. Details of the openwork carving showing boys holding branches of peach and persimmon (left), persimmon and lotus (right)

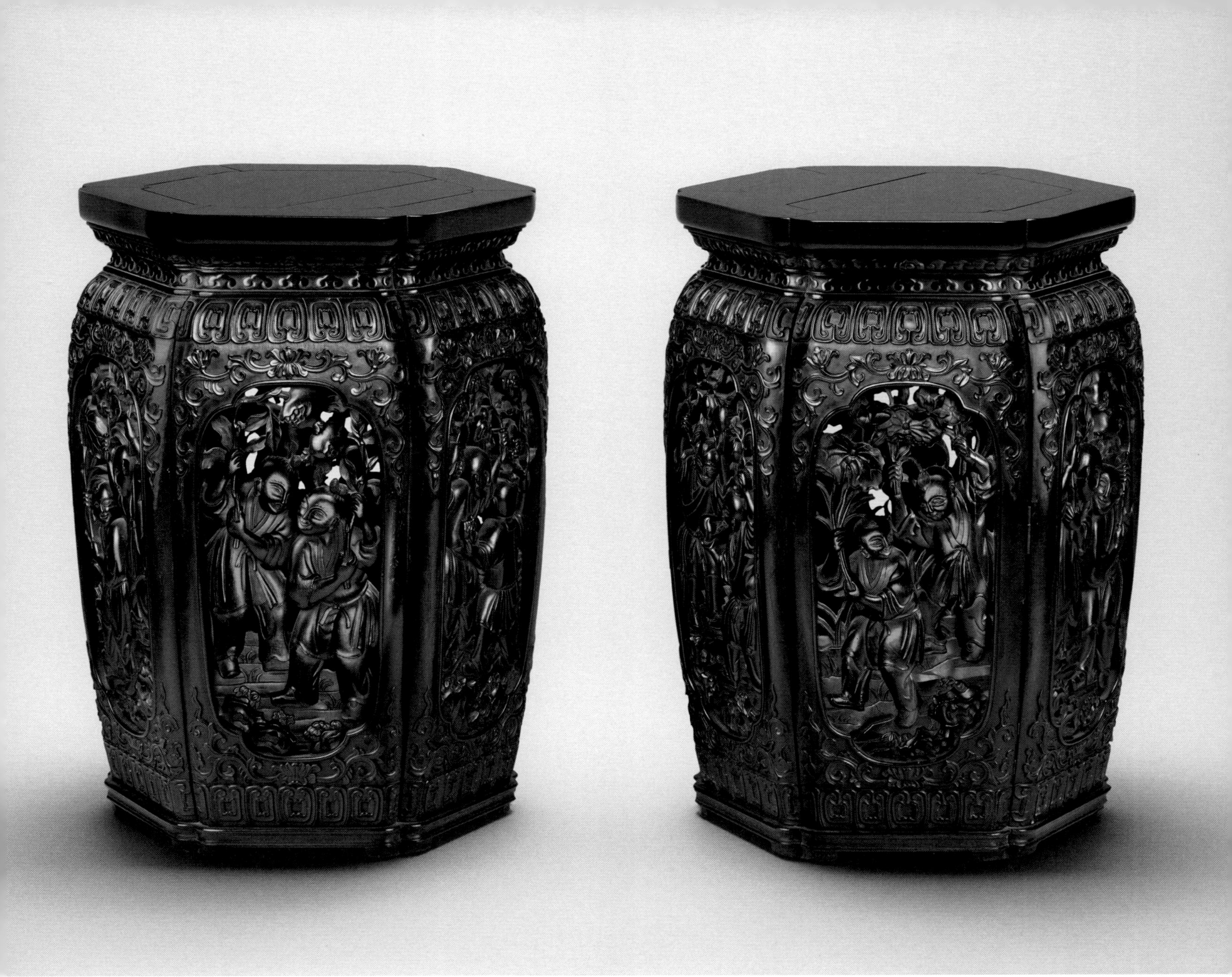

Xiwangmu, the Queen Mother of the West, who grew the fruit in her garden; it conferred immortality when eaten.[3] The lotus expresses wishes for peace and harmony. Overall, the design functions as a rebus conveying wishes for many successful, wealthy, happy, and long-lived sons. The borders around the edge of the seat are made up of the longevity fungus, called *ruyi* (literally, "as you wish"), thus reinforcing the message.

The stools are made from *zitan*, a dense wood with a characteristic dark purplish color, finely textured grain, and lustrous appearance. Considered one of the rarest and most precious woods in Chinese furniture making, it was used for much of the Qing imperial palace furniture. Given the material of these stools and the high quality of the designs,[4] it is likely that they were made in the imperial workshops.[5] HK

1. Fang 2004, 112.
2. Fang 2004, 148–49.
3. Fang 2004, 143.
4. The design of the scrolling floral motifs in particular resembles *yangcai* (foreign colors) enameled porcelain, so called because its decoration incorporated Western painting techniques. *Yangcai* enameled porcelain with Western-inspired decoration was especially favored by the Qianlong emperor. For examples with similar Western-style flower scrolls and lotus lappets, as on these stools, see Taipei 2008, nos. 8, 74.
5. A stool similar in size and decoration is in the Palace Museum, Beijing; see Zhu 2002, no. 82. The Philadelphia stools were once in the imperial collection (see p. 22 above).

88

Panels from a Scholar's Study

Qing dynasty (1644–1911), Qianlong period (1736–95), late 18th century
Wood with lacquer and gilded decoration (*miaojin*)
9 feet 7 inches x 20 feet 10¹⁄₁₆ inches x 17 feet 9⅞ inches (292.1 x 635.2 x 543.2 cm)
Each panel 6 feet 9 inches x 23 inches (205.7 x 58.4 cm)
Gift of Wright S. Ludington in memory of his late father, Charles H. Ludington, 1929-30-1

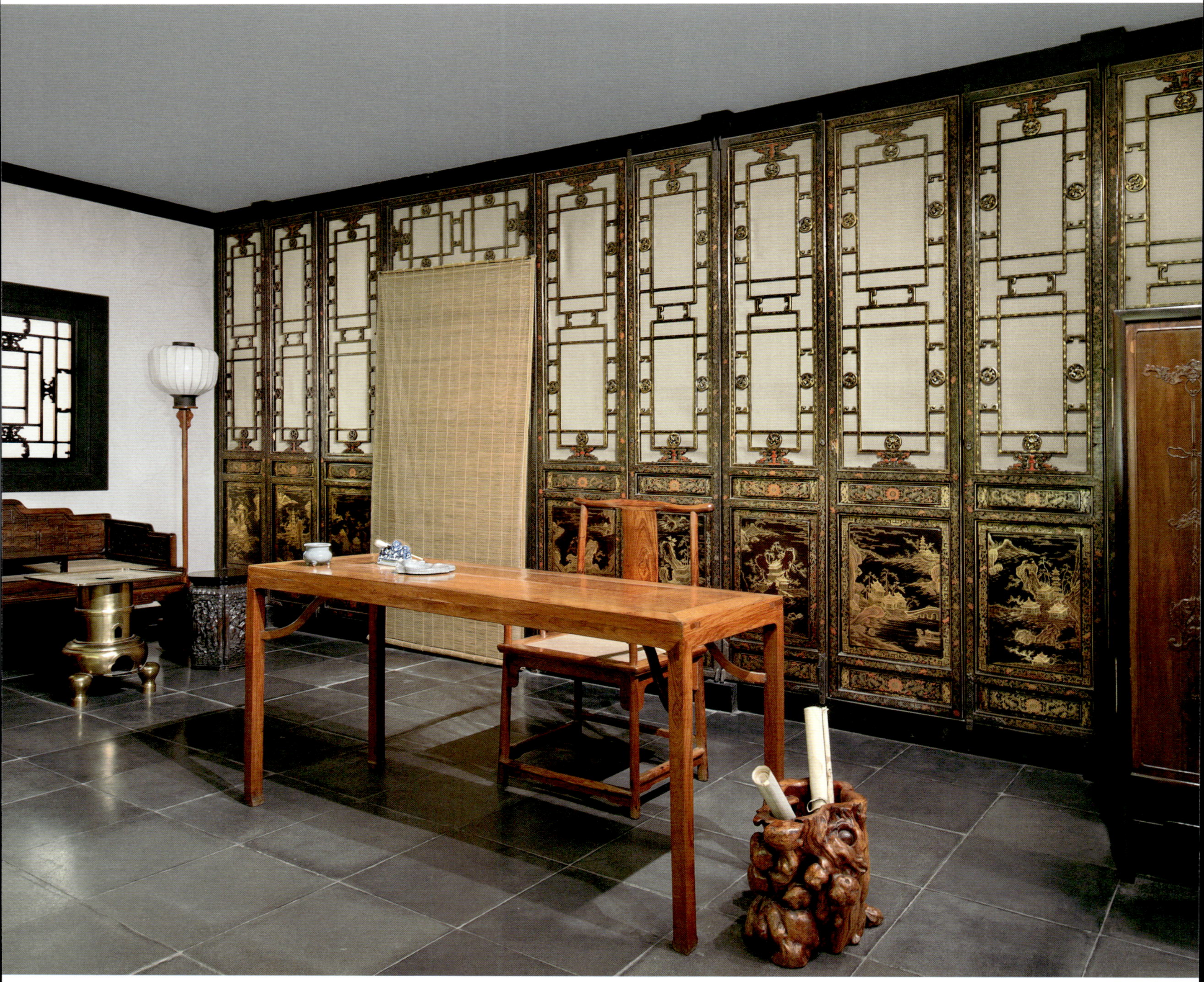

a

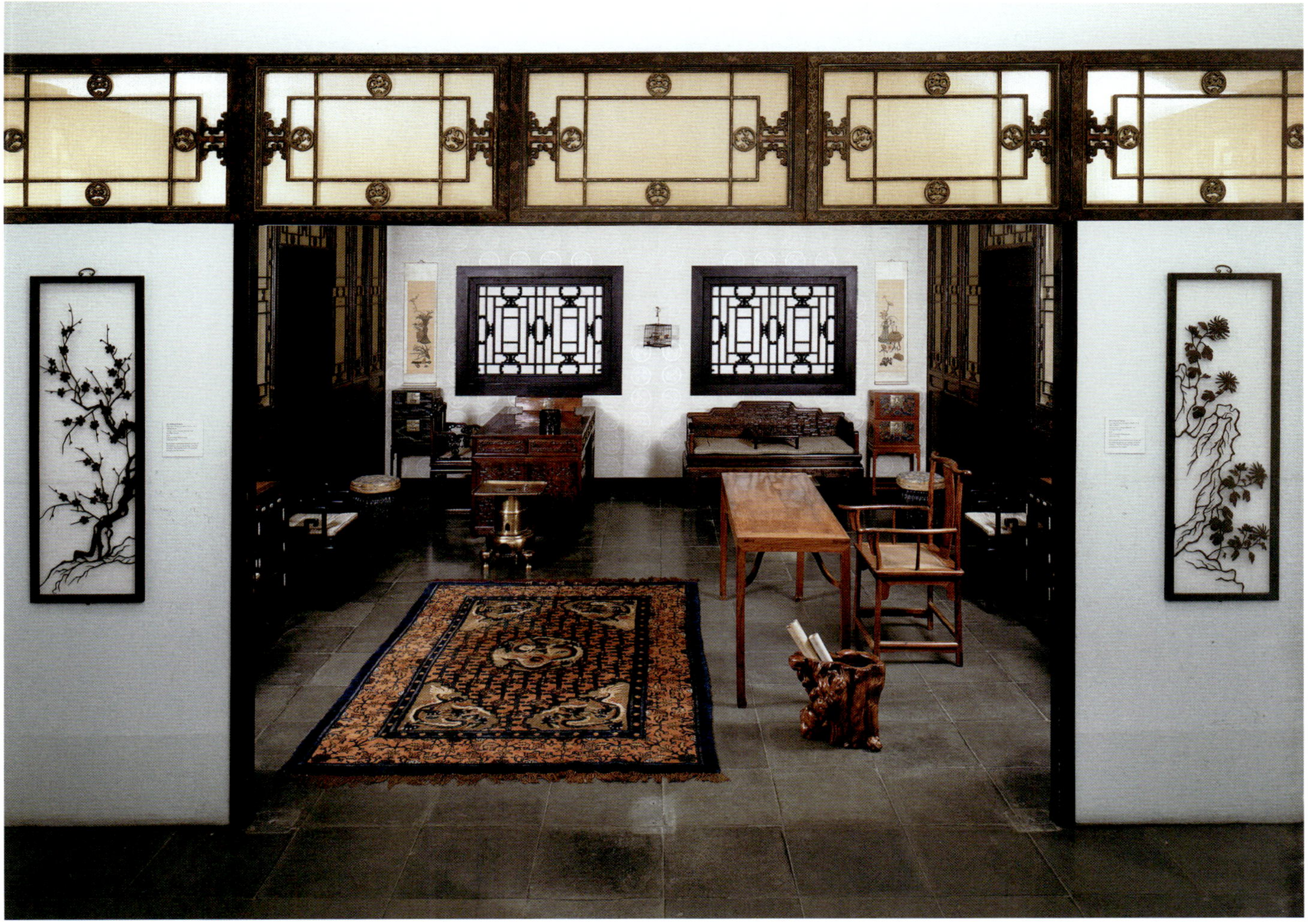

b

These eighteen elaborately decorated, lacquered and gilded wood panels once formed a scholar's study in the residence of a member of the imperial family or a high-ranking official.[1] Such rooms, installed with furniture and other accoutrements to create a quiet, private retreat for a learned scholar-bureaucrat as an escape from his official duties, were typically located in the innermost part of a dwelling. Each long "wall" in this example has alternating sets of fixed or hinged door panels that could be opened or closed for privacy and air circulation, with the longest wall (a) punctuated by a doorway that once led to an adjoining room. The panels are elaborately decorated on both sides of the solid bottom sections with landscape scenes depicting multistoried palace pavilions set amid towering rock formations, distant mountains, trees, and water (c, d); the open latticework top sections each had a fabric backing that allowed light in (since replaced).[2] The rocky landscapes are in the style of the dramatic paintings of mountains and pavilions created by professional artists such as Yuan Jiang (act. 1723–35) and his nephew Yuan Yao (act. c. 1740–80), who served at the imperial court and whose distinctive rocky outcrops imitated the style of monumental landscape painters of the Northern Song dynasty (960–1127), such as Guo Xi (c. 1000–1090).

Created using the traced-gold (*miaojin*) technique, each wood panel was first covered in black lacquer; the designs were then painted on and built up in additional layers to create low relief decoration colored with various natural pigments, after which the panels were placed in a warm, humid room to cure or set the lacquer. The design was then "traced" on the lacquer using very fine gold powder applied with cotton balls.[3] Also known as *yangqi*, or "foreign style," this technique became popular during the reign of the Yongzheng emperor (1723–35), who especially appreciated and collected Japanese-style gold and

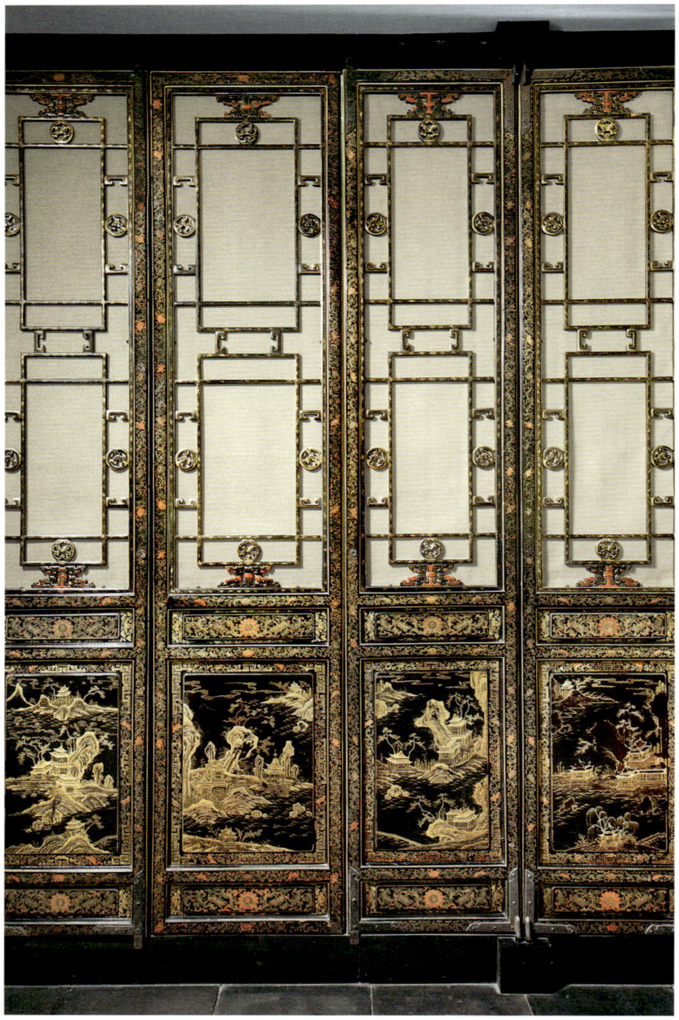

c

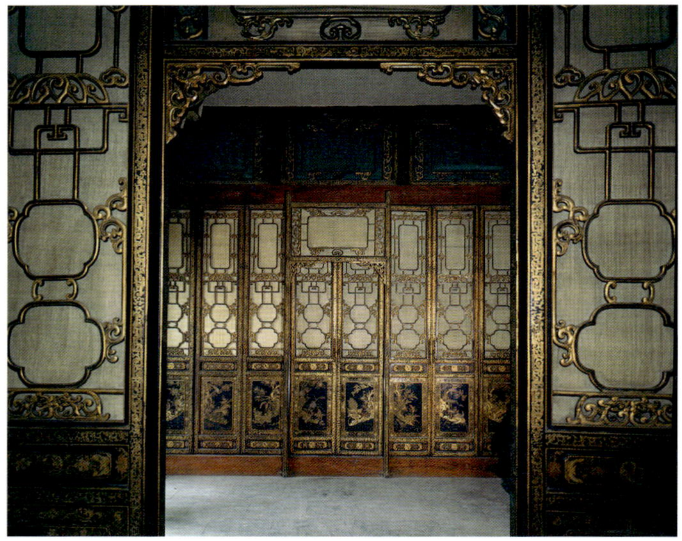

Fig. 69. Lacquered and gilded paneling from the Palace of Established Happiness (*Jianfu gong*), Forbidden City, Beijing

silvered lacquer (*maki-e*), renowned for its use of extensive amounts of gold.[4] The traced-gold lacquer technique continued into the reign of the Qianlong emperor (1736–95), when it was used to decorate interior paneling for rooms; furniture such as thrones, couch beds, chairs, tables, and wardrobes; and objects for the scholar's study, including bookshelves, display cabinets,[5] and incense stands.

Comparison with the finely executed and intricately decorated lacquered and gilded paneling in the Palace of Established Happiness (*Jianfu gong*; fig. 69)—the Qianlong emperor's favorite retreat in the Forbidden City, where he built his first private garden in 1742 and kept many of his treasured artworks[6]—suggests that the museum's more simply rendered panels most likely came from an official's residence. The room had higher ceilings than is indicated in the museum's reconstruction, as a row of horizontal openwork lattice panels, some of which have been placed at the front of the scholar's study (b) in the museum's installation, would have been fitted on top of the vertical panels. HK

1. They were purchased by Horace H. F. Jayne on his trip to the Orient in 1928, and were described as "from Chih Pei Lo Fu, Peking." See Jayne's accounts of his "Oriental Trip, 1928," Registrar's file, Philadelphia Museum of Art.
2. Other translucent materials, such as inlaid glass panels, embroidered textiles, and paintings and calligraphy mounted on silk, were also used as backings for the openwork lattices in the Forbidden City; Gugong bowuyuan gu jianzhu guanli bu 2007, 109.
3. This is according to the Annotated "Lacquer Decoration," which describes techniques of lacquer in the Ming dynasty; see Wang 1998, 87.
4. Examples of Chinese copies of this Japanese technique made during the Yongzheng period are in the Palace Museum, Beijing; illustrated in London 2005–6, 262–3, nos. 175, 176.
5. London 2005–6, 296, no. 221.
6. Gugong bowuyuan gu jianzhu guanli bu 2007, 134–40. Landscapes in the Japanese style decorate the Lodge of Emerald Clouds (*Cuiyun guan*) in the Palace of Many Splendors (*Chonghua gong*), the residence of the Qianlong emperor when he was still a prince; see http://en.dpm.org.cn/collections/architecture/architecture/28.html. Some works of art were also stored there; Cheng 2010, 251.

d

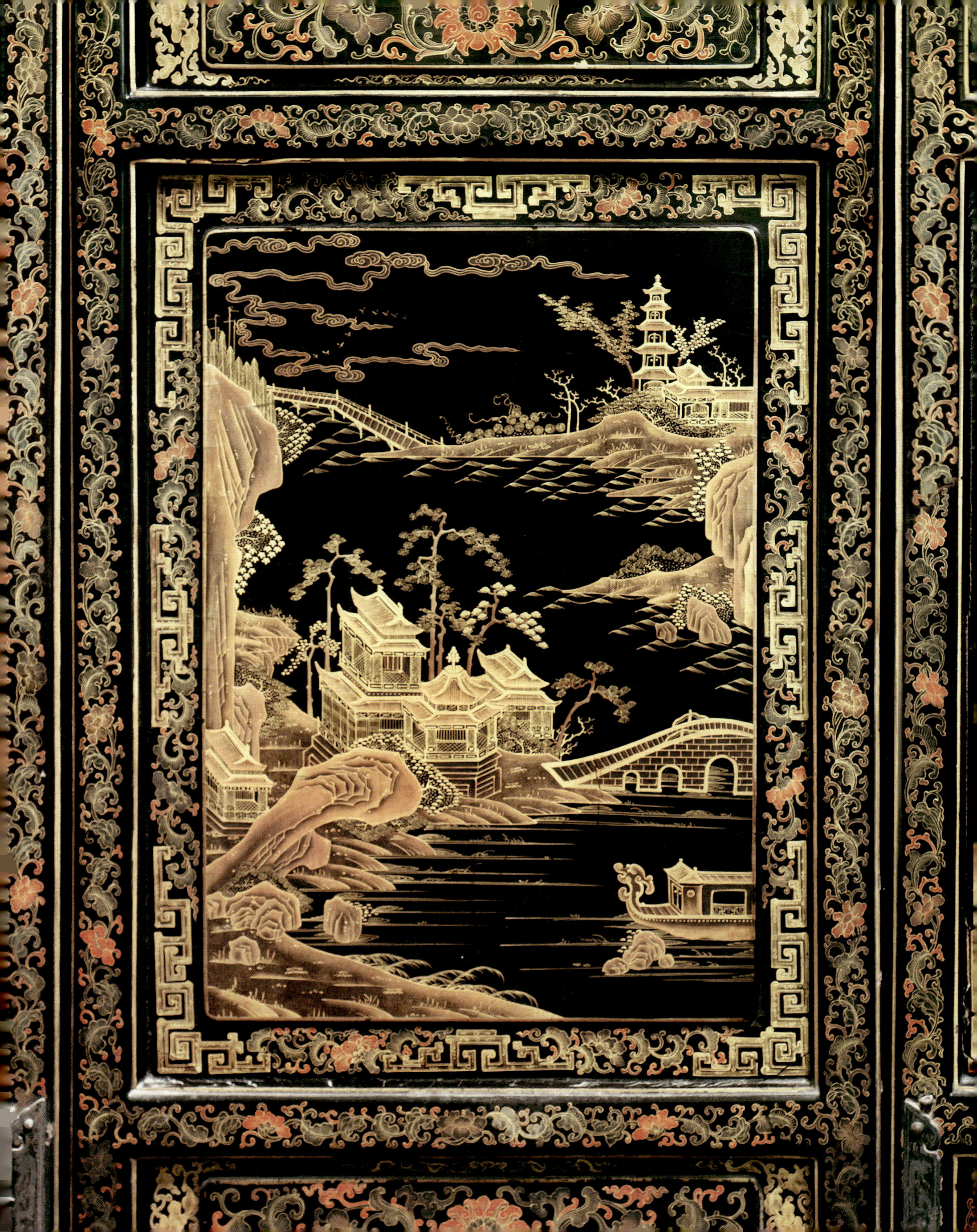

89

Celestial Bird with Covered Vases

Qing dynasty (1644–1911), Qianlong period (1736–95)
Rock crystal (quartz)
4⁹⁄₁₆ x 5 x 1⁹⁄₁₆ inches (11.6 x 12.7 x 4 cm)
Gift of Major General and Mrs. William Crozier, 1944-20-212a–d

A celestial bird (*tianji*) supports two bronze-form covered vessels with auspicious decoration in this small rock-crystal carving, most likely displayed in a scholar's study. Since at least the Ming dynasty (1368–1644), curios and other meaningful "playthings" appreciated for their aesthetic beauty and associations with ancient traditions were popular with scholar-collectors. This trend continued in the Qing dynasty and at court, where the early Qing emperors were well versed in literati culture. At no time was this inclination more prevalent than during the Qianlong emperor's rule. With the imperial workshops at his command, the Qianlong emperor commissioned numerous works of art for his study and enjoyment.

This carving has transformed a ritual vessel form into an object of pure ornament, conveying not only good wishes for happiness, health, and wealth—expressed by the bats decorating the sides of the two-handled globular vase—but also longevity, as conveyed by the finial on the cover of the taller vase, shaped like a *lingzhi* fungus (see nos. 22, 24, 42–44). Vessels in the form of a celestial bird with blunt beak, webbed feet, and luxuriant plumage and supporting an archaic wine vessel (*zun*) were collected by the court in different mediums, including jade, porcelain, and cloisonné enamel.[1]

The use of rock crystal in Chinese art is fairly limited.[2] That it was considered a Western material is evident from the Kangxi emperor's (Qianlong's grandfather) reliance on the skill of Jesuit missionaries at court to establish imperial glassworks, where crystal was also worked.[3] Archives from the Qing imperial workshops responsible for the production of objects for use by the imperial family show limited quantities of rock-crystal carvings made during Qianlong's reign, such as small figurines, water containers, seal-paste boxes, brush washers, and other accoutrements for the scholar's study.[4]

This carving is one of a group of forty-seven rock-crystal carvings collected by Major General and Mrs. William Crozier when they lived in Beijing in the late 1920s, which they donated to the museum in 1944 (see p. 26). Some of the vessels in the collection are extremely large, and while they carry Qianlong marks are most likely creations of the later nineteenth century or Republican period (early twentieth century), when many craftsmen, no longer working for the imperial court, continued to create high-quality works in imperial style for the market. Many are fashioned from flawless crystal, including the rock-crystal ball in the museum's collection (fig. 70), among the largest known.[5] Other, smaller rock-crystal balls, often placed on elaborate metal stands, were collected by Westerners in the early twentieth century,[6] attesting to their appeal abroad. HK

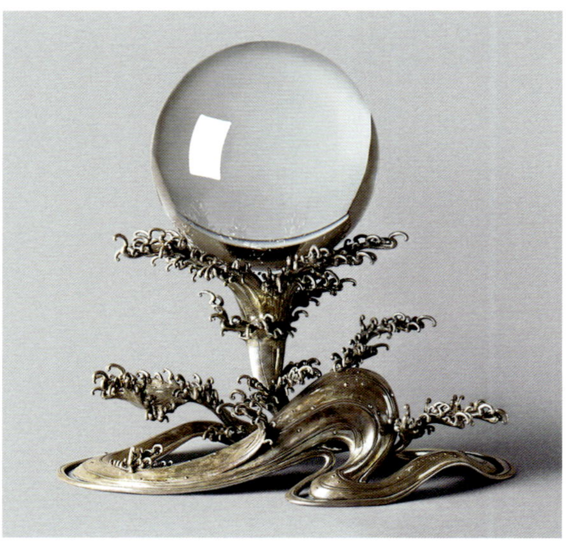

Fig. 70. Crystal Ball. 19th–early 20th century. Rock crystal (quartz) with silver stand; diam. of ball 8¹¹⁄₁₆ inches (22 cm). Philadelphia Museum of Art. Gift of Major General and Mrs. William Crozier, 1944-20-2a,b

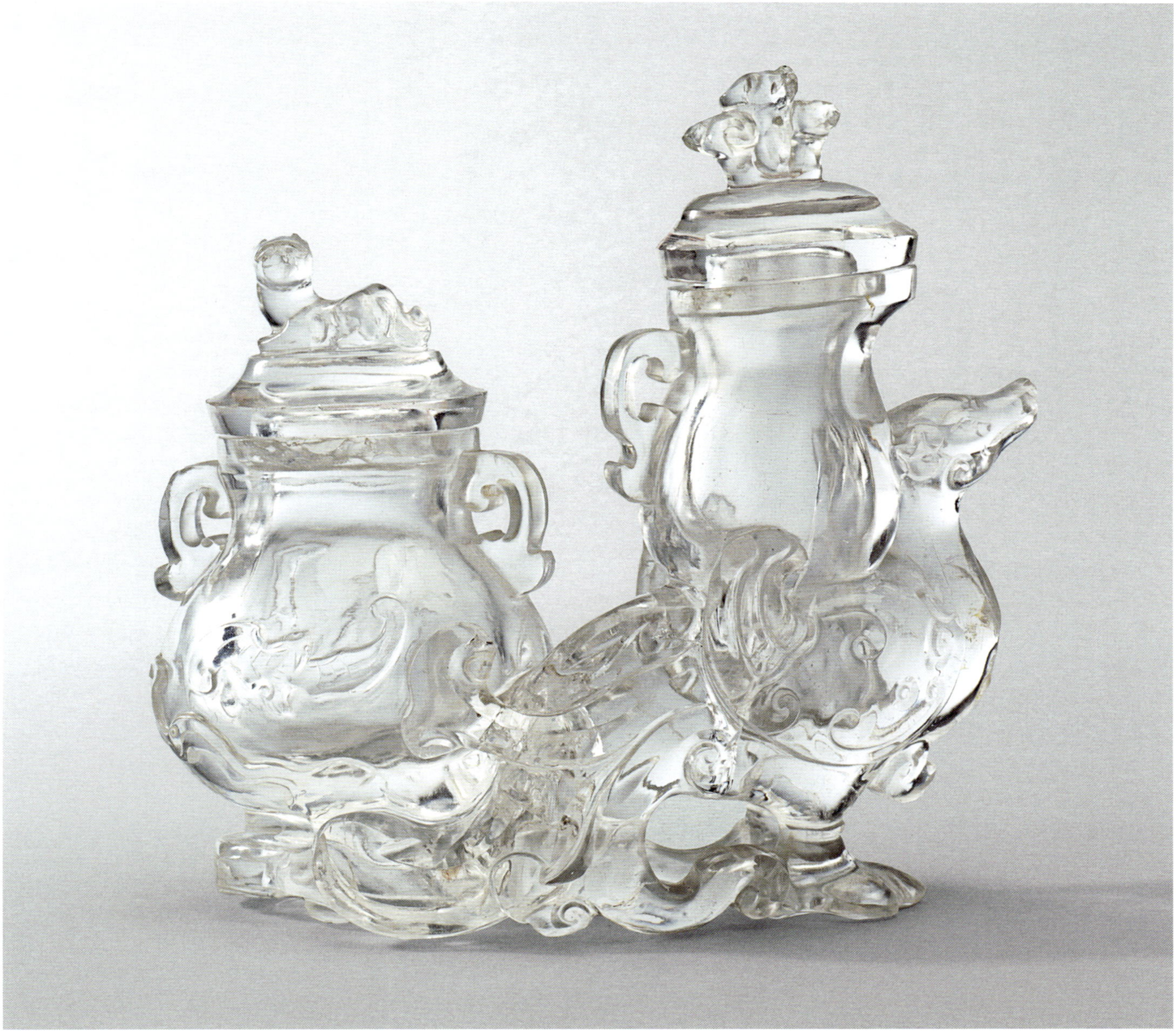

1. An example of a rock-crystal carving of a similar small size, also showing a bird but only a single vase form, is illustrated in Zhang and Gugong 2011, vol. 3, 45, no. 14. Larger cloisonné, jade, and rock-crystal versions are published on the Palace Museum's website: https://www.dpm.org.cn/collection/enamel/230184; www.dpm.org.cn/collection/jade/230176 and 230175.
2. Found in small amounts in China, rock crystal was used from ancient times, mainly for beads and ornaments, and was also found in Buddhist reliquaries.
3. Crystal carving, like glass production, employed similar lapidary techniques. In 1696, the Kangxi emperor ordered the building of a glass house, an imperial glass workshop, which one or two workmen from the imperial glassworks were able to make from glass and crystal. See Lam 2005, 59–60; Curtis 2001.
4. See Xianggang and Zhongguo 2005, 47 (Qianlong, 48th and 49th year, or 1783–84), 246.
5. Larger flawless crystal balls are in the National Museum of Natural History, Washington, DC; Crow Collection, Dallas; and the University of Pennsylvania Museum, Philadelphia, the latter of which may have come from the same lapidary, as it too has a similar Japanese silver wave-form stand. Sold by John Wanamaker to the Penn Museum, it was thought to have once been in the imperial palace of the Dowager Empress Cixi, who controlled China from 1861 to 1908; however, this remains an unsubstantiated claim. See https://www.penn.museum/collections/highlights/asian/crystalball.php.
6. One on a gilded bronze lotus-form stand is in the Winthrop collection, Harvard University Museums, Cambridge, MA (1943.55.24), and another on a Japanese silver double-dragon stand that was purchased from the Seisuke Ikeda collection of Japanese and Chinese art in 1904 by Jane Lathrop Stanford and is in the Canton Arts Center collection, Stanford University, CA (JLS.9304.B).

90
Dog Cage

Qing dynasty (1644–1911), late 18th–19th century
Gilded cast copper alloy with cloisonné enamels, jade rings, wood frame
45½ x 32 x 24¾ inches (115.6 x 81.3 x 62.9 cm)
Gift of the Friends of the Philadelphia Museum of Art, 1964-205-1

This impressive cage is decorated in cloisonné enamel along all four sides and on the wheel rims with designs of five-clawed dragons set against scrolling lotuses.[1] The extravagant decoration, further embellished with highly prized opaque "mutton fat" white jade rings, suggests that it once graced the private quarters of a sumptuous palace. On each side of the domed top, pairs of gilded confronting three-clawed dragons are depicted amid enameled clouds, while along the top horizontal frame below the dome are gilded bronze lion masks with curled manes fitted with hooks below the mouths, possibly to suspend a curtain; along the bottom, two of the lion masks have thick ring handles issuing from the mouths to attach cords for pulling the wheeled cage. An arched opening at the front would have been closed with a grille, using four loops at the sides to hold it in place; its shape echoes the onion-form finials at each corner of the cage and the central, large, bell-shaped finial, which are reminiscent of Mughal design elements popular in the Qianlong period (1736–95) and later. Another practical feature is the wood base lined with a silk cushion, which conveniently slides out from the back for ease of cleaning.

This elaborate mobile kennel was most likely made for a small dog such as a Pekingese, a breed that was already in the imperial court in the nineteenth century.[2] Dogs were favored pets of court ladies and were treated royally at the Qing court, supposedly living in pavilions with marble floors, sleeping on silk cushions, and cared for by eunuchs. They even had silk brocade outfits made with their name on the inside lining.[3]

During the Qing dynasty a number of large cloisonné objects, such as vases, fish bowls, incense burners, garden seats, and floor and table screens, were made to furnish the many interior spaces of the Forbidden City. The eighteenth century saw extraordinary, exotic inventions in cloisonné enameling, as seen in this unique cage and two large containers supported by pairs of foreign-looking attendants, one in the State Hermitage Museum, Saint Petersburg, and the other in the Victoria and Albert Museum, London, where it is documented to have come from the imperial Summer Palace (Yuanming yuan) in Beijing.[4] During this time cloisonné enamel workshops were set up in Beijing at the Summer Palace and in the Forbidden City, as well as at Guangzhou, Yangzhou, and Suzhou, though most of the imperial wares were made in Beijing and Guangzhou.[5] HK

1. Cloisonné enamel was first produced in China in the Yuan dynasty (1271–1368) as a result of foreign influence. Strips of metal wire called *cloisons* in French (hence the term *cloisonné* enamel) were soldered to the metal surface in the desired design before colored enamel paste was packed into the cells and then fired to fuse the enamels together. This process was repeated several times to completely fill the cells, after which the surface of the object was polished down to reveal the wire edges, which were then gilded and burnished. See New York 2011, 4–6.
2. Illustrated by the famous incident of a Pekingese taken by the British army during the 1858 Anglo-French looting of the Summer Palace in Beijing and given to Queen Victoria; see "The 99th (Lanarkshire) Regiment 1824–1881," The Wardrobe: Home of the Infantry Regiments of Berkshire and Wiltshire, http://www.thewardrobe.org.uk/.
3. See Li and Chen 2016, 218, no. 92, for a silk brocade outfit made for an imperial pet dog.
4. The lobed basin in the State Hermitage Museum (JIM-499) is illustrated in their online collection; the rectangular covered ice chest in the Victoria and Albert Museum, London (no. 255&A-1876) can be found online as well.
5. Li and Chen 2016, 431.

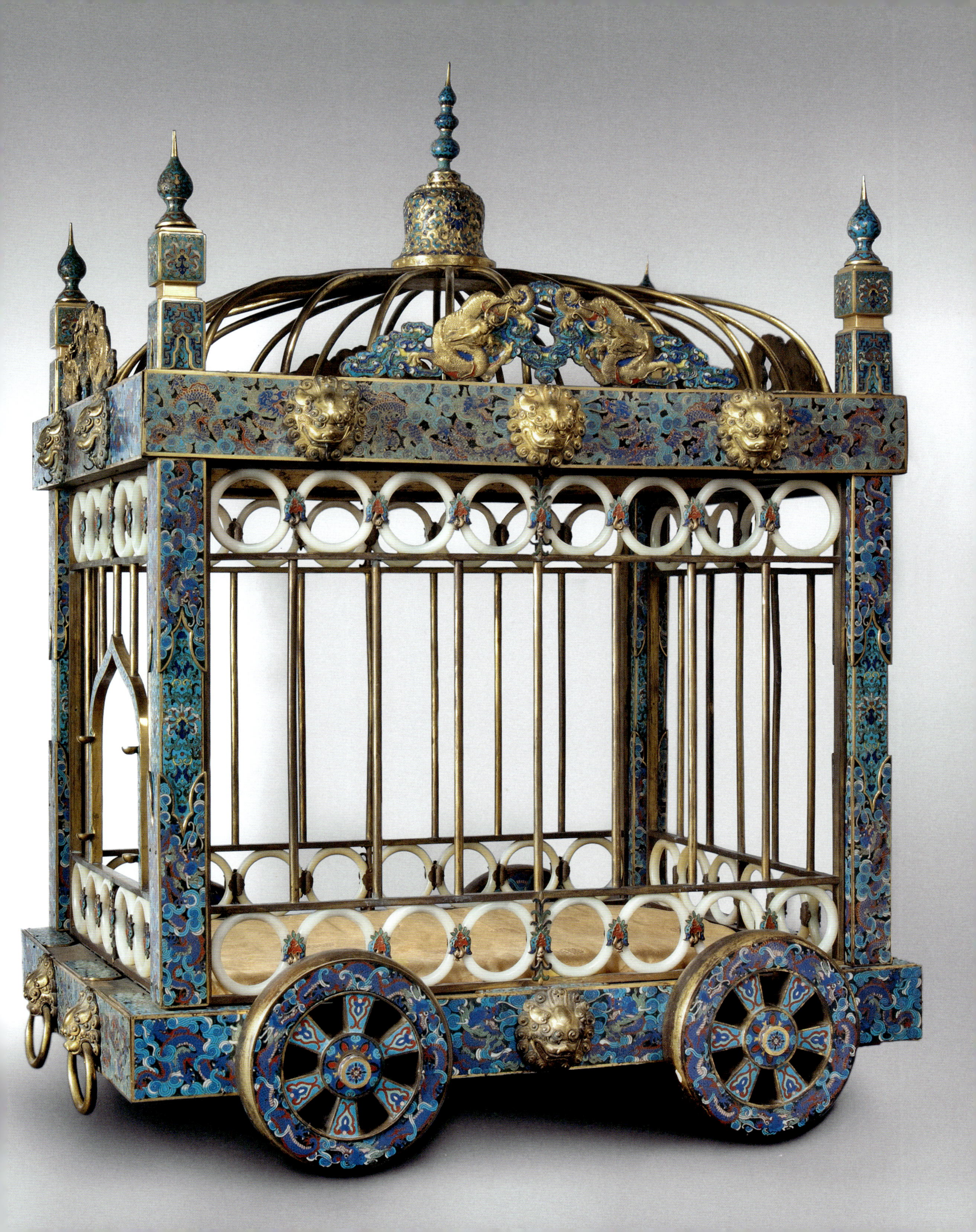

91

Warrior Opera Costume

Qing dynasty (1644–1911), Qianlong period (1736–95) or Jiaqing period (1796–1820)
Silk satin with gold leaf on paper-wrapped thread in couching and basket-weave couching stitches, and with appliques of silk lampas with gold leaf on paper strips, silk lampas with gold leaf on paper-wrapped thread, embroidered silk satin and silk velvet; plaited silk cord; metal-framed glass studs and plaques; gilded brass buttons; painted silk twill lining
50½ x 68 inches (128.3 x 172.7 cm)
Gift of Mrs. Henry W. Breyer, Sr., 1950-4-1

This opera garment was created for the role of a *wusheng*, a military character noted for acrobatics and singing in a natural voice. It was one of the standard *sheng*, or male roles. The exquisite workmanship and attention to detail in this costume, made for an imperial palace troupe, is quite different from the flashy styles created for the numerous private and metropolitan troupes that arose during the nineteenth and twentieth centuries.[1]

The Qing court inherited the popular opera called *Kunqu*, with its use of vernacular language and sophisticated aria lyrics and its libretti based on romances, histories, and legends. Four character types predominated: male (*sheng*), female (*dan*), painted-face (*jing*), and clown (*chou*), often preforming in ensembles.[2] Despite local and regional variations, a distinctive feature of all Chinese opera since at least the sixth century has been its multifaceted nature, combining a variety of speech forms, song, mime, dance, slapstick, and acrobatics with generous displays of visual splendor.[3]

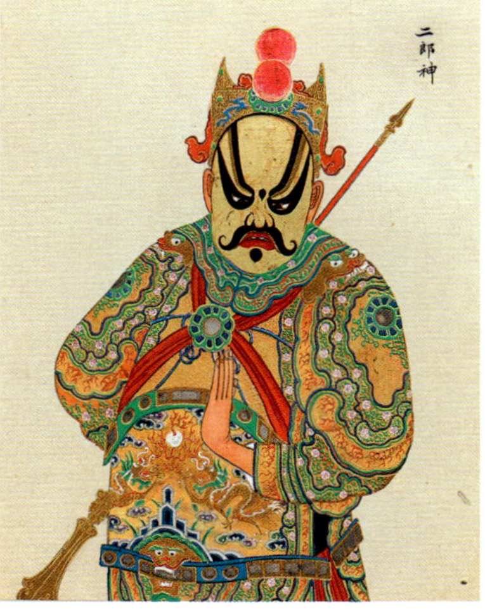

Fig. 71. *Erlang Shen*, divine Daoist warrior (leaf two of fifty, right image), from *One Hundred Portraits of Peking Opera Characters*. Qing dynasty, probably Guangxu period (1875–1908). Ink, color, and gold leaf on silk, mounted in an album of fifty leaves; image 10⅜ x 8¼ inches (26.4 x 21 cm). The Metropolitan Museum of Art, New York. Rogers Fund, 1930 (30.76.299b)

The Qianlong emperor took a particular interest in opera, having been exposed to the court and private troupes of the capital, as well as those of other regions, during his various inspection tours of the south. In honor of the emperor's eightieth birthday in the autumn of 1790, the imperial salt commissioner of Zhejiang province brought an opera troupe from the neighboring Anhui province to Beijing.[4] The performance style in Anhui differed from *Kunqu* practices, emphasizing accurate enunciation with elegant projection and a nuanced singing style accompanied by intricate ornamentation. The Anhui troupe caused a sensation, and other southern troupes soon arrived at the capital. There the Anhui style absorbed elements of popular local performance practices, resulting in a new opera form called *Jingju* (also known as Peking or Beijing opera; fig. 71).[5]

The Qianlong emperor's fondness for the newly evolving art form is reflected in the expansion of the court drama unit from one hundred to one thousand employees. The *Neiweifu* (Imperial Household Department) ordered fabrics and the tailoring of costumes for imperial troupes from the imperial silk factories. JV

1. Bonds 2008, 31–36.
2. Li 2010, 36–37; Wong 2002, 289–96.
3. Yung 2002, 279.
4. "Hui Opera's Future in Mist," *China Daily: Ethnic Groups in China*, August 12, 2009, accessed August 10, 2017, http://www.chinadaily.com.cn/ethnic/2009-08/12/content_8561968_2.htm.
5. Pian 2002, 281–87.

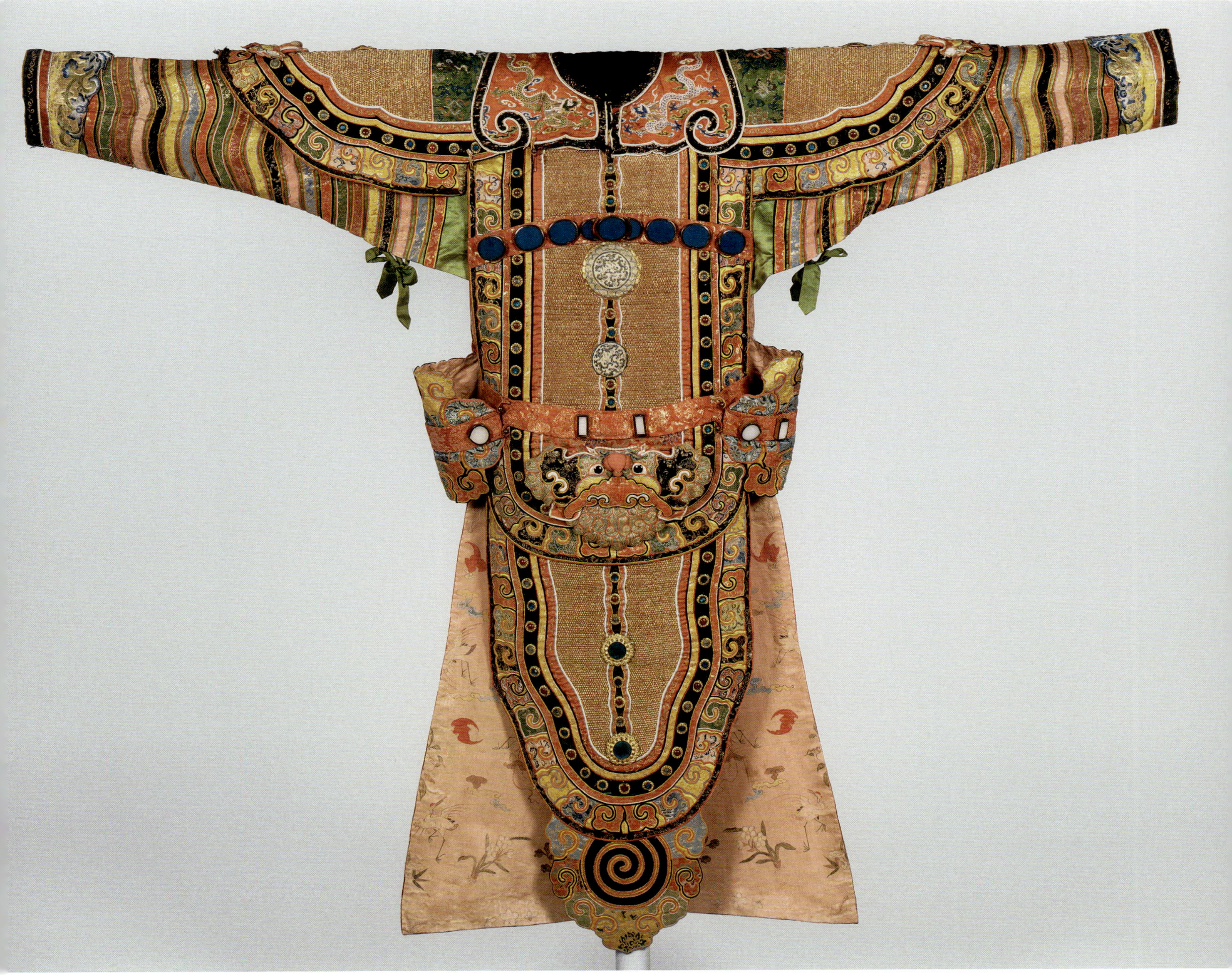

92

Daoist Vestment (*Jiangyi*)

Qing dynasty (1644–1911), Jiaqing period (1796–1820)
Silk satins embroidered with floss silk in satin and chain stitch, with couched silk cord and gold leaf on paper-wrapped thread, gold leaf on paper appliqué
L. 53 inches (134.6 cm)
Purchased with the George W. B. Taylor Fund, 1967-144-1

Many of the worship practices in Daoism involve the celebrants visualizing themselves rising to the heavens to meet with the gods or bringing the energies of various celestial bodies down into themselves. Since most ancient Daoist deities were star gods thought to dwell in different parts of the heavens, it is fitting that the back of this priest's garment depicts that realm. The actions of the priest, with such a celestial "map" on his back, thus evoked the union of heaven and earth in the sacred space of the Daoist altar (fig. 72). The *jiangyi* (literally, "crimson mantle") continues to be worn by the highest ranking Daoist priests (*daozhang*), who conduct rites calling to the gods of the pantheon, presenting petitions to them and seeking their forgiveness for wrongdoing.[1]

At the center of the garment's back is a tower, representing the home of the gods. Surrounding it are colored circles signifying the twenty-eight lunar mansions, the constellations through which the moon passes during its annual rotation around the earth. Above, three gold half-circles supported by clouds represent the Three Terraces, the stars near the Northern Dipper (or Big Dipper) in what the ancient Chinese considered the most important part of the sky; the Three Terraces were linked to the emperor's three highest ministers. Flanking these are symbols of the sun and moon. The five roundels on the robe back are filled with auspicious symbols (dragons, butterflies, and emblems of the Eight Immortals). At the hem, billows and waves depict the universal ocean that surrounds the earth, while the sleeves are bordered by the eight trigrams of the *I Ching* (or *Book of Changes*), symbolizing the various combinations of *yin* and *yang* in the world.[2]

The design of the five roundels and layout of the main body of this robe can also be found on two other vestments worked on green silk satin, one in Chicago,[3] and the other in Minneapolis.[4] Although the borders of these three finely wrought vestments vary, their similarities argue for a single workshop. JV

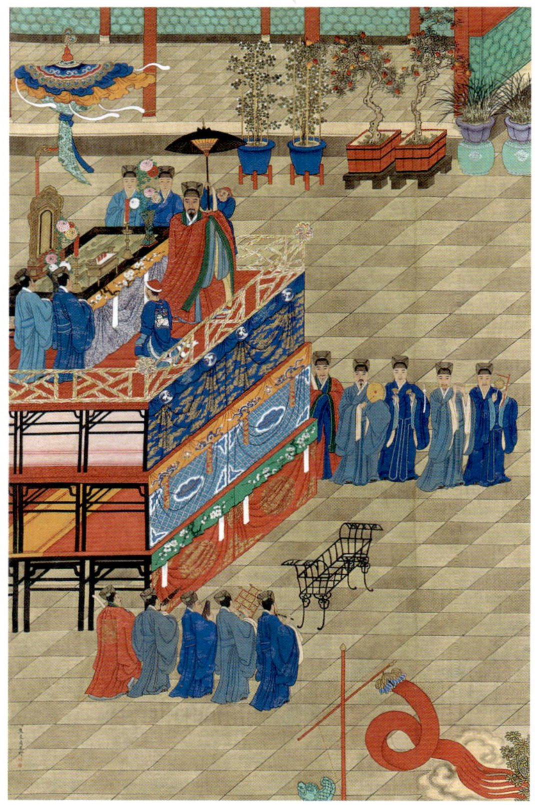

Fig. 72. Attributed to Jiao Bingzhen (act. c. 1689–1726). *The Yongzheng Emperor's Nephew at a Daoist Ceremony for the Recovery of His Father*. Qing dynasty, 1723–26. Ink and color on silk, 140³⁄₁₆ x 63⅜ inches (356 x 161 cm). Freer Gallery of Art and Arthur M. Sackler Gallery, Smithsonian Institution, Washington, DC. Purchase—Smithsonian Collections Acquisition Program and partial gift of Richard G. Pritzlaff, S1991.99

1. Maruyama 2008, 456–57.
2. Chicago and San Francisco 2000–2001, 195–99.
3. Vollmer 2000, 67.
4. Jacobsen 2000, vol. 1, 386–87.

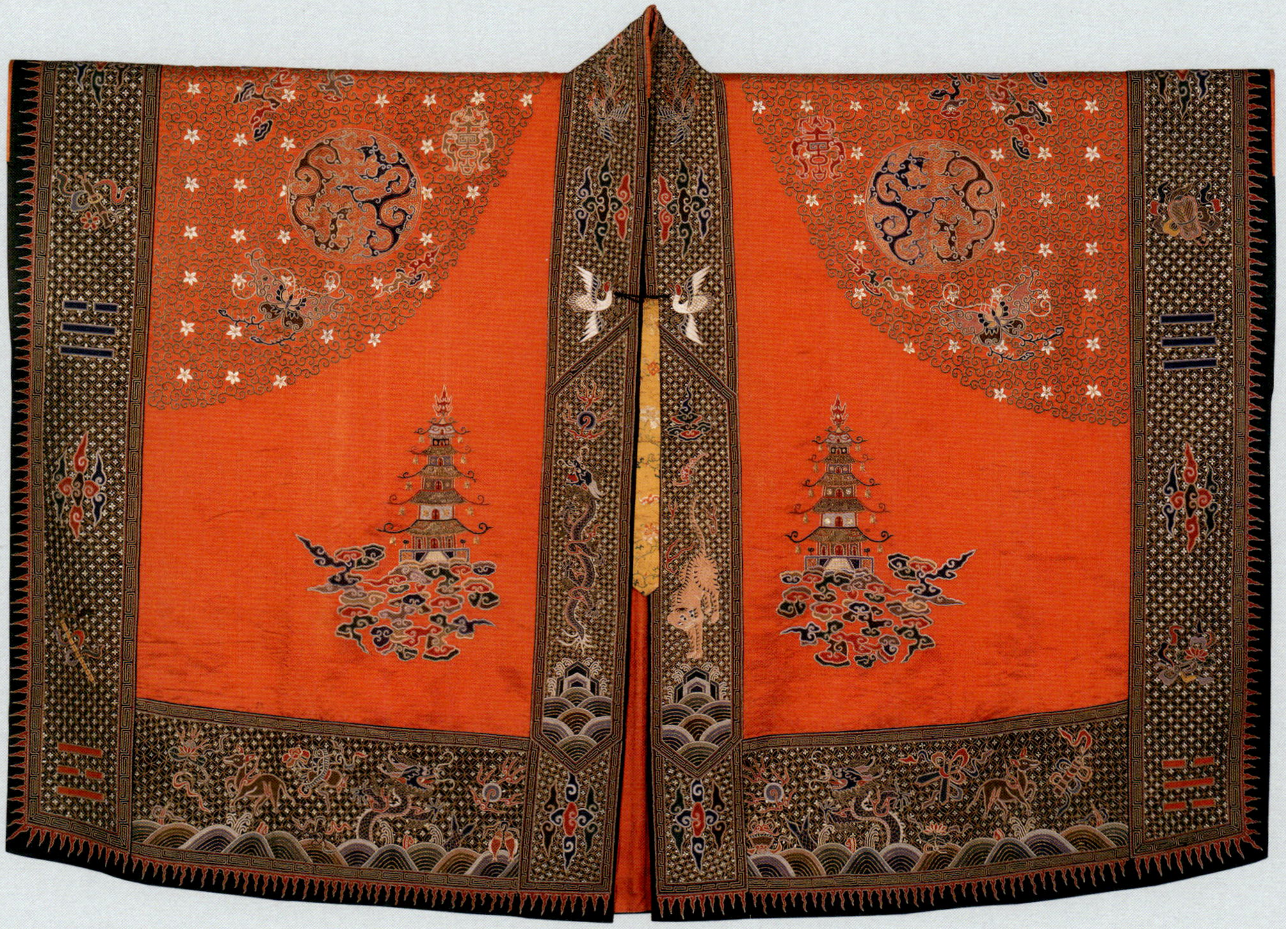

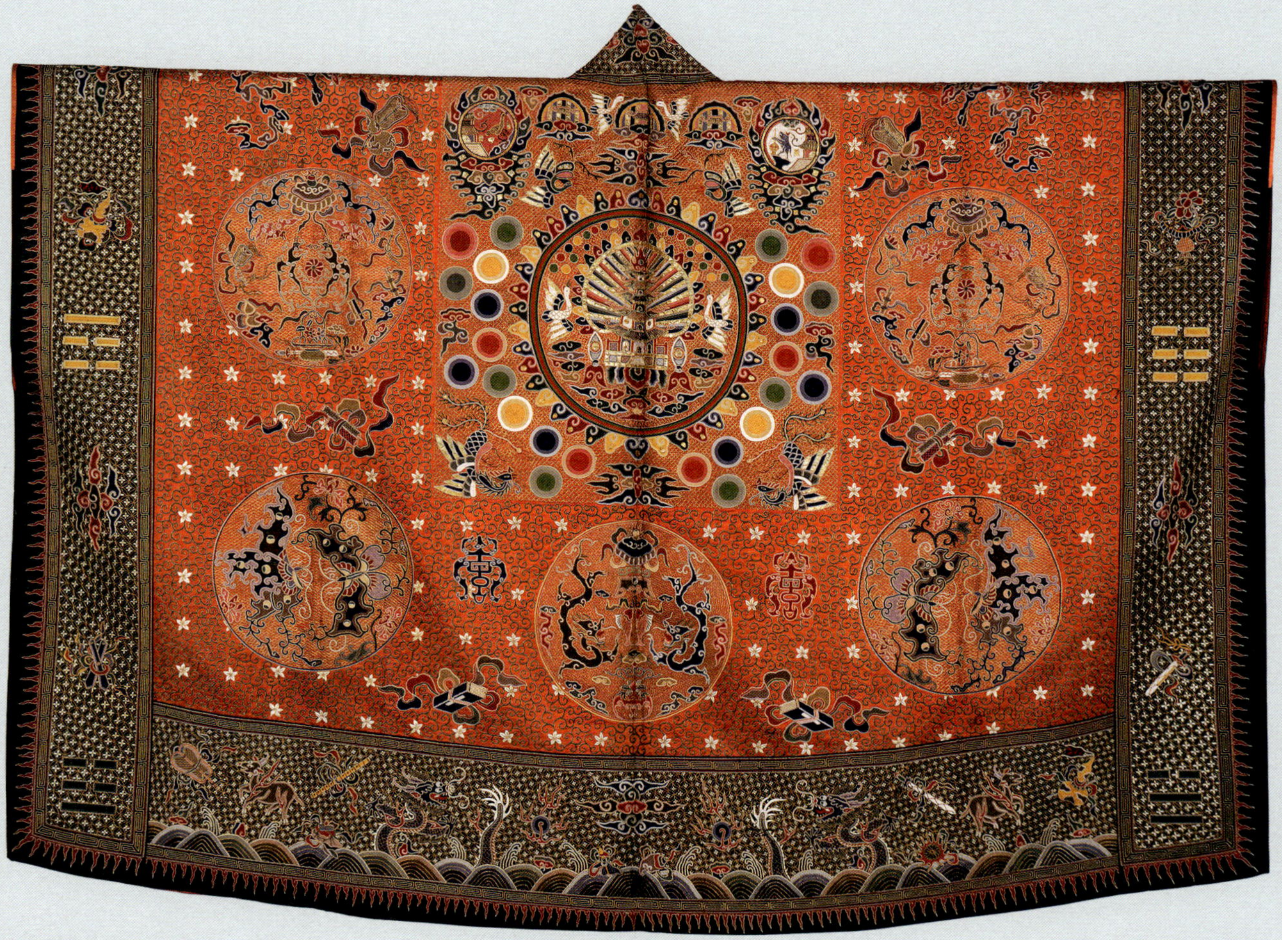

93

Hat Ornament of a *Junwang* (Prince of the Second Rank)

Qing dynasty (1644–1911), possibly Jiaqing period (1796–1820)
Gold, pearls, and spinel ruby
5 5/16 x 1 3/4 inches (13.5 x 4.5 cm)
Gift of the Friends of the Philadelphia Museum of Art, 1970-6-1

Special hats had always been an essential component of Chinese court attire, but took on new significance when the Manchu emperor ascended the Dragon Throne in 1644. New regulations concerning court attire were issued, with a dome-shaped, fur-faced cap characteristic of the pre-conquest Manchu wardrobe prescribed as the official hat for winter wear, and a conical sunshade made of woven finely split bamboo specified for summer; a jeweled finial and red silk floss tassel decorated the crown of both hats. Finials topped with tall, pointed jewels appeared on hats for formal wear (*chaoguan*) worn by all ranks of court officials and officers, while simple spherical jewels or buttons were used on hats for semi-formal wear (*jiguan*) for both nobility and officials.[1]

Hat finials were coded with information about rank. The finials of the imperial clan were lavishly embellished with large "eastern pearls"—freshwater pearls from the Sungari, Yalu, and Amur rivers associated with the Manchu homeland. The formal court hat ornaments for the emperor and crown prince included thirteen pearls set in three tiers of gold filigree with an intricate design featuring twelve dragons. For the emperor, the pearl at the apex was a very large "precious pearl"; for the crown prince, an eastern pearl. The number of tiers, pearls, and dragons decreased for lower-ranking officials, and the large pearls at the apex were replaced with rubies for sons of the emperor down to the ninth rank of nobility (fig. 73). This rare surviving finial (shown here larger than life-size), with its two tiers of gold filigree featuring two dragons and a spinel ruby at the apex, includes eight eastern pearls, appropriate for an imperial prince of the second rank (*duoluo junwang*). JV

1. Dickinson and Wrigglesworth 2000, 98–114.

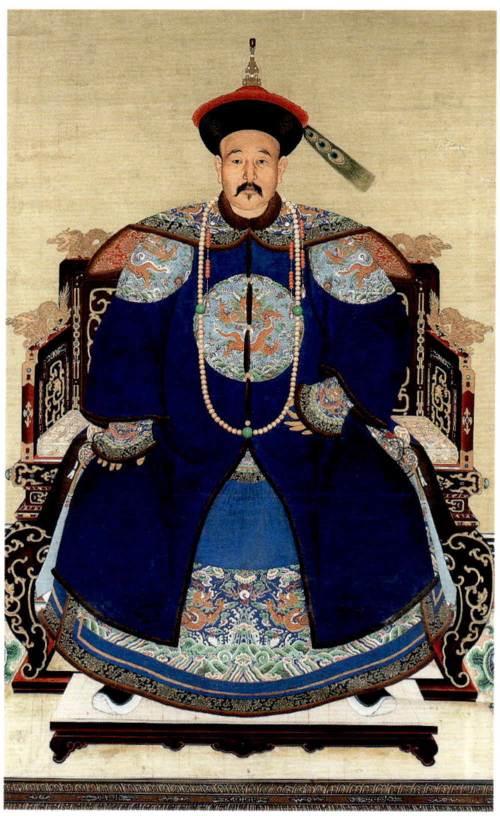

Fig. 73. Posthumous Portrait of a Prince of the First Rank (possibly Shi Wenying, brother-in-law to the Qianlong emperor). Qing dynasty, possibly Jiaqing period, late 18th century. Ink and color on silk, mounted as a hanging scroll; 81 1/2 x 44 3/16 inches (207 x 112.2 cm). Minneapolis Institute of Art. Gift of Ruth and Bruce Dayton, 2002.12.2.1

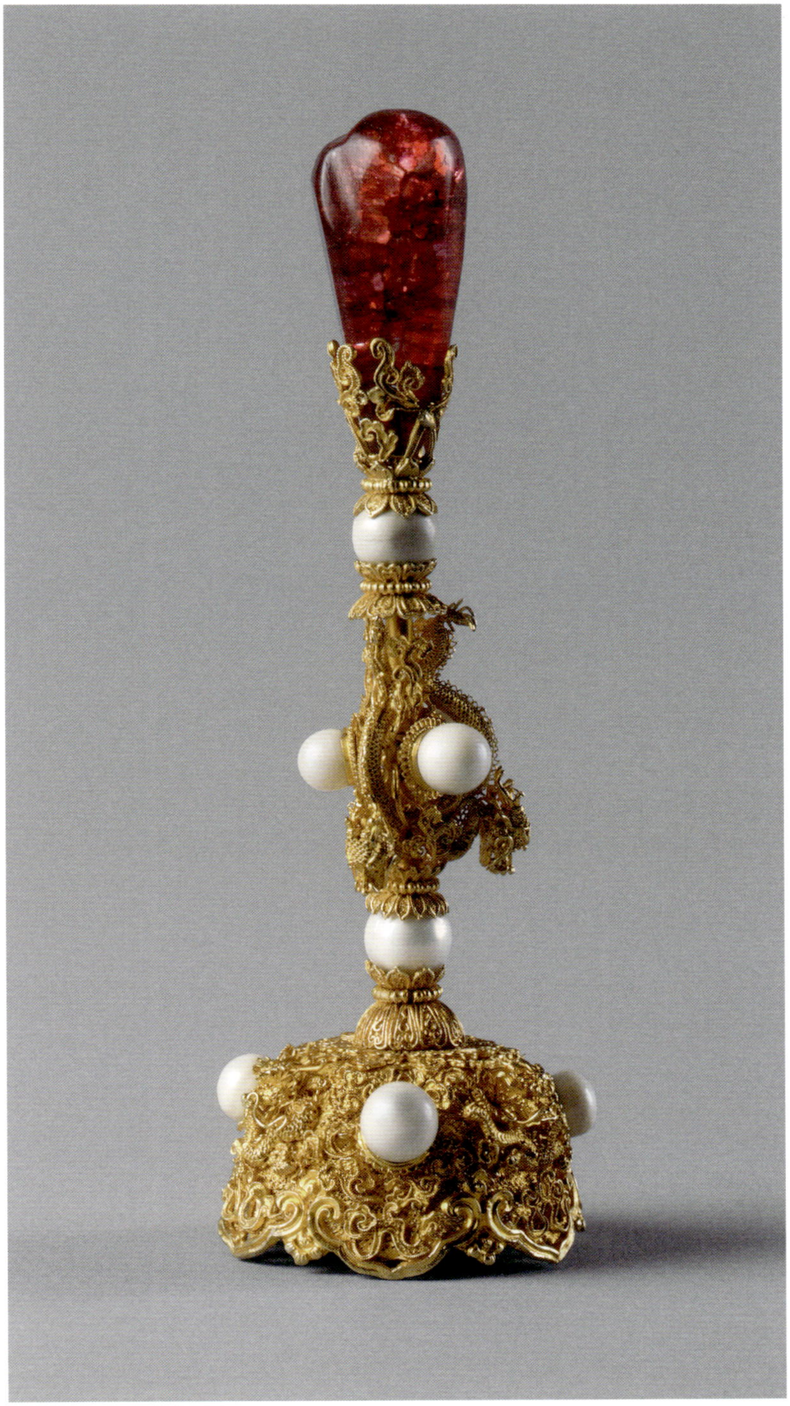

94

Tea Table with Figures in a Chinese Formal Garden

Qing dynasty (1644–1911), Daoguang period (1821–50), c. 1839
Wood with lacquer and gilded decoration
31 11/16 x 35 5/8 inches (80.5 x 90.5 cm)
Gift of Mrs. Joseph H. Burroughs, 1940-34-1

Americans entered the lucrative China trade in 1784, when the former privateer the *Empress of China* made her first voyage to Canton (present-day Guangzhou), and found the goods their European counterparts sought: tea, porcelains, silks, and other "exotic" items. By the early nineteenth century large quantities of lacquerwares were being exported to Europe and America to satisfy the taste of the growing middle class. Chinese craftsmen created Western-style pieces decorated in Chinese designs specifically for export, including dressing tables, desks, screens, sewing boxes, fans, games boxes, and tea caddies.[1]

The round tea table with a top that tilted up was a favorite furniture form in colonial America, where it became fashionable in the early 1700s. The "Orientalized" version shown here consists of a circular hinged tabletop mounted on a turned stand resting on a four-footed base, the feet carved to look like furry paws. The whole is covered in black and red lacquer, and the design finely painted in various shades of gold. Areas where the gold has worn off reveal the vermillion lacquer layer underneath.[2] Represented at the center of the tabletop is a Chinese formal garden bordering a lake, with bridges, boats, and pavilions where people are gathered to play music, recite poetry, and engage in other pleasurable activities. Around the central scene is a band of boldly rendered auspicious motifs in low relief that include boys pulling a cart full of cash (signifying wealth), a seated sage, bats (symbolizing happiness and good fortune), birds, butterflies, antiques, and three goats.[3] The outermost border integrates the ubiquitous Chinese design of confronting dragons facing a flaming pearl between smaller areas of lions, butterflies, birds, and flowers, all on a diaper-pattern ground.

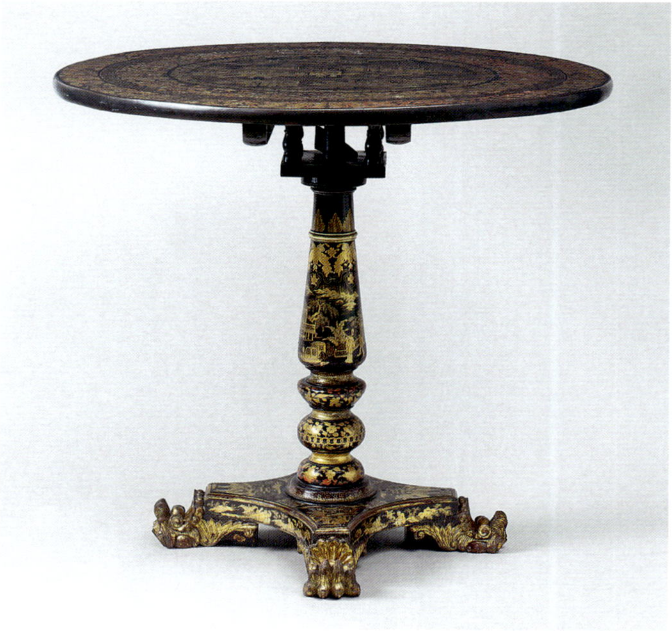

The fine execution and detailing of the painted decoration and the table's overall good condition, indicating the care taken to preserve it, suggest its superior quality among Chinese export lacquerwares. The piece was made for the Philadelphian John A. Lewis while he was in China in 1839 working for his father, John Frederick Lewis.[4] He and his brother took over the family China-trade business, located at Walnut and Front streets in Philadelphia, when their father died in 1858. HK

1. For examples of a dressing table, screen, and another round tea table with a tilting top, see Petisca et al. 2016. For a sewing box and a fan, see Hong Kong 1993, nos. 107, 108.
2. Most lacquered furniture pieces made for export were covered in a few layers of black lacquer. After tracing a drawing of the intended gilded design on top of the black lacquer, vermilion and orpiment were used to outline the motifs, which were then painted in red-pigmented lacquer, with gold dust applied before the lacquer had dried completely; see Petisca et al. 2016, 88.
3. Three (*san*) goats (*yang*) symbolize the saying *san yang kai tai*, a wish for prosperity in the new year; for a fuller explanation, see London 2005–6, 469, no. 299.
4. For the history of the Lewis (originally Ludwig) family, see Philadelphia 1984, 172; for the tea table, 177, no. 182.

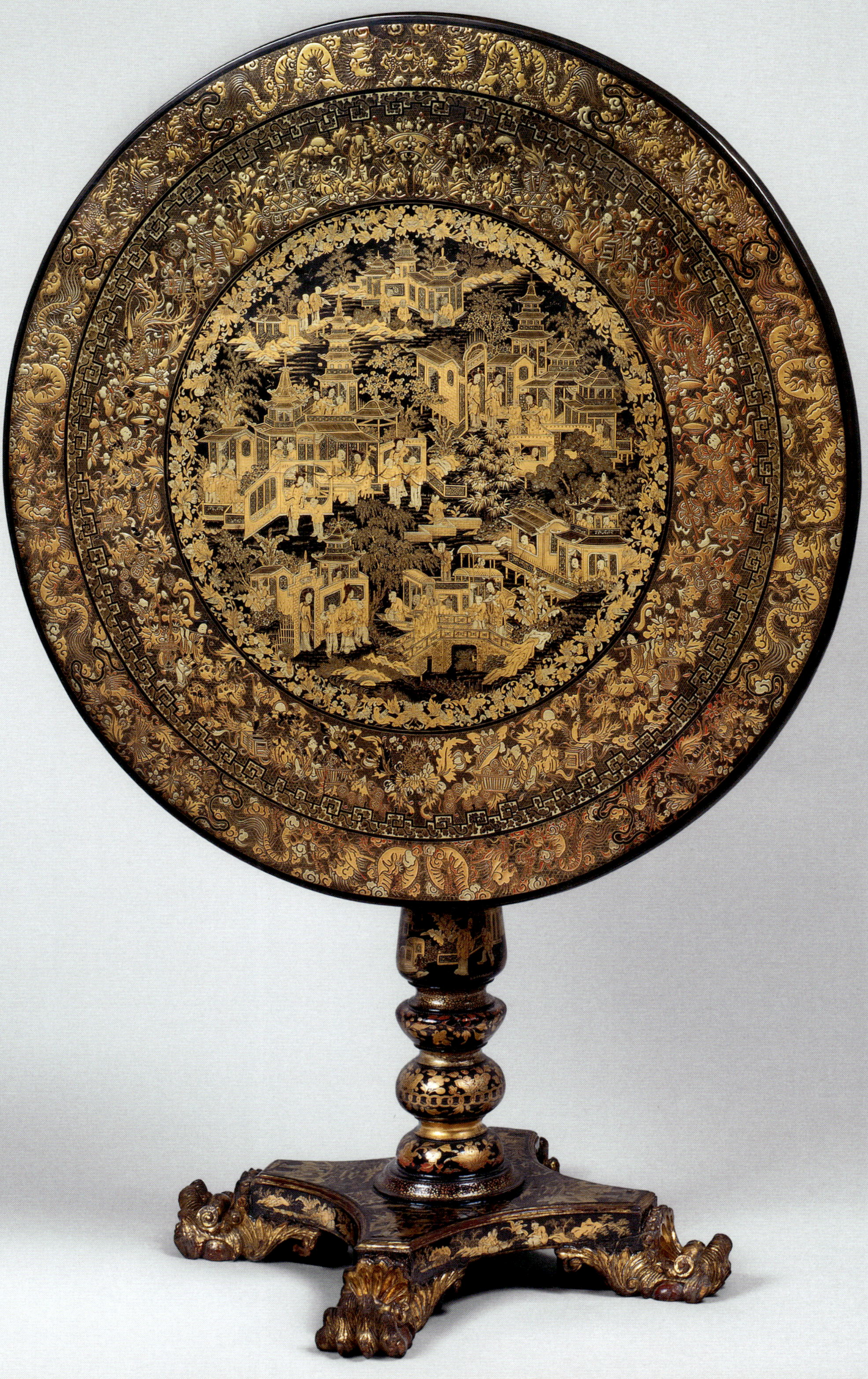

95

Woman's Informal Court Vest

Qing dynasty (1644–1911), Guangxu period (1875–1908), c. 1890s
Silk tapestry weave (*kesi*), silk lampas ribbon and binding with floss silk and gold leaf on paper-wrapped thread; chased gilded brass buttons
L. 28½ inches (72.4 cm)
The Samuel S. White 3rd and Vera White Collection, 1967-30-334

Nineteenth-century textiles made for ritual and administrative functions in the waning years of the old imperial order often lack vitality and precision, but those produced for the private court of the Empress Dowager Cixi (1835–1908) reflect a resurgence of creativity and aesthetic achievement. During the last half of the nineteenth century Cixi had far-reaching influence over the course of the Qing dynasty.[1] She served as regent to two emperors when they were still minors, and as advisor to her nephew the Guangxu emperor (r. 1875–1908).

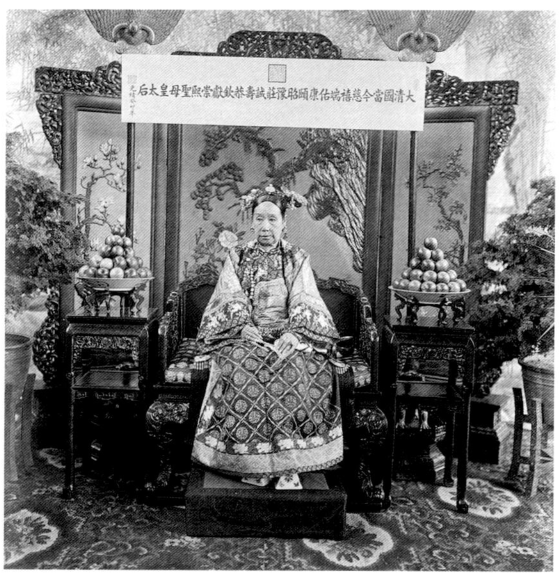

Fig. 74. Xunling (1874–1943). Cixi, Empress Dowager of China. Qing dynasty, 1903. Glass plate negative, 9½ x 7 inches (24.1 x 17.8 cm). Photographs, Freer Gallery of Art and Arthur M. Sackler Gallery Archives, Smithsonian Institution, Washington, DC. Purchase, FSA A.13 SC-GR-252

This tapestry woven vest (*beixin*), with its bold floral design, is typical of the prodigious quantities of gorgeous garments made for the Empress Dowager Cixi (fig. 74). The narcissus decorating the vest is a symbol of good fortune and prosperity and a much-beloved flower of the Chinese (or lunar) New Year, suggesting that the garment was made specifically for these celebrations.

Yu Deling, better known in the West as Der Ling (1885–1944), was a Western-educated lady-in-waiting to Empress Dowager Cixi. In her memoir, *Two Years in the Forbidden City*, she describes the obsession with dress at the court, detailing Cixi's morning toilet and describing the process of selecting a robe for her to wear for a specific occasion from among dozens of choices. But perhaps the most revealing account is of preparations for a trip from the Summer Palace to the Forbidden City in the summer of 1903. Although planning for a stay of only four or five days, the court lady responsible for organizing the dowager empress's robes packed more than fifty of them into yellow-painted wood trays measuring 4 by 5 by 1 foot. In addition, there were hats, jewels, and a wide range of accessories. In the end, fifty-six trays were sent ahead of the empress's procession.[2]

This robe's blue and white design against a vivid yellow field evokes the imperial porcelains decorated in underglaze cobalt with overglaze yellow enameled grounds, such as the sixteenth-century Zhengde dish illustrated in this volume (see no. 40). JV

1. See Chang 2014.
2. Der Ling 1911, 67, 128–29.

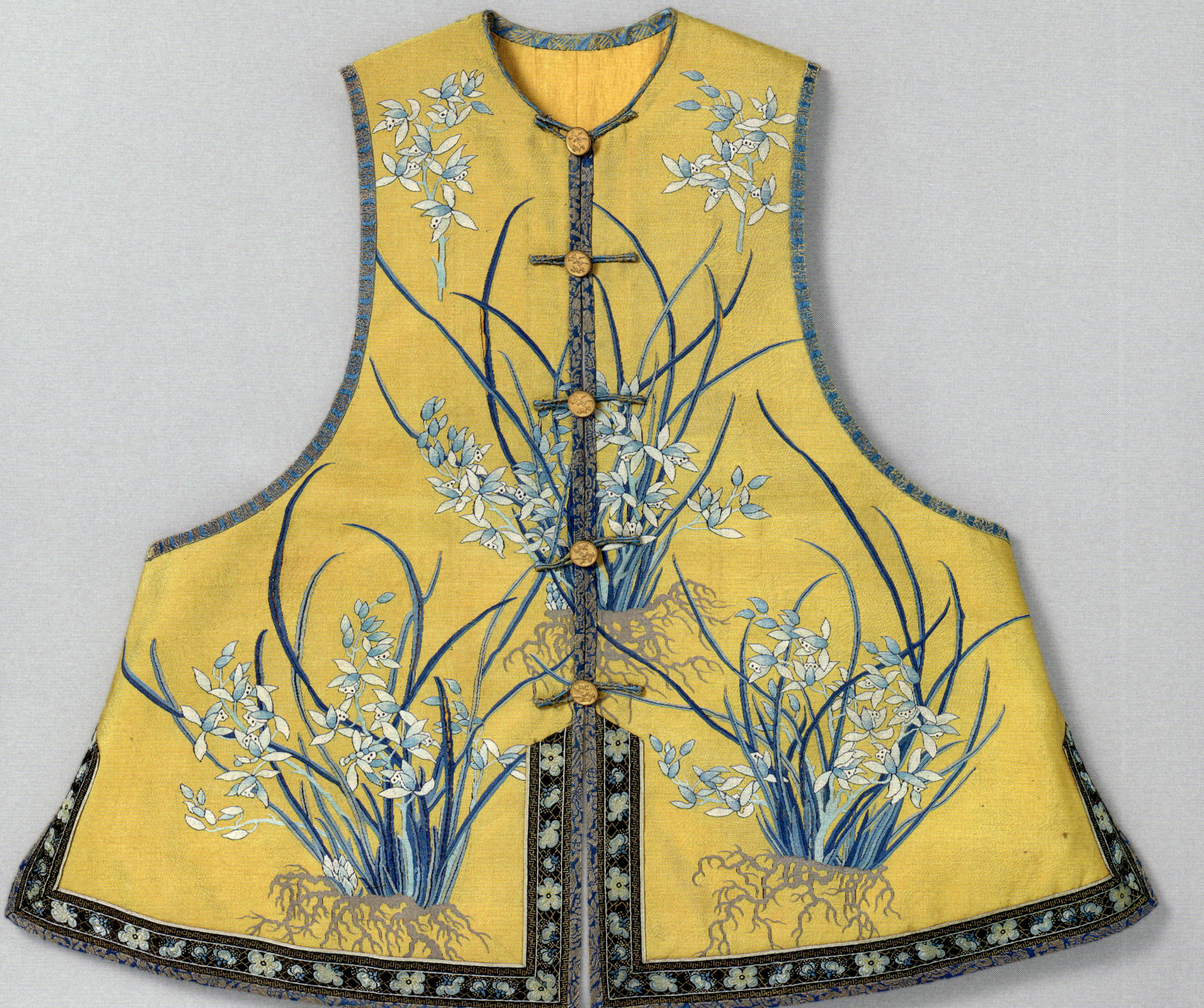

96

Ai Weiwei (b. 1957)
Hanging Man, 1986 and 2014

Edition 5 of 5
Steel, wood (*huali*)
17¾ x 15¾ x 1½ inches (45.1 x 40 x 3.8 cm)
Purchased with funds contributed by Marion Boulton Stroud in memory of Anne d'Harnoncourt and in honor of Timothy Rub, Gail Harrity, Carlos Basualdo, John Tancock, and Innis Shoemaker, 2015-62-1a,b

The wide-ranging work of the artist and political activist Ai Weiwei encompasses fine art, architectural projects, curatorial investigations, and social activism.[1] *Hanging Man* is one of Ai's early works, made when he was living in New York from 1982 to 1993. He became interested in Western artists while studying at the Parsons School of Design, where he enrolled shortly after arriving in the city. Here, a wire coat hanger is bent into the profile of Marcel Duchamp (1887–1968),[2] an artist who profoundly influenced not only Ai but a generation of Chinese artists. By reusing a functional object, Ai references Duchamp's concept of the readymade, of which *Bicycle Wheel* and *Fountain* are two of the most famous examples.[3] Through Duchamp, Ai realized that the most important aspect of a work of art is the idea behind it, and that artists are not required to fabricate a work of art themselves. This understanding profoundly shaped his subsequent works, notably the Neolithic and Han-dynasty Chinese earthenware jars that he splashed with color or painted with the Coca-Cola logo, and the Ming- and Qing-dynasty furniture that he deconstructed and re-created with the help of skilled Chinese craftsmen.[4]

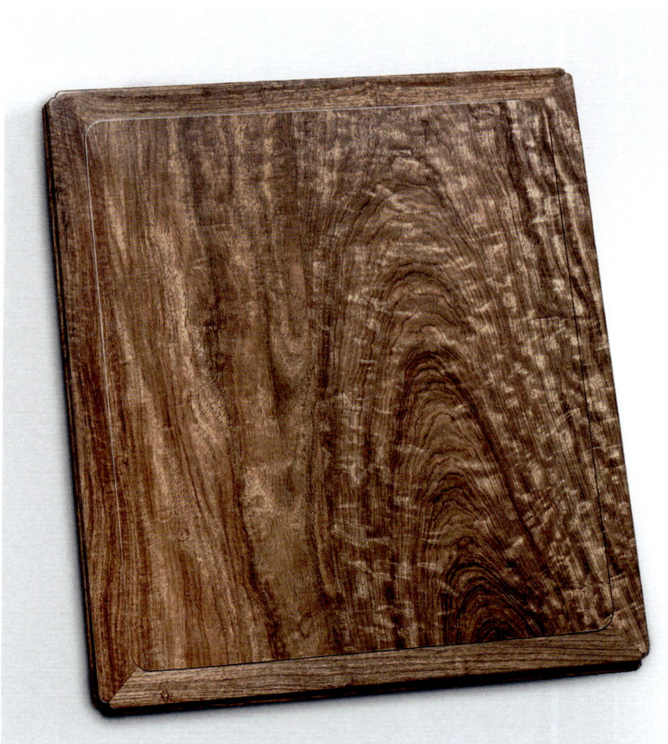

Fig. 75. Cover of the *huali* box of *Hanging Man*

In 2014 Ai placed a coat hanger that he had earlier fashioned into Duchamp's profile (1986) within a custom-made box fashioned from *huali* wood (fig. 75),[5] a prized hardwood popular in Chinese furniture production from the late Ming to the early Qing dynasty (16th–18th centuries). The new work was inspired by his fondness for Chinese furniture and was a further nod to Duchamp, who often housed documentary materials and miniature works in boxes. The piece is especially relevant in the context of the Philadelphia Museum of Art, which holds the largest Duchamp collection in the world. HK

1. Son of the painter and revolutionary poet Ai Qing, Ai Weiwei grew up in exile in Xinjiang during the Cultural Revolution. He attributes this difficult period and the influence of his father to opening up a world of ideas that led him to become a conceptual artist; see Washington et al. 2012–14, 10. Ai worked at the Beijing Film Academy for several years and in 1979 was a co-founder of The Stars, China's first group of avant-garde artists. In 1981 he left for the United States, arriving first in Philadelphia to study English and then settling in New York.
2. He first used a coat hanger in this way in *Profile of Duchamp: Sunflower Seeds* (1983), in which the coat hanger forming the profile of Duchamp was partially filled with sunflower seeds (the seeds would resurface in later work); illustrated in Beijing and Berlin 2009–12, 47.
3. See the entry by Carlos Basualdo on Duchamp's *Fountain* in Philadelphia Museum of Art 2014, 342. A later version of *Bicycle Wheel* (the original was from 1913) is in the Museum of Modern Art in New York (595.1967.a–b).
4. Washington et al. 2012–14, 83–89.
5. A purplish-red hardwood with a slight fragrance, *huali* originated in southern China and was prized in Chinese furniture. During the Tang dynasty (618–907) it was sourced from Vietnam and Hainan Island, and in the fifteenth century from Guangdong province; see Wang 1986, 16.

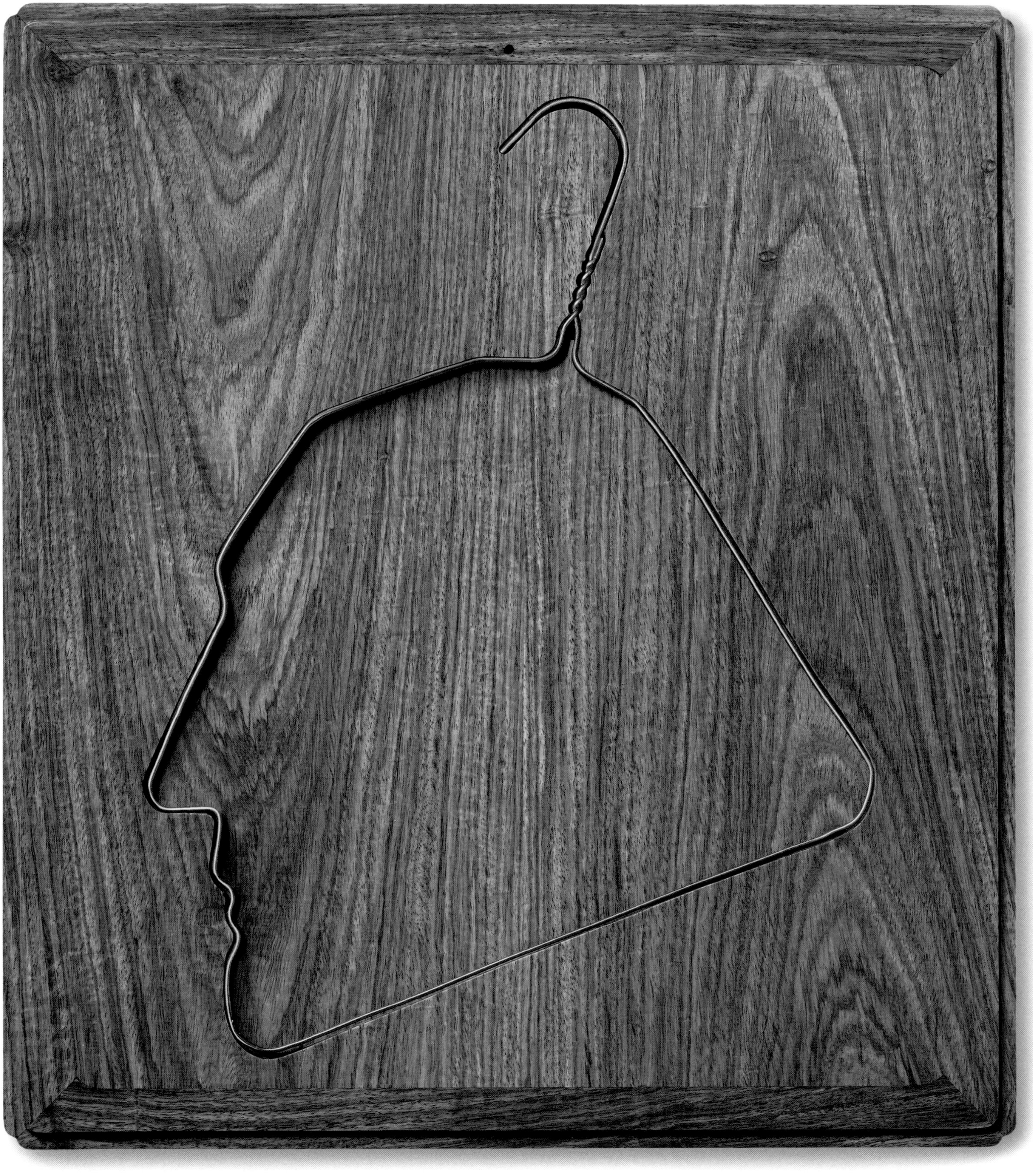

97

Zhang Huan (b. 1965)
To Raise the Water Level in a Fish Pond, 1997

Chromogenic print
Image 27 x 40½ inches (68.6 x 102.9 cm)
Purchased with the Hunt Corporation (formerly Hunt Manufacturing Co.) Arts Collection Program, 1999-33-1

In 1997, while living in Beijing, Zhang Huan invited some forty migrant workers to take part in a performance piece set in a shallow fish pond. After the anonymous participants had spread out in the pond, the artist waded in to direct the "act" of raising the water level.[1] The premise is sensible, given the laws of physics, but the futility of the performance seems to undercut the collective effort documented in the photograph. The somber expression of the artist, who carries the son of one of the workers on his shoulders, contrasts with the more impassive faces of his co-performers,[2] intensifying the curiously disconcerting effect of the image.

One of the themes Zhang had in mind when selecting the locale and the all-male group for this performance was the symbolism of water, which, according to the artist, has traditionally been associated with life and femininity in Chinese culture. However, this provocative work is open to multiple readings, such as reflecting on the relationship between man and nature or the social costs of China's drastic modernization efforts.[3]

A native of Anyang in Henan province, Zhang studied drawing and painting from age fourteen and completed graduate study in oil painting at the Central Academy of Fine Arts in Beijing in 1993. By that time he had already developed an interest in performance art, which he continued to experiment with in Beijing while struggling to make ends meet and evading the obstructions of local police. In 1998 he immigrated to the United States following a landmark exhibition at the Asia Society in New York, where his work, including this photograph, was prominently displayed.[4]

Zhang Huan's performance pieces often feature a heightened sense of corporeality,[5] which he sees as his preferred communication strategy, noting that "the corporeal self is the most essential component in my works. But the way my body is presented in an artwork and the message it carries is entirely determined by my mind."[6] This mind-centered approach is based in the artist's Buddhist thinking, which has spurred him to challenge and manipulate his own physical existence as well as the phenomenological world, ultimately to imbue his art with an aura of spirituality. DL

1. The artist described the process on his website, http://www.zhanghuan.com, accessed December 1, 2017.
2. The workers' impassive expressions have been noted by Peter Barberie. See Philadelphia Museum of Art 2014, 412.
3. According to Wu Hung, reflecting on the precipitous transformation of China was an essential aspect of Chinese contemporary art beginning in the 1990s. See Wu and Wang 2010, 198.
4. See New York, San Francisco, and Seattle 1998–2000.
5. See Yu Yeon Kim's essay "Intensified Corporeality," in Zhang and Dziewior 2003, 26–30.
6. This quotation is excerpted from an interview with the artist, translated and cited in New York 2013–14, 66.

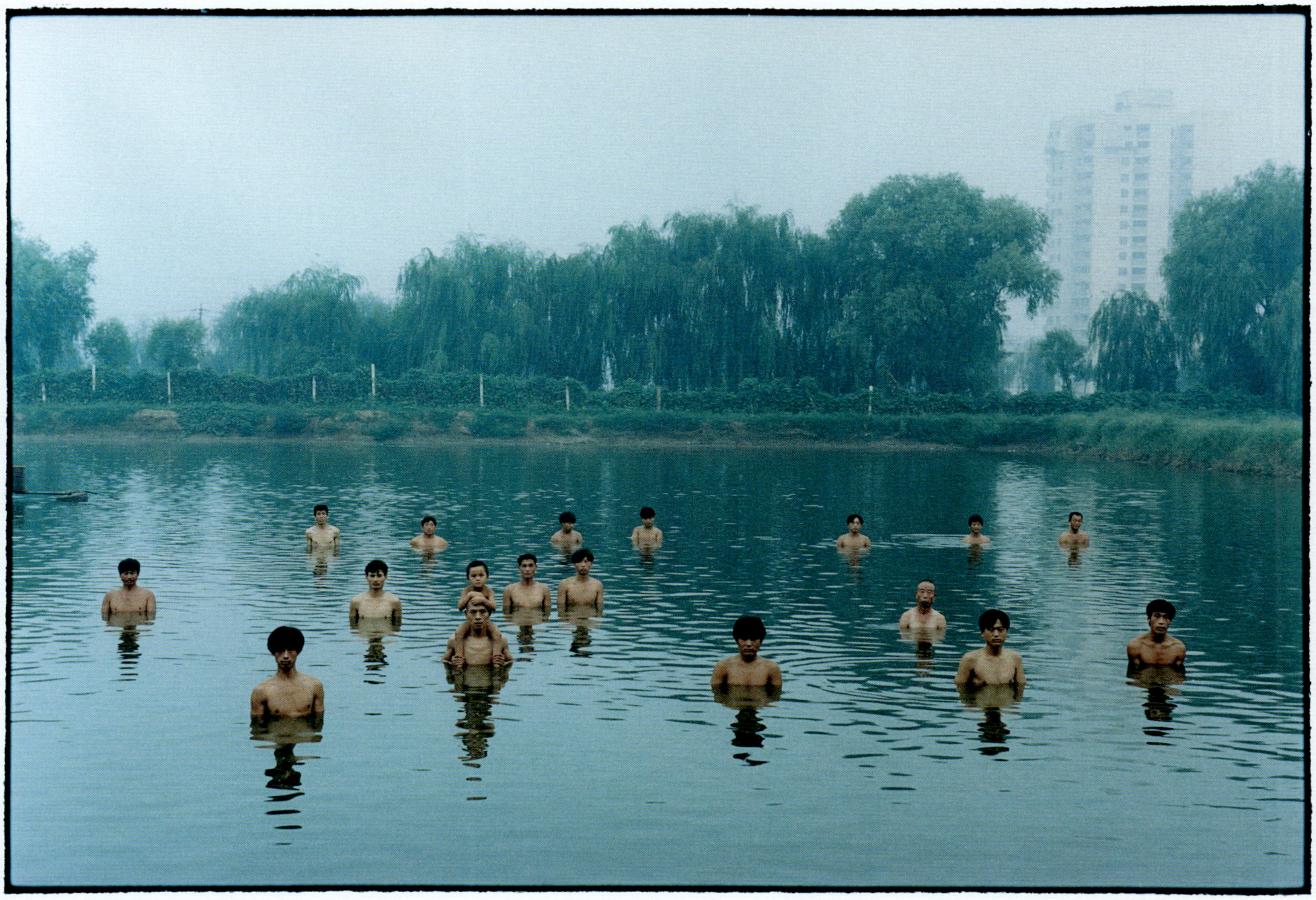

98

Zheng Chongbin (b. 1961)
Descending from the Above, 2016

Ink and acrylic on *xuan* paper, mounted on a wood frame
6 feet 2 13/16 inches x 8 feet 10 5/16 inches (190 x 270 cm)
Purchased with funds contributed by June and Simon K.C. Li, 2017-24-1

Composed with the traditional materials of Chinese black ink, brush, and *xuan* paper, this ink abstraction celebrates materiality, geometry, and gesture by illuminating the nature of perception and its connection to the physical world around us. In classical ink painting, the most direct form of self-expression is achieved through brushwork, line, and ink. Instead of imposing his own vision onto the medium, Zheng Chongbin introduces "egoless gestures" through a range of non-brush actions (dropping, throwing, tearing, folding), allowing the medium itself to speak.[1] By breaking down the constraints of ink with the introduction of white acrylic—a "white ink" that gives depth and space[2]—he expands his visual vocabulary. He loads the watered paper with ink and acrylic to expose the vision of the medium in order to explore the deconstruction of light and space and the phenomenon of energy, material, and the *qi* (resonance) of ink. Working with *xuan* paper, which has substance and body, he connects the flat surface of a painting with the physical space by cutting, arranging, and overlapping sections of painted surfaces to create structures and planes in three dimensions.[3]

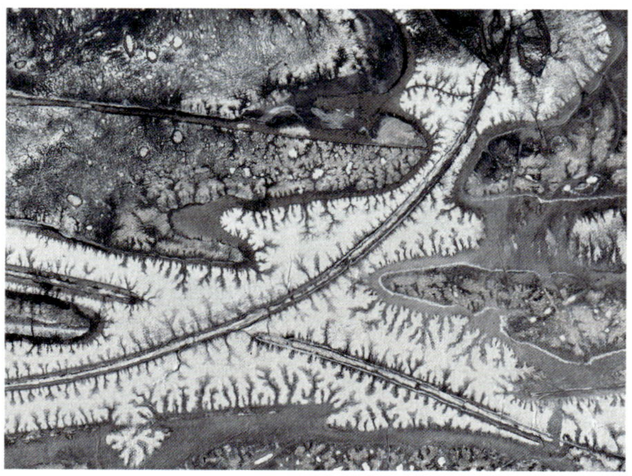

Fig. 76. Detail of fractals in the central area of the second-to-right panel of *Descending from the Above*

This large, imposing work suggests a landscape seen from high above, in bird's-eye view. The beauty of these natural forms is that they elicit from each viewer his or her own personal and meaningful reaction. Zheng is particularly fascinated by fractals (fig. 76), which reveal the processes of nature as a dynamic force in the world. In taking a Western-modernist philosophical approach and deconstructing the language of traditional ink painting in this work, he bridges East and West—in technique, materials, and conception.

Zheng Chongbin is classically trained in Chinese ink painting, having graduated in 1984 from the Zhejiang Academy of Fine Arts (now the China Academy of Fine Arts) in Hangzhou.[4] He taught at the academy for several years and showed nationally before being awarded an international fellowship to the San Francisco Art Institute, where he earned his Master of Fine Arts in 1991. He has spent the past few decades working on the phenomenological and materialist approach to ink painting employed in *Descending from the Above*. HK

1. See "The Classical Originals of Contemporary Abstraction," in Erickson et al. 2014, 37.
2. See "Selections from Artist Interviews," in Erickson et al. 2014, 98.
3. "Selections from Artist Interviews," 99.
4. Zheng's use of materials is clearly influenced by his classical training.

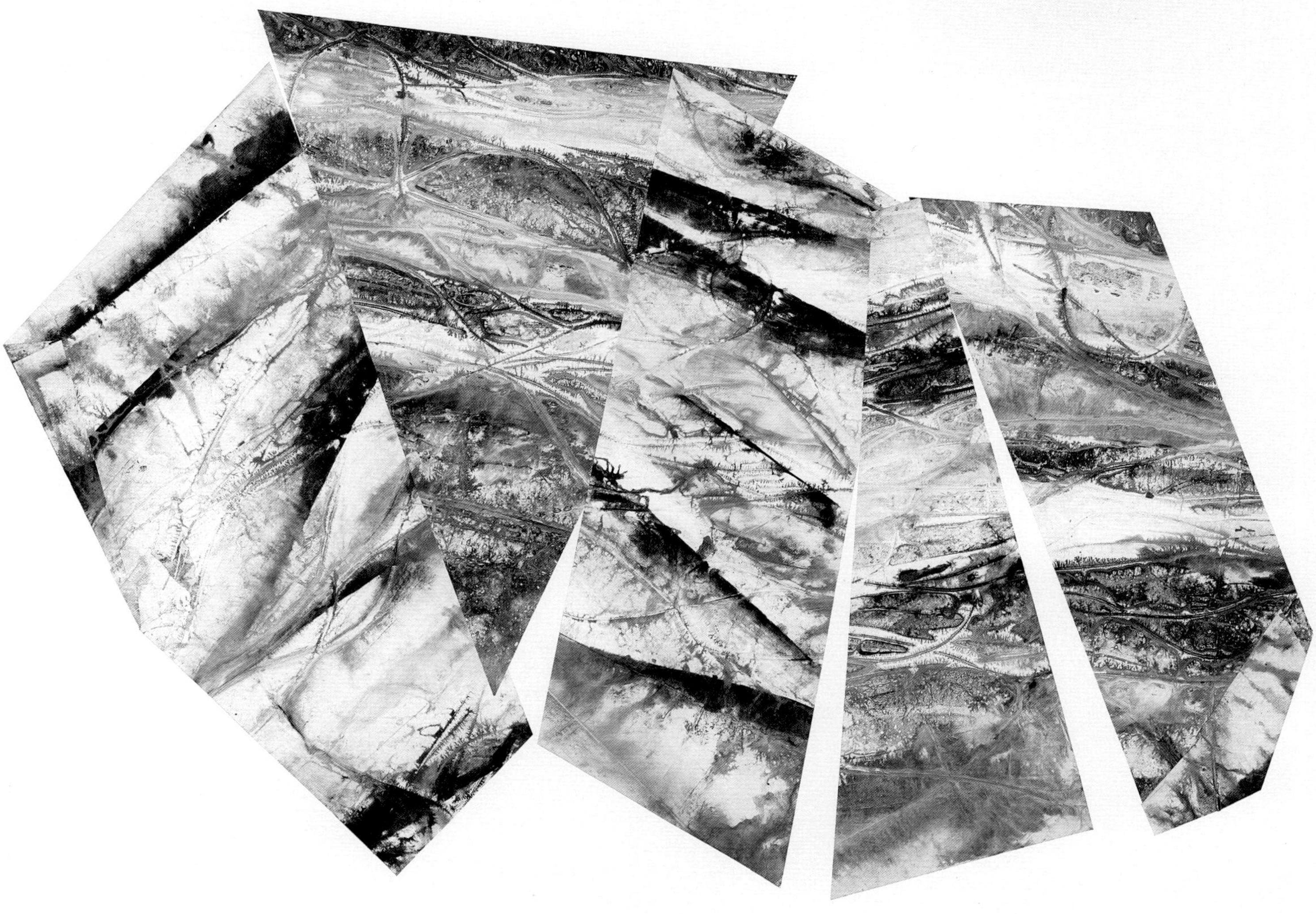

DOCUMENTATION

1
Ritual Disc (*Bi*)
1944-20-497a,b

Published: Lü et al. 2017, 322.

2
Silk Fragments from Noin Ula, Mongolia
1934-2-2, 1934-2-6

Exhibited: Oakland 1941 (no cat.); Los Angeles, Cleveland, and Detroit 1944, 1, pl. 1 (1934-2-2).
Published: Blum 1997, 164, no. 301 (1934-2-6).

3
Votive Stele
1927-20-2

Published: Sirén 1925, vol. 1, 64–65; vol. 3, pl. 242; Sirén et al. 1925, 79; Ingram 1929, 24–25; Jayne 1933, 38.

4
***Admonitions to the Monks* (*Subcommentary on the "Quadripartite Prātimokṣa" by Śramaṇa Hui*)**
1968-227-1

Exhibited: Philadelphia 1971, no. 19.
Published: Hui and Mair 1984, 327–32; Lü et al. 2017, 206–7; Morita 2017, 4.

5
Architectural Tile from Xiudingsi Pagoda
1929-17-3

Published: Kinoshita 2017, 5, fig. 11.

6
Musicians on Horseback
1923-21-146-50

Published: Philadelphia Museum of Art 2014, 8; Lü et al. 2017, 18–21.

7
Pair of Tomb Guardian Creatures *(Zhenmushou)*
1923-21-5, 1923-21-6

Exhibited: Philadelphia 1969 (no cat.).
Published: Lü et al. 2017, 32–33 (1923-21-5), 34–35 (1923-21-6).

8
Tomb Guardian Warrior
1923-21-24

Published: Lü et al. 2017, 30–31.

9
Tomb Figure of a Bactrian Camel
1964-9-1

Published: Philadelphia Museum of Art 1995, 27; Philadelphia Museum of Art 2014, 8–9; Lü et al. 2017, 26–27.

10
Panel and Posts from a House-shaped Sarcophagus
1931-50-3, 1931-50-5, 1931-50-11

Published: Roberts 1940, 23.

11
Funerary Mask
2012-53-1

Exhibited: Philadelphia 2013 (no cat.).
Published: Lü et al. 2017, 286–87.

12
Bodhisattva
1925-53-10

Published: Jayne 1926, 165; Sirén 1927, 8; Sickman 1939, 15; Sickman and Soper 1971, 190; Philadelphia Museum of Art 2014, 15; Lü et al. 2017, 350–51.

13
Wine Bottle
1923-21-272

Published: Lü et al. 2017, 44–45.

14
Brush Washer
1944-20-95a,b

Published: Henan 2008, 245, no. 70, col. pl. 23:1; Philadelphia Museum of Art 2014, 20; Lü et al. 2017, 48.

Inscribed with a poem by the Qianglong emperor (see fig. 29); for the translation, see p. 62.

15
Pillow with Phoenix and Peony Blossoms
1957-26-3

Published: Lü et al. 2017, 54–55.

16
Pillow with Confucian Scholar, Buddhist Monk, and Daoist Priest
1957-26-1

Exhibited: Indianapolis et al. 1980–81, 134–35, pl. 55.
Published: Lee 1957, 76–77; Riddell 1979, 59; Philadelphia Museum of Art 1995, 28; Liu 2004, 46; Ni 2008, 132; Ma 2013, 201, fig. 4; Philadelphia Museum of Art 2014, 22; Lü et al. 2017, 60–61.

The original inscription on the base, now worn away, recorded the year of its making; see Lee 1957.

17
Flower-form Cup
1978-41-1

Published: Philadelphia Museum of Art 1995, 28; Philadelphia Museum of Art 2014, 20; Lü et al. 2017, 323.

18
Flower-form Dish
1974-29-1

Published: Lü et al. 2017, 362–63.

Seal mark on underside of base.

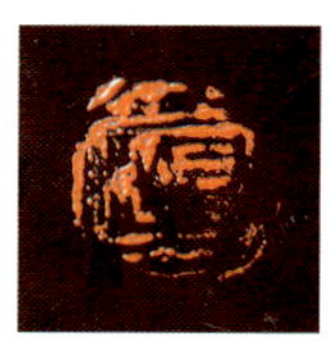

19
Lady beneath Tall Bamboo
1929-40-29a,b

Exhibited: Berkeley, New Haven, and Saint Louis 1985, 253.
Published: Cahill 1962, 57–58, no. 24; Liu 2009, 104; Li 2016, 46; Lü et al. 2017, 210–11.

20
Palace beneath Lofty Pines
1929-40-35

Published: Li 1871 (2002), vol. 12, 15–16; Li 2016, 46; Lü et al. 2017, 212–13.

21
Three Fish
1929-40-2

Exhibited: London 1935–36, no. 949, pl. 80; Richmond 1954–55 (no cat.); Philadelphia 1969 (no cat.); Cincinnati 2009–10, no. 74.
Published: Jayne 1929, 4. pl. 1; Gombrich 1984, 111, fig. 100; Lü et al. 2017, 208–9.

22
Possibly Sun Jue (act. c. 1225–27)
Female Immortals
1929-40-48a,b

Exhibited: Chicago and San Francisco 2000–2001, 334, no. 127.
Published: Huang X. 2012, 182–83; Philadelphia Museum of Art 2014, 23; Li 2016, 47; Lü et al. 2017, 214–15.

Inscribed by the artist: *Gengyin sui Sun Jue hua* (Painted by Sun Jue in the year of Gengyin).

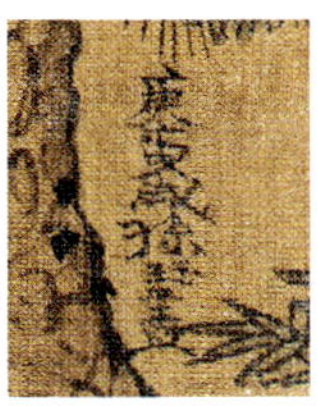

23
Octagonal Jar with the Eight Immortals
1964-58-1

Exhibited: Cleveland 1968, no. 83; Indianapolis et al. 1987–88, 202–3, no. 82; New York 2010–11, 271, fig. 293.
Published: Philadelphia Museum of Art 1995, 29; Philadelphia Museum of Art 2014, 43; Lü et al. 2017, 80–81.

24
Pouring Vessel with *Lingzhi* Fungus
1944-20-145a,b

Exhibited: Philadelphia and Chicago 1949–50, no. 12; Cleveland 1968, no. 168, pl. 169.
Published: Mayuyama 1960, no. 74; Lü et al. 2017, 72–73.

25
Gourd-shaped Vase with Scrolling Peonies
2016-55-1

Not previously exhibited or published.

26
Guanyin Seated in Royal Ease
1925-53-11

Not previously exhibited or published.

27
Bottle with Flowers of the Four Seasons
1952-30-1

Exhibited: Philadelphia and Chicago, 1949–50, no. 22.
Published: Suzuki 1972–73, vol. 5, 245; Lü et al. 2017, 82–83.

28
Covered Box with the Three Friends of Winter
1953-1-1a,b

Exhibited: San Marino 2006 (no cat.).
Published: New York 1991–92, 33, fig. 12; Philadelphia Museum of Art 2014, 31; Lü et al. 2017, 364–65.

Six characters incised on underside of box: *Da Ming Yongle nian zhi* (Made in the Yongle period of the great Ming dynasty).

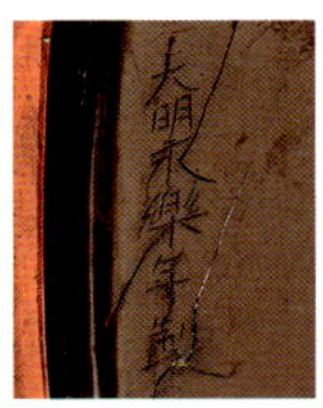

29
Dish with Beribboned Bouquet
Promised gift

Not previously exhibited or published.

30
Conical Bowl with the Three Friends of Winter
1984-116-1

Exhibited: Philadelphia and Chicago, 1949–50, no. 28; San Marino 2006 (no cat.).
Published: Tokyo 1977, pl. 28; Philadelphia Museum of Art 1995, 30; Pegg 2005, 2–8; Lü et al. 2017, 84–85.

31
Ewer with Five-clawed Dragons
1950-118-1

Exhibited: London 2014–15, 85, fig. 65.
Published: Lu 2011, 64; Philadelphia Museum of Art 2014, 31; Harrison-Hall 2017, 194, no. 1; Lü et al. 2017, 290–91.

32
Basin with Five-clawed Dragons
1950-74-1

Exhibited: San Francisco 1939, 39, no. 198; London 2014–15, 85, fig. 66.
Published: Philadelphia Museum of Art 2014, 31; Lü et al. 2017, 288–89.

33
Set of Ten Volumes of the Sutra *The Great Perfection of Reason*
1974-200-1a–k

Published: Xu 2018, 344–47.

Dated to the 11th month, 11th day, 5th year of the Zhengtong reign (1440).

34
Coffered Ceiling from Zhihuasi (Temple of Transforming Wisdom)
1930-38-1a–n

Published: Liu 1932, 22–24; Jayne and Lee 1958, 29–32; Hammond 2001, 193; Philadelphia Museum of Art 2014, 30; London 2014–15, 35, fig. 13; Lü et al. 2017, 372–73; Kinoshita 2018.

35
Mural Fragment of *Deva* from a Buddhist Assembly
1925-98-1

Published: Malenka and Price 1997, 127–37; Lü et al. 2017, 276–79.

36
Roundel for an Empress
1940-4-749

Published: Blum 1997, 167, no. 310; Lü et al. 2017, 396–97.

37
Dish with Gardenias
1944-20-347

Exhibited: New York 1970–71, 59, no. 31.
Published: Lü et al. 2017, 92–93.

Six-character underglaze-blue reign mark within double circle: *Da Ming Hongzhi nian zhi* (Made in the Hongzhi period of the great Ming dynasty).

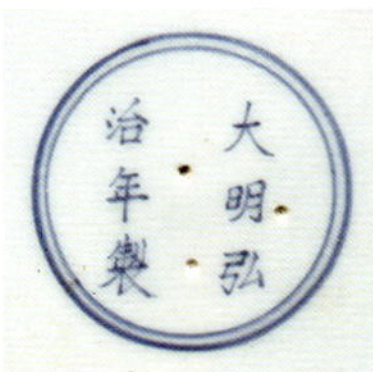

38
Insignia Badge for an Imperial Censor
1940-4-745

Published: Blum 1997, 166, no. 307.

39
Hexagonal Candleholder with Persian Script
1944-38-1

Exhibited: Philadelphia and Chicago 1949–50, no. 102, cover illus.; New York 1970–71, 62, no. 34.
Published: Lü et al. 2017, 98–99.

Six-character underglaze-blue reign mark within double circle: *Da Ming Zhengde nian zhi* (Made in the Zhengde period of the great Ming dynasty).

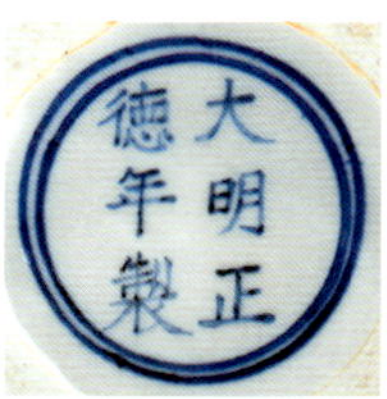

40
Imperial Yellow Dish
1946-49-1

Published: Lü et al. 2017, 102–3.

Six-character underglaze-blue reign mark within double circle: *Da Ming Zhengde nian zhi* (Made in the Zhengde period of the great Ming dynasty).

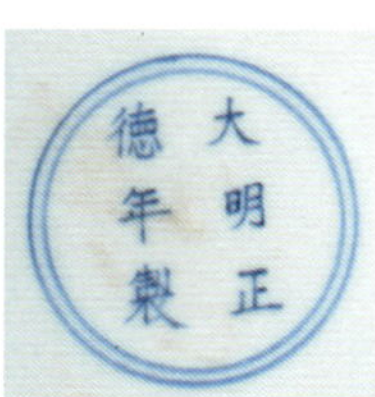

41
Qiao Bin (act. 1481–after 1500)
Guanyin, Bodhisattva of Compassion
1923-21-441

Exhibited: Princeton 2010–11 (no cat.).
Published: Hsu 2012–13, 42, fig. 6; Philadelphia Museum of Art 2014, 40; Lü et al. 2017, 358–59.

Inscribed on left side of base: *Shanxi Zezhou Yangcheng xian Baijianli Wang Xing jian zai Doucun juzhu. Da Ming Zhengde er nian er yue [. . .] fa xin she cai zao shang mo* (Wang Xing of Baijian community, Yangcheng county in Zezhou district, Shanxi province, currently residing in Dou village [vowed] to donate money for the making [of this statue]. Offering the ink [i.e., writing with brush and ink] in the second month of the second year of the Zhengde period in the Great Ming; translation based on Hsu 2012–13); above the firing hole: *Guanying tang* (Guanyin Hall).

Inscribed on right side of base: *Ben xian zai cheng dai zhao Qiao Bin zao ji er* (It is recorded that [this statue was] made by Qiao Bin, a *daizhao* [craftsman] residing in this county; translation based on Hsu 2012–13); above the firing hole: *Tongji miao* (Tongji Temple).

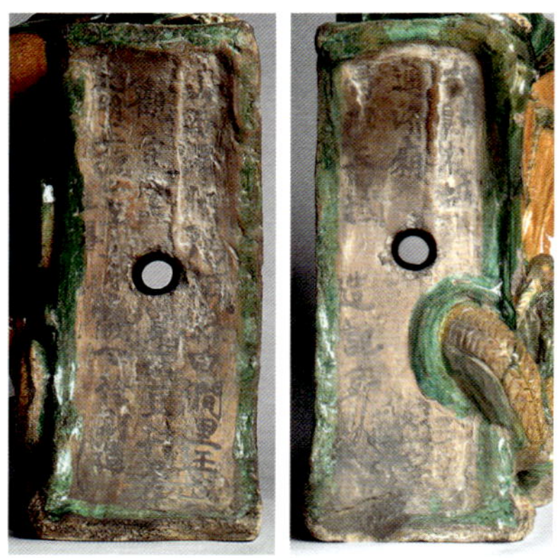

42
Gourd-shaped Vase with Dragons, Phoenixes, and Cranes
1882-727

Exhibited: Philadelphia and Chicago, 1949–50, no. 110.
Published: Barber 1909, 66; Philadelphia Museum of Art 2014, 33; Lü et al. 2017, 106–7.

Six-character underglaze-blue reign mark: *Da Ming Jiajing nian zhi* (Made in the Jiajing period of the great Ming dynasty).

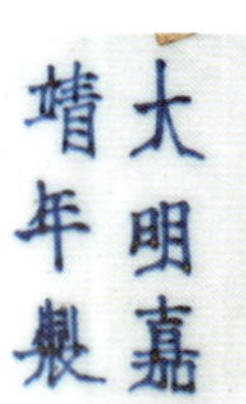

43
Square Dish with Peonies and Chrysanthemum
1882-1313

Published: Lü et al. 2017, 114–15.

Six-character underglaze-blue reign mark: *Da Ming Jiajing nian zhi* (Made in the Jiajing period of the great Ming dynasty).

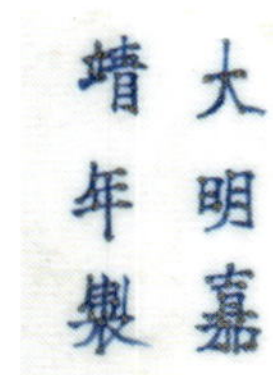

44
Jar with Dragons and *Shou* Characters
1944-20-78a,b

Published: Lü et al. 2017, 104–5.

Six-character underglaze-blue reign mark on neck: *Da Ming Jiajing nian zhi* (Made in the Jiajing period of the great Ming dynasty).

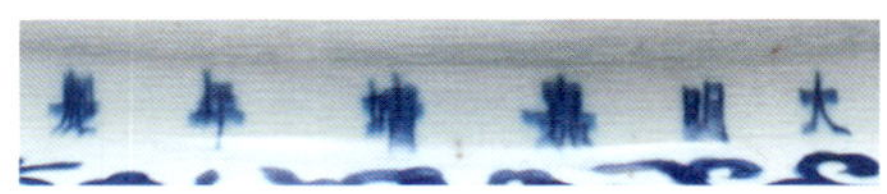

45
Jar with *Shou* Characters
1944-20-83a,b

Not previously exhibited or published.

Six-character underglaze-blue reign mark within double circle: *Da Ming Jiajing nian zhi* (Made in the Jiajing period of the great Ming dynasty).

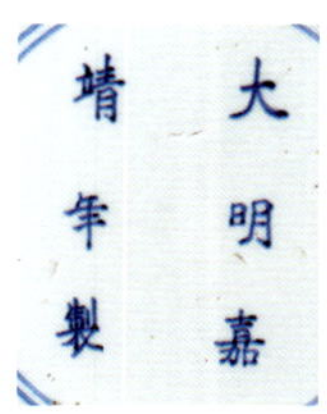

46
Lobed Dish with Cloud Scrolls
1979-55-2

Exhibited: Philadelphia 1980 (no cat.).
Published: Lü et al. 2017, 366–67.

47
Faceted Vase with Morning Glories
1944-20-292a,b

Exhibited: Philadelphia and Chicago, 1949–50, no. 121.
Published: Philadelphia Museum of Art 2014, 58–59; Lü et al. 2017, 116–17.

Apocryphal six-character underglaze-blue reign mark within double circle: *Da Ming Xuande nian zhi* (Made in the Xuande period of the great Ming dynasty).

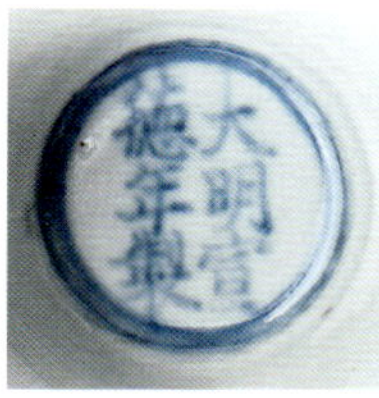

48
Tribute Giraffe with Attendant
1977-42-1

Exhibited: London 2014–15, 260–61.
Published: Wilson 1992, 23; Watt 2008, 112; Ebrey 2010, 211; Los Angeles and Houston 2011–12, 118, fig. 106; Lü et al. 2017, 246–47.

49
Round-back Armchairs (*Quanyi*)
1971-12-1, 1971-12-2

Published: Lee 1963, no. 7; Lü et al. 2017, 380–81.

50
Xu Wei (1521–1593)
Sixteen Flowers
1968-29-1

Exhibited: Philadelphia 2014 (no cat.).
Published: Liang 1977, 98–99; Ishikawa et al. 1986, no. 17; Philadelphia Museum of Art 1995, 31; Yen 2004, 36–37; Philadelphia Museum of Art 2014, 45; Lü et al. 2017, 230–31; Shao and Xu 2018, 14–29.

Seal marks of the artist: *Tian chi shan ren*; *Qing teng dao shi*; *Xiang guan zhai*.

51
Seated Luohan
2013-74-1

Published: Lü et al. 2017, 360–61.

52
Chen Dao, Cao Xi, and Zhou Shichen (act. late 16th–early 17th century)
Orchids and Rocks
1968-9-1

Exhibited: San Marino 2006 (no cat.).
Published: Goepper 1963, pl. 29; Lü et al. 2017, 238–41.

Signed inscriptions by Chen Dao, Chen Zaikang, Xi Kongyang, Cao Xi, Zhang Xuan, Zhu Zhideng, Zhou Shichen, and Xu Rudeng, respectively.

Seal marks of the artist Zhou Shichen: *Bingzhong*; *Zhou Shichen*.

53
Lobed Cup Stand
1969-260-1a,b

Not previously exhibited or published.

For another cup stand of the same type in the museum's collection (1969-260-2a), see Lü et al. 2017, 292–93.

54
Seated Twins of Union and Harmony, Hanshan and Shide
1944-20-324a–c

Published: Lü et al. 2017, 128–29.

Seal marks of the potter impressed on figures' backs: *Zhang Shoushan* [double-gourd mark]; *Zhang Shoushan yin* (seal of Zhang Shoushan) [square mark].

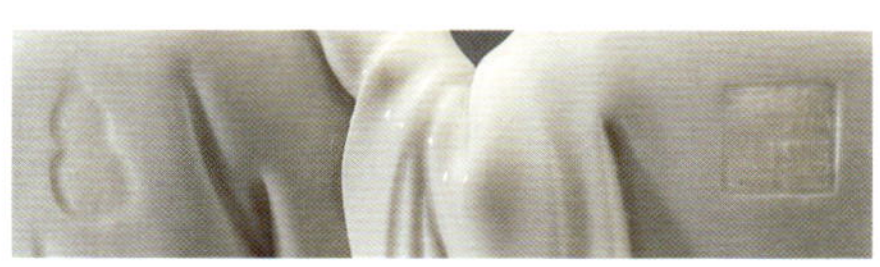

55
Games Table
1958-158-1

Published: Lee 1963, no. 14; Ellsworth 1971, 254, pl. 73; Beurdeley 1979, 96; Lo 2004, 101, fig. 8:6; Lü et al. 2017, 376–77.

56
Reception Hall from the Palace of Duke Zhao (Zhaogongfu)
1929-163-1

Published: Jayne 1929, 4–15; Jayne 1940, 2–15; Roberts 1940, 22; Philadelphia Museum of Art 1995, 33; Proser, Malenka, and Price 2004, 5–47; Philadelphia Museum of Art 2014, 56–57; Kinoshita 2017, 6, fig. 13.

57
Insignia Badge for an Imperial Noble or Military Officer
1940-4-731

Published: Cammann 1979, cover illus.; Blum 1997, 166, no. 308; Philadelphia Museum of Art 2014, 52; Lü et al. 2017, 410–11.

58
Liu Du (act. c. 1628–75)
Landscapes
1929-40-82a–e

Published: Suzuki 1974, 36, nos. 28, 29; Lü et al. 2017, 250–51.

Inscribed by the artist: *Gengxu chun sanyue wei Zongwen citan shuzheng Qiantang Liu Du* (Dedicated to the Poet Zongwen by Liu Du from Qiantang in the spring, the third month of the Gengxu year).

Seal marks of the artist: *Liu Du; Shuxian*.

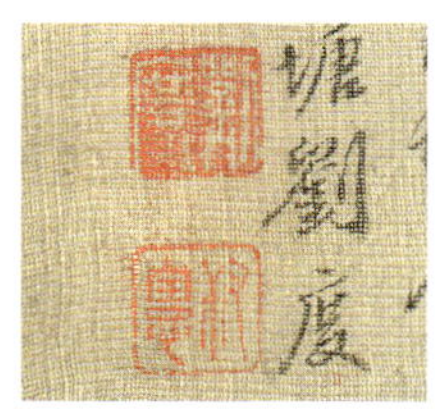

59
Large Imperial Yellow Bowls
1989-75-1, 1989-75-2

Published: Lü et al. 2017, 138–39.

Six-character underglaze-blue reign marks in double circle: *Da Qing Kangxi nian zhi* (Made in the Kangxi period of the great Qing dynasty).

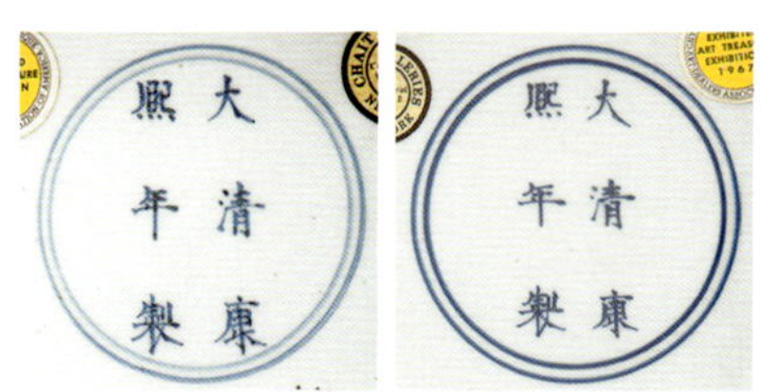

60

Scholar's Desk Implements: Vase, Brush Washer, and Water Coupe
1955-50-51, 1977-255-1a,b, 1955-50-52

Exhibited: Philadelphia 1956 (no cat.).
Published: Fujioka et al. 1956, pl. 50 (water coupe), pl. 51 (vase); Lee 1956, pl. 9; Lü et al. 2017, 132–33 (vase), 134–35 (water coupe).

Six-character underglaze-blue reign marks: *Da Qing Kangxi nian zhi* (Made in the Kangxi period of the great Qing dynasty).

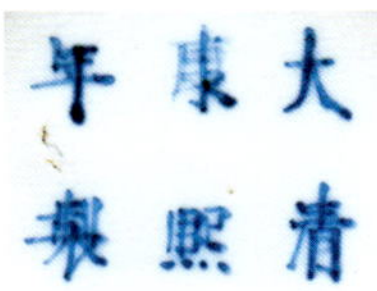

(vase)

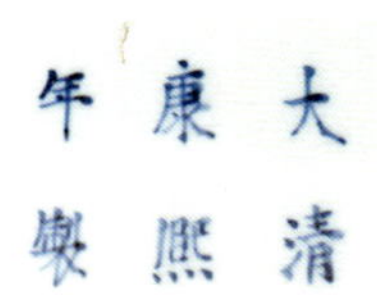

(water coupe)

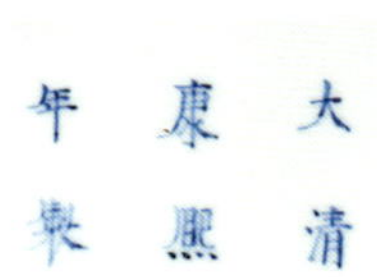

(brush washer)

61

Bowl with Incised Dragons and Enameled Flowers
1925-27-37

Published: Lü et al. 2017, 144–55.

Six-character underglaze-blue reign mark in double circle: *Da Qing Kangxi nian zhi* (Made in the Kangxi period of the great Qing dynasty).

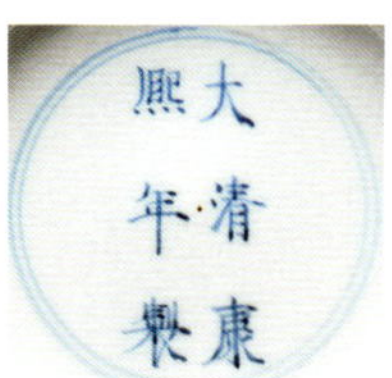

62

Phoenix-tail Vase
1955-50-99

Exhibited: London 1935–36; Glasgow 1937 (no cat.); Philadelphia 1956 (no cat.).
Published: Hobson 1931, no. 136. pl. 27; Lee 1956, pl. 4; Ayers and Sato 1983, vol. 15, 15, no. 4; Philadelphia Museum of Art 1995, 34; Philadelphia Museum of Art 2014, 58–59; Kinoshita 2017, 9, fig. 19.

Partial painted inventory mark $^{N1}_{I}$ on base indicates the vase was once in the collection of Augustus the Strong (1670–1733) in Dresden.

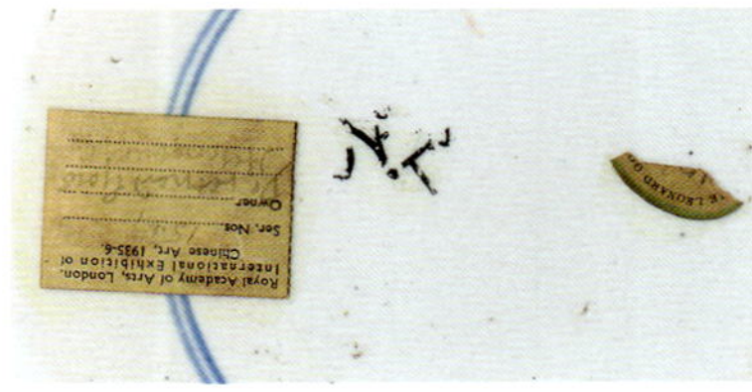

63

Covered Jar with *Qilin*, Lion, and Elephant
1955-50-75a,b

Exhibited: London 1935–36, no. 1663; Glasgow 1937 (no cat.); Philadelphia 1956 (no cat.); Philadelphia 2010–11 (no cat.).
Published: Hobson 1931, no. 149, pl. 32; Lee 1956, pl. 3; Lü et al. 2017, 152–53.

Partial painted inventory marks on base (left) and inside lid (right) indicate the jar was once in the collection of Augustus the Strong (1670–1733) in Dresden, Germany. According to Hobson (1931, 44), the inventory number reads $^{N4}_{I}$.

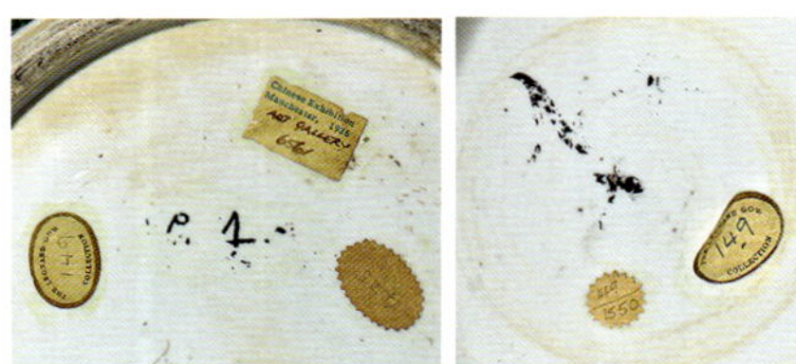

64

Phoenix-tail Vase with the Battle of Sishui Pass
1955-50-84

Exhibited: London 1935–36; Glasgow 1937 (no cat.); Philadelphia 1956 (no cat.).
Published: Hobson 1924, pl. 3; Hobson 1931, no. 120, pl. 20; Lü et al. 2017, 154–55.

Painted seal mark on neck of vase: *Zhuju* (Bamboo Studio).

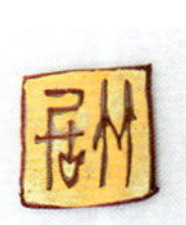

65

Large Bowl with Illustrations of Tilling and Weaving
1955-50-170

Exhibited: Glasgow 1937 (no cat.); Philadelphia 1956 (no cat.).
Published: Hobson 1931, no. 182; Lü et al. 2017, 160–61.

The inscriptions about rice cultivation and silk production are each followed by two gilded iron-red seal marks: (top seal) *Mushiju* (Wood and Stone Studio [a private workshop]).

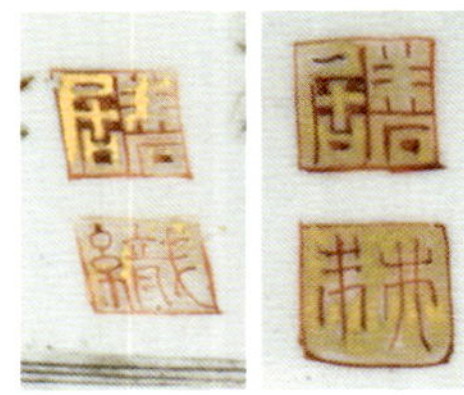

Underglaze-blue mark on base.

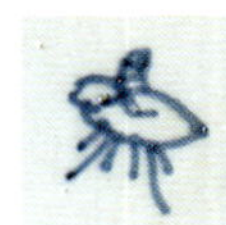

66

Wine Cups with Roosters, Hens, and Chicks
1944-20-463, 1944-20-464

Published: Lü et al. 2017, 149.

Six-character underglaze-blue reign marks in double square: *Da Qing Kangxi nian zhi* (Made in the Kangxi period of the great Qing dynasty).

67

Oxblood Glazed Bowl
1944-20-39a,b

Published: Lü et al. 2017, 136–37.

68
Snuff Bottles
a) 1944-20-586
b) 1944-20-551
c) 1944-20-550
d) 1944-20-553
e) 1944-20-558

Published: Lee 1979, 10–13; Philadelphia Museum of Art 2014, 58–59 (b); Lü et al. 2017, 295 (a), 329 (b), 328 (c), 331 (d), 330 (e).

a) Inscribed in red enamel on base: *Kangxi yu zhi* (Made by imperial command of the Kangxi emperor).

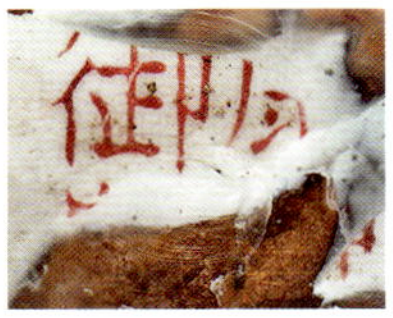

b) Carved four-character mark on base: *Qianlong nian zhi* (Made in the Qianlong period).

c) Inscribed in blue enamel on base: *Qianlong nianzhi* (Made in the Qianlong period).

d) Inscribed in blue enamel on base: *Qianlong nianzhi* (Made in the Qianlong period).

e) Inscribed in blue enamel on base: *Qianlong nian zhi* (Made in the Qianlong period).

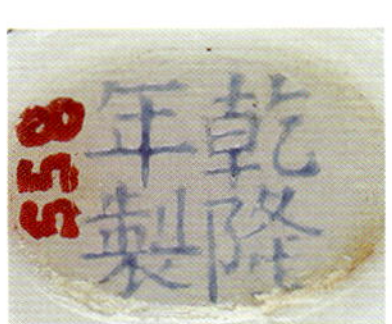

69
Manggūri (Mang Huli; Mongolian-Manchu, 1672–1736)
Portrait of a Manchu Lady
1970-259-2

Exhibited: Berkeley 2013, 56–57.
Published: Yu 2002, 63–69; Philadelphia Museum of Art 2014, 76; Lü et al. 2017, 256–57.

Seal marks of the artist: *Mang Huli*; *Zhuoran*.

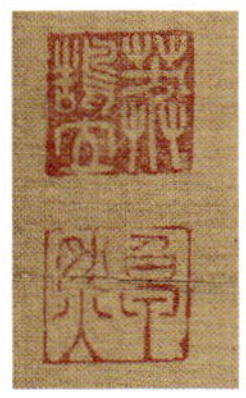

70
Faceted Vase with Morning Glories
1944-20-831

Published: Lü et al. 2017, 174–75.

Six-character underglaze-blue reign mark in double circle: *Da Qing Yongzheng nian zhi* (Made in the Yongzheng period of the great Qing dynasty).

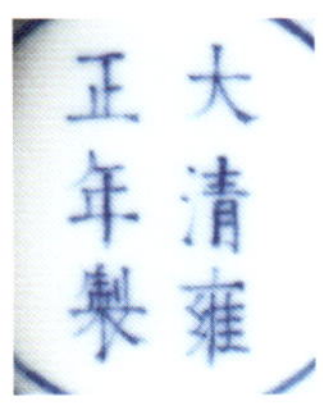

71
Saucers with Floral Blossoms
1944-20-287a,b, 1944-20-288a,b

Not previously exhibited or published.

Six-character underglaze-blue reign marks in double circle: *Da Qing Yongzheng nian zhi* (Made in the Yongzheng period of the great Qing dynasty).

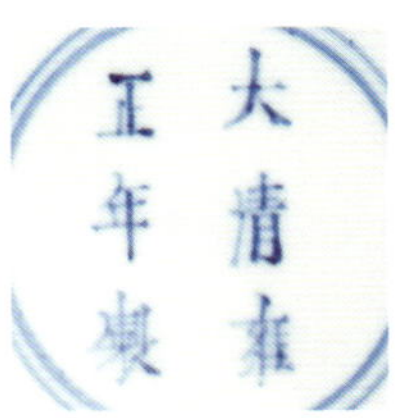

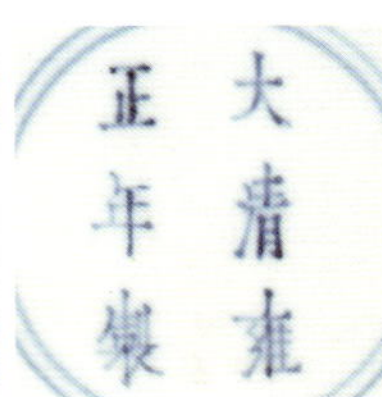

72
Conical Bowl with Floral Medallions
1925-27-36

Published: Lü et al. 2017, 170–71.

Six-character underglaze-blue reign mark in double circle: *Da Qing Yongzheng nian zhi* (Made in the Yongzheng period of the great Qing dynasty).

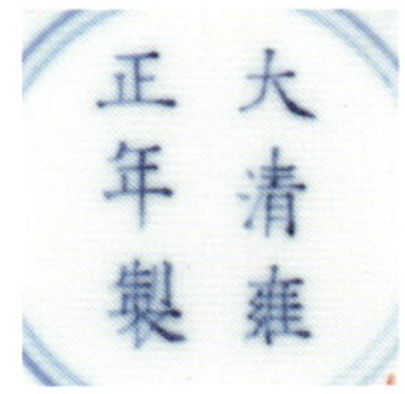

73
Pair of Hexagonal Lanterns
1955-50-105, 1955-50-106

Exhibited: London 1935–36; Glasgow 1937 (no cat.); Philadelphia 1956 (no cat.).
Published: Hobson 1931, no. 413, pl. 84; Fujioka et al. 1956, no. 88; Lee 1956, pl. 8; Lü et al. 2017, 178–79.

74
Huang Shen (1687–after 1768)
Lady Carrying a Zither
1929-40-139

Published: Lü et al. 2017, 258–59.

Seal marks of the artist: *Huang Shen*; *Gongmao*.

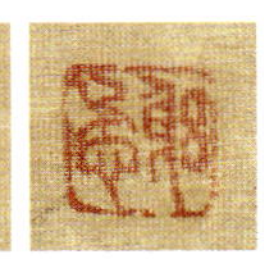

75
Cup in the Form of a Half Peach
1905-201

Exhibited: New York 1977–78, 70–71.
Published: Barber 1911, 17–23, no. 34; Lü et al. 2017, 180.

76
Cup and Saucer with Roman Mythological Figures
1899-804a,b

Published: Lü et al. 2017, 298–99.

77
Dragon Robe Opera Costume
1951-29-6

Published: Cammann 1979, 2–19; Blum 1997, 169, no. 315; Lü et al. 2017, 400–401.

78
Pair of Compound Wardrobes
1940-7-1a–c, 1940-7-2a–c

Published: Philadelphia Museum of Art 1995, 32; Philadelphia Museum of Art 2014, 41; Kao et al. 2017; Lü et al. 2017, 382–83.

79
Tea-dust Glazed Bottle
1882-1577

Published: Lü et al. 2017, 182–83.

Six-character reign mark impressed on base: *Da Qing Qianlong nian zhi* (Made in the Qianlong period of the great Qing dynasty).

80
Vessel in the Form of a Bird on Wheels
1909-41

Exhibited: Philadelphia 1969 (no cat.); New York 2011, 89, no. 89.
Published: Lü et al. 2017, 318–19.

Four-character reign mark incised on vase rim: *Qianlong nian zhi* (Made in the Qianlong period).

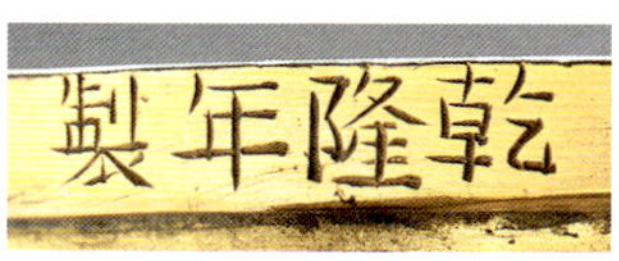

81
Devotional Hanging (*Thangka*)
1960-131-5

Exhibited: Philadelphia 2005 (no cat.); Philadelphia 2011–12 (no cat.).
Published: Kramrisch 1960, no. 68.

Inscribed in ink on the verso in Chinese, Mongolian, Manchurian, and Tibetan, the four official languages of the Qing dynasty.

Tibetan: [This] single image of Amitayus [*tshe dpag med*] was created by sewing many pieces of cloth, which are held together at their edges, at the urging of the revered [Bejing Lama] the *lcang skya Hutuktu* [*Rolpa'i Dorje*] who was imperially commanded to do so in the second month of the 26th year [1761] of [the Qianlong Emperor,] the one who defends the heavens.

Chinese: On the third day of the second month of the 26th year [1761] of [the Qianlong Emperor,] the one who defends the heavens. One fine silk embroidered image of Amitayus [Chinese here... was made] as the Emperor imperially commanded the *lcangs skya hutkutu* [*Rolpa'i Dorje*] to do.

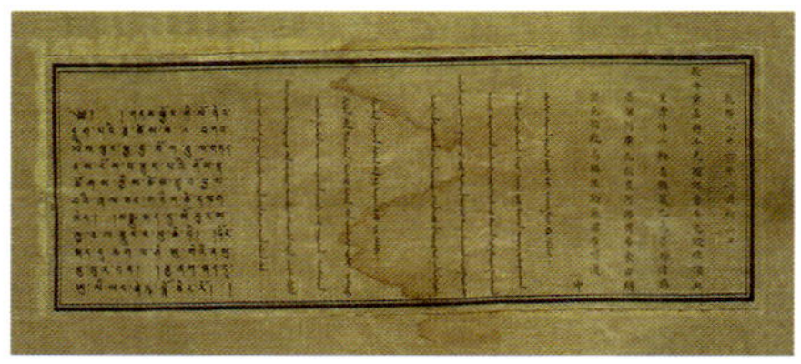

82
Yokeback Armchair for Guanyin
1988-27-72

Published: Tian 2001, 93; Tian 2003, 145–46; Lü et al. 2017, 388–89.

Inscribed on reverse of back splat: *Pumen dashi Da Qing Qianlong sishiyi nian gui yue li Xin'an dizi Cheng Dianwen zhu* (The Bodhisattva Guanyin; made in the eighth month of the forty-first year of Qianlong period; donated by the disciple Cheng Dianwen of Xin'an).

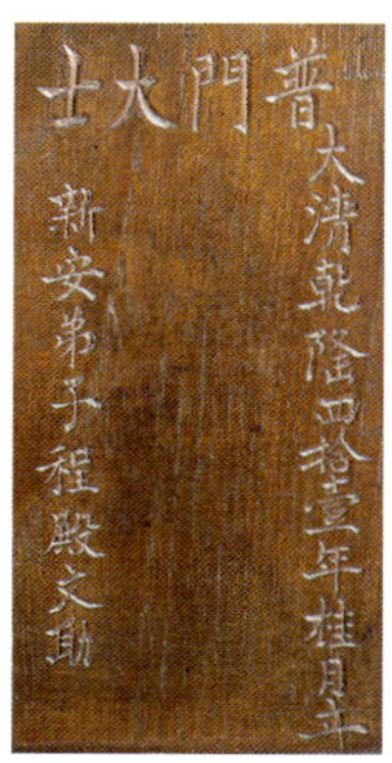

83
Semi-formal Court Robe
1983-15-1

Exhibited: Philadelphia 1990 (no cat.).
Published: Lü et al. 2017, 404–5.

84
Luo Ping (1733–1799)
Flowering Plum Branch
1983-26-1

Published: Lü et al. 2017, 260–61.

Seal marks of the artist: *Luo Ping*; *Liang feng dao ren*.

85
Hua Guan (1740–c. 1822)
Elegant Gathering Honoring the Studio of Inebriating Ink
1967-173-1

Published: Lü et al. 2017, 264–71.

Inscribed by the artist: *Renzi chun sanyue Xishan Hua Guan jin xie* (Carefully painted by Hua Guan of Xishan in the spring, the third month in the Renzi year).

Seal mark of the artist: *Hua Guan*.

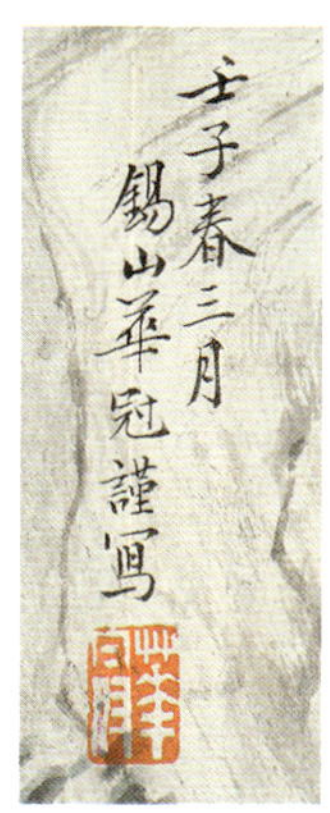

86
English-style Bookcase
1970-109-1

Exhibited: Philadelphia 1984, 84.

Inscribed on central panel: *vBH* (initials of original owner, Andreas Everardus van Braam Houckgeest).

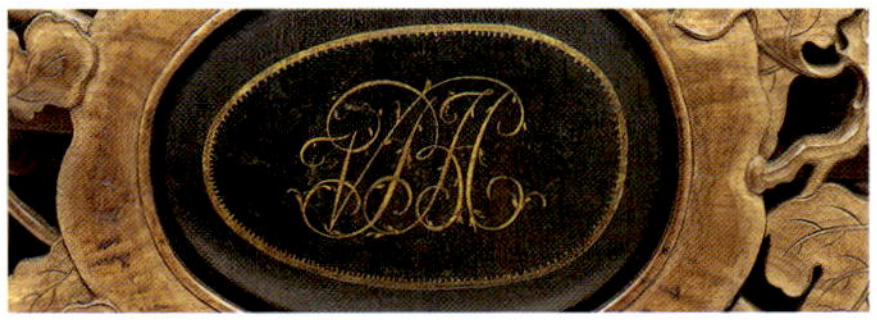

Manuscript label pasted on inside back: *Purchased of Mr. Andrew Edvardus Van Braam Houckgest 8th. May. 1798.*

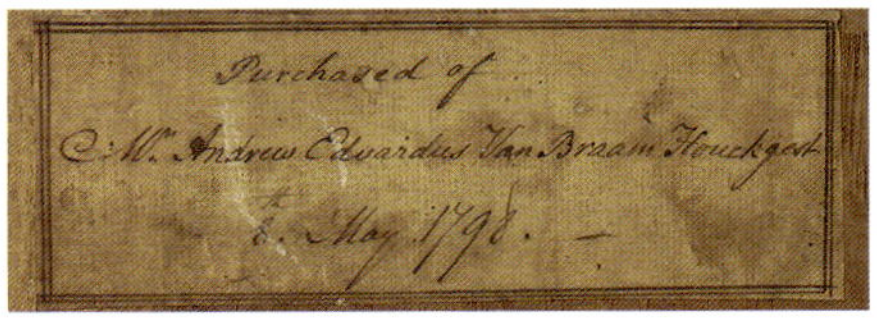

87
Pair of Hexagonal Stools
1946-85-1a,b, 1946-85-2a,b

Published: Lee 1963, no. 12; Lü et al. 2017, 390–91.

88
Panels from a Scholar's Study
1929-30-1

Published: Roberts 1934, 65–66; Jayne and Lee 1958, 33–35; Philadelphia Museum of Art 1995, 35; Philadelphia Museum of Art 2014, 73; Kinoshita 2017, 4, fig. 7.

89
Celestial Bird with Covered Vases
1944-20-212a–d

Published: Hu 1944, 12, no. 36; Lü et al. 2017, 336–37.

90
Dog Cage
1964-205-1

Published: Philadelphia Museum of Art 1995, 34; New York 2010–11, 55, fig. 3.34; Philadelphia Museum of Art 2014, 70; Lü et al. 2017, 320–21.

91
Warrior Opera Costume
1950-4-1

Published: Blum 1997, 173, no. 325; Lü et al. 2017, 402–3.

92
Daoist Vestment (*Jiangyi*)
1967-144-1

Exhibited: Philadelphia 1979–80.
Published: Cammann 1979, 12–14; Philadelphia Museum of Art 1995, 78; Blum 1997, 174, no. 326; Lü et al. 2017, 398–99.

93
Hat Ornament of a *Junwang* (Prince of the Second Rank)
1970-6-1

Exhibited: Philadelphia 1974 (no cat.).
Published: Lü et al. 2017, 412–13.

94
Tea Table with Figures in a Chinese Formal Garden
1940-34-1

Exhibited: Philadelphia 1984, 177, no. 182.

95
Woman's Informal Court Vest
1967-30-334

Exhibited: Philadelphia 1979–80, no. 17.
Published: Cammann 1979, 11; Blum 1997, 171, no. 320; Philadelphia Museum of Art 2014, 81; Lü et al. 2017, 408–9.

96
Ai Weiwei (b. 1957)
***Hanging Man*, 1986 and 2014**
2015-62-1a,b

Not previously exhibited or published.

97
Zhang Huan (b. 1965)
***To Raise the Water Level in a Fish Pond*, 1997**
1999-33-1

Exhibited: Philadelphia 2007 (no cat.); Philadelphia 2015 (no cat.).
Published: Philadelphia Museum of Art 2014, 412–13.

98
Zheng Chongbin (b. 1961)
***Descending from the Above*, 2016**
2017-24-1

Not previously exhibited or published.

REFERENCES

EXHIBITIONS

Beijing 2015
Shengshi fenghua: Da Qing Kangxi yuyao ci [Porcelain wares: From the imperial kiln in the Kangxi period of the Qing dynasty]. Capital Museum, Beijing, 2015. Catalogue. Beijing: Beijing chubanshe, 2015.

Beijing (Chen) 2015
Yuyao mima: Mingdai huangjia ciqi tezhan [Imperial kiln code: Special exhibition on imperial porcelains from the Ming dynasty]. Beijing, 2015. Catalogue by Chen Jianming. Beijing: Zhonghua shuju, 2015.

Beijing 2016
Da Yuan san du [The capital cities of Yuan dynasty]. Capital Museum, Beijing. Catalogue. Beijing: Kexue chubanshe, 2016.

Beijing and Berlin 2009–12
Ai Weiwei: 1981–1993 / New York 1983–1993. Three Shadows Photography Art Centre, Beijing, opened January 2009; Martin-Gropius-Bau, Berlin, October 14, 2011–March 18, 2012. Catalogue by John Tancock and Stephanie Tung. Beijing: Three Shadows Press, 2010; Berlin: Wuppertal Distanz Berlin Gestalten, 2011.

Berkeley 2013
Beauty Revealed: Images of Women in Qing Dynasty Chinese Painting. Berkeley Art Museum and Pacific Film Archive, University of California, September 25–December 22, 2013. Catalogue by James Cahill et al. Berkeley: University of California, Berkeley Art Museum and Pacific Film Archive, 2013.

Berkeley, New Haven, and Saint Louis 1985
Bones of Jade, Soul of Ice: The Flowering Plum in Chinese Art. University Art Museum, Berkeley, CA, January 23–March 24, 1985; Yale University Art Gallery, New Haven, CT, April 18–June 16, 1985; Saint Louis Art Museum, July 12–September 8, 1985. Catalogue by Maggie Bickford. New Haven: Yale University Art Gallery, 1985.

Cambridge 2009
The Immortal Stone: Chinese Jades from the Neolithic Period to the Twentieth Century. Fitzwilliam Museum, Cambridge, January 27–May 31, 2009. Catalogue by James C. S. Lin. London: Scala, 2009.

Cambridge 2012
The Search for Immortality: Tomb Treasures of Han China. Fitzwilliam Museum, Cambridge, May 5–November 11, 2012. Catalogue edited by James C. S. Lin. New Haven: Yale University Press, 2012.

Cleveland 1968
Chinese Art under the Mongols: The Yüan Dynasty, 1279–1368. Cleveland Museum of Art, October 2–November 24, 1968. Catalogue by Sherman E. Lee and Wai-kam Ho. Cleveland: Cleveland Museum of Art, 1968.

Cleveland and New York 1997–98
When Silk Was Gold: Central Asian and Chinese Textiles. Cleveland Museum of Art, October 19, 1997–January 4, 1998; Metropolitan Museum of Art, New York, March 3, 1998–May 17, 1998. Catalogue by James C. Y. Watt and Anne E. Wardwell. New York: Metropolitan Museum of Art, 1997.

Chicago and San Francisco 2000–2001
Taoism and the Arts of China. Art Institute of Chicago, November 4, 2000–January 7, 2001; Asian Art Museum of San Francisco, February 21–May 13, 2001. Catalogue by Stephen Little and Shawn Eichman. Chicago: Art Institute of Chicago; Berkeley: University of California Press, 2000.

Cincinnati 2009–10
Decoded Messages: The Symbolic Language of Chinese Animal Painting. Cincinnati Art Museum, October 9, 2009–January 3, 2010. Catalogue edited by Hou-mei Sung. New Haven: Yale University Press, 2009.

Florence 2007–8
China at the Court of the Emperors: Unknown Masterpieces from Han Tradition to Tang Elegance (25–907). Palazzo Strozzi, Florence, October 12, 2007–January 20, 2008. Catalogue edited by Sabrina Rastelli. Florence: Fondazione Palazzo Strozzi, 2008.

Glasgow 1937
Glasgow Art Galleries and Museums, 1937. No cat.

Groningen 2011–12
Famille Verte: Chinese Porcelain in Green Enamels. Groninger Museum, June 26, 2011–June 17, 2012. Catalogue by Christiaan J. A. Jörg. Groningen: Groninger Museum, 2011.

Hong Kong 1993
2000 Years of Chinese Lacquer / Zhongguo qi yi erqian nian. Oriental Ceramic Society of Hong Kong and Art Gallery, Chinese University of Hong Kong, September 24–November 21, 1993. Catalogue by Hu Shih-chang, Yip Shing Yiu, and Teo Kheng Chong. Hong Kong: Oriental Ceramic Society of Hong Kong; Art Gallery, Chinese University of Hong Kong, 1993.

Hong Kong 1995
Qing ci cui zhen: Qingdai Kang Yong Qian guanyao ciqi [Qing imperial porcelain of the Kangxi, Yongzheng, and Qianlong reigns]. Art Gallery, Chinese University of Hong Kong, 1995. Catalogue by Song Boliang, Cheng Shaozhong, and Peter Lam. Nanjing: Nanjing bowuyuan; Hong Kong: Xianggang zhongwen daxue wenwuguan, 1995.

Hong Kong 1999
Adornment for the Body and Soul: Ancient Chinese Ornaments from the Mengdiexuan Collection / Jin cui liu fang: Mengdiexuan cang Zhongguo gudai shiwu. University Museum and Art Gallery, University of Hong Kong, 1999. Catalogue by Emma C. Bunker, Julia M. White, and Jenny F. So. Hong Kong: University Museum and Art Gallery, University of Hong Kong, 1999.

Hong Kong 2005
Wu se qiong xia: Zhuyuetang cang Yuan Ming Qing yidaoyou ciqi [Shimmering colors: Monochromes of the Yuan to Qing period; The Zhuyuetang collection]. Art Museum, Chinese University of Hong Kong, March–September 2005. Catalogue by You Xuehua. Hong Kong: Xianggang Zhongwen daxue wenwuguan, 2005.

Hong Kong 2007–8
Ji xia qing shang: Huaihaitang cang Qingdai yuyao ciping [Ethereal elegance: Porcelain vases of the imperial Qing, the Huaihaitang collection]. Art Museum, Chinese University of Hong Kong, November 11, 2007–March 30, 2008. Catalogue edited by Peter Lam. Hong Kong: Xianggang Zhongwen daxue wenwuguan, 2007.

Hong Kong 2012–13
Ji xia ming dao: Huaihaitang cang Mingdai zhong wan qi guanyao ciqi [Enlightening elegance: Imperial porcelain of the mid to late Ming, the Huaihaitang Collection]. Art Museum, Chinese University of Hong Kong, December 1, 2012–April 21, 2013. Catalogue edited by Lai Suk Yee. Hong Kong: Xianggang Zhongwen daxue wenwuguan, 2012.

Indianapolis et al. 1980–81
Freedom of Clay and Brush through Seven Centuries in Northern China: Tz'u-chou Type Wares, 960–1600 A.D. Indianapolis Museum of Art, November 17, 1980–January 18, 1981; China House Gallery, New York, March 16–May 24, 1981; Denver Art Museum, June 27–August 9, 1981; Cleveland Museum of Art, August 5–September 6, 1981. Catalogue by Yataka Mino. Indianapolis: Indianapolis Museum of Art, 1981.

Indianapolis et al. 1987–88
Ice and Green Clouds: Traditions of Chinese Celadon. Indianapolis Museum of Art, January 28, 1987–March 27, 1988; traveled. Catalogue by Yutaka Mino and Katherine R. Tsiang. Indianapolis: Indianapolis Museum of Art, 1986.

London 1935–36
The Chinese Exhibition. Royal Academy of Arts, London, November 28, 1935–March 7, 1936. Catalogue [*A Commemorative Catalogue of the International Exhibition of Chinese Art*] by Leigh Ashton, Basil Gray, R. L. Hobson, and Oscar Raphael. London: Faber and Faber, 1936.

London 2005–6
China: The Three Emperors, 1662–1795. Royal Academy of Arts, London, November 12, 2005–April 17, 2006. Catalogue edited by Evelyn S. Rawski and Jessica Rawson. London: Royal Academy of Arts, 2005.

London 2014–15
Ming: 50 Years That Changed China. British Museum, London, September 18, 2014–January 5, 2015. Catalogue edited by Craig Clunas and Jessica Harrison-Hall. London: British Museum Press, 2014.

Los Angeles and Houston 2011–12
Gifts of the Sultan: The Arts of Giving at the Islamic Courts. Los Angeles County Museum of Art, June 5–September 5, 2011; Museum of Fine Arts, Houston, October 23, 2011–January 15, 2012. Catalogue by Linda Komaroff. Los Angeles: Los Angeles County Museum of Art, 2011.

Los Angeles, Cleveland, and Detroit 1944
2000 Years of Silk Weaving. Los Angeles County Museum, January 9–February 29, 1944; Cleveland Museum of Art, March 18–April 16, 1944; Detroit Institute of Arts, May 12–June 4, 1944. Catalogue. New York: E. Weyhe, 1944.

Münster 2008
The Monochrome Principle: Lacquerware and Ceramics of the Song and Qing Dynasties. Museum für Lackkunst, Münster, Germany, January 18–March 8, 2008. Catalogue edited by Monika Kopplin. Translation of *Prinzip Monochrom: Lack und Keramik der Song- und Qing-Zeit*. Munich: Hirmer, 2008.

New York 1945
Costumes from the Forbidden City. Metropolitan Museum of Art, New York, March 6–May 1945. Catalogue by Alan Priest. New York: Metropolitan Museum of Art, 1945.

New York 1970–71
Ming Porcelains: A Retrospective. China House Gallery, New York, October 29, 1970–January 31, 1971. Catalogue by Suzanne G. Valenstein. New York: China House Gallery, China Institute in America, 1970.

New York 1977–78
I-Hsing Ware. China House Gallery, New York, October 28, 1977–January 29, 1978. Catalogue by Terese Tse Bartholomew. New York: China House Gallery, China Institute in America, 1977.

New York 1991–92
East Asian Lacquer: The Florence and Herbert Irving Collection. Metropolitan Museum of Art, New York, November 22, 1991–February 23, 1992. Catalogue by James C. Y. Watt and Barbara Brennan Ford. New York: Metropolitan Museum of Art, 1991.

New York 2002
Blanc de Chine: Divine Images in Porcelain. China Institute Gallery, New York, September 19–December 7, 2002. Catalogue by John Ayers and Yuan Bingling. New York: China Institute Gallery, 2002.

New York 2010–11
The World of Khubilai Khan: Chinese Art in the Yuan Dynasty. Metropolitan Museum of Art, New York, September 28, 2010–January 2, 2011. Catalogue by James C. Y. Watt et al. New York: Metropolitan Museum of Art, 2010.

New York 2011
Cloisonné: Chinese Enamels from the Yuan, Ming, and Qing Dynasties. Bard Graduate Center, New York, January 26–April 17, 2011. Catalogue edited by Béatrice Quette. New York: Bard Graduate Center, 2011.

New York 2012
Theater, Life, and the Afterlife: Tomb Décor of the Jin Dynasty from Shanxi / Shengsi tongle: Shanxi Jin dai xiqu zhuandiao yishu. China Institute Gallery, New York, February 9–June 17, 2012. Catalogue edited by Shi Jinming and Willow Weilan Hai Chang. New York: China Institute Gallery, 2012.

New York 2013–14
Ink Art: Past as Present in Contemporary China. Metropolitan Museum of Art, New York, December 11, 2013–April 6, 2014. Catalogue by Maxwell K. Hearn and Wu Hung. New York: Metropolitan Museum of Art, 2013.

New York 2017
Age of Empires: Art of the Qin and Han Dynasties. Metropolitan Museum of Art, New York, April 3–July 16, 2017. Catalogue by Zhixin Jason Sun. New York: Metropolitan Museum of Art, 2017.

New York et al. 1977
Chinese Ceramics from Japanese Collections: T'ang through Ming Dynasties. Asia House Gallery, New York, April 29–June 26, 1977; Seattle Art Museum, July 14–August 21, 1977; Kimbell Art Museum, Fort Worth; Asian Art Museum of San Francisco. Catalogue by Seizō Hayashiya and Henry Trubner. New York: Asia Society, 1977.

New York, Cologne, and Zurich 2006–7
Gilded Splendor: Treasures of China's Liao Empire (907–1125). Asia Society and Museum, New York, October 6–December 31, 2006; Museum für Ostasiatische Kunst, Cologne, Germany, January 26–April 22, 2007; Museum Rietberg, Zurich, May 13–July 15, 2007. Catalogue edited by Hsueh-man Shen. New York: Asia Society, 2006.

New York, San Francisco, and Seattle 1998–2000
Inside/Out: New Chinese Art. Asia Society Galleries, New York, September 15, 1998–January 3, 1999; San Francisco Museum of Modern Art, February 26–June 1, 1999; Tacoma Art Museum and the Henry Art Gallery, Seattle, November 18, 1999–March 7, 2000. Catalogue edited by Minglu Gao. San Francisco: San Francisco Museum of Modern Art, 1998.

Oakland 1941
Mills College, Oakland, CA, October–November 1941. No cat.

Oxford 1988
Iron in the Fire: The Chinese Potter's Exploration of Iron Oxide Glazes. Ashmolean Museum, University of Oxford, May 10–June 19, 1988. Catalogue by John Ayers, Margaret Medley, and Nigel Wood. London: Oriental Ceramic Society, 1988.

Philadelphia 1956
Inaugural Exhibition. Philadelphia Museum of Art, 1956. No cat.

Philadelphia 1969
The Animal Kingdom. Philadelphia Museum of Art, March 13–April 16, 1969. No cat.

Philadelphia 1971
Chinese Calligraphy. Philadelphia Museum of Art, September 25–November 7, 1971. Catalogue by Tseng Yu-ho Ecke. Philadelphia: Philadelphia Museum of Art, 1971.

Philadelphia 1974
A Decade of Gifts. Philadelphia Museum of Art, May 12–June 16, 1974. No cat.

Philadelphia 1979–80
The Delights of Fine Fashion. Philadelphia Museum of Art, September 29, 1979–February 10, 1980. Catalogue. Philadelphia: Philadelphia Museum of Art, 1979.

Philadelphia 1980
Oriental Acquisitions, 1970–1980. Philadelphia Museum of Art, February 8–April 20, 1980. No cat.

Philadelphia 1984
Philadelphians and the China Trade, 1784–1844. Philadelphia Museum of Art, July 1–September 23, 1984. Catalogue by Jean Gordon Lee. Philadelphia: Philadelphia Museum of Art, 1984.

Philadelphia 1990
Fabric and Fashion: A Decade of Acquisitions. Philadelphia Museum of Art, February 11–March 25, 1990. No cat.

Philadelphia 2005
Mongols, Manchus, and Monks: The Art of Tibetan Diplomacy. Philadelphia Museum of Art, May 7–November 6, 2005. No cat.

Philadelphia 2007
Contemporary Art on Paper. Philadelphia Museum of Art, February 10–April 22, 2007. No cat.

Philadelphia 2010–11
Porcelain for the Emperor: Chinese Ceramics of the Kangxi Reign (1662–1722). Philadelphia Museum of Art, August 7, 2010–September 5, 2011. No cat.

Philadelphia 2011–12
The Natacha Rambova Collection of Lamaist Art. Philadelphia Museum of Art, September 2011–April 2012. No cat.

Philadelphia 2013
First Look: Collecting for Philadelphia. Philadelphia Museum of Art, July 13–September 8, 2013. No cat.

Philadelphia 2014
Making a Classic Modern: Frank Gehry's Master Plan for the Philadelphia Museum of Art. Philadelphia Museum of Art, July 1–September 1, 2014. No cat.

Philadelphia 2015
Take Two: Contemporary Photographs. Philadelphia Museum of Art, August 22–November 15, 2015. No cat.

Philadelphia and Chicago 1949–50
Ming Blue-and-White: An Exhibition of Blue-Decorated Porcelain of the Ming Dynasty. Philadelphia Museum of Art, October 29–December 4, 1949; Art Institute of Chicago, December 21, 1949–February 5, 1950. Catalogue introduction by Jean Gordon Lee. Philadelphia: Philadelphia Museum of Art; Chicago: Art Institute of Chicago, 1949 [separately printed].

Princeton 2010–11
Green, Amber, Cream: Forgotten Art of a Ceramic Workshop in Shanxi, China. Princeton University Art Museum, Princeton, NJ, September 25, 2010–January 9, 2011. No cat.

Richmond 1954–55
Masterpieces of Chinese Art. Virginia Museum of Fine Arts, Richmond, November 19, 1954–January 2, 1955. No cat.

San Francisco 1939
Pacific Cultures: Department of Fine Arts, Division of Pacific Cultures, Golden Gate International Exposition. San Francisco, February 18–October 29, 1939 [also May 25–September 29, 1940]. Catalogue by Langdon Warner et al. San Francisco: Golden Gate International Exposition, 1939.

San Francisco 2006
Hidden Meanings: Symbolism in Chinese Art. Asian Art Museum of San Francisco, October 7–December 31, 2006. Catalogue by Terese Tse Bartholomew [*Hidden Meanings in Chinese Art*]. San Francisco: Asian Art Museum, 2006.

San Francisco, Indianapolis, and Saint Louis 2008–9
Power and Glory: Court Arts of China's Ming Dynasty. Asian Art Museum of San Francisco, June–September 2008; Indianapolis Museum of Art, October 2008–January 2009; Saint Louis Art Museum, February–May 2009. Catalogue by He Li and Michael Knight. San Francisco: Asian Art Museum—Chong-Moon Lee Center for Asian Art and Culture, 2008.

San Marino 2006
Chrysanthemums on the Edge: Plants in Chinese Art. Huntington Chinese Garden, San Marino, CA, August–December 2006. No cat.

Seattle 2000
Porcelain Stories: From China to Europe. Seattle Art Museum, February 7–May 7, 2000. Catalogue by Julie Emerson, Jennifer Chen, and Mimi Gardner Gates. Seattle: Seattle Art Museum, 2000.

Seattle et al. 2001–2
Ancient Sichuan: Treasures from a Lost Civilization. Seattle Art Museum, May 10–August 12, 2001; Kimbell Art Museum, Fort Worth, September 30, 2001–January 13, 2002; Metropolitan Museum of Art, New York, March 4–June 16, 2002; Royal Ontario Museum, Toronto, August 2–November 10, 2002. Catalogue edited by Robert Bagley. Seattle: Seattle Art Museum, 2001.

Sydney 2016
Tang: Treasures from the Silk Road Capital. Art Gallery of New South Wales, Sydney, April 9–July 10, 2016. Catalogue edited by Cao Lin. Sydney: Art Gallery of New South Wales, 2016.

Taipei 1998
Mingdai Xuande guanyao jinghua tezhan tulu [Catalogue of the special exhibition of selected Hsüan-te imperial porcelains of the Ming dynasty]. National Palace Museum, Taipei, 1998. Catalogue by Liao Baoxiu. Taipei: Guoli Gugong bowuyuan, 1998.

Taipei 2003
Gu se: Shiliu zhi shiba shiji yishu de fanggu feng [Through the prism of the past: Antiquarian trends in Chinese art of the sixteenth to eighteenth century]. National Palace Museum, Taipei, 2003. Catalogue by Li Yumin. Taipei: Guoli Gugong bowuyuan, 2003.

Taipei 2006–7
Da guan: Bei Song Ruyao tezhan [Grand view: Special exhibition of Ju ware from the Northern Song dynasty]. National Palace Museum, Taipei, December 25, 2006–March 25, 2007. Catalogue by Lin Boting. Taipei: Guoli Gugong bowuyuan, 2006.

Taipei 2008
Huali caici: Qianlong yangcai [Stunning decorative porcelains from the Qianlong reign]. National Palace Museum, Taipei, 2008. Catalogue by Liao Baoxiu. Taipei: Guoli Gugong bowuyuan, 2008.

Taipei 2009
Yongzheng: Qing Shizong wenwu dazhan [Harmony and integrity: The Yongzheng emperor and his times]. National Palace Museum, 2009. Catalogue by Feng Mingzhu. Taipei: Guoli Gugong bowuyuan, 2009.

Taipei 2012
De jia qu: Qianlong huangdi de taoci pinwei [Obtaining refined enjoyment: The Qianlong emperor's taste in ceramics]. National Palace Museum, Taipei, 2012. Catalogue by Yu Peijin. Taipei: Guoli Gugong bowuyuan, 2012.

Taipei 2015–16
Shen bi dan qing: Lang Shining lai hua sanbai nian tezhan [Portrayals from a divine brush: A special exhibition on the tricentennial of Giuseppe Castiglione's arrival in China]. National Palace Museum, Taipei, October 6, 2015–January 4, 2016. Catalogue by Marco Musillo and He Chuanxin. Taipei: Guoli Gugong bowuyuan, 2015.

Tokyo 1977
Tōyō No Sometsuke [Far Eastern blue-and-white porcelain]. Mitsukoshi, Tokyo, August 16–28, 1977. Catalogue by Hayashiya Seizō. Tokyo: Nippon Keizai Shimbunsha, 1977.

Washington et al. 2012–14
Ai Weiwei: According to What? Hirshhorn Museum and Sculpture Garden, Washington, DC, October 7, 2012–February 24, 2013; Indianapolis Museum of Art, April 5–July 28, 2013; Art Gallery of Ontario, Toronto, August 31–October 27, 2013; Pérez Art Museum, Miami, November 28, 2013–March 16, 2014; Brooklyn Museum, April 18–August 10, 2014. Catalogue by Mami Kataoka, Charles Merewether, and Kerry Brougher. Munich: Prestel, 2012.

PUBLICATIONS

Ayers 1974
Ayers, John. *The Baur Collection, Geneva: Chinese Ceramics*. Vol. 4, *Painted and Polychrome Porcelains of the Ch'ing Dynasty*. Geneva: Collections Baur, 1974.

Ayers 1999
Ayers, John. *Chinese Ceramics in the Baur Collection*. 2 vols. Geneva: Baur Collection, 1999.

Ayers 1999–2000
Ayers, John. "The 'Peachbloom' Wares of the Kangxi Period (1662–1722)." *Transactions of the Oriental Ceramic Society* 64 (1999–2000): 31–50.

Ayers and Sato 1983
Ayers, John, and Sato Masahiko. *Shin* [Ch'ing dynasty]. Vol. 15 of *Sekai tôji zenshû* [Ceramic art of the world]. Tokyo: Shogakukan, 1983.

Barber 1909
Barber, Edwin Atlee. "Chinese Porcelains." *Bulletin of the Pennsylvania Museum* 7, no. 28 (October 1909): 61–67.

Barber 1911
Barber, Edwin Atlee. "So-Called 'Red Porcelain' or Boccaro Ware of the Chinese, and Its Imitations." *Bulletin of the Pennsylvania Museum* 9, no. 34 (April 1911): 17–23.

Barnhart et al. 1997
Barnhart, Richard M., et al. *Three Thousand Years of Chinese Painting*. New Haven: Yale University Press; Beijing: Foreign Languages Press, 1997.

Beijing wenbo jiaoliu guan 2005
Beijing wenbo jiaoliu guan, Beijing Zhihuasi guanli chu. *Gucha Zhihuasi* [The ancient Zhihua temple]. Beijing: Beijing yanshan chubanshe, 2005.

Benard 2004
Benard, Elisabeth. "The Qianlong Emperor and Tibetan Buddhism." In *New Qing Imperial History: The Making of Inner Asian Empire at Qing Chengde*, edited by James A. Millward et al., 123–35. Abingdon, Oxfordshire: Routledge, 2004.

Berger and Yuan 2005
Berger, Patricia, and Yuan Hongqi. "Ritual." In *China: The Three Emperors, 1662–1795*, edited by Evelyn S. Rawski and Jessica Rawson, 116–27. Exh. cat. London: Royal Academy of Arts, 2005.

Beurdeley 1979
Beurdeley, Michel. *Chinese Furniture*. Translated by Katherine Watson. Tokyo and New York: Kodansha International, 1979.

Bieberly 2013
Bieberly, Rebecca M. "'Seeing' the 'Ordinary' at Lingyan Temple in Eleventh-century China." PhD diss., University of Michigan, 2013.

Blum 1997
Blum, Dilys E. *The Fine Art of Textiles: The Collections of the Philadelphia Museum of Art*. Philadelphia: Philadelphia Museum of Art, 1997.

Blumenfield 2002
Blumenfield, Robert H. *Blanc de Chine: The Great Porcelain of Dehua*. Berkeley, CA: Ten Speed Press, 2002.

Bonds 2008
Bonds, Alexandra B. *Beijing Opera Costumes: The Visual Communication of Character and Culture*. Honolulu: University of Hawai'i Press, 2008.

Brook 2014
Brook, Timothy. "Commerce: The Ming in the World." In *Ming: 50 Years That Changed China*, edited by Craig Clunas and Jessica Harrison-Hall, 254–91. Exh. cat. London: British Museum Press, 2014.

Cahill 1962
Cahill, James. *The Art of Southern Sung China*. New York: Asia House Gallery, 1962.

Cahill 1982
Cahill, James. *The Distant Mountains: Chinese Painting of the Late Ming Dynasty, 1570–1644*. A History of Later Chinese Painting, 1279–1950, vol. 3. New York: Weatherhill, 1982.

Cahill 1994
Cahill, James. *The Painter's Practice: How Artists Lived and Worked in Traditional China*. New York: Columbia University Press, 1994.

Cai 1998
Cai Hongsheng. "Haba gou yuanliu" [A history of Pekingese dogs]. In *Tang dai Jiuxinghu yu Tujue wenhua* [The Sogdians and Turkic culture during the Tang period], 211–20. Beijing: Zhonghua shuju, 1998.

Cammann 1942
Cammann, Schuyler V. R. "Notes on the Development of Mandarin Squares—Some Newly Discovered Ming Textiles." *Bulletin of the Needle and Bobbin Club* 26, no. 1 (1942): 2–28.

Cammann 1944
Cammann, Schuyler V. R. "The Development of the Mandarin Square." *Harvard Journal of Asiatic Studies* 8, no. 2 (Autumn 1944): 71–130.

Cammann 1979
Cammann, Schuyler V. R. "Costume in China, 1644 to 1912." *Philadelphia Museum of Art Bulletin* 75, no. 326 (Fall 1979): 3–19.

Chang 2014
Chang Jung. *Empress Dowager Cixi: The Concubine Who Launched Modern China*. New York: Anchor Books, 2014.

Chen 2008
Chen Huixia. *He guang ti cai: Gugong cang qi* [Carving the subtle radiance of colors: Treasured lacquerware in the National Palace Museum]. Taipei: Guoli Gugong bowuyuan, 2008.

Cheng 2010
Cheng, Yen-Wen. "Tradition and Transformation: Cataloguing Chinese Art in the Middle and Late Imperial Eras." PhD diss., University of Pennsylvania, 2010.

Chou and Chung 2015
Chou, Ju-hsi, and Anita Chung. *Silent Poetry: Chinese Paintings from the Collection of the Cleveland Museum of Art*. Cleveland: Cleveland Museum of Art, 2015.

Clunas 2005–6
Clunas, Craig. "The Other Ming Tombs: Kings and Their Burials in Ming China." *Transactions of the Oriental Ceramic Society* 70 (2005–6): 1–16.

Coulter and Turner 1997
Coulter, Charles Russell, and Patricia Turner. *Encyclopedia of Ancient Deities*. Jefferson, NC: McFarland, 1997.

Crossman 1991
Crossman, Carl L. *The Decorative Arts of the China Trade: Paintings, Furnishings, and Exotic Curiosities*. Revised edition of *The China Trade* (1972). Woodbridge, Suffolk: Antique Collectors' Club, 1991.

Curtis 1993
Curtis, Emily Bryne. "European Contributions to the Chinese Glass of the Early Qing Period." *Journal of Glass Studies* 35 (1993): 91–101.

Curtis 2001
Curtis, Emily Byrne. "A Plan of the Emperor's Glassworks." *Arts Asiatiques* 56 (2001): 81–90.

Dai and Lu 1987
Dai De and Lu Bian. *Da Dai Liji* [Book of rites with commentaries of Dai De]. Reprint, Shanghai: Shanghai guji chubanshe, 1987.

David 1971
David, Sir Percival, ed. and trans. *Chinese Connoisseurship: The Ko Ku Yao Lun, The Essential Criteria of Antiquities*. London: Faber and Faber, 1971.

Der Ling 1911
Der Ling. *Two Years in the Forbidden City*. New York: Moffat, Yard, 1911.

Dickinson and Wrigglesworth 2000
Dickinson, Gary, and Linda Wrigglesworth. *Imperial Wardrobe*. Rev. ed. Berkeley, CA: Ten Speed Press, 2000.

Donnelly 1969
Donnelly, P. J. *Blanc de Chine: The Porcelain of Têhua in Fukien*. New York: Praeger, 1969.

Du Boulay 1995
Du Boulay, Anthony. "The Taft Collection of Chinese Porcelains." In *The Taft Museum: Its History and Collections*, edited by Edward J. Sullivan and Ruth K. Meyer, vol. 2, 567–699. New York: Hudson Hills, 1995.

Duyvendak 1939
Duyvendak, J. J. L. "The True Dates of the Chinese Maritime Expeditions in the Early Fifteenth Century." *T'oung Pao*, 2nd ser., 34, no. 5 (1939): 341–413.

Ebrey 1981
Ebrey, Patricia Buckley, ed. *Chinese Civilization and Society: A Sourcebook*. New York: Free Press, 1981.

Ebrey 2010
Ebrey, Patricia Buckley. *The Cambridge Illustrated History of China*. New York: Cambridge University Press, 2010.

Eckfeld 2005
Eckfeld, Tonia. *Imperial Tombs in Tang China, 618–907: The Politics of Paradise*. London: Routledge, 2005.

Egan 1994
Egan, Ronald. *Word, Image, and Deed in the Life of Shi Su*. Harvard-Yenching Institute Monograph Series 39. Cambridge, MA: Council on East Asian Studies, Harvard University, 1994.

Ellsworth 1971
Ellsworth, Robert Hatfield. *Chinese Furniture: Hardwood Examples of the Ming and Early Ch'ing Dynasties*. New York: Random House, 1971.

Erickson et al. 2014
Erickson, Britta, et al. *Zheng Chongbin: Impulse, Matter, Form / Zheng Chongbin: Zhan wu shu*. Beijing: Ink Studio, 2014.

Fang 2004
Fang Jing Pei. *Symbols and Rebuses in Chinese Art: Figures, Bugs, Beasts, and Flowers*. Berkeley, CA: Ten Speed Press, 2004.

Fong 1987
Fong, Mary H. "T'ang Line-Engraved Stone Reliefs from Shensi." *Ars Orientalis* 17 (1987): 41–71.

Fong 1990
Fong, Mary H. "Dehua Figures: A Type of Chinese Popular Sculpture." *Orientations* 21, no. 1 (January 1990): 42–48.

Fong 1991
Fong, Mary H. "Antecedents of Sui-Tang Burial Practices in Shaanxi." *Artibus Asiae* 51, no. 3/4 (1991): 147–98.

Fong 1992
Fong, Wen C. *Beyond Representation: Chinese Painting and Calligraphy, 8th–14th Century*. Princeton Monographs in Art and Archaeology 48. New York: Metropolitan Museum of Art; New Haven: Yale University Press, 1992.

Frick 2008
Frick, Patricia. "Gentle Forms and Quiet Colours: The Perfection of Song Lacquerware." In *The Monochrome Principle: Lacquerware and Ceramics of the Song and Qing Dynasties*, edited by Monika Kopplin, 22–45. Exh. cat. Munich: Hirmer, 2008.

Fujioka et al. 1956
Fujioka Ryōichi et al. *Shinchō hen* [China: Ch'ing dynasty and Annamese and Thai ceramics]. Edited by Zauhō Kankōkai et al. Tokyo: Kawade Shobō, 1956.

Garner 1970
Garner, Harry M. *Oriental Blue and White*. London: Faber and Faber, 1970.

Garner 1971
Garner, Harry M. "The Export of Chinese Lacquer to Japan in the Yuan and Early Ming Dynasties." *Archives of Asian Art* 25 (1971–72): 7–28.

Garner 1979
Garner, Sir Harry M. *Chinese Lacquer*. Boston: Faber and Faber, 1979.

Geng 1993
Geng Baochang. *Ming Qing ciqi jianding* [Connoisseurship of Ming and Qing porcelain]. Beijing: Zijincheng chubanshe, 1993.

Geng 2000
Geng Baochang. *Qinghua youlihong* [Blue and white porcelain with underglaze red]. Gugong bowuyuan cang wenwu zhenpin quanji. 3 vols. Hong Kong: Shangwu yinshuguan, 2000.

Geng and Lü 2009
Geng Baochang and Lü Chenglong. *Za youcai, susancai* [Miscellaneous enameled porcelains, plain tricolored porcelains). Shanghai: Shanghai kexue jishu chubanshe, 2009.

Goepper 1963
Goepper, Roger. *The Essence of Chinese Painting*. Translated by Michael Bullock. London: Lund Humphries, 1963.

Gombrich 1984
Gombrich, E. H. *The Story of Art*. Oxford: Phaidon, 1984.

Gu 1987
Gu Sili, ed. *Yuan shi xuan* [Selected poems from the Yuan dynasty]. Vol. 3. 1987. Reprint, Beijing: Zhonghua shuju, 1994.

Gu and Liu 2005
Gu Fang and Liu Yunhui. *Zhongguo chutu yuqi quanji* [The complete collection of jades unearthed in China]. Vol. 14, *Shaanxi*. Beijing: Kexue chubanshe, 2005.

Gu and Song 2005
Gu Fang and Song Jianzhong. *Zhongguo chutu yuqi quanji* [The complete collection of jades unearthed in China]. Vol. 3, *Shanxi*. Beijing: Kexue chubanshe, 2005.

Gu and Yang 2005
Gu Fang and Yang Lixin. *Zhongguo chutu yuqi quanji* [The complete collection of jades unearthed in China]. Vol. 6, *Anhui*. Beijing: Kexue chubanshe, 2005.

Guan 2012
Guan Shanming [Simon Kwan]. "Tixi wen yang fenqi chuyi" [Tentative proposal for the different periods of *Tixi* pattern]. In *Zhongguo gudai qiqi yantaohui lunwen ji* [Proceedings of conference on ancient Chinese lacquer], edited by Chan Kuen On [Chen Juan'an], 59–70. Hong Kong: Xianggang Zhongwen daxue wenwuguan, 2012.

Guang 1971
Guang Lin. "Beijing chutu de jijian Mingdai qinghua ciqi" [A few Ming dynasty blue-and-white porcelains excavated from Beijing]. *Wenwu* 6 (1972): 64–66.

Gugong 2008
Gugong bowuyuan. *Qinggong xiqu wenwu* [Cultural relics of traditional opera of the Qing dynasty]. Vol. 55 of *Gugong bowuyuan cang wenwu zhenpin quanji* [The complete collection of treasures of the Palace Museum]. Hong Kong: Shangwu yinshuguan, 2008.

Gugong 2009
Gugong bowuyuan. *Hebei Quyang Xiudesi yizhi chutu fojiao zaoxiang* [Buddhist figures unearthed at the site of Xiude Temple in Quyang, Hebei province]. Vol. 7 of *Gugong bowuyuan cangpin daxi: Diaosu* [Compendium of collections in the Palace Museum: Sculpture]. Beijing: Zijincheng chubanshe, 2009.

Gugong and Jingdezhen 2015
Gugong bowuyuan and Jingdezhen shi taoci kaogu yanjiu suo. *Mingdai Hongwu Yongle yuyao ciqi: Jingdezhen yuyao yizhi chutu yu Gugong bowuyuan cang chuanshi ciqi duibi* [Imperial porcelains from the reigns of Hongwu and Yongle in the Ming dynasty: A comparison of porcelains from the imperial kiln site at Jingdezhen and the imperial collection of the Palace Museum]. Beijing: Gugong chubanshe, 2015.

Gugong bowuyuan gu jianzhu guanli bu 2007
Gugong bowuyuan gu jianzhu guanli bu, ed. *Gugong jianzhu neiyan zhuangxiu: Gugong jingdian* [Architecture and decoration of the Forbidden City: Classics of the Forbidden City]. Beijing: Zijincheng chubanshe, 2007.

Guoli gugong bowuyuan 1971
Guoli gugong bowuyuan. *Gugong falangqi xuancui* [Masterpieces of Chinese enamel ware in the National Palace Museum]. Taipei: Guoli gugong bowuyuan, 1971.

***Gugong shuhua tulu* 8, 1991**
Gugong shuhua tulu [Catalogue of painting and calligraphy at the National Palace Museum] 8. Taipei: Guoli gugong bowuyuan, 1991.

Hammers 2011
Hammers, Roslyn Lee. *Pictures of Tilling and Weaving: Art, Labor, and Technology in Song and Yuan China*. Hong Kong: Hong Kong University Press, 2011.

Hammond 2001
Hammond, Kenneth J. "Beijing's Zhihua Monastery: History and Restoration in China's Capital." In *Cultural Intersections in Later Chinese Buddhism*, edited by Marsha Weidner, 189–208. Honolulu: University of Hawai'i Press, 2001.

Handler 1993
Handler, Sarah. "Cabinets and Shelves Containing All Things in China." *Journal of the Classical Chinese Furniture Society* 4, no. 1 (1993): 4–29.

Handler 2001
Handler, Sarah. *Austere Luminosity of Chinese Classical Furniture*. Berkeley: University of California Press, 2001.

Handler 2005
Handler, Sarah. *Ming Furniture in the Light of Chinese Architecture*. Berkeley, CA: Ten Speed Press, 2005.

Harrison-Hall 2001
Harrison-Hall, Jessica. *Catalogue of Late Yuan and Ming Ceramics in the British Museum*. London: British Museum Press, 2001.

Harrison-Hall 2017
Harrison-Hall, Jessica. *China: A History in Objects*. London: Thames and Hudson, 2017.

Hasebe 1973
Hasebe Gakuji, ed. *Toji* [Ceramics]. Vol. 5 of *Chugoku Bijutsu* [Chinese art in Western collections]. Tokyo: Kodansha, 1973.

Haufler 2014
Haufler, Marsha. "Beliefs: Miracles and Salvation." In *Ming: 50 Years That Changed China*, edited by Craig Clunas and Jessica Harrison-Hall, 204–53. Exh. cat. London: British Museum, 2014.

Hay 2010
Hay, Jonathan. "Seeing through Dead Eyes: How Early Tang Tombs Staged the Afterlife." *RES: Anthropology and Aesthetics* 57–58 (Spring–Autumn 2010): 16–54.

Hebei 1996
Hebei sheng kaogu yanjiu suo. "Hebei Xuanhua Liao Zhang Wenzao bihua mu fajue jianbao" [A report on the excavation of Zhang Wenzao's tomb from the Liao dynasty in Xuanhua, Hebei]. *Wenwu* 9 (1996): 14–46.

Hebei 2001
Hebei sheng kaogu yanjiu suo. *Xuanhua Liao mu bihua* [Liao mural tombs at Xuanhua]. Beijing: Wenwu chubanshe, 2001.

Henan 2008
Henan sheng wenwu kaogu yanjiu suo. *Baofeng Qingliangsi Ru yao* [Ru wares of Qingliangsi in Baofeng]. Zhengzhou shi: Daxiang chubanshe, 2008.

Henan and Anyang 1983
Henan sheng wenwu yanjiusuo, Anyang diqu wenwu guanli weiyuanhui, and Anyang xian wenwu guanli weiyuanhui. *Anyang Xiudingsi ta* [Pagoda at Xiuding temple, Anyang]. Beijing: Wenwu chubanshe, 1983.

Hobson 1924
Hobson, R. L. [Robert Lockhart]. "Chinese Porcelain in the Collection of Mr. Leonard Gow–IX." *Burlington Magazine for Connoisseurs* 45, no. 259 (October 1924): 186–93.

Hobson 1931
Hobson, R. L. [Robert Lockhart]. *Catalogue of the Leonard Gow Collection of Chinese Porcelain*. London: George W. Jones at the Sign of the Dolphin, 1931.

Holzwarth 2005
Holzwarth, Gerald. "The Qianlong Emperor as Art Patron and the Formation of the Collections of the Palace Museum, Beijing." In *China: The Three Emperors, 1662–1795*, edited by Evelyn S. Rawski and Jessica Rawson, 41–53. Exh. cat. London: Royal Academy of Arts, 2005.

Howard and Ayers 1978
Howard, David, and John Ayers. *China for the West: Chinese Porcelain and Other Decorative Arts for Export Illustrated from the Mottahedeh Collection*. 2 vols. London: Sotheby Parke Bernet, 1978.

Hsu 2012–13
Hsu, Eileen Hsiang-ling. "Green, Amber, and Cream: The Forgotten Art of 'Liuli' Glazed Ceramics in Ming China." *Record of the Art Museum, Princeton University* 71–72 (2012–13): 36–55, 57.

Hu 1944
Hu Shih. "The Crozier Collection Part 1: Rock Crystals." *Philadelphia Museum Bulletin* 40, no. 203 (November 1944): 3–30.

Hu 1954
Hu Jigao. "Nanjing nanjiao Yingtai Sishan Ming Jin Ying mu qingli ji" [Record of the excavation of the Ming tomb of Jin Ying at Sishan, Yingtai in the southern suburbs of Nanjing]. *Wenwu cankao ziliao* 12 (1954): 64–74.

Huai'an 2011
Huai'an shi bowuguan cang Ming Qing shuhua jingpin ji [Huai'an City Museum collection of Ming and Qing painting and calligraphy]. Beijing: Wenwu chubanshe, 2011.

Huaihua and Tongdao 1984
Huaihua diqu wenwu gongzuodui and Tongdao xian wenhuaju. "Hunan Tongdao faxian nan Ming kucang yinqi" [Silver vessels discovered in a Southern Ming hoard in Tongdao, Hunan]. _Wenwu_ 2 (1984): 88–92.

Huang 2003
Huang Nengfu, ed. _Zhongguo Nanjing yunjin_ [Nanjing brocade of China]. Nanjing: Nanjing chubanshe, 2003.

Huang 2004
Huang Ximing. "Jin pu yu hu, qi chuang linglong—Qinggong neiting geshan" [Golden knocker, jade door, and exquisite silk window: Partition board of Qing dynasty inner court]. _Zijincheng_ 2 (March–April 2004): 51–54.

Huang S. 2012
Huang, Susan Shih-Shan. _Picturing the True Form: Daoist Visual Culture in Traditional China_. Harvard East Asian Monographs 342. Cambridge, MA: Harvard University Asia Center, 2012.

Huang X. 2012
Huang Xiaofeng. "Kanhua zhibing: Chuan Song ren 'Guanhuatu' yanjiu" [Healing illness by viewing paintings: Research on the drawing of Song people viewing paintings]. _Meiyuan_ 4 (2012): 68–80.

Hubei and Zhongxiang 2007
Hubei sheng wenwu kaogu yanjiusuo and Zhongxiang shi bowuguan. _Liangzhuang wang mu_ [Mausoleum of Prince Liang Zhuangwang]. 2 vols. Beijing: Wenwu chubanshe, 2007.

Hucker 1958
Hucker, Charles O. "Governmental Organization of the Ming Dynasty." _Harvard Journal of Asiatic Studies_ 21 (December 1958): 1–66.

Hui and Mair 1984
Hui, Sramana, and Victor H. Mair. "The Complete Text of Śramaṇa Hui's _Subcommentary on the Quadripartite Prātimokṣa (Ssu-fen chieh-pen shu)_." _Journal of the American Oriental Society_ 104, no. 2 (April–June 1984): 327–32.

Hutt 1987
Hutt, Julia. "Chinese Influence on the Japanese Lacquer Tradition." In _Style in the East Asian Tradition_, Colloquies on Art & Archaeology in Asia 14, edited by Rosemary E. Scott and Graham Hutt, 197–216. London: School of Oriental and African Studies, University of London, 1987.

Ingram 1929
Ingram, Isabel. "The Sirén Collection of Chinese Sculpture—II." _Pennsylvania Museum Bulletin_ 25, no. 130 (December 1929): 24–33.

Ishikawa et al. 1986
Ishikawa Jun, Iriya Yoshitaka, Nakata Yūjirō, and Kohara Hironobu. _Jo I, Tō Kishō_ [Xu Wei and Dong Qichang]. Bunjinga suihen. Chūgoku hen 5 [The fine collection of literati painting: China volume 5]. Tokyo: Chūō Kōronsha, 1986.

Jacobsen 2000
Jacobsen, Robert D. _Imperial Silks: Ch'ing Dynasty Textiles in the Minneapolis Institute of Arts_. 2 vols. Minneapolis: Minneapolis Institute of Arts, 2000.

Jacobsen and Grindley 1999
Jacobsen, Robert D., and Nicholas Grindley. _Classical Chinese Furniture in the Minneapolis Institute of Arts_. Edited by Sarah Callaghan. Minneapolis: Minneapolis Institute of Arts, 1999.

Jackson and Hugus 1999
Jackson, Beverley, and David Hugus. _Ladder to the Clouds: Intrigue and Tradition in Chinese Rank_. Berkeley, CA: Ten Speed Press, 1999.

Jayne 1926
Jayne, Horace H. F. "Special Exhibition of Chinese Art." _Pennsylvania Museum Bulletin_ 21, no. 103 (May 1926): 165–68.

Jayne 1929
Jayne, Horace H. F. "A Collection of Chinese Paintings Given with an Interior for Their Exhibition." _Pennsylvania Museum Bulletin_ 24, no. 128 (May 1929): 4–15.

Jayne 1933
Jayne, Horace H. F. "Exhibition of the Art of China." _Pennsylvania Museum Bulletin_ 28, no. 152 (January 1933): 37–39.

Jayne 1940
Jayne, Horace H. F. "The New Oriental Wing." _Philadelphia Museum Bulletin_ 35, no. 185, (March 1940): 2–15.

Jayne and Lee 1958
Jayne, Horace H. F., and Jean Gordon Lee. "Handbook of the Far Eastern Wing." Special issue, _Philadelphia Museum Bulletin_ 53, no. 256 (Winter 1958).

Jiang 2010
Jiang Qiqi. "Tang Sancai." PhD diss. University of Oxford, 2010.

Jing 1996
Jing Anning. "The Eight Immortals: The Transformation of T'ang and Sung Taoist Eccentrics during the Yüan Dynasty." In _Arts of the Sung and Yüan: Papers Prepared for an International Symposium_, edited by Maxwell K. Hearn and Judith G. Smith, 213–29. New York: Metropolitan Museum of Art, 1996.

Kao et al. 2017
Kao, Wei, Kate Duffy, Hiromi Kinoshita, Peggy Olley, and Behrooz Salimnejad. "A Pair of Qing Dynasty Lacquer Clothes Wardrobes in the Collection of the Philadelphia Museum of Art: Conservation and Analysis." _Wooden Artifacts Group Specialty Postprint_ for a presentation given at the American Institute for Conservation (AIC) Annual Meeting in Chicago, June 1, 2017. http://www.conservation-us.org/docs/default-source/periodicals/wooden-artifacts-group-postprints-2017.pdf.

Kerr 1991
Kerr, Rose, ed. _Chinese Art and Design: The T. T. Tsui Gallery of Chinese Art_. London: Victoria and Albert Museum, 1991.

Kerr 2000
Kerr, Rose. "What Were the Origins of Chinese _Famille Rose_?" _Orientations_ 31, no. 5 (May 2000): 53–59.

Kerr 2001
Kerr, Rose. "'A Passionately Immoderate and Incurable Addiction to Buying Porcelain': The Collection of Augustus the Strong at Dresden." _Orientations_ 32, no. 9 (November 2001): 39–44.

Kerr 2011
Kerr, Rose. "A Reverence for the Past: Influences from Chinese Antiquity." In _Cloisonné: Chinese Enamels from the Yuan, Ming, and Qing Dynasties_, edited by Béatrice Quette, 81–103. Exh. cat. New York: Bard Graduate Center, 2011.

Kerr and Ayers 2002
Kerr, Rose, and John Ayers et al. _Blanc de Chine: Porcelain from Dehua_. Chicago: Art Media Resources, 2002.

Kerr and Wood 2004
Kerr, Rose, and Nigel Wood. _Science and Civilisation in China_. Vol. 5, _Chemistry and Chemical Technology_, pt. 12, _Ceramic Technology_. Cambridge: Cambridge University Press, 2004.

Kingery and Vandiver 1985
Kingery, W. D., and P. B. Vandiver. "The Eighteenth-Century Change in Technology and Style from the Famille-Verte Palette to the Famille-Rose Palette." In _Technology and Style_, edited by W. D. Kingery and Esther Lense, 363–81. Ceramics and Civilization 2. Columbus, OH: American Chemical Society, 1986.

Kinoshita 2004
Kinoshita, Hiromi. "Hybridity and Conquest: Patterns of Liao (AD 907–1125) Khitan Tomb Burial." In _Cultural Interaction and Conflict in Central and Inner Asia_, edited by Michael Gervers, Uradyn E. Bulag, and Gillian Long, Toronto Studies in Central and Inner Asia Society 6, 129–44. Toronto: Asian Institute, University of Toronto, 2004.

Kinoshita 2006
Kinoshita, Hiromi. "Burial Practices of the Liao (907–1125) Khitan Elite: A Reflection of Hybrid Culture." PhD diss., University of Oxford, 2006.

Kinoshita 2017
Kinoshita, Hiromi. "Feicheng yishu bowuguan de Zhongguo guancang" [The Chinese collection at the Philadelphia Museum of Art]. In _Haiwaicang Zhongguo gudai wenwu jingcui: Meiguo Feicheng yishu bowuguan juan_ [Selected treasures of Chinese artifacts collected overseas: Philadelphia Museum of Art, National Museum of China international exchange series], edited by Lü Zhangshen, 1–12. Hefei: Anhui meishu chubanshe, 2017.

Kinoshita 2018
Kinoshita, Hiromi. "Making Visible the Invisible: An Early Ming Coffered Ceiling at the Philadelphia Museum of Art." _Arts of Asia_ 48, no. 3 (May–June 2018): 94–102.

Knauer 1998
Knauer, Elfriede Regina. _The Camel's Load in Life and Death: Iconography and Ideology of Chinese Pottery Figurines from Han to Tang and Their Relevance to Trade along the Silk Routes_. Akanthus crescens 4. Zurich: Akanthus, 1998.

Kondō and He 1997
Kondō Hidemi and He Qingxian. "*Tuhui baojian" jiaokan yu yanjiu* [Study of the "Precious Mirror of Painting"]. Nanjing: Jiangsu guji chubanshe, 1997.

Krahl 1986
Krahl, Regina, with Nurdan Erbahar. *Chinese Ceramics in the Topkapi Saray Museum Istanbul: A Complete Catalogue*, edited by John Ayers. 3 vols. London: Sotheby's Publications, 1986.

Krahl 2005
Krahl, Regina. "The Yongzheng Emperor: Art Collector and Patron." In *China: The Three Emperors, 1662–1795*, edited by Evelyn S. Rawski and Jessica Rawson, 242–69. Exh. cat. London: Royal Academy of Arts, 2005.

Krahl and Harrison-Hall 2009
Krahl, Regina, and Jessica Harrison-Hall. *Chinese Ceramics: Highlights of the Sir Percival David Collection*. London: British Museum, 2009.

Kramrisch 1960
Kramrisch, Stella. "The Art of Nepal and Tibet." Special issue, *Philadelphia Museum of Art Bulletin* 55, no. 265 (Spring 1960).

Kuhn 1998
Kuhn, Dieter. *How the Qidan Reshaped the Tradition of the Chinese Dome-Shaped Tomb*. Wurzburger Sinologische Schriften. Heidelberg: Edition Forum, 1998.

Kuhn 2008
Kuhn, Dieter. "The Social Background to the Rise of Monochrome Wares in Song Civilization (960–1279)." In *The Monochrome Principle: Lacquerware and Ceramics of the Song and Qing Dynasties*, edited by Monika Kopplin, 8–21. Exh. cat. Munich: Hirmer, 2008.

Lam 2003–4
Lam, Peter Y. K. "Lang Tingji (1663–1715) and the Porcelain of the Late Kangxi Period." *Transactions of the Oriental Ceramic Society* 68 (2003–4): 27–49.

Lam 2005
Lam, Peter Y. K. "Three Studies on the Glasshouse of the Qing Imperial Household Department." In *Guang ning qiu shui: Qing gong zaobanchu boliqi* [Luster of autumn water: Glass of the Qing imperial workshop], edited by Zhang Rong, 28–83. Exh. cat. Beijing: Zijincheng chubanshe, 2005.

Lam 2005–6
Lam, Peter Y. K. "The Dating of Imperial Kangxi Ceramics." *Bulletin of the Oriental Ceramic Society of Hong Kong* 14 (2005–6): 51–66.

Lau 2004
Lau, D. C. *Mencius*. London: Penguin, 2004.

Lee 1956
Lee, Jean Gordon. "The Caspary Memorial Gift of Chinese Porcelains to Philadelphia." *Far Eastern Ceramic Bulletin* 8, no. 4 (December 1956): 1–8.

Lee 1957
Lee, Jean Gordon. "A Dated Tz'u Chou Pillow." *Archives of the Chinese Art Society of America* 11 (1957): 76–77.

Lee 1963
Lee, Jean Gordon. "Chinese Furniture Collection." *Philadelphia Museum of Art Bulletin* 58, no. 276 (Winter 1963): 41–80.

Lee 1979
Lee, Jean Gordon. "The History of the Snuff Bottle Collection in the Philadelphia Museum of Art." *Journal of the International Chinese Snuff Bottle Society* 11 (Winter 1979): 10–13.

Lee and Hu 1993
Lee King-tsi and Hu Shih-chang. "On Chinese *Tixi* Lacquer." *Orientations* 24, no. 9 (September 1993): 65–68.

Legge 1991
Legge, James. *The Chinese Classics, with a Translation, Critical and Exegetical Notes, Prolegomena, and Copious Indexes*. 5 vols. (in 4 vols). Reprint, Taipei: SMC Publishing, 1991. First published Hong Kong and London, 1861–72.

Leidy 2015
Leidy, Denise Patry. *How to Read Chinese Ceramics*. New York: Metropolitan Museum of Art, 2015.

Leidy and Strahan 2010
Leidy, Denise Patry, and Donna Strahan et al. *Wisdom Embodied: Chinese Buddhist and Daoist Sculpture in the Metropolitan Museum of Art*. New York: Metropolitan Museum of Art, 2010.

Li 1871 (1997)
Li Zuoxian. *Shuhua jianying* [Reflections on painting and calligraphy]. 1871. Reprinted in *Zhongguo lidai shuhua yishu lunzhu congbian*, ed. Xu Juan, vols. 35–36. Beijing: Zhongguo dabaike quanshu chubanshe, 1997.

Li 1871 (2002)
Li Zuoxian. *Shuhua jianying* [Connoisseurship of calligraphy and painting]. Xu xiu Siku quanshu, 1085–1086 [Continuation of compilation: Complete library in four sections, 1085–1086]. 1871. Reprint, Shanghai: Shanghai guji chubanshe, 2002.

Li 1897
Li Yufen. *Ouboluo shi shuhua guomu kao* [Examination of paintings and calligraphy from the Ouboluo Studio]. 4 vols. Beijing: Wenkui tang, 1897.

Li 1992
Li Xianqi. "Henan Yanshi Tang Liu Kai mu" [Tang tomb of Liu Kai at Yanshi, Henan]. *Wenwu* 12 (1992): 21–33.

Li 1994
Li Dejin. "Technology of Longquan Ware Manufacturing." In *New Light on Chinese Yue and Longquan Wares: Archaeological Ceramics Found in Eastern and Southern Asia, A.D. 800–1400*, edited by Chuimei Ho, 85–99. Hong Kong: Centre of Asian Studies, University of Hong Kong, 1994.

Li 1996
Li He. *Chinese Ceramics: A New Comprehensive Survey from the Asian Art Museum of San Francisco*. New York: Rizzoli, 1996.

Li 2010
Li Ruru. *The Soul of Beijing Opera: Theatrical Creativity and Continuity in the Changing World*. Hong Kong: Hong Kong University Press, 2010.

Li 2016
Li Diandian. "Provenance of Prominence: The Simkhovitch Collection of Chinese Paintings at the Philadelphia Museum of Art." *Orientations* 47, no. 3 (April 2016): 42–49.

Li and Chen 2016
Li Yongxing and Chen Shen. "Adaptation and Innovation: The Imperial Cloisonné Collection." In *The Forbidden City: Inside the Court of China's Emperors*, edited by Wen-chien Cheng and Shen Chen, 429–32. Exh. cat. Toronto: Royal Ontario Museum, 2016.

Li and Yang 1991
Li Guoxiang and Yang Chang, eds. *Ming shilu leizuan: shewai shiliao juan* [A compilation of historical materials from the veritable records of the Ming: Materials on foreign affairs]. Wuhan: Wuhan chubanshe, 1991.

Li, Bower, and He 2010
Li, Zhiyan, Virginia L. Bower, and Li He, eds. *Chinese Ceramics from the Paleolithic Period through the Qing Dynasty*. New Haven: Yale University Press, 2010.

Liang 1977
Liang Yicheng. *Xu Wei de wenxue yu yishu* [The literature and art of Xu Wei]. Taipei: Yiwen yinshuguan, 1977.

Liang 2007
Liang Zhu, ed. *Liang Zhuang wang mu* [Mausoleum of Prince Liang Zhuang]. 2 vols. Beijing: Wenwu chubanshe, 2007.

Liao 2000
Liao Baoxiu. *Gugong cangci daxi: Xuande zhi bu* [A compendium of ceramics in the collection of the National Palace Museum, Xuande ware I]. Taipei: Guoli Gugong bowuyuan, 2000.

Liscomb 2016
Liscomb, Kathlyn. "How the Giraffe Became a *Qilin*: Intercultural Signification in Ming Dynasty Arts." In *The Zoomorphic Imagination in Chinese Art and Culture*, edited by Jerome Silbergeld and Eugene Y. Wang, 341–78. Honolulu: University of Hawai'i Press, 2016.

Little 1992
Little, Stephen. "The Arhats in China and Tibet." *Artibus Asiae* 52, nos. 3–4 (1992): 255–81.

Litzenburg 2003
Litzenburg, Thomas V., Jr., with Ann T. Bailey. *Chinese Export Porcelain in the Reeves Center Collection at Washington and Lee University*. London: Third Millennium, 2003.

Liu 1932
Liu Dunzhen. "Beiping Zhihuasi Rulaidian diaocha ji" [Site investigation report on the Buddha Hall at Beiping's Monastery of Transforming Wisdom]. *Zhongguo yingzao xueshe huikan* 3, no. 3 (September 1932): 1–69.

Liu 1997
Liu Jiu'an. *Song Yuan Ming Qing shuhuajia chuanshi zuopin nianbiao* [Dates of existing works by painters of the Song, Yuan, Ming, and Qing dynasties], vol. 1. Shanghai: Shanghai shuhua chubanshe, 1997.

Liu 2004
Liu Tao. *Song Liao Jin jinian ciqi* [Dated ceramics of the Song, Liao, and Jin periods]. Beijing: Wenwu chubanshe, 2004.

Liu 2009
Liu Jiuzhou. *Chong xian: Bajitang cang Song Yuan huihua yanjiu* [Painting is the message: Studies of Song and Yuan paintings in the Bajitang collection]. Hangzhou: Zhejiang renmin meishu chubanshe, 2009.

Lo 2004
Lo, Andrew. "Double Sixes, Holding Spears, and the Long March: Games of the Backgammon Family in China." In *Asian Games: The Art of Contest*, edited by Colin Mackenzie and Irving Finkel, 97–104. Exh. cat. New York: Asia Society, 2004.

Lo 2009
Lo, Hui-Chi. "Political Advancement and Religious Transcendence: The Yongzheng Emperor's (1678–1735) Deployment of Portraiture." PhD diss., Stanford University, 2009.

Lo, Lai, and Ip 1986
Lo, K. S., Lai Suk Yee, and Ip Wing Chi. *The Stonewares of Yixing from the Ming Period to the Present Day, with an Index of Potters, Artistic Collaborators, and Collectors*. London: Sotheby's Publications; Hong Kong: Hong Kong University Press, 1986.

Lu 2011
Lu, Pengliang. "Beyond the Women's Quarters: Meaning and Function of Cloisonné in the Ming and Qing Dynasties." In *Cloisonné: Chinese Enamels from the Yuan, Ming, and Qing Dynasties*, edited by Béatrice Quette, 63–79. New York: Bard Graduate Center, 2011.

Lu et al. 1992
Lu Fusheng et al., eds. *Zhongguo shuhua quanshu* [Compendium of Chinese calligraphy and painting]. Vol. 10. Shanghai: Shanghai shuhua chubanshe, 1992.

Lü et al. 2017
Lü Zhangshen et al., eds. *Haiwai cang Zhongguo gudai wenwu jingcui: Meiguo Feicheng yishu bowuguan juan* [Selected treasures of Chinese artifacts collected overseas: Philadelphia Museum of Art, National Museum of China international exchange series]. Hefei: Anhui meishu chubanshe, 2017.

Ma 2013
Ma Xiaoqing. "Song Jin Yuan Cizhou yao baidi heihua cizhen de fazhan yanbian" [The evolution of black on white decorated Cizhou pillows during the Song, Jin, and Yuan dynasties]. In *Cizhou yao ciqi yanjiu* [The research on porcelain of Cizhou kiln], ed. Feng Xiaoqui, 197–205. Beijing: Gugong chubanshe, 2013.

Malenka and Price 1997
Malenka, Sally, and Beth A. Price. "A Chinese Wall Painting and a Palace Hall Ceiling: Materials, Technique, and Conservation." In *Conservation of Ancient Sites on the Silk Road: Proceedings of an International Conference on the Conservation of Grotto Sites*, edited by Neville Agnew, 127–38. Los Angeles: Getty Conservation Institute, 1997.

Mao 2014
Mao Qiujin. *Mo xiang fo yin: Dunhuang xiejing shufa yanjiu* [Fragrance of ink and sound of Buddha: Research on the calligraphy of sutra in Dunhuang]. Beijing: Beijing daxue chubanshe, 2014.

Maruyama 2008
Maruyama Hiroshi. "*Guanfu*." In *The Encyclopedia of Taoism*, vol. 1, edited by Fabrizio Pregadio, 455–57. London: Routledge, 2008.

Mayuyama 1960
Mayuyama Junkichi, ed. *Chinese Ceramics in the West: A Compendium of Chinese Ceramic Masterpieces in European and American Collections*. Translation of *O-Bei shuzo Chugoku toji zuroku*. Kyoto: Mayuyama Ryūsendō, 1960.

Mertz and Itoh 2010
Mertz, Mechtild, and Itoh Takao. "Analysis of Wood Species in the Collection." In *Wisdom Embodied: Chinese Buddhist and Daoist Sculpture in the Metropolitan Museum of Art*, by Denise Patry Leidy and Donna Stahan et al., 216–19. New York: Metropolitan Museum of Art, 2010.

Meskill 1963
Meskill, Johanna Margarete Menzel. *The Chinese Civil Service: Career Open to Talent?* Boston: Heath, 1963.

Miller 2009
Miller, Harry. *State versus Gentry in Late Ming Dynasty China, 1572–1644*. New York: Palgrave Macmillan, 2009.

Morita 2017
Morita, Miki. "An Overview of North American Collections." *IDP [International Dunhuang Project] News* 49–50 (Summer 2017): 1–7. http://idp.bl.uk/archives/news_current/news_current.a4d.

Mu 2002
Mu Qing. *Dingci yishu* [The art of Ding ceramics]. Shijiazhuang: Hebei jiaoyu chubanshe, 2002.

Naquin 2000
Naquin, Susan. *Peking: Temples and City Life, 1400–1900*. Berkeley: University of California Press, 2000.

Ni 2008
Ni Yibin. *Kantu shuoci* [Interpreting narrative scenes on Chinese porcelains]. Beijing: Zhonghua shuju, 2008.

Nie 2004
Nie Chongzheng, ed. *Jing Tang liang Song huihua: Huaniao zoushou* [Painting from the Jin dynasty, Tang dynasty, and Northern and Southern Song dynasties: Flowers, birds, and beasts]. Hong Kong: Shangwu yinshuguan, 2004.

Owen 2016
Owen, Stephen, ed. and trans. *The Poetry of Du Fu*. 6 vols. Boston: De Gruyter, 2016.

Pang 1909
Pang Yuanji. *Xuzhai minghua lu* [Record of famous paintings from Xuzhai's collection]. Shanghai, 1909.

Pang 1924
Pang Yuanji. *Xuzhai minghua xulu* [Supplement of the Record of famous paintings from Xuzhai's collection]. 1924. Reprinted in *Zhongguo lidai shuhua yishu lunzhu congbian*, ed. Xu Juan, vol. 20. Beijing : Zhongguo dabaike quanshu chubanshe, 1997.

Pankova 2016
Pankova, Svetlana. "Unearthed Early Silks from the Silk Road in Russia (3rd century BC–4th century AD)." In *The Silk Road: A Road of Silk*, edited by Zhao Feng, 54–66. Shanghai: Donghua University Press, 2016.

Pearlstein 1984
Pearlstein, Elinor. "Pictorial Stones from Chinese Tombs." *Bulletin of the Cleveland Museum of Art* 71, no. 9 (November 1984): 302–31.

Pegg 2005
Pegg, Richard A. "Three Friends of Winter: Chinese Art from the Ming Dynasty (1368–1644)." *Oriental Art* 55, no. 2 (2005): 2–8.

Petisca et al. 2016
Petisca, Maria João, et al. "A Hint of Orient in an Americana Collection: Investigations into Chinese Export Furniture at Winterthur Museum." *Studies in Conservation* 61, issue suppl. 3 (2016): 85–90. http://www.tandfonline.com/doi/full/10.1080/00393630.2016.1227113.

Philadelphia Museum of Art 1995
Philadelphia Museum of Art. *Philadelphia Museum of Art: Handbook of the Collections*. Philadelphia: Philadelphia Museum of Art, 1995.

Philadelphia Museum of Art 2014
Philadelphia Museum of Art. *Philadelphia Museum of Art: Handbook*. Philadelphia: Philadelphia Museum of Art, 2014.

Pian 2002
Pain, Rulan Chao. "Peking Opera: *Jingju*." In *The Garland Encyclopedia of World Music*, vol. 7, *East Asia: China, Japan, and Korea*, edited by Robert C. Province, Yosihiko Tokymaru, and J. Lawerence Witzleben, 281–87. New York: Routledge, 2002.

Pierson and McCausland 2003
Pierson, Stacey, and S. F. M McCausland. *Song Ceramics: Objects of Admiration*. London: School of Oriental and African Studies, 2003.

Ponlop 2006
Ponlop, Dzogchen. *Mind beyond Death*. Ithaca, NY: Snow Lion Publications, 2006.

Pope 1956
Pope, John Alexander. *Chinese Porcelains from the Ardebil Shrine*. Smithsonian Publication 4231. Washington, DC: Smithsonian Institution, Freer Gallery of Art, 1956.

Pope 1981
Pope, John Alexander. *Chinese Porcelains from the Ardebil Shrine*. 2nd ed. London: Sotheby Parke Bernet, 1981.

Pressreader 2017
Pressreader.com, s.v. "*Yongle Beizang, Beijing's Tripitaka Block-printing.*" Translated by Wang Xiaohua. http://www.pressreader.com/china/beijing-english/20170427/281509341082683.

Proser 2000
Proser, Adriana. "The Carved Rock Crystals of Emperor Qianlong." *Magazine Antiques* 157, no. 3 (March 2000): 448–55.

Proser, Malenka, and Price 2004
Proser, Adriana G., Sally Malenka, and Beth A. Price. *Painted Splendor: The Context and Conservation of a Chinese Reception Hall in the Philadelphia Museum of Art*. Bulletin of the Philadelphia Museum of Art 92, nos. 389–90. Philadelphia: Philadelphia Museum of Art, 2004.

Rawski 1998
Rawski, Evelyn S. *The Last Emperors: A Social History of Qing Imperial Institutions*. Berkeley: University of California Press, 1998.

Rawson 1995
Rawson, Jessica. *Chinese Jade: From the Neolithic to the Qing*. London: British Museum Press, 1995.

Rawson 2005
Rawson, Jessica. "The Qianlong Emperor: Virtue and the Possession of Antiquity." In *China: The Three Emperors, 1662–1795*, edited by Evelyn S. Rawski and Jessica Rawson, 272–305. Exh. cat. London: Royal Academy of Arts, 2005.

Riddell 1979
Riddell, Sheila. *Dated Chinese Antiquities, 600–1650*. London: Faber and Faber, 1979.

Roberts 1934
Roberts, Laurance P. "The Chinese Scholar's Study." *Pennsylvania Museum Bulletin* 29, no. 161 (March 1934): 65–66.

Roberts 1940
Roberts, Laurance P. "Chinese Palace and Galleries." In "Special Oriental Art Issue for the New Chinese, Indian, and Persian Galleries in Philadelphia," *Art News* 38, no. 27 (April 6, 1940): 22–25, 31.

Robinson 2013
Robinson, David M. *Martial Spectacles of the Ming Court*. Cambridge, MA: Harvard University Asia Center, 2013.

Rong 1999
Rong, Xinjiang [trans. Valerie Hansen]. "The Nature of the Dunhuang Library Cave and the Reasons for Its Sealing." In "Nouvelles études de Dunhuang: Centenaire de l'École française d'Extrême-Orient," ed. Jean-Pierre Drège, special issue, *Cahiers d'Extrême-Asie* 11 (1999–2000): 247–75.

Rösch 2007
Rösch, Petra. *Chinese Wood Sculptures of the 11th to 13th Centuries: Images of Water-Moon Guanyin in Northern Chinese Temples and Western Collections*. Stuttgart: Ibidem Verlag, 2007.

Royal Ontario Museum 1992
Royal Ontario Museum. *Homage to Heaven, Homage to Earth: Chinese Treasures of the Royal Ontario Museum*. Toronto: University of Toronto Press, 1992.

Sargent 2012
Sargent, William R. *Treasures of Chinese Export Ceramics from the Peabody Essex Museum*. Salem, MA: Peabody Essex Museum, 2012.

Shaanxi 1972
Shaanxi sheng bowuguan and Liquan xian wenjiaoju. "Tang Zheng Rentai mu fajue jianbao" [Brief excavation report of the Tang dynasty tomb of Zheng Rentai]. *Wenwu* 7 (1972): 33–44.

Shaanxi 2003
Shaanxi sheng kaogu yanjiusuo. *Xi'an Beizhou An Qie mu* [Northern Zhou tomb of An Qie in Xi'an]. Beijing: Wenwu chubanshe, 2003.

Shanxi 1980
Shanxi Yungang shiku wenwu baoguansuo. *Huayansi* [Huayan temple]. Beijing: Wenwu chubanshe, 1980.

Shanxi 2000
Shanxi sheng kaogu yanjiusuo, ed. *Tangdai Xue Jing mu fajue baogao* [Excavation report of the Tang dynasty tomb of Xue Jing]. Beijing: Kexue chubanshe, 2000.

Shanghai Museum 1998
Shanghai bowuguan. *Shanghai bowuguan cang Kangxi ci tulu* [Kangxi porcelain wares from the Shanghai Museum collection]. Shanghai: Shanghai bowuguan chubanshe, 1998.

Shangraw 1986
Shangraw, Clarence F. "Chinese Lacquers in the Asian Art Museum of San Francisco." *Orientations* 17, no. 4 (April 1986): 22–41.

Shao and Xu 2018
Shao Yan and Xu Li. "Feicheng yishu bowuguan cang Xu Wei huahui dazhou yanjiu" [Research on a large floral painting by Xu Wei in the collection of the Philadelphia Museum of Art]. *Meishu Yanjiu* 175 (January 2018): 14–29.

Sheng 2017
Sheng, Angela. "Chinese Silks That Circulated among People North and West: Implications for Technological Exchanges in Early Times?" In *Silk: Trade and Exchange along the Silk Roads between Rome and China in Antiquity*, edited by Berit Hildebrandt with Carole Gillis, 104–23. Oxford: Oxbow Books, 2017.

Shih 2002
Shih, Jen Lang. "The Perpetuity of the Dharma: A Study and Translation of *Da Aluohan Nantimiduoluo Suoshuo Fazhu Ji*." PhD diss., University of California, Berkeley, 2002.

Shih 2005
Shih Ching-fei. "A Record of the Establishment of a New Art Form: The Unique Collection of 'Painted Enamels' at the Qing Court." In *Art in China: Collections and Concepts* 7 (2005): 1–39. University of Heidelberg and the National Palace Museum International Symposium (Bonn, November 21–23, 2003). urn:nbn:de:bsz:16-opus-57056.

Sickman 1939
Sickman, Laurence. "Notes on Later Chinese Buddhist Art." *Parnassus* 11, no. 4 (April 1939): 12–17.

Sickman and Soper 1971
Sickman, Laurence, and Alexander Soper. *The Art and Architecture of China*. The Pelican History of Art, Z10. Harmondsworth, Eng.: Penguin Books, 1971.

Sirén 1925
Sirén, Osvald. *Chinese Sculpture from the Fifth to the Fourteenth Century: Over 900 Specimens in Stone, Bronze, Lacquer, and Wood, Principally from Northern China*. London: Ernst Benn, 1925.

Sirén 1927
Sirén, Osvald. "Studien zur chinesischen Plastik der Post-T'angzeit." *Ostasiatische Zeitschrift* 14, nos. 1–2 (1927): 1–20.

Sirén 1940
Sirén, Osvald. "Chinese Marble Sculptures of the Transition Period." *Bulletin of the Museum of Far Eastern Antiquities* [*BMFEA*] (Stockholm) 12 (1940): 473–96.

Sirén et al. 1925
Sirén, Osvald, et al. *Documents d'art chinois de la Collection Osvald Sirén*. Ars asiatica 7. Paris and Brussels: G. van Oest, 1925.

Steinhardt 1997
Steinhardt, Nancy Shatzman. *Liao Architecture*. Honolulu: University of Hawai'i Press, 1997.

Steinhardt 2002
Steinhardt, Nancy Shatzman. *Chinese Architecture*. The Culture and Civilization of China. New Haven: Yale University Press, 2002.

Stevens 1998–99
Stevens, Keith. "Images of Sinicised Vedic Deities on Chinese Altars." *Journal of the Hong Kong Branch of the Royal Asiatic Society* 38 (1998–99): 51–56.

Suzuki 1972–73
Suzuki Kei. *Chugoku bijutsu* [Chinese art in Western collections]. 5 vols. Tokyo: Kodansha, 1972–73.

Suzuki 1974
Suzuki Kei. *Ri Tō, Ba En, Ka Kei* [Works of Li-tang, Ma-yuan, Hsia-kuei]. Vol. 2 of *Suiboku-bijutsu taikei* [Complete collection of Japanese and Chinese Suiboku paintings through the centuries]. Tokyo: Kōdansha, 1974.

Swart and Till 1990
Swart, Paula, and Barry Till. "The Xiudingsi Pagoda: A Buddhist Architectural Masterpiece Unveiled." *Orientations* 21, no. 5 (May 1990): 64–76.

Teiser 1999
Teiser, Stephen F. "The Spirits of Chinese Religion." In *Religions of China in Practice*, edited by Donald S. Lopez, Jr., 3–40. Princeton, NJ: Princeton University Press, 1999.

Tian 2001
Tian Jiaqing. *Ming Qing jiaju ji zhen* [Notable feature of the main schools of Ming and Qing furniture]. Hong Kong: Sanlian shudian, 2001.

Tian 2003
Tian Jiaqing, ed. *Ming Qing jiaju: Jianshang yu yanjiu* [Ming Qing furniture: Connoisseurship and research]. Beijing: Wenwu, 2003.

Toh 2000
Toh Hoong Teik. "Shaykh ʿÂlam: The Emperor of Early Sixteenth-Century China." *Sino-Platonic Papers* (University of Pennsylvania, Philadelphia) 110 (October 2000): 1–20.

Tsai 1996
Tsai, Shih-shan Henry. *The Eunuchs in the Ming Dynasty*. New York: State University of New York Press, 1996.

Vainker 2012
Vainker, Shelagh. "Northern Song Lacquer." In *Zhongguo gudai qiqi yantaohui lunwen ji* [Proceedings of a conference on ancient Chinese lacquer], edited by Chen Juan'an, 31–40. Hong Kong: Xianggang Zhongwen daxue wenwuguan, 2012.

Van Braam Houckgeest 1798
Van Braam Houckgeest, André Everard. *An Authentic Account of the Embassy of the Dutch East-India Company to the Court of the Emperor of China in the Years 1794 and 1795*. Translated from the original of M. L. E. Moreau de Saint-Méry. 2 vols. London: Printed for R. Phillips, 1798.

Vinograd 1992
Vinograd, Richard E. *Boundaries of the Self: Chinese Portraits, 1600–1900*. Cambridge: Cambridge University Press, 1992.

Vollmer 2000
Vollmer, John E. "Clothed to Rule the Universe: Ming and Qing Dynasty Textiles at the Art Institute of Chicago." In *Clothed to Rule the Universe: Ming and Qing Dynasty Textiles at the Art Institute of Chicago*, 12–79. Exh. cat. Chicago: Art Institute of Chicago, 2000.

Vollmer 2002
Vollmer, John E. *Ruling from the Dragon Throne: Costume of the Qing Dynasty (1644–1911)*. Berkeley, CA: Ten Speed Press, 2002.

Vollmer and Simcox 2009
Vollmer, John E., and Jacqueline Simcox. *Emblems of Empire: Selections from the Mactaggart Art Collection*. Edmonton: University of Alberta Press, 2009.

Wan 2007
Wan, Maggie C. K. "Jiajing Emperor and His Auspicious Words." *Archives of Asian Art* 57 (2007): 95–120.

Wan 2009
Wan, Maggie C. K. "Building an Immortal Land: The Ming Jiajing Emperor's West Park." *Asia Major*, 3rd ser., 22, no. 2 (2009): 65–99.

Wan 2012
Wan, Maggie C. K. "Xiyuan dongtian: Jiajing yuyong ciqi de daojiao wenshi" [Grotto-heaven in West Park: Daoist motifs on Jiajing imperial porcelains]. In *Ji xia ming dao: Huaihaitang cang Mingdai zhong wan qi guanyao ciqi* [Enlightening elegance: Imperial porcelain of the mid to late Ming, the Huaihaitang collection], edited by Lai Suk Yee, 42–61. Exh. cat. Hong Kong: Xianggang zhongwen daxue wenwuguan, 2012.

Wan and Wang 2011
Wan Shuxun and Wang Limin. *Quyang shi diao* [Stone sculptures from Quyang]. Beijing: Kexue chubanshe, 2011.

Wang 1986
Wang Shixiang. *Classic Chinese Furniture: Ming and Early Qing Dynasties*. Translated by Sarah Handler and Wang Shixiang. London: Han-Shan Tang, 1986.

Wang 1998
Wang Shixiang. *Xiushilu jieshuo* [The annotated "Lacquer Decoration"]. Beijing: Wenwu chubanshe, 1998.

Wang 1999
Wang Liying. *Wucai doucai* [Porcelain in polychrome and contrasting colors]. Vol. 38 of *Gugong bowuyuan cang wenwu zhenpin quanji* [The complete collection of treasures of the Palace Museum]. Hong Kong: Youxian gongsi, 1999.

Wang 2002–3
Wang Jianhua. "Emperor Yongzheng and His Pastimes." *Transactions of the Oriental Ceramic Society* 67 (2002–3): 1–11.

Wang 2012
Wang Guangyao. "Jiajing Wanli shiqi yuyao zhidu de bianhua ji yuyao ciqi nianpu" [The changing system of imperial kilns and the imperial kiln production chronology during the Jiajing and Wanli reigns]. In *Ji xia ming dao: Huaihaitang cang Mingdai zhong wan qi guanyao ciqi* [Enlightening elegance: Imperial porcelain of the mid to late Ming, the Huaihaitang collection], edited by Lai Suk Yee, 62–74. Exh. cat. Hong Kong: Xianggang zhongwen daxue wenwuguan, 2012.

Wang and Evarts 1995
Wang Shixiang and Curtis Evarts. *Masterpieces from the Museum of Classical Chinese Furniture*. Chicago: Chinese Art Foundation, 1995.

Watt 2008
Watt, James C. Y. "The Giraffe as the Mythical *Qilin* in Chinese Art: A Painting and a Rank Badge in the Metropolitan Museum." *Metropolitan Museum Journal* 43 (2008): 111–15.

Weitz 2011
Weitz, Ankeney. "The Vocabulary of Fashion: Word-Image Play in Southern Song Painted Fans." *National Palace Museum Bulletin* 44 (October 2011): 39–48.

Weng 2012
Weng Yu-Wen. "Hui liu zhu fan—Zhende guanyao ciqi suo jian Yisilan feng" [Recurring Islamic influence on Zhengde imperial porcelain designs]. In *Ji xia ming dao: Huaihaitang cang Mingdai zhong wan qi guanyao ciqi* [Enlightening elegance: Imperial porcelain of the mid to late Ming, the Huaihaitang collection], edited by Lai Suk Yee, 12–25. Exh. cat. Hong Kong: Xianggang zhongwen daxue wenwuguan, 2012.

Wilson 1992
Wilson, Samuel M. "The Emperor's Giraffe—Not Every Powerful Country Chooses World Domination." *Natural History* 101, no. 12 (December 1992): 22–25.

Wilson 2004
Wilson, Ming. *Chinese Jades*. Far Eastern series. London: V&A Publications, 2004.

Wong 2002
Wong, Isabel K. F. "Kunqu." In *The Garland Encyclopedia of World Music*, vol. 7, *East Asia: China, Japan, and Korea*, edited by Robert C. Province, Yosihiko Tokymaru, and J. Lawerence Witzleben, 289–96. New York: Routledge, 2002.

Wood 1999
Wood, Nigel. *Chinese Glazes: Their Origins, Chemistry, and Recreation*. Philadelphia: University of Pennsylvania Press, 1999.

Wu 2010
Wu Hung. *The Art of the Yellow Springs: Understanding Chinese Tombs*. London: Reaktion Books, 2010.

Wu and Li 2006
Wu Bin and Li Yingjian, eds. *Shenyang gugong bowuyuan yuancang wenwu jingcui: Huihua juan xia* [Selected treasures from the collections of cultural relics in the Palace Museum in Shenyang: Painting], vol. 2. Shenyang: Wanjuan chuban gongsi, 2006.

Wu and Wang 2010
Wu Hung, with Peggy Wang, eds. *Contemporary Chinese Art: Primary Documents*. New York: Museum of Modern Art, 2010.

Xianggang and Zhongguo 2005
Xianggang zhongwen daxue wenwuguan and Zhongguo diyi lishi dang'an guan, eds. *Qinggong neiwufu zaobanchu dang'an zonghui* [Complete compilation of the archival materials of the Qing dynasty imperial workshops]. Beijing: Renmin chubanshe, 2005.

Xie 2013
Xie Mingliang. "Tang yong zhaji" [Notes on Tang dynasty tomb figures]. *Gugong wenwu yuekan* 361 (April 2013): 58–67.

Xu 1984
Xu Ke, ed. *Qing bai lei chao* [Categorical copies of Qing history] 13. 1984. Repr. Beijing: Zhonghua shuju, 2003.

Xu 2015
Xu Xiaodong. "Europe–China–Europe: The Transmission of the Craft of Painted Enamel in the Seventeenth and Eighteenth Centuries." In *Goods from the East, 1600–1800: Trading Eurasia*, edited by Maxine Berg, 92–106. Houndmills, Basingstoke, Hampshire: Palgrave Macmillan, 2015.

Xu 2018
Xu Zheng. *Meiguo Feicheng yishu bowuguan cang sichou jingmian yanjiu* [A study of the collection of sutra covers at the Philadelphia Museum of Art]. Shanghai: Donghua daxue chubanshe for Zhongguo sichou bowuguan, 2018.

Xu and Nanjing 2003
Xu Huping and Nanjing bowuyuan. *Zhongguo Qingdai guanyao ciqi: Gongting zhen cang* [The official kiln porcelain of the Chinese Qing dynasty: Treasures in the royalty]. Shanghai: Shanghai wenwu chubanshe, 2003.

Xu and Sun 1995
Xu Bingkun and Sun Shoudao. *Dongbei Wenhua* [Northeast culture]. Zhongguo diyu wenhua daxi [Compendium of Chinese regional culture]. Shanghai: Shanghai yuandong chubanshe, 1995.

Yang 1999
Yang Jingrong. *Yanse you* [Color-glazed porcelain]. Vol. 37 of *Gugong bowuyuan cang wenwu zhenpin quanji* [The complete collection of treasures of the Palace Museum]. Hong Kong: Shangwu yinshuguan, 1999.

Yang 2001
Yang Boxian. *Fahaisi bihua* [Mural paintings from Fahai temple]. Beijing: Zhonguo minzu sheying yishu chubanshe, 2001.

Yang 2004
Yang, Xiaoneng. *New Perspectives on China's Past: Chinese Archaeology in the Twentieth Century*. 2 vols. New Haven: Yale University Press, 2004.

Yang 2010
Yang Danxia. "A Study of Hua Guan's Life and Work in Beijing." *Gugong bowuyuan yuankan* 148, no. 2 (2010): 26–47.

Yang 2011
Yang Zhishui. *She hua zhi se: Song Yuan Ming jin yin qi yanjiu* [The color of opulence: Research on silver and gold wares from the Song, Yuan, and Ming dynasties] 3. Beijing: Zhonghua shuju, 2011.

Yang 2016
Yang Zhishui. "Gongzhuang bianjin shang pinting: Mao nü gushitu kao" [Courtly attire thoroughly changed but still graceful: Examining pictorial representations of the story of Maonü]. In *Wuzhong kanhua* [Understanding pictures in the light of objects], by Yang Zhishui, vol. 7 of *Huishilou ji* [The collective writings of Yan Zhishui], 41–50. Beijing: Renmin meishu chubanshe, 2016.

***Yangzhou* 1998**
Yangzhou huapai shuhua quanji: Huang Shen [The comprehensive collection of paintings of the Yangzhou school: Huang Shen]. Tianjin: Tianjin renmin meishu chubanshe, 1998.

Yen 2004
Yen, Shou-chih [Isaac]. "Xu Wei's Zahua: A Study of Genres." PhD diss., Yale University, 2004.

Yu 1967
Yu Yingshi. *Trade and Expansion in Han China: A Study in the Structure of Sino-Barbarian Economic Relations*. Berkeley: University of California Press, 1967.

Yu 1974
Yu Anlan, ed. *Huashi congshu* [Collection of works on the history of painting]. Reprint, Taipei: Wenshizhe chubanshe, 1974.

Yu 2002
Yu Hui. "Shiba shiji fuwu yu jingcheng wangfu huangdi de renwu huajia" [Figure painters who served aristocratic households and mansions of eunuchs in the 18th century]. *Gugong bowuyuan yuankan* 6 (2002): 63–69.

Yu 2005
Yu Hui, ed. *Jing Tang liang Song huihua: Renwu fengsu* [Painting from the Jin, Tang, Northern, and Southern Song dynasties: Figures and customs]. Hong Kong: Shangwu yinshuguan, 2005.

Yü 2001
Yü, Chün-fang. *Kuan-yin: The Chinese Transformation of Avalokitśvara*. New York: Columbia University Press, 2001.

Yung 2002
Yung, Bell. "Chinese Opera: An Overview." In *The Garland Encyclopedia of World Music*, vol. 7, *East Asia: China, Japan, and Korea*, edited by Robert C. Province, Yosihiko Tokymaru, and J. Lawerence Witzleben, 275–80. New York: Routledge, 2002.

Zhang 2004
Zhang Songlin. *Zhongguo gudai zhenmu shenwu* [Ancient Chinese guardian creatures]. Beijing: Wenwu chubanshe, 2004.

Zhang 2016
Zhang Dewei. "Where the Two Worlds Met: Spreading a Buddhist Canon in Wanli (1573–1620) China." *Journal of the Royal Asiatic Society* 26, no. 3 (July 2016): 487–508.

Zhang and Dziewior 2003
Zhang Huan and Yilmaz Dziewior. *Zhang Huan*. Ostfildern-Ruit: Hatje Cantz, 2003.

Zhang and Gugong 2011
Zhang Li and Gugong bowuyuan. *Gugong bowuyuan cangpin daxi: Falangqi bian* [Compendium of collections in the Palace Museum: Enamels). 4 vols. Beijing: Zijincheng chubanshe, 2011.

Zhao et al. 1976–77
Zhao Erxun et al., eds. *Qing shi gao* [Draft history of the Qing dynasty]. 1976–77. 536 volumes in 48 [paginated consecutively]. Reprint, Beijing: Zhonghua shu ju, 2008.

Zheng 2006
Zheng Binglin. "Wan Tang Wudai Dunhuang diqu *Dabanruojing* xinyang yu difang zhengquan de guanxi" [The relationship between *Mahaprajnaparamita Sutra* and local polities in Dunhuang during the later Tang and Five dynasties]. *Pumen xuebao* 34 (July 2006): 1–19.

Zhongguo 1988
Zhongguo meishu quanji bianji weiyuanhui, ed. *Zhongguo meishu quanji: Diaosu bian* [Collection of Chinese art: Sculpture series]: *Yuan Ming Qing diaosu* [Yuan, Ming, and Qing sculpture] 6. Beijing: Remin meishu chubanshe, 1988.

Zhongguo 1999
Zhongguo gudai shuhua jiandingzu, ed. *Zhongguo huihua quanji 8, Yuan 2* [Comprehensive collection of Chinese paintings 8, pt. 2, Yuan dynasty]. Beijing: Wenwu chubanshe, 1999.

Zhongguo 2001
Zhongguo shehui kexueyuan kaogu yanjiusuo. *Yanshi Xingyuan Tang mu* [Tang tombs in Xingyuan, Yanshi]. Beijing: Kexue chubanshe, 2001.

Zhou 2014
Zhou Lili. *Qingdai Yongzheng—Xuantong Guanyao ciqi* [Qing dynasty—Yongzheng to Xuantong imperial porcelains]. Shanghai: Shanghai renmin chubanshe, 2014.

Zhu 1998
Zhu Boqian. *Longquan yao qingci* [Celadons from Longquan kilns]. Taipei: Yishujia chubanshe, 1998.

Zhu 2002
Zhu Jiajin, ed. *Ming Qing jia ju (xia)* [Furniture of the Ming and Qing dynasties (vol. 2)]. Gugong bowuyuan cang wenwu zhenpin quanji [The complete collection of treasures of the Palace Museum series]. Hong Kong: Shangwu yinshuguan, 2002.

Zhu 2010
Zhu Yuping. *Yuandai qinghuaci* [Yuan dynasty blue-and-white porcelains]. Shanghai: Shanghai kexue jishu chubanshe, 2010.

SELECTED INDEX